Student Teaching:

Early Childhood Practicum Guide

3rd Edition

Student Teaching:
Early Childhood Practicum Guide

3rd Edition

Jeanne M. Machado, Emerita
San Jose City College

Helen Meyer-Botnarescue, Ph.D.
California State University—Hayward

Contributor:
Kathy Kelley, Instructor
Chabot College
Hayward, California

Delmar Publishers

 I(T)P® International Thomson Publishing

Albany • Bonn • Boston • Cincinnati • Detroit • London • Madrid
Melbourne • Mexico City • New York • Pacific Grove • Paris • San Francisco
Singapore • Tokyo • Toronto • Washington

NOTICE TO THE READER

Cover Design: The Drawing Board

Delmar Staff
Senior Editor: Jay Whitney
Associate Editor: Erin J. O'Connor
Project Editor: Timothy Coleman
Editorial Assistant: Glenna Stanfield
Production Coordinator: Sandra Woods
Art and Design Coordinator: Carol Keohane

COPYRIGHT © 1997
by Delmar Publishers
a division of International Thomson Publishing Inc.
The ITP logo is a trademark under license.

Printed in the United States of America

For more information, contact:

Delmar Publishers
3 Columbia Circle
Box 15015
Albany, New York 12203-5015

International Thomson Editores
Campos Eliseos 385, Piso 7
Col Polanco
11560 Mexico D F Mexico

International Thomson Publishing Europe
Berkshire House 168-173
High Holborn
London, WC1V7AA
England

International Thomson Publishing GmbH
Königswinterer Strasse 418
53227 Bonn
Germany

Thomas Nelson Australia
102 Dodds Street
South Melbourne, 3205
Victoria, Australia

International Thomson Publishing Asia
221 Henderson Road
#05-10 Henderson Building
Singapore 0315

Nelson Canada
1120 Birchmount Road
Scarborough, Ontario
Canada, M1K5G4

International Thomson Publishing–Japan
Hirakawacho Kyowa Building, 3F
2-2-1 Hirakawacho
Chiyoda-ku, Tokyo 102
Japan

2 3 4 5 6 7 8 9 10 XXX 01 00 99 98 97

Library of Congress Cataloging-in-Publication Data

Machado, Jeanne M.
    Student teaching: early childhood practicum guide / Jeanne M. Machado.
    Helen Meyer-Botnarescue: contributor, Kathy Kelley. — 3rd ed.
        p.   cm.
    Includes bibliographical references and index.
    ISBN 0-8273-7619-7
    1. Student teaching—Handbooks, manuals, etc. 2. Early childhood
education—Curricula. 3. Lesson planning. I. Meyer-Botnarescue, Helen.
II. Kelley, Kathy. III. Title
LB2157.A3M28 1996   96-13121
370'.7'33—dc20   CIP

CONTENTS

SECTION 1
Orientation to Student Teaching

SECTION 2
Programming

SECTION 6
Parents

SECTION 7
Knowing Yourself and Your Competencies

SECTION 8
Professional Concerns

SECTION 9

Infant/Toddler Placements

PREFACE

Student Teaching: Early Childhood Practicum Guide is designed for students who are assuming teaching responsibilities under guided supervision. Student teaching is a memorable, individual struggle to put theory into practice. It is a synthesizing experience from which each student emerges with a unique professional style. This text attempts to help each student teacher reach that goal.

Many aspects of teaching that affect the student teacher, both now as a student and later as a professional, are discussed. The topics are diverse, including, among others, teaching the "special" child, dealing with parents, principles of classroom management, interpersonal communication skills, observation and assessment (of both children and student teachers), values clarification, and a selection of trends and issues in early childhood education. Each topic is discussed in detail, using case studies and applying theories.

All of the chapters offer learning objectives, chapter summaries, suggested activities, review questions, and a list of resources. Numerous tables, charts, and illustrations reinforce the textual material.

Special emphasis on problem resolution and teachers' critical thinking skills has been added to this edition. We have enhanced the area dealing with guidance and expanded it to encompass the larger concerns of classroom management. Also enhanced are the chapters concerning what it means to be a professional and promoting quality care.

Recognition of the present shortage of teachers in preschools and child care settings, the increasing number of already employed student teachers, and the cultural diversity existing in both child groups and among staff are reflected in text readings. We have attempted to provide student teachers with increased insight into their values and instructional goals through small and large group exercises.

It is the authors' wish that this text guide student teachers in their studies and in the practical application of the knowledge acquired. *Student Teaching: Early Childhood Practicum Guide* will serve as a useful reference tool for teaching tips and problem-solving techniques as the student enters the professional world.

Comments of former student teachers begin the chapters. These personal revelations may provide insight and reading enjoyment.

Note: Associate degree or certificate program graduates preparing to work with children from birth through age five in private or public preschool and child care settings will find discussing the topics in Chapter 20 valuable. Baccalaureate degree early childhood majors completing a credentialing program and headed for employment in public or private school systems may wish to select only those trends and issues applicable to the elementary schools in their respective states. However, the issues of an "antibias," multicultural curriculum, the "back to basics" thrust, computer use with young children, language and literacy, and authentic assessment are as valid for elementary school programs as they are for preschool ones.

ACKNOWLEDGMENTS

The authors wish to express their appreciation to the following individuals and institutions for their contributions to this text.

Reviewers

Charlotte Madison
University of Connecticut
Stoors, Connecticut

Barbara Payne Shelton
Villa Julie College
Stevenson, Maryland

Rosemary Wolfe
Anne Arundel Community College
Crofton, Maryland

Illustrations and Photos

Nancy Martin
Jayne Musladin
Jody Boyd
The parents of photographed children

Individual Assistance

The director and staff of the San Jose City College and Evergreen Valley College Child Development Centers, and enrolled student teachers.
Barbara Kraybill, Director, Afterschool Programs, Livermore, CA.

Preschools, Centers, and Elementary Schools

San Jose City College Child Development Center
Evergreen Valley College Child Development Center
Young Families Program, San Jose, CA
California State University Associated Students' Child Care Center
Pexioto Children's Center, Hayward, CA
Parent-Child Education Center, Hayward, CA
Festival Children's Center, Hayward, CA
Jackson Avenue School, Livermore, CA
Harder School, Hayward, CA
St. Elizabeth's Day Home, San Jose CA
Donnelly Headstart, Donnelly, ID
Cascade Elementary School, Cascade, ID
Redeemer Lutheran Church Child Development Center, Redwood City, CA

We also wish to express our appreciation to We Care Day Treatment Center, Concord, CA, for permission to photograph attending children.

Students, Instructors, and Professors
San Jose City College
Evergreen Valley College
California State University, Hayward
Intern Students and Taiwanese preschool teachers attending National Hispanic University

◄ ABOUT THE AUTHORS ►

The authors of this text, Jeanne M. Machado and Helen Meyer-Botnarescue, are actively involved in child care and teacher training programs. Jeanne received her M.A. degree from San Jose State University and a Vocational Life Credential from University of California, Berkeley. She has experience as an early childhood education instructor and department chairperson at San Jose City College and Evergreen Valley College. As a past president of two professional associations—Northern California Association for the Education of Young Children (Peninsula Chapter) and California Community College Early Childhood Educators—Jeanne is deeply involved in early childhood teaching issues. Her text *Early Childhood Experiences in the Language Arts* is currently in its fifth edition.

Helen Meyer-Botnarescue received her Ph.D. from the University of Alabama. She also received a Life Credential in Psychology. Currently, Helen is a professor of education in the Department of Teacher Education at California University, Hayward. In addition, she serves as coordinator of the Early Childhood Education master's program. She is advisor to the campus Early Childhood Center. Helen is an active member of five professional organizations: California Professors of Early Childhood Education and Child Development, an affiliate group of the National Association of Early Childhood Teacher Educators; the California Association for the Education of Young Children, a branch of the National Association for the Education of Young Children; the World Organization for Preschool Education (OMEP); and the Association for Childhood Education International (ACEI). She has served on the governing board of the National Association of Early Childhood Teacher Educators, has been an active member of and presenter at Congresses sponsored by the Organisation Modiale pour l'Éducation Préscolaire (OMEP), and currently is president of the California Association for Childhood Education, the state affiliate of ACEI.

CHAPTER

1

Introduction to Student Teaching Practicum

OBJECTIVES

After studying this chapter, the student will be able to:

- Identify some important goals of a student teaching experience.
- Describe the relationships and responsibilities of student teacher, cooperating teachers, and supervisors.
- List three professional conduct considerations for student teachers.

Comments of student teachers after their first week in the classroom.

On the first day of student teaching I was very excited. I felt nervous and tried my best to fit in as though I had been there many times. I memorized all the children's names before the day was over.

May Valentino

I worked hard to get into this final class in the training program. I did it part-time going evenings after a full day of work with young children. My college supervisor insisted I student teach at a center away from my job. I resented it but found I was able to grow, gain new skills, see quality I'd never experienced.

Janice Washington

Student teaching is both a beginning and an end. It begins a training experience that offers the student a supervised laboratory in which to learn. New skills will develop, and the student will polish professional skills already acquired. The student teacher's vocational "know-how," feelings, motivations, values and attitudes, uniqueness, abilities, talents, and possible limitations are examined through self-analysis, observation, and consultation with others. As the final step in a formal training program offering a certificate, degree, license, or credential, student teaching completes a period during which exposure to theory and practical application has occurred. It requires the synthesizing of all previous coursework, training, workshops, and background experience.

Congratulations! You have satisfied all the prerequisites for student teaching. Now you will assume teacher responsibilities and duties with young children and become a member of a professional teaching team.

One of the culminating phases of your professional preparation for teaching, your student teaching provides opportunities to try your wings if you are not presently employed. If employed, the student teaching experience will sharpen and expand already acquired competencies.

TRAINING GUIDELINES

The National Association for the Education of Young Children has taken the lead in advocating training guidelines for the preparation of teacher education programs in both associate of arts degree programs and in four- and five-year bachelor's and advanced degree programs. *Guidelines for Preparation of Early Childhood Professionals: Associate, Baccalaureate, and Advanced Levels* (1994) suggests that training programs provide opportunities to apply knowledge and skills in working with children in a variety of field experiences with increasing levels of interaction with children. Each graduating student is expected to have successfully completed a supervised practicum experience or alternative equivalent during which the student assumes major responsibility for a full range of teaching and care-

giving duties for a group of young children. Skills, knowledge, and attitudes gained prepare the student to demonstrate the knowledge and competencies required to meet state licensing requirements and/or permits, certificates and/or credentials.

INITIAL FEELINGS

Many students approach student teaching with mixed feelings of trepidation and exhilaration. The challenge presents risks and unknowns, as well as opportunities for growth, insights, and increased self-awareness. Student teaching will be memorable. You will cherish and share with others this "growing stage" of your development as a person and teacher.

Everyone who comes to the field of early childhood brings some kind of relevant experiences with young children, experiences that form a foundation on which to construct teaching theory and practice (Jones, 1994).

THE MECHANICS OF STUDENT TEACHING

Student teaching (sometimes called practicum or field experience) in an early childhood program involves three key people—the student teacher, the cooperating teacher who is responsible for a group of young children, and a supervisor who is a college instructor or teacher trainer. The cooperating teacher models teaching techniques and practices, and the supervisor observes and analyzes the development of the student teacher's skills. Perrodin (1966) defines the roles of these three key people as follows:

Student
Teacher— A student experiencing a period of guided teaching during which the student takes increasing responsibility for the work with a given group of learners over a period of consecutive weeks. (Other terms used: practice teacher, apprentice teacher, intern.)

Cooperating
Teacher— One who teaches children or youth and who also supervises student teaching and/or other

professional laboratory experiences. (Other terms used: supervising teacher, laboratory school teacher, critic teacher, master teacher, directing teacher, resident teacher.)

College/
University
Supervisor— The college representative responsible for supervising a student teacher or a group of student teachers. (Other terms used: off-campus supervisor, resident supervisor, clinical teacher, teacher trainer.)

● KEY PARTICIPANTS PLAY A ROLE IN STUDENT TEACHER DEVELOPMENT

Personality, settings, child groupings, the commitment and professionalism of individuals, and many other factors contribute and influence the quality and variety of training opportunities. Key participants (student teacher, cooperating teachers, college and university supervisors) each play a role in student teacher development.

Each student teacher is responsible for serious effort. We have all met people who have a desire and knack for getting all possible from a given situation. Their human "antennae" are actively searching, receiving, and evaluating! As a student teacher, you will guide much of your own growth. Your cooperating teacher and college or university supervisor will support and reinforce your commitment to learn. Your increasing skill will depend, in part, on you.

Cooperating teachers, as a first duty, must fulfill the requirements of their positions. Child instruction is paramount. Student teacher direction and guidance is an additional task for which they may or may not be compensated. Even in laboratory school settings educating and caring for children supercedes the training of student teachers, which is seen as an auxiliary function.

The college or university supervisor's role includes being responsive to a student's concerns, encouraging, understanding, being sensitive and supportive, as well as being serious and rigorous in promoting each student teacher's attention to professional high standards of performance and timely completion of responsibilities. Your supervisor will take an active interest in your career development, and in your existing and growing skills and competence.

Jones (1986), speaking about the role of a campus laboratory instructor who supervises student teachers, suggests:

> If I were a preschool lab instructor supervising students' work with children, I'd challenge more, because the student in that setting has responsibilities as a teacher as well as learner. . . .
>
> To be a learner, I think, is to have a chance to mess about, try things out, make mistakes. Practice and self-correction go a long way.

● BEFORE PLACEMENTS

College and university departments and individual college instructors (supervisors) have developed guidelines for selecting placement sites long before the first days of student teaching practicum classes. Some colleges and universities endeavor to canvas widely their community preschools and centers to recognize those meeting their training standards as certified student practicum placement sites. Decisions involve selection of the best training site(s) for students, considering the constraints of their particular situations. Selection criteria may depend on location, placement staff experience and training, licensing and accreditation of a placement school or center, law, willingness and ability of administrators and staff to carry out procedures and responsibilities, as well as other factors.

A number of group and individual consultations have taken place as supervising college and university instructors set the scene for student teacher experiences, activities, assignments, and evaluation procedures. Informational written material, including a student teacher and cooperating teacher handbook, may have been designed and produced. The handbooks attempt to cover all facets of training and need to be read carefully and kept handy.

The student teacher should recognize that decisions concerning the number of classroom or center placements per semester (quarter or training period) have already been established. In some communities a wide variety of child classrooms are available and possible. In other areas placement classrooms are few or limited.

Colleges and universities may offer early childhood education training programs that can include preparation for diverse teaching specialties. Infant–toddler teacher and school-age teacher (before and after primary school) are two new areas provided within traditional early childhood or child development training programs. Some colleges and universities make student teacher placements in both private and public kindergartens or elementary school classrooms where students assume assistant teacher or aide duties.

Student teaching classes are offered at baccalaureate degree granting colleges and universities (both private and public). Students enrolled in these classes are completing course work to fulfill state credentialing requirements, and possibly, an advanced degree such as a master of arts degree in education that includes teacher certification. Student teachers at primary grade level usually function as practicing teachers with full responsibility for their assigned classrooms while under the supervision of their assigned cooperating teachers. Rarely do student teachers at prekindergarten level immediately assume full teaching responsibilities. More commonly, they gradually perform an increasing amount of duties, program planning, and instruction and work their way up to total teacher responsibilities while still under their cooperating teacher's supervision. Employed student teachers are often asked to leave their employment classrooms so this type of growth experience is possible.

The Currently Employed Student Teacher

For the currently employed student teacher the logistics of putting in unpaid hours at another child center may seem an undue hardship, yet many will welcome the opportunity to gain insight into another teacher's competencies and profit from the professional consultation that occurs. In some training programs one may have to become a day student instead of a night student to enroll in a student teaching class. College and university supervisors are sometimes able to work out placements that allow a student to student teach at her place of employment. This unfortunately can deprive one of the chance to work in a quality early childhood model.

Most employed teachers find they go back to their own classrooms with new ideas or strategies that change teaching for the better (Wood, 1994).

Increasingly, students entering early childhood work start classes after employment because of trained early childhood teacher shortages. Most experience results in some kind of learning, but it may not be college-level learning or meet professional standards (Fyfe, 1994).

Learning and Growth

Being a unique individual, each student teacher has developed his own learning style. Life and school experience has molded how you see yourself and how you proceed toward knowing and accomplishing new knowledge or skill. Hopefully your student teaching class will offer diverse ways to learn and also give structured aid in the form of clear guidelines, directions, and suggestions by both your instructor and your cooperating teacher. You will no doubt work alone at times and also in small and large groups.

A portion of your time will be spent in pondering what you have read and experienced. You will observe closely other adults in child classrooms and try to gauge the outcomes of their behaviors. You will also become an avid watcher of yourself and the reactions of others to you. As M. Carter and D. Curtis (1994) explain, effective teaching requires continual analysis, adjustment, reflecting, and refocusing. Growth will build and proceed on what you already know as you take tentative and then firm steps in new directions.

Part of the joy of teaching is experimenting, innovating, and inventing new approaches. These new ways always will be offered after judging whether they mesh with your basic conclusions considering what is safe and developmentally appropriate for young children. You have already internalized goals. They stand behind your daily interactions with children and their families. Child self-esteem and self-reliance rate high with most student teachers, as does child self-selected direction and discovery.

Empathy

Most cooperating teachers and college supervisors have themselves been student teachers at the beginning of their own careers. Their feelings tend to be empathetic and supportive while at the same time they expect a serious student attempt to develop competency. They provide counseling and assistance.

The whole student teaching experience can be viewed as a miniature world, a slice of life, a human laboratory that will be full of memorable events, including the ups and downs all student teachers ex-

perience. Every student ideally comes to a clarification of self in relation to people and situations designed to provide quality care and educationally sound environments for young children. New insights concerning values, goals, cultures, self-realization, and other important life issues are attained.

Student Teacher Progress. If the student completes student teaching duties and responsibilities successfully, the student receives recognition of teaching competency. Observation and analysis of the student's performance, followed by consultation with the teaching team, is an integral part of student teaching. There is a wide variety of methods of observation and analysis. Written observations, narratives, checklists, rating scales, and videotapes are common. Many supervisors focus upon child, group, and adult reaction to student teacher/child and student teacher/adult interaction. (See figures 1-1 and 1-2.)

Figure 1-1 Student teachers may be required to present activity ideas to other student teachers.

Figure 1-2 Exchange student teachers from Taiwan also present activity ideas to their peers.

How should student teachers view their progress and learning in a student teaching class? Rasinski (1989) observes:

> Students can no longer be viewed as passive recipients of knowledge dispensed by teachers; rather, students need to be perceived as active and responsible participants in their own education, relying on their own knowledge and experience to contextualize the educational process.

A child care center is seen as a growing place for everyone, not only for the student teacher. Every human who enters the class can grow from each experience. It is presumed that all adults—even the cooperating teacher and supervisor—are unfinished products. Each participant is viewed as a combination of strengths and talents, with the possibility of expanding. A caring and supportive relationship between the student teacher, the cooperating teacher, and the supervisor is crucial to this growth process. Most supervisors and cooperating teachers respect the differences in the talents and backgrounds of student teachers. Although the training sessions and classes are the same, there are dissimilar, as well as similar, values, attitudes, and past experiences. Cooperating teachers are uniquely individual; the differences in their personalities and teaching techniques are readily apparent. Diversity is the one similarity to be expected among cooperating teachers.

Many students are eventually hired by training sites if they have demonstrated competent teaching methods.

Placement sites differ in so many respects that comparing them may be like comparing the proverbial oranges and apples. But an attempt to list possible training advantages appears in figure 1-3. The

Staff:
- is highly qualified, professional, degreed
- has experience with previous student teachers
- gives frequent feedback, advice, and/or suggestions
- is supportive, empathetic, accepting
- has prepared clear, written student teacher procedures and guidelines
- has time and opportunity to observe student teachers
- is committed to recognition and enhancement of student teacher skills
- communicates often, with clarity and respect
- has planned a developmentally appropriate environment and program
- provides learning opportunities and prefers students work through new or perhaps difficult situations, yet offers help when appropriate
- is able to encourage and maintain a team spirit
- includes specialized personnel

Program:
- is individualized, developmentally appropriate, and culturally sensitive
- reflects respect for children, parents, teachers, community, and volunteers
- is varied, interesting, and current
- attempts to provide for children's and families' needs
- ensures children's safety and welfare

Facilities (and Supplies):
- are appropriate and adequate
- are professionally planned and maintained
- include audiovisual teaching aids
- include library and resource material for student teaching
- contain features and provisions for children and adults with physically limiting conditions
- have observation and conference areas
- allow student participation in food preparation and service activities
- allow room and outdoor environments to be changed and/or altered by student teacher(s) attempting to provide additional child activities and/or different play and learning opportunities

Children:
- are enrolled who are of particular ages, backgrounds, language diversity, and so on, to provide student teacher with training experiences that will lead to a teaching specialization

Administration of the School or Center:
- is open and committed to student teacher training
- is supportive and expert
- has promoted and acquired accreditation by the National Association for the Education of Young Children
- has developed a working cooperative spirit and liaison with a variety of community groups, agencies, and resources.

Figure 1-3 Possible training advantages in selected placement sites, classrooms, and centers.

figure is based on the authors' experiences and may differ from what exists at your placement site. It may help you to understand the placements of other student teachers in your class.

ORIENTATION

Introductions, tours, oral and written guidelines, instructions and informational data, and completing forms are all part of student teaching orientation meetings. Remembering names and taking notes is advisable. First impressions are important, and "body language" will send many messages to others.

Introductions and tours enable the student teacher to become familiar with people and settings, and help reduce anxieties. Anxieties may increase when responsibilities and requirements are described. Supervisors and cooperating teachers may require the completion of various assignments. Keeping each in order may mean coding or keeping different folders or binders. A datebook or daily appointment calendar is also recommended since many important meetings, appointments, and deadlines will occur. As always, the newness, the attention required for details, and the amount of information to remember and read may produce stress temporarily. Creating a buddy system with other student teachers can be helpful.

Forms, Forms, Forms

Various informational written materials provide helpful guidelines for orientations. They are categorized as follows:

Supervisor
- Supervisor's course guide sheet
- Supervisor's student teacher placement responsibilities (figure 1-4)
- Supervisor's tips, aids (figure 1-5)
- Supervisor's assessment forms
- Supervisor's forms for cooperating teachers (figure 1-6)

Center
- Parents' guide and policy statement

1. Be prompt and prepared.
2. If you are ill on your assigned days, call your supervisor and cooperating teacher as close to 8 a.m. as possible.
3. If you must be absent, phone ahead and let your school know you are unable to be there that day. Preferably, let the school know ahead of time if there will be an unavoidable absence during your student teaching asignment.
4. Remember, the cooperating teacher depends on your services as a fellow teacher.
5. Sign in and out if required.
6. Consult with your supervisor on lesson planning when help is needed.
7. Make an appointment with your supervisor to discuss class-related questions or problems.
8. Remember to avoid conversations that label children or deal with confidential information.
9. Sign in the lesson plan book at least one week in advance if your cooperating teacher or supervisor requests it.
10. Complete assignments.
11. Complete your student teacher file, and take it to the director's office as soon as possible. (Included in this file are TB clearance, personal data sheet, rating sheets, return envelope.)
12. Be sure to have your fingerprint card and background check completed prior to beginning your first observation and/or student teaching assignment.
13. Please see and do what needs to be done without direction. Ask questions. Assume as much teaching responsibility as you can handle.

Figure 1-4 Sample of student teacher responsibilities.

1. Get your TB and criminal background clearances to your center's director as soon as possible. (Note: This is not required in some states.)
2. Leave your belongings in the place provided.
3. Sign in.
4. Enter the children's room quietly, wearing your nametag.
5. Look for emergency room evacuation plans (posted on wall).
6. Consider child safety. Watch and listen for rules and expectations.
7. Actively involve yourself helping staff and children. See what needs to be done. Ask only what is necessary of staff after saying hello or introducing yourself. (Do not interrupt an activity. Wait until the cooperating teacher is free.)
8. Let the staff handle child behaviors that are puzzling on first days.
9. Write down any questions concerning children, programs, and routines that baffle you, and discuss them with your supervisor.
10. If you are sick on your scheduled day, call both your supervisor and your cooperating teacher.
11. Keep a brief diary of your activities, feelings, perceptions, etc. You may want to buy a pocket-sized notebook.

Figure 1-5 Sample of trainer's tips for student teacher's first days.

- Center newsletter
- Policy for visitors and observers
- Children's records

Cooperating Teacher
- Student teacher assignments, responsibilities rating sheet

- Children's daily schedule
- Children's names (with pronunciation guides if necessary)
- Student teacher rating sheets
- Staff meeting dates and times (optional)
- Placement classroom guidelines for student teachers (figure 1-7)

1. Let your student take as much responsibility as possible.
2. Give feedback on progress if possible.
3. Written tips, hints, and suggestions on lesson plans are helpful.
4. Let your student teacher work out the "tight" spots when possible. You may want to set up a signal to indicate when the student wishes you to step in and remedy the situation.
5. Gauge your student's ability. (Some student teachers may be able to handle a full morning's program from the beginning.) Each student needs the experience of handling the group.
6. Discuss the student teacher's performance in confidence after the activity. Some suggestions while an activity is occurring may be necessary for child or equipment safety.
7. Your student teacher may ask you for a letter of reference.
8. Peer evaluations have been assigned. This means perhaps that another student teacher may observe and rate the student assigned to you. This may happen twice during the semester.
9. Please call the student's supervisor if a difficulty or question arises.
10. Rate the student on the last week of participation. A rating sheet is part of your student teacher's folder. The student will remind you a week in advance.
11. The student teacher has been instructed to consult with you on lesson plan activities. If you want the activities to deal with particular curriculum areas or themes, this is your choice. The student has been told to abide by your wishes.
12. Your student's Personal Data Sheet has information concerning special interests and background, etc.
13. The student's supervisor will visit periodically to give the student feedback on competencies and possible growth areas.
14. Frequent conferences help the student obtain a clear picture of skill progress.
15. Near the end of the student teacher's assignment, the college/university supervisor will schedule a three-way conference with you, your student teacher, and the supervisor for the closing student teacher evaluation.

Thank you for taking on the extra work involved in having a student in your classroom.

Figure 1-6 Sample of supervisor's written instructions to cooperating teachers.

The following forms are common to student teaching. Many must be on file before the student's first working day.

- Class schedule (location, rooms, and times of any additional courses)
- Student teacher sign-in sheets (to keep track of arrival, departure, and volunteer and assigned work hours)
- Tuberculin (TB) clearance (mandatory in many states)
- Staff information form, personnel record
- Personal background form (figure 1-8)
- Physical examination, physician's report
- Criminal background clearance

Criminal History and Background Check

An increasing number of states are requiring a criminal history and background inquiry prior to a student teacher field placement. All paid and volunteer staff are required to comply and receive clearance, which then is placed in the child care facility's or school's personnel files.

● PROFESSIONALISM

You may want to skip ahead and read the Code of Ethics provided in the Appendix.

Extra attention to teacher conduct is required because of the age and vulnerability of young children and the influence a teacher may have with parents. Katz and Ward (1978) remind us:

In any profession, the more powerless the client is in relation to the practitioner, the more important the practitioner's ethics become. That is to say, the greater the necessity for internalized restraints against abusing that power.

Early childhood practitioners have great power over young children, especially in day care centers.

Suggestions for guiding behavior:
1. Redirect behavior in a positive way whenever possible (e.g., feet belong on the floor).
2. Do not give a choice when one does not exist.
3. Give help only when it is needed.
4. Do not be afraid to limit or channel destructive behavior.
5. Help the children understand by explaining.
6. Encourage children to use their words during peer disagreements.
7. Inform the children a few minutes ahead of the next activity to come. ("It's three minutes until clean-up/snack.")
8. Watch for situations that may be explosive, and step in. Try to let the children settle problems themselves. If they cannot, redirect them.
9. Remember, an ounce of prevention is worth a pound of cure.

Inside:
1. Playdough stays in the creative activities room.
2. Parents have been asked not to send their children with toys, except on sharing days.
3. Running is for outside; walking is for inside.
4. Encourage children to pour their own drinks from the pitchers provided. This will probably mean frequent spills so sponges should be available on all tables. Have children pass things to each other.

Outside:
1. Adults need to distribute themselves throughout the center and the playground, rather than grouping together. Your attention should be on the children, observing them so you can be ready to step in when guidance is needed.
2. Children are to climb up the ladder and slide down on their bottoms when using the slide.
3. All sand play and sand toys must be in the designated area.
4. Remind the children that water from the fountain is for drinking. Sand and cornmeal should be kept away from the water fountain to avoid clogging.
5. Help children park wheeled toys along the fence before going in. Please keep the gate area clear.
6. All wheeled toys have a specific use and should be used properly.

Figure 1-7 Sample of child center guidelines for student teachers.

Practitioners' superior physical power over young children is obvious. In addition, practitioners have virtually total power over the psychological goods and resources of value to the young in their care.

Teachers face moral and ethical dilemmas daily. A student teacher strives to do the right action rather than the expedient action in each situation encountered. This may be more difficult than it sounds:

Situations in which doing what is right carries high probability of getting an award or being rewarded may not require a code of ethics as much as situations rife with risks (e.g., risking the loss of a job or a license to practice, facing professional alienation or even harsher consequences). (Katz and Ward, 1978)

When you reach the level of student teaching, others presume you have a certain amount of educational background and some degree of professional skill. Some parents may feel you are an expert in child rearing and may try to seek your opinion(s) on a wide variety of developmental issues. You will need to direct these parents to your cooperating teacher, who may refer them to the director or other staff, who, in turn, may refer them to professionally trained individuals or community resources.

As a student teacher you represent a profession. As a professional, you are asked to abide by certain regulations, including a professional conduct code. Confidentiality is an integral part of this code as it protects children and families, and it

PERSONAL DATA SHEET

NAME _____

ADDRESS _____ CITY _____

PHONE _____ MESSAGE PHONE # _____ EMERGENCY PHONE # _____

CAR yes_____ no _____

FAMILY DATA (optional)

HEALTH _____

EXPERIENCES WITH CHILDREN   (past employment, volunteer, family, etc.)

_____

_____

_____

COLLEGE _____ year _____ major _____

COURSES in early childhood major not presently completed

_____

_____

Previous college work related to student teaching

_____

_____

Presently Employed _____ Where _____

Hours _____ Duties _____

_____

SPECIAL INTERESTS _____

_____

WHAT WOULD YOU LIKE YOUR COOPERATING TEACHER TO KNOW ABOUT YOU? _____

_____

HOBBIES AND SPECIAL TALENTS OR SKILLS _____

_____

CAREER GOALS _____

Figure 1-8 Sample of personal background form.

should be maintained at all times. Staff meetings and individual conferences are conducted in a spirit of mutual interest and concern for the children's and adults' welfare and the center's high standards. At such conferences, student teachers are privy to personal information that should not be discussed elsewhere.

This point needs to be stressed: Student teachers can become so involved with classroom happenings and individual children that they inadvertently discuss privileged information with a fellow student teacher or friend, or within the center in earshot of a parent or another individual. One can easily see how this might happen and cause irreparable damage.

Classes of student teachers are frequently reminded by their instructors/supervisors that real child and family names cannot be used in seminar/class discussions.

The student teacher's appearance, clothing, and grooming contribute to a professional image. Fortunately, comfortable, functional clothing, which allows a student teacher to perform duties without worrying about mobility or messy activity supervision, is relatively inexpensive (figure 1-9). Many supervisors suggest a pocketed smock or apron and a change of shoes.

Figure 1-9 Student teachers assist this cooperating teacher in a group movement activity.

Responsibilities

A clear picture of the responsibilities of the student teacher, cooperating teacher, and supervisor will help students make decisions about handling specific incidences as professionals. As a general rule, it is better to ask for help than to proceed in any questionable situation that goes beyond one's responsibilities and duties (barring emergency situations that call for immediate action). (See figures 1-10 and 1-11.)

Exposure to Bloodborne Pathogens

You will be instructed at your placement site about exposure to child blood, skin, eye, and mucous membrane secretions and other potentially infectious materials and will be provided with protective gloves and equipment. Should a classroom situation occur, cooperating teachers will prefer to handle the incident. Discuss this with your cooperating teacher. Privacy laws protect parents who do not wish to disclose child conditions; therefore, it is wise to follow exposure guidelines strictly. The Occupational Safety and Health Administration, via the Occupational Safety and Health Acts of 1970 and 1992, recognizes the need for child care worker training and protections. Each center (there are a few exceptions) by law must develop a written exposure control plan, provide protective clothing and equipment, give employees information and training, and provide vaccine and medical help to exposed employees. Centers will instruct student teachers concerning who gives first aid.

It is suggested that each student teacher consult their private physician regarding the advisability of hepatitis B vaccination.

Student's Responsibilities
- Attendance and promptness
- Performance and completion of all assignments and duties
- Working with a minimum of direction
- Translating theory into performance

College/University Supervisor's Responsibilities
- Conducting orientations
- Clearly outlining duties, responsibilities, and class assignments
- Arranging and monitoring placements
- Observing progress and confirming strengths and talents
- Providing feedback
- Helping students develop individual plans for future growth
- Working as a liaison between cooperating teacher and student, consulting frequently as a team member
- Becoming aware of cooperating teacher's assigned tasks for student teacher
- Serving as a resource and modeling when possible
- Evaluating student's competencies

Cooperating Teacher's Responsibilities
- Orienting student teacher to room environment, schedules, class rules, and children
- Serving as a model of philosophy, teaching style, and teaching technique
- Clearly outlining student teacher expectations, duties, and assigned work
- Answering questions
- Giving feedback on observations when possible
- Providing ideas for child activities and materials
- Increasing the student teacher's opportunity to gain and sharpen skills by giving increased responsibilities when appropriate
- Following agreed-upon tasks

Responsibilities of All
- Maintaining professional conduct
- Communicating ideas and concerns; seeking aid when in doubt
- Gaining new skills and sharpening existing skills
- Working as supportive, caring team members

Figure 1-10 Responsibilities.

Student Teaching in a Kindergarten or Primary Grade in a Public or Private Elementary School. When you are assigned to student teach in a kindergarten or primary grade classroom, your first days will involve you in many of the same activities as when you were assigned to student teach in a prekindergarten.

You will want to drive or walk around the neighborhood in which the school is located and observe in more than the one classroom. Most elementary schools have staff handbooks. You will be given a copy and be expected to read it. A handbook will contain vital information such as the school calendar, a list of the school board members, and the date their term ends. The names of the school principal, secretary, nurse, librarian, head maintenance person, community liaison person, and so on, will be listed. School rules and regulations will be presented. In reading the handbook, you will have a firm idea of policies you would be expected to follow during your student teaching period.

Different colleges and universities have different ways in which student teaching is arranged. In some states which have certification for nursery/kindergarten/primary (NKP) teaching, you may have three different placements—one at a preschool, another at the kindergarten level, a third in a primary grade. Other states require only two experiences—one at preschool, a second at either kindergarten or primary level. In some certification programs, all theory and methods classes precede a one-semester, 12-week, all-day student teaching experience. Other programs integrate some of the theory and methods courses with short observation assignments lasting for approximately four weeks. Again, these precede a major student teaching assignment that most typically covers one academic semester. In California, early childhood education is an "emphasis" appended to the multiple subject (elementary) credential; colleges and universities with similar state-approved programs must provide student experiences at both primary and intermediate grade levels in addition to an experience in a preschool. Assignments, then, often involve a short practicum-observation in a preschool, often only in the mornings (sometimes paid experience may be substituted), another assignment in the intermediate grades (usually grade four), and a final longer assignment of approximately 12 to 15 weeks, all day, in a kindergarten or primary grade. Colleges and universities with NCATE (National Council for the Accreditation of Teacher Education)-approved programs must meet NAEYC (National

In accepting the role of a cooperating teacher to_____
                                                                         (student's name)

I agree to perform the following:

1. Orient the student to all school child safety procedures, school policies, staff handbook, and other pertinent particulars concerning the operation of school or classroom.
2. Read all written material and become acquainted with all facets of the student teaching situation including time lines, deadlines, training objectives and goals, tasks and responsibilities of both the student and myself.
3. Meet with the student teacher at least weekly at regular times for consultation, progress evaluation, and planning.
4. Schedule periodic meetings with the student's college supervisor, and immediately contact college supervisor as the need arises.
5. Observe and offer clear, honest opinions of student strengths and training needs to promote student's growth in teaching and human interaction skills and competency.
6. Be open to questions, providing a professional example and communicating directly to student concerning daily problems, matters, and concerns.
7. Develop procedures that record student's actual attendance hours in classroom.
8. Complete the formal exit evaluation of the student that details student's level of competence and suggests future growth areas.

As a training model you directly contribute to teaching excellence and professional recognition of our career field.

Please sign below and return to the College Supervisor before _____

Cooperating teacher   _____   date _____

        school   _____

        address _____

        phone # _____   message phone # _____

        fax #   _____   e mail # _____

Figure 1-11 Example of contract listing cooperating teacher training tasks, procedures, and responsibilities.

Association for the Education of Young Children) guidelines, and you must have at least two weeks of full-time teaching during your final experience.

In student teaching assignments that cover only one semester, you probably will have only one college/university supervisor. Most supervisors are chosen for their expertise; most are former primary grade teachers themselves. In colleges and universities with programs that include short practica or observation periods prior to student teaching, you may well have more than one college/university supervisor. (Some of these practica or short observation periods may not be directly supervised; the college may rely upon the cooperating teacher or principal for any supervision that is needed.) Having different supervisors can provide you with the benefit of exposure to more than one type of supervision technique. One supervisor may stress the need to see lesson plans as you are teaching. Another, schooled in clinical supervision techniques, may focus on the communication and questioning strategies you use. A third may watch your interactions with your pupils.

Student teaching assignments are usually made very carefully. Cooperating teachers are chosen for their expertise as well as for their willingness to help train a student teacher (figure 1-12). Many states require any cooperating teacher to have had at least three years of experience prior to being considered;

most principals will choose their most competent teachers for this role.

Having an "expert" cooperating teacher can be both a boon and a headache. You may feel that you will never be that proficient and become discouraged. Talk about these feelings in your seminar group, with your college/university supervisor, and with your cooperating teacher. Chances are she knows exactly how you feel. She has been there. Sometimes, a truly "expert" cooperating teacher is reluctant to turn over the class to you. Again, honesty in communicating with him and your college/university supervisor is critical. Once in a while, inevitably, a placement has to be changed. Sometimes philosophic differences are the problem; sometimes reluctance to allow you to teach is the difficulty. Always remember, though, you are in the school to learn—placements are made with excellent cooperating teachers with that in mind.

Learn and have fun!

● STUDENT TEACHING GOALS

The most important goal of student teaching is to gain adequate (or better) teaching competence. The acquisition of skills allows the completion of training and new or continued employment.

Specific objectives vary but they generally are concerned with understanding children, planning

and providing quality programs for children and families, acquiring technical teaching skills, and personal and professional development. A list of common student teacher objectives follows:

- Increasing awareness of a child's and family's individuality
- Building rapport
- Understanding ethnicity, neighborhood values, and individual group cultural values
- Identifying a child's needs
- Promoting child growth and development
- Identifying the goals of instruction
- Acquiring an individual teaching style
- Offering a child activities and opportunities
- Applying theory and past experiences to present situations
- Preparing interesting classroom environments
- Assuming a teacher's duties and responsibilities
- Learning school routines
- Developing self-confidence
- Evaluating effectiveness
- Growing personally and professionally
- Acquiring communication skills
- Experimenting and creating
- Using creative problem-solving techniques
- Guiding child behavior appropriately
- Establishing and maintaining working relationships
- Assessing strength and endurance
- Understanding supportive family services
- Developing a personal philosophy of early childhood education
- Participating in advocacy efforts
- Learning state guidelines, standards, and laws

Shaplin (1965) cites an additional important goal:

Teachers must learn to analyze, criticize, and control their own behavior.

Figure 1-12 Consultation with the cooperating teacher sets the stage for growth.

Individual goals reflect each student teacher's idea of professional conduct and skill and how each feels about the kind of teacher and person she would like to become. Teachers constantly make choices in agreement with their values and goals.

Your Personal Philosophy

From your readings on early childhood education and your observations and interactions with teachers and trainers, you have formed your own ideas regarding the "best" early childhood education, the "right" teaching techniques and methods, and the "proper" room environments. You have opinions on the why, what, where, when, who, and how of group programs for young children. As you student teach, you will revise your philosophy based upon new experiences with children, adults, and different schools and child centers.

Student Teacher Observational Record Keeping

Busy cooperating teachers are usually quite interested in daily observations and student teacher written accounts of child incidents and happenings. It gives cooperating teachers an "outside opinion." This may be the first perception by another adult that they have heard concerning child behavior they are trying to trace or evaluate themselves.

It takes only a few minutes a day for student teacher record keeping, unless a cooperating teacher has assigned more lengthy observation exercises. Any notes are confidential and should be guarded closely. One can easily understand the danger apparent if a student teacher leaves observational notes lying around! Anecdotes are jotted down quickly with the date and time, and differ from records of accidents, injuries, or illnesses noted during the day. The latter are detailed and necessary for school record keeping; each school or center has its own specific form or format.

Student Journals (Logs)

Many training programs require the student teacher to begin a journal (log) of their experiences and feelings during the student teaching. Supervisors periodically monitor journal entries (or student tape recordings) to keep on top of student growth, work actions, concerns, feelings, questions, and needs. It is suggested that student teachers make at least one five-minute daily entry (written or taped) on participation days while impressions are fresh. Some college supervisors give suggestions for recorded topics:

- personal views, insights, expressions
- classroom dilemmas
- feelings about all aspects of the classroom
- insights concerning the philosophy of the cooperating teacher
- relationships with particular children
- perceptions of student teacher skills
- what's going well; what isn't
- staff relationships
- areas student pinpoints for self-growth
- ways the student has overcome a problem
- new ideas to improve instruction and how they worked
- why it would be great (or not) to be a child in this classroom
- special children's needs
- children's interests
- planned activities
- unscheduled activities
- favorite spots in classroom
- difficult times of day

Journal entries are dated in lefthand margins.

Some college supervisors write in the student's journal, giving supportive assistance or encouragement. A journal is really used as a communication device and promotes shared understandings and intimacy. Follow-up conferences may concentrate on student progress.

Your completed journal will be cherished and shared with others.

SUMMARY

The student teaching experience is the last step in a training sequence for early childhood teachers. Three key participants—the student teacher, the cooperating teacher, and the supervisor—form a team enabling the student teacher to gain new skills and sharpen previously acquired teaching techniques.

Student teaching involves the integration of all former training and experience. The cooperating teacher and supervisor guide, model, observe, and analyze the student teacher's progress in an assigned classroom as the student teacher assumes greater responsibilities with children and their families. Initial orientation meetings and written requirements and guidelines acquaint the student teacher with expectations and requirements. The student teaching experience is unique to each training institution, yet placement in a children's classroom with a supervisor's analysis of competency is common to all.

A caring, supportive atmosphere helps each student teacher attain established goals and helps develop the student teacher's personal style and philosophy.

SUGGESTED ACTIVITIES

A. Read all of the following student teacher goals. Give each a priority from 1 to 5, number 1 being the highest. Name two goals other than those listed that are important to you.

Understanding children

Learning teacher's duties

Understanding minority groups

Developing self-confidence

Evaluating effectiveness

Developing rapport with children

Acquiring an individual teaching style

Gaining experience

Experimenting and creating

Gaining guidance ability

Applying theories and ideas to practice

Clarifying individual philosophy

Personal growth and development as a professional

Discovering what parents view as important

B. Read the following essay by Patricia Pruden Mohr (from California Child Development Centers' Administrators Association Newsletter). Which ideas and/or phrases do you feel are important? Discuss with the class how this description relates to centers or schools where you have observed or have been employed.

Philosophy for a Children's Center

A philosophy statement for a children's center is a critical starting point. It presents the ideal toward which a staff and parents strive. It establishes a basic premise from which all activities of the center emanate. It's a returning point, a centering, in time of crisis.

Here then is a philosophy adhered to by one center. Perhaps it will facilitate you in the development or reassessment of yours.

The Children's Center is designed to create an environment of trust where people can grow emotionally, intellectually, socially, and physically. The people of the Center are those children and adults who participate in its program. Each person is a learner, each a teacher, each a valued individual.

What a young child experiences is what s/he will learn. There is that of the young child in all of us. The Center is a learning place, a place to experience oneself in relationship to others and to the environment. The Center is a place of feeling, a place where the individual and his or her feelings are accepted and valued. The Center is a place of wonder that provides the opportunity to question, to explore, to succeed, to celebrate. It is a sharing environment based on the premise that each of us has a unique gift to share—the gift of self. The Center is a pluralistic environment that has a commitment to support ethnic, economic, and social similarities and differences.

Each of us is here together to experience, to learn, to support one another in the experience that is life. Each person has a right to experience him/herself as a person of worth who participates in determining his/her own destiny as much as s/he is able without causing harm to self or others. Each person has the obligation to recognize, respect, and support the rights of others. Each person has the right to move at his or her own pace honoring his/her individual development rate. The Children's Center is designed to support the search for direction of children and adults who participate in the program and to permit each person to set the design of his/her own becoming.

C. Cut a large gingerbread figure out of paper. With crayons, illustrate your feelings toward student teaching at this point of the experience—the first days. Pin the figure to your blouse or shirt, and silently walk around the room studying others' gingerbread figures. In groups of two, discuss your interpretations of each gingerbread figure. Discuss similarities and differences between your gingerbread figure and others. Briefly discuss your discoveries with the class. (Figures can be pasted to a large chart, then posted.)

D. Interview a practicing teacher. Discuss the teacher's experiences while student teaching.

E. a. What resentments might you hold concerning the requirement that you be placed in a classroom other than your employment classroom? If unemployed, what resentments would you expect others already employed to express?

b. What are the possible problems that an employed student teacher faces when his director or other staff has not had preservice training? How might they be handled?

Discuss with classmates.

F. If you were to describe yourself using a self-designed logo or a popular song title, what would it be?

G. As you enter this student teaching experience, try to describe briefly who you are, what you do, and any individual unique teaching perspectives or life experiences you might hold. Share with a classmate.

H. Think about the perfect placement classroom for you. What would that classroom have that would aid your teaching potential? Include staff, children, and setting particulars on your listing. Share during a class discussion.

I. Make an anonymous listing of those "happenings" during your first class meeting(s) with other student teachers, instructor(s), and cooperating teachers that made you feel at home, included, welcome, relaxed and part of the group. Give the list to your instructor to share with the student teaching group.

J. Describe how you will keep all assignment deadlines, important information, telephone numbers, office hours, and other student teacher materials organized and handy.

K. Role play with a fellow student teacher how you will behave when meeting your cooperating teacher and your assigned school's staff members and how you will introduce yourself. If you've already met with your cooperating teacher, describe what you might change about that meeting if you had the power to do so.

L. Would you prefer that your state licensing law require criminal background clearance, finger printing, and emotional and/or psychological screening of individuals who will work with young children? Discuss with classmates. Report key ideas to total training group.

M. Read and discuss the following with a group of classmates. Report the group's reactions to whole class.

There was a world of difference between student teaching and daily work environments (employment site). The lab school was rich in staff role models and materials. The community (employment site) program was ill-equipped with both. At the lab school, there was [sic] almost enough wheel toys for each child to have one, while at the child care center, about a dozen children vied for the opportunity to ride one working vehicle. It was almost impossible to translate what I was learning at the university into practice at my job because the basic ingredients were so different. Discouragement and frustration were the result. (Whitebook, 1994)

REVIEW

A. Choose the statements that describe what you feel are important goals of a student teaching experience.

1. The student teacher increases the quality of the children's daily program.
2. The student teacher evaluates the cooperating teacher's style.
3. The student teacher becomes aware of vocational skill and strengths and weaknesses.
4. The student teacher develops unique capabilities.
5. The student teacher gains practical experience.
6. The three key members stimulate each other's growth through supportive, caring interactions.
7. The centers reduce costs by working with training programs.
8. The student teacher is another expert with whom parents can consult regarding their child's progress.
9. Communities benefit when early childhood teacher training produces well-trained, competent teachers.

B. Select the answer that best completes each statement

1. Student teaching practices and procedures are
   a. very similar when one compares different teacher training programs.
   b. as different as pebbles in a pile.
   c. uniform and dictated by state law.
   d. different at training institutions and agencies but always involve five key individuals.

2. The individual who is supposed to gain the most new skills through student teaching is
   a. the student teacher, but the cooperating teacher's and supervisor's new skills may surpass the student's skills.
   b. the child.
   c. the supervisor, who has learned each student teacher's unique way of performing duties.
   d. the reader of this text.
   e. impossible to determine.

3. Being observed and analyzed during student teaching means
   a. being watched and criticized.
   b. self-evaluation and evaluation of others will take place.
   c. others will try to pinpoint the areas where the student teacher needs to sharpen skills.
   d. parents, directors, and all members of the adult team will evaluate student competency.
   e. children's behavior will determine ratings of student teacher competency.

4. In most states, the record which must be completed before the student teacher works with children is the student teacher's
   a. health history.
   b. personal history.
   c. bonding agreement.
   d. insurance clearance.
   e. TB clearance.

5. Professional conduct can mean
   a. insisting that a child say please and thank you.
   b. dressing appropriately with attention to personal hygiene.
   c. speaking candidly to a parent about the limitations of a cooperating teacher's method.
   d. none of these.

REFERENCES

Carter, M., & Curtis, D. (1994). *Training teachers: A harvest of theory and practice.* St. Paul: Redleaf Press.

Fyfe, B. (1994). Assessing experiential learning for college credit. In J. Johnson & J. McCracken (Eds.), *The Early Childhood Career Lattice: Perspectives on Professional Development.* Washington, DC: National Association for the Education of Young Children.

National Association for the Education of Young Children. (1984). *Guidelines for preparation of early childhood professionals: Associate, baccalaureate, and advanced levels.* Washington, DC: Author.

Jones, E. (1986). *Teaching adults.* Washington, DC: National Association for the Education of Young Children.

Jones, E. (1994). Constructing professional knowledge by telling our stories. In *The early childhood career lattice: Perspectives on professional development.* J. Johnson and J. McCracken (Eds.) Washington, DC: National Association for the Education of Young Children.

Katz, L., & Ward, E. (1978). *Ethical behavior in early childhood education.* Washington, DC: National Association for the Education of Young Children.

Perrodin, A. F. (1966). *The student teachers' reader.* Chicago: Rand McNally and Co.

Rasinski, T. V. (1989). Reading and the empowerment of parents. *The Reading Teacher, 43*(3), 226–231.

Shaplin, J. (1965) Practice in teaching. In *Breakthrough to better teaching. Harvard Educational Review.* Montpelier, VT: Capitol City Press.

Whitebook, M. (1994). At the core: Advocacy to challenge the status quo. In J. Johnson & J. McCracken (Eds.), *The early childhood career lattice: Perspectives on professional development.* Washington, DC: National Association for the Education of Young Children.

Wood, C. (1994). Responsive teaching: Creating partnerships for systemic change. *Young Children, 50*(1), 21–28.

RESOURCES

National Association for the Education of Young Children. (1985). *Guidelines for early childhood programs in associate degree granting institutions.* Washington, DC: Author.

National Association for the Education of Young Children. (1986). *Guidelines for early childhood programs in 4- and 5-year baccalaureate and advanced degree granting institutions.* Washington, DC: Author.

2

Placement—First Days on the Teaching Team

After studying this chapter, the student will be able to:

- Describe preplacement activities and considerations.
- Identify pertinent information to be obtained on a student teacher's first day.
- Pinpoint three activities a student teacher can use as an introduction, to learn the children's names, or develop rapport with the children.
- Identify three valuable skills for staff meetings.

On my first day of student teaching I was scared and nervous . . . shaking in my boots. Not knowing where things were made me feel unsure. It was a good thing that I had a compassionate cooperating teacher; she put me at ease and directed me so I could begin to find my own way.

Felicia Martinez

I'm employed at the school where I did part-time student teaching. I was so glad when my college supervisor insisted I be assigned to another school. I was able to see different methods.

Charlotte Zinger

I worried a lot during student teaching about children becoming attached to me, more friendly and affectionate than I observed they were with the cooperating teacher. My cooperating teacher and I had no problem with this after I bravely asked about it. Children are able to form bonds in different ways with different teaching personalities.

Connie Mock

● PREPARING FOR YOUR FIRST DAYS

Before your first day of student teaching, you have been given your cooperating teacher's name and the school's address, and you may have attended orientation meetings for student teaching at your placement site. Your first working day is near. You have either an "on campus" or "off campus" child center or school assignment.

A stroll through the neighborhood where the children live will help you discover something about them. Observe the community, its businesses, its recreation, its uniqueness. A close look will tell you many things. What type of transportation brings the child to school? Where do the parents work? Try to think about family life in this community. Notice the people and the types of neighborhood activities. As Riley and Robinson (1980) point out:

> Places, people, and the processes of a community can be thought of as a significant part of the environments that support learning. (p. 9)

Soon you will be trying to understand the children from this neighborhood. Your visit will serve as an initial frame of reference. Do not overlook the opportunity to observe this community's resources for planning child activities. Perhaps a construction site is an interesting possibility for a field trip or an orchard or park holds treasures to be discovered.

Within an on-campus laboratory school placement, you may have previously participated in the children's program and perhaps completed observation assignments. The center and its staff and children may be familiar. You will now assume the role of student teacher. Take a new look at the campus and the resources of the campus community.

If you have been told to meet with the director or principal of the school, call to make an appointment. Plan to have the meeting at least 15 minutes before you are scheduled to be in the classroom. Ask about available staff parking. Remember to avoid parent parking spots or drop-off areas.

It is time to dust off the resource idea files and books you have collected during your training since you may be using them to plan activities. Choose a short activity to offer on your first day, even if it has not been assigned. Brush up on fingerplays or short songs to be used as "fill-ins" or transitions. If they are not memorized, put them on cards that slip into a pocket. It's important for you to be prepared to step in with an activity if you are asked to do so.

Some good ideas for first-day activities that have worked well for other student teachers are as follows:

- A nametag-making activity
- A puppet who tells a short story about his or her name, introduces the student teacher, and wants to know the children's names
- A favorite book or tape recording to discuss
- A simple food preparation activity
- An art or craft activity that uses children's names
- A collage or chart that shows interesting things about a student teacher's life
- A collection of photographs that are important to the student teacher
- A game made by the student teacher that involves children's names and places in their community
- A bean bag activity that uses children's names
- A flannelboard story
- A new song or movement activity
- A "my favorite" chart on which the student teacher shows three favorite objects and then writes the children's favorite things next to their names.
- A storytelling experience, figure 2-1
- An activity involving a particular student teacher skill, e.g. musical instrument, dance, carpentry
- A tape recording of school or neighborhood sounds to guess and discuss

Last-minute Preparations

Activities that can be easily carried and quickly set up work best. Get the necessary materials together the night before your class. If you received a set of classroom rules and a schedule of routines and planned activities, study it beforehand.

Think about clothing. Make sure it will be comfortable and appropriate. A smock, shirt, or apron with pocket will hold a small notebook, pen, tissues, and other small necessities. You should wear shoes that will protect your toes and help keep your balance and speed on the playground.

● MEETING WITH THE ADMINISTRATOR

It is customary to meet with the administrator before going to the classroom. At that time, the

Figure 2-1 A student teacher with a planned storytelling aid.

student teacher's records will be added to the personnel file. The file usually includes a TB clearance, a physical examination form, an emergency form, a personal background form, cooperating teacher guidelines (hints), and rating sheets from the supervisor.

Some topics you might discuss are the procedures for storing your coat and personal items, sign-in and sign-out requirements, and miscellaneous details. You might be introduced to the secretarial staff begore you are directed to your classroom. Gordon-Nourok (1979) mentions the following as possible subjects for this first meeting with the administrator.

- The general plan of classes under the administrator's domain
- The administrator's philosophy about what a school should be and how it should be run
- Staff members and their special skills
- The children attending the school
- The degree of parent participation
- The center's or school's community involvement
- The administrator's expectations of a student teacher

Meyer (1981) suggests each student teacher should be introduced to the total staff and become familiar with all activities of the school where assigned. Regulations, handbooks, school policies, teaching responsibilities, and privileges need to be spelled out and followed by a tour of the facility. If a calendar or schedule of school happenings and events is available, it will contain valuable information for the student teacher.

Student teachers usually make a good impression with an administrator (and staff) when they look a person directly in the eyes, speak clearly with confidence, and smile.

● YOUR CLASSROOM

There probably will be time for a smile and a few quick words with your cooperating teacher. Your introduction to the children can wait until a planned group time. Introduce yourself briefly to other classroom adults when you are in close proximity. Your cooperating teacher may ask that you observe instead of participate. Otherwise, actively participate in supervising and interacting with the children. Pitch in with any tasks that need to be done.

Ask questions only when necessary; jot down others on a pad of paper, which you should carry with you. Use your judgment as to where you are needed most. Do not worry about assuming too much responsibility; your cooperating teacher will let you know if you are overstepping your duties. New student teachers tend to hold back and wait to be directed. Put yourself in the teacher's place. Where would the teacher direct you to supervise or assist children when the teacher is busy with other work? Periodically scan the room to determine whether you are needed elsewhere.

Supplies

Familiarize yourself with storage areas to minimize the need to ask questions about the location of equipment and supplies. Check with your cooperating teacher when he is not involved with children or parents. Make your inspection when you are free from room supervision. Become familiar with yard storage also. During team meetings, you should inquire about your use of supplies for planned activities.

Child Records

Some early childhood centers will allow student teachers access to child and family records; others will not. Knowing as much as possible about each child increases the quality of your interaction. Remember that confidentiality should be maintained at all times if permission to review the records is granted. During this review, you may wish to make note of any allergies, specific interests, and special needs of each child. For example:

Roberto—eats no milk, cheese, or dairy products

Clorinda—needs pink nap blanket

Jake—likes horses

Pierre—occasionally gets leg cramps

Lei Thien—uses toothbrush with own special paste

Each child's file may contain the following:

- Emergency information
- Health history and record
- Physical examination form
- Application form and family or child history
- Attendance data
- Anecdotal records, specimen records, figure 2-2; timed observation records, assessments; and conference notes

Emergency Procedures

Acquaint yourself with the location and use of first aid supplies. For emergencies such as fire, earthquake, and storms, become familiar with evacuation plans showing exit routes. Most states require that these plans be posted. Enforce all health and safety rules. If you have any questions regarding health and safety, be sure to note them so they can be discussed.

Opening

Be aware of how children and parents are greeted upon arrival. What activities or choices are available for child exploration? A keen observer will notice which children separate and make the transition from parent to center with ease, and which

Child Observed   *Melissa*
Child's Age   *4 years*
Setting   *Preschool classroom*
Time   *9:20 to 9:30*
Activity   *Free play*

Objective Behavioral Description	Interpretations
9:20–9:22 Melissa arrives about 35 minutes late; puts her coat in her cubby. She stands in the doorway of main classroom and looks around; remains motionless for ½ minute, moving only her eyes as she glances briefly at other children and their activities.	Melissa seems shy, almost withdrawn. From moment of arrival, she seemed reluctant to enter into things. May be because she didn't want to come in first place.
9:22–9:24 M. Finally walks toward reading area on far side of room from cubbies. Moves slowly at first, scraping the toe of her right foot at each step, for about 5 feet. She passes by the puzzle table where 2 children are seated; no communication exchanged. She now walks more briskly to a table with some books lying on it. Tina, Ralph, and Morton are seated at the table; Ralph and Morton are sharing a book, Tina is watching them "read." Melissa says nothing to the three children as she sits down.	Melissa still seems uncertain; even her motor behaviors seem restricted; she walks slowly, shuffling, as though unsure of herself and of her relationship with the other children or her environment. Seems to have trouble deciding what to do. Not at all communicative; makes no overtures to any of the children who were "available" for such.
9:24–9:29 Ralph and Morton don't look up or acknowledge Melissa in any way. Tina says, "Hi, Melissa, wanna read a book with me?" M. cocks her head to one side and says softly, "I don't know how to read." T. replies "We can look at the pictures." M. looks over toward the big block area and without looking at T., says "OK." Tina smiles broadly and goes to a shelf containing a number of books. M. picks up one of the books and flips slowly through the pages. T. returns with a book and says "I like this one, let's look at this one." M. merely nods; T. sits down close to M., but M. moves slightly, keeping a distance of about 6–8 inches between her and T.	Tina is outgoing and friendly as Melissa approaches; M. is still uncommunicative; still seems shy and uncertain; speaks softly as though afraid of being heard. Tina persists in spite of M.'s lack of enthusiasm. M. also seems distractable or inattentive. She shies away from T.'s efforts to get close physically. Tina moves at a quick pace—much more energetic than M.
9:29–9:30 Ralph looks up and says "Hey, you two, wha'cha doin?" T. tilts her head upward, thrusts out her chin slightly and says "Never mind, we're busy." M. says nothing, but gets up from the table and walks slowly toward big block area. Morton still reads.	Tina is much more outgoing and sure of herself than M. T. didn't interact too much w/Ralph and Morton; may have felt left out of their activity. T. definitely seemed pleased to see M.; displayed no unfavorable response to M.'s "unsocial" behavior. T.'s response to Ralph quite assertive, but in a friendly way; almost like she claimed Melissa as her playmate, maybe in retaliation for the two boys ignoring her earlier. M. still seems uninterested, even uncertain of what to do.

Figure 2-2 Specimen record. (Bentzen, 1993)

classroom adults contribute to the classroom's atmosphere or tone.

Dismissal Procedures

Be aware that each center or school has a policy regarding adults who can remove a child from the classroom at a session's close or any other time. You should not release children to arriving adults. This is your cooperating teacher's responsibility. Make sure adults coming to pick up children are directed to talk with the child's teacher before exiting.

Seeing Where You Are Needed

Cooperating teachers overwhelmingly state they appreciate student teachers who are watchful and notice where they are most needed. This is difficult for new student teachers unless they consciously endeavor to know "the lay of the land." Figure 2-3 attempts to help you focus on aspects of the classroom program, its enrolled children, procedures, and interactions.

Observing at Your Placement Site

During your first days and weeks you will learn a lot about your placement school. Answering the questions in figure 2-3 will make you aware of the factors or features that make your placement unique. Discuss any concerns with your college supervisor. Your supervisor may advise you to consult with your cooperating teacher or urge you to keep your conclusions and judgments to yourself.

Pitfalls

During the first days of work, it is not unusual for the student teacher to acquire some bad habits unconsciously . It helps to be aware of these pitfalls in advance.

During class time, avoid having extended social conversations or small talk with other adults, and seeking the company of other adults as a source of support. Use your breaks for this purpose if necessary.

Refrain from talking about children in their presence. Avoid the tendency to label a child. Keep your judgments and/or evaluations to yourself, and save questions for staff meetings.

Introductions

Group time is introduction time. Children are quiet and attentive. Your cooperating teacher may ask you to introduce yourself. You might start by saying, "My name is Miss Smith. I'm a teacher, and I'm going to be here every day until December." Your face and body language should express acceptance and warmth. Alternatively, you might do a short "hello" activity that emphasizes your name.

—says "hello" with a finger . . .
—says "hello" with a hand . . . (Julius, 1978)

Facilities
  Where are materials and supplies stored?
  Are storage areas organized?
  Where are exits? How do windows open, lights work, temperature controls operate?
  How do doors open?
  What is the classroom layout? Traffic patterns?
  What school area or rooms have specific functions? House particular staff?
  What is the play yard's appearance, equipment, built-ins?
  Where are the safety controls, fire extinguisher, alarm, etc.?
  Is any safety hazard apparent?
  Are there special building features for individuals with physical handicapping conditions?

Children
  What individual physical characteristics are apparent?
  What is the multicultural composition of the group?
  What activities are popular?
  Can all children in room be viewed from one spot in the room?
  Do all children seem to lose themselves in play?
  What kinds of play exist? Solitary? Cooperative? Other?
  What languages are spoken?
  Does any child seem uncomfortable with adults?
  What seems to be the group's general interest, general behavior?
  Are there any children who need an abundance of teacher attention?
  Are there any children with special needs?

Teaching Behaviors and Interactions
  Are children "with" teachers?
  How is guidance of child behavior undertaken?
  Are all children supervised?
  What style of teaching seems apparent?
  Are feelings of warmth and acceptance of individuality shown?
  If you were a child in this room, how might you feel?
  Do teachers show enthusiasm?

Program
  Does an atmosphere exist where children and teachers share decision making and show respect for individual differences?
  Are children exploring with teachers more often than being directed by them?
  What are the planned activities?
  Is there small group or large group instruction?
  Is it developmentally appropriate program?
  How do activities begin and end?
  Is program based on child interest?
  Does lots of dialogue exist among children? Among children and adults?
  Are the children "tuned in" or "out"?
  How are children moved from one activity to the next?

Overall First Impressions
  What immediate questions would you like answered about the classroom?
  What emotions have occurred as you observed?
  What were your first impressions of the classroom?

Figure 2-3 Knowing your classroom.

Continue the activity using your elbow, arm, and other body parts, and finish by using your whole body to say hello. Then invite the children to repeat the entire activity with you.

If you have prepared an activity, briefly describe and check with the cooperating teacher regarding the best time to offer it.

● BEGINNING DAYS

Your first few working days are going to be both exciting and exhausting. Many factors contribute to the situation. The Kraft and Casey (1967) comments that follow, though dated, are still relevant today!

The induction of the student into actual teaching is a delicate and critical process. Unfortunately, no procedure exists that would guarantee universal success because many uncontrollable factors must be considered. The attitude of the student, the classroom climate, the inclination of the cooperating teacher, and the time of year are but a few of the many factors.

Kraft and Casey list the following four guidelines for beginning days:

1. The student teacher should be gradually inducted into the responsibilities of actual teaching.
2. The plan of inducting the student teacher will be from the easy to the difficult, the simple to complex, from observation to participation, and to long-term teaching.

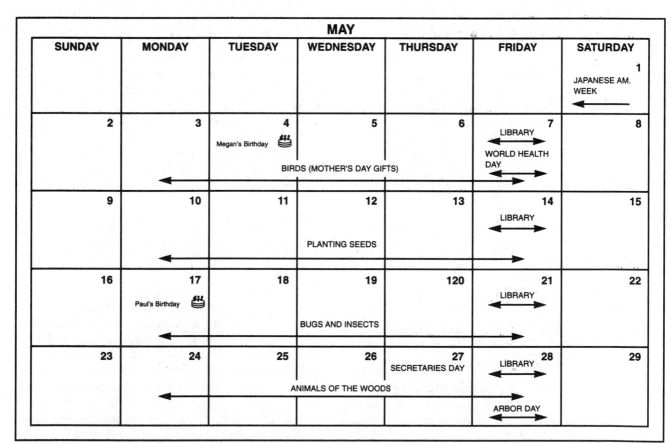

Figure 2-4 Sample of a class calendar (preschool level).

Student Teacher _____	Week _____

Cooperating Teacher _____   Conference Time with Cooperating Teacher _____

STUDENT TEACHER RESPONSIBILITIES

Time	Monday	Tuesday	Wednesday	Thursday	Friday

Figure 2-5 Sample of a student teacher weekly activity sheet.

3. The student teacher is to be thought of as a distinct personality, capable of growth, sensitive to success and failure, and deserving of help and consideration.

4. The student-teaching activities should be conducted in as natural and typical a situation as possible. (Kraft & Casey, 1967)

After-Session Conferencing

At team meetings, after important issues are discussed, your cooperating teacher and other staff adults will be interested in the questions and impressions you have developed after the first sessions. Be prepared to rely on your notes or journal. They are useful in refreshing your memory. Wasserman (1992) refers to these team conferences as debriefings when participants compare ideas, hypothesize, and make assumptions calling for the cognitive processing of information.

This meeting is also an appropriate time to clarify your cooperating teacher's expectations during your next few work days. If a class calendar, figure 2-4, is available, it will aid your activity planning. Most schools have their own system of planning activities. You may be asked to schedule your own activities at least one week in advance on a written plan.

Ask for suggestions on the theme of your next week's activities. The cooperating teacher may want you to stay within the planned subject areas or may give you a wide choice. Copies of a student teacher weekly activity sheet, figure 2-5, can be made and given weekly to the cooperating teacher. Its development may be a joint effort. Ask about the best time to consult with your cooperating teacher.

BECOMING A TEAM MEMBER

You will become aware of each staff member's function and contribution to the operation of your assigned classroom. Nonteaching staff support educational efforts and realization of the center's goals, figure 2-6.

You are now a member of an important team of people. In addition to your own growth and development, one of your major goals as a team member is to add to the quality of young children's experiences, figure 2-7. This involves teamwork. Teamwork takes understanding, dedication, and skill. Your status and acceptance as a member of the team will be gained through your own efforts.

For purposes of this field of study, teams are those people employed or connected with the daily operation of an early childhood center who work to achieve the goals of that center. They include paid and volunteer staff and parents. Understanding the duties and responsibilities of each team member will help you function in your role.

● GOALS OF THE TEAM AND PROGRAM

Knowing the goals of instruction helps you understand how your work contributes to the realization of the center's or school's goals. If a copy is available, you should read and review the center's or school's program handbook, which usually lists the program philosophy and goals. In your activity planning and preparation, you will have a chance to offer the children growth experiences, one of the prime goals of the center or school. Team meetings will help you realize how the planned activities relate to the center's or school's goals. The feeling of team spirit is enhanced when your efforts reinforce or strengthen the efforts of other members.

Thomson, Holmberg, and Baer (1978) describe team discussion-evaluation meetings:

> In most teacher-training programs, great importance is attached to the practicum's end-of-day conferences. These conferences generally include how the day went, how particular children behaved, and what plans should be made for the next day. It is also a time for the master teacher to evaluate the student teacher's activities and recommend improvement.

When feedback is given consistently, constructively, and with meaningful interpretation, it often does change and influence a student teacher's performance.

Team Meetings

Team meetings often include only the staff members associated with child instruction. Since staff meetings are new to student teachers, they are full of learning opportunities. Attend staff meetings if your student teaching schedule permits. The extra time involved will be well spent. To make these meetings as successful as possible, and to make them work for you, there are several things you can do before, during, and after the meeting.

Figure 2-7 Adding to the quality of a child's experience is one of your major goals as a student teacher.

Do the following staff members exist at your placement center?

	Yes	No	Names
1. Clerical staff	____	____	_____
2. Food service personnel	____	____	_____
3. Maintenance staff	____	____	_____
4. Bus drivers	____	____	_____
5. Community liaisons	____	____	_____
6. Heath or nutrition staff	____	____	_____
7. Consultants or specialists	____	____	_____
8. Classroom aides	____	____	_____
9. Volunteers	____	____	_____
10. Others?	____	____	_____
In what capacity?			_____

Figure 2-6 Checklist of nonteaching support staff.

Before

- Mark the time, date, and place of the meeting on your calendar.
- Clarify your role. Are you a guest, an observer, or an active participant?
- Get a copy of the meeting agenda and study it. Jot down notes to yourself.
- Make sure you understand the purpose of the meeting.
- Bring your notes and notebook.
- Review your notes from the last meeting you attended.
- Arrive on time.
- Prepare to stay for the entire meeting.

During

- Listen attentively.
- Take notes, particularly when the discussion concerns student teachers.
- Participate and contribute when appropriate.
- Help staff members reach their objectives.
- Don't ask redundant questions—meetings are long enough as it is!
- Watch interactions between individuals.
- Look for preferences in teaching tasks expressed by others.
- Stay until end of meeting.

The more understanding you possess concerning individuals and group dynamics the better prepared you will be to function as an effective team member. As you become "one of them" it's highly likely you will modify and change your initial thoughts and feelings.

After

- Mark the date of the next meeting.
- Complete your responsibilities.
- Prepare to report back at next meeting.

Ask yourself the following questions:

- Do common bonds exist?
- Was satisfaction of individual needs apparent?
- Is there shared responsibility in achieving group goals?
- Was group problem solving working?
- Are members open and trusting?
- Are individual roles clear?
- Did you notice cooperation and real ideas?
- Do members know each others' strengths?
- Was the meeting dominated by one or a few?

Staff Behaviors

A number of behaviors may be exhibited during staff interactions. Some of these can be evaluated as positive team behaviors because they move a team toward the completion of tasks and handling of responsibilities. The following is a summary of supportive and positive staff behaviors.

- Giving or seeking information; asking for or providing factual or substantiated data
- Contributing new ideas, solutions, or alternatives
- Seeking or offering opinions to solve the task or problem
- "Piggybacking," elaborating, or stretching another's idea or suggestion; combining ideas
- Coordinating activities
- Emphasizing or reminding the group of the task at hand
- Evaluating by using professional standards
- Motivating staff to reach decisions
- Bringing meeting to a close and reviewing goals; making sure everyone understands the expected outcome
- Recording group ideas and progress

During staff meetings, individual staff members sometimes exhibit attitudes and sensitivities that soothe and mediate opposing points of view. Some examples follow:

- Encouraging, praising, respecting, and accepting diverse ideas or viewpoints

- Reconciling disagreements and offering "a light touch" of humor to help relieve tension
- Compromising
- Establishing open lines of communication
- Drawing input from silent members
- Monitoring dominance of discussion

Some staff behaviors can be viewed as inhibitors of team process. For a list of such behaviors, see figure 2-8.

Collaboration

At your employment you may feel isolated and long for conversations with other professional care givers. You may look back and fondly remember student teaching as a collaborative teaching time. Regular discussions with peers help teachers sustain their self-reflection and learn the value of different approaches (Carter & Curtis, 1994). Tight budgets at some programs decrease staff interaction and allow minimal sharing between staff members. Staff consultation can unfortunately be viewed as a luxury item cutting into profits or other priorities.

Carter (1995) describes a strategy that builds a "community culture" among teachers in any partic-

ular child care facility. The elements of this community culture are shared values and resources, traditions, and a sense of collective history developed by living together daily, caring for one another, sharing goals, and mediating conflicts. Not seen as static in nature, community culture is viewed as changing and transforming.

Staff meetings are crucial to developing this type of team culture and begin to happen when sharing, reflection, and collaboration are present and when individual teaching styles are accepted and treasured. Usually ground rules concerning staff meeting participation and decision making have been ironed out through group discussion and agreement. Trying to build a school's community culture challenges staffs to honor individual and ethnic diversity. Fortunate indeed is a student teacher who is assigned to a facility where individuality is welcomed as a new part of a dedicated-to-excellence program.

● WORKING RELATIONSHIPS

Your relationship with your college supervisor ideally will become, as Hilliard (1974) proposes, "close, continuing, prolonged contact . . . under conditions that maximize feedback." You'll need feedback relevant both to children's learning and development and to how your own behavior and interactions promote or impede that learning and development.

Your relationship with other staff members depends on your communication and respect for the contributions of each staff and team member, figure 2-9. Being friendly and taking the initiative in meeting each person will give you a real sense of belonging. You have much in common and often will be combining efforts. Members of other staff may often be able to answer your questions, as well as provide valuable insight.

Find out whether you can add agenda items at staff meetings. Staff meetings offer wonderful training opportunities. Each group of people is unique. The skills and talents staff members possess in group communication can be observed. Things to ask include:

- aggression
- putting others down
- sarcastic humor
- crediting oneself with ideas of others
- being negative
- stubbornness
- blocking progress
- being irrelevant
- side conversations
- never contributing
- seeking recognition
- not attending
- interrupting
- monopolizing conversation
- constantly telling fears, troubles, insecurities
- pleading for special interests
- a "sky-is-falling" stance
- exhibiting false anger or emotion

These characteristics bog down teamwork and often create strained relationships that destroy staff spirit.

Figure 2-8 List of inhibiting behaviors during staff meetings.

Figure 2-9 Working together on a joint project strengthens a relationship.

• Does everyone have input into decisions that affect them?
• Is it all right to disagree?
• Can individual like or dislike of team tasks be expressed?
• Does delegating take place?
• Is staff growth important?
• Is group problem solving working?
• How is consensus reached?
• Can responsibilities change from person to person?

Gutwein (1988) believes communication is an active people process rather than a language process. Any two people perceive any given situation from a different frame of reference. Adult conflict and differences exist in most centers. Staff members interested in resolution need to be willing to discuss different perceptions. Conflict usually is tied to individual philosophies that can change as people are exposed to life experiences. Gutwein notes that conflict does not have to dissolve friendships when people view mat-

ters as mutual problems with solutions. She believes giving and receiving criticism is a trait few people possess, regardless of their educational level. She suggests the following framework in conflict situations:

1. Define the problem or conflict.
2. State the problem or conflict.
3. Check individual interpretations and perceptions with the facts.
4. Brainstorm possible solutions until agreement has been reached.

Note: When "defining and stating" as well as brainstorming takes place, a good tactic is to write items on a large chalk board or chart paper.

Chapters 9 and 10 are devoted to interpersonal communication skill development, and problem-solving techniques.

As a student teacher, you may have a clearer picture of the student teacher/cooperating teacher relationship than you do of the relationships among the assistant teacher, aide, parent, and student teacher. Usually student teachers, aides, and volunteers work under the cooperating teacher, who makes the ultimate decisions regarding the workings of the classroom. Moving from assistant to co-teacher, a student teacher is the closest to the status of assistant or volunteer and assumes greater responsibility as time passes. Because of the changing role and increasing responsibilities, clear communication is a necessity.

Observing Children

From the first day, you will start to observe the unique characteristics of enrolled children. You will constantly monitor behaviors and conjecture causes for behaviors and underlying needs. Unconsciously or consciously you will begin to sort children into loose groupings that change daily in an almost unlimited number of ways. More noticeable characteristics will be the first to be recognized and, as you gain additional experience, subtle differences and similarities.

You will experience differing emotions with each child as you observe and interact. Many of the children will become memorable as children in your first class, as ones who taught you something about all children, or something about yourself.

Your fresh observational perspective offers cooperating teachers the luxury of hearing another teacher's conjectures. Bentzen (1993) believes the interpretations and explanations of child behaviors that teachers make hold an inherent danger:

> Interpretation or explanation, then, involves attempts to identify the cause of some behavior or event; to assign motives to an individual; to determine the objectives of a behavior: in short, to provide additional information that might make your objective descriptions more meaningful than they would otherwise be.

> This third aspect of observation is possibly the most dangerous part of the observation process, for it is at this point that you apply your values and attitudes to the child's behavior, characteristics, and personality. Evaluation refers to placing a value on, or judging worth of, something. Unfortunately, it is all too easy to make hasty judgments or to form stereotypes about someone.

Parent Contacts

Upon your first meeting with parents, they may wonder who you are or immediately accept you as another classroom adult worker. Read their faces and introduce yourself if they seem interested. Be friendly and open rather than talkative. Mention your student teacher status and your training program. Remember: In this meeting, as in all others, you are representing the early childhood teaching profession.

Every classroom has a "feeling tone," that is, it projects a certain atmosphere that creates feelings and perceptions in the minds and hearts of those who enter. Your classroom, no doubt, was designed and furnished with children in mind but possibly includes a parent corner or an area making parents also feel at home or welcome.

Parents may see you as an expert and ask advice. You should refer these parents to your cooperating teacher.

In today's busy world some parents will looked rushed and anxious to get their child out the door.

Others you observe will take time to touch base with their child and teachers before leaving. All parents will appreciate your knowing the location of their child's belongings and what needs to be taken home, and also your aid in promoting the child's transition back into parental care. Activities planned for parent pick-up times should allow children to easily stop and finish.

Portfolio Development (Preschool Level)

You may be required to put together a representative collection of your training accomplishments. The portfolio represents who you are, what skills and competencies you possess, and what experiences have been part of your training. Because CDA (Child Development Associate) training, a national training program, includes portfolio development, the collection of such materials has become increasingly required. Students usually find this collection valuable in future job interviews.

Student Portfolios

Your portfolio is a record of your growth and accomplishments in student teaching. It is a visual display of teaching competencies, projects, planned activities, and student-child interactions. It may include "befores" and "afters" or specialized student talents and abilities. It can include a vast number of diverse visual, audio, and written materials, including:

- Supervisory comments
- Rating sheets and evaluations
- Letters of recommendation
- Projects
- Examples of child work
- Class papers
- Photographs
- Lesson plans
- Activities offered and units created
- Discovery center creations
- Classroom schedules
- Examples of specializations
- Certificates, awards, and other commendations

- Parent letters or comments
- Designed room arrangements
- Videotapes
- Classroom instructional materials created
- Any other items that display teaching ability or competency

Supervisors can cite examples of employed graduates who secured employment by letting a prospective employer review the graduate's portfolio.

The formatting of portfolios differs from one institution to another, but written materials usually include articulation of learning outcomes, reflections or related experience, and documentation for each area of learning to be assessed.

SUMMARY

Before your first day of student teaching, it is a good idea to get an understanding of the children's environment by acquainting yourself with the school's neighborhood and community. Also, you may wish to plan an activity to introduce yourself on the first day.

Active classroom interaction, as well as asking questions, should typify your first days. You can obtain necessary information concerning your work from the cooperating teacher when both you and the cooperating teacher have no supervision responsibilities. If you feel you require additional background information on the children, find out whether their records can be made available to you.

It is helpful to become acquainted with other staff members. They can offer answers and insight that can aid your adjustment to the center. In time, you will develop smooth working relationships and earn team status and acceptance. This type of relationship will work well when it is time for you to participate in team meetings. Meetings are important vehicles for learning, and they will be a part of your future employment. You will be able to understand how each staff or team member contributes to the goals of a particular child center through observation, interaction, and a review of job descriptions.

SUGGESTED ACTIVITIES

A. Invite the director of your placement center to discuss particulars of past experiences with student teachers.

B. Make an appointment with your cooperating teacher to develop a calendar of student teaching activities. Pinpoint tentative dates and times for your part of the program.

C. In small groups discuss the positive and negative aspects of being able to review children's records.

D. Complete the requests in figure 2-10 and prepare a daily teaching responsibilities list similar to figure 2-11.

E. Where are the following?

Director's or principal's office _____

Health facilities _____

Food service area _____

Children's eating area _____

Children's sleeping area _____

Children's bathrooms _____

Storage for your belongings _____

Teachers' restrooms _____

Teachers' rest area or lounge _____

Fire alarm _____

Fire extinguisher _____

Teachers' lunchroom or eating area _____

---

1. Make a rough map of your classroom and yard.
2. Briefly describe the group. Identify children about whom you would like additional information.
3. List names of staff members.
4. Describe your relationship with your cooperating teacher during your first days.
5. Describe available materials and equipment. Do you feel they are adequate and satisfactory in all aspects?
6. What are some memorable experiences of your first days?

Figure 2-10 Placement observation form.

Three-year-olds—Morning program

8:00–8:30   Check to see that room is in order and materials are on proper shelves. Check snack supplies. Check day's curriculum. Know what materials are needed.

8:30–8:45   **Arrival of Children**
- Greet each child and parent.
- Help children locate their lockers.
- Help children with nametags.
- Help children initiate an activity.

8:30–9:20   **Free-play Time Inside**—Art, block play, dramatic play, manipulative materials, science, math, housekeeping area, language arts.
- Supervise assigned area. Proceed to another area if there is no child in your area.
- Interact with children if you can. Be careful not to interfere in their play.
- Encourage children to clean up after they finish playing with materials.
- Manipulative materials, including playdough and scissors, must stay on the table.
- Be on the child's level. Sit on the floor, on a chair, or kneel.
- Children wear smocks when using paint or chalk. Print children's names on their art work in upper left corner.
- Give five-minute warning before clean-up time.

9:20–9:30   **Transition Time**—Clean up, wash hands, use bathrooms. Sing a clean-up song. Help with clean-up. Guide children to bathroom before coming to group. All children should use the bathroom to wash hands and be encouraged to use the toilet.
- Place soiled clothes/underpants in plastic baggies, and place them in children's cubbies.
- Children flush the toilet.
- Let them wash hands, using soap.
- Bathroom accidents should be treated matter-of-factly.
- Use word "toilet."
- Help children with their clothes but remember to encourage self-help skills.

9:30–9:45   **Large Group**—Assist restless children. Leave to set up snack if it is your responsibility. Put cups and napkins around table. Make sure there are sufficient chairs and snack places.
- Teacher of the week leads group time.
- Other teachers sit behind children, especially those that are restless.

- Show enthusiasm in participating with the activities.

9:45–10:00   **Snack**
- There should be one teacher at each table.
- Engage in conversation.
- Encourage self-help skills. Provide assistance if needed.
- Encourage children to taste food.
- Demonstrate good manners such as saying please and thank you.
- Help children observe table manners.
- Children should throw napkins in trash can.
- If spills occur, offer a sponge. Help only if necessary.
- Quickly sponge down tables.

10:00–10:45   **Outside Play**—Check children and cubbies to make sure children are wearing outside clothing if the weather is cold. If a child does not have sufficient clothing, check the school supply of extra clothing.

                 Outside Activities—Tricycles, sand toys, climbing equipment, balls, etc.
- Supervise all areas. Spread out. No two teachers should be in one spot unless all children are there.
- Help children share toys, take care of the equipment.
- Always be alert to the physical safety of the child.
- When necessary, remind them that sand is to be kept in the sandbox.
- Water faucet is operated only by adults or when there is adult supervision.
- Children may remove shoes during warm weather only.
- If raining, children must stay under the shelter.
- Teachers should refrain from having long conversations with each other. Attention should be on the children all the time.
- Bring tissue outside to wipe noses if needed.
- Give five-minute warning to clean up and go inside.
- Children must help return toys to the storage room.

10:45–11:00   **Clean up, Use Bathroom, Prepare for Small Group**
- Children go to assigned small groups.
- Each child sits on a carpet square.
- Extra teachers should sit behind children to quiet them when needed.

Figure 2-11 Guide to daily teaching responsibilities.

11:00–11:20	**Small Group**—Transitional activities include flannelboard stories, discussion with visual aids, games, filmstrip if applicable, songs, and finger-plays. Teacher puts children's rest mats out.	11:30	**Departure** • Get children's art work to take home and put in their cubbies. • Help children with coats, shoes, etc. • See children off.
11:20–11:30	**Rest Time** • Children lie on mats. • Quiet music is played. • Children do not have to be perfectly still as long as they do not bother other children. Whisper to restless children and tell them it is a quiet time. • Teacher tells the children to get up and turns on lights. Children fold blankets, rugs, or mats and put them in their cubbies.	11:30–12:00	**End of Morning Session**—Help with clean-up. Double-check that all areas are clean and all materials are in their correct places. Share any observations with teachers, and solicit their observations and feelings during your team meeting.

NOTE: This daily guide is typical of guides used in a morning prekindergarten laboratory school placement for student teachers. A similar guide can be developed for any placement site by a student teacher once room schedules are known.

Figure 2-11 (continued).

Staff telephone _____

   Available to you? _____

Teachers' workroom or preparation area _____

Cot storage _____

Maintenance equipment storage _____

Teachers' protective clothing or gloves _____

Water for adults _____

Washer and dryer _____

Conference room _____

Staff parking area _____

Other important areas _____

_____

F. Discuss the following:

  1. "The student teacher has the same responsibilities for attendance and punctuality as a regularly employed teacher."

  2. "The student teacher is obligated to notify the administrator of cooperating school immediately or, if possible, well in advance of his or her scheduled appearance in school" (Meyer, 1981).

G. Obtain a copy of your placement school's disaster plan. Bring to class to discuss.

H. Keep a separate folder to contain a summary of all meeting discussions that mention you as a student teacher and any aspect of your work.

I. In groups of four or five, develop a chart that pinpoints behaviors leading to smooth relationships between team members. Do the same for those behaviors that lead to awkward relationships.

J. In groups of five or six, take turns role playing the following situations. The rest of the class can serve as an audience to determine each role. Students can choose their roles from the list in figure 2-12.

Situation A: Part of the staff wants to give up the staff room and turn it into a dance studio for the children. Others see such renovation as a waste of valuable space.

Situation B: Some staff members wish to try fund raising to increase their salaries. Other staff members are not interested and think it is a poor idea.

Situation C: The janitor is doing a terrible job maintaining the building even though many requests have been made to improve conditions. The janitor happens to be the preschool owner's son. The owner never attends team meetings. The staff members are baffled as to what step to take next.

Constant shoulder crying	Seeking information	Adding irrelevant ideas
Encouraging and praising	Offering new suggestions or solutions	Using sarcastic humor
Serving as an audience for ideas	Asking for opinions	Mediating opposing positions
Recording	Evaluating teamwork	Stubborn and resistant
Compromising	Calling on team to move toward decisions	Horseplay
Aggressively attacking	Making sure all understand outcome of team discussions	Interrupting often
Side conversationalist	Monopolizing discussion	Pleading for special interests

Figure 2-12 Roles for suggested activity exercise.

K. Rate each of the following items on a scale of 1 to 5. Discuss the results as a group.

1 strongly agree	2 mildly agree	3 cannot decide	4 mildly disagree	5 strongly disagree

Staff status is not earned. There is always a pecking order.	Food service people are usually held in high regard by early childhood teachers.	Ethnic and cultural differences are the cause of most staff disagreements.	Children are affected by staff spirit.
One staff member may be responsible for enthusiastic staff meetings.	Giving dignity and respect to each job is the key to positive staff relationships.	Maintenance staff and teaching staff have few interactions at most early childhood centers.	It would be a good idea for staff members to trade positions for one day.
Meetings should be evaluated.	Aides and assistants in the classroom regard student teachers as threatening.	Cooperating teachers do not see student teachers as co-teachers.	The student teacher is the only one who is observed and evaluated.
It is easy to get along with staff.	Speaking up in staff meetings can be scary.	Most student teachers are used to participating in meetings and group efforts.	It would be a good idea to post a student teacher's photograph in the lobby of a preschool.
There are some people who just will not talk at meetings.	A golden rule in staff relationships is to leave an area as orderly as you found it.	All staff members should be on a first name basis.	Food and coffee can help break barriers at staff or other meetings.
Close consideration of a meeting should be given.	Everything that is said in a meeting is confidential.	The children's progress is the subject of most meetings.	Individuals should rate themselves on both the quantity and quality of their input at meetings.

L. The following guidelines for staff meetings have been adopted for Lone Tree School staff meetings. React to the listing and add to the list if you choose.

Tasks are shared.

Individual likes and dislikes are recognized and accepted.

Diverse opinions are expected.

Interrupting is avoided.

Our goal is consensus.

Put-downs are unacceptable.

Planned meetings have beginning and ending times.

Meeting notes are taken and made available for reference.

Staff meetings are evaluated.

A summary of the meeting is distributed to all meeting attendees and absent members.

REVIEW

A. List four considerations in preparing for your first day as a student teacher.

B. Describe two activities you might plan for your first day as a student teacher. List two reasons you selected these activities.

C. Read "How to Get the Most Out of Practice Teaching," (figure 2-13). Write a one-minute summary of the area about which you are most anxious. What can you do to overcome this anxiety and prepare?

---

1. Be clear about your expectations. You are there to learn. Don't be shy about trying new techniques and making mistakes. Let your supervisor know through words and actions that you expect to be given responsibilities and feedback that will enable you to learn.

2. Ask questions. Don't be afraid of sounding ignorant. You are there to learn. When work schedules do not permit time for questions, you may need to arrange to arrive early, stay late, or write your questions and submit them to your supervisor.

3. Use your best judgment. When faced with uncertain situations, use your best judgment and ask for clarification of rules later.

4. Be professional. Arrive on time; be prepared to work. Let your supervisor know your schedule and the times you can be expected to be at school. Call if you are late or absent. Offer to make up the time.

5. Respect the teacher's need to give first priority to the children and parents. The teacher may not have time to take you on a guided tour. Use your time—observe, get to know the children, and study the environment. Familiarize yourself with locations of toilets and fire exits, and look to see where equipment is kept. Study the daily routine.

6. Look for a need and fill it. Make a mental note of the times a teacher might appreciate your assistance. Offer to redirect children, plan a project, hold a restless child on your lap, or simply step in to free the teacher for something else. Don't wait to be asked.

7. Make yourself a welcome addition to the staff. Schools are busy places. Don't wait for others to make you feel welcome. Learn the names of children, parents, and members of the staff. Smile; be friendly. Your job is to fit in quickly and be of help. Do your share—and more.

8. Contribute something positive to the school. Look for ways in which you can help improve the school: suggesting a new curriculum idea, repairing a piece of equipment, leaving something that will be appreciated.

9. Model yourself after effective teachers. Watch good teachers interact with parents and children. Listen to what they say and watch how they behave. Adapt their styles to your own.

10. Avoid socializing with other adults. Supervising teachers sometimes complain that students just "stand around and talk to each other" even when they have been assigned to specific areas to observe or supervise. Even when children are playing happily, stay alert for potential problems.

11. Avoid staff politics. Do not get involved in the problems of staff members. Taking sides may close off opportunities for you to learn.

12. Withhold judgment about the school and staff. Don't jump to conclusions about "good" or "bad" teaching. A few short visits can be misleading. Keep an open mind. The techniques you have learned in lab school or have read about in a book may not work in every situation.

13. Learn from your experiences. Replay in your mind the things you did that were effective. Ask for evaluations and suggestions for how you can improve.

Figure 2-13 How to get the most out of practice teaching (prekindergarten level) (Hess & Croft, 1989).

D. Rate the following student teacher meeting skills in order of priority from 1 to 10, number 10 being the highest. You may give equal points to items if necessary.

- Speaking one's mind
- Listening
- Being prepared
- Following through
- Asking questions
- Staying the whole meeting
- Not interrupting
- Bringing notes
- Giving solutions
- Suggesting innovations
- Giving data
- Taking notes

E. List the staff members at your preschool center or elementary school.

F. Describe why regularity of meetings is important to student teachers.

G. List student teacher behaviors that can contribute to smooth relationships with other staff members.

H. Identify some of your placement site's program goals in the following child development areas.

- Academic—intellectual—cognitive
- Social—emotional development and behaviors
- Physical development and skill
- Creative potential development
- Language development
- Multicultural understanding
- Self-help skills

I. Develop a freehand line chart that represents levels of responsibility at your placement center. Begin with person(s) who directs, owns, or administers at the top level, and work down to yourself. Add this to your journal.

REFERENCES

Bentzen, W. R. (1993). *Seeing young children: A guide to observing and recording behavior* (2nd ed.). Albany, NY: Delmar Publishers.

Carter, M. (January 1995). Building a community culture among teachers. *Child Care Information Exchange, 104*, pp. 52–54.

Carter, M., & Curtis, D. (1994). *Training teachers: A harvest of theory and practice.* St. Paul: Redleaf Press.

Fyfe, B. (1994). Assessing experiential learning for college credit. In J. Johnson and J. McCracken (Eds.), *The early childhood career lattice: Perspectives on professional development.* Washington, DC: National Association for the Education of Young Children.

Gordon-Nourok, E. (1979). *You're a student teacher!* Sierra Madre, CA: Southern California Association for the Education of Young Children.

Gutwein, B. (1988). Providing preschool inservice training to increase communications and teamwork spirit. *Practicum II Report.* Nova University.

Hess, R. D., & Crofts, D. J. (1989). *Teachers of young children* (5th ed.). Boston: Houghton-Mifflin.

Hilliard, A. G. (1974). Moving from abstract to functional teacher education. In B. Spodek (Ed.), *Teacher Education.* Washington, DC: National Association for the Education of Young Children.

Julius, A. K. (November 1978). Focus on movement: practice and theory. *Young Children,* 19.

Kraft, L., & Casey, J. R. (1967). *Roles in off-campus student teaching.* Champaign, IL: Stipes Publishing Co.

Meyer, D. E. (1981). *The student teacher on the firing line.* Saratoga, CA: Century Twenty-One Publishing.

Riley, R. D., & Robinson, B. E. (November 1980). A teaching learning center for teacher education. *Young Children, 36,* 9.

Thomson, C. L., Holmberg, M. C., & Baer, D. M. (1978). An experimental analysis of some procedures to teach priming and reinforcement skills to preschool teachers. *Monographs of the Society for Research in Child Development, 43*(4, Serial No. 176), 1–66.

Wasserman, S. (1992). *Serious players in the primary classroom.* New York: Teachers College Press.

3

A Student Teacher's Values

OBJECTIVES

After completing this chapter, the student will be able to:

- Define the role of personal values in teaching.
- Describe how values influence what happens in the classroom.
- Describe how the activities the student teacher enjoys reflect personal values.
- List at least five values that guide the student teacher's lessons and activities.

I've learned that I am a rather biased person rather than the enlightened minority group member I thought I was. Understanding and accepting this was my first step toward change. I've had to analyze the origins of my attitudes.

Felicia Arii

I like a well organized, tidy classroom. My cooperating teacher likes the three-ring circus approach to classroom activity which offers plenty of child choices. I suspect my supervisor chose to place me here to broaden my horizons, to "loosen me up" so to speak, and it's happening. I can tolerate clutter and minor confusion better.

Bobbette Ryan

It bugs me to have to be addressed as Miss Penny, but it's a long-time practice at my placement school. I think it's a hang up from some old television kid's show. I tried to explain it at a teacher's meeting but they said it was traditional to be called Miss Blank, Mrs. Blank, etc. It's probably a trivial concern for I feel this is an excellent, quality preschool in most all other respects.

Penny Soto

My cooperating teacher had very definite attitudes concerning the celebration of Halloween. When she explained how she felt, I had a new view. Now I'm feeling it's good to question if some traditional celebrations add to the quality of children's lives.

Mannington Lee

KNOWING YOURSELF AND YOUR VALUES

We will begin this chapter with an exercise. On a separate sheet of folded paper, number the spaces from 1 to 20. Then list, as quickly as possible, your favorite activities. Do this spontaneously; do not pause to think.

Now go back and code your listed activities as follows.

- Mark those activities you do alone with an *A*.
- Mark those activities that involve at least one more person with a *P*.
- Mark with an *R* those activities that may involve risk.
- Mark those in which you are actively doing something with a *D*.
- Mark with an *S* those activities at which you are a spectator.
- Mark activities that cost money with an *M*.
- Mark activities that are free with an *F*.
- Mark with a *Y* any activity you have not done for one year.

Now that you have coded your activities, what have you learned about yourself? Are you more a spectator than a doer? Do you seldom take risks? Did you list more than one activity in which you have not participated for more than one year? Do you frequently spend money on your activities, or do most of your activities cost little or nothing? Were any of your answers a surprise? We hope you learned something new about yourself.

Let us try another exercise. Complete the following sentences as quickly as possible.

1. School is . . .
2. I like . . .
3. Children are . . .
4. Teaching is . . .
5. Little girls are . . .
6. I want . . .
7. Childen should . . .
8. Little boys are . . .
9. Parents are . . .
10. Teachers should . . .
11. I am . . .
12. Fathers are . . .
13. I should . . .
14. Mothers are . . .
15. Teachers are . . .
16. Parents ought to . . .
17. School ought to . . .
18. Aggressive children make me . . .
19. Shy children make me . . .
20. Whiny children make me . . .

Did you find this activity easier or more difficult than the first? This exercise is less structured than the first. You had to shift your thinking from statement to statement. We hope it made you take a thoughtful pause as you were forced to shift your thinking as verbs changed from simple or declarative to the more complex conditional or obligatory forms. Present tense forms such as "is" or "are" encourage concrete, factual responses. With the conditional "should" or obligatory "ought," your response may have become more a reflection of what you feel an ideal should be. In addition, with the present tense, a response is usually short whereas with the conditional "should" or obligatory "ought," you may have used more words to explain your response.

Look at your answers. Do you find you have different responses depending upon whether the present tense, the conditional tense, or the obligatory form of the verb was used? What do these differences tell you about yourself?

THE ACQUISITION OF VALUES

Let us reflect on how we acquire our values. Logically, many of our values reflect those of our parents. As children, we naturally absorbed our first values through observing our parents and family members and direct parental teaching figure 3-1. Few children are even aware that they are being influenced by their parents; they take in parental attitudes and values through the processes of observation and imita-

Figure 3-1 Family teachings and traditions influence children. They absorb values through observation and imitation. (Courtesy of Nancy Martin)

tion. We want to be like our fathers and mothers, especially since they appear to have the power over the rewards we receive. Smiles when we do something of which they approve, hugs, and "that's right" said over and over shape our behavior so that we begin to accept what our parents accept.

Why are you attracted to the profession of teaching? Is there a teacher in your family? Does your family place a value on learning? Did you enjoy school yourself? Were your parents supportive of school when you were young? The chances are that you answered positively to at least one of these questions. One reason many people teach professionally is that they truly enjoyed being a student themselves, figure 3-2. Learning has been fun and often easy. As a result, an education is highly valued. Teachers frequently come from families in which the profession was valued not because it pays well but, more likely, for the pleasure received in working with young children and the intangible experience of influencing young lives.

One problem many teachers face is accepting negative attitudes from parents or caregivers who do not place similar values upon education. It is difficult to relate to them. You need to remember that some parents may come from cultures where educational opportunities were denied. In addition, some parents

may feel that an education never did them any good; they may be products of education systems that failed them. These parents have different values than you. What can you do? The start always is to show, through your actions (they speak louder than words), that you care for their children and that you want to help their children. Assuming that the parents want their children to have better opportunities, that they want the best for their children, you can earn the parents' respect and cooperation.

On a separate sheet of paper judge the following as true or false.

1. Your ethnic background wasn't an issue when you were a child.
2. Your neighborhood was multicultural.
3. People treat you differently because of your ethnic heritage.
4. You were financially secure most of your childhood.
5. Religion is important in your life.
6. You're proud of your racial group.
7. Life was full of hope rather than despair in childhood.
8. You've been the object of discrimination.
9. Your ethnic group is minimally understood by most Americans.
10. Your identity, sense of self, is well formed.

Figure 3-2 Teachers often value education because they received pleasure and reward from learning activities. (Courtesy of Nancy Martin)

Many of our most enduring values were formed through contact with our family when we were too young to remember. Others were acquired through repeated experience. Let us use an example. Assume that you were raised in the city and lived in apartment houses your entire life. Because you never had a yard of your own, you have had little experience with plants beyond the potted variety. You are now renting a house with a yard, and you enjoy puttering around in the garden. Because your experiences with gardening have been pleasurable, you have acquired a positive value for it. If your experiences had been bad, you could have acquired a negative value just as easily.

Krathwohl's Hierarchy   One way of looking at the acquisition of values is to look at Krathwohl's taxonomy (1984). Krathwohl and his associates were interested in looking at the "affective domain," or the field of knowledge associated with feelings and values. Krathwohl arranged the affective domain into a hierarchy as follows:

1. Receiving (attending)
2. Responding
3. Valuing
4. Organization
5. Characterization by a value or value complex.

For you, as a teacher of young children, the first three levels are the most important. Suppose you had not been willing to receive the stimulus of potted plants being a pleasure to see? Being aware of the aesthetics of having plants and enjoying their presence is the first sublevel of receiving—becoming sensitive. Becoming interested in them and enjoying their beauty moves one beyond mere awareness to the next sublevel—willingness to receive. There is a third sublevel of receiving—controlled or selected attention. What does this mean? How is this demonstrated? Looking at potted plants and remarking on their growth, need for water, and flowers are all examples of selected attention.

If you saw that the plant needed water and proceeded to water it, you have moved to the second level of the hierarchy—responding. If you water the plant after being asked to do so, you have reached the first sublevel—acquiescence in responding. If you do it without being asked, you are at the second sublevel—willingness to respond. Noting satisfaction in the growth of the plant because you have been a part of its care moves you into the third sublevel of responding—satisfaction in response.

Valuing, the third level, also has sublevels. The first is acceptance of a value. When you buy your own potted plants, for example, you are revealing a value. You like potted plants enough to buy and care for them. The second sublevel is showing a preference for a value. For example, if you chose to rent a house with a yard instead of an apartment because of the opportunity to work in the yard, you have shown preference for a value. Taking care of the yard then moves you into the third sublevel—commitment. (From Awareness to Action, Project Wild, 1986, Western Regional Environmental Education Council.)

Let us now study these three levels of value in more specific terms. Try the following exercise (adapted from Biehler & Snowman, 1990). Write your answers on a separate sheet of paper.

Receiving (attending)—The learner becomes sensitized to the existence of certain phenomena and stimuli.

1. Awareness: What types of awareness do you want your students to have? For example, do you want them to be aware of the books in the classroom? List those things you want the children to become aware of.

2. Willingness to receive: What types of tolerance do you want your students to develop? For example, do you want your students to sit quietly and listen when you read a book to them? Describe the behavior you hope to see from your students regarding their willingness to receive.

3. Controlled or selected attention: List the things you want the students to recognize that are frequently ignored by trained observers. For instance, do you want your students to recognize the predictability or pattern of repetition in a story?

Responding—The learner does something with the phenomena.

1. Acquiescence in responding: What habits of responses do you want to encourage? Do you want your students to respond to your questions about the story you just read?

2. Willingness to respond: List the voluntary responses you want to encourage. Do you want the students to ask their own questions about a story as you read it?

3. Satisfaction in response: List the habits of satisfaction you want your students to develop. Do you want them to respond with smiles, excitement, or laughter to the story? Do you want them to listen with anticipation, predicting the outcome with pleasure and enthusiasm?

Valuing—The learner displays consistent behavior reflecting a general attitude.

1. Acceptance of a value: List the types of emotional acceptance you want your students to develop. Do you want your students to go voluntarily to the book corner to "read" the same book you just read to them?

2. Preference for a value: What values do you want your students to develop to the point of actively identifying with the stimulus? Do you want them to urge other children in the class to "read" the story? Do you want to see them choose this book to "read" while role playing school and you as teacher?

3. Commitment: List the behaviors you want your students to develop that will enable you to decide whether they are committed to the stimulus. Do you want them to check out the book from the class to take home? Do you want them to take out the book from the local library? Do you want them to go to the book corner at least three times each week? What evidence of commitment to your stimulus are you looking for?

We will not continue further with this exercise since you may not know if the students have absorbed your stimulus into their values system until after they move on from your class. For yourself, however, go back over this exercise and ask yourself the following:

1. Why did I choose that particular example as the stimulus I wanted my students to receive and respond to?

2. What does this reveal about my own values system?

3. Is this value a part of *me*, a part of my character?

If you cannot answer these questions, we suggest that you go back and repeat the exercise with another stimulus. For example, your choices may range from some facet of the curriculum—storytime and books—to some facet of behavior—paying attention, sharing toys, not fighting, among other possibilities.

● YOUR VALUES

Why is it important for you as a student teacher to be aware of your values? We hope that you already know the answer. In many ways, the answer lies in what Rogers (1966) calls congruence. Self-knowledge should precede trying to impart knowledge to others. By looking closely at your values, you will be able to develop a philosophy of teaching more easily. Your particular life stories can be the starting point for reflection and dialogue (Jones, 1994).

Let us move on to another exercise. On a separate sheet of paper, trace the above figure. In the top left-hand section, draw a picture of what you believe is your best asset. Next to it in the top right-hand section, draw a picture of something you do well. In the middle left-hand section, draw a picture of something you would like to do better. In the middle right-hand section, draw a picture of something you want to change about yourself. In the bottom left-hand section, draw a picture of something that frightens you. In the bottom right-hand section, write five adjectives which you would like other people to use to describe you. Look at your drawings and think about what your *affective* responses were to this exercise. Did you find it easier to draw a picture of something that frightens you? Was it easier to draw than to list five adjectives? Did you feel more comfortable drawing or writing your responses? What does this say about you? Were you able to write the first two or three adjectives quickly and then forced to give some thought to the remaining two?

Some of us have more difficulty handling compliments than negative criticism; thus, we find it easier to draw a picture of something we do well. Some of us have negative feelings about our ability to draw anything; being asked to do an exercise that asks for a drawn response is a real chore. Did you silently breathe a sigh of relief when you came to the last part of the exercise and were asked for a written response? Does this suggest that you are more comfortable with words than with nonverbal expressions?

If you are more at ease with words, what are the implications regarding any curriculum decisions you might make? Would you be inclined to place a greater emphasis on language activities than on art activities especially those involving drawing? If you can deal more easily with the negative aspects of yourself than with the positive aspects, what are the implications for your curriculum decisions? Is it possible that you would find it easier to criticize, rather than compliment, a student? Is it possible that you are inclined to see mistakes rather than improvements? Think about this. How do the activities you enjoy reflect your personal values and thus influence your classroom curriculum, figure 3-3? Go back to the first exercise you completed in this unit. What were the first five activities you listed? List them on a separate piece of paper. Next to this column, write five related classroom activities. Does your list look something like this?

Activity	Related Curriculum Activity
Playing the piano	Teaching simple songs with piano accompaniment
Jogging	Allowing active children to run around the playground
Skiing	Climbing, jumping, gross motor activities

Figure 3-3 Activities we enjoy may influence classroom curriculum choices. (Courtesy of Nancy Martin)

PERSONAL VALUES AND ACTIVITIES

What is the relationship between activities and personal values? It seems obvious that we would not become involved in an activity that did not bring us some reward or pleasure; we have to be motivated. Usually that motivation becomes intrinsic because significant people in our lives provided an extrinsic reward, usually a smile or compliment. Given enough feedback in the form of compliments, we learn to accept and even prize the activity.

Many of us want to teach young children because we genuinely like them. When did we learn this? Some teachers, as the oldest of many siblings, learned to care for and enjoy being with younger brothers and sisters. Others had positive experiences from babysitting.

Perhaps we want to teach young children because they are less threatening than older children. In addition, young children are often more motivated to please the adults in their lives than teenagers.

Attitudes toward or against something are often formed when we are so young that we do not know their origin. We only know that we have a tendency to like or dislike something or someone. Because these attitudes arouse a strong *affect*, or feeling for or

Figure 3-4 Student teachers from different ethnic groups may find their values challenged at times.

against, they can influence our values. People of different backgrounds who do not share similar ideals often find their values being challenged, figure 3-4.

Other student teachers in your class (group) will demonstrate individual degrees of teaching experience, background knowledge, teaching skill, and technique. You are urged not to compare what you have to offer children with what you perceive others possess but rather that you stretch and advance in your own directions.

We urge you to be thoughtful, open minded, and reflective concerning your training experiences, stepping back at times to think about your conclusions and experiences in child classrooms and to participate in discussions that clarify and enlighten.

● ETHICS

Katz (1992) defines ethics as a set of statements that helps us to deal with the temptations inherent in our occupations. Ethics may also help us to act in concert with what we believe to be right rather than what is expedient. Making decisions in the best interests of children and their families may take courage and commitment to professional excellence. One may risk losing a job, license, or other serious consequences by sticking to one's ethical standards.

Child care workers have considerable power over children's daily lives and general welfare and often are seen as experts by parents. This occupational situation enables them to impact and influence lives, self-esteem, and so on. They also can possibly cause short- and long-term damage.

Speaking of the power a teacher exerts over children in care, Stephens (1994) notes the following:

> I possess tremendous power to make a child's life miserable or joyous. I can be a tool of torture or an instrument of inspiration. I can humiliate or humor, hurt or heal. In all situations it is my response that decides whether a crisis will be escalated or de-escalated, a child humanized or de-humanized.

The National Association for the Education of Young Children (NAEYC) published its Code of Ethical Conduct and Statement of Commitment in 1989. (See Appendix). Ward (1992) notes:

> The members of a profession monitor themselves from within. They take appropriate steps to ensure the ethical basis of programs, goals, and directions. They critique themselves and their field.

NAEYC's (1991) Code of Ethical Conduct should be studied by all who make daily decisions in their work with young children and families. It is included in the Appendix.

SUMMARY

In this unit we discussed the relationship between attitudes and values and the curriculum choices that are made as a result. We also discussed how values and attitudes are formed. We included several learning exercises; their aim was to help you define more clearly some of your personal values.

SUGGESTED ACTIVITIES

A. Complete the following exercise in small groups. Discuss the process involved in making your decisions. What did you learn about yourself and your peers as a result?

1. Following your cooperating teacher's directions, you have always placed your purse and coat in the teachers' closet. The closet is locked after the teacher, aide, and any parent volunteers have arrived in the child center or primary grade classroom. Only the teacher and aide have keys. One day after you have left the center/school and stop at a store to buy a few groceries before going home, you discover that $10.00 is missing from your wallet; only a five and a one dollar bill remain. Your immediate reaction is . . .

2. You are a student teacher in a preschool classroom for four-year-old children. One day Mike arrives with a black eye and wearing long sleeved sweater in spite of the pleasant weather. He winces when you approach him to give him a good morning hug. When you ask him what's wrong, Mike shakes his head "no" and doesn't answer.

   Later in the day, as the weather has turned sunny and warmer, you are able to persuade Mike to remove his sweater. Almost immediately, you notice bruises on his left arm. Quickly, you report to your cooperating teacher. "Sarah, would you come and look at Mike? I think he's been abused. What are the procedures we should follow?"

   Sarah replies, "Leave it to me; I'll talk to Mrs. R. (the director). She needs to know about possible child abuse and she'll take care of it."

   By the time the children are being picked up by their parents, no one from either Child Protective Services or from the police have arrived to look at Mike or interview you.

   What should you do?

3. You have recently been hired as the afternoon kindergarten teacher at the ABC School. The DEF District policy stipulates that the morning teacher assists the afternoon teacher and vice versa. You feel that this will provide you with wonderful support from the older, more experienced morning teacher, Mrs. Sexton.

On your first day of work in late August, you are surprised to see that there are no interest centers arranged in the kindergarten room. There are only five tables with six chairs at each; a book shelf; and two desks for the teachers.

"Mrs. Sexton," you inquire, "don't we have blocks, easels, or play house materials?"

"We have the reading workbooks on the shelf over here," she responds, "and the math workbooks on the shelf by the desk. DEF District has a curriculum for kindergarten that we follow; haven't you read it?"

You confess that although you received the district guidelines two days before when you were hired, you had not had enough time to read through them.

"Well," Mrs. Sexton says, "you'll see that there are specific goals in reading and math that we must reach this year. The children all have their workbooks and we use direct teaching to achieve the goals. By the way, you do know that Mrs. Maier (the principal) expects you to have your lesson plans ready for her perusal on Friday of each week and you do understand that DEF District uses the five-step lesson plan format?"

You begin to have doubts about having accepted the position, but you need a job to pay off the student loans you had acquired while going through college. You know that this classroom is not "developmentally appropriate" according to NAEYC guidelines. You hope, however, that maybe you can at least do more developmentally appropriate activities in your afternoon class. You decide to spend some money borrowed from your parents to buy some unit blocks and you visit the local public library for some picture books for an in-class library. You also visit the local teacher supply house to price items like unifix cubes, play house materials, and an easel and paint. You estimate that you may be able to afford different items with each month's paycheck.

You remain in the classroom late on the day before school opens to arrange a "reading corner" with the books from the library and you shift the book shelf to form a protected corner. You place two large beanbag chairs you used at college in the "reading center." Then, you bring in the blocks and place them in the opposite corner of the room on a shelf you also had in college. A carpet you retrieved from the city's once-a-month clean up day is placed in the block area to reduce noise.

When school opens the next day, Mrs. Sexton exclaims, "What have you done to my room? You had no right to change anything!"

What do you do now?

4. A parent of one of the three-year-olds in the parent participatory preschool where you are student teaching has formed a close relationship with you; you are both about the same age; you both have experienced financial stresses you've shared. One day, Ms. Sharif confesses that she's just discovered she's pregnant again (she has a baby as well as the three-year-old in your class) and that she's thinking of having an abortion. What is your reaction?

5. At your center/school, teachers, aides, and student teachers alike customarily place their respective lunches in the refrigerator in the teachers' lounge. One day when you go to pick up your lunch bag, it is missing. You ask those people in the lounge if they have seen it and no one says that she or he has. Wondering if perhaps you had left the bag in your car, you check only to discover that it is not there. Puzzled, you wonder if you might have left the bag on the kitchen table at home. Upon returning to your apartment, however, you do not find the lunch. You begin to wonder if one of the people at the center/school, having forgotten their own lunch, "borrowed" yours. Your immediate action is . . .

6. In preparing an art lesson, you have purchased 25 pounds of white clay. (It does not represent a large capital outlay; total cost was less than $15.00.) When you introduce the activity to the children at your table, you are surprised to discover that a large chunk of the clay has been cut away. Knowing you have enough for the lesson, you continue with the demonstration. You supervise the interested children who have begun to pound and shape their pieces of clay. After they have placed their sculptures on the drying rack, you begin to work with the next interested group. At the end of the day, you ask your cooperating teacher if she had taken a piece of the clay. (You had placed it in an unlocked cupboard where art materials are typically stored.) When she says, "No," you begin to wonder who might have.

B. Write a paragraph on how you have been influenced by stereotyping and what you have done to counter this. How has this use of stereotyping affected your attitude toward that person who used it? Why?

C. In one column, list as many characteristics of an effective teacher as you can think of. In a parallel column, check those characteristics you feel you already possess. Then, for one minute, using the above listed characteristics, describe what you believe most parents will want you to be like and how you perceive yourself to be.

D. Read, react, discuss.

. . . we must also work with ourselves until we come to the place where we realize that there are many right ways to live, many right ways to solve problems, many right ways to look at the world. Our homes and educational settings must become true celebrations of option and choice that allow children to appreciate the beauty of individual styles—especially their own. (Manfredi-Petitt, 1994)

E. Read #1. Discuss with a group of peers. React to following:

What teacher behaviors could result if this stereotypical view of Asian-American children is believed? What is the reality?

1. Asian-Americans are generally stereotyped as successful, law-abiding, and high-achieving minorities. The success of many Asian-American students has created a new "model minority" stereotype. They have been described in popular and professional literature as "whiz kids" and as "problem free" (Feng, 1994).

   Read #2 and discuss. What teacher values could influence their work with Asian-American children?

2. "Most Asian-American parents teach their children to value educational achievement, respect authority, feel responsibility for relatives, and show self-control. Asian-American parents tend to view school failure as lack of will and to address this problem by increasing parental restrictions. Asian-American children tend to be more dependent, conforming, and willing to place family welfare over individual wishes than are other American children" (Feng, 1994).

   Self-effacement is a trait traditionally valued in many Asian cultures. Asian children tend to wait to participate, unless otherwise requested by the teacher. Having attention drawn to oneself, for example, having one's name put on the board for misbehaving, can bring considerable distress. Many Asian children have been socialized to listen more than speak, to speak in a soft voice, and to be modest in dress and behavior. (Feng, 1994)

F. Read, react, and discuss with a small group of classmates the following:

   Often in the college classroom, preservice teachers express confusion about the "proper" racial terminology for a particular group. They ask, for example, "Should I say 'black' or 'African American'? 'Latino' or 'Hispanic'? 'Indian' or 'Native American'?" (Boutte, LaPoint, & Davis, 1993)

G. Role play the following situations.

   A. As the parent (grandparent, foster parent, significant adult) of a child attending the school, identify the concerns you may have and any possible curriculum changes you would like to see. Note: This is the first parent meeting of the school year.

   You may choose to be any of the following:

   1. Mother of attending child who is from an inner city housing project.

   2. Mother of attending child who is ethnically different from most of the other children enrolled in the school.

   3. Grandmother of attending child who cares for child evenings while mother works a night shift job.

   4. Mother, recovering alcoholic, who is afraid social workers may be spying on her child at school in order to decide whether the child belongs in the father's custody.

   5. Newly arrived immigrant father who speaks limited English.

   B. As the teacher (aide, volunteer), describe and briefly outline a handout you would distribute to the above parents to help them become more involved in the curriculum.

   You may choose to be:

   6. Teacher of the class.

   7. Teacher's paid aide who lives in the children's neighborhood.

   8. Senior citizen who volunteers at the school and who also lives in the neighborhood.

REVIEW

A. List five personal values.

B. Write an essay describing how the values you listed in review question A influence what you do in the classroom.

REFERENCES

Biehler, R. F., & Snowman, J. (1990). *Psychology applied to teaching* (6th ed.). Boston: Houghton Mifflin.

Boutte, G. S., LaPoint, S., & Davis, B. (November 1993). Racial issues in education: Real or imagined? *Young Children, 49*(1), 19–23.

Feng, J. (June 1994). Asian-American children: What teachers should know. *ERIC Digest*, EDO-PS-94-4.

Jones, E. (1994). Constructing professional knowledge by telling our stories. In J. Johnson & J. McCracken (Eds.), *The Early Childhood Career Lattice: Perspectives on Professional Development.* Washington, DC: National Association for the Education of Young Children.

Katz, L. G. (1992). Ethical issues in working with young children. In *Ethical Behavior in Early Childhood Education.* Washington, DC: National Association for the Education of Young Children.

Krathwohl, D. R., Bloom, B. S., & Masia, B. B. (1984). *Taxonomy of educational objectives: The classification of educational goals. Handbook II: Affective domain.* New York: David McKay.

Manfredi-Petitt, L. A. (November 1994). Multicultural sensitivity: It's more than skin deep! *Young Children, 50*(1), 72–73.

Rogers, C. R. (1966). To facilitate learning. In M. Provus (Ed.), *Innovations for time to teach.* Washington, DC: National Education Association.

Stephens, K. (January 1994). Bringing light to darkness: A tribute to teachers. *Young Children, 49*(2), 44–46.

Ward, E. H. (1992). A code of ethics: The hallmark of a profession. In *Ethical Behavior in Early Childhood Education* (pp. 17–26). Washington, DC: National Association for the Education of Young Children.

RESOURCES

Carter, M., & D. Curtis. (1994). *Training teachers: A harvest of theory and practice.* St. Paul: Redleaf Press.

Derman-Sparks, L. (1989). *Anti-bias curriculum: Tools for empowering young people.* Washington, DC: National Association for the Education of Young Children.

Ethical behavior in early childhood education (expanded edition). (1992). Washington, DC: National Association for the Education of Young Children.

Feeney, S., & Kipnis, K. (1989, 1996). The National Association for the Education of Young Children: Code of ethical conduct. *Young Children, 45*(1), 24–29; reprinted in *Young Children, 51*(3), 57–60.

Greenberg, H. M. (1969). *Teaching with feeling.* New York: Macmillan.

Jones, E. (1986). *Teaching adults,* Washington, DC: National Association for the Education of Young Children.

Kowalski, T. J., Weaver, R. A., & Henson, K. T. (1990). *Case studies on teaching.* New York: Longman.

Rogers, C. R., & Freiberg, H. J. (1994). *Freedom to learn* (3rd ed.). New York: Merrill/Macmillan.

Simon, S. (1993) *In Search of Values: 31 Strategies for Finding Out What Really Matters Most for You.* New York: Warner Books.

Willis, S. (September 1993). Multicultural teaching: Meeting the challenges that arise in practice, *ASCD Curriculum Update,* 1.

CHAPTER

4

Review of Child Development and Learning Theory

OBJECTIVES

After studying this chapter, the student will be able to:

- Identify four major child development theories that influence early childhood education.
- Describe how children learn.
- List five ways in which the student teacher can help a child learn.

I'm attracted to some children more than to others. I purposely try to spend equal time with and give equal attention. The active child's the hardest.

Mia Mendonca

One of my instructors said "the hardest thing about being a teacher is figuring out how individual children learn." During student teaching I found many learn quickly from other children, some learn by doing something over and over again, and some learn by observing and asking questions. I found if I wanted to teach something, I definitely had to capture their attention first. I often did this by being enthusiastic.

Doreen Liu

Play really is the work of the young child. They become so focused, so serious, so excited at times. It's great fun to accompany them, to watch their enthusiasm and sense of wonder.

Shelby Ochoa

THEORIES OF CHILD DEVELOPMENT

Historical Background

Historically, three theories of child development have been prevalent in developing educational programs for young children: the *nativist*, the *nurturist*, and the *interactionist*.

The nativist tradition, based upon the philosophy of Rousseau (1742/1947), takes the view that children are like flowers, unfolding in a natural way. Out of the nativist tradition has developed the concept of children's natural development or maturation as the determinant of their ability to learn with little direction from adults (parents or teachers). Gesell, Ilg, and Ames (1974), as maturationists, best exemplify the nativistic point of view. The traditional nursery school of the 1920s, 1930s, and 1940s, and still seen today in some programs, is based upon this nativistic philosophy.

Another variant of the nativist tradition can be seen in the psychoanalytic theories of Freud and Erikson (1963). Erikson stressed his concept of the eight psychosocial stages of human development and posited a specific task to be resolved at each stage. For example, the task of infancy is the resolution of *basic trust* in comparison to mistrust; for toddlers, the task of *autonomy* as compared to shame and doubt. During the preschool years, the task is *initiative* in comparison to guilt; and for elementary school-age children, *industry* as opposed to feelings of inferiority. The concepts that the major tasks of toddlers and preschoolers are autonomy and initiative have evolved into the philosophy of child-directed learning seen in such programs as some of the traditional preschools and Montessori programs.

The nurturist tradition, based upon the philosophy of Locke (Braun & Edwards, 1972), looks at development from the point of view that the minds of children are a *tabula rasa* or blank slate. From the nurturist tradition have evolved the behavioristic programs. The concept that children are much like Locke's "blank slate" upon which adults "write," or "impress" learnings, started models such as DARCEE and DISTAR, which best exemplify this model in practice. Both of these programs have received considerable reaction and disagreement. Some traditional teacher-directed elementary school programs also exemplify the nurturist or behaviorist philosophy.

Interactionists view development and learning as taking place in the interactions between children and their respective environments. Programs exemplifying this point of view are those of the constructivists. Jean Piaget (1952), although influenced by Rousseau's concept of children as active explorers of their respective environments, extended the concept of natural unfolding by maintaining that children create their own knowledge as they interact with their social and physical environments. "Piaget calls this interaction *assimilation* and *accommodation*, and *equilibration*" (Seefeldt & Barbour, 1993). Programs based upon the Piagetian point of view are best exemplified by Lavatelli (1973), High/Scope (Hohmann, Banet, & Weikart, 1979), and Kamii-DeVries (1978). In each of these programs Piaget's theory is translated in somewhat different ways: Lavatelli tends to emphasize the structural aspects; High/Scope, the relationship between the theory and children's spontaneous activities; and Kamii-DeVries, the constructivist aspects.

What Student Teachers Should Know

It has been said that a teacher training program is successful if its graduates know just one thing well—how children learn. Current learning theory is based upon views of human development that differ among experts. The concept that each child is a unique individual who learns in his or her own way further complicates the issue. How does a beginning teacher begin to understand how children learn?

There is a basic knowledge about children's learning that forms the base upon which theories have been built. Hendrick (1985 & 1993) has identified the following:

- Children pass through a series of stages as they grow.
- Children learn things a step at a time.
- Children learn best through actual experiences.
- Children utilize play to translate experience into understanding.

- Parents are the most important influence in the development of the child.

- The teacher must present learning within a climate of caring. (p. 5)

Stevens and King (1976) have compared five different views of learning and development, see Appendix. Program models differ based on the bias of each theory. According to the stimulus-response theory, education is a series of stimuli planned by the teacher to which the children respond. The nature of the learning process is seen as observable changes in behavior. Stimulus-response theorists define learning as a more or less permanent change in behavior (Stevens & King, 1976).

In contrast, the traditional approach by maturationists emphasizes discovery by the child. This approach is the basis of learning at the traditional nursery school and play school. The approach of cognitive theorists, notably Piaget and Montessori, has led to programs such as the Weikart cognitively oriented curriculum. The studies of Erikson, a psychosexual interactionist, are less concerned with cognitive development and more concerned with social-emotional development. Emphasis is placed on social interaction and discovery (Stevens & King, 1976). In view of these different approaches to child development, it is obvious that no one theorist has the final word on how children learn.

Figure 4-1 Nonverbal behavior tells us this child is concentrating and learning.

● HOW DO CHILDREN LEARN?

Learning occurs as a child interacts with the environment using the five senses: seeing, hearing, touching, tasting, and smelling. Some theorists say there is a sixth sense, the kinesthetic, or the sense of where the body is in relation to space.

Look at a baby; offer a new toy. What does the baby do? The baby looks it over carefully, shakes it to see if it makes any noise, puts it in the mouth, and turns it over and over in the hands. It seems that the baby uses all of the senses to discover all there is to know about the toy. Look at a young child. Look at how the child is concentrating, figure 4-1; the child stares intently, and grasps the blocks carefully. We may assume the child is listening closely, with the mouth

open and tongue pressed against the teeth to help concentration. All of these actions show us that the child is learning. A learning sequence may proceed as follows:

- The child attends and records.

- The child experiences and explores.

- The child imitates actions, sounds, words, and so on. The child becomes aware of similarities and differences and/or matching events.

- The child responds appropriately to actions and words. Discusses and questions.

- The child talks about what has been learned or discovered.

- The child remembers and uses knowledge.

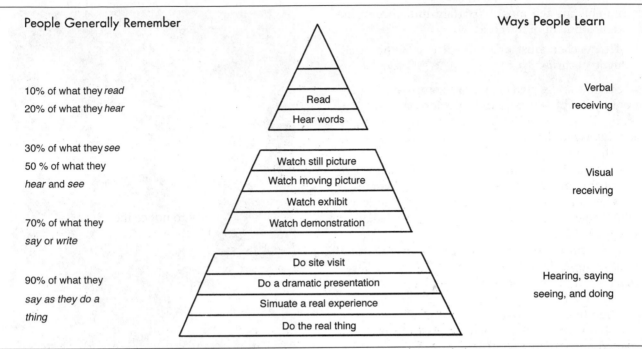

People Generally Remember   Ways People Learn

10% of what they *read*   Read   Verbal
20% of what they *hear*   Hear words   receiving

30% of what they *see*   Watch still picture
50 % of what they   Watch moving picture   Visual
hear and *see*   Watch exhibit   receiving

70% of what they   Watch demonstration
say or *write*

                                        Do site visit
90% of what they   Do a dramatic presentation   Hearing, saying
                                   Simuate a real experience   seeing, and doing
say as they do a
                                       Do the real thing
thing

Figure 4-2 How people learn. (Reprinted with permission from Diane Trister Dodge (1993). *A Guide for Supervisors and Trainers on Implementing the Creative Curriculum for Early Childhood* (3rd ed.). Washington, DC: Teaching Strategies, Inc. Based on Edgar Dale, "Cone of Experience." [Adapted from *Audiovisual Methods in Teaching* (3rd ed., 1969). New York: Holt, Rinehart and Winston, Inc., p. 107.])

When something is learned, the child may respond with appropriate nonverbal behavior. The child may point to, show, or do what has been discovered, figure 4-2. In addition, the child may name or talk about what has been learned and may apply the knowledge.

Discussions of child learning usually include the following:

- If a child's action receives positive reinforcement immediately, there is a strong possibility that the act will recur.
- If a child's action receives negative feedback or is ignored, repetition of the act will be discouraged.
- Habit behavior is difficult to change.
- Periodic positive reinforcement is necessary to maintain children's favorable actions.
- The motivation level may increase persistence in learning tasks.

- For each child, all classroom experiences have a "feeling tone," ranging from pleasant to neutral to unpleasant.
- Motivation may contain a degree of tension, which may aid or inhibit success.
- There are two types of motivation: intrinsic and extrinsic motivation. Intrinsic motivation is acting a certain way because it feels good or right. Extrinsic motivation is acting a certain way because it is dictated by a particular situation or person.

The emotions that exist within individuals during experiences may enhance or retard how much learning takes place. Infants and children have anxiety levels ranging from overload (extreme agitation or excitement) to underload (boredom) in life situations. If overwhelmed, the infant will tune out and turn away. Learning is best accomplished when anxiety is low and the excitement about finding out and knowing is high—but not too high!

A teacher's technique or way of interacting, which includes pressuring, embarrassment, or increasing a child's self-doubt or feeling of inadequacy, can limit child learning. Student teachers unfortunately may only need to look back into their own schooling experiences to find examples they do not want to repeat.

On the other hand, we all remember teachers who accepted our ideas as important contributions, smiled when they were with us, appreciated our perhaps feeble attempts, noticed our efforts, and made us feel unique and special.

What else do early childhood educators know about child learning?

1. Children have curiosity and are motivated to know and find out about what has captured their attention or what they have experienced.

2. Knowledge is constructed internally when children move, act, explore, and talk about the environment and life experiences with other children and adults.

3. A social-emotional feeling tone is present in most all learning situations and is accompanied by shared narrative that is meaningful to the child.

4. Questions are welcomed and answers are thought provoking, leading to discovery.

Problem Solving

In a rapidly changing world, the ability to solve problems becomes a survival skill. Felton and Henry (1981) believe "problem solving is really a synthesis of convergent and divergent thinking skills, of classification, patterning and evaluation skills." To become a more effective problem solver, the child must:

1. have a general knowledge of the properties of objects

2. have the ability to notice incongruities or inconsistencies and define the problem (the "what is wrong here")

3. have the ability to think of new and unconventional functions for familiar objects

4. have the ability to generate many possible solutions

5. have the ability to evaluate various solutions

6. have the ability to implement a solution he/she thinks will best fulfill the requirements of solving the problem. (p. 3)

Early childhood student teachers need to analyze whether problem solving (figure 4-3) is a priority in their planning and daily interactions with young children.

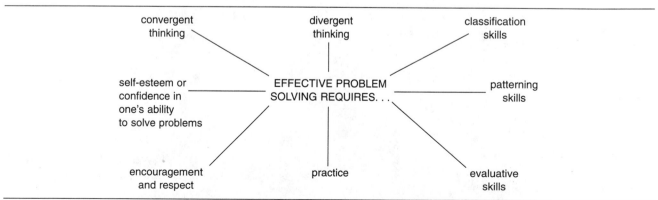

Figure 4-3 Effective problem-solving skills. (From "Think Power" by Victoria Felton and Joan Henry. Presentation at the National Association for the Education of Young Children Conference, November 6, 1981.)

Learning Modalities

Recent studies have tried to identify children who learn more efficiently through one sense or modality than through others. A child who enjoys looking at books and notices your new clothes may be a visual learner as opposed to the child who listens intently during storytime and is the first to hear a bird chirping outside the window. The latter child may be an auditory learner, figure 4-4. The child who enjoys playing with materials of different textures—for example, fingerpaint, clay, feelie-box games—may be a kinesthetic learner, one who learns best through touch and body motion, figure 4-5. Many children are visual learners, but most, especially preschoolers, use a combination of all the senses to gather impressions. A teacher can expect greater retention of knowledge if all senses are involved.

Learning Styles

In addition to learning from the use of their senses, or learning modalities, children also learn from the adults in their lives. Traditionally, some children learn as apprentices to their parents. The Native American child's parents may model a particular type of learning mode, as do parents of many other cultures.

Some children, however, demand more attention as they learn than others. The terms *field sensitive* and *field independent* can be used to describe certain types of children. Field-sensitive children like to work with others and ask for guidance from the teacher. They have difficulty completing an open-ended assignment without a model to follow. The field-sensitive child waits until the other children begin an art lesson to see what they are doing, and then starts to paint. The field-independent child, in contrast, prefers to work alone, is task oriented, rarely seeks guidance from the teacher, and prefers open-ended projects. The field-independent child will try new activities without being urged to do so. In terms of learning, this child enjoys the discovery approach best. Study the rating forms, figures 4-6 and 4-7, for each type of child. Which children at your center or school are field sensitive or field independent?

Figure 4-4 Children who enjoy listening activities may be auditory learners.

Figure 4-5 Children who enjoy playing with materials of different textures may be kinesthetic learners.

Learning Styles and Learning

Since the publication of H. Gardiner's book, *Frames of Mind*, in 1983, there has been a new look at the influence of learning style on how children learn. Gardiner posited seven types of intelligences—linguistic, logico-mathematical, spatial, bodily-kinesthetic, musical, interpersonal, and intrapersonal. Gardiner (1988), rightfully perhaps, accuses schools of teaching only to those children with linguistic and logico-mathematical intelligence and largely ignoring the other five types.

In *Multiple Intelligences: The Theory in Practice* (1993), Gardiner includes selections by educators who have tested his theory in both preschool and elementary school classrooms. Of particular interest to early childhood student teachers are chapter 6, "The Emergence and Nurturance of Multiple Intelligences in Early Childhood: The Project Spectrum Approach," and chapter 7, "The Elementary Years: The Project Approach in the Key School Setting."

Co-authored by Mara Krechevsky, the Project Spectrum approach describes an assessment and related curriculum approach developed at the Eliot Pearson Children's School at Tufts University. Children as young as four were already found to have developed learning style preferences. Because the project began in the 1986–1987 school year, early follow-up research has shown that "[t]he working styles for the five children remained relatively consistent over the one- to two-year follow-up period" (p. 103).

The Key School is a public elementary school in the inner city of Indianapolis. Initially stimulated by their reading of *Frames of Mind*, eight teachers from Indianapolis approached Gardiner for training on how to implement his theory in their school. After two years of work, the Indianapolis school district allowed the teachers to open Key as a public "options" school. Patricia Bolanos, one of the original teachers, is now principal. The success of the school can be seen in action on "The Creative Spirit," Part I,

FIELD-SENSITIVE OBSERVABLE BEHAVIORS

Instructions: Evaluate the child for each behavior listed below by placing a check in the appropriate column.

Child's Name _____ Grad _____ School _____ Date _____

Observer's Name _____

Situation (e.g., art, block play, etc.) _____

FREQUENCY

FIELD-SENSITIVE OBSERVABLE BEHAVIORS	Not True	Seldom True	Sometimes True	Often True	Almost Always True
RELATIONSHIP TO PEERS					
1. Likes to work with others to achieve a common goal					
2. Likes to assist others					
3. Is sensitive to feelings and opinions of others.					
PERSONAL RELATIONSHIP TO TEACHER					
1. Openly expresses positive feelings for teacher					
2. Asks questions about teacher's tastes and personal experiences; seeks to become like teacher					
INSTRUCTIONAL RELATIONSHIP TO TEACHER					
1. Seeks guidance and demonstration from teacher					
2. Seeks rewards which strengthen relationship with teacher					
3. Is highly motivated when working individually with teacher					
CHARACTERISTICS OF CURRICULUM WHICH FACILITATE LEARNING					
1. Performance objectives and global aspects of curriculum are carefully explained					
2. Concepts are presented in story format					
3. Concepts are related to personal interests and experiences of children					

Figure 4-6 Field-sensitive child rating form. (Developed by H. Krueger and M. Tenenberg for Instructional Strategies Class, California State University, Hayward, 1985.)

FIELD-INDEPENDENT OBSERVABLE BEHAVIORS

Instructions: Evaluate the child for each behavior listed below by placing a check in the appropriate column.

Child's Name   Grad   School   Date

Observer's Name

Situation (e.g., art, block play, etc.)

	FREQUENCY				
FIELD-INDEPENDENT OBSERVABLE BEHAVIORS	Not True	Seldom True	Sometimes True	Often True	Almost Always True
RELATIONSHIP TO PEERS					
1. Prefers to work independently					
2. Likes to compete and gain individual recognition					
3. Task oriented; is inattentive to social environment when working					
PERSONAL RELATIONSHIP TO TEACHER					
1. Rarely seeks physical contact with teacher					
2. Formal; interactions with teacher are restricted to tasks at hand					
INSTRUCTIONAL RELATIONSHIP TO TEACHER					
1. Likes to try new tasks without teacher's help					
2. Impatient to begin tasks; likes to finish first					
3. Seeks nonsocial rewards					
CHARACTERISTICS OF CURRICULUM WHICH FACILITATE LEARNING					
1. Details of concepts are emphasized; parts have meaning of their own					
2. Deals with math and science concepts					
3. Based on discovery approach					

Figure 4-7 Field-independent child rating form. (Developed by H. Krueger and M. Tenenberg for Instructional Strategies Class, California State University, Hayward, 1985.)

which was shown on the Public Broadcasting System in 1993, and in the enthusiasm of the teachers, students, and parents who vie for the opportunity to place their children at Key.

Sternberg (1985, 1988) is another theorist who has taken a different look at the construct of intelligence. He states that intelligence is composed of three basic parts: conceptual, creative, and contextual. The intelligence most frequently rewarded in schools is the conceptual type, involving the ability to process information such as that from class lectures and textbooks.

Perhaps one of the more thorough looks at learning style, especially in relation to providing teachers with ideas for how to teach to children with different styles or ways of processing information in the classroom, has been the work of McCarthy (1987). In establishing her 4MAT system, she provides the reader with a succinct, easy to read and understand summary of many of the ways of looking at learning style, including research on the Myers-Briggs Inventory, the Gregorc Student Learning Styles, Kolb's Experiential Learning, and others. Many of these are based on the work of Carl Jung (1976), who suggested that there were four ways in which people perceive and process information: feeling, thinking, sensing, and intuiting.

One of the reasons that some methods of teaching to learning styles have not been addressed in schools is because they are difficult to evaluate and too much emphasis has been placed on discrete, item-to-item, day-to-day evaluation. Another reason is related to our own biases as teachers; we teach in the way we learn best. Many teachers are strong visual, experiential learners.

Frederick J. Moffett's poem "Thus A Child Learns" gives additional advice for dealing with the process of learning:

Thus a child learns, by wiggling skills through his fingers and toes into himself; by soaking up habits and attitudes of those around him, by pushing and pulling his own world.

Thus a child learns; more through trial than error, more through pleasure than pain, more through experience than suggestion, more through suggestion than direction.

Thus a child learns; through affection, through love, through patience, through understanding, through belonging, through doing, through being.

Day by day the child comes to know a little bit of what you know; to think a little bit of what you think; to understand your understanding. That which you dream and believe and are, in truth, that which becomes the child.

As you perceive dully or clearly; as you think fuzzily or sharply; as you believe foolishly or wisely; as you dream drably or goldenly; as you bear false witness or tell the truth—thus a child learns.

Preschool, kindergarten, and primary grade teachers, using the statements in figure 4-8, can observe their respective students and learn more about their children's preferred learning styles. (For other learning style questionnaires, see the Appendix.)

Temperament

Children also reveal different temperaments. These also can determine how a child relates to the environment. Examine figure 4-9, which lists the characteristics of temperament. Where do you fit on the lines between the extremes? Are you more or less active? Are your body rhythms regular or irregular? Do you tend to be impulsive or cautious in making decisions? Do you see yourself as an adaptable person? Do you have a quick or slow temper? Are you generally an optimist or a pessimist? Are you easily distracted, or could the house burn down around you when you are reading a good book? Your answers to these questions describe your temperament.

Chess and Thomas (1986) have undertaken longitudinal studies looking at nine characteristics of temperament identified by Thomas, Chess, Birch, Hertzig, and Korn (1963) and further investigated by Soderman (1981). Their studies suggest that there are three general types of children, depending on where they fall on the nine characteristics: the easy-to-get-along-with child; the "difficult" one; and the slow-to-warm-up child. Children who are easy to get along with have moderate activity levels

	Yes	No

In the classroom the child:
1. Usually chooses to play/work in a quiet area.
2. Usually chooses to play/work in the noisier areas.
3. Prefers to work/play with music in the background.
4. Becomes distracted if music is played in the background.
5. Is able to concentrate even if others near her are talking or are noisy.
6. Prefers to work/play near window areas or in brightly lighted ones.
7. Usually chooses to play/work at a table or desk.
8. Usually chooses to play/work on the floor, a couch, or beanbag chair.
9. Concentrates for longer periods of time in the morning.
10. Often appears more tired in the morning than in the afternoon.

In relating to adults and/or peers, the child:
1. Prefers to work/play alone.
2. Prefers to play/work with only one friend.
3. Works/plays better if the teacher/peer helps.
4. Likes clear directions regarding how to complete any specific task.
5. Prefers to play/work with several friends.
6. Looks to teacher/peers to reinforce directions as a project is being completed.
7. Frequently starts a project but seldom finishes.
8. Has difficulty following spoken directions unless a demonstration, with a model, is given.
9. Notices whenever teacher or friends have a new haircut or are wearing something new.
10. Follows spoken directions easily.

Figure 4-8 Observation checklist to assess child's preferred learning style.

and regular rhythmicity. They are moderate in decision making, adaptable, slow to anger (without being so slow that they do not assert themselves when appropriate), both quick and slow to respond depending upon the situation, and more optimistic than pessimistic. They tend to have low levels of distractibility and lengthy attention spans. These children may also be more field independent than field sensitive. The behavior of children who are difficult to handle goes to extremes. The children have fast activity levels and irregular rhythmicity.

They are cautious, nonadaptable, quick to anger (temper tantrums), generally negative, and easily distracted. They have short attention spans. Children who are slow to warm up tend to be so cautious in making a decision that they will often wait for a decision to present itself before they move. They are slow to respond, have low adaptability levels, and are generally more pessimistic.

You should be aware that there are no good or bad temperaments; there are only different ones, figure 4-10. Take another look at where you fall on the line between the extremes. Generally, you will have difficulty relating to children at opposite extremes from yourself. For example, if your body rhythms are very regular, you may have less patience toilet training a child who does not have regular body rhythms. This can happen because you may not understand why the child is not regular like yourself. If you are a trusting, optimistic person, it may be difficult to relate to the suspicious, cautious child. The teacher with a lengthy attention span and low level of distractibility may have less patience with the child who is easily distracted and has a short attention span. In planning, the teacher may feel that an activity will take 15 minutes only to discover that this child flits through it in three minutes.

What is the teacher's role in working with children of different temperaments? First, be careful not to label a child with a different temperament as good or bad. Second, take a cue from the characteristics, and plan the lessons accordingly. The child with a short attention span can learn to lengthen it. Give the child activities that can be completed quickly at first. Look to see what activities the child prefers. Then plan an activity that will take a little longer to finish and encourage the child to remain with it. Gradually, you can persuade the child to attend to the activity for a longer period of time.

All teachers soon realize that children do not accomplish the lesson or skill at the same speed, and they differ in the amount of time and attention they devote to activities. The number of repetitions needed for children to memorize or know varies. In general, the memory of an experience will become stronger each time it is encountered.

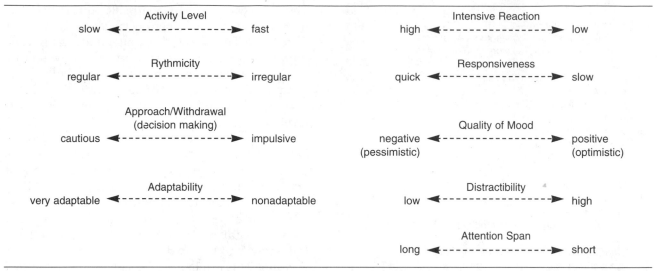

Activity Level		Intensive Reaction	
slow ⟷ fast		high ⟷ low	

Activity Level
slow ◄------------► fast

Rythmicity
regular ◄------------► irregular

Approach/Withdrawal
(decision making)
cautious ◄------------► impulsive

Adaptability
very adaptable ◄------------► nonadaptable

Intensive Reaction
high ◄------------► low

Responsiveness
quick ◄------------► slow

Quality of Mood
negative ◄------------► positive
(pessimistic)   (optimistic)

Distractibility
low ◄------------► high

Attention Span
long ◄------------► short

Figure 4-9 Temperament in clinical practice. (Updated from Temperament and Behavior Disorders in Children, by S. Chess and A. Thomas. New York: Guildford, 1986.)

Figure 4-10 Children's temperaments vary and must be responded to individually.

Self-Esteem and Learning

After much research in the 1960s and 1970s on the relationship of self-esteem to learning, the 1980s saw little being done. A new interest has emerged in the 1990s, however, and researchers are again impressed with the interrelationships between how children view themselves and their abilities to learn. Initial work by Coopersmith (1967), Bandura (1977), and others has shown that children who perceive of themselves as capable and competent and who have a feeling of belongingness (in terms of the classroom atmosphere) are more likely to do well in school than those who do not. For teachers, then, the task is clear—we need to help children feel that they are competent and valued as persons, have control over their own behavior, can make valid choices within the classroom structure, and with the development of self-respect can learn to respect others. We must be aware of any hidden biases we might hold and learn to treat all of our children fairly, honestly, and to encourage individual responsibility (Curry & Johnson, 1990, pp. 146–147). Our curricular goals must value the thinking processes children use as well as any product; we need to emphasize what Katz and Chard (1989) call dispositions, such as "curiosity, resourcefulness, independence, initiative, responsibility, and other positive dispositions" (p. 30).

Some self-esteem curricula have been developed, such as Magic Circle, Quest, and Tribes. Preschools, day-care programs, and elementary schools using these programs have reported increased interest in cooperation and learning among their children.

Teachers familiar with the need for children to see themselves as capable and belonging to their classroom group often provide opportunities within the curriculum as a whole for building self-esteem. These teachers offer children viable choices, utilize cooperative learning groups, and modeling, among other techniques, to boost children's self-esteem, figure 4-11.

Levels of Representation

According to Piagetian theory, children represent the real world at four levels and progress from the lowest to highest levels in thinking abilities. H. Draper and M. Draper (1979) have reviewed these levels as follows:

Figure 4-11 Children are allowed to choose child-authored books during silent reading (first grade classroom).

1. Object Level—Learning about the real thing by interacting with the real object. For example, Janet learns about the telephone by touching it, dialing, listening to someone talk through it, listening to the ring, and seeing others actually use it.

2. Index Level—The second level is called the index of the real object. This level requires the use of one or more of the five senses. Either some part of the real thing or a sound, smell, or taste from it alerts the child to what the real object is. For example, the child hears the telephone ringing. The child who has had a lot of object experiences with the real telephone does not have to see it to know that the ring refers to the telephone.

3. Symbol Level—Only after the child has had ample experience at the object and index levels will that child use symbols. Only then will the child be able to represent the real object with a symbol such as a picture. The picture is not the real thing and there is no sound, smell, or taste coming from it. But often after adequate experience at both the object and index levels, the child will recognize a picture. The child recognizes the picture of the telephone and knows that it represents the real thing. The adult world is full of symbols. It is easy to assume that children can use pictures and other symbols such as drawings to represent real things. Observe children closely and you will see that they do not always see pictures as adults do. A hat may look like a cap to a child, or a bat may look like a stick. A drawing of a round face may look like a cookie. Only after we know children understand the object and index levels can we expect them to represent reality by the use of symbols.

4. Sign Level—This fourth level is the use of a sign such as a word to represent the real thing. The word telephone will mean little to a child who does not know how to read. Many children learn their own names—signs which refer to them. Even though they cannot read, many young children begin to recognize signs if they have lots of experience with them. Have you ever heard a mother say to the father in front of the young child, "We will have c-o-o-k-i-e-s

(spells it aloud) after lunch," and the child says, "Mom can I have a cookie now?" They have heard this sign used enough to know what it refers to even though they cannot see, touch, smell, or taste the cookies.

Piaget (Slavin, 1994) posited four stages of representation.

1. Sensorimotor Stage (birth to age two or three)—Starting at birth, infants and toddlers during the sensorimotor stage learn primarily through their senses—seeing, hearing, touching (manipulating), smelling, and tasting. Remember the example of the baby with the new toy?

2. Preoperational Stage (age two or three to eight or nine)—At this stage, beginning with the development of language approximately at age two, the preschooler develops what Piaget terms "preconcepts" and learns by using his intuition. Thus, a three-year-old child makes typical mistakes in conceptual learning and may call a cow, seen for the first time, by the name of the only large animal with which he has knowledge, "horsie."

Adults can see the children's intuition at work as they make grammatical errors in overgeneralizing plurals. For example, "mouse" becomes "mouses" just as "house" becomes "houses." "Foot" becomes "foots" or "feets." "I don't have no more cookies" becomes standard emphasis for the three year old, the use of the double negative being normal usage.

Piaget often called children in the preoperational stage "perception bound," meaning that they are limited by what they can see, hear, touch, manipulate, and so on, and that they have difficulty seeing comparisons when differences are dramatic. A child at this stage may not understand that a chihuahua and a great dane are both dogs. One two year old, for example, called a Scottie dog a "funny cat" as her only acquaintance with small furry black animals had been her own large female Persian cat.

3. Concrete Operational Stage (ages six to eight to age 11 and even to adulthood)—At this stage the child begins to be able to form classifications, to see the similarities among categories despite their differences. All dogs and all cats, for example, become "animals." Birds that fly, such as sparrows and cardinals, can be grouped with chickens and, sometimes with difficulty, ducks and geese.

Also during the concrete operational stage, the child begins to understand the principles of conservation, essential to the understanding of mathematics. These are the development of understanding that the mass of clay does not change even if it is rolled into an elongated shape or left in a ball; that the liquid in a tall, thin glass is the same as that in a short, fat glass; that area does not change if there are the same number of objects placed on a field, even though one field looks more crowded because the objects are scattered and the other field seems to have more area because the objects are aligned along one side.

4. Formal Operational Stage (age 11 to adulthood)—According to Piaget, during this final stage in intellectual development, the child begins to be capable of abstract thinking. At this stage the child can formulate hypotheses and learns to monitor his own thinking (metacognition).

A contemporary of Piaget, much of the research developed by Vygotsky (Berk & Winsler, 1995) was kept unknown to Western psychologists and educators by the Union of Soviet Socialist Republics (USSR). After *perestroika* and the break-up of the USSR, many of the former Soviet researchers came to the United States and a wide distribution of Vygotsky's research has become available.

Vygotsky saw learning as taking place through social contact and the development of what he termed "private speech." Children talk to themselves, either silently or vocally, in the attempt to internalize learning, monitor themselves, and solve problems. Vygotsky emphasized the importance of language in the development of socially shared cognition in which adults, or peers, assisted the child to move ahead in her development by noticing what the next logical step might be. The term *zone of proximal development* was applied to the adult's or peer's recognition of when the child needed assistance and when she did not. This assisted learning is called scaffolding.

Understanding Vygotsky's theory in teaching has led to the emphasis on cooperative learning, scaffolding or assisted learning, and teaching children to use private speech to help in their problem solving. A teacher might notice that a child is having difficulty placing one piece of a puzzle in the right place and suggest that the piece be rotated. A peer familiar with the same puzzle might do the same. Likewise, a teacher might suggest that the child verbalize as he is putting the pieces into the puzzle, saying such words as, "I see the yellow piece here and I see more yellow there; maybe the piece fits in here."

STUDENT TEACHER INTELLIGENT BEHAVIOR

Costa (1991) suggests that there are several characteristics of intelligent behavior displayed by children. These behaviors apply to adults as well. In this case, student teachers can gain insight into their own behaviors. Costa notes that these are suggested intelligence characteristics and are not meant to represent a complete listing. He urges teachers to discover additional indicators through "kid-watching and self-analysis."

Costa's characteristics of intelligent behavior follow:

1. Persistence: Persevering when the solution to a problem is not immediately apparent
2. Decreasing impulsivity
3. Listening to others with understanding and empathy
4. Using flexibility in thinking
5. Metacognition, defined as awareness of one's own thinking
6. Checking for accuracy and precision
7. Questioning and problem posing
8. Drawing on past knowledge and applying it to new situations
9. Using precision in language and thought rather than confused, vague, and imprecise language to express ideas (This includes using complete sentences, providing supportive evidence for ideas, elaborating, clarifying, and defining terminology in written and oral expression.)
10. Using all the senses
11. Displaying ingenuity, originality, insightfulness, and creativity
12. Displaying wonderment, inquisitiveness, curiosity, and the enjoyment of problem solving; displaying a sense of efficacy as a thinker

Other indicators of intelligent behaviors Costa mentions that are not found in the above listing are a sense of humor and ethical/moral reasoning.

SUMMARY

Four identified theories currently influence decisions and views about child learning. Individuality in learning is apparent; children learn at different rates and learn from different techniques. The teacher's understanding of child development and learning theory, and the idea of how children will learn best, should serve as the basis for the children's guidance and growth.

The senses gather information that is stored mentally and is under continual revision as new situations are met. There is a definite sequence to the learning processes, and teachers need to be aware of individual styles and preferred learning modality to make the experience easier for each child. Many learning behaviors seen in early childhood remain our preferred learning styles throughout our lives.

SUGGESTED ACTIVITIES

A. In groups of three or four, discuss the usual methods of motivating children to try new materials or experiences.

B. Rate the following situations as A (appropriate; justified by current learning theory) or I (inappropriate). If appropriate, cite the theory that supports the answer. Discuss your choices with four or five others in a class group meeting.

1. Marilee, a student teacher, encounters two children who want to learn to tie their shoes. Since she realizes shoe tying is a complex skill, she says, "When you're a little bigger, you'll be able to do it."

2. Thien, a student teacher, would like to tell a group of three-year-olds about the country of his birth, Vietnam. However, Thien realizes they probably would not be able to grasp the concept of a foreign country so he presents a simple Vietnamese song he learned as a child instead.

3. A cooperating teacher presents an activity in which she names and appreciates children who give correct answers.

4. Toni notices Mike and Eduardo are using the toy razors to shave their legs. She redirects their play, asking them to shave their faces like their fathers do.

5. Elena notices that Tilly, an independent child, always hides when inside time is announced. She decides to interest Tilly in an indoor activity before inside time is called to avoid having to find Tilly and coax her in.

6. Johnny refuses to attend any group activities. Laura suspects that he has had negative experiences at previous group times, and decides to make group time so attractive Johnny will want to join in. Laura has planned an activity with large balloons that children sit on and pop.

7. Lisa, Garrett, and Thad often gather at the reading corner and read new books. Stephanie Lynn, the student teacher, sees this as an example of intrinsic motivation.

8. Bud notices that his cooperating teacher always calls on each child by name in any conversation at group or discussion times.

9. Carolyn, a student teacher, feels she needs only to set out activities for the children and they will select the ones they need for their intellectual growth.

10. Gregorio, age three, has just poured water on the floor. The student teacher approaches, saying, "You need to tell me why you poured water on the floor."

11. Carlos says he hates carrots. Susan, the student teacher, tells him she likes them.

12. A child whines, "You know, so tell me!" Joanne, the student teacher, is reluctant to give a direct answer because she feels the child should explore the toy and find out for himself which puzzle piece fits. "Try turning the piece," she suggests.

13. Upon driving to her assigned preschool, Margo notices a street barricade. When the first parent arrives, she asks what is happening.

14. There is a new child in the classroom. This child has a tattoo which fascinates other children. The cooperating teacher feels it is best not to ask the child about it at group time since it might embarrass the newcomer. When a child asks about it, she answers, "I can see you're really interested in the mark you see on our new friend's arm."

15. In Mrs. Clements's preschool, the children select activities, and they have the choice of attending group times or engaging in other quiet activities.

C. In groups of three, act out a teaching/learning situation (two children, one teacher) based on one of the four major theories discussed in this chapter. Have other groups guess which theory you chose to role play.

D. Divide the class into four groups. Have each group write a description of the furnishings and arrangements found in the classroom that adhere to the four major theories previously discussed.

E. Read and discuss the following story. What are the implications for early childhood educators?

The Top of the Class

Once upon a time, the animals decided they must do something heroic to meet the problems of a "new world." So they organized a school. They adopted an activity curriculum which consisted of running, climbing, swimming, and flying. To make it easier to administer the curriculum, all the animals took all the subjects.

The duck was excellent in swimming. In fact, he was much better than the instructor. However, the duck received only a passing grade in flying. He was doing poorly in running also. Consequently, he had to stay after school to practice running. After a while, his webbed feet were so badly worn, he was only average in swimming. But average was acceptable in school, so nobody worried about it except the duck.

The rabbit started at the top of the class in running, but had a nervous breakdown because of so much make-up work in swimming.

The squirrel was excellent in climbing but was very frustrated in flying class when the teacher made her start from the ground up instead of from the treetop down. She also developed charley horses from over-exertion, and only earned a C in climbing and a D in running.

The eagle was a problem and had to be disciplined severely. In the climbing class, he beat all the others to the top of the tree but insisted on using his own method to get there.

At the end of the year, an abnormal eel that could swim very well and run, climb, and fly only a little had the highest average and was valedictorian.

The prairie dogs stayed out of school, and fought the tax levy because the administration would not add digging and burrowing to the curriculum. They apprenticed their child to a badger, and joined the groundhogs and gophers to start a private school.

F. Think back to your first days in your assigned classroom. What elements made the classroom feel safe and comfortable for you the adult? What cooperating teacher actions made you feel "at home," capable, and encouraged? Did you feel that you would learn something and do well in student teaching? Were there situations in which you felt like an outsider? What events, features, would you replicate in your future classrooms to have children feel part of the group, capable, and at ease? Discuss with your training class.

G. With a small group of fellow student teachers discuss student teaching situations that have called for intelligent action and how you or others in your student teaching assignment proceeded or behaved. Share significant conclusions with the total class.

REVIEW

A. Choose the best answer to complete each statement.

1. Beginning teachers should
   a. have a clear idea of how children learn best because research has discovered the learning process.
   b. realize that there are a number of learning theories.
   c. expect children to learn in their own unique ways, making similarities between the children's learning patterns insignificant.
   d. look to their own experiences for clues on child learning.
   e. None of these.

2. A theory is someone's attempt to
   a. gain fame.
   b. help instructors teach.
   c. make sense of a vast series of events.
   d. control others.
   e. make others think like the theorist.

3. It is generally accepted that children should
   a. be grouped according to ability.
   b. be grouped according to age.
   c. be asked to practice and recite learnings.
   d. play because it promotes learning.
   e. be exposed to planned group times that teach survival skills.

4. When one hears that children pass through stages in their development, it means that

a. all the children pass through stages in an orderly, predictable way.

b. children should tour buses and theaters.

c. there seem to be phases in growth that teachers and parents can expect.

d. most children will return to previous stages at times.

e. All of these.

5. Children generally remember a concept best when

a. they see a picture of the concept.

b. they watch a demonstration of the concept by the teacher.

c. they hear the teacher describe the concept.

d. they use the concept in the discovery center.

e. All of these.

6. Gardiner believes that in elementary schools, teachers too often teach only to children with

a. logico-mathematical and intrapersonal intelligences.

b. logico-mathematical and spatial intelligences.

c. logico-mathematical and linguistic intelligences.

d. logico-mathematical and bodily-kinesthetic intelligences.

e. logico-mathematical and interpersonal intelligences.

7. According to research into temperament, the easy-to-get-along-with child has the following characteristics:

a. a regular rhythmicity, an easy adaptability, a positive quality of mood, a low distractibility, and a long attention span.

b. a regular rhythmicity, an easy adaptability, intense reactions to environmental stimuli, and a negative quality of mood.

c. an irregular rhythmicity, a fast activity level, an easy adaptability, a negative quality of mood, and a long attention span.

d. a regular rhythmicity, a negative quality of mood, high distractibility, a long attention span, and intense reactions to stimuli.

e. a regular rhythmicity, a cautious approach to decision making, adaptability, a negative quality of mood, and a long attention span.

8. Field-sensitive children tend to

a. want to work and play alone.

b. seek reinforcement frequently from the teacher.

c. like to work and play in small groups.

d. tend to like math and science better than concepts related to personal interests.

e. b and c.

f. a and d.

9. Costa suggests that among the intelligent behaviors displayed by children (and adults) are any of the following:

a. persistence.

b. impulsivity.

c. questioning and problem posing.

d. flexibility in thinking.

e. a, b, and c.

f. a, c, and d.

10. Children with a strong sense of self-esteem generally

a. do poorly in school.

b. do well in school.

c. are resourceful.

d. are dependable.

e. a and b.

f. c and d.

B. List any accepted learning theories you feel were excluded from this unit. Cite your source (text, individual, etc.).

C. Define convergent thinking, divergent thinking, symbol level, and sign level.

REFERENCES

Bandura, A. (1977). *Social learning theory.* Englewood Cliffs, NJ: Prentice-Hall.

Berk, L. E., & Winsler, A. (1995). *Scaffolding children's learning: Vygotsky and early childhood education.* Washington, DC: National Association for the Education of Young Children.

Braun, S. J., & Edwards, E. P. (1972). *History and theory of early childhood education.* Worthington, OH: Jones.

Chess, S., & Thomas, A. (1986). *Temperament in clinical practice.* New York: Guilford.

Coopersmith, S. (1967). *The antecedents of self-esteem.* San Francisco: Freeman.

Costa, A. L. (1991). The search for intelligent life. In *Developing minds: A resource book for teaching thinking.* Alexandria, VA: Association for Supervision and Curriculum Development.

Curry, N. E., & Johnson, C. N. (1990). *Beyond self-esteem: Developing a genuine sense of human value.* Washington, DC: National Association for the Education of Young Children.

Draper, H., & Draper, M. (1979). *Studying children.* Peoria, IL: Bennett.

Erikson, E. (1963). *Childhood and society.* New York: Norton.

Felton, V., & Henry, J. (November 6, 1981). Think power. Presentation at the annual conference of the National Association for the Education of Young Children.

Gardiner, H. (1983). *Frames of mind: The theory of multiple intelligences.* New York: Basic Books.

Gardiner, H. (1988). Beyond the IQ: Education and human development. *National Forum 68, 27,* pp. 4–7.

Gardiner, H. (1993). *Multiple intelligences: The theory in practice.* New York: Basic Books.

Gesell, A., Ilg, F. L., & Ames, L. B. (1974). *The child from five to ten.* New York: Harper & Row.

Hendrick, J. (1985, 1993). *Total learning for the whole child.* Columbus, OH: Merrill/Macmillan; New York: Merrill/Macmillan.

Hohmann, M., Banet, B., & Weikart, D. (1979). *Young children in action.* Ypsilanti, MI: High/Scope Press.

Jung, C. G. (1976). *Psychological types.* Princeton, NJ: Princeton University Press.

Kamii, C., & DeVries, R. (1978). *Physical knowledge in preschool education: Implications of Piaget's theory* Englewood Cliffs, NJ: Prentice-Hall.

Katz, L. G., & Chard, S. C. (1989). *Engaging children's minds: The project approach.* Norwood, NJ: Ablex.

Lavatelli, C. (1973). *Piaget's theory applied to an early childhood curriculum.* Boston: American Science and Engineering.

McCarthy, B. (1987). *The 4MAT system: Teaching to learning styles with right/left mode techniques.* Barrington, IL: Excel.

Piaget, J. (1952). *The origins of intelligence.* New York: International Universities Press.

Rousseau, J. J. (1947). L'Emile ou l'education. In O. E. Tellows and N. R. Tarrey (Eds.), *The age of enlightenment.* New York: F. S. Croft (First published, 1742).

Seefeldt, C., & Barbour, N. (1993). *Early childhood education: An introduction* (3rd ed.). New York: Merrill/Macmillan.

Slavin, R. E. (1994). *Educational psychology: Theory and practice,* 4th ed. Boston: Allyn & Bacon.

Soderman, A. K. (November 6, 1981). *Marching to a different drummer: A look at temperament in the development of personality.* Presentation at the annual conference of the National Association for the Education of Young Children.

Sternberg, R. (1985). *Beyond IQ: A triarchic theory of human intelligence.* New York: Cambridge University Press.

Sternberg, R. J. (1988). *The triarchic mind: A new theory of human intelligence.* New York: Viking.

Stevens, J. H., Jr., & King, E. W. (1976). *Administering early childhood programs.* Boston: Little, Brown.

Thomas, A., Chess, S., Birch, H. G., Hertzig, M. E., & Korn, S. (1963). *Behavioral individuality in early childhood.* New York: New York University Press.

RESOURCES

Barron, J. B., & Sternberg, R. J. (1987). *Teaching thinking skills: Theory and practice.* New York: Freeman.

DeVries, R., & Kohlberg, L. (1990). *Constructivist early education: Overview and comparison with other programs.* Washington, DC: National Association for the Education of Young Children.

Mosston, M., & Ashworth, S. (1990). *The spectrum of teaching styles: From command to discovery.* New York: Longman.

Rieber, R., & Carton, A. S. (Eds.). (1987). *The collected works of L. S. Vygotsky, Vol. 1, Problems of general psychology* (N. Minick, Trans.). New York: Plenum.

Sternberg, R., & Wagner, R. (1986). *Practical intelligence: Nature and origins of competence in the everyday world.* Cambridge: Cambridge University Press.

Vygotsky, L. S. (1934, 1986). *Thought and language* (A. Kozulin, Trans.). Cambridge, MA: MIT Press.

5

Activity Planning

After studying this chapter, the student will be able to:

● Complete a written activity or lesson plan form.

● Identify three ways of assessing child interest.

● List criteria for child activity planning.

● Describe the benefits of written activity/lesson plans.

● Identify factors to consider when planning settings for teacher-guided activities.

Many children seem to be typical and average at first. Then you experience their unique diversity. Many are about the same size but inside they are just wired differently.

Jo Beth Scrivani

I found I tried to teach too many things in my activities. Then I focused upon teaching a few things. I'll never forget the day the children practiced dialing 911, our local telephone emergency number. Luckily my cooperating teacher suggested I put something in the parent newsletter the week before. I found out quickly that many children didn't know their address.

Lindsay Hauser

The most memorable part of student teaching has been the daily experience in my placement classroom. The lessons I have learned and the information shared has been a storehouse that will take years to exhaust.

Being forced to write lesson plans has helped me with my planned classroom activities. It has also widened the activities I present in my employment classroom. I'm more aware of my own capabilities and knowledge.

Judy Mabie

My first day of student teaching was easy. My cooperating teacher didn't ask much of me, so I made a point of being helpful, handing out papers so she could continue talking, etc. Later she said, "If you have any ideas of things you'd like to do, feel free. . . ." That filled me with dread. I didn't know what to do with first graders, and I was hoping she'd clue me into the sorts of things we'd be doing the next few weeks so I'd be able to figure out how to fit in. I remember thinking that the kids seemed older, bigger than I expected, but I was soon reminded of their age when they were trying to do any reading or writing.

Fononga Pahula

● IDENTIFYING CHILD INTERESTS

You will plan, prepare, and present classroom activities. The teaching day contains structured (teacher-planned) and unstructured (child-chosen) activities. The cooperating teacher's philosophy, the school's philosophy, the identified program goals, and classroom setting determine the balance between child-chosen activities and teacher-planned activities. In activity-centered classrooms, or those with a Piagetian view, student teachers arrange room centers to invite and promote child discovery and learning. "Every time we teach a child something, we keep him from reinventing it. On the other hand, every time a child discovers it himself, it remains with him for the rest of his life" (Piaget, in the film *Patron:Piaget In New Perspective*).

Jones (1986) describes a classroom based on an open-classroom model where children choose the majority of their own activities:

Adults are responsible for structuring an environment full of developmentally appropriate choices, helping children choose among the possibilities, and enriching their experience by joining in it and building on it.

and

unique events keep happening. . . . Good curriculum emerges out of those unique events.

Using Child Interest and Improvising

Teaching is a complex task requiring continual on-the-spot decision making (Carter & Curtis, 1994). Carter and Curtis believe master teachers have certain qualities that distinguish them from teachers who depend on curriculum activity books, follow the same theme plans year after year, or struggle daily to get the children involved in anything productive. They possess a set of attitudes and habits of mind to respond to classroom dynamics and multiple needs of children with the readiness of an improvisational artist.

An example of the above master teacher mindset can be seen in the actions of one student teacher (Fredrica) in the following:

A book about cats was brought to school by a child. After being previewed, Fredrica shared the book with a group of the child's friends. Susan, a four-year-old, went to the scrap paper and craft table later in the afternoon and cut long paper nails for one hand. She then asked Fredrica for tape to secure them to her fingers. They again looked at the book's illustrations to see if long cat nails were visible. Susan enjoyed meowing, pretending to scratch a tree trunk, and climbing the outdoor structure. Other children wished to cut and color cat nails of their own. Fredrica supplied materials. Soon a number of children were pretending to be cats! Fredrica was prepared to intervene if nails were used aggressively. The following day Fredrica set up a discovery area which included taped domestic animal sounds, cat figures to manipulate, and pictures of different house cat varieties. Poems about cats were part of story times. A cat visited school and cat care particulars were listed by the children on a wall chart printed with child ideas. Fredrica and the children explored how the cats' sharp nails helped cats climb trees in one activity, and how cats use their nails to protect themselves in another.

You will be searching for activity ideas that will interest and challenge the group of children to which you are assigned. Observing children's play choices and favorite activities will give you ideas, figure 5-1. Children's conversations provide clues as to what has captured their attention. (You can make comments in your pocket notebook concerning individual and group curiosity and play selections.) Watch for excitement among the children. What were they eager to try? Was considerable time spent exploring or concentrating on an experience? (See figure 5-2.) Holt (1964) emphasizes that teachers need to be aware of children's interests.

We can begin by thinking of ourselves not as teachers, but as gardeners. A child's mind, like a flower, is a living thing. We can't make it grow by sticking things on it any more than we can make a flower grow by gluing on petals and leaves. All we can do is surround the growing mind with what it needs for growing and have faith that it will take what it needs and will grow. Our job as teachers is not to get the child to learn what we want but to help him learn what he wants. Go back into your own experiences as

Figure 5-1 Trying on hats is fun and is an interesting activity idea.

ucators realize the importance of teacher interaction in classrooms. Child-initiated activities and social communication take place in many learning situations, particularly with three-, four-, and five-year olds. Collaborative meaning-making happens constantly. O'Loughlin hopes the present emphasis on constructivism will consider and incorporate children's culture, race, class, learning histories, gender backgrounds, language, and the reality of teacher as power figure into the early childhood field's recommended teaching model.

The National Association for the Education of Young Children's [NAEYC's (1988)] *Developmentally Appropriate Practice in Early Childhood Programs Serving Children from Birth through Age 8* has been highly praised and acclaimed as the field's most respected guide to child activity planning. Developed through the efforts of many individuals and groups under

a child and learn from them. Remember your enthusiasm for certain activities and your discovery and avid participation in others.

● CONSTRUCTIVISM AND DEVELOPMENTALLY APPROPRIATE PRACTICE

It's difficult to read any written material dealing with early childhood curriculum development and pedagogy that doesn't mention:

- child-centered
- child-initiated
- active learning
- constructivist, and
- developmentally appropriate

The first two terms are self-explanatory. Constructivism, a cognitive-developmental notion, has direct roots within the structuralism that underlies Piaget's theory of intellectual development (O'Loughlin, 1991). A constructivist takes the position that learners must have experiences with hypothesizing and predicting, manipulating objects, posing questions, researching answers, imagining, investigating, and inventing for new constructions to be developed (Fosnot, 1989). Early childhood ed-

Figure 5-2 Discovering together is an enjoyable aspect of teaching. (Courtesy of Nancy Martin)

NAEYC's leadership, it has been widely accepted though it is not without its critics. O'Loughlin (1991) has listed what he believes to be the essence of Developmentally Appropriate Practice's recommended pedagogy:

- The curriculum is integrated so that children's learning in all traditional subject areas occurs primarily through projects and learning centers that teachers plan and that reflect children's interests and suggestions. Teachers guide children's ideas, responding to their questions, engaging them in conversation and challenging their thinking.

- The curriculum is integrated so that learning occurs primarily through projects, learning centers, and playful activities that reflect current interests of children. . . .

- Teachers use much of their planning time to prepare the environment so that children can learn through active involvement with each other, with adults and older children serving as informal tutors, and with materials. Many learning centers are available for children to choose from. . . . Errors are viewed as a natural and necessary part of learning. Teachers analyze children's errors and use the information obtained to plan curriculum instruction.

- Individual children or small groups are expected to work and play cooperatively or alone in learning centers and on projects that they usually select themselves or are guided to by the teacher. Activity centers are changed frequently so children can have new things to do.

- Learning materials and activities are concrete, real and relevant to children's lives. Objects children can manipulate and experiment with, such as blocks, cards, games, woodworking tools, arts and crafts materials, and scientific equipment are readily accessible. Tables are used for children to work alone or in small groups. A variety of work places and spaces is provided and flexibly used.

It's O'Loughlin's (1991) opinion that:

> Two points are worthy of note. First, in order to brighten the halo round developmentally appropriate education, traditional education is presented as a uniformly bleak, authoritarian, punitive form of pedagogy, and as the polar opposite of developmentally appropriate education. Second, it is notable that in all of the foregoing there is virtually no mention of the *purpose* of education. The focus, instead, is almost exclusively on method, with content assumed to be unproblematic. The curriculum needs to be built around items of interest to children is repeated often enough, but what does that mean? Do children always know what interests them, and what happens if a teacher wants to teach something educationally sound but initially uninteresting to children? The more serious question, of course, is *in whose interest* schooling takes place. The NAEYC statement does not address this issue directly but some insights can be gained from examining their proposals regarding curriculum. At the core of their proposal is the notion that curriculum should be integrated across disciplines. The issue of interdisciplinary integration is not addressed in its own right, however, but rather through presentation of recommendations in specific curriculum areas.

Schools and teachers who believe traditional education has proved its merits over the years, parents who want traditional teacher-planned and directed learning activities and curriculum, and educators who feel their group of young children is far from the mainstream and require specific experiences before first grade are faced with a dilemma! Can their center's or school's curriculum be completely developmentally appropriate and based only on child interests?

This text includes a section on student-teacher-written activity plans to aid students whose training program mandates this requirement. We believe that in trying to expand already noted child or group interest, written lesson planning, skill and practice is useful and necessary. Also, we think most teachers often wish to attempt teaching something they believe educationally sound and valuable because of some school or societal happening important to children's growth.

In general, it is easier at the preschool level and private kindergarten and primary grades to teach with learning center activities. Most states limit the number of children per teacher in preschools to 12 to

15. Many private schools limit the number of children in kindergarten and primary classrooms to 20 to 25. In public school kindergarten and primary grade classrooms where the number of children can be as high as 30–35, DAP (Developmentally Appropriate Practice) can be difficult, and the teacher-centered, more authoritarian approach often becomes necessary.

As more and more states have begun to look critically at their programs in early childhood (birth to age eight), the question of what is developmentally appropriate to the learning abilities and styles of young children becomes a major issue. What is meant by the term *developmentally appropriate practice*? In 1988, the National Association for the Education of Young Children published its definitive explanation in a book entitled, *Developmentally Appropriate Practice in Early Childhood Programs Serving Children from Birth through Age 8. Developmentally Appropriate Practice* evolved from a perceived need articulated by other early childhood professionals, principally Elkind in his books, *The Hurried Child:Growing Up Too Fast and Too Soon* (1986) and *Miseducation:Preschoolers at Risk* (1987). Other researchers (the International Reading Association, 1986; Williams & Kamii, 1986; and Hirsch-Pasek & Hyson, 1988) confirmed many of the concerns that kindergarten and primary education in the United States was not developmentally appropriate and that children experienced feelings of anxiety and/or boredom in classes that were principally teacher-directed, work-sheet-oriented, and driven by end-of-the-year testing.

Their concerns soon attracted the attention of several states. California, for example, appointed a Kindergarten Task Force to look at curriculum practices in the state's kindergartens. The result, *Here They Come, Ready or Not!* (1988), has sparked renewed concern about how young children learn and what are appropriate curricular practices. In 1989, the National Association of State Boards of Education reconfirmed what is developmentally appropriate in their publication, *Right from the Start*. A simple definition is that developmentally appropriate practice provides "learning activities suitable for a child's age, stage of development, and interests" and is appropriate for the group's age as a whole (Seefeldt & Barbour, 1993).

Another consideration in defining the terms is that the "curriculum is designed to develop children's knowledge in all developmental areas—physical, social, emotional, and intellectual—and to help children learn how to learn—to establish a foundation for lifelong learning" (Bredekamp, 1988, p. 67).

ACTIVITY RESOURCES

Files, resource books, and activity ideas you collected during training will now come in handy. Research books that describe child activity ideas. You will have to discern whether the ideas fit your group. Teachers' and children's magazines often have timely seasonal activity planning ideas.

Draw upon your own creative abilities. All too often student teachers feel that tried and true ideas are superior to what they invent. The new and novel activities you create will add sparkle and uniqueness to your teaching. Do not be afraid to draw from and improve a good idea or change successful activities your children have already enjoyed. Some classroom activities are designed because of an overabundance of scrap or donated material. Take another look at materials in storage that are not receiving much attention or have been forgotten. Perhaps these can be reintroduced in a clever, new way.

CURRICULUM AREAS

Most preschool curriculums include: arts and crafts; music and movement; language; science; large and small motor skill development; cooking and nutrition activities; numbers and measurement; perceptual motor activities; health and safety activities; social learnings; multicultural awareness activities; and plant and animal study. Primary classrooms often follow district-approved guidelines.

Newly evolving areas of study with different degrees of acceptance include: anti-bias, economics and consumer awareness; ecology and energy study; moral and ethical values; the study of changing sex role responsibilities; the study of changing family patterns; introduction to photography; introduction to computers; gardening and preserving activities; and structured games.

Academic programming at prekindergarten and kindergarten levels is programming that seems pushed down from above and is of great concern to the field of early childhood education. This type of programming usually requires young children to sit passively for long periods of listening or requires learning by rote memorization and is consequently inappropriate. In planning activities you will be striving to provide for active exploration integrated with each child's previous out-of-the-classroom experiences. You will attempt to match age-appropriate developmental needs and characteristics of the group with activities. Children will explore, manipulate, converse, move about, play, and freely talk about what is happening and what it means to them. Activities will provide for heterogeneous child abilities.

Your placement classroom will have planned activities and may use a learning center-thematic approach, and you will be asked to start planning and presenting activities.

Your planned activities may attempt to meet the special needs of culturally and linguistically diverse students as well as those of other students with special needs.

At prekindergarten level you'll plan for abundant child play. Schickendanz (1989/1990) notes "the preschool program pendulum once again swings back to play," and "children can learn a lot of academics while they play." She urges teachers to:

> be skillful, clever, and in tune with preschoolers' minds. They must take adult-oriented goals and fit them into a child's world. As one wise teacher once said to me, I know what I must teach children, but I depend on them for ideas about how to do it.

Your previous early childhood education training courses have promoted your sensitivity to and awareness of cultural pluralism. Activities and interactions with children are designed to eliminate practices and materials that discriminate on the basis of race, sex, age, ethnic origin, language, religion, or handicapping conditions.

U.S. education has joined the war on drugs by increasing program planning that includes drug abuse prevention. Early childhood programs need to face, as Oyemade and Washington (1989) point out, the fact that some families have barriers to economic security, good health, good education, a nice home, and a safe neighborhood:

> Some families have more barriers to overcome to achieve these dreams than others. Some have to fight poverty, crowded housing, inadequate health care, crime, illiteracy, unemployment, and/or ethnic stereotypes as they struggle to achieve their dreams of self-sufficiency.

The social-emotional emphasis in activity planning has gained additional status through the work of Elliot (1993) and Marcon (1994). The social skills involve cooperation, assertion, responsibility, empathy, and self-control and are viewed as keys to both acceptable behavior and academic achievement.

Parent-child interaction, particularly the quality of personal relationships and parent discipline techniques, seems to contribute to potential child drug use. The function of teachers in developing self-discipline in attending children and providing children with the logical consequences of their actions during daily contacts is in itself part of a drug abuse prevention program.

In developing curriculum, remembering that each class is unique, each child individual, is mandatory. What is or is not learned depends on classroom materials and interactions between adults and children and/or children and other children as they attempt to understand what is experienced and how it relates to them and others.

Look at your placement classroom in a different way. What do children seem to be learning? What have they already mastered? What line of learning could be extended by provision of materials or a planned activity? The answers to these questions may help your ability to customize your activities.

Being Aware

On any given day certain classroom events and happenings evolve naturally as children react to the weather, the setting, the choices set out, activities, people encountered, and so on. The dynamics and personalities present influence children. Student teachers need to be curious, watchful, and ready to support child discoveries, rather than closely focused on planned, teacher-directed efforts. Noticing child pursuits gives additional data for activity planning and discovery center topics.

Daily Schedules

Daily time schedules alert teachers to that day's planned happenings. Children's needs dictate what takes place. Food, rest, and toileting times are inserted in time slots. Active periods alternate with quiet ones. Group times include announcements of that day's particular events and activities and recognize and welcome each child's presence.

With a schedule teachers and children know what comes next. Teachers plan in advance for necessary room settings, materials, equipment, furniture, and staffing needs. Each center and school decides on the flexibility of its daily schedule, and most deviate often when the unexpected occurs and children can profit from a newly created activity. Schools are rarely slaves to schedules but rather capitalize on unplanned learning opportunities or immediately revise a schedule when planned activities in some way fizzle or fail to capture interest.

Play and Learning

A commonly heard saying in early childhood literature, "Play is the work of the young child," should be coupled with "Play is learning." Children use play to translate experience to understanding. Teachers often see in the child's play the reenactment of behaviors the child has viewed in others. Behaviors that may be puzzling or significant in their lives are "tried on for size." They step inside the other person's shoes and seemingly gain insight through the reliving.

In children's random and investigative play, discoveries are made. Happenings are tested, retested, varied, and extended. Focus may be keen and, at times, they are eager to talk about what they understand and experience.

Peers often function as tutors or providers of information. Adults observe, supply, talk about, encourage, and appreciate, without interfering except when safety is a factor. Adults do ask provocative questions and give suggestions but guard against inflicting their own directions or intentions concerning the child's choice of play.

All of the following may be part of play episodes:

- exploring
- experimenting
- comparing
- ordering
- classifying
- imitating
- verbalizing
- organizing
- discovering
- questioning
- creating
- problem solving and other thinking skills

● HOW WHOLE LANGUAGE INSTRUCTION FITS INTO ALL ACTIVITY PLANNING

The whole language movement has emphasized the need for prekindergarten teachers to realize language learning is a natural part of young children's play and exploration.

Listening, speaking, becoming aware of print and books happens throughout a preschool day. Advocates of whole language methods urge teachers to help young children discover the functional use of language and the integrated nature of the language arts in meaningful settings. McCallum (1989) hopes teachers of young children realize:

- Language develops in a social context.
- Language development has an affective base.
- Language development happens in functional and meaningful contexts.
- Language growth is a developmental process.
- Language development is an active process tied to almost every human endeavor. Thought-conceptualization occurs in real time and space.
- Literacy instruction should be child centered versus teacher centered.

Language will be involved with whatever you plan for young children. Teaching strategies can facilitate emerging literacy, both functional and literary.

An early childhood program involves continual child interactions with pleasurable, quality picture books read by enthusiastic adults skilled in discussing and expanding child interest and enjoyment. With familiarity and repetition and access to a book collection, children explore, notice book features, start to pretend to read, join in the reading, predict outcomes, look for picture clues, feel at home with print, read to themselves, and usually glide naturally into reading on their own. This sounds easy but takes time and planned actions on the adult's part. Many homes offer this type of literary background to young children and couple book reading with pencil (crayon) and paper home activities. These homes are usually verbal environments where conversations about joint parent-child happenings abound. All preschoolers do not experience this backdrop for literacy development. Some have experienced a similar home environment in a language other than English and can be very literate in that language and culture. English literacy development at school is usually designed along the same lines described in the enriching homes above.

Other children have arrived at school with limited or spotty experiences with books, print, or conversationally interested adults. The center or school attempts to supply a rich language and literature program that not only introduces picture books but also print and its functional use, nursery rhymes, classic word and movement activities (finger and body play), music with words, listening experiences and games, poetry, puppetry, storytelling, mechanical language aids (computers, books with tapes, language master, projectors, among others), and additional language activities all offered with supportive, skilled, word-providing teachers. Most schools believe language pervades all school happenings and take clues from child preferences, interests, and pursuits in developing their curriculum. Teachers become subtle opportunists who engage in daily conversations, question and provide suggestions, and

provide materials and environments that lead to child discovery and further exploration and activity.

Wasserman (1992) helps the teacher's language interactions by describing a language interaction process (adult-child) she calls play/debrief/replay. The teacher's questions are, What happened? What did you notice? and What did you think about that? The verbal responses the child offers come from firsthand happenings with the environment and its materials and from peer associations. Teachers can then reflect, expand, extend with further discussion, and ask additional honest questions from an interested co-explorer's perspective.

A variation of Wasserman's questioning interaction sequence with young beginning-to-be-verbal preschoolers might sound like, What's that? What did you see? How do you think that person felt? and What happened? Child responses may be partially nonverbal, and reenacted in the child's actions and movement.

Early childhood teachers inclined to use a whole language approach should realize whole language instruction need not exclude phonics. In recent years teachers' exclusive use of whole language instruction has been increasingly criticized as end of the year test scores have dropped.

Instructing Non-English-Speaking Children

There are two opposing positions concerning a teacher's need to be fluent in a child's home language to be able to plan an effective curriculum for a particular child. Kuster (1994) advocates that teachers become fluent in the attending children's language and knowledgeable about their culture. Others cite what has been traditional and historic in education in the United States: a standard-English-speaking teacher using standard English. Each early childhood program will plan instruction based on its own opinion. It is commonplace today, however, to find as many as 12 different languages being spoken by the children in one classroom.

Types of Activities

Planned activities can promote child growth through child/teacher discussion and interaction.

Important factors that need consideration in the planning and preparation of any activity are:

- Child safety
- The goal or objective of the activity
- Appropriateness to children's ages, experiences, and skill levels
- Setting environment and its comfort, lighting, and sound level
- Number of children and adults
- Duration and time of day
- Materials, furnishings, objects to be used
- Expense
- Clean-up provisions
- Transition to next activity
- Nonsexist and nonracist language; appropriate values

It is generally agreed that activities for young children should:

- Capture and hold their attention
- Provide opportunities for active involvement with minimal time spent waiting
- Provide firsthand sensory experiences and explanations when necessary
- Allow for discovery and pursuit of interests
- Give children a sense of confidence in themselves and their learning competence
- Be connected to past experiences so they can bridge the gap between what they already know and the new experience. However, activities should not be too closely related so as to slow down the child's learning due to boredom. Also, activities should not stretch beyond the child's capacity for learning; this could result in feelings of frustration and a sense of boredom.
- Add to the quality of their lives
- Be of a reasonable duration
- Fit into quiet and active periods and be planned according to noisy or quiet locations
- Provide for individual differences
- Have clearly stated directions and expectations if necessary

- Be flexible enough to provide for unexpected child interests
- Be intellectually stimulating

McCracken (1995) reminds teachers of four goals which she believes are at the heart of professional teaching practices:

- Instill trust
- Promote independence
- Foster friendships
- Encourage success

Marcon (1994) states:

> If you are going to provide a preschool program for children, do so only if it can be individualized to match children's levels of development and natural approaches to learning. Child-initiated, active learning approaches win hands down in both the short and the long term. Pushing children too soon into "formalized academics" may actually backfire when demands of the later childhood grades require children to do more independent thinking.

Multicultural Recognition

In student teaching classes the students enrolled may well represent a wide spectrum of different, diverse values and cultural outlooks or a relatively narrow, limited perspective. Child classrooms are increasingly multicultural in most parts of the United States while some remain only barely ethnically and culturally diverse. In both cases your assumptions about adults and enrolled children will need careful examination as you strive to embrace, appreciate, and respect cultural and ethnic similarities and differences. Offering a child a curriculum that ensures dignity to diverse groups will be a challenging teaching task.

Written Activity Plans

Activity plans are useful devices that encourage student teachers to thoroughly think through the different parts of their planned activities. They help beginning teachers foresee possible problems and find solutions. With adequate preparation through written planning, the student teacher can approach each planned activity with a degree of confidence and security. Cooperating teachers and supervisors often contribute ideas on the student's written plans or consult with the student, making plans a team effort. Written plans are a starting point from which actual activity flows, depending on the children's reception and feedback. Monitoring the children's interest is a teaching task, figure 5-3, and will often result in improvising and revising the activities to suit their needs.

> A teacher needs to observe students during instruction to identify those who have the greatest difficulty becoming actively engaged. However, simply to identify them is not enough. The teacher must determine the reasons for their lack of participation and how to evoke more active participation. Students may be uninvolved for different reasons—boredom, anxiety, fatigue, personal problems, inability to understand the instruction, or involvement in matters unrelated to the classroom. Sometimes the teacher's interest in students and their needs or "private attention" can improve motivation and involvement. (Levin & Long, 1981, p. 12)

Figure 5-3 Monitoring chidren's interest in a planned activity is one of the teacher's tasks.

Figure 5-4 shows one classroom's weekly plan. This particular classroom was staffed with one full-time teacher, one part-time assistant, and three high school volunteers. Since the classroom was organized into learning centers and a wide variety of basic materials was always available to the children, it notes only additions in materials or special projects to be started or continued (Schickendanz, York, Stewart, & White, 1977). This plan indicates which adult is responsible for which room area or activity. Written lesson plans proceed one step farther and isolate a teacher's or student teacher's plan for what will happen during a specific time block and in a specific location.

The activity plan guide in figure 5-5 is one of many possible forms that can be used by student teachers. It is appropriate for most, but not all, planned activities. Storytimes, fingerplays, flannelboard stories, songs, and short-duration activities usually are not written in activity plan form. Activity plan titles are descriptive, such as Sink and Float, Making Farmers' Cheese, or Tie Dyeing. They quickly clarify the subject of the planned experience.

Filling in the curriculum area space sometimes leads to indecision. Many early childhood activities are hard to categorize. Subjects seem to fall into more than one area. Use your own judgment and designation; it is your plan!

Identification of materials, supplies, and tools comes next. Some activities require visual aids and equipment for teachers as well as those materials used by children. Make sure you, as the student teacher, know how to use visual aids and do simple repairs on them. Estimating exact amounts of necessary materials helps calculate expenses and aids preparation. You will simply count out the desired quantities. Student teachers generally know what classroom supplies are available to them and what they will have to supply themselves.

The location of a planned activity has much to do with its success. The following questions can help decide the best location.

- What amount of space will children need?

- What room or outdoor features (e.g., windows,

Area \ Day	Monday	Tuesday	Wednesday	Thursday	Friday
Math	Chart worms eaten by turtle.				
Science	(Steve)		(Steve) Tubes, corks, water, and food coloring.		
Language Arts			(Sara) Write Dictation.		
House Area	(Ted) Add materials for table.	(Ted) Applesauce- Sharon & Tom.	(Ted)	(Ted)	(Ted)
Blocks	Add transportation toys.				
Art Table	Object printing.		Add new objects for printing.		
Music	Resonating bells.			(John)	
Story	(Jan) (Steve)	(Ted)	(Ted)	(Ted) (Susan)	(Ted) (Jan)
Group Time	(Jan)	(Jan)	(Jan)	(Jan)	(Jan)
Outdoor Play	Old tires for rolling down hill.		Visiting goat.		
Trips or Visitors					
Snack	Celery and peanut butter.	Applesauce.	Juice and crackers.	Tapioca pudding.	Juice and raisins.

Figure 5-4 Sample of a prekindergarten teacher's weekly plan sheet. (From Schickendanz *et al.*, *Strategies for Teaching Young Children*, © 1977, p.15. Reprinted by permission of Prentice Hall, Inc., Englewood Cliffs, NJ.)

water, flat floor, storage or drying areas, rug, lighting, grass, shade) are necessary?

- Will electrical outlets be necessary?
- Will noise or traffic from adjacent areas cause interference?
- Will one adult be able to supervise the location?

Self-help and child participation in clean-up, if necessary, need consideration. Activities that actively engage children and invite exploration suit young children's needs. Random set-ups can lead to confusion and conflict over work space and supply use. A good set-up helps a child work without help and promotes proper respect for classroom supplies and equipment and consideration for the work of others. Each set-up reflects a teacher's goals and philosophy of how children best learn.

Student teachers usually begin planning for small groups and then tackle larger groups and the total room activity plans. A number of fascinating early childhood activities call for close adult supervision and can happen safely or successfully only with a few children at a time. Instant replays or ongoing activities may be necessary to accommodate all interested children. Waiting lists are useful in these cases, and children quickly realize they will be

1. Activity title _____
2. Curriculum area _____
3. Materials needed _____
   _____
   _____
4. Location and set-up of activity _____
5. Number of children and adults _____
6. Preparation _____
   _____
   _____
   _____
7. Specific behavioral objective _____
   _____
   _____
   _____
   _____
8. Developmental skills necessary for success _____
   _____
9. Getting started _____
   _____
   _____
10. Procedure (step by step) _____
    _____
    _____
11. Discussion (key concepts, attitudes, facts, skills, vocabulary, etc.) _____
    _____
    _____
    _____
    _____
    _____
12. Apply (or additional practice of skill or learning) _____
    _____
13. Clean-up _____
14. Terminating statement _____
15. Transition _____
16. Evaluation: activity, teacher, child _____
    _____
    _____
    _____
    _____
    _____
    _____
    _____
    _____

Figure 5-5 Activity plan guide.

called when it is their turn, figure 5-6. The number of children on activity plan forms could read, "Two groups of four children," for example.

Preparation sections on lesson plans alert the student teacher to tasks to be completed prior to actual presentation. This could include making a number of individual portions of paste, moving furniture, mixing paint, making a recipe chart, or a number of similar teacher activities. Preparation includes attention to features that minimize child waiting and decrease the need for help from the teacher.

Writing Lesson Plans for Elementary Schools. There are several ways, each based upon a different theoretical model, to approach a lesson plan. One of the more popular models, and one based upon behavioristic theory, is the six-step lesson plan, a direct instruction model. Popularized by Hunter (1984), and used in many elementary schools, the six-step plan consists of:

1. Review of previously learned material,
2. Statement of objectives for the lesson,
3. Presentation of new material,
4. Guided practice with corrective feedback,

Figure 5-6 These children may need to take turns touching the rabbit.

5. Independent practice with corrective feedback, and
6. Periodic review, with corrective feedback if necessary. (Gunter, Estes, & Schwab, 1990, p. 73)

As teachers of young children, however, the Hunter model is not necessarily the "developmentally appropriate" one. More applicable to our students is the cooperative learning model. Slavin (1983, 1987, 1988) has looked extensively at cooperative learning and has conducted research that indicates its efficacy. Some of the steps included in this model will look familiar. As in any lesson plan, a cooperative learning lesson begins with

A statement of the "performance objective" (written in terms of observable behaviors, such as, "Students will explore in cooperative learning groups a lesson on health and safety. As they participate in the activity, they will discover why cooperative learning groups are helpful. We will allow 30 minutes for group time.").

Step 1: Anticipatory set: A motivational question or statement, intended to pique student interest, such as, "Wouldn't it be neat if someone else helped you with your homework?"

Step 2: Instruction: Generally beginning with a follow-up question or statement to the "anticipatory set" one and intended to motivate further student curiosity, the instruction step involves listing any materials needed and the procedures to be followed.

Example (following from the above question):

Materials needed: Health texts and additional related reference materials from in-classroom library.

Motivation statement: "Today we are going to look at a way that you can help each other get ready for your health and safety test. I know you'd rather do this by yourselves . . . No? . . . OK, Let's try this then . . . "

Procedures: A step-by-step look at what happens next. "Please do not move until I ask you to. The first thing I'm going to do is to put you into six groups with five people in each group. Each group will study one of the parts you need to know for our health test tomorrow. This way no one group has to do it all. How does this sound? Each group will report its findings to the class as a whole, and I'll write down all the important facts you'll need for the test on the board." (The student teacher arranges the groups heterogeneously with a leader being designated for each group. Other roles, such as recorder [appointed for his or her handwriting ability], researchers [usually more than one who look up in books, notes, encyclopedias, and so on, any material relating to the subject they are to present to their peers], may be designated by the student teacher or, in groups accustomed to the process of cooperative learning, chosen by the students in the group. The critical difference in cooperative learning as opposed to what has often been called a group project is that each student in the group has a clearly defined role; no one student has to feel responsible for doing all the work of the group to receive the approval of his or her peers or a group grade. In the example illustrated here, students would not be receiving a grade; however, it is possible that some reward would be given to the best group report by the rest of the students in the class. In another example, each member of the group might grade both himself or herself and also each member of the group. In this way, the student teacher is able then to arbitrate in cases of disagreement.)

Step 3: Guided practice: At this point, the student teacher circulates from group to group and checks to see that each group has the materials it needs and that each student in the group is working. She or he may have to intervene in a group having difficulty, praise a group working smoothly, assist a student researcher with an idea of how to obtain more information about the topic under study, and so on. In this example, each group studies one aspect of the material to be learned for the test rather than all of the material. When the groups report back to the class, notes on all important concepts will be written on the chalkboard and copied by each individual student for further study at home. (If the class has had practice in taking part in a jigsaw lesson, studying for the test could also be handled as a jigsaw.)

Step 4: Closure: As the time for the lesson draws to a close, the student teacher alerts the groups to the end of the group study period and the need to prepare for their reports to the class as a whole. If the reports are to be presented on the same day, as in this example they should be, the student teacher possibly needs to have the groups make their respective presentations after a recess. So closure might consist of the following reminder:"In 10 minutes it'll be time for recess. When we come back, we'll have our oral reports from each group. Recorders, make sure your notes are legible. Reporters, be sure to read the recorder's notes so you can ask for clarification on any words you're unsure about."

Step 5: Independent practice: After recess ends and the oral reports have been given, the student teacher will need to remind the class that they are responsible for information in the reports from each group. (The student teacher should carefully print all essential information on the board as the reports are presented and have the cooperating teacher circulate to make sure that each student copies them down.) At the end of the oral reports, the student teacher should then remind the class, "For homework tonight, I want you to study the notes you took during the group reports. Remember, we're going to have a test on the information tomorrow." Homework, in this example, is independent practice. (A thank-you to Colleen Sequeira, student teacher at California State University, Hayward, during the 1989–1990 academic year, for this third grade lesson plan.)

In our lesson plan above, the cooperative learning model is an example from the social learning family and recognizes that children often learn best from one another, especially in some cultures.

Other models for lesson planning include concept attainment, concept development, synectics, and inquiry, among others. A student teacher should keep in mind that sometimes the purpose of a lesson will dictate what type of plan she will use. In many mathematics lessons, for example, the student teacher may want to use the social learning model as students frequently can better explain a process to a peer than can an adult. Paired learning teams are another variant of the social learning model. Inquiry lends itself well to science, especially when the student teacher wants his class to explore a scientific phenomenon.

For example, fall and why it is called fall might be introduced to first-graders by a walk through the school grounds with each student having a paper bag to collect interesting objects they observe. After a return to the classroom, the student teacher might ask students to cover their desks with newspaper and place on the desk the items they have collected. Using brainstorming as a technique, the student teacher might then ask students to tell him what they have collected. After writing and sketching each named item on the board, the student teacher could ask student pairs to try, in a five-minute period, to group or classify the listed objects. Then after listing (and drawing) examples of the classifications on the board, the student teacher might want to ask students what any two or more groups might have in common in an attempt to enable students to develop hierarchical categories, a difficult task for primary grade children. This sort of lesson models concept development as a part of the inquiry process. One typical answer in one first grade class

has been, "We found all these things on the ground." The conclusion that Fall is named because items have fallen on the ground is fairly obvious. A follow-up art lesson involves the children making Fall "sculptures" with their materials by inserting various pieces into a clay base.

GOALS AND OBJECTIVES

Planned and unplanned activities and experiences have some type of outcome. Written student teaching plans include a section where outcomes are identified. This serves as the basis for planning and presentation and all other form sections.

Cooperating teachers and supervisors differ in requiring activity plans with specific behavioral or instructional objectives. Instructional objectives are more general in nature and may defy measurement. Examples of specific behavioral objectives (SBO) and instructional objectives (IO) follow:

SBO: When given four cubes of different colors (red, blue, green, and purple), the child will point to each color correctly on the first try when asked.

IO: The child will know four colors—red, blue, green, and purple.

SBO: When given a cut potato, paper, and three small trays of paint, the child will make at least one mark on the paper using a printing motion.

IO: The child will explore a printing process.

SBO: After seeing the teacher demonstrate cutting on a penciled line and being helped to hold scissors with the thumb and index finger, the child will cut apart a two-inch strip of pencil-lined paper in two out of five attempts.

IO: The child will learn how to cut on a line.

Note: Written specific behavioral objectives use verbs which clearly describe observable behavior, figure 5-7.

It is best for beginning teachers to accomplish one objective per activity, do it thoroughly and well, and keep the activity short and lively. Student teachers tend to plan activities involving multiple concepts or skills. Usually, none of these skills is accomplished because of the amount and diversity of

ask	count	hold	paint	return	take
attempt to	cut	jump	paste	say	tell
choose	dry	look at	pick	select	touch
close	empty	make motions	point to	sequence	turn
collect	explore	mark	pour	show	use
color	find	mix	put hand on	sing	use two hands
comment	finish	nail	put in order	solve	wait
complete	follow two directions	name	remove	sponge off	wash
contribute	guess	open	replace	state a favorite. . .	weigh

Figure 5-7 Verbs used in writing specific behavioral objectives.

learning. Objectives of any kind may or may not always be realized. Evaluation sections analyze whether the student teacher achieved what he or she set out to do. Centers with clearly defined objectives, combining their teaching team's efforts, have a greater chance of realizing their objectives.

DEVELOPMENTAL SKILLS

Each activity builds upon another. A child's skill and knowledge expands through increased opportunity and experience. Knowing the children's developmental skills makes student teachers aware of their capacities and levels. The ability to sit and focus for a period of minutes can be the requirements in a planned preschool activity, and having the ability to pick up small objects can be part of another. Planning beyond children's capacities may occur because of the student teacher's eagerness to enrich the children's lives and try out different ideas. A close look at the children's achievements and abilities will help the student teacher plan activities that are successful for both the children and himself. Levin and Long (1981) comment upon prerequisite skills in relation to new learning.

> Each new learning task requires some cognitive prerequisites on the part of the student. These prerequisites help students relate new ideas, skills, or procedures to what they already know, and better understand the instruction. (p. 6)

Getting Started

Some student teachers find a lesson plan outlined on a 3 × 5 card and kept on the lap or in a pocket acts as a cue card reminding them step-by-step how the activity unfolds. Planning a first statement that motivates children by creating a desire to know or do increases their attention. Motivational statements need to be studied for appropriateness. Statements that create competition ("The first one who . . . ") or are threatening ("If you don't try it, then . . . ") cause unnecessary tensions. Appropriate motivational statements strike a child's curiosity and often stimulate the child to action or exploration.

> John brought a special pet. I think you'll want to see him.
>
> There are some new items in the collage box for pasting today. Where have you seen a shiny paper like this?
>
> Today you'll be cooking your own snack. Raise your hand if you've seen your mom or dad make pancakes.
>
> Do you remember the sound our coffee can drums made yesterday? There's a bigger drum with a different sound here today. Let's listen.

Focusing activities such as fingerplays, body movement actions, or songs are often used as a "getting started" routine. If planned, this is written in the "getting started" section of the lesson plan. Many teachers find helpful the practice of pausing briefly for silence that signals that children are ready to find out what will happen next. The following types of statements are frequently used.

> When I hear the clock ticking, I'll know you're listening . . . .

If I see your eyes, I can tell you're ready to find out what we're going to do in the art center today. Martin is ready, Sherry is ready . . . .

Lowering the volume of one's voice motivates children to change their behaviors so they can hear. This creates a hushed silence, which is successful for some teachers. Enthusiasm in a teacher's voice and manner is a great attention getter. Children are quick to notice the sparkle in the teacher's eyes or the excitement in the voice tone, stress, and/or pitch, figure 5-8.

During an activity's first few minutes, expectations, safety precautions, and reminders concerning class or activity rules should be covered if necessary. Doing so will avoid potential activity problems.

Procedure

If an initial demonstration or specific instruction needs expressing, this can be noted and written briefly in a step-by-step fashion. Since involvement is such an important aspect for the young child's learning, active, rather than passive, participation is part of most planned activities.

Figure 5-8 The teacher's enthusiasm is contagious.

This section of the plan outlines sequential happenings during the activity. Student teachers must identify important subcomponents chronologically. The student teacher mentally visualizes each step and its particular needs and actions.

Discussion

Although teacher discussion and questioning is appropriate for many child activities, it can be intrusive in others. When deeply involved, children do not usually benefit from a break in their concentration. Other activities lead to a vigorous give-and-take, question-and-feedback format that helps children's discovery and understanding.

The following questions clarify the written comments that may be included in this lesson plan section.

1. What key points, concepts, ideas, or words do you intend to cover during conversation?
2. What types of questions, inquiries, or voluntary comments might come from the children?
3. Are you going to relate new material to that which was learned previously?

Application

Sometimes an activity leads to an immediate application of a new knowledge or skill. If the idea of a circle was introduced or discovered, finding circular images or objects in the classroom can immediately reinforce the learning. Repetition and practice are key instruments in learning.

Evaluation

Hindsight is a valuable teaching skill. One can evaluate many aspects of a planned and conducted activity. Goal realization, a close look at instructional techniques or methods, and student teacher actions usually come under scrutiny. The following questions can aid activity and self-evaluation:

1. Was the activity location and set-up appropriate?
2. Would you rate the activity as high, middle, or low in interest value and goal realization?
3. What could improve this plan?
4. Should a follow-up activity be planned?

5. Was enough attention given to small details?

6. Did the activity attempt to reach the instructional objectives?

7. Was the activity too long or too short?

8. If you planned to repeat the activity how would you change it?

9. Were you prepared?

10. Which teacher/child interactions went well? Which ones went poorly?

11. Was the size of the group appropriate?

12. Was the activity a success with the children?

13. Were my reactions to boys and girls nonsexist?

14. Was the activity above, at, or below the group's developmental level?

15. What did you learn from the experience?

16. What seemed to be the best parts of the activity?

17. Did you learn anything about yourself?

18. How good were you at helping children put into words what they experienced or discovered?

19. In what way(s) do you now know more about the children involved in the activity?

Evaluation and comments from others will add another dimension. Team meetings usually concentrate on a total day's happenings but may zero in on the student's supervised areas and planned activities.

Other Activity Plan Areas

Many activity plans pay close attention to clean-up. Usually, both children and adults clean up their shared environment. Drying areas, housecleaning equipment, and hand washing can be important features of a plan, figure 5-9.

Terminating statements summarize what has been discovered and enjoyed and tie loose activity ends together, bringing activities to a satisfying group conclusion.

> After watching Roddie, the hamster, eat today, Leticia noticed Roddie's two large teeth. Sam plans to bring some peanut butter on toast for Roddie tomorrow to see if he likes it. Ting wants to telephone the pet

Figure 5-9 Clean-up time is an important step in activity planning.

store to ask the storekeeper what hamsters eat. We decided to get a library book about hamsters to find out. Our list shows Roddie nibbled on celery and lettuce today.

Transitions

Transitions are defined as statements that move children in an orderly fashion from one activity to the next.

> After you've placed your clay pot on the drying rack, you can choose to play in the block area or the yard.
>
> Raise your hand if you're wearing long pants that touch your shoes. If your hand is up, get your jacket and meet Carol near the door. Raise your hand if you're wearing a belt today.
>
> Suzette, I can see you're finished. If you look around the room, you'll see something else you may want to do. Bill is in the loft reading to Petra and Alphonso.

Promoting Cognitive Skills

You know from child development classes that young children often rely heavily on what they see. As Jones (1986) explains:

> . . . if a line is longer, there must be more. Young children think differently than they will when they are older. That's important to remember if you're working with them. Observe, ask questions, get a sense of what this child understands and when he's ready to move to a new level of understanding. But if you try to *make* him understand, he may learn your words, but he won't *know* what they mean. Teaching requires patience.

When you interact, you can expect some children will begin to pause, reflect, consider and try out more than one idea, and will begin to attend to more than one factor. Many tasks or experiences presented to young children are purposely open-ended, with different ways available to proceed. Many activities promote diverse and individual courses of action or ways of using, or thinking about, or creating. These types of activities promote reflective thinking and child planning.

The dialogues teachers have with young children often involve imagining, observing, predicting, brainstorming, creative problem solving. Discussions can be lively. Child answers are accepted and further discussions welcomed and promoted. Child comments are based on child experience, consequently correct in light of what the child knows.

In the preschool and lower primary grades, a teacher may ring a bell five minutes before recess. A teacher may also remind children of what is expected, as in, "Be sure to put away your math manipulatives; try to finish your stories with Mrs. Chandler in the writing center. The rest of you need to shelve your books and get ready." Another teacher may blink the classroom lights; still another may play a few chords on the piano. You will want to try different techniques to decide what works best for you.

Warnings or alerting bells, and whistles, are used with large groupings of older children. Teachers of young children use softer signals sufficient to gain the attention of small groups.

Using Community Resources

The whole community is a learning resource for young children's activities. Each neighborhood has unique features and people with special talents and collections. Industries, businesses, and job sites may provide field trip opportunities, resource speakers, or activity material "giveaways." Cultural events and celebrations, ethnic holidays, parks and recreation areas, and buildings easily integrate into the school's activities and promote a "reality-based" children's program.

Pitfalls

The biggest pitfall for the student teacher is the tendency to stick to the plan when children's feedback during the activity does not warrant it. Teachers should take their cues from the children's interests and encourage their growth. Expanding the children's interests can mean spending additional time, providing additional opportunities and materials. In some cases, it can mean just talking if the children want to know and do more.

If children's interests cut into other activities, some activities can be postponed. Others may be revised to fit into the schedule. The unforeseen is always happening. It sometimes captures and holds the children's attention. Getting the children to refocus on a planned activity may mean having to clear the children's minds of something more important to them.

Teachers usually try to relate unexpected occurrences to the planned activity. For example, "That was a loud booming noise. We can listen for another while we finish shaping our bread before it goes into the oven." If efforts to refocus fail, a teacher knows the written plan has been preempted.

A real teaching skill involves using unplanned events to promote identified specific curriculum objectives or objectives that were not even considered but are currently timely and important.

One of the difficulties in using Hunter's five-step lesson plan is its inflexibility. In working with young children, a teacher must, above all, be flexible.

Going out on a Limb

In planning activities and reviewing results, expect successes and failures. You may well experience more growth from your "duds"! They will need analyzing and could stimulate your creativity. Don't forget that taking risks (within safety limits of course) and trying new ideas and new ways of doing things may temporarily create uncertainty but also may offer challenge, excitement, and growth. Approaching child curriculum in unique ways is part of the fun of teaching. When college and university supervisors and cooperating teachers see students branching out in new directions, they see serious effort. To grow, adults, like children, explore, experiment, fail, create, invent, talk about, and follow their own curiosities.

Teaching Tips

As mentioned before, your enthusiasm while presenting the lesson plan must be emphasized. When your eyes sparkle and your voice sounds excited about what you and the children are accomplishing, the children will probably remain interested and focused. Your level of enthusiasm needs to be genuine and appropriate.

You will be eager to start the activities you have designed. You will be anxious to see whether you have captured the children's attention and stimulated their developmental growth. When you feel that the group joins in your excitement and discovery, no other reward is necessary.

Look for the unexpected to happen during your activities. Children will see things that you do not, ask unexpected questions, and make statements you will find a challenge to understand. Listen closely to the children's responses. If you cannot understand them, probe further. More often than not, you will understand the wisdom of their thoughts that are based on their unique past experience.

Do not panic when a child corrects you or you do not have an answer. Develop a "we'll find out together" attitude. A teacher who has all the answers often fails to notice the brilliance, charm, and honesty of children.

Room Environments

Looking closely at room environments will be a challenging aspect of student teaching. You may be asked to "take over" a particular area, redesign, re-

structure it, or create a new interest, or discovery area. In other classrooms, the cooperating teacher may not wish anything moved or "improved." In this case you cannot help but evaluate its arrangement.

You will be looking at child behaviors affected by physical surroundings and notice popular and unpopular room areas. Problem room areas may be immediately apparent, figure 5-10. Some room spaces will appear designed for special purposes, accommodating the need(s) of one or many children.

Experimentation in placement of furniture, equipment, and supplies is an ongoing teacher task in most classrooms. Prekindergarten classrooms may change dramatically from week to week, depending on a course of study. Many pieces of preschool furniture have been designed for multi-use flexibility and utmost mobility.

Effective classroom arrangements do not just happen. They are a result of much hard work and planning (Reddy and Lankford, 1987). Considerable thought and observation of child play pursuits is involved. Because of budget (usually lack of it) creative solutions to classroom environments abound.

Phillips (1987) describes some of the goals of most early childhood teachers who scrutinized the classroom environments:

> The physical environment is safe, orderly, and contains varied and stimulating toys and materials organized into appropriate activity areas.

Student teachers will find some room areas need their constant attention! Analyzing the possible provoking factors may lead to one reason or many, including the room arrangement itself, furnishings, activities, set-ups (the way individual activity materials are arranged), storage, supplies or lack of them, and clean-up provisions.

Greenman (1989) suggests "a rich, responsive learning environment" or room areas that allow children to plan and explore independently, and can allow staff to focus on "prime times" which he defines as one-to-one caring and learning moments that lie at heart of healthy development. Room arrangements, he feels, regulate behavior(s) and, by dividing space into clear boundaries and

Figure 5-10 Does there appear to be a storage problem in this preschool room?

traffic patterns, help to control child crowding and wandering.

Greenman also promotes sensory and motor aspects of room environments:

> Build sensory learning into the environment. Within a coordinated tasteful aesthetic, use different textures, lighting, colors, temperatures or breezes, views or angles of visions.
>
> and
>
> Build motor learning into the environment. Furniture and equipment that encourage or allow climbing up or over, moving around, through, over, under, etc.

In some placement classrooms student teachers may notice and recognize the cooperating teacher's priorities and individuality. A musically inclined teacher's room might have considerable space devoted to children's experiences and exploration of music-related activities. Another child center or classroom may emphasize gardening activities both indoors and outdoors, and so on. You are probably already aware of your own favorite instructional areas, and envision your own future classroom that will incorporate your own creative ideas.

Note: Student teachers can obtain *Developmentally Appropriate Practice in Early Childhood Programs Serving Children Birth through Age 8* (No. 224) from National Association for the Education of Young Children, 1509 16th St. N.W., Washington, DC 20036.

SUMMARY

Planning, presenting, and evaluating activities are a part of student teaching. Written activity plans are usually required and encourage student teachers to examine closely all aspects of their curriculum. Guidelines and criteria for planning activities promote overall success. Consultation with teachers often aids in the development of written plans.

Learning objectives can be written as instructional objectives or in measurable specific behavioral objective terms.

A number of lesson plan forms exist; this text provides one suggested form. Preparing a written plan allows for greater student teacher confidence and less stress, and averts potential problems. A lesson plan is only a starting point and has the flexibility to change or be discontinued during its presentation, depending on interest and need among the children.

Many planned activities do not need to be put into lesson plan form because of their simplicity or their focus on creative expression. Lesson plans are a beginning teacher's attempt to be thoroughly prepared.

SUGGESTED ACTIVITIES

A. Collect and compare lesson plan forms.

B. Invite practicing teachers to discuss the merits of written lesson plans.

C. React to the following statement.

"A tidy classroom seems to be the number one priority for many student teachers who come to us from that college!"

D. In groups of two to four, identify which activity plan section needs greater attention by the student teacher in the following situations.

1. Danielle is presenting an activity with her collection of seashells. She has repeatedly requested that children look while she explains the details of the shells. Most of the children who started the activity are showing signs of disinterest.

2. Francisco introduced a boat-floating activity that has children excited to try it. The children start pushing, shoving, and crowding.

3. Dean prepared an activity with airplanes landing on a tabletop landing strip. Children are zooming loudly and running about the room, interfering with the work of others. The situation is getting out of hand.

4. Claire's activity involves making a greeting card. Many children are disappointed because Claire has run out of the metallic paper used for her sample card. Others are requesting help because their fingers are sticky with glue.

5. Kate's activity making cinnamon toast works well until Joey burns his finger on the toaster oven.

6. Spencer has given a detailed verbal explanation of how the children should finish the weaving project he has introduced. However, the children seem to have lost interest.

7. During Jackie Ann's project, paint gets on the door handles, and the children are unable to turn on the faucets because of slippery hands.

8. Boris and Katrina have combined efforts during an activity. They have spent 10 minutes returning the area to usable condition for the next activity.

E. In groups of two to three, write up a plan using a form similar to figure 5-5. Fill in those lesson plan sections that seem to fit your idea. Give it to your instructor for comments.

F. Using the criteria in this unit, rate the following student teacher statements or actions as A (appropriate), U (unsure), or I (inappropriate). Briefly state why you judged any inappropriate actions as such.

1. Miko offers an activity that involves a demonstration by two local karate experts.

2. Children are assisted in making and frying donuts.

3. The children are making Mother's Day cards. John asks, "Can I make a Mother's Day card for my dad?" Tisha responds, "Father's Day is next month. We'll do it then, Josh."

4. "In just a minute you'll be able to shake our butter-making jar. Mick's turn is first, then Alfie, Christa, Dana, Martin, and Ali."

5. "Sure you can do it," Cantrell, the student teacher, says. The planned activity involves drawing and cutting a boat before pasting it on the class mural.

6. "Let me show you how this works," Rob says during his planned activity. "This handle goes up, then the lid opens. You reach in for the small box. It opens if you push down. Now I'll tell you how this one opens. It has a key. First, I'll put it here in the lock. Lucy, what did you say? Well, I wish you could try it, but these are very valuable boxes so today you can watch, and I'll show you."

7. "Here's the way pieces of wood are sanded to make them smooth. You'll have your own piece of wood and your own sandpaper to use. Feel your wood. How does it feel? Rough and scratchy? Does your hand slide across it easily? Feel this one now."

G. In groups of five or six, discuss why many activities are not prepared in written lesson plan form. Share key ideas with the total group.

H. React to the following briefly in writing then share with classmates. List main points.

1. "Every time I see Carlton (student teacher) he seems to be in the housekeeping area with a chef's hat on!" (parent to cooperating teacher).

2. "It's very distracting to be in a play area with a group of kids and still have to monitor the whole room. It's like the kids notice I'm not giving them my full attention" (student teacher to cooperating teacher).

3. "Why do I have to run around gathering all this stuff for the wagon repair shop child discovery area my resident teacher wants? The kids are perfectly happy with the present housekeeping area!" (student teacher to supervisor).

I. Role play the following situation:

Mrs. A., a college student teacher supervisor, visits many preschool classrooms. When she enters Mrs. B.'s classroom, most of the children immediately start asking questions about who she is, what she's doing, what's in her purse, whose mother/grandmother is she, and so on. Some children rub their hands over her fuzzy dress. Others embrace her leg and lean on her. Mrs. A. rarely has this happen and wants to discuss it with Mrs. B. and the student teacher, Miss C. assigned to the classroom. She has also noticed classroom equipment and furnishings and the behavior of classroom adults.

Mrs. A. wishes Mrs. B. and Miss C. would become more aware of attending children's needs and interests, the classroom, and the school's planned program. So she starts her after school discussion with "I'd like to know more about the children in your class and how they spend their day. Could you fill me in?"

Role players:

• Mrs. A., college student teacher supervisor

• Mrs. B., cooperating teacher

• Miss C., student teacher

After the situation is role played, write another opening line for Mrs. A.

Discuss what dynamics you think might be present and what may account for the children's behavior. If you were the student teacher, how would you proceed and what child reaction would you predict for your planned activities?

J. In small groups, list on a wall chart possible ways to complete the sentence below. Share your list with the total group.

Social skill area planning has recently received greater emphasis in early childhood curriculum planning because . . . .

REVIEW

A. List two ways to identify children's interests.

B. Write three examples of motivational statements for activities you plan to present or could present.

C. Define:

Curriculum

Transition

Specific behavioral objective

Motivation

D. Write three examples of specific behavioral objectives.

E. Write three examples of transitional statements.

F. Match items in Column I with those in Column II.

I	II
1. curriculum area	a. ethnic dance group
2. specific behavioral objective	b. "Those with red socks can wash their hands before lunch."
3. transitional statement	c. four out of five times
4. motivational statement	d. "Snails have one foot which slides along on a slippery liquid which comes from the snail."
5. an activity plan criterion	e. nutrition
6. set-up	f. has three parts
7. community resource	g. "Have you ever touched a bird's feathers?"
8. performance criterion	h. too many concepts attempted
9. summary statement	i. paper left, then patterns, crayons, scissors at far right on table
10. pitfall in student teacher lesson planning	j. child safety

G. Write your feelings concerning written activity plans.

REFERENCES

Bredekamp, S. (Ed.). (1988). *Developmentally appropriate practice in early childhood programs serving children from birth through age 8.* Washington, DC: National Association for the Education of Young Children.

California State Department of Education. (1988). *Here they come, ready or not!* Report of the School Readiness Task Force.

Carter, M., & Curtis, D. (1994). *Training teachers: A harvest of theory and practice.* St. Paul: Redleaf Press.

Elkind, D. (1986). *The hurried child: growing up too fast and too soon.* New York: Knopf.

Elkind, D. (1987). *Miseducation: Preschoolers at risk.* New York: Knopf.

Elliot, S. N. (1993). *Caring to learn: A report on the positive impact of a social curriculum.* Greenfield, MA: Northeast Foundation for Children.

Fosnot, C. T. (1989). *Inquiring teachers, inquiring learners: A constructive approach for teaching.* New York: Teachers College Press.

Greenberg, F. (1990). Why no academic preschool? (Part 1). *Young Children, 45,* 70–80.

Greenman, J. (1989) Living in the real world. *Child Care Information Exchange, 67,* pp. 49–50.

Gunter, M. A., Estes, T. H., & Schwab, J. H. (1990). *Instruction: A models approach.* Boston: Allyn & Bacon.

Hirsch-Pasek, K., & Hyson, M. (1988). Academic environments in early childhood. Grant funded by the Spencer Foundation.

Holt, J. (1964). *How children fail.* New York: Dell Publishing Co.

Hunter, M. (1984). Knowing, teaching, and supervising. In P. L. Hosford (Ed.), *Using What We Know About Teaching.* (pp. 175–176) Alexandria, VA: Association for Supervision & Curriculum Development.

International Reading Association, Early Childhood and Literacy Development Committee. (1986). Literacy development and pre-first grade. *Young Children, 41,* 10–13.

Jones, E. (1986). *Teaching adults.* Washington, DC: NAEYC.

Kuster, C. A. (1994). At the Core: Language and cultural competence. In J. Johnson & J. McCracken (Eds.), *The Early Childhood Career Lattice: Perspectives on Professional Development.* Washington, DC: National Association for the Education of Young Children.

Levin, T., & Long, R. (1981). *Effective instruction.* Alexandria, VA: The Association for Supervision and Curriculum Development.

Marcon, R. A. (November 1994). Doing the right thing for children: Linking research and policy reform in the District of Columbia public schools. *Young Children, 50*(1), 8–20.

McCallum, R. D. (November 1989). Whole language versus direct instruction. Paper presented at California Reading Association Conference, San Jose.

McCracken, J. B. (August 1995). Image building: A hands-on developmental process. *Child Care Information Exchange, 104,* pp. 48–55.

National Association of State Boards of Education, Task Force on Early Childhood Education. (1989). *Right from the start.* Alexandria, VA.

O'Loughlin, M. (1991). Beyond constructivism: Toward a dialectical model of the problematics of teacher socialization. Paper presented at the Annual Meeting of the American Educational Research Association, Chicago, April 3–7.

Oyemade, U. J., & Washington, V. (July 1989). Drug abuse prevention begins in early childhood. *Young Children, 44*, 5, 6–12.

Patron: Piaget in new perspective. New York: Parents Magazine Films, Inc.

Phillips, D. (1987). *Quality in child care*, Washington, DC: National Association for the Education of Young Children.

Reddy, N., & Lankford, T. (July 1987). Rotating classrooms in child care. *Child Care Information Exchange, 56*, pp. 39–41.

Schickendanz, J. A. (December 1989/January 1990). Where's the teacher in a child-centered classroom? *Reading Today, IRA, 7*, 3.

Schickendanz, J. A., York, M. E., Stewart, I. S., & White, D. (1977). *Strategies for teaching young children.* Englewood Cliffs, NJ: Prentice-Hall, Inc.

Seefeldt, C., & Barbour, N. (1993). *Early childhood education: An introduction* (3rd ed.). Columbus, OH: Merrill.

Slavin, R. E. (1983). *Cooperative learning.* New York: Longman.

Slavin, R. E. (1987). Cooperative learning and the cooperative school. *Educational Leadership, 47*, 7–13.

Slavin, R. E. (1988). The cooperative revolution catches fire. *The School Administrator, 44*, 9–13.

Wasserman, S. (1992). *Serious players in the primary classroom.* New York: Teachers College Press.

Williams, C. K., & Kamii, C. (1986). How children learn by handling objects. *Young Children, 42*, 23–27.

RESOURCES

Charlesworth, R. (1989). Behind before they start? Deciding how to deal with the risk of kindergarten failure. *Young Children, 44*, 5–13.

Colletta, A., & Colletta, K. (1987). *Preschool curriculum activities library.* West Nyack, NY: Center for Applied Research in Education, Inc.

Greenberg, F. (1990). Why no academic preschool? (Part 1). *Young Children, 45*, 70–80.

Harms, T., Clifford, R., & Cryer, D. (1988). *Introduction to the early childhood environmental rating scale.* Wolfeboro, NH: Teachers College Press (multimedia package).

Hunt, J. McV. (1974). *Reflections on a decade of early childhood education.* Urbana, IL: ERIC Clearinghouse in Early Childhood Education.

Katz, L., & Chard, S. (1989). *Engaging the minds of young children: The project approach.* Norwood, NJ: Ablex.

Krough, S. (1990). *The integrated early childhood curriculum.* New York: McGraw-Hill.

Planning guide to the preschool curriculum. (1991). Mt. Rainier, MD: Gryphon House.

Whitebook, M., Howes, C., & Phillips, D. (1989). *Who cares? Child care teachers and the quality of care in America.* Berkeley, CA: Community Child Care Employees Project.

Wingert, P., & Kantrowitz, B. (April 1989). How kids learn. *Newsweek*, pp. 4–10.

Wright, M. (1988). *Compensating education in the preschool.* Ypslanti, MI: 1983 High Scope.

Instruction—Group Times, Themes, and Discovery Centers

After studying this chapter, the student will be able to:

- Plan a group activity.
- Discuss factors that promote group time success.
- Describe a teaching unit (theme) approach to early childhood instruction.
- Cite two possible benefits and limitations of theme-centered curriculums.
- Outline preparation steps in theme construction.

Thinking up unit themes wasn't difficult. Collecting what I needed, that was a problem. A teacher needs a giant storeroom, an adequate budget, and a place to keep materials and supplies for child exploring.

Rowena Singson

My supervisor suggested I plan activities in areas of my own personal interests. Since I'm an avid needlework enthusiast, I planned an activity in which I taught simple stitchery. The children (even the boys) loved doing sewing. Some went on to do long-term projects.

Amanda St. Clair

I like watching the expressions on children's faces during small group activities. They all want to do each activity, and they have a hard time waiting for their turn. Before I started student teaching my employment school never had small group times. Now children really look forward to doing new activities.

Vicole Phipps

I was given a small group within 10 minutes in my cooperating teacher's classroom. I appreciated being thrown in at once because I had little time to be overwhelmed. It reminded me of the "sink-or-swim" method my father used when he taught us to swim.

Kim Canas

I can remember by the end of the day I was completely exhausted. I remember how surprised I was when we did a week's worth of carefully planned ideas (activities) in the first day. I remember feeling panic-stricken; what am I going to do tomorrow?

Calli Collins

● WORKING WITH GROUPS

Group times are covered in detail in this chapter as student teachers frequently need help in planning and conducting them. The authors don't intend to suggest planned group gatherings are the best or most efficient vehicles for child learning. Play and spontaneous child activity offer equally excellent opportunities.

Group Size

More and more early childhood teachers prefer planning and working with small groups of young children within their classrooms. Consequently, large groups consisting of the total class may only happen when a group is formed early in the morning or at closing. These larger child groups tend to facilitate information passing rather than instruction. Think about your former training classes and classroom discussions and your feelings about group meetings and consultations in your own training classes. Most teachers admit they were comfortable offering their ideas and felt "listened to" when groups were kept small, figure 6-1.

Figure 6-1 Every child is focused on this planned activity.

Instructional Goals

A number of things can happen when a student teacher tries to ascertain what program goals control the content of instruction and program at his or her placement site. Finding out exactly what and why each child's activities and experiences are planned can range from easy to downright impossible. Goals can be nebulous and nonexistent, poorly or well stated. Instructional goal setting is a complex, time-consuming process, which involves staff, parents, and community. If your placement site has a written statement of instructional goals and priorities, read it thoroughly. Then try to determine if programming reflects stated goals. Questioning one's cooperating teacher during student-cooperating teacher meeting times can be an eye-opening experience. One of the hardest questions for cooperating teachers to answer may well be identifying what they are attempting to teach, or how daily group times reflect goals and child interests and needs.

You may want to discuss with your cooperating teacher how she/he integrates child-initiated, informal, hands-on activities with the trend, sometimes a demand from parents and/or the director, for academically structured lessons.

Instructional Trends

A new sensitivity to instructional content and a teacher's group leading skills and technique has come about with the early childhood field's focus on "empowering" young children, multicultural education, and antibias curriculum [National Association for the Education of Young Children (NAEYC)]. The content and scope of many programs are increasingly considering the difference between multicultural instruction and what Derman-Sparks (1989) termed tourist curriculum. Tourist curriculum's definition by Derman-Sparks (1989) follows:

> Tourist curriculum is both patronizing, emphasizing the "exotic" differences between cultures and trivializing, dealing not with the real-life daily problems and experiences of different peoples, but with surface aspects of their celebrations and modes of entertainment.
> and
> Children "visit" non-white cultures and then "go home" to the daily classroom, which reflects only the

dominant culture. The focus on holidays, although it provides drama and delight for both children and adults, gives the impression that that is all "other" people, usually people of color, do. What it fails to communicate is understanding.

Student teachers must be careful, however, in trying too hard to provide a multicultural curriculum based solely upon the ethnicity of the children in their classroom. One day, an eight-year-old Pakistani boy was heard to lament, "I am not Pakistani; I am a child!" (*First Call for Children*, A UNICEF Quarterly, July-September, 1993, p. 11).

When analyzing holiday curriculum or planned activities Carter and Curtis (1994) use the following questions:

- What does this teacher want children to learn from this curriculum?

- How does the teacher think children learn?

- What are the sensory aspects of this curriculum?

- What values are promoted?

- How do these curriculum plans draw on the children's daily lives and experiences?

Promoting Children's Language Usage during Group Times

National literacy concerns have focused many educators' attention on young children's oral competency and comprehension. Some schools and school districts clearly attend to these areas of needed strength.

Goodman (1986) believes more and more teachers of young children should offer instruction involving children's functional use of language, language that purposefully helps them satisfy their own needs. He urges:

> Let the readiness material, the workbooks, and the ditto masters gather dust on the shelves. Instead, invite pupils to use language. Let them talk about things they need to understand. Show them it's all right to ask questions and listen to the answers, and then to react or ask more questions.

Children's language learning, Goodman points out, is difficult when children are distracted from what they are trying to say by the teacher focusing on how it is said. Some schools prefer to have instant replays or two concurrent groups to preserve the intimacy of a small group. Instructional intent is often dissimilar. Some group times are conducted mainly for roll call and announcing information about the day's special activities. Others may handle classroom problems, offer new learnings, literature, and music, or combine features. The student teacher can attempt to duplicate the cooperating teacher's group time or discuss and plan, with the cooperating teacher's approval, another type.

Carter and Curtis (1994) remind teachers that we must help children inquire more than acquire.

Successful Group Times

It pays to think about and analyze elements that promote success. Student teachers will tend to imitate their cooperating teachers' group times and carry techniques into their own future classrooms.

Identifying the purpose of group times precedes their planning. During these times, the children not only learn but draw conclusions about themselves as learners. The following teacher skills during planned group times are considered important:

- Preserving each child's feeling of personal competence as a learner

- Strengthening each child's idea of self-worth and uniqueness

- Promoting a sense of comfortableness with peers and the teaching team

- Helping children gain group attendance skills, such as, listening to others, offering ideas, taking turns, and so on.

- Helping children to want to find out about the world, its creatures, and diversity; helping children to preserve their sense of wonder and discovery

- Promoting children helping others

Child Characteristics and Group Times

How can group time become what you would like it to be? Go back in your memory to age and stage characteristics. Group times are based upon what a teacher knows about the children for whom activities are planned. The children's endurance, need for movement, need to touch, enjoyment of singing, chanting, ability to attend, and other factors are all taken into consideration. The dynamics of the group setting and the children affect outcomes. Two children seated together could mean horsing around. Maybe some children have sight or hearing problems. Perhaps there is a child who talks on and on at group times. All situations of this nature should be given planning consideration.

Planning

The following are guideline questions you might ask yourself when planning a small group activity:

- How will you promote child self-help and independence?
- Why will or how will children be motivated to want to know, discover, and/or find out about planned group subject matter?
- How will you minimize waiting?
- Will your materials attract them?
- Are materials or tools to be shared? How will children know?
- If a demonstration is necessary before children proceed, will materials be temptingly close to children during the demonstration?
- How does your setting provide for active participation?
- Clean up? Who? How?
- How will children know what's to happen next or where to go?

Whether it is group time or any other time during the day, you will want to promote discussion and elicit children's ideas. Lively interchanges promote comprehension and clarify what everyone is experiencing. Most often discussions pursue what is of interest to children, and teachers find that one topic leads to another.

Student teachers often plan their group times with other adults. The following planning decisions are usually discussed:

- Which adults will lead? Which adults will be aides?
- When and where? How long? How will the children be seated?
- What will be the instructional topics, activities, and goals?
- How many adults and children will attend?
- Will there be one presentation or instant replays?
- What materials or audiovisuals will be needed?
- Who will prepare needed materials?
- How will children be gathered?
- In what order will events happen?
- Can the children actively participate?
- Will a vigorous activity be followed with a slow one?
- Will children share in leading?
- How will the results of group time be reviewed or tied together if necessary?
- How will children leave at the conclusion?

There seem to be distinct stages of group times. For example, there is the gathering of children and adults. This then leads to a focusing of the children's attention. There is a joint recognition of the persons present at group time. At that point, someone begins to lead and present the activity. This is followed by the children participating and reacting. In the final stage of group time, there can be a brief summary and then a disbanding.

Building Attention and Interest

Teachers use various methods to gather the children and get their attention.

- A signal like a bell or clean-up song helps to build anticipation.

  "When you hear the xylophone, it's time to . . . "
- A verbal reminder to individual children lets them know that group time is starting soon.

  "In five minutes we'll be starting group time in the loft, Tina. You need to finish your block building."

In order to help the children focus, the teacher might initiate a song, fingerplay, chant, or dance in which all perform a similar act. Many group leaders then build a sense of enthusiasm by recognizing each child and adult. An interesting roll call, a "selecting nametags" activity, or a simple statement like "Who is with us today?" are good techniques. Children enjoy being identified.

"Bill is wearing his red shirt, red shirt, red shirt . . . Bill is wearing his red shirt at group time today. Katrina has her hair cut, hair cut . . . "

To build motivation or enthusiasm, some teachers drop their voice volume to a whisper. Others "light up" facially or bodily, showing their enthusiasm. The object is to capture interest and build a desire in the children to want to know or find out. Statements like:

"We're now going to read a story about . . . "

or

"You're going to learn to count to six today . . . "

do not excite children. In contrast, statements like:

"There's something in my pocket I brought to show you . . . "

or

"Raise your hand if you can hear this tiny bell . . . "

build the children's interest and curiosity. Tone of voice and manner will be a dead giveaway as to whether wonder and discovery is alive in the teacher. Teachers use natural conversation. Presenting materials or topics (of an appropriate age level) close to the heart of the presenter is a key element. Experiences from one's own love of life can be a necessary ingredient. New teachers and student teachers should rely on their own creativity and use group times to share themselves.

Practice

If memorized songs, fingerplays, or chants are part of the group time, practice is necessary. Time spent preparing and practicing will promote a relaxed presenter. Lap cards may be used as insurance if the leader forgets under pressure.

Practice sessions often alert the student teacher to whether most of the group time activity is led by the teacher and children do little more than listen. If so, there is time to redesign the activity.

Feedback

A student teacher's group time awareness and verbalizations promote goal realization and success. Feedback from children and adults needs to be monitored while presenting. For example, seeing a child hesitate may cue the presenter to repeat and emphasize words. It is worthwhile to see what really interests the children and spend additional time with that activity. Sometimes, even the best group time plans are discarded, revised, and another created based on feedback.

Recognition

One technique that helps recognize individuality is giving credit to each child's idea. "John says he saw a fox in the woods, Mike thinks it was a wolf, and Debbie says it looked like a cat." Bringing a child back to focus by naming him or asking a question is common. "Todd, this dog looks like your dog, Ranger," or "Todd, can you show us . . . ?"

Guidance

Handling child behaviors during group time can distract a student teacher and upset the sequence of thought. Quick statements, such as "If everyone is sitting down, you will be able to see" or "Mei-Lee and Josh are waiting for a turn," help curb distracting behaviors. A group leader can be very grateful for an alert aide or assistant teacher to handle group or individual behaviors so the group time can proceed.

Transitions

To end group times, a transition statement or activity is used. The transition statement should create an orderly departure rather than a thundering herd or questionable ending. There are thousands of possibilities for disbanding the group one by one. Some examples are

"Raise your hand if your favorite ice cream is chocolate. Alfredo and Monica, you may choose which area in the room you are going to now."

"People with curly hair stand up."

"Put your hand on your stomach if you had corn-flakes for breakfast. If your hand is on your stomach, walk to . . . "

"Peter, Dana, and Kingston, pretend you are mice and quietly sneak out the door to the yard."

Evaluation

If time and supervision permit, you should analyze your group activity after you have relaxed and reflected on its particulars. Hindsight is valuable now. If possible, you might consider videotaping your group time. This offers tremendous growth opportunities. Listen closely to the supervisor's and cooperating teacher's objective comments and suggested improvements.

● THEMATIC TEACHING

The theme approach to child program planning is popular in many early childhood centers and classrooms. A theme includes a written collection of activity ideas on one subject, idea, or skill such as a picture book, butterflies, homes, neighborhood, kindness, friendship, biking, trees, or family, among others. Activities within the theme encompass a wide range of curriculum areas including art, music, numbers, science, small and large motor development, etc. A theme's course of study involves a day, week, or longer period; one week is typical. Though usually pre-planned, themes can be developed after a child's or group's interest is recognized. Themes differ from teacher to teacher and school to school; each offers a unique collection and presentation of activities.

Possible Instructional Benefits

There are a number of reasons for using the theme approach in young children's instruction. Some major ideas are as follows:

- A theme tackles instruction through a wide variety of activities that reinforce child learning as the same new ideas, facts, skills, and attitudes are encountered through different routes. Discovery and deductions happen in varied activities, keeping classrooms enthusiastic and alive.

- The classroom environment can be "saturated" with activities and materials on the same subject.

- A theme approach lets children gather, explore, and experience the theme at their own pace and level of understanding because of the number of choices in room activities and materials.

- Planned group times offer shared experiences and knowledge.

- Teachers can identify and gather theme materials for future use, saving time and energy.

- Teachers can guide child discovery better through knowledge gained from their own research during theme preparation and construction.

- Community resources can provide classroom materials, and community uniqueness is incorporated into instruction.

- The teacher collects and develops audiovisuals and "real objects," figure 6-2.

- A theme can evolve from the unplanned and unexpected, giving curriculum flexibility.

- The teacher's and children's creativity and resourcefulness are encouraged and challenged.

- Once the environment is set, the teacher is free to help uninvolved individuals and interact intimately with the highly focused children.

Figure 6-2 The subject of butterflies is a possible study theme that will interest the children. (Courtesy of San Jose City College Child Development Center)

- The classroom environment becomes a dynamic, changing, exciting place for both children and adults, figure 6-3.
- A theme can provide a security blanket for new teachers outlining a plan for one week's activities.

Elementary Grades

The integrated curriculum is the second component listed in Bredekamp's *Developmentally Appropriate Practice* (1987). And in presenting examples of what is meant by integration, Bredekamp states, "The goals of the language and literacy program are for children to expand their ability to communicate orally and through reading and writing, and to enjoy these activities" (p. 70). The popularly known "whole language" approach accomplishes these goals. The teacher might read part of a stimulating story to the class and ask the children what they think will come next. After listening to several examples of what might come and writing them on the chalkboard, the teacher might then assign the students to cooperative groups to write their own endings. Children who may have difficulty reading or writing because of a learning disability may be good at generating ideas or illustrating the final product. As briefly explained in the previous section, it is also important to understand that cooperative groups have been shown to be remarkably effective for children of all ability levels.

Figure 6-3 Class pets can lead to a theme on animals.

Another way to integrate across the curriculum is to use a theme approach. Such topics as dinosaurs or the family are immensely popular and can be introduced with a book where children are asked to write their own version or to write a sequel. An in-class library can house several books about dinosaurs or families that children can use for reference and for enjoyment. The books should encompass several different grade levels so each student can have the opportunity to read independently. In listening and writing and reading activities, "whole language" again is used. Spelling and mechanics are an integrated part of the final stories the children write and illustrate. (Each cooperative group needs to have a good editor, maybe two creative thinkers, at least one logical sequential thinker to keep her or his peers on target, and a good illustrator.) After groups have created book covers and flyleaf synopses, the creative teacher will then teach students bookbinding. Finally, card pockets can be affixed to the inside covers and students can check out the efforts of their peers. Students can also be invited to go to another class and share their stories, a very real self-esteem booster. This process is the essence of "whole language."

How would the theme of "family" relate to the other curricular areas? Let us look at a first-grade social studies example, "We Are All Unique and Special":

Reading, including Language Arts: Reading and writing about the children's own families. Telling stories about family traditions, special events, favorite foods, and so on.

Art: Illustrating their stories about their families.

Math: Counting the number of girls and boys in the class; graphing the results. Counting the number with various different characteristics—eye color, hair color, wearing something red, and so forth; graphing the results; and posting them on the bulletin board. Counting the number of siblings in each student's family; preparing a graph of the results. Predicting the number of siblings a new child coming to the class would most likely have.

Science: As an extension of eye color, hair color, skin color, have students talk to parents and grandparents, if available, about where their ancestors lived. (Be sensitive about the child who is living in a foster family. Perhaps you would want to contact the foster mother and father initially before beginning this assignment.) Bring a globe into the classroom and post a world map for children to use. Have them point out where their grandparents and great-grandparents lived. Use colored thread and map pins for each child to place on the map to indicate where their grandparents or ancestors came from. Have the children stretch a thread from one area of the map to the area where your school is located. Talk about the weather where they live. Talk about what the weather must be like where their grandparents and great-grandparents lived. Have books available in your in-class library that illustrate life in several different parts of the world. Have the children look at styles of dress, housing, foods being sold in markets. Have them compare these to their lifestyles. Do not expect first graders to be able to understand concepts related to cultural anthropology; you could expect them to understand that those families who lived near the equator had darker skin, eyes, and hair than those who lived near the Arctic areas. It may then be possible to talk about how we are all unique and, at the same time, we are all alike. (Based upon materials and suggestions in Project Reach.)

One way of planning a thematic unit is to use a process called "webbing." In making a web, the student teacher is laying out the central theme of the plan and illustrating how the pieces fit together in a diagram that might resemble a spider web, thus the name. Webbing provides the student teacher with a picture of how one topic integrates across curricular areas. For example, a web for a third grade unit based on the book, *The Big Wave*, by Pearl Buck, might look like figure 6-4.

Possible Limitations or Weaknesses

Critics of thematic teaching mention several limitations of this type of program.

- Once developed, thematic units tend to become a teacher-dictated curriculum.

- A reliance on this crutch produces dated programs.
- Themes may not be closely evaluated or critically analyzed for appropriateness during construction.
- Theme teaching promotes the copying of teaching techniques rather than the developing of individual styles.
- A dependence on commercial materials can add expense and lose child interest.
- Thematic unit teaching promotes the idea that preplanned units are a preferred way to teach.
- Themes often overlook geographic, socioeconomic, and cultural factors.
- Themes impose one child's or teacher's interest upon the whole group.
- Thematic units may be used to compare teachers.

Thematic Subsections

This analysis of a thematic unit is provided for student teachers who may need to compile a written unit. Some of you will not be required to do so, and your preparation for unit or thematic teaching will not be this detailed. Nevertheless, what follows will be helpful to those intending to try this type of instructional approach.

Thematic units may have many subsections. Based on teaching preferences and teacher decisions, each section is either present or absent. Subsection listings contain a description of contents:

- *Title page* includes theme identification, writer's credit line, ages of children, classroom location, and descriptive and/or decorative art.
- *Table of contents* lists subsections and beginning pages.
- *Instructional goals description* contains writer's identification of concepts, ideas, factual data, vocabulary, attitudes, and skills in the unit.
- *Background data* are researched background information with theme particulars useful in updating adults on the subject. Technical drawings and photos can be included.
- *Resource list* includes teacher-made and commercial materials (names and addresses) and/or sup-

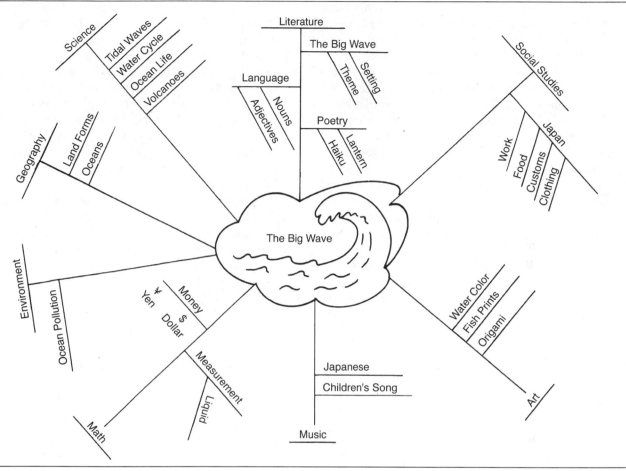

Figure 6-4 Curriculum web for third grade based on Pearl Buck's story *The Big Wave*. (A thank-you to Sharon Ridge, third-grade teacher, Flood School, Ravenswood School District)

plies. Also contains audiovisuals, community resources, consultants, speakers, field trip possibilities, and inexpensive sources of materials.

- *Weekly time schedule* pinpoints times and activities, supervising adults, and duration of activity.
- *Suggested activities* use activity plans, procedure descriptions, and/or plans for room settings, centers, and environments.
- *Children's book lists* identify children's books related to the theme.
- *Activity aids* describe patterns, fingerplays, poems, storytelling ideas, recipes, chart ideas,

teacher-made aids and equipment, ideas and directions, and bulletin board diagrams.

- *Culminating activities* offer suggestions for final celebrations or events that have summarizing, unifying, and reviewing features.
- *Bibliography* lists adult resource books on theme.
- *Evaluation* contains comments concerning instructional value, unit conduct, and revisional needs.

How to Construct a Thematic Unit

Initial work begins by choosing a subject. Then data are collected and researched. Next, brainstorming (mental generating of ideas) and envisioning "saturated" classroom environments take place. Instructional decisions concerning the scope of the proposed child course of study are made. The search for materials and resources starts. Instructional goals and objectives are identified, and activities are created. A tentative plan of activities is compiled and analyzed. After materials, supplies, and visual aids have been made or obtained, a final written plan is completed. The unit is conducted, concluded, and evaluated. Each aspect of instruction is assessed. Notes concerning unit particulars are reviewed, and unit revisions, additions, or omissions are recorded. The unit's written materials are stored in a binder for protection. Other items may be boxed.

Units can be an individual, team, or group effort. Developing a unit during student teaching creates a desired job skill and may aid in preparing for the first job. A written theme, finished during student teaching, can display competency and become a valuable visual aid for job interviews.

Saturated Environment

Thinking up ways to incorporate a unit's theme into the routine, room, yard, food service, wall space, and so on means using your creativity. Background music, room color, the teacher's clothing, and lighting can reflect a theme. The environment becomes transformed. Butterfly-shaped crackers, green cream of wheat, special teacher-made theme puzzles, face painting, and countless other possibilities exist. Do not forget child motor involvement, and child and adult enactment of theme-related concepts and skills.

Room Areas and Instructional Images

During student teaching a study of your placement classroom's physical layout and equipment is a growing opportunity. You may be asked to do an assessment of the popularity and efficiency of different classroom areas. Looking at traffic patterns, bottlenecks, and trouble spots often will alert you to room arrangements that affect child play and behavior. All classroom areas are learning areas whether they are called so or not.

Identify hidden or blind spots where it's difficult to monitor and supervise children. Student teachers begin to grow the proverbial eyes in the backs of their heads during student teaching. Being aware of classroom ebb and flow means frequently "panning" the room is in order and expected.

Rearranging a classroom area is a frequent student teacher assignment. Some resident teachers will not want radical new arrangements, or indeed any changes at all! Others will ask you to design new room centers, and eventually restructure the total classroom.

Derman-Sparks (1989) suggests you look closely at the attending child population's ethnic and cultural diversity and judge the appropriateness of your classroom's images, equipment, and furnishings, figure 6-5.

Discovery (Learning) Centers

Room areas that suggest specific types of play and exploration are sometimes called discovery

---

If the population of the class is predominantly

- *children of color*—more than half, although not all, of the images and materials in the environment should reflect their background in order to counter the predominance of white, dominant cultural images in the general society.

- *poor children* (white and children of color)—a large number of images and materials should depict working-class life in all its variety in order to counter the dominant cultural image of middle- and upper-class life.

- *white children*—at least one-half of the images should introduce diversity in order to counter the white-centered images of the dominant culture.

- *differently abled children*—children deserve learning about gender and cultural diversity as well as about the capabilities of people with special needs. A large number of images should depict children and adults with disabilities doing a range of activities.

If there are a few children who are different from the rest of the group, then take care to ensure that those children's background is amply represented along with representations of the majority groups in the class.

Figure 6-5 A closer look at classroom images. (Reprinted with permission from Louise Derman-Sparks and the A.B.C. Task Force)

centers. A theme or topic connected to the room area may identify a discovery center as the insect corner, train station, weighing and measuring place, or tortilla factory.

Student teachers are often given the assignment of developing a new room area or changing an existing one. Again children's interests will provide clues to the possible popularity of a proposed teacher-developed discovery center. An increasing number of programs are recognizing the value and worth of children's self-selected pursuits. The teacher's role is changing from initiator to facilitator with themes more frequently emerging from the children's own play and interests. Teachers design and supply classroom areas with materials and space for child exploration and experimentation. Once child interest in a particular area is achieved, the teacher's new role includes being both a provider of additional and supplemental materials and also a thoughtful co-explorer who promotes discovery, obstacle resolution, and problem solving as a facilitor rather than a leader. The teacher may weave in and out of the picture as in his judgment he feels it is appropriate. One might also think of the teacher as a watchful opportunist who realizes there is a fragile line between invading child play and helping children sustain interest and gain additional information. During this type of child-teacher interaction the teacher encourages children's verbalizing and representing their ideas and experiences with other media, therefore, further "cementing and reinforcing" new ideas and learning.

Usually discovery centers are a self-selected child activity. They can be designed to be open only at specific times when an adult helper is available.

Instructional goal setting precedes discovery center planning, and child discovery is enhanced through thoughtful teacher analysis of possible materials and child exploration.

There is considerable teacher time and activity (usually unpaid) spent collecting items for classroom centers. Many times teachers are delighted with the receptiveness they find in securing donated items from parents and community. After the teacher explains that it is for child classroom use, many individuals willingly help.

Some discovery centers seem to be immediately popular with children. Interest may wane or continue, so monitoring of centers and possibly adding new features is a part of the teaching task.

Planning for Play

You will most likely be asked to plan and set up varied play opportunities, including providing well-equipped play areas with abundant materials for props. The importance of child make-believe play is not overlooked in child-appropriate curriculums. At times you will join child play with small groups and individual children and make believe yourself, carefully avoiding directing, overpowering, or stifling child initiative and control. Most often you will zip in and out providing additional materials, redirecting damage or aggression, asking leading questions that might add depth while still being interested, enthusiastic, supportive, communicative, responsive, warm, and understanding—no easy teaching task!

Designing New Room Areas: Items to consider when planning a new classroom area include:

- classroom traffic patterns
- attractiveness
- what it will look like at children's eye level
- aesthetics
- age-appropriateness
- multiethnic representation
- whether it is inviting and participatory
- comfort, lighting, and heating
- sound level
- adjacent room centers or areas
- access to clean-up
- whether it is nonsexist
- adult staffing
- ambiance (overall effect)

SUMMARY

Each classroom's group times differ in intent and purpose. Student teachers plan and present group instruction after carefully analyzing goals and the group's particular dynamics, needs, and learning level. Many decisions affect the smooth, successful flow as different stages evolve. Technique, preparation, presentation, and goal realization are all factors that should be evaluated.

Thematic unit teaching is a popular instructional approach, figure 6-6. However, there are different views of the benefits and limitations of unit teaching. Construction of a teaching unit includes theme identification, research, decisions concerning instructional objectives, activity development in a wide range of curriculum areas, and gathering of materials, supplies, and teaching aids. Each thematic unit is a unique collection of activities planned for a specific group of young children, and should take into consideration their particular geographic, socioeconomic, and cultural setting. The choice of unit sequence and subsectioning is up to the indi-

Figure 6-6 A collection of books related to a theme's topic is often provided.

vidual. After a thematic unit is presented, it should be evaluated by the writer for improvement.

SUGGESTED ACTIVITIES

A. Plan and present a group time activity. Use figure 6-7 as a guide.

1. Topic?	6. Materials?
2. Time and place?	7. Preparation and practice?
3. Number of children?	8. Sequence?
4. Adults present?	9. Evaluation?
5. Goals?	

Figure 6-7 Group time planning guide.

B. List the advantages in conducting a group time with seven to 10 children rather than 15 to 20 children.

C. Visit a student teacher's classroom to observe group instruction. Time its length. Analyze its goals and success. Keep your ideas confidential.

D. In groups of five to six, discuss ways to increase children's active participation during group instruction.

E. In groups of five to six, develop a list of themes you feel would interest the children at your placement site.

F. After the class has been divided in half, select either the "pro" or "con" views of unit teaching as an instructional approach. Use 20 minutes to plan for a debate in a future class.

G. Interview three practicing teachers concerning their views of unit teaching.

H. With a group of three others, identify five instructional objectives for the following themes: friendship, pets, automobiles, things that taste sweet, grandparents.

I. Develop a unit individually, in pairs, or with a group of others. Prepare copies to present to the class, and discuss sharing and trading units.

J. Examine figures 6-8 and 6-9, and develop a flow-chart on the concepts of boats, vehicles, houses, or a subject of your own choosing.

Note: Figure 6-8 represents a kindergarten teacher's instructional approach on the theme "our town." Bayman cites the following readings as instrumental to her quest to "letting go" and trying a project approach to instruction.

Katz, L. (1989). *Engaging children's minds: The project approach.* Norwood, NJ: Ablex.

Hemlich, J. E., & Helman, S. D. (1986). *Semantic mapping: Classroom applications.* Newark, DE: International Reading Association.

Workman, S., & Anziano, M. C. (January 1993). Curriculum webs: Weaving connections from children to teachers. *Young Children, 48*(2), 4–9.

REVIEW

A. List considerations for group instruction planning.

B. Describe five important considerations when a student teacher is planning to conduct a 20-minute group time with 15 four-year-olds.

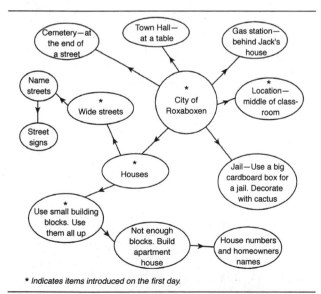

* Indicates items introduced on the first day.

Figure 6-8 Semantic map for construction of Roxaboxen. (From "An Example of a Small Project for Kindergartners that Includes Some 3R's Learning," by Aroti G. Bayman. *Young Children, 50*(6), September 1995, pp. 27–31.)

C. Complete the following statements.

1. Two ways to improve a teacher's skills in conducting groups are . . . .

2. Activities which approach the same knowledge through art, music, science, cooking, measurement activities, and language activities can reinforce . . . .

3. A "saturated" environment might be described as . . . .

4. Using a thematic unit developed in another section of the country is probably . . . .

D. List possible thematic unit subsections.

E. Identify the items listed below as subsection (S) or part of a subsection (P).

1. child activities
2. child skill level
3. adult/child ratio
4. teacher evaluation
5. weekly time schedule
6. furniture and comfort
7. child safety
8. index
9. culminating activity
10. table of contents
11. artistic decoration
12. description of instructional goals
13. resource list
14. cultural values
15. background data
16. audiovisuals and real objects
17. title page
18. balance of curriculum areas
19. book lists
20. bibliography

F. List what you believe are two benefits and two limitations of theme teaching.

G. Describe the use of thematic unit teaching in your future teaching responsibilities.

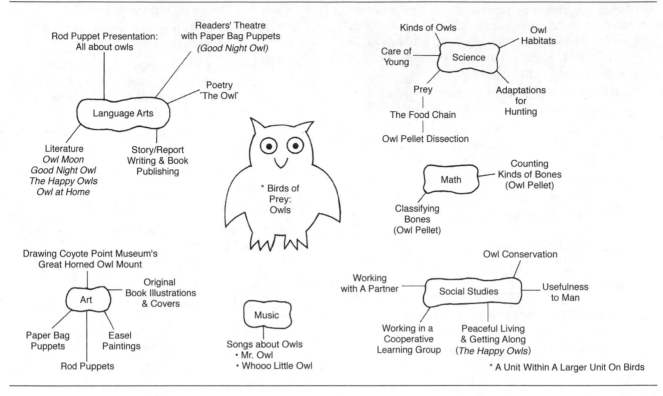

Figure 6-9 Curriculum web for first grade. (A thank-you to Janet Conn, first-grade teacher, Flood School, Ravenswood School District)

H. Describe a classroom discovery center for city-dwelling four-year-olds. Why is the theme appropriate?

I. Discuss what types of knowledge might be "discovered" in a classroom discovery center.

J. Describe resources for thematic units.

REFERENCES

Bredekamp, S. (Ed.). (1987). Developmentally appropriate practice in early childhood programs serving children from birth through age 8 (exp'd. ed.). Washington, DC: National Association for the Education of Young Children.

Carter, M., & Curtis, D. (1994). *Training teachers: A harvest of theory and practice.* St. Paul: Redleaf Press.

Derman-Sparks, L., & The A.B.C. Task Force. (1989). *Anti-Bias Curriculum.* Washington, DC: National Association for the Education of Young Children.

Goodman, K. (1986). *What's whole in whole language.* Portsmouth, NH: Heinemann.

RESOURCE

Spiegel, D. L. (November 1989). Content validity of whole language materials. *The Reading Teacher, 43,* 2, pp. 168–169.

CHAPTER

7

Classroom Management Goals and Techniques

OBJECTIVES

After studying this chapter, the student will be able to:

- List the five major management areas.
- Discuss the effects of the classroom environment on children's behaviors.
- Define the role of the guidance function in the management of the classroom.
- List and describe five common guidance techniques.
- Identify the different behaviors children display when resisting adult authority.
- Analyze what guidance techniques work best and state why.

I once heard in a beginning class what one teacher tried when a child picked up a large tree branch and brandished it threateningly at other children. The teacher went to the child and said "What a marvelous branch, could I hold it?" That led into a discussion about the branch hurting someone, and the child's deciding it needed to be given to the custodian. The teacher later had the custodian carry it in at a small group time for discussion. The child received attention and status for considering the safety of others.

I tried this technique with a child who'd picked up a play ground rock. It worked well for me, too. I'm sure it won't always work but it might work most of the time.

Peter Mills

109

CLASSROOM MANAGEMENT

What comes to your mind when you hear the words *classroom management*? Many student teachers, indeed many teachers themselves, associate the phrase with another word, *discipline*. Classroom management goes far beyond discipline, although the guidance function is certainly a part of what is involved in managing the classroom. Classroom management, in the fullest sense of the meaning of the phrase, involves five separate prongs: (1) the physical arrangement of the classroom(s); (2) curriculum choices; (3) time management; (4) managing classroom routines; and (5) the guidance function. Guidance, in turn, has two facets (1) managing routine behavior problems and (2) managing serious behavior problems.

The Physical Arrangement of the Classroom

What is the "best" arrangement for a preschool classroom? Questions such as the following should be considered:

- Where should blocks be located? Are they easy to reach?
- Where should an art area be located? on a easy-to-clean floor area? near a water supply?
- Should there be a clothesline on which to hang paintings?
- Is the dramatic play area attractive? Are there enough changes of clothing to stimulate a variety of roles?
- Is there a quiet corner where children can look at books (figure 7-1)?
- Is there plenty of space, especially outside, for active play?
- Do children have an opportunity to climb, run, and ride wheeled toys without endangering each other's safety?
- Given an empty room of 20 feet by 30 feet, where should different areas be located? How can the teacher define each?

Look at figure 7-2. Is this the best possible arrangement this first grade teacher could have made? What flaws can you see? Was the teacher wise in placing the reading area next to the water fountain? Where should the math manipulatives be stored? Given the configuration of the desks, what circulation problems might you anticipate? Can you think of what you might do should your cooperating teacher allow you to rearrange this classroom? You may want to discuss this with your fellow student teachers.

Now look at figure 7-3. Is this the best possible arrangement for this preschool play yard for three- and four-year-olds? Can you point out any possible areas of difficulty related to the placement of the play equipment in the yard? Was it wise of the person who designed the yard to have placed the sand area by the water spigot and fountain? Should the storage shed be located where it is? Is the paved area for wheeled vehicles large enough and stimulating enough? Again, you may want to discuss this play yard arrangement with your peers and describe any changes you may feel would be justified and why.

Figure 7-1 A book can be enjoyed in a quiet, comfortable area.

Curriculum Choices

Each choice you make regarding curriculum is another part of classroom management. First, choose the materials you will set out for children to explore. Second, decide which materials, such as scissors and glue sticks, can be used only under your direct supervision. Third, decide how you will equip the dramatic play center or the discovery center. Fourth, develop colorful bulletin board displays that are informative and attractive. Finally, decide which materials are used every day and which materials change after children have had ample opportunity to explore them. Keeping children adequately motivated with new curricular choices while retaining those materials children clearly love both contribute to effective classroom management.

Time management

Time is a limited source. Time management involves more than simply following a schedule. It also involves observing each child closely and understanding when one child may need to use the toi- let or when another may need to be redirected from playing with a child with whom he or she has had altercations in the past. Time management means you know how long children in your care can sustain interest. Choose books for story time that not only pique the children's interests but also are short enough to sustain their attention. Time management means planning activities that are neither too long nor too short and giving children more opportunities to engage in activities. Sometimes there never seems to be enough time to accomplish everything that we would like to do.

At the elementary school level, time management also means "time on task." How much time is actually spent on learning activities? In one study of time allotted to mathematics in a second grade classroom, students were actively engaged in learning math only 60 percent of the total time. What happened to the other 40 percent? Some of the time was spent in reminding students to get out the math manipulatives they were to use that day. Some of the time was spent with the student teacher reprimand-

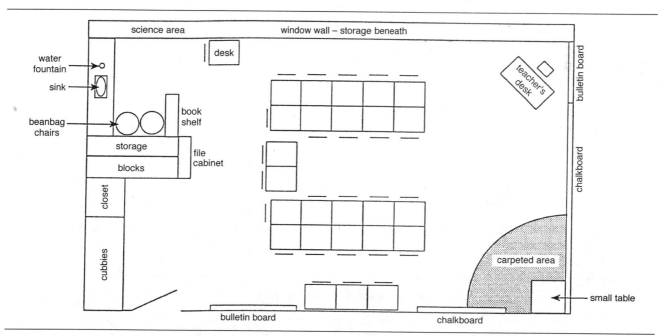

Figure 7-2 Why might the arrangement of this first grade classroom lead to management problems?

ing students who were not paying attention. In fact, he had to remind some students three times to take the manipulatives off the shelves where they were stored. How might he have better used the time? One simple solution to the loss of attention while some students were slow to go to the shelves for the manipulatives would have been to have designated only one student from each table group to be the "materials manager" for that day.

Time management also means wise use of your own time: Try to balance your work, preparation, home and family, relaxation, and recreation times. Set priorities and try not to become so overwhelmed with preparation for school that you have no time for other things.

Managing Classroom Routines

For student teachers, it is essential to your success that you observe carefully your cooperating teacher's routines. Should you want to introduce a change in routine, clear it with your college supervisor first; then check with cooperating teacher. One

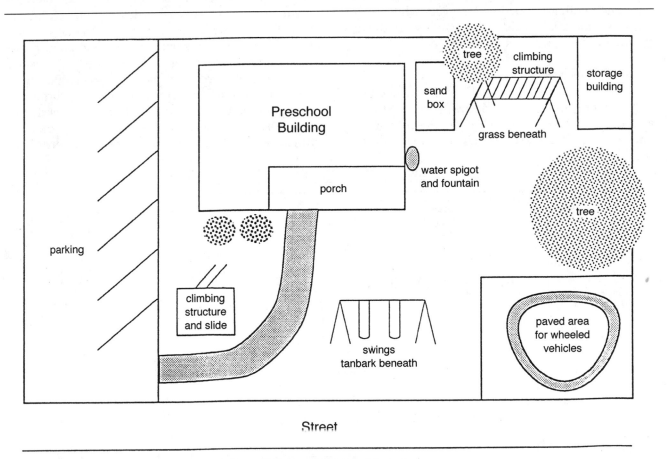

Head Start Play Yard

Figure 7-3 What might be the possible problems with the arrangement of this preschool play yard?

may say no, but another may suggest that you try but that you be aware of what a change in the routine may do to two or three of the children. Always remember that, for some children, routines offer predictability and, therefore, safety.

THE GUIDANCE FUNCTION IN CLASSROOM MANAGEMENT

When we think of the guidance function and its role in classroom management, what do we mean? Guidance can be the act of guiding; it can mean leadership or directing someone to a destination or goal. In the classroom, guidance is the teacher's function in providing leadership. In particular it is the act of assisting the child to grow toward maturity. This is the major goal.

Managing Routine Behavior Problems

What is meant by "routine behavior problems"? Can any misbehavior be considered routine? Obviously, two-year-old children may present several "routine behavior problems" as they struggle with trying to establish their autonomy. But it isn't just two-year-olds who struggle with autonomy. To a certain extent, all children struggle with it. What do you see then? You see children who push against the limits, the boundaries. When you first take over the class from your cooperating teacher, you will often see children who seem to misbehave deliberately. You ask them to come to the circle time area and some children say no. You ask others to pick up the blocks and replace them on the shelves prior to snack time; again, you hear, "No" and/or, "Why should I?" and/or, "I don't want any snack today."

So, what is the student teacher to do? One set of guidelines is the four c's: consistency, considerateness, confidence, and candor. What is meant by consistency? Consistency of adult behavior, consistency of expectations, consistency of limits and rules. Consistency means that you understand yourself well enough that you can respond to children in a fair and impartial manner. It also means reliability; your behavior does not change from day to day and remains reasonably predictable to the children. For children, there is safety in knowing that the adults in their lives are predictable. Such reliability gives children feelings of security and safety. This becomes especially important when you, as a student teacher, are responsible for children who may be inconsistent and unpredictable.

The second c is considerateness. This means that you are considerate of the children you teach and of the adults with whom you work. You respect the children and are aware of their needs, their likes, and dislikes. You are considerate by taking time to listen, even to the child who talks constantly. It means watching all of the children closely and noting which child needs an extra hug and which one needs to be removed from a group before a temper tantrum erupts. All of these actions show children that you care and will help you establish a warm relationship with them. Considerateness helps to build rapport.

The third c is confidence. You need confidence to make decisions that reflect careful thought on your part, decisions that are free of bias and based on all evidence. Confidence implies that you realize you like some children better than others, and you know why you react differently to identical actions involving different children. Confidence is knowing when to stand up for your opinions and decisions and when to compromise. It means understanding when to be silent, knowing that waiting is the more mature action to take.

Candor, the fourth c, means that you are open and honest in your actions with the children, your fellow workers, and yourself. It means being frank and fair; you may inevitably "put your foot in your mouth," but you will gain a reputation for being honest in your relations with others. Candor is the ability to admit a mistake and being unafraid to apologize.

The four c's can perhaps be spelled CARE. As Rogers and Freiberg (1994) wrote, good teachers possess three qualities: congruence, acceptance of others, and empathy. These can easily be expanded to four: congruence, acceptance, reliability, and empathy, figure 7-4.

Congruence is Rogers's term for understanding yourself. Always remember that with truly great teachers, their teaching is such an extension of themselves that you see the same person whether that

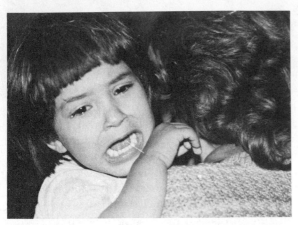

Figure 7-4 Student teaching offers many opportunities to show children you CARE.

person is in the classroom, the office, the home, or the supermarket. These people radiate self-confidence in knowing who they are and what they want from life. It is sometimes difficult for the student teacher to copy the congruent teacher, for the methods the teacher uses are so much a part of that person that the student teacher may not be able to emulate. This is related to the second goal of guidance—knowing yourself.

What you as a student teacher must learn is what methods are congruent with your inner self. The best methods are always those that seem natural to use, those that are an extension of how you feel about yourself.

Acceptance in the Rogerian sense means truly caring about each child you teach. It means all children deserve your respect regardless of how they act. The aggressive, "acting-out" child is just as deserving of your acceptance as the star pupil of the class.

As mentioned, reliability means that your children know you and the routine for the class. Being reliable also implies fairness.

According to Rogers, empathy implies being able to place yourself in the child's shoes, of seeing from that perspective. It is the ability to see that the hostile, aggressive child may need love and acceptance more than the happy, easygoing child. Empathy also means knowing that the happy child needs

attention even though it is not demanded. Learn to be empathetic; it is worth the effort.

Let us assume that you have learned how to CARE. Does that mean you will not have any behavior problems? Does that mean you will automatically have rapport with all your children? Of course not. It only means that you can, perhaps, understand children's behavior more easily and plan to teach self-discipline to those who need to learn.

● CHILD EMPOWERMENT

Your previous classes no doubt dealt with the issue of child choice and responsibility for behavioral actions. Empowering children in classrooms can mean giving them the opportunity to think about and guide their own actions, therefore allowing them to choose between possible actions in any given situation. Naturally all child group living arrangements have rules to guard the safety of children and limit behaviors unpleasant to others.

It may be all too easy for a student teacher to "do everything" for children. It makes the student teacher appear busy and productive, in control, active rather than passive. Giving choices within limits takes time and is usually more work, and sometimes creates room disorder. Is it easier to pass out paper at art times or have children help themselves? Easier to write names on the children's papers than to ask children if they want to write their own names on their work? Easier to promote children's taking turns as group leaders or helpers or doing the task yourself? Most teachers answer it is easier to do it oneself, but sharing tasks and promoting children's experiences and self-esteem are the preferred and most educative practices.

Teachers strive to make rules consistent and clear. There are times during classroom life when a child cannot choose. These times are not presented as choices. As adults we usually abhor, avoid, and sometime rebel in situations in which we lose our autonomy; so do young children.

The authors felt an update and review at this point in your student teaching would be useful. Unfortunately there is no magic formula. This text aims to both provide you with the possible "whys" (chapter 8) of children's behavior and techniques used successfully by professional early childhood teachers.

Character Guidance

Ryan (1993) points out that schools and teachers unconsciously and consciously attempt to educate children:

- To be concerned about the weak and those who need help;
- To help others;
- To work hard and complete tasks as well as they are able and promptly;
- To control violent tempers;
- To work cooperatively;
- To practice good manners;
- To respect authority;
- To respect the rights of others;
- To help resolve conflicts;
- To understand honesty, responsibility, and friendship;
- To balance pleasure and responsibilities; and
- To ask themselves and decide what is the right thing to do.

Student teachers may experience many classroom adult-child learning situations that are also guidance situations and may be concerned with one or more of the above listed goals of the guidance function in classroom management.

Helping Children Understand and Express Emotions and Feelings. Researchers have attempted to identify stages in children's understandings of their own emotions and the language and actions children use to express emotions. One major conclusion derived from these studies is that conversations about feelings provide an important context for learning about emotions and how to manage them (Kuebli, 1994). In everyday interactions teachers have the opportunity to help children gain insight into emotions, their own and those of others, and develop socially acceptable expression.

Kuebli suggests:

- Evaluating the classroom climate for staff acceptance of children's expressions of feelings and also the appropriate adult responses.
- Considering classroom features and settings where emotions and children's reflections on feelings can be experienced. Well-stocked play centers and adults who prompt vicarious exploration can be part of the dramatic play area.
- Providing art materials conducive to emotional response and where adults promote "talking about" and child reflections concerning emotional happenings.
- Using story books dealing with emotions, asking children how they would feel in a similar situation, and discussing causes and consequences.
- Using audiovisual equipment. Children can recreate emotions they have seen. Then, they can dramatize a situation for themselves and discuss the choices children have made in responding to their own and others' emotions.
- Dealing with children's quarrels and disputes in a way that develops child understanding. Giving children time to tell their respective sides without interruption. Teachers can reflect back and ask for clarification while also urging each child to examine his personal contribution to the conflict. Talking about how they feel and what could be done differently next time helps children manage feelings rather than suppressing or denying them.

Staffing almost always determines how much time individual teachers have to spend on children's disputes. Student teachers may play a special preventive and interactional role in social, emotional development and supplement the cooperating teacher's efforts.

Rules

Wherever you work with children there will be rules. Some will be unique, for schools and centers vary immensely in physical structures and staffing patterns. Even economics can influence rules for children. In an earlier chapter you were asked to read any written rule statement in existence at your placement site. By now you have probably discovered rule revisions and rules unique to your classroom that were not included, so-called unwritten rules. Rules are not secret! To be effective each child needs a clear picture of the teacher's expectations of classroom behavior. Any new rules need to be discussed with the children.

All rules in an early childhood center, kindergarten, or primary classroom are related to four basic categories of actions: (1) children will not be allowed to hurt themselves; (2) children will not be allowed to hurt others; (3) children will not be allowed to destroy the environment; and (4) everyone helps with the clean-up tasks. Another category also enters the picture when group instruction begins: (5) children will not be able to impact other children's access to instruction. In other words, they cannot interrupt, hamper, impede, or delay the smoothness or flow of the educational program by disruptive actions(s).

Student teachers need to closely examine rules. If rules become picky or ultraspecific, it often indicates an overuse of teacher power. One student teacher shared with her student teaching class an incident where a child was admonished for eating his "pusher" first at lunchtime. The student teacher could not understand what a "pusher" was or, second, why the adult was interfering with the child's choice of what he wished to consume first. She found a "pusher" was the adult's word for a piece of bread. Another student teacher shared another unbelievable center mealtime rule: children were not to eat just the frosting off their cupcakes at a center she observed. You will keep tabs on whether rules are reasonable and/or too numerous as you student teach.

A student teacher is an authority figure, one who assures rules are followed for the safety and welfare of all concerned. Authority figures expect that there may be occasions of child anger, for the teacher's action(s) can block a child from her desire or goal. It is not realistic to expect enrolled children will always be happy with you.

Age of Child

Some loose guidelines will be discussed next concerning guidance techniques for children of dif-

ferent ages. Teachers of infants and toddlers find that techniques that require the physical removal of objects or the child from a given situation are used more frequently, although words always accompany teacher action. During preschool years teachers often focus on changing environmental settings, or their instructional (planned) program, or the way they interact or speak in order to help preschoolers with rule compliance. It is common in preschool, pre-kindergarten, and lower elementary school grades to have teacher-child and teacher-group discussion about classroom rules and the reason(s) behind rules, then classroom "trouble spots" or difficulties, are solved together. Teachers are still the ultimate authority but children have a greater feeling and understanding that rules protect everyone. Rules become "our rules" rather than "the teacher's rules."

● CLASSROOM MANAGEMENT TECHNIQUES

Now let us look at specific techniques you might use to manage some of the problems you will encounter in any classroom. At the same time, do not forget the broader meaning of the term *guidance*.

In its narrower sense of classroom or behavior management, guidance refers to those things you do to teach or persuade the children to behave in a manner of which you approve. There are many ways to manage behavior but there are six which have proven to be more effective than others: (1) behavior modification; (2) setting limits and insisting they be kept; (3) labeling the behavior instead of the child; (4) using the concept of logical consequences; (5) teacher anticipation and intervention; and (6) conflict resolution.

Behavior Modification

In terms of behavior modification, it is important to be objective. The term has acquired a negative connotation that is unfounded. Everyone uses behavior modification, whether it is recognized or not, from turning off the lights when children are to be quiet to planning and implementing a behavior modification plan. See the Appendix for a behavior modification plan.

Setting Limits

Rules must be stated, repeated, and applied consistently. The aggressive, acting-out child must often be reminded of these rules over and over again. You may have to repeatedly remove the acting-out child from the room or to a quiet area in the room. You may have to insist firmly and caringly that the child change the negative behavior. A technique that works one day, removing the child to a quiet corner, may not work the next. A technique that works on one child may not work on another.

There are several difficulties facing the student teacher regarding behavior management. One of the difficulties is the problem of developing a repertoire of techniques with which you are comfortable. A second difficulty is developing an awareness or sensitivity to children so that you can almost instinctively know which technique to use on what child. The third difficulty is understanding, usually through the process of trial and error, what techniques are congruent with your self-image. If you see yourself as a warm and loving person, do not pretend to be a strict disciplinarian. The children will sense your pretense and will not behave.

Perhaps the most critical error made by many student teachers is confusing the need to be liked by the children and the fear of rejection with their need for limits. As a result, the student teacher may fail to set limits or interfere in situations, often allowing the situation to get out of hand. When the student teacher must finally intervene, the student teacher may forget to CARE; he or she may fail to be congruent and not accept the child causing the problem. The student teacher may not be consistent from day to day or child to child and may not take the time to develop empathy.

The children, in contrast, know perfectly well the student teacher's need to be liked, but they do not know whether the student teacher can be trusted. Trust is acquired only when the children discover that the student teacher CAREs. It is more important that the children respect, rather than love, the student teacher. In fact, no child can begin to love without having respect first.

It is easier to explain your limits at the beginning of your student teaching experience than to make any assumptions that the children know them. They know what limits your cooperating teacher has established, but they do not know that you expect the same. In order to reassure themselves that the limits are the same, they test them. This is when you must insist that your rules are the same as the cooperating teacher's. You will have to repeat them often. Most children will learn rapidly that your expectations are the same. Others will have to be reminded constantly before they accept them.

Labeling the Behavior

What is meant by the phrase "labeling the behavior, not the child"? Essentially, we are referring to what Gordon (1974) calls "I" messages in contrast to "you" messages. In an "I" message, you recognize that it is your problem rather than the child's. For example, if one of your three-year-olds accidentally spills the paint, you are angry, not because the child spilled the paint, but because you do not want to clean up the mess. Unfortunately, you may lash out at the child and say something like "For goodness sake! Don't you ever look at what you're doing?" or "Why are you so clumsy?" The result is that the child feels that spilling the paint is the child's fault when it is possible that it is your fault. The paint may have been placed too close to the child. The spilled paint is your problem, not the child's. How much better to say something like "I really hate to clean up spilled paint!" This is what is truly annoying you, not the child. Even children can understand a reluctance to clean up a spill. How much better it would have been to label the behavior, not the child.

There are times, of course, when you will honestly feel you do not like the child, and it is especially important then to let the child know that it is the behavior you do not like, rather than the child. Continue to look for other times when you can give an honest compliment. Do not try to use positive reinforcement unless the child's behavior warrants it. All children know whether they deserve a compliment; do not try to fool them.

Sending "I" messages is a technique that even young children can learn. As the teacher, you can ask children to say "I don't like it when you do that!" to other children instead of shouting "I don't like you!" By labeling the action that is disliked, the child who is being corrected learns what is acceptable behavior without being made to feel bad. The children who are doing the correcting also learn what is acceptable. Eventually, they also learn how to differentiate between who a child is and how the child behaves. It is a lesson even adults need to practice.

Logical Consequences

Developed by psychiatrist Rudolf Dreikers, the concept of logical consequences is based upon his long association with family and child counseling. Eventually relating his theories of family-child discipline to the classroom, his landmark books, *Psychology in the Classroom* (1968), *Discipline without Tears* (co-authored with P. Cassel, 1972), and *Maintaining Sanity in the Classroom* (co-authored with B. Grunewald and F. Pepper, 1982) introduced teachers and administrators to his concepts of natural and logical consequences.

For example, a natural consequence of not coming to dinner when called might be the possibility of eating a cold meal. In the classroom setting, however, natural consequences are not easily derived, so logical consequences are generally used instead.

Dreiker's key ideas relate to his beliefs that all students want recognition; and, if unable to attain it in ways teachers would call "socially acceptable," children will resort to four possible "mistaken goals": *attention getting*, *power seeking*, *revenge seeking*, and *displaying inadequacy*. To change the behavior, then, teachers need first to identify the student's mistaken goal. This is accomplished by recognizing student reaction to being corrected.

If the student is seeking attention, he or she may stop the behavior but then repeat it until he or she receives the desired attention. If seeking power, he or she may refuse to stop or even may escalate the behavior. In this case, a teacher may want, in as much as possible, to ignore the behavior in order not to provoke a power struggle with the student. Or

the teacher may want to provide the student with clear-cut choices, "You may choose to go to the 'time out' area until you feel able to rejoin the group or you may go to the math center and work on the tangrams." A student wanting revenge may become hostile or even violent; a teacher may have no recourse but to isolate the student or send him or her to the office. A student displaying inadequacy may refuse to cooperate, participate, or interact unless working one-to-one with the teacher.

To change student behavior, Dreikers has several suggestions, some that reinforce what has already been said: provide clear-cut directions of your expectations of the students; develop classroom rules cooperatively with them, especially those related to the logical consequences for inappropriate behaviors. Logical consequences should relate as closely as possible to the misbehavior, so the students can see the connection between them (Charles, 1992, p. 74).

> Demond, a second grade student, just sits in class when it's time for math. Given a set of problems to finish after a demonstration at the board, he lowers his head, refusing to look at you when you suggest that he should begin working. Fifteen minutes later, he still has not begun to respond. What does Demond's mistaken goal appear to be? If you identify it as inadequacy, you might say, "Demond, I know you can do this lesson. Take a look at the first problem. What does it ask you to do?"
>
> One way to avoid the problem altogether might be to ask your cooperating teacher if you might pair the students for learning tasks or group them in blocks of four where the primary rule is "Three before me," a technique that means that students are responsible for teaching each other before they raise their hands for help from you.

For a more complete look at the concept of natural and logical consequences, you may want to look at chapter 5 of Charles's *Building Classroom Discipline*, 4th edition (1992); chapter 8 in Fields and Boesser's *Constructive Guidance and Discipline* (1994); pp. 84–86 in Marion's *Guidance of Young Children*, 4th edition (1995); and chapter 8 in Miller's *Positive Child Guidance* (1990).

Marion stresses four points if the use of logical consequences is to be successful: "the adult has delivered an I-message; the consequence is 'logically' related to the unsafe or inappropriate behavior; the consequence is one the adult can really accept and that the child would likely view as fair; the consequence is well timed" (p. 85). She illustrates each point with concrete examples that are easy to follow and understand. For example, if a child has repeatedly left toys and a bicycle in the driveway and the parent has had to move them to park or bring the car into the garage, the parent first would state an I-message followed by the logical consequence should the behavior repeat itself. "I can't park the car with all the toys lying around. So I'll put them in the shed if you decide not to pick them up tomorrow" (p. 85). In this situation, the parent has stated her point of view and a logical consequence should the child repeat the behavior; the child would probably view the consequence as fair, certainly more fair than if the parent had said, "If you can't pick up your toys from the driveway, I may run over them another time."

You may also wish to look at Gartrell's *A Guidance Approach to Discipline* (1994), in which he suggests three levels of mistaken behavior instead of Dreiker's four. Gartrell urges teachers to drop ideas about "misbehavior," which connotes willful wrongdoing, and look at inappropriate child behavior as "mistaken." In the process of learning such complex life skills as cooperation, conflict resolution, and acceptable expression of strong feelings, children, like all of us, make mistakes. Taking this view helps teachers see their role as mediators, problem solvers, and guides.

Gartrell (1994) offers three levels of mistaken behavior, figure 7-5. Level three behavior, survival behavior, is difficult for the teacher to accept because of its nonsocial and, at times antisocial, aspect. Strong needs result from psychological and/or physical pain beyond the child's ability to cope and should be interpreted as a cry for help. At level three would be the one or two or three children who misbehave because they have a need to exert power or are expressing hostility; these children typically would be misbehaving with the cooperating teacher as well as with you as their student teacher.

Motivational source	Relational pattern	Level of mistaken behavior
Desire to explore the environment and engage in relationships	Encountering	One: Experimentation
Desire to please and identify with significant others	Adjustment	Two: Socially influenced
Inability to cope with problems resulting from health conditions or the school or home environment	Survival	Three: Strong needs

Figure 7-5 Common sources of motivation, relational patterns, and levels of mistaken behavior (Courtesy of Delmar Publishers [Gartrell 1994, 38]).

Suggested (level three) techniques include:

- Non-punitive intervention;
- Building a positive child-teacher relationship;
- Gathering more information by observing;
- Seeking additional information through conversations with the child, parents, and caregivers;
- Creating a coordinated individual guidance plan with other adults through consultation; and
- Implementing, reviewing, and modifying the plan as necessary.

Gartrell believes that level two, socially influenced mistaken behavior, is based in pleasing others, peers and/or adults. Children exhibiting this behavior seek high levels of teacher or peer approval; they seem to lack self-esteem and the strength to use their own judgment. The teacher's task is to nudge the child toward autonomy and observe whether one child or a group is involved in the mistaken behavior. A common problem to many student teachers is such a strong desire to be liked by the children that classroom rules are assumed and/or relaxed. The result is children's misbehavior because they have not yet learned to respect the student teacher and the student teacher's failure to understand that respect has to precede liking. At level two, then, the behavior becomes intentional.

Gartrell (1994) suggests that class meetings are a useful technique in handling level two behaviors. The children are asked for their suggestions for how any given problem might be resolved. The teacher then monitors progress and, if needed, calls additional meetings. Teacher follow-up is necessary to acknowledge progress and new appropriate behavior and to provide reminders concerning agreed-upon guidelines.

At level one, Gartrell (1995) suggests that young children may misbehave simply to experiment. The children who, unintentionally, are testing the limits of classroom rules when the student teacher takes over from the cooperating teacher are displaying level one mistaken behaviors—they are experimenting to see whether the student teacher has the same rules as the cooperating teacher. Disagreements over toys also fall into this category. Gartrell (1995) states:

> [T]he teacher responds in different ways to different situations. Sometimes he may step back and allow a child to learn from experience; other times he will reiterate a guideline and, in a friendly tone, teach a more appropriate alternative behavior.

Depending upon the situation, Gartrell (1995) offers the following suggestions to teachers:

- Increased levels of teacher firmness are necessary with level two and three mistaken behaviors, with the element of friendliness retained.
- Serious mistaken behaviors occur when life circumstances make children victims.
- Aggression is a nonverbal request for help.
- In guidance situations the victim (wronged child) gets attention first and the teacher assists calming down.
- Empathy building is done by pointing out the victim's hurt.
- Stating that the teacher won't let anyone be hurt at school is necessary.
- Child-teacher discussions about how the problem could be avoided in the future take place.

Incident of mistaken behavior	Motivational source	Level of mistaken behavior
Child uses expletive	Wants to see the teacher's reaction	One
	Wants to emulate important others	Two
	Expresses deeply felt hostility	Three
Child pushes another off the trike	Wants trike; has not learned to ask in words	One
	Follows aggrandizement practices modeled by other children	Two
	Feels the need to act out against the world by asserting power	Three
Child refuses to join in group activity	Does not understand teacher's expectations	One
	Has "gotten away" with not joining in	Two
	Is not feeling well or feels strong anxiety about participating	Three

Figure 7-6 Classifying similar mistaken behaviors by level (Courtesy of Delmar Publishers [Gartrell 1994, 49]).

- Asking how the aggressor could help the hurt child feel better is an appropriate technique.
- Assisting the aggressor to choose a positive activity is another teacher endeavor.

See figure 7-6 for additional information showing how similar behaviors could be classified at different levels.

Important to remember is that the goal of discipline is to help children learn to assume greater responsibility for their own behavior. This is best accomplished by treating them with respect; distinguishing between what students do and who they are as persons; setting limits from the very beginning and consistently applying them; keeping demands simple; responding to any problems quickly; letting students know that mistakes, once corrected, are forgotten; and CARE-ing.

Anticipating Behavior or "With-it-ness"

The technique that takes time and experience to learn is anticipating aggressive behavior and intervening before the situation erupts, figure 7-7. By studying patterns in the child's behavior, you can learn to anticipate certain situations. Many children are quite predictable. Some children can be in a social atmosphere for only a short time before being overwhelmed by the amount of stimuli (sights, sounds, and actions), and reacting in a negative way. If you conclude, from observing a child, that the child can play with only one other child before becoming aggressive, you can take care to allow that child to play with only one child at a time. If you know that another child really needs time alone before lunch, you can arrange it. Likewise, if you know a third child becomes tired and cross just before it is time to go home, you can provide some extra rest time for that child.

Learning to anticipate behavior is not easy. You will require much practice. Keep trying; it is worth the effort, and the children will be happier.

Conflict Resolution

As Wheeler (1994) points out, past pedagogy has viewed child-child conflicts and confrontations

as undesirable and has urged teachers to intervene or use preventive measures. Newer theory supported by current research suggests growth in social skill is acquired when peer conflict resolution strategies enable children to solve problems without adult help.

Conflict resolution includes physical and verbal tactics that can be both aggressive and nonaggressive (Wheeler, 1994). Verbal interactions to resolve a conflict may be child statements opposing the other child's actions or verbalization, such as saying, "No! Don't," "I had it first," "My turn" or "My toy!" "Stop that," or similar statements, or can be forms of verbal negotiation, clever reasons to support one child's position and more mature and complex reasoning attempts to solve the problem. Children can agree on their own to seek teacher help.

Teachers who observe child disputes will notice the following resolutions:

- one party leaves or gives up or gives in; and/or
- a satisfying, mutually acceptable plan of action is reached through verbal interaction that can in-

Figure 7-7 Intervening is sometimes necessary to promote sharing and prevent disagreements. (Courtesy of Jim Clay)

clude compromises, give-and-take actions, negotiations, dickerings, and alternatives.

They will also notice that a teacher still needs to monitor and step in to encourage and support conflict resolution, especially with younger preschoolers who use physical aggression in disagreements. Teacher generated solutions simply are held off to give children the opportunity to gain skill in using verbal conciliatory behavior that can lead to nonviolent, satisfying, cooperative play, peaceful conflict resolution, and the resumption of child-child play or partnership.

Wheeler (1994) offers these suggestions to teachers:

- Teachers need to be aware of children's intentions. Is this conflict one that the children are truly trying to resolve, or is it verbal play? Teachers should help children make clear their own understanding of the conflict.

- Children's ability to resolve conflicts increases as their verbal competence and ability to take other perspectives grow. If the children involved in a dispute are verbal and empathetic, teachers should let them try to work things out themselves.

- Teachers' decisions to intervene should be made after they observe the issues of children's conflicts. Possession issues and name-calling generate less discussion than issues about facts or play decisions.

- Children who explain their actions to each other are likely to create their own solutions. In conflicts characterized by physical strategies and simple verbal oppositions, teachers should help children find more words to use.

- Teachers should note whether the children were playing together before the conflict. Prior interaction and friendship motivate children to resolve disputes on their own.

- Teachers can reduce the frustration of constant conflict by making play spaces accessible and providing ample materials for sharing.

- Children often rely on adults who are frequently happy to supply a "fair" solution. Teachers should give children time to develop their own resolutions and allow them the choice of negotiating, changing the activity, dropping the issue, or creating new rules.

- Many conflicts do not involve aggression, and children are frequently able to resolve their disputes. Teachers should provide appropriate guidance, yet allow children to manage their own conflicts and resolutions.

Gartrell (1994) also urges early childhood teachers to use conflict resolution as a guidance technique. Conflict resolution involves teaching children positive alternative and socially acceptable ways to solve problems. Many of the suggestions Gartrell mentions are covered in the previous discussion of Gartrell's views on logical consequences and need not be repeated here.

ADDITIONAL MANAGEMENT STRATEGIES

Child behavior may always remain puzzling and challenge your efforts to help each child learn socially acceptable behaviors. A review of common strategies used by other teachers may be helpful. Naming strategies, describing them, and discussing when they are most appropriate and effective will sharpen your professional guidance skills.

In this chapter thus far, you have studied goals and techniques, the origins of behavior, and ways to promote self-control in children. One goal in guiding child behavior is the idea that the child will learn to act appropriately in similar situations in the future. This can be a slow process with some behaviors, speedy with others. There is a change from external "handling" of the child, to the child monitoring his or her own progress, and then acting and feeling that it is the right thing to do.

Environmental Factors

It is easy to conclude that it is the child who needs changing. A number of classroom environmental factors can promote inappropriate child behaviors in group situations. A dull variety of activities, an "above comprehension" program, meager and/or frustrating equipment, and a "defense-producing" teacher elicit behavior reactions to unmet needs. Close examination of the classroom environment may lead to changing causative factors rather than attempts to change child behavior. School programs, room environments, and teaching methods can fail the children rather than the children failing the program.

As a student teacher, you should carefully examine the relationship between the classroom environment, the daily program, your teaching style, and children's reactions. Fortunately, your training program has developed your teaching skill as well as an understanding of quality environments. An analysis of your placement may lead you to discover that child appeal is lacking. Rearranging and/or creating new areas may add interest. Remember, however, that any changes need the cooperating teacher's approval.

Rapport

This is an important element of guidance. Trying to develop rapport, trust, a feeling relationship with each child can be tricky. Mitchell, the active, vigorous explorer, may be hard to keep up with—even talk with! He may prefer the company of his peers, so how can one establish rapport? When it does happen you will be aware of the "you're OK I'm OK" feeling, and experience pleasure when he says "I enjoy being with you" with his eyes. Children respond to straightforward "honest talking" teachers in a positive way.

Same Behavior, Different Strategy

Child individuality can still result in unexpected reactions. The boy who finally swings at another child after letting others grab his toys and the child who slugs at every opportunity are performing the same act. You will decide to treat each incident differently. The age of children, their stage of growth, and the particulars of the situation will be considered. You have already learned that what works with one will not necessarily work with another. You will develop a variety of strategies,

focus often on the child's intent, and hypothesize underlying causes.

You will be able to live with child rejection, come to expect it, and realize it is short-lived. Act you will, and react the child will. Sometimes you will choose to ignore behavior and hope it goes away. You will find ignoring is appropriate under certain conditions.

Using Proximity

Many times the teachers' physical presence will change a child's behavior. When the teacher becomes interested in a child's activity and asks questions concerning what the child is trying to accomplish, it may head off undesirable child behavior.

Other Common Strategies

Stating rules in a positive way serves two purposes. It is a helpful reminder and states what is appropriate and expected. "Feet walk inside, run outside" is a common positive rule statement. Statements such as "Remember, after snack you place your cup on the tray and any garbage in the waste basket" or "books are stored in your desk before we go to lunch." These clearly indicate the students' tasks.

Cause and effect and factual statements are common ways to promote behavior change. "If you pick off all the leaves, the plant will die." "Sand thrown in the eyes hurts." "Here's the waiting list; you'll have a turn soon, Mark." Each of these statements gives information and helps children decide the appropriateness or realize the consequences of their current actions.

Using *modeling* to change behavior entails pointing out a child or teacher example:

"The paint stays on the paper. That's the way, Kolima."
"See how slowly I'm pouring the milk so it doesn't spill."
"Nicholas is ready, his eyes are open, and he is listening."

These are all modeling statements, figure 7-8.

Always using the same child as a model can create a "teacher's pet." Most teachers try to use every

Figure 7-8 "See how carefully Kathy is using the glue" is an example of a modeling statement. (Courtesy of Jody Boyd)

child as a model. When children hear a modeling statement, they may chime in "me, too," which opens the opportunity for recognition and reinforcement of another positive model. "Yes, Carrie Ann, you are showing me you know how to put the blocks in their place on the shelf."

Redirection is a behavioral strategy that works by redirecting a child to another activity, object, or area.

> "Here's a big, blue truck for you to ride, Sherilyn."
> "While you're waiting for your turn, Kathleen, you can choose the puzzle with the airplane landing at the airport or the puzzle with the tow truck."
> "I know you would have liked to have read one of the dinosaur books, Bokko, during SSR [sustained silent reading period], but they're all taken. Since you like trains and airplanes, why don't you read one of these two books instead?"
> "Mieko, while you're waiting for Tina and Maria to finish the Spill 'n Spell game, why don't you and Jennifer look at some of the other games we have on the shelf and choose another one?"

These are redirection statements.

Statements like "Let's take giant steps to the door. Can you stretch and make giant steps like this?" and "We're tiptoeing into snack today; we won't hear anyone's footsteps" may capture the imagination and help overcome resistance. The key to redirection is to make the substitute activity or object desirable. A possible pitfall is that every time the child cannot have her way the child may get the idea that something better will be offered. Offering a pleasurable alternative each time a difficulty arises may teach the child that being difficult and uncooperative leads to teacher attention and provision of a desirable activity or object.

Younger preschoolers (two- and three-year-olds) intent on possessing toys and objects usually accept substitutions, and their classrooms are equipped with duplicate toys to accommodate their "I want what he has" tendency.

In kindergarten and the primary grades, however, the use of redirection can indicate to children that they have an opportunity to make a second or third choice when blocked on their first.

Giving a choice of things you would like the child to do appeals to the child's sense of independence. Some examples are:

> "Are you going to put your used napkin in the trash or on the tray?"
> "Can you walk to the gate yourself or are we going to hold hands and walk together?"
> "You can choose to rest quietly next to your friend or on a cot somewhere else in the room."

Setting up direct communication between two arguing children works as shown in the following:

> "Remember, Matti, we agreed that class would line up promptly when the bell rang. You have a choice now either to line up quickly or to be the last student to leave for recess."
> "Use your words, Xitlali. 'Please pass the crackers.'"
> "Look at his face; he's very unhappy. It hurts to be hit with a flying hoop. Listen, he wants to tell you."

Taking a child by the hand and helping confront another to express the child's wishes or feelings lets the child know you will defend his or her rights. It also lets the child know that you care that rules are observed by all.

Marshall (1995) cautions teachers to remove "I like the way . . . ." statements in teacher attempts to praise or reinforce child behavior. She points out that using "I likes" focus the child on whether the teacher likes them rather than the learning task. As examples of more appropriately worded teacher statements Marshall suggests the following:

> "Let's see who is ready to listen to the story."
> "Latasha is ready to learn about frogs."
> "Remember to find a place where you can be comfortable, where no one will disturb you."
> "You've made a 4. What do you think of it? Compare it with the 4 on the wall."
> "Let's sing our Good Morning song while Erlinda and Duane finish putting their things away so we can start sharing."

Self-fulfilling statements such as "You can share, Molly. Megan is waiting for a turn" and "In two minutes, it will be Morris's turn" intimate it will happen. Hopefully, you will be nearby with positive reinforcement statements, helping the child decide the right behavior and feel good about it. *Positive reinforcement* of newly evolving behavior is an important part of guidance. It strengthens the chances that a child will repeat the behavior. Most adults will admit that, as children, they knew when they were doing wrong, but the right and good went unnoticed. The positive reinforcement step in the behavior change process cannot be ignored if new behavior is to last. Positive attention can be a look of appreciation, words, a touch, or a smile. Often a message such as "You did it" and "I know it wasn't easy" is sent.

Calming-down periods for an out-of-control child may be necessary before communication is possible. Rocking and holding help after a violent outburst or tantrum. When the child is not angry anymore, you will want to stay close until the child is able to become totally involved in play or a task.

Ignoring is a usable technique with new behaviors that are annoying or irritating but of minor con-

sequence. Catching the adult's attention or testing the adult's reaction may motivate the behavior. One can ignore a child who sticks out the tongue or says "you're ugly." Treating the action or comment matter-of-factly is ignoring. Answering "I look ugly first thing in the morning" usually ends the conversation. You are attempting to withhold any reaction that might reinforce the behavior. If there is definite emotion in the child's comment, you will want to talk about it rather than ignore it. Children can be taught the ignoring technique as well when they find someone annoying them.

When all else fails, the use of *negative consequences* may be appropriate. Habit behavior can be most stubborn, and may have been reinforced over a long period. Taking away a privilege or physically removing a child from the group is professionally recognized as a last-resort strategy.

Isolation involves the common practice of "benching" an aggressive elementary-age student, sending him or her to a desk segregated from the rest of the class at the extreme front or back of the classroom, or short periods of supervised chair-sitting for a preschooler.

Teachers need to be careful not to shame or humiliate the child in the process. Statements such as "You need to sit for a few minutes until you're ready to . . ." allow the child an open invitation to rejoin the group and live up to rules and expectations. The isolation area needs to be supervised, safe, and unrewarding. Teachers quickly reinforce the returning child's positive, socially acceptable new actions.

Removal of privilege can restrict the child's use of a piece of play equipment or use of a play area for a short period. After the "off-limits" time, the child is encouraged to try again, with a brief positive rule statement to remind the child of limits.

Using statements that accept the child's reasons for actions show the child you recognize his/her need or desire. "You want to play with the puzzle." This is followed by "*but* Brianna is using the horse puzzle now." The comment helps the child realize others' rights. Saying "Soon it will be your turn" or "I'll tell you when it's your turn" can encourage children to wait and delay gratification. A teacher might add "You can wait while Brianna finishes or choose another puzzle to work while you're waiting." This indicates your confidence in the child's ability to wait. You will constantly try to increase each child's independence and growing decision-making ability and must stay close enough to the situation to assure that what you stated will happen.

Your goal is promoting each child's self-controlled behavior, behavior that satisfied his unique personal needs and yet allows membership and inclusion into today's society. Encourage the development of the child's self-concept as a valued, worthwhile, capable and responsible person.

Violent Play

Television, current events, young children's observations of older children, and community occurrences often influence the initiation of violent, aggressive play actions. The student teacher is faced with an immediate decision concerning children's safety and the prudence of allowing (which can be seen as approving) this type of play. Most teachers feel deeply about peaceful solutions to individual and world problems. New curriculums have been purposely designed by some early childhood professionals to promote peace and acquaint young children with the brotherhood of humanity concept.

Experienced teachers know that even if guns and other play weapons are not allowed at school, some children will still fashion play guns from blocks or other objects and engage in mock battles or confrontations.

Schools and centers make individual decisions concerning gun, super hero, and war play. It is best for student teachers to question their cooperating teacher if such play develops. Of course, an unsafe situation is stopped immediately and talked about later.

Child Strategies

Child strategies to remain in control are natural and normal. Rules can be limiting. Crying, whining, pleading, screaming, and arguing are common.

Anger, outrage, and aggression may occur. Suddenly going deaf, not meeting adults' eyes, running away, holding hands over ears or eyes, becoming stiff, or falling to the ground may help the child get what is wanted. The child may also use silence, tantrums, changing the subject, bargaining, name-calling, threats to tell someone, or threats to remove affection. Even "talking them to death" or ignoring rules are not uncommon strategies. Much of the time, young children function in groups, showing consideration for others. Empathetic and cooperative interaction of preschoolers within classrooms leads adults to admire both their straightforward relationships and their growing sensitive concern for others.

Managing Serious Behavior Problems

Many of the techniques and strategies already described may help you with children who display serious behavior problems. What do we mean by the phrase "serious behavior problems"? Depending on the age of the child, serious problems range from biting and hitting by a two-year-old to super hero play that is physically aggressive to destroying another child's work and other aggressive behaviors, such as fighting on the play yard, by four- to eight-year-olds. And, please do not overlook the overly quiet child who tries to disappear into the background of the classroom and/or play yard. He or she may need as much help as the overly aggressive child. What should you try to do?

First of all, you want to defer to your cooperating teacher; he or she may have already developed plans to help the child develop more socially appropriate behaviors. Additionally, the cooperating teacher may ask you to speak to the school psychologist, who may be seeing the child once or twice a week; or talk to the PIP (Primary Intervention Program) consultant working with the child; or even sit in on a parent conference with the school's student study team. All of these resource people may give you some more ideas of how to work more effectively with the child in question.

Sandor, a student teacher in a third grade classroom, was faced with a male child, Rory, who was getting into fights during the first recess of every day. Upon his return to the classroom, the principal would call over the intercom, "Rory, please come to the office at once!" The result of this behavior was that Rory inevitably missed at least half of the mathematics lessons that were taking place after the first recess. Sandor discussed the problem with Ms. Olivados, his cooperating teacher. She reassured him that Rory's behavior was not new and suggested that Sandor might observe Rory during the next morning's recess and try to determine why Rory got into fights with the other children.

Following Ms. Olivados's suggestion, Sandor accompanied the class to the first recess the next day. Rory went with two or three other boys from his class to a corner of the play yard; Sandor discretely followed. Suddenly, Rory yelled, "You can't call my mother that!" and hit Derek, the boy standing next to him. Sandor intervened by placing himself between the two and asked, "What did you say, Derek?"

The boy answered, "Oh, we were just playing the dozens; Rory knows that! and besides his mother is a _____!"

"How do you know that?" Sandor asked Derek.

"Oh, everybody knows," replied Derek, who attempted to kick Rory from under Sandor's arm.

"What do you think you might do instead of calling each other names or calling your mothers names?" Sandor asked both boys.

Neither boy replied, and the bell announcing the end of recess sounded before Sandor was able to take the discussion any further. Both Derek and Rory continued to yell at each other as they lined up to go back to the classroom.

Sandor again placed himself between the two boys in the line to prevent any further hitting or kicking. Upon reentering the classroom, Ms. Olivados noticed the angry faces of Rory and Derek and Sandor's distraught one. Before she could ask what had happened, the intercom clicked on and the principal said, "I want Rory C. and Derek K. in my office immediately!"

What might Ms. Olivados and Sandor try tomorrow to prevent further altercations between Rory and Derek?

How might we look at Rory's misbehavior? What might be his mistaken goal, according to Dreikers? Does Rory seem to be vying for attention? for power? for revenge? It seems clear that he's not acting from a sense of inadequacy. Looking at Gartrell's levels of mistaken behavior, at what level of mistaken behavior does Rory's behavior appear to be?

Should you conclude that Rory's mistaken goal is revenge and/or power in his relationship with Derek, what intervention might be the best one to try? Should Sandor keep the boys separated during recess? Should Rory and Derek be involved in a role reversal exercise? Should Mrs. Olivados involve the principal? the school's PIP professionals? What might be most appropriate?

GUIDANCE TECHNIQUES USED IN ELEMENTARY SCHOOLS

Assertive Discipline

Many elementary schools use a form of behavior management called assertive discipline (L. Canter, 1976; L. Davidman & P. Davidman, 1994). While an inappropriate technique for preschools, assertive discipline has been widely used in elementary school settings. Assertive discipline has been shown to work best when an entire school staff is committed to using the technique. In assertive discipline teachers must initially set their classroom rules (best done at the beginning of the year, elicited from the children themselves, and posted prominently in the classroom). Teachers must consistently apply the rules and learn to use "I" messages indicating their displeasure or pleasure. "I don't like it when someone interrupts another student, Aisha." "I like the way you are all listening politely to Mustapha." Consequences of misbehavior must be clearly understood and consistently applied. At the first incidence, the teacher places the child's initials on the board in a place reserved and consistently used for assertive discipline markings. At the second incidence of misbehavior, a check mark goes by the child's name, and a specific and reasonable consequence is related to it. This may be having to remain in the room during a recess or having to move to an isolated area of the classroom. After a second check, the consequence may be a phone call to the student's parent(s) and a request for a conference. After the third check, the child is generally sent to the office, the parent(s) is called and notified that the child must serve detention the next day or that the child must serve an in-house suspension. (This may involve assigning the child to another classroom, attended only by other in-school suspension students. The students are expected to complete assignments their teachers send with them, and the classroom is monitored by either a special teacher or a teacher assistant.) The child is usually assigned to the in-house suspension class until the parent(s) makes an appointment for a conference with the teacher and principal.

Crucial to the success of assertive discipline is following through with the predetermined consequences; empty threats cannot exist.

While assertive discipline has been highly successful, it has also been criticized. Canter, however, maintains that the "assertive teacher is one who *clearly and firmly communicates needs and requirements to students, follows those words with appropriate actions, responds to students in ways that maximize compliance, but in no way violates the best interests of the students*" (Charles, 1992, p. 106, emphasis in the original).

Glasser's Model

Another classroom management model commonly used in elementary schools is the Glasser model (1985). Glasser strongly believes that students have unmet needs that lead to their behavior difficulties and that if teachers can arrange their classes in such a way that these needs are met, there will be fewer control problems. Student needs are identified as (1) the need to belong, (2) the need for power, (3) the need for freedom, and (4) the need for fun. By breaking the class into small learning teams, the teacher is able to provide students with a sense of belonging, with motivation to work on behalf of the group, with power to stronger students in helping weaker ones, with freedom from over-reliance on the teacher for both weaker and stronger ones, and with friends for all students, shy and outspoken. Two precautions: groups should be heterogeneously arranged and groups should be changed at regular

or irregular intervals. (Changes might occur as units or themes change, or they might change every six weeks. The teachers should decide for themselves which tactic works best in their respective classroom.)

SUMMARY

Throughout this chapter, you have been able to formulate an idea of the scope of the guidance function. Remember that in actuality everything you do—planning activities, arranging the environment, planning the length of activities, planning how much direction you will provide—is part of the guidance function.

Another part is managing behavior. In this chapter you were given two cues to use in managing behavior: the four c's of consistency, considerateness, confidence, and candor; and CARE—be congruent, acceptable, reliable, and empathetic. In addition, six specific techniques were explained: behavior modification, limit setting, "I" messages, logical consequences, anticipating behavior, and conflict resolution. Try them; experiment with others of your own. Discover which techniques work best for you and analyze why they work best.

Helping children satisfy needs in a socially acceptable way and helping them feel good about doing so is a guidance goal. Classroom environments can promote self-control, especially when rapport, caring, and trust are present. Examination of behavior—its intent and circumstances—may lead student teachers to different plans of action with different children. There is no "recipe" for handling guidance problems. A review of common strategies was contained in this chapter. They are as follows: positive rule statements; cause and effect and factual statements; modeling; redirection; giving a choice; setting up direct communication; self-fulfilling statements; positive reinforcement; calming-down periods; ignoring; and negative consequences.

Children's strategies to circumvent rules and limits cover a wide range of possible actions; yet, an obedience to rules and sensitivity to others is pres-ent most of the time. Check your responses to figure 7-9, Analysis checklist in establishing a well-managed elementary school classroom, and you will be doing OK.

SUGGESTED ACTIVITIES

A. Read Carl R. Rogers's "To Facilitate Learning." Write a review of the major points Rogers makes regarding the qualities of a good teacher. How do you feel you compare on these points?

B. Read C. M. Charles's *Building Classroom Discipline*. Choose one of the techniques and present it to your peers, cooperating teacher, and supervisor for discussion.

C. From the Charles book, describe one of the techniques that you have used successfully to change behavior. In your student teaching seminar, share the experience with your peers.

D. Analyze your placement classroom's rules. Do many rules fall into the four basic areas mentioned in this chapter? Are there any rules which need a new category?

Students' Aptitudes	Instructional Treatments	Learning Outcomes
What do I know about the general developmental characteristics of the students I am teaching?	In what varieties of ways can I present instruction on a topic?	Do I consider both cognitive and affective learning outcomes for my students?
What cognitive development abilities can I expect them to exhibit?	What types of learning tactics and strategies can I teach?	Do the cognitive outcomes include higher-level thinking skills as well as basic knowledge?
Which learning style does each student seem to prefer?	What is the best way to organize and sequence the presentation of a lesson?	Do I explicitly share these learning outcomes and their purpose with students
What social/emotional characteristics must I consider?	How can I present instruction at an appropriate ability level—for students to achieve success with effort?	Do I connect these outcomes to students in meaningful ways?
What are the social behaviors that each student exhibits?	How can I present instruction that will be interesting and motivate students?	Do I specify how students will be assessed on their mastery of the outcomes?
What are the academic strengths and weaknesses that each student possesses?	What textbooks and other instructional materials best engage students in active learning?	Is my system of grading a valid evaluation of the content students have learned?
What are the special needs of students that I must take into account?	How can I help students better understand the connections between topics?	Do I provide nongraded formative evaluation to students to monitor their progress?
Who has influence on the students? Their peers? Their parents? Their teachers?	How can I help students develop problem-solving skills?	Do I allow multiple opportunities for students to achieve the learning outcomes?
What ethnic and cultural factors influence the way students communicate with others?	How can I instruct students at higher levels of cognition?	
What are the interests of each student?	How can I plan instruction that fosters creativity?	
What level or degree of prior knowledge does each student possess of a subject?	How can I maintain high expectations for all students?	
	How can I help students attribute their success to their abilities and efforts?	

Figure 7-9 Analysis checklist in establishing a well-managed elementary school classroom.

E. Write your own definition of aggression, assertion, and cooperation as they apply to child conflicts. Discuss your definitions with a small group of classmates. In your discussion answer the following:

- Is aggressive behavior normal behavior?

- When does it emerge?

- What socially productive alternatives do adults attempt to teach?

- What anger management techniques are familiar to you?

- How is cooperation fostered in young children?

- When is assertion appropriate?

Compare your definition with definitions found in the Appendix.

F. Go back to your own childhood. What techniques did you use to avoid punishment when you'd broken a family rule? What parental guidance techniques (or punishment) still remain vivid today? What guidance techniques used on others have you observed that created strong emotions in you? If you received but one unforgettable message from your parents concerning your behavior as a child, what was that message? Report the message to total group.

G. Dewayne, a student in your kindergarten room, is in his usual negative mood. During morning planning time, he refuses to choose what interest center he will go to during the morning center choice period. Your reaction is to offer him a choice between the manipulatives center and the story-telling one. Dewayne tells you to f—— off. Your anger aroused, you are tempted to send him to the office immediately; instead you say quietly, "Dewayne, we don't use the 'f' word at school." He glares at you defiantly, and you realize that the other students are looking expectantly at you to see what you'll do next.

According to Dreikers, what does Dewayne's mistaken goal appear to be? Discuss with your peers what responses might be most effective.

H. Read the following:

Mrs. X, the college supervisor, visited Miss Y at her preschool placement classroom, a church-related preschool program. The yard looked spacious and well equipped. Miss Y was a paid employee doing her student teaching at her place of employment. She was also a member of the church that operated the program.

Mrs. X entered a small hallway with a desk and wall phone, then approached the doorway to the classroom and hesitated. Miss Y motioned her supervisor to enter.

A free play period was in progress. Children were busy at small desks or playing in groups. One child stood by the wall seemingly trying to push himself against it. Children looked at Miss Y frequently as if checking for some signal. Two small girls wanted to lean against Miss Y and followed her around the room. One patted Miss Y's arm periodically. The telephone in the hall rang. Miss Y went to answer leaving Mrs. X, her college supervisor, in the room.

After a minute or so a boy tried to grab a toy, another boy was running back and forth across the top of a small desk. The boy attempted to push the grabber away. He knocked over both the desk and the other child. Miss Y entered in time to see the child falling.

"We don't hit," she said sternly, "You know what happens now." The child who pushed said, "He did it," pointing to a third child. Other children seemed tense and frightened. The boy, hugging the wall, turned and faced it. Miss Y picked up the boy who had pushed the child, who tried to grab his toy, and headed toward the door. One girl put her head down on a desk and covered her eyes.

At this point, Mrs. X said, "It was an accident." Miss Y put the child down and said, "Mrs. X said it was an accident."

After watching another half hour, Mrs. X could finally consult with Miss Y on the play yard, for another teacher had come on duty. Asking Miss Y to step to an area where they wouldn't be overheard, she said "I can see this school uses spanking. How do you feel about that policy?" Miss Y answered,

"Oh it works very well. I don't have but rare acts of hitting now, and I've noticed the children are much more affectionate toward me." Mrs. X asked, "You've been present in classes where guidance techniques were studied. Was spanking a recommended technique?" "No, but it sure works well!" the student teacher answered. "You've seen no child behavior that bothers you?" Mrs. X asked. "No," Miss Y answered. "Have you noticed children accusing other children of things they might have done themselves?" (Mrs. X had seen this a number of times during her observation.) "Well, that always happens. I did it myself when I was a child." "Did you know spanking was against the law in preschools in this state?" Mrs. X asked. "Yes, but we have a form parents sign approving spanking," Miss Y answered. "My director and I think spanking works." "Can I give you permission to break the law and speed at 70 miles per hour?" asked Mrs. X. "No, I don't think that would work," answered Miss Y. "Can parents give you permission to break the law?" Mrs. X asked. "Well they have," retorted Miss Y.

After a discussion in which Mrs. X asked for another meeting, she left the school. Later in the day Mrs. X telephoned the licensing agency responsible for licensing Miss Y's place of employment.

Discuss this story with three to four classmates. Report key ideas, observations, conclusions to the total class.

I. Plan a discussion group with a small group of four-year-olds. (Have a picture of a child who might want to join these children's classroom handy.) Start your discussion with "We have a rule in our classroom. The rule is we ask for a turn if we want a toy someone else has chosen to use." Here's a picture of Suzy (or any other appropriate name). She wants to come to school with us. What will Suzy need to know about our classroom? If Suzy plays in the block center what should we tell her? If Suzy wants to join us at snack time, what should we tell her?" Share the results of your discussion group with classmates.

J. In the following management situations, write down your first impulse and your first probable statements and actions.

1. Tonette says Renata pushed her down. You've observed the incident and Renata just happened to trip Tonette as she ran to pick up the ball.

2. Conner is large and muscular. He delights in terrifying other children by standing directly in their path. He rarely physically hits, pushes, or touches the children he is frightening. You see Conner standing in front of the outside water faucet intimidating children who wish to drink.

3. Rogerio is telling your aide she's ugly and fat. The aide, being new, is distressed.

4. Scott cries every time he is not chosen to be first in line or when some other child gets a "handing out supplies" job he wants. You want Geoff to go to the aquarium to feed the fish. Scott's crying because Geoff got the job. Geoff turns to Scott and says, "OK, stop it, you can do it."

5. Sierra's on a painting binge. It's time to clean up. You've told her it's clean up time. "No way," says Sierra as she threatens you with a wet paint brush.

K. Now go back to the situations in J (1–5), but think about the child's needs, feelings, and point of view. Is there any way for the child to solve the inherent difficulty in the situation? Are there setting or time factors teachers could manipulate so the same problem doesn't happen again?

What are your inner feelings in each situation? Discuss with a small group.

REVIEW

A. List four classroom factors which might promote inappropriate child behaviors.

B. Complete this statement.

The reason teachers may use different techniques in guiding aggression is . . .

C. 1. List four positive rule statements.

2. List four redirection statements.

3. List four modeling statements.

D. List six strategies a child may use to "get around" an adult who has just announced that it is time for all the children to come inside.

E. Select the answer that best completes each statement.

1. Roberta, a student teacher, feels sure a textbook or a practicing teacher will be able to describe guidance strategies that work. Roberta needs to know that

a. children are different but the same strategies work.

b. teachers handle behaviors based upon examples their parents and teachers modeled in their own childhood.

c. there are no techniques that always work.

d. books and practicing teachers agree on best methods.

e. None of these.

2. Withholding of privilege is

a. a technique that may work.

b. used before rule statements.

c. not very effective.

d. a rather cruel punishment.

e. All of these.

3. When a teacher notices inappropriate child behavior, the teacher should immediately realize that

a. parents created the behavior.

b. children may need to learn school rules.

c. the teaching technique is ineffective.

d. the director should be consulted.

e. None of these.

F. Complete the following statements. Analyze your responses and discuss them with your peers and supervisor. What have you learned about yourself?

1. The ideal classroom should . . .

2. When a fight breaks out, I want to . . .

3. As a teacher, I want to . . .

4. Aggressive children make me . . .

5. Shy children make me . . .

6. Children who use bad language ought to be . . .

7. Little boys are . . .

8. Little girls are . . .

9. Whiny children make me . . .

10. Stubborn children make me . . .

G. Describe conflict resolution techniques.

REFERENCES

Canter, L. (1976). *Assertive discipline: A take-charge approach for today's educator.* Seal Beach, CA: Canter & Associates.

Charles, C. M. (1992). *Building classroom discipline* (4th ed.). New York: Longman.

Davidman, L., & Davidman, P. (1994). *Teaching with a multicultural perspective: A practical guide.* New York: Longman.

Dreikers, R. (1968). *Psychology in the classroom.* New York: Harper & Row.

Dreikers, R., Grunewald, B., & Pepper, F. (1982). *Maintaining sanity in the classroom.* New York: Harper & Row.

Fields, M. V., & Boesser, C. (1994). *Constructive Guidance and discipline: Preschool and primary education.* New York: Merrill/Macmillan.

Gartrell, D. (1994). *A guidance approach to discipline.* Albany, NY: Delmar.

Gartrell, D. (July 1995). Misbehavior or mistaken behavior? *Young Children, 50*(5), 27–34.

Glasser, W. (1985). *Control theory in the classroom.* New York: Perennial Library.

Gordon, T. (1974). *T.E.T.: Teacher effectiveness training*. New York: David McKay.

Kuebli, J. (March 1994). Young children's understanding of everyday emotions. *Young Children, 49*(3), 36–47.

Marion, M. (1995). *Guidance of young children* (4th ed.). Englewood Cliffs, NJ: Merrill/Prentice Hall.

Marshall, H. H. (January 1995). Beyond "I like the way . . ." *Young Children, 50*(2), 26–28.

Miller, D. F. (1990). *Positive child guidance*. Albany, NY: Delmar.

Rogers, C. (1966). To facilitate learning. In Provus, M. (Ed.). *Innovations for time to teach*. Washington, DC: National Education Association, pp. 419–443.

Rogers, C., & Freiberg, H. (1994). *Freedom to learn* (3rd ed.). New York: Merrill/Macmillan

Ryan, K. (November 1993). Mining the values in the curriculum. *Educational Leadership, 51*(3), 16–18.

Wheeler, E. J. (September 1994). Peer conflicts in the classroom. *ERIC Digest*, EDO-PS-94-13.

RESOURCES

Gartrell, D. J. (January 1987). More thoughts . . . Punishment or guidance. *Young Children, 42*(2), 55–61.

Paley, V. G. (1984). *Boys & Girls: Superheroes in the doll corner*. Chicago: University of Chicago Press.

Wittner, D. S., & Honig, A. S. (July 1994). Encouraging positive social development in young children. *Young Children, 49*(5), 4–12.

Analyzing Behavior to Promote Self-Control

After studying this chapter, the student will be able to:

- Identify what motivates children to act as they do.

- Analyze behavior using Erikson's psychological theory of development and its relationship to the development of self-control.

- Recognize the similarities as well as the differences among children of differing cultural backgrounds and how these relate to differences observed in their behaviors.

- Identify two phases of development which are critical in terms of developing self-control according to Burton White.

- Discuss the relationship between the guidance function and the ability of the child to learn self-control.

My most memorable day of student teaching was the day one of my most active, talkative students managed to sit still for ten minutes. I dropped a note on his desk telling him I appreciated his hard work.

Lara Trillo

The hardest part of student teaching involved the children's understanding that I would enforce rules. I hated it when children cried or threw a wingding. A teacher is an authority figure. Children will not always like you.

Ke-Chang Wang

I had been warned by the previous student teacher that a certain child would make my life miserable. I gleaned the best information on "power-seeking" children from a management book I knew. Lucky for me, I over-prepared because the child was not nearly as difficult as I anticipated.

Catherine Millick

My placement classroom was a Montessori school. Each child automatically pushed his chair under the table when he got up. It was habit behavior. They also returned each child "game" activity to its own special place on shelves. It's the first classroom where I've worked where children picked up after themselves so effortlessly. I wish my placement had started in the fall so I could have seen how my cooperating teacher accomplished it.

Marlis McCormick

To analyze the behavior of any child, you, as the student teacher, need to remember two important concepts:

1. All behavior is meaningful to the child, even that which an adult might call negative.
2. All behavior is reinforced by the environment (people, places, and things).

Let us begin this chapter by looking at some of the typical reinforcers of behavior. Perhaps the easiest ones to understand are physiological in nature: the need to eat when hungry, drink when thirsty, sleep when tired, dress warmly when cold, stay out of the sun when hot, and so forth. It is less easy to understand the psychological ones, although they control more of our actions.

● ERIKSON'S THEORY OF PSYCHOSOCIAL DEVELOPMENT AND ITS RELATION TO SELF-CONTROL

Erikson's (1993) theory of psychosocial development is relevant to our understanding of behavior and self-control. According to Erikson, there are four different stages the child goes through from birth into elementary school age. Each stage has its developmental task to achieve, figure 8-1.

First Stage of Development

For the infant (birth to approximately one and one-half to two years), the task is to develop basic trust. If the infant is fed when hungry, changed when wet, dressed to suit the weather, and given much love and attention, the infant will learn that adults can be trusted. The infant who is not fed regularly and feels rejected or neglected may learn that adults cannot be trusted.

Look at a small baby. What do you see? If the child is younger than six months, you will notice almost immediately that this infant is constantly using the senses and the mouth. The presentation of a toy brings a multiple reaction. The child puts it into the mouth, tastes it, takes it out of the mouth, looks at it, turns it over in the hands, shakes the toy, listens to see if it will make a noise, and holds the toy to the nose to see if it smells. The child uses all of the senses to understand this toy that has become a part of the immediate environment, figure 8-2. Eyes (seeing), mouth (taste), hands (touch), nose (smell), and ears (hearing) all come into action, figure 8-3.

What does this have to do with learning self-control? Think about the interaction between the infant and the toy, as well as between the infant, toy, and significant adult, usually the mother. Think also about why the infant uses all of the senses to learn about a new toy or, indeed, about anything in the environment. Why is learning about one's surroundings important? When one learns about the environment, one feels safe in that environment and learns to control it. Can you see why it is important for the infant to sense some control over the environment? How does the child feel when experiencing cause and effect relationships? What does the child learn from tasting, shaking, looking at, and manipulating an object? The child is learning that he or she has some influence upon what is happening. It is this feeling of influence or control that is important to the child's learning of self-control.

Think about what can happen if the child feels no control over the environment. Suppose the significant adult in the infant's life holds out a new toy toward the child, shakes it in front of the eyes, and, as the infant reaches for it, takes it away? Suppose the infant reaches for an object over and over only to have it always withdrawn? How long do you think the child will continue to reach? The child will ultimately stop trying. The child will also learn to feel helpless and not in control over the environment. This child, then, will have difficulty in acquiring self-control. This is the child who becomes either underdisciplined or overdisciplined.

Experiencing some influence on the environment leads the child to understand that he or she affects the environment. An awareness of cause and effect relationships develops in this manner.

Second Stage of Development

As the child becomes mobile and begins to talk, the child enters the second stage of development. Erikson calls this the autonomy stage. Two-year-old children are motor individuals; they love to run,

Age	Task	Outcome ("Good Me")	Outcome ("Bad Me")
0–1 year	Acquiring a sense of BASIC TRUST	Child develops the ability to TRUST the significant adults in her life	Child develops a sense of MISTRUST in all adults and a sense of HOPELESSNESS
	PARENTAL/CAREGIVER ROLE:	Meeting physical needs, nurturing emotional and social needs; providing stimulation of intellectual and language needs; providing unconditional LOVE	
1–3 years	Acquiring a sense of AUTONOMY	Child develops SELF CONTROL and will power; learns give and take (leadership-follower roles)	Child develops SELF DOUBT and a sense of SHAME
	PARENTAL/CAREGIVER ROLE:	Emotional support; firm, but gentle, limit setting; gradual granting of freedom; consistency in expectations and in establishing boundaries; providing simple choices	
3–5 years	Acquiring a sense of INITIATIVE	Child develops a sense of direction and purpose; is unafraid to explore new or changed settings	Child feels a sense of GUILT; becomes uneasy with new settings; only involves self in activities he knows well
	PARENTAL/TEACHER ROLE:	Communication; joint problem solving; sharing of values and ideals; continued emotional support	
6–12 years	Acquiring a sense of INDUSTRY	Child learns that he is competent; experiments with methods to become competent; fully develops leadership-follower roles	Child develops feelings of incompetence and INFERIORITY; lacks understanding of leadership-follower roles
	TEACHER/PARENTAL ROLE:	Encouraging realistic goals; helping child become open to criticism; accepting criticism from child; answering child's questions; being open to all kinds of questions from child	

Figure 8-1 Erikson's developmental stages.

climb, ride, move, move, and move. They are so active, they almost seem like perpetual motion machines! The developmental task of the two-year-old toddler is learning autonomy and self-discipline. It is this age in particular that is so trying for both the parents and preschool teachers.

Learning Autonomy. (Its contrast is shame and doubt.) This stage coincides with two physiological events in the toddler's life: the ability to crawl and walk and learning how to use the toilet.

There has been much written about the problems of training a child to use the toilet. Many parents, day care workers, and family day care providers do not understand that most children will essentially train themselves, especially if given an appropriate model such as an older sibling who is toilet trained or a loving, caring parent who anticipates the child's need to use the toilet and, in an unthreatening way, sits the child on the seat and compliments the child upon success. The adult needs to allow the child to look at, and even smell, what his body has produced. It is not uncommon for toddlers to play with their bowel movements, an action sure to bring down upon them the wrath of the adult. What needs to be remembered is that the child is pleased and curious about what the body has done. Instead of becoming angry, adults

Figure 8-2 Infants and toddlers will thoroughly explore whatever captures their attention.

should understand the child's interest, stating simply that the playing is not approved and direct attention to playing with clay, for example, as a substitute.

Problems arise when adults overreact to the child's playing with fecal matter. Many parents who try to toilet train what appears to be a stubborn, willful child fail to understand that the child is simply attempting to develop control—over the parent, in part, but over her own self as well.

At this time, the child reinforces the sense of having an effect on the environment. Assume that the toddler, as an infant, was allowed some degree of freedom in which to crawl and explore safely, that within this safe environment the infant had a variety of toys and objects with which to play and manipulate and a loving adult to supervise. This infant then becomes an active, curious toddler, ready to expand his or her environment. Assume also that the parents, early childhood educators, and family day care providers with whom this toddler comes into contact continue to provide a safe environment in which the child can explore. What is the child then learning? At this particular age, the child is continually learning that he or she has control over the immediate environment. The child can learn only when given practice in self-control. In order to allow for practice, the environment must be physically

safe, stimulating, and offer choices.

It is this third factor—offering choices—that is critical in terms of helping a child acquire self-control. Even an infant crawling around in a playroom can make choices about which toys he or she will play with and when. As the child begins to feed himself or herself, the child can make a choice between slices of apple or orange as a snack. The toddler can make the choice between two shirts that may be laid out. In the center setting, the toddler can easily make the choice between playing with clay or climbing on a play gym. As we talk about older infants and toddlers, we are also talking about allowing the child a choice between two alternatives chosen by the adult, figure 8-4. The young child cannot handle a choice of six different activities; this is overwhelming. Too much choice is as bad as none. In either case, one child may become confused, anxious, and angry while another will withdraw and do nothing.

But one concern we, the parents and teachers (caregivers), have is that the young toddler often seems to be breaking limits deliberately. We fail to understand that one of the ways the child can be reassured that we care is repeatedly to test the limit to

Figure 8-3 "This is so much fun to touch!"

Figure 8-4 "Shawn, you can choose to hold the squash or place it here on the table."

see if we really mean what we say. What sometimes happens is, that on days when we are rested and time is plentiful, we tolerate behavior that would not be tolerated under different circumstances.

If it is OK to throw a ball to another child, why is it wrong to throw a rock? If it is OK to run down the driveway in one instance, why is it wrong in another? (Boundaries are not understood very well, especially since the child can go somewhere with supervision but not without it). In the toddler's mind, these are seen as inconsistencies regarding adult expectations. The child cannot differentiate safe from unsafe, so for parents and preschool teachers/day care workers, it means repetition of rules and limits. Eventually, of course, the child does learn. "I don't go down the driveway without holding Mom's hand" or "I don't leave the yard unless Miss Jan holds my hand."

For some parents and teachers/day care workers, the two-year-old child becomes too difficult to handle in a caring way. Two courses of action are frequently taken. Some parents confine the child rather than tolerate the need to explore. As a result, the

child's basic motor needs are squelched, and the child becomes fearful and distrustful of his or her motor abilities. The child also learns to feel guilty about the anger felt toward the adults. Since these adults are still responsible for the child's primary care (food, water, love), the child feels that there must be something wrong with him if the adults inhibit the natural desire to explore. Thus, the child feels guilty and learns to be ashamed of the anger and represses it. In the classroom, this child is the timid, shy, fearful one with poor motor abilities due to a lack of opportunities to practice them.

Other parents may refuse to assert their responsibilities and allow the child to do anything. (Think of how terrifying it is for the child to have such power over the parents!) As a result, the child's behavior becomes progressively worse until the parents finally have had enough and resort to punishment. A different result may be a child who fights against any kind of limits and becomes shameless in attempting to do the opposite of what an adult expects or wants, especially regarding motor restrictions. Just as the physically restrained child learns to feel ashamed and guilty, so does the unrestrained child. This child really wants to have reasonable limits set but cannot accept them without a struggle. This struggle of wills makes the unrestrained child feel just as guilty as the overly restrained child. Both children lack the inner controls that the emotionally healthy child has developed. Both lack self-discipline; the overly restrained child through a lack of opportunities to practice, the under-restrained child through a lack of learning any standards.

In the primary school setting, difficulties with autonomy can be seen in two very different types of behavior: overconfidence, willingness to try anything (the more outrageous, the better), frequently unrealistic expectations of physical prowess, students who appear to have leadership qualities but who become angry if thwarted in their attempts and who may then heap scorn on ideas that originally might even have been theirs; or a lack of confidence, students who continually ask if they are completing an assignment the way you want them to, students who seem to need additional cues before starting a creative writing or art project such as checking what their peers are doing before beginning their own work.

Third Stage of Development

The next stage roughly approximates the usual preschool years of three to five. Erikson believes that the developmental task of the preschooler is to develop initiative, to learn when to do something by oneself and when to ask for help. The result of practice in asserting one's initiative results in a self-confident, cheerful child.

Again, as with the overly restrained toddler, the five-year-old who has been denied a chance to exert initiative learns instead to be ashamed. The child learns that any self-made decisions are of no importance; the adults in the child's life will make decisions. For example, if the child attempts to dress without help, the parents are likely to criticize the result. "Your shirt's on backwards. Don't you know front from back?" Sometimes the correction is nonverbal; the parent or teacher will simply reach down toward the child, yank the T-shirt off the arms, turn it, and put the arms back through the sleeves. The child learns that he or she does not know how to dress and eventually may stop trying altogether. As the teacher, you then see a child of six or seven who cannot put on a jacket without help, who mixes left and right shoes, and who often asks, "Is this the way you want me to . . . ?" This child needs constant reassurance that the assigned task has been completed the way the adult wants it done. Given an unstructured assignment, such as a blank piece of paper on which to draw, this child looks first to see what the other children are doing. Because the child has no self-confidence, the child frequently comes to you for ideas.

The under-restrained toddler grows to be an under-restrained school-age child and becomes your most obvious classroom problem. This child enters preschool like a small hurricane, spilling blocks, throwing down a difficult puzzle, and tearing a neighbor's drawing because it is "not as good" as the child's own. This child is the one who pushes another off the tricycle to ride it and grabs the hammer from another when the child wants to use it.

The under-restrained child is also undersocialized. This child has never learned the normal "give and take" of interpersonal relationships, and does not know how to take turns or share, figure 8-5. This child has had few restrictions regarding what to do, when to do it, and where. At the same time, this child often wanted the parents, caregivers and teachers to tell him or her what to do and what not to do. A word of caution: Some perfectly normal children who have little or no preschool experience will act like the undersocialized child simply because they lack experience. They learn rapidly, however, and some become quite acclimated to classroom procedures and rules. The under-restrained, under-socialized child does not learn rules and procedures easily and continually pushes against any restrictions. At the same time, this child often wants parents, caregivers, and teachers to tell him or her what to do and what not to do.

Remember: The child who is most unloved is also the one most in need of your love. What are some of the ways you can help this child? Use the

Figure 8-5 Learning to wait for his turn is not easy.

four c's and CARE. It is difficult to accept this child; all children deserve your respect and acceptance regardless of how unlikable they may be. In fact, this particular child will probably sense your dislike; therefore, it is important to be scrupulously fair. Do not allow yourself to be caught in the trap of assuming that this child will always be the guilty party in every altercation. It does not take other children long to realize that they have the perfect scapegoat in their midst; it is too tempting for them to break a rule and blame it on the child who is expected to break rules. Remember to be firm. The under-restrained child needs the security of exact limits. They should be repeatedly stated and enforced. This is the child you will constantly need to remind of the rules and of his or her need to adhere to them as do the others in the class.

Ask your cooperating teacher about the child's family background. You are likely to discover there is little security. Bedtime may occur whenever the child finally falls asleep, whether it be on the floor in front of the television, on the couch, or in bed with an older brother, sister, or cousin. You may discover that mealtimes are just as haphazard. Breakfast may come at any time in the morning and only if there is food in the house. You may find out that family members eat as they each become hungry. This child may open a bag of potato chips for breakfast and eat whatever can be found in the refrigerator for dinner. Sometimes the child's only meal is the one served at school. Life, for this child, simply is not very safe or predictable. Mom may or may not be home when the child returns from school. Dad may come home and may work or not as the opportunity presents itself. There may be no one primary caretaker for this child. It is even possible that this child has always been an unwanted child and has been sent from relative to relative or from foster home to foster home.

In terms of Erikson's theory, this child, being unwanted, may never have learned to trust. This possibility is easy to check. As you try to be friendly, does this child's behavior worsen? As you reach out, does the child draw away and/or wince? Think of the consequences of not being wanted. If the child perceives that no one, especially the significant adults in the child's life, likes her, how can the child learn to like herself? How can the child learn to love without first receiving love from others, preferably from the significant adults in the child's life? The child cannot do these things. An unwanted, unloved child is a real challenge to any caring teacher. Because the child feels so little self-worth, attempts at friendliness on your part will be seen as weakness. To deal with this child you first will have to acquire a tough skin. This child has learned how to "read" adult behavior. This is the child's form of protection. This child knows what you are going to do before you even do it. On the other hand, the child's behavior will seem less predictable to you. One day the child will obey the rules of the classroom; another day the child will not. This youngster will make friendly overtures to another child in the morning and kick that same child in the afternoon. The child will help a group of peers build a city with the blocks, only to knock them down when the project is finished.

You will have to repeat the limits and rules continuously. You will continually have to physically remove this child from the center of action to a quiet corner or room. There is no magic wand that can change this child overnight. In fact, you have to remember that it has taken two, three, or four years to shape the child into the person you are seeing. It make take weeks, even months to change the child. In rare cases, it may even take years.

Uncaring, neglectful families may have been warm and loving, and this child may have learned how to trust at least in part. Still, if this child has not resolved Erikson's second task of early childhood, learning autonomy, the child may frequently get into trouble. Never having learned how to set limits, this child is constantly going beyond the limits. The roof is off limits? This child finds a way to climb on the roof. The kitchen is off limits? This child continually goes to the kitchen. The child will continue the escapades even if an injury results. The child accepts hurt as the correct punishment. In fact, this child seeks punishment. When you speak to the child's family, the answer often given is, "Just give him a good spanking. He'll behave then!"

Similar behaviors may be exhibited by the child who is overindulged at home and smothered with attention. This child expects to be the "center of action" at school.

Children with this type of behavior test every resource you have. Again, remember to use the four c's and to CARE even though it may be difficult. Repeat the limits and expectations over and over. Physically remove the child whenever necessary; isolation sometimes works best.

Another technique is to say what the child is thinking, figure 8-6. "You want me to tell you that I hate you, but I'm not going to." Sometimes the shock of hearing you put into words what the child is thinking is enough to change the behavior. It may work for a day, anyway. You will have to do this repeatedly. When the child hits another, you can say, "You expect me to yell at you for hitting Joey. Well, I'm not going to. I'm going to ask you to sit here with me until you think you can go back with the other children. You know we do not hit in this room." Insist again that limits be respected; the child must follow the rules just like everyone else.

Speak to the parents but be careful. Try not to speak down to them or in an accusing manner. Try to use the "I want to help your child" approach.

Figure 8-6 "Janine, I know you'd like to tease Robbie by taking his toy."

Most parents want to help their children; however, many do not know how. You may have to explain why you have limits and rules and suggest that the parents have some limits for the child at home. You may have to give many tips to some parents, and you will have to be tactful and show them that you care. If you sense a noncaring attitude, you can easily understand why the child has problems. In this case, you will have to work with the child only, but keep trying.

One technique that sometimes works with the aggressive, underdisciplined child is to "call" the child on the behavior. What is meant by "call"? One way to look at interactions between two or more children is to find the underlying motivators. Does this sound familiar? Some children are motivated by a desire to control, for they have learned that their own safety lies in their ability to control their environment. This can provoke a tug of war between the child's need to control and yours. At this point, there is no sense in trying to reason, especially verbally. Simply isolate the child, repeat the rules or limits, and leave. Tell the child as you leave that you know what the child is doing and why. Be specific. "I'm not going to argue with you" or "Sit here until you feel ready to rejoin us."

Be prepared to understand that you will not be successful with every child. There will always be one or two children who will relate better to another teacher.

Once in a while you will see a child who is so psychologically damaged that the regular classroom may not be an appropriate setting. The child may be underfed, poorly clothed, uncared for, and unloved. Erikson would suggest that this child has never resolved the task of basic trust as an infant, much less having resolved the task of autonomy and initiative. Being unwanted and unloved makes it extremely difficult for a child to acquire any sense of self-worth.

As the teacher, your job is to provide the kind of environment in which the child is able to resolve these early developmental tasks, even if the child has not yet done so. It is never too late to learn to trust or to develop autonomy; it is never too late to satisfy the deficiency needs so that the growth needs can be encouraged.

Fourth Stage of Development

For school-age children there is probably no more important task than to learn that they are capable of learning. Erikson called this stage industry and its negative outcome, inferiority. Unfortunately, some children who have progressed through the earlier stages of development smoothly and who enter school trusting in others, knowing the give-and-take expected of group life, feeling confident in their own abilities, stumble when they reach kindergarten and first grade.

For some children the fine motor tasks of writing manuscript, shaping numerals, and coloring within specified lines are difficult. They may then learn that they do not have the abilities rewarded by their teachers.

School, instead of being a place of joy and learning, may become a place where children fail. Inferiority is the obvious result. A secondary result can be that the child develops feelings of helplessness. Successful students generally believe that they are responsible for their successes and attribute any failures to lack of effort. Unsuccessful students, however, often attribute successes to luck and failures to factors beyond their control or to lack of ability (Dweck, 1975; Abramson, Seligman, & Teasdale, 1978). The unfortunate consequence in students who feel helpless is that they often give up and stop trying. It then becomes extremely difficult for teachers to change the behavior.

In a classroom that offers developmentally appropriate materials for children to interact with actively there is no difficulty with industry. A developmentally appropriate classroom is likely to have centers to allow for active exploration and enough physical space to allow for movement opportunities at different times. For example, it may have a carpeted reading area with pillows where children can go to look at and "read" books; a science area with "attractive junk" to handle; floor space for the children who may wish to work on the floor; a math center with cuisinaire rods, unifix cubes, tangrams, and other manipulatives; a writing area, managed by an aide or parent volunteer where children can dictate stores or write and illustrate their own; and so on. In the classroom with many options for working alone, in pairs, or in cooperative groups, children discover that learning is enjoyable and industry is then the result.

● BURTON WHITE AND SELF-CONTROL

White (1975) divides the child's first three years into seven phases, each with its unique characteristics, needs, and preferred child-rearing practices.

Phase I: Birth to six weeks

Phase II: Six weeks to three and one-half months

Phase III: Three and one-half to five and one-half months

Phase IV: Five and one-half to eight months

Phase V: Eight to 14 months

Phase VI: 14 to 24 months

Phase VII: 24 to 36 months

According to White, during Phase I the primary needs of the infant are to feel loved and cared for, and to have the opportunity to develop certain skills such as holding up the head while on the stomach and tracking objects held eight to 24 inches from the face. The newborn baby does not need much stimulation other than a change of position from back to stomach to the mother's arms.

During Phase II, helping the infant achieve certain skills such as holding up the head becomes more important than during Phase I. Phase II infants also need hand-eye activities such as crib devices.

Phase III infants have attained head control and are beginning to attain torso control. At this age, the child learns to turn from stomach to back and back to stomach. Also, the child's leg muscles are strengthened. Infants at Phase III enjoy being held so they can press their feet against a lap and practice standing. They are quite social and respond to tickling and smiling with their own coos and smiles. The infants "soak up" all the attention from family and strangers alike and respond easily.

Phase IV infants begin to show an understanding of language. *Mama, daddy, bottle,* and *eat* may all be understood by the child. The child cannot say the words but can respond, indicating a knowledge of the words. Phase IV babies are beginning to develop real motor skills such as sitting independently, getting up on hands and knees, and rocking. A Phase IV child may even pull to a standing position. Phase IV babies need freedom in which to move and practice these growing skills. They can also grasp toys quite well and need suitable small objects with which they can practice picking up and holding. Toys such as crib devices to kick at, stacking toys, stuffed toys, balls to pick up, objects that are two to five inches in size so they cannot be swallowed all help the Phase IV child learn about the world and gain mastery over the immediate environment.

During Phase V, the infant usually comes into direct conflict with significant adults for the first time. This is due to the child's growing mobility. Soon there is no area in the house or center that is safe from the child's active exploration. Knick-knacks, books, ashtrays, electric cords, pots and pans, utensils, and pet food dishes are stimuli to the active Phase V child and bring the child into conflict with the parents or caregivers.

It is at this age that the child begins to develop self-control. It is important that the child has a child-proof area in which to play. Parents, early childhood teachers, and family day care providers need to know that the Phase V child can be safe from harm in that area.

If the Phase V child does not get into trouble, the Phase VI child will. At this point, mobility has been established. Phase VI children can walk and begin to run, climb, ride, push and pull objects, reach for and pull down, and talk. "No" becomes a favorite word, mostly because they hear it so often. Mama, Daddy, bye bye, and baby are spoken. The Phase VI child begins to pay less attention to the people in the environment and to spend more time looking, listening, practicing simple skills, and exploring.

It is the exploring that causes difficulty for both the Phase V and the Phase VI child. Most houses and yards are not childproof. Children will pull

Figure 8-7 Children develop the ability to assume the roles of both leader and follower. (Courtesy of Steve Howard)

flowers off stems, grab dirt pebbles and throw them, toddle down driveways and out into streets, climb up ladders, and push and pull at furniture. This struggle to experiment with growing motor skills comes into continued conflict with parental and center needs for the child's safety. Instead of complimenting the climber who has mastered the front steps and is now crying to be picked up so he or she can start over, we may scold the child, saying the steps are off limits. The Phase V and Phase VI child simply cannot comprehend this. It would be more beneficial to our peace of mind and the child's need to climb if a portable gate is placed across the third stair and the child is allowed to practice going up and down. If the child falls down the three steps, he or she will not be hurt and will approach the climb more carefully the next time.

Self-control grows from experiences like these. The Phase V and Phase VI child will become an autonomous, able Phase VII preschooler if allowed to experiment with what the body can do and is given opportunities to practice growing motor skills. As a Phase VII preschooler, the child will be able to:

- Get and hold the attention of adults
- Use adults as resources after first determining that a job is too difficult

- Express affection and mild annoyance
- Lead or follow peers (see figure 8-7)
- Compete with peers
- Show pride in accomplishments
- Engage in role-playing activities
- Use language with increasing competence
- Notice small details or discrepancies
- Anticipate consequences
- Deal with abstractions
- See things from another person's viewpoint
- Make interesting associations
- Plan and carry out complicated activities
- Use resources effectively
- Maintain concentration on a task while simultaneously keeping track of what is going on (dual focusing)

According to Burton White, most babies grow at essentially the same rate until Phase V. Most family environments provide reasonable positive experiences for Phase I through Phase IV children. As mentioned, conflicts arise as the child's mobility increases. As a teacher of young children, you must provide the kind of environment in which the children have as much opportunity as possible to grow and learn about their environment and themselves.

Self-esteem and Self-control

Although much of the research on self-esteem was completed in the late 1960s and throughout the 1970s, the 1990s are bringing about a renewed interest. With the noticeable changes in families that have occurred in the past 20 years due to the problems of divorce and subsequent single-parenthood, mobility, the rise in the incidence of substance abuse, remarriage and "blended" families, teenage parenthood, smaller family size, homelessness, the two working-parent family, and difficulties with child care and/or after-school care, child caregivers and teachers are seeing more and more stressed and even "damaged" children. Characteristic of these children is low self-esteem. Children of divorced parents typically blame themselves for the divorce,

a phenomenon that exists even in the most "friendly" of divorce cases. Children raised in single-parent homes, over 90 percent of them headed by a woman, often live in reduced circumstances. It is well known that most single-parent females are not able to command the salaries that the single-parent male can; the result has been the feminization of poverty and the consequent cost to children living in poverty—housing if any, in less desirable and often more dangerous neighborhoods, little medical or dental care, insufficient clothing for the weather conditions, lack of proper nutrition, just simply lack of care in too many instances. What you see in the classroom then is the damage to these children's self-esteem—parents too stressed, too busy, and too often suffering from low self-esteem themselves to parent their children properly or nourish their children's self-esteem. One word of caution: not all single parents are overstressed; some children are less stressed after a divorce between parents who constantly argued than before; some single-parent women do earn substantial salaries, are emotionally and psychologically healthy, and are able to build their children's self-esteem. As always, be careful of using stereotypes.

In his landmark research, Coopersmith (1967) cited three home factors that contribute to children's feelings of self-esteem: (1) unconditional acceptance of the child (although not necessarily accepting all of the child's behaviors), (2) setting clear expectations for behavior and consistently reinforcing the need for adherence to them, and (3) respecting the child's need for initiative within the set limits. Some children you see today in child care and school may have been accepted only when they did exactly what their parents demanded of them; tired from working, other parents have abdicated their job as parents and have allowed the children essentially to raise themselves or have allowed the TV to raise them; still other parents feel threatened by their children's desires for autonomy and initiative and do not respect the need to exert their wills. (See research by Loeb, Horst, & Horton, 1980, for more information on the relationship between self-esteem and parental child-rearing styles.)

For the caregiver and teacher working with "damaged" children with low self-esteem, the task is to attempt to provide the missing elements of acceptance, clearly defined limits, and respect for the child's need to assert autonomy and practice initiative within those limits. If this sounds like CARE-ing, it should.

Self-control can be defined as the ability to resist the inappropriate and act responsibly. Acting responsibly includes respecting the rights of others, showing compassion, being honest and at times exhibiting courage. It entails dealing effectively with anger and other strong emotions and having patience.

The following suggestions for promoting children's social development and skill are cited by Wittmer & Honig (1994):

- Value and emphasize consideration for others' needs.

- Model prosocial behaviors.

- Label and identify prosocial and antisocial behaviors.

- Attribute positive and social behaviors to each child.

- Notice and positively encourage prosocial behaviors, but do not overuse external rewards.

- Acknowledge and encourage understanding and expression of children's feelings.

- Facilitate perspective- and role-taking skills and understanding others' feelings.

- Use victim-centered discipline and reparation. Emphasize consequences.

- Help children become assertive concerning prosocial matters.

- Encourage means-ends and alternative-solution thinking in conflict situations.

- Use Socratic questions to elicit prosocial planning and thoughtfulness and recognition of responsibility.

    "How does that help you?"

    "How is that helping the group?"

- Provide specific behavioral training in social skills such as listening, using nice talk, using brave talk, saying thank-you, asking for help, greeting others, waiting one's turn, offering help, asking someone to play, and sharing.

- Respond to and provide alternatives to aggressive behaviors.

- Offer children choices.

- Provide opportunities for social interactions through play. Pair "social isolates" with sociable children.

● MASLOW'S HIERARCHY OF NEEDS AND ITS RELATION TO SELF-CONTROL

Maslow (1968) attempted to develop a hierarchy of needs by which people are motivated.

- Growth Needs

    Self-actualization needs

    Aesthetic needs

    The need to know and understand

- Deficiency Needs

    Esteem needs

    The need to belong and be loved

Figure 8-8 When mom leaves, there may be a period of uneasiness.

Safety needs

Physiological needs

Maslow grouped these needs according to whether they were "deficiency" needs or "growth" needs; whether or not the individual was growing in a positive direction. For anyone to grow positively, Maslow felt that the deficiency needs must be filled in order for the growth needs to be met.

The implications for the children you teach are multiple. The child who is hungry, cold, and, more importantly, unloved, may not be able to grow and learn as we would wish. This child may be afraid to grow for fear of losing the known. Regardless of how inclement and/or unwholesome that child's current environment may be, there is a certain safety in the known. For this child, growth can be full of anxiety.

Anxiety and fear in the child are often seen in the classroom as opposites. One fearful, anxious child will withdraw physically from the environment, figure 8-8. The child may cling to the mother or the teacher, refuse to try a new activity, and limit participation to what the child knows and can do best. Another fearful, anxious child will lash out verbally or physically, sometimes both.

Maslow's hierarchy of needs is another way of looking at what motivates behavior. The child who is hungry, poorly clothed, and unloved may have difficulty in becoming self-actualized. The same child may have difficulty in developing the natural desire to explore, know, and understand the environment. The overtly aggressive child and the fearful child are both underdisciplined or undisciplined.

In studying Maslow's hierarchy of needs, remember that if one goal is to help the child become self-actualizing, the child's deficiency needs must be met. The child's belongingness, love, and esteem needs must be met. Belongingness carries the implication of family identity, of belonging to a particular adult or group, and feeling that one is a part of this group. There is psychological safety in having a group to belong to. This group is the one that takes care of the physiological needs and makes sure that

the environment is safe. This group also allows the growing child to develop self-esteem.

How is self-esteem developed? According to Maslow, it is developed in interaction with the important people in the environment. Look at the following sequence of events: It is morning. The infant cries; the mother goes to the crib, smiles, speaks softly to the baby, and picks the baby up. She changes the diaper, goes to the kitchen to warm a bottle or sits down in the rocking chair to nurse. As the infant feeds, she coos and speaks to the child and plays with the hand. What is the infant learning? Besides learning that this mother is reliable and loving, the baby is learning that he is important to the mother. Later, the child turns over from the stomach onto the back. The mother smiles, claps her hands, and says, "My, aren't you getting big! How smart you are to turn over!" The child is learning that he is physically competent. Self-esteem is developed through the continual interaction between the parent, day care workers, and child. Every time you give positive attention to the child, and smile, and notice achievements, you are helping to build the child's self-esteem.

The child from this type of environment will have no difficulty in becoming self-actualized. In contrast, the child whose home environment has not provided for these deficiency needs will have difficulty. For this child, you will need to provide those experiences that the child has missed: attention to physiological needs, safety needs, and the need to belong. The loving early childhood teacher or family day care provider can do much to help the child whose own family group has been unable to help.

Children are remarkably resilient; they can survive situations that seem almost impossible. Even given a poor beginning, if a child comes into contact with a warm, loving, accepting adult, the child will be able to self-actualize. Children who seem invulnerable or untouched by negative family environments (alcoholism, criminality, poverty, and/or mental illness) are also those children who, during their first year, had at least one significant adult in their lives who cared (Werner & Smith,

Figure 8-9 This child is exploring his environment.

1982). This adult could be trusted, thus enabling the children to resolve the question of basic trust. According to Werner and Smith, these children are able to find other adults to whom they can relate in terms of resolving the other tasks of early childhood. These adults meet the children's deficiency needs so that they can self-actualize in spite of negative environments.

How does self-actualization relate to self-control? One aspect of self-actualization *is* self-control. The child who is able to self-actualize is able to make choices and accept leader or follower roles and has a good sense of self, figure 8-7. Having a sense of self enables the child to be assertive when appropriate or to accept directions from another.

Implications for Teachers

To summarize theorists' suggestions regarding the promotion of self-control, let us briefly look at each. Erikson relates self-control with resolving the question of autonomy, the task of toddlers. According to Maslow, self-control relates to the resolution of deficiency needs and the beginnings of self-actu-

alization. Burton White's theory indicates that self-control develops as the child passes from Phase V to Phase VI in a healthy, positive environment with caring, loving parents. The child who has gained mastery over the environment gains self-control, figure 8-9. Self-esteem theory would suggest that self-control is related to self-worth and that, when provided with acceptance, respect, and clearly stated classroom rules, the children who feel good about themselves will also exhibit self-control. Often the parents of these children begin changing and showing interest when their children begin to feel good about themselves.

Sometimes words like *empower* and *belonging* are used to indicate that teachers who empower their students and provide them with a sense of belonging are also teaching students self-control. Empowerment means allowing children control over certain aspects of the classroom life, for example, choices of which learning center they want to study at or what the logical consequences might be for breaking certain classroom rules. And given an opportunity to feel a part of the classroom group satisfies the universal need to belong.

What does this mean to you as a teacher? First, you will need to provide the kind of environment where the children feel safe. Second, you must also provide the kind of personal environment where the children can grow positively. You must use guidance techniques and recognize, through keen observation, which children need more help than others to learn self-control.

What is meant by saying that you must provide for a safe environment? The physical arrangement of the rooms must be safe. It also means consistency of behavior expectations and predictability regarding the schedule and your own behavior. You must remember to use the four c's of discipline. You must CARE so that the psychological climate is warm and loving. It means recognizing a child's developmental level in terms of self-control.

If the child has not learned to be autonomous, you will need to provide the kinds of opportunities that allow the child to practice. As mentioned, it means providing guided choices and allowing practice in decision making. Does the child have a low self-image? Is the child's need to belong unfulfilled? You will need to provide success experiences for this child and a lot of tender, loving care (TLC as it has been called). If this child has at least a sense of belonging in class, this is a start.

Is this a negative-acting child who appears to be at Burton White's Phase V and Phase VI stages? What has happened to this child? Most likely, if you check with the parents or other primary caretakers, you will find that the child's attempts to explore at Phase V were thwarted. This child was not encouraged to explore the physical environment and master newly emerging motor abilities. This is the child who becomes too fearful or shy or too aggressive. This child needs opportunities to explore and use motor abilities but needs to be told the limits over and over. This child must be urged ever so gently to try again.

Self-control, or self-discipline, is learned only through the initial imposition of controls from the significant adults in the child's life and the opportunity to practice the child's own controls secondarily.

Self-respect

Young children often want to share accomplishments with peers and caretakers. Requests to "Look at me, teacher!" pervade daily teacher-child interactions and help children respect themselves if given teacher attention. Many children take satisfaction in their appropriate behavior and accomplishments and notice the inappropriate behavior of peers. Teachers deal with children's failures to act in line with their own developing good conscience as children move toward greater self-control. When classrooms model respect, compassion, and concern for others, children gain self-control and self-respect with greater ease. Teachers genuinely try to be the sort of people they hope children will become.

Talking through complications or problem situations with children is one way to help them understand the consequences of different choices. Story discussions also bring to light what choices and consequences occurred for story characters. Most teachers attempt to draw from children what choices existed in life situations and what consequences might follow. This promotes the child's own ability to reflect.

● A CASE STUDY TO ANALYZE

Let us look at a sampling of behavior, and see if you can apply any of the theories. More importantly, see whether knowing theory helps in teaching the child.

Chris is a five-year-old whose mother brings him to school during the spring registration period. School policy invites spring registrants to attend class with the current children for a part of the morning session. You noted when he was enrolled that his mother looked much older than the others. Under "Reason for Enrollment," the mother wrote, "To give me a rest, and to give Chris a chance to be with children his own age."

Later, in your initial conference with her, Chris's mother confessed, "You know, Chris was such a surprise to his father and me! After 20 years of being married, we never thought we'd ever have children. I thought I was going through the 'change,' you know, when I found out I was pregnant. What a shock! My husband and I lead such busy lives, you can imagine what having a baby did!"

Upon further investigation, you discover that Chris was carried full-term, the delivery was normal, and his arrival home was uneventful. Chris's mother assured you that her son had always been well cared for. "After all, my husband has a good income from his business (he's a CPA), and I used to run his office before Chris came. I'm a financial secretary, you know, and a good one."

When you asked about Chris's eating habits and sleeping patterns, she responded, "Well, of course, Chris doesn't have many regular habits. According to Mattie, our housekeeper, Chris eats when he wants to. Mattie takes care of Chris while my husband and I work. We don't see too much of him, you know, especially during tax season. But Mattie assures me Chris eats well, and I know he sleeps well when he finally goes to bed.

Upon further questioning, you find out that Chris "has a TV in his bedroom and usually falls asleep with it on. My husband or I turn it off when we go to bed."

Later, the mother volunteers, "Chris is such an active child that his father and I sometimes go nuts on the weekends. We tried locking Chris in his bedroom. That worked until he found out how to open his window screen and crawl out. Can you imagine that? And, only three years old at the time. I can tell you we paddled him good for that!"

You wonder what Chris's behavior is going to be like when he comes for his scheduled visit. When Chris arrives with the housekeeper, unfortunately, your worst fears are realized. In less than 10 minutes he has knocked down a castle Jaime and Roberto had been working on for more than 20 minutes, has run to the easels, grabbed the paint brush from Anya's hand, and, to her cries of dismay, smeared her painting. Then, he has opened the hamster cage and none too carefully has searched through the wood shavings in the cage for the sleepy animal. At this point, you've had enough and intervene.

Why do you think Chris acts the way he does? What hypotheses or educated guesses can you make? Was he a wanted child? Do his basic physiological needs seem to be met? (The answer to that question is obvious. Chris is clean, well dressed, and large for his age. He shows no signs of malnutrition.) Moving to the next level on Maslow's hierarchy, safety needs, you can only guess at this point. Looking at his rather awkward large motor coordination and lack of ease in handling his body, it becomes apparent that Chris does not seem comfortable in the physical environment. Moving to the third level, the need to belong and be loved, you are no longer so sure. Chris parted from his housekeeper as soon as he came into the room.

However much he may have been used to being left with the housekeeper, it was obvious that she did nothing to restrain him. Her only remark was, "Good lord! Sometimes he used to act like that when I took him to visit at my friend's house. Now I don't even try to take him any more."

Upon intervening, you took Chris's arm firmly, closed the door to the hamster cage, and said, "You'll be able to play with Sebastian next Fall. But, first, you will have to learn how. In our kindergarten we respect each other's work, and we don't disturb others when they are busy. Look at me when I talk to you. You have a choice of going to the clay table where you can pound on the clay and make something you'd like to make. Or, you can come to the workbench over by the door and drive some nails into some pieces of scrap wood or make a wood sculpture."

Looking at the fourth level of the Maslow hierarchy, do you think Chris has feelings of self-esteem? Is it likely that a child who destroys other children's work has good self-esteem? The answer is no. What are the chances then of Chris being able to self-actualize? At this point, they are probably not too good. Chris is a typical underdisciplined child, cared for in a material way but not in a loving way.

What would Erikson's theory reveal? Has Chris resolved the tasks of infancy, toddlerhood, and preschool? Is he ready to work on the task of school-aged children? Is it possible that, before Chris became an active crawler, his mother did love and accept him. She had reported a normal delivery and a healthy baby. In telling of his birth, she commented about what a pretty baby Chris was, and how she and her husband used to take him everywhere because he'd go to sleep anywhere as long as he was in his bassinet. You suspect that it was only after Chris began to crawl that he began to pose problems. You feel that Chris probably has some level of basic trust.

Autonomy, though, is another question. You already know that Chris was locked in his bedroom so his parents could rest. When asked, Chris's mother admitted that she generally kept him confined to the playpen while in the house or yard. "I couldn't have him get into my collection of miniatures or into his father's rose garden!" When asked if Chris had space in the yard for a swing set or other play equipment, Chris's mother said, "Heavens, no! My husband and I like to entertain in our yard in the summer; we can't have play equipment cluttering it up!"

It seems apparent that Chris has not had the kind of gross motor experiences of most preschoolers. In fact, you already noted during Chris's visit that he ran awkwardly as though he did not have much practice running in the past. Another observation was that Chris's mother took off his jacket for him; the boy did not do it for himself. When asked whether Chris dressed himself, his mother stated, "Oh, no. I always put his clothes on for him." When asked if Chris chose what to wear, she replied, "No. Chris wouldn't know what to choose! He'd end up with a blue plaid shirt and his green overalls when he ought to be wearing his gray pin-striped shirt and black jeans!"

You realize that Chris has had little experience in making the usual choices common to many kindergarteners. Has he resolved the questions of autonomy or initiative? It seems unlikely. What does this mean for you in terms of having Chris in your kindergarten? First, it means a lot of close watching, restating rules, calm insistence of acceptable behavior, and gradual choices. You know it also means a lot of tactful, gentle education for Chris's parents.

● CULTURAL DIFFERENCES

How do cultural differences reflect in analyzing student behaviors? The most important factor to remember is to avoid using stereotypes. All Asians are not quiet, nor are they all straight-A students, nor are Asians from one single-cultural group. All African Americans are not inner-city dwellers nor do they all speak nonstandard English. All Hispanics are not Mexican or Puerto Rican or Cuban; they come from as many different separate Hispanic cultures as do Africans, Asians, or Europeans. Among Native Americans you will note the same great variations depending upon individual cultural backgrounds. It is important for you as future teachers to remain as open-minded as possible, not to use the kind of thinking that can ascribe to culturally different students behaviors that may not apply to them as individuals.

In observing children and families from cultures other than your own, the most important factor in establishing a good relationship with the family is to remain open-minded. Listen carefully to what a parent may say; even if you disagree, try to place yourself in the parent's shoes, to see from their perspective. Parents from India typically greet another person with clasped hands and a bow of the head. To offer to shake hands is simply not appropriate. One teacher related that when she held a conference with one of her Afghan parents, the father had to be addressed through a male teacher: he made it clear that it was inappropriate for him to speak directly to his child's female teacher. A parent from Japan will often bow to his child's teacher; it is a sign of respect. A Latino mother may not look you straight in the eyes as she may feel that to do so connotes disrespect. Parents from Vietnam may have different names and legally be married (Berger, 1994).

Certainly one reason for the existence of stereotypes is that when we don't have the information, we rely upon the news media, and typically television, for the "facts." But "bad" news sells more than "good" and stories of homicides, robberies, and assaults abound. Since many more of these occur in inner cities than in suburbs, the stereotype develops that since the inner city or barrio or wherever the violence is happening has more African Americans or Latinos or people of color living within its confines, all people of that particular race or ethnic group must be violent or prone to violence.

We need to remember that the first African Americans to come to what is now the United States came with Columbus and Coronado, and many more arrived, as did many whites, as indentured servants. It was only later historically that they were brought as slaves (Banks, 1984). We need also remember that Latinos had settled in the Southwestern parts of the United States before the first Puritans settled in Massachusetts. If there is any one thing you should always remember about children from minority families in your classroom it is to recognize their diversity (Berger, 1994). For some excellent ideas of how to avoid stereotyping and bias in your classroom, look at Sparks's (1989) book, *The Anti-Bias Curriculum: Tools for Empowering Children.*

SUMMARY

In this chapter we have presented several different theories to help you analyze children's behaviors, together with suggestions to implement in your attempt to help children learn self-control. Among theorists mentioned were Erikson, Maslow, the self-concept theorists, and White.

In terms of the Erikson tasks, the one most closely related to self-control is autonomy. If resolved during toddlerhood, teachers see a child who knows how to play/work within the prescribed limits in any classroom, who understands both leadership and follower roles, who knows when to ask for help or when he can do a task by himself. Ideas for teachers to implement in the classroom for children who have incompletely resolved autonomy were also given—allowing choices and reminding children of limits and rules are two.

Maslow believed that self-control evolved out of self-esteem (as do the self-concept theorists) and self-actualization. Thus everything a teacher can do to build self-esteem and a feeling of belongingness in the classroom, and, again, to allow choices all will lead to children with good self-control.

White focuses on infants during their first explorations with mobility, an event that usually comes between eight and 24 months. Given appropriate toys and the freedom to explore within safe limits, active babies and toddlers develop into healthy, happy preschoolers.

Finally, we presented you with the case study of a child, Chris, and gave some suggestions, related to the different theories, to analyze his behavior and develop and implement some management strategies.

SUGGESTED ACTIVITIES

A. Read Burton L. White's *The First Three Years of Life*. Give close attention to chapters 6 and 7. Discuss your readings with your peers, cooperating teacher, and supervisor.

B. Read Erik Erikson's *Childhood and Society*. In particular, read those chapters covering the first four stages of psychosocial development. Write a review of your reading and discuss it with your peers and supervisor.

C. You are concerned because Tahira, a student in your third grade room, is frequently absent. A bright-eyed, eager-to-learn child, she does poorly on tests; and, when she turns in her homework, it is often incomplete. Your cooperating teacher also has been concerned, and she suggests that you attend a conference she has arranged with Tahira's mother to help you understand. At the conference, you discover that Mrs. Bhas often keeps Tahira home to take care of her younger brothers and sister whenever one or more of them are ill. You explain that it is important for the child to be in school but Mrs. Bhas demurs, "Tahira is my oldest girl; she knows she is supposed to help me. I work and it's Tahira's duty to take care of her younger brothers and sister after school or when they are sick. Education is important for my boys but not for my girls. It is only important that they have a good marriage arranged for them."

In view of Mrs. Bhas's cultural expectations for her daughter, what might you do? How might you try to convince her that you think a third grader is too young to babysit or that a girl needs an education as much as a boy? Do any of the theories discussed in our chapter help you in understanding your dilemma about Tahira?

Applying Erikson's theory might indicate the satisfactory completion of basic trust, but is autonomy or initiative an expectation of Tahira by Mr. and Mrs. Bhas? It is more likely that being quiet and obedient (i.e., doing as mother and father ask) are cultural practices more valued by her parents than are independence, exploration, and curiosity. One approach you might take is to ask Mrs. Bhas what her occupation is to determine whether or not an education is needed. Unfortunately, her response could be, "We own several motels in town and my job, and Tahira's and her sister's on the weekends, is to see that linens are changed, beds are made, and rooms are cleaned." It might be possible to find someone of the Bhas's own culture to explain the importance of education to them.

Using Maslow's hierarchy might point out the satisfactory completion of the deficiency needs, but interference with Tahira's "need to know and understand" by her culture.

D. Observe one child in your classroom closely and analyze the child's level of self-control. Discuss your observations regarding whether you feel the child has resolved the task of autonomy, feels competent, and is becoming self-actualized. State specific actions that reinforce your conclusions.

E. Close your eyes as a fellow student teacher reads the following:

A Visualization

Sometimes visualizing what you're attempting to do in classroom management situations is helpful. Imagine a large metropolitan train station where at the moment every child is happily playing. Imagine each child as a different kind of railroad car. All of a sudden the box car and the coal car are becoming increasingly noisy and agitated and rolling out of the station to a destination called Violence. The agitation can represent lots of different feelings including anger, frustration, fear, jealousy, anxiety, and other negative feelings. You, the railway security officer, aren't sure exactly how each car is feeling. You think it's best if the box car and coal car go to different destinations than Violence. Down in Violence lots of hurtful things happen like hair pulling, biting, hitting and pushing, and so on. At times you notice friends of box car or coal car want to ride down to Violence too, ending up with many beaten up and crushed cars. Sometimes a car comes out of Violence unscathed and rolls back into the station ready to roll out to Violence with another car destined to become beaten or broken.

Your goal is to have cars in conflict buy tickets to Negotiation and/or Problem Solving, a shorter trip and closer destination. You are willing to buy a ticket to either of these destinations and help the cars think of innovative solutions where both will ride back to the station with needs satisfied. You may be able to stop cars headed toward Violence before car feelings get heated up. You're ready to get them on the track to Negotiation and Problem Solving quickly. You've found you are usually able to promote agreement in these destinations by:

1. Verbally stating a problem exists
2. Stopping aggressive acts
3. Holding the conflict object if there is one
4. Drawing out in words the feeling of the nonaggressor. Drawing out the feeling of the aggressor
5. Reflecting back the expressed feelings to both parties
6. Describing and stating both sides of the conflict
7. Verbally drawing solution ideas from both sides until a satisfactory solution is discovered. Offering a solution when a stalemate occurs
8. Promoting agreement on a solution
9. Congratulating parties on offering solution ideas
10. Monitoring both parties while they work through the agreed plan
11. Stating that the conflict solution has been accomplished

This process is also suggested for adult conflict situations in chapter 10.

How do the suggested techniques promote child self-control?

F. Read the following from Kathleen Grey (1995). Discuss with a group of classmates. Try to answer the questions posed in the second paragraph.

A teacher is trying to reinforce the behavior of a child who has voluntarily carried out a classroom rule.

She says to him, "Good job, Tom! You're doing just what you're supposed to do, aren't you? You're always such a good boy." The message to Tom is not about his intrinsic worth, but about his value *when he does what his teacher wants him to.* If Tom's teacher truly wants to affirm Tom's intrinsic worth, as he expressed it through his desire to participate competently in classroom culture, she might say, "I saw you carry all the dirty paint brushes to the sink, Tom. You had to make three trips to get them all! I sure appreciate your help."

If Tom regularly hears the unspoken message in the first scenario, how is he likely to apply it to himself? How do you think this message will affect his ability to make judgments for himself? Would he have a different sense of his competence if he regularly received the message in the second sample?

G. Read the following and react:

Young children are often helped by a playful, imaginative approach when feelings are hard to face (Zavitkovsky, Baker, Berlfein, & Almy, 1986).

Can you remember any life situations when a teacher or adult helped a child overcome or face fear using this approach?

REVIEW

A. According to Erikson, what are the first four stages of psychosocial development? What are the tasks associated with each?

B. Read the following description of behavior. Then answer the question at the end.

Cindy, an only child, is a bright-eyed, small, three-and-a-half-year-old attending your day care center for the first time. Her family recently moved to your community. Her mother and father are both teachers in local school districts. Her mother reported that Cindy's birth was normal, and she has had no major health problems. Coming to your day care center will be her first experience with children her own age except for religious instruction school.

Cindy appears to like day care very much. She is a dominant child despite her small size, and rapidly becomes one of the leaders. She plays with just about all of the toys and materials supplied at the center. Her favorite activities, however, appear to be the playhouse and easel painting when inside, and either the sandbox or swings when outside. She occasionally gets into arguments with her peers when they no longer accept her leadership. Cindy has difficulty resolving these conflicts and frequently has a tantrum when she is unable to have her own way.

1. Would you suggest that Cindy has basic trust? What evidence suggests this?
2. Do you think Cindy has resolved the task of autonomy? What evidence suggests that?
3. Erikson would suggest that Cindy's task at age three and one-half is to learn to use initiative. What evidence is there in the brief description of her behavior that suggests she is going through this phase of development in a positive or negative way?
4. Using Maslow's hierarchy of needs, at which level would you place Cindy? Why?

C. List the seven phases of development that occur during the child's first three years according to Burton White.

D. Read Harter's 1983 article, "Developmental Perspectives on the Self-System," and discuss with your peers and supervisor. What are the implications for teachers in terms of self-concept theory and self-control?

E. List five characteristics of an autonomous, six-year-old child with positive self-esteem.

F. Rate each of the following actions with a plus (+) if it would help a child develop self-control or a minus (–) if it would not. If the action would neither help nor hurt, rate it with an x.

1. Smiling each morning when the child enters
2. Picking up and isolating the child who is fighting
3. Spanking the child
4. Setting strict limits and frequently reminding the child of them

5. Asking the child who is fighting to please stop

6. Moving toward a group of arguing children

7. Complimenting the child when successful at a new task

8. Applying the same standards to all the children

9. Gently persuading the child

10. Pairing a shy child with an outgoing one

11. Ridiculing a naughty child

12. Redirecting the attention of a child engaged in a potentially dangerous activity

REFERENCES

Abramson, L., Seligman, M., & Teasdale, J. (1978). Learned helplessness in humans: Critique and reformation. *Journal of Abnormal Psychology*, *67*, 49–74.

Banks, J. A. (1984). *Teaching strategies for ethnic studies.* Boston: Allyn & Bacon.

Berger, E. H. (1994). *Parents as partners in education: The school and home working together* (4th ed.). Columbus, OH: Merrill/Macmillan.

Coopersmith, S. (1967). *The antecedents of self-esteem.* New York: W. H. Freeman.

Dweck, C. (1975). The role of expectations and attributions in the alleviation of learned helplessness. *Journal of Personality and Social Psychology*, *4*, 474–485.

Erikson, E. H. (1993). *Childhood and society* (reprint of 2nd ed.). New York: Norton.

Grey, K. (July/August 1995). Not in praise of praise. *Child Care Information Exchange*, #104, 56–59.

Loeb, R. C., Horst, L., & Horton, P. J. (1980). Family interaction patterns associated with self-esteem in preadolescent boys and girls. *Merrill-Palmer Quarterly*, *26*, 203–217.

Maslow, A. H. (1968). *Toward a psychology of being* (2nd ed.). Princeton: Van Nostrand Reinhold.

Sparks, L. D. (1989). *The anti-bias curriculum: Tools for empowering young children.* Washington, DC: National Association for the Education of Young Children.

Werner, E., & Smith, R. S. (1982). *Vulnerable but invincible: A longitudinal study of resilient children and youth.* New York: McGraw-Hill.

White, B. L. (1975). *The first three years of life.* Englewood Cliffs, NJ: Prentice-Hall.

Wittmer, D. S., & Honig, A. S. (July 1994). Encouraging positive social development in children. *Young Children*, *49*(5), 4–12.

Zavitkovsky, D., Baker, K. R., Berlfein, J. R., & Almy, M. (1986). *Listen to the Children.* Washington, DC: National Association for the Education of Young Children.

RESOURCES

Barclay, K. H., with Breheny, C. (September 1994). Letting children take over more of their own learning: Collaborative research in the kindergarten classroom. *Young Children*, *49*(6), 27–32.

Chang, H. N.-L. (1993). *Affirming children's roots: Cultural and linguistic diversity in early care and education.* San Francisco: A California Tomorrow Publication.

Chaskin, R. J., & Rauner, D. M. (Guest Eds.) (May 1995). A Kappan special section on youth and caring. *Phi Delta Kappan*, *76*(9), 665–719.

Children's Defense Fund. (1995). *The state of America's children Yearbook.* Washington, DC: Author.

Comer, J. P., & Poussaint, A. F. (1975). *Black child care.* New York: Pocket Books.

Critical Perspectives on Diversity. (Summer 1993). *The Educational Forum, A Kappa Delta Pi Publication*, *57*(4), Entire issue.

Curry, N. F., & Arnaud, S. H. (May 1995). Personality difficulties in preschool children as revealed through play themes and styles. *Young Children*, *50*(4), 4–9.

Dembo, M. H. (1994). *Applying educational psychology* (5th ed.). New York: Longman.

Dweck, C. (1986). Motivational Process affecting learning. *American Psychologist*, *41*, 1040–1048.

Educating yourself about diverse cultural groups in our country by reading. (March 1993). *Young Children*, *48*(3), 13–16.

Enriching classroom diversity with books for children, in depth discussion of them, and story-extension activities. (March 1993). *Young Children*, *48*(3), 10–12.

Furman, R. A. (January 1995). Helping children cope with stress and deal with feelings. *Young Children*, *50*(2), 33–41.

Gibson, J. T., & Chandler, L. A. (1988). *Educational psychology: Mastering principles and applications.* Boston: Allyn & Bacon.

Good, T. L., & Brophy, J. E. (1990). *Educational psychology: A realistic approach.* New York: Longman.

Harter, S. (1983). Developmental perspectives on the self-system. In P. Mussen (Ed.), *Handbook of Child Psychology* (4th ed., Vol. 4). New York: Wiley.

Heath, H. E. (July 1994). Dealing with difficult behaviors—teachers plan with parents. *Young Children, 49*(5), 20–27.

King, E. W., Chapman, M., & Cruz-Janzen, M. (1994). *Educating young children in a diverse society.* Boston: Allyn & Bacon.

Kotloff, L. J. (March 1993). Fostering cooperative group spirit and individuality: Examples from a Japanese preschool. *Young Children, 48*(3), 17–23.

Kuebli, J. (March 1994). Research in review: Young children's understanding of everyday emotions. *Young Children, 49*(3), 36–47.

Multicultural Education—Materials published by Kappa Delta Pi, 1976–94. (Summer 1994). *Kappa Delta Pi Record, 30*(4), 168–169.

Neugebauer, C. (Ed.). (1992). *Alike and different: Exploring our humanity with young children.* Washington, DC: National Association for the Education of Young Children. (Originally published by Exchange Press, Redmond, WA).

Pines, M. (January 1979). Super kids: The myth of the vulnerable child. *Psychology Today.*

Ramsey, P. G. (September 1995). Research in review. Growing up with the contradictions of race and class. *Young Children, 50*(6), 18–22.

Saracho, O. N., & Spodek, B. (1983). *Multicultural experience in early childhood education.* Washington, DC; National Association for the Education of Young Children.

Sigel, I. (1985). *Parental belief systems: The psychological consequences for children.* Hillsdale, NJ: Erlbaum.

Slavin, R. E. (1994). *Educational psychology* (4th ed.). Boston: Allyn & Bacon.

Stevenson, H., Azuma, H., & Harkuta, K. (1986). *Child development in Japan.* New York: W. H. Freeman.

Stone, S. J. (Annual Theme Issue, 1995). Empowering teachers, empowering children. *Childhood Education, 71*(5), 294–295.

Werner, E. E. (1979). *Cross-cultural child development.* Monterey, CA: Brooks/Cole.

Whiting, B., & Whiting, J. W. M.(1975). *Children of six cultures.* Cambridge, MA: Harvard University Press.

CHAPTER

9

Common Problems of Student Teachers

OBJECTIVES

After studying this chapter, the student will be able to:

- Identify five common student teacher problems related to interpersonal communication.
- List areas of possible conflict between student teachers, supervisors, and cooperating teachers and their relationship to interpersonal communication.
- Describe the goals of interpersonal communication during the student teaching experience.
- Identify communication skills that aid in sending and receiving verbal and nonverbal messages.
- Define "authenticity" of communication.
- Describe the atmosphere necessary for promoting student teaching growth.

I was convinced my cooperating teacher didn't like me! I don't take criticism well. After hearing the same comment from different team members, I realized they were trying to help me.

Jean Hamilton

Many of the parents of my placement classroom's children don't speak English. Some are new, struggling immigrants. My cooperating teacher makes all feel welcome. We've a classroom corner where tea and coffee is served and parents can sit and chat at pickup time on sunny days. It's a good idea.

Margaret Hanneford

This chapter is not intended to solve all problems encountered during student teaching. It will probe possible reasons for difficulties, especially those related to communication, and help alert the student to possible courses of action. Knowing that problems are going to occur is stress reducing. You will relate more strongly to some ideas in this chapter than to others. Knowledge may help you escape some problems, confront others, and cope with ones that cannot be changed. Open communication with others—cooperating teacher, college supervisor, children—is often the key.

● KINDS OF PROBLEMS

Do you know of any human relationship that is problem-free and always smooth sailing? Student teaching, involving close human interaction and communication, is no exception. Pressures, feelings, desires, needs, risks, and possible failures are inherent.

Stress

During the first days and weeks of student teaching, stress arises usually from student teachers' desire to become good practicing teachers and feelings of self-doubt and lack of confidence. As you grasp the challenges through watching your cooperating teacher and attempt to put your own theory into practice, the task seems monumental. Fuller (1969), who summarized 11 studies related to the concerns of teacher education students, pinpointed three sequential stages in teacher training: (1) focus on self or self-protection; (2) focus on pupils (children); and (3) focus on outcomes of teaching.

Anxiety

An early focus on oneself may produce anxiety. A student teacher can feel uncomfortable until there is a clear feeling of exactly what is expected (Danoff, 1977). One can react to stress in a number of ways. In student teaching, reactions could be:

- Becoming defensive
- Concentrating energies on passive, shy children
- Fear of being "unloved" if you discipline

- Becoming extremely authoritative—giving directions in every situation
- Talking too much
- Looking for fault in others
- Becoming overly critical of the student teaching situation
- Withdrawing into busy work or room maintenance
- Seeking additional written or oral guidelines, figure 9-1
- Organizing tasks into time blocks
- Clearly outlining assignments on a calendar, file, or binder system
- Seeking the supervisor to communicate anxieties
- Using stress-reduction techniques

The first eight reactions can lead to immediate additional difficulties. The other reactions confront and possibly reduce tension. Anxiety may occur when there are changes in life. Change for student teachers occurs with their increasing responsibilities.

Figure 9-1 Are there guidelines about student teacher telephone calls at your placement school?

Clear, authentic communication of feelings, done with skill and sensitivity, is not often taught at either home or school. The student teaching experience puts student teachers, children, and other adults in close human contact and adds the anxiety-producing procedure of observing and assessing the student teacher's competency development. If you have already acquired the abilities of speaking openly and frankly without alienating, being a skillful listener, and receiving and accepting suggestions, this unit will serve as a review, perhaps giving additional insights and communication techniques.

Keirsey and Bates (1984) offer advice to individuals seeking to understand and communicate with others:

> If I do not want what you want, please try not to tell me that my want is wrong.
>
> Or if I believe other than you, at least pause before you correct my view.
>
> Or if my emotion is less than yours, or more, given the same circumstances, try not to ask me to feel more strongly or weakly.
>
> If you will allow me any of my own wants, or emotions, or beliefs, or actions, then you open yourself, so that some day these ways of mine might not seem so wrong, and might finally appear to you as right—for me.
>
> People are different in fundamental ways. They want different things (pp. 1–2).

The importance of relating and communicating with others in childhood work cannot be overestimated. A study by Oberg (1992) points out that connections between people are psychological, cultural, and political. Many early childhood teachers face cultural diversity daily. This necessitates increased awareness, sensitivity and communication skill.

> I was so anxious the first day my supervisor came to observe me in my third grade placement that the example I placed on the board to illustrate multiplication as an easy way to add was totally wrong! And to make matters worse, Marcia (my fel-low student teacher in the classroom next door) was also observing!
>
> (A thank-you to Suzanne Cady, student teacher, California State University, Hayward, fall quarter 1990, for sharing, from her journal, this as her most memorable experience).

Typically this feeling disappears with experience.

> I found out that my supervisor was so supportive and understanding of my anxieties when she came to observe me that I no longer was afraid to see her come in. I even goofed on a tangram demonstration and was able to laugh with my students when they pointed out my mistake!
>
> (Another thank-you to Suzanne Cady for sharing this thought from her journal.)

Sometimes extreme reactions to student teaching happen.

> The situation is complicated by biases and stereotypes each of us may have about the teaching role. You may find yourself saying, "All teachers are bad . . . I will save these children and protect them from the teacher. I will do the opposite of what she does . . ." Or you may say, "All teachers are wonderful, superior people . . . I will copy the words, phrases, voice quality, and gestures of this teacher. Then I, too, will be marvelous" (Danoff, Breitbart, & Barr, 1977).

Even extreme feelings can be accepted as natural and to be expected. Once accepted, there is the chance to move on and get past them or at least cope.

> First of all, students can expect to feel inadequate when they begin participating in the school and probably for some time after that. They cannot possibly be prepared for all that may happen. No one can give instructions that will cover everything, certainly not in the time there may have been for preparation. Of course, students will not feel sure of what is expected of them or of what they are supposed to do. The teacher who is guiding them may not be sure of these things herself, as she does not know them yet or know what is possible for them. What we can do about the feeling of inadequacy at this

point is to feel comfortable about having it (Read & Patterson, 1980).

Another common panic feeling during first days is expressed in the following:

> The material in Introductory Educational Psychology courses has slipped from memory. How is all that stuff about learning theory going to help you survive tomorrow? Gone are all the professors who told you of the excitement, challenge, and satisfaction of teaching (Brooks, 1978).

You will find it is possible to be excited, eager to try your ideas and activities, eager to develop your own teaching style, and still be somewhat apprehensive. Hendrick (1975) states, "One of the outstanding characteristics of beginning teachers is the caring and involvement that they bring with them to their work." These will promote their success in student teaching.

A contrast to the anxious approach to student teaching is the relaxed, confident one. Danoff, Breitbart, and Barr (1977) suggest this happens after your first successes. Self-confidence and self-esteem are important primary goals of student teaching. They evolve in student teachers as they do in children through actions resulting in success and through the feedback received from others. A strong feeling of success through child interactions is described by Read and Patterson (1980):

> A child's face lights up when he sees us come into the room, and we know that our relationship with him is a source of strength. He is seeing us as someone who cares, who can be depended on, and who has something significant to give him. It makes us feel good inside to be this kind of person for a child. It gives us confidence. (See figure 9-2.)

Hints for dealing with anxiety suggest trying not to worry about being the teacher and, instead, reflect on teachers you liked and why (Brooks, 1978). Another method is to relax and treat children your own way, the way you really think about them. This will give you the confidence required to

Figure 9-2 "Come and see what I just made, teacher!" (Courtesy of Nancy Martin)

give more, try more, and be more effective (Lewis and Winsor, 1968).

Not only will you enjoy your developing confidence, but your cooperating teacher will also be pleased. One cooperating teacher described her memorable experiences in the following:

> My best experience has been throwing a student teacher into a classroom teaching situation despite reservations and lack of confidence on the part of that student teacher and seeing him emerge as a capable, confident, successful teacher (Tittle, 1974).

Putting student teaching in perspective and being able to laugh at one's self, help reduce anxiety. This is something each student teacher needs to consider.

Time Management

For some student teachers time management is a continual problem. A date book, file, or pocket and desk calendar help. Organization is a key element. Devise a system that puts what you need within reach; it will save time. Plan ahead and break large tasks into small, specific pieces. Use daily lists and give tasks priorities. Think of "must do first," medium priority, and "can wait" categories. Do not waste time feeling guilty. Working with a colleague or friend is a strategy that often gets difficult tasks accomplished.

SEEKING HELP

It is difficult for some student teachers to ask for help or suggestions. The risk involves having either the cooperating teacher or supervisor realize one's limitations. Therefore, student teachers sometimes turn to other student teachers. Trust is an important element in this dilemma. Fortunately, one builds trust through human reaction and seeking help usually becomes easier as time passes.

As Meyer (1981) states:

> Conferences can help. Feel free to request a conference at any time you feel a particular need to do so.

It is important to seek help quickly in many instances and to use consultation times and meetings to pick the brains of others and seek assistance.

> The biggest threat to good communication is that the student teacher believes that any questions they ask the supervising teacher will reflect a lack of preparation which might be interpreted as not being motivated. (Brooks, 1978).

The role of both the supervisor and cooperating teacher includes on-site support and advice, figure 9-3. Katz (1972) notes that a beginning teacher needs encouragement, reassurance, comfort, guidance, instruction in specific skills, and insight into the complex causes of behavior. Stevens and King (1976) point out that in the English primary school system, it is the usual practice that a beginning teacher receives advice and supportive assistance on a daily basis throughout the first full year of teaching!

The Half-A-Teacher Feeling

During their experiences, many student teachers are led to feel either by the children, cooperating teachers, or other staff members, that, because of their position, they are not quite students and not quite teachers yet. Because of this "neither-here-nor-there" attitude, student teachers are not always treated as figures of authority. Read the poem in fig-

Figure 9-3 Seeking advice and assistance becomes easier as time passes. (Courtesy of Nancy Martin)

STATUS

This room is hers
This is her class–
This much is established
Clearly . . .
And,
As if by decree,
I am classified,
Categorically,
As an "almost,"
A "not-quite,"
A neophyte,
Labeled simply
"Wait-and-see."
But —
What else can
A student teacher be?

Figure 9-4 "Status" by Anthony Tovatt. (Reprinted by permission of the publisher, *The Indiana Teacher*, Jan. 1958, 102:207.)

ure 9-4. It may bring a knowing smile. "My worst experience took place because the children in many instances did not recognize me as a teacher but referred to me as a student teacher" (Tittle, 1974). Some student teachers have had the experience of being treated as a "go-fer." "I do not think that a student teacher should be made to do what a teacher is not required to do. I hate being given errands and 'dirty work' to do just because I'm a student teacher!" (Tittle, 1974). Sometimes early in student teaching, a strong team feeling has not been developed. Its development is critical for all involved. It may be best to consult with one's supervisor first. Cooperating teachers have a number of factors to consider in relinquishing control of their classroom. Often they feel uneasy about their routines and classroom behavior standards being threatened. They also may feel they are asking too much too soon of their student teachers and may be unclear of their role in giving assignments. It may be difficult for cooperating teachers to interchange their roles and become co-teachers instead of lead teachers. They can also be worried about child safety.

Cooperating teachers get a real sense of teaming with student teachers as the semester progresses. Tittle describes her finest experience as follows:

> My best experience was with a student teacher who adjusted to classroom routines and was so perceptive that she would anticipate without my having to ask her to do things. As a result, we worked as a team and the pupils really accomplished a great deal.

Guidance

Student teachers often find that the children will obey the rules when the cooperating teacher is present or asks but not when *they* ask them. Children test and question the authority of a new adult. Student teachers tend to force issues or completely ignore children when classroom rules are broken. These situations may be temporarily troublesome to student teachers. In time, the children will realize that the student teacher means what is said. Consistency and firmness will win out.

When student teachers feel they cannot deal with these situations, they tend to stay close to self-controlled or affectionate children. This type of behavior indicates a possible withdrawal from the total room responsibility.

Attachments

At times a child may form a strong bond with a particular student teacher. The child may be inconsolable for a period after the student teacher's departure. Most students worry about this behavior and their supervisor's and cooperating teacher's reactions to it. It is an important topic for team meetings.

Male student teachers can have a unique experience during student teaching based on children's past experiences or lack of experiences with males. After a short period, the children will see the male student teacher as just another teacher with his own individuality. If not, further study of the child or children is in order.

Philosophic Differences

Student teaching provides the student teacher with a growing experience. Sometimes the cooperating teacher's view of child education and how children learn is quite similar to the student's; in other placements, it is not. An understanding of methods, techniques, curriculums, and goals and objectives of classrooms is the task of the student. When conflicting views are present in a supportive atmosphere, they are respected. Student teachers can gain a chance to clarify their own ideas when confronted with differing ones. New and diverse views result in the growth and clarification of a student's idea of what is best for children and families.

It is disconcerting and uncomfortable for both students and cooperating teachers when their teaching styles clash. Open discussion, particularly if it is done in a caring way that preserves the dignity of each teacher's opinions, is the best course of action.

Students should not surrender their philosophical values but tenaciously retain what they feel is best for children. Every wave of newly trained preschool and primary school teachers has its own contribution to make. The old or established way is always subject to questions in education. Practicing teachers continue to try innovative approaches; some are used in a complete or modified form, others once tried are discarded. Thoughtfulness and open-mindedness help student teachers as does an "all win" attitude. Remember: Everybody learns and grows!

Personality Conflicts

Whether or not you believe everyone has their own "vibes," you probably readily admit that you work much better with some people than with others. Tittle (1974) describes one of her experiences:

> I had a student teacher who was very cold. She did an excellent job of teaching, but seemed to have created a wall between myself and the class by her very presence. I do not mind a student teacher that cannot teach a lesson. That comes with experience and I can help her.

Communication skill is critical in working relationships. Fortunately, student teaching is only a temporary assignment. Most difficult situations can at least become bearable through open communication.

Being Held Back

Very often, student teachers are not given the opportunity to work with children as much as they would like. As a result, they can become frustrated and feel that their potential for growth as teachers is being stifled. This can also happen when a cooperating teacher steps in during an activity or incident and assumes the student cannot handle the situation. These occurrences reduce the student's opportunity to work out of tight or uncomfortable spots. In the first example the student is not allowed to start; in the second, to finish.

The student needs to know the "why's" behind the cooperating teacher's behavior; the cooperating teacher needs to grasp the student's feeling. Neither can happen without communicating.

> Your master teacher is not able to read your mind. The only way he is going to know the things you are worried about, any feeling of inadequacy or uncertainty you may have, as well as your positive feelings, is to tell him (Gordon-Nourok, 1979).

A special agreed-upon signal can be used by student teacher to alert the cooperating teacher to a student teacher's need for help, immediate consultation, or suggestion.

Time and Energy

Time seems to be a problem for many students—enough time and organization of time. Cooperating teachers sometimes complain that students are not prepared, are tardy, or are unreliable. Working while student teaching limits the hours necessary for the preparation of activities. Student teachers must learn to manage their time. This involves planning ahead and analyzing task time lengths. Poor time management increases tension, destroys composure, and creates stress. Only the student teacher can make adjustments to provide enough time and rest necessary for student teaching. Standards of teacher training are rarely relaxed for just one individual. Figure 9-5 offers time management hints.

One-Day Wonders

One way to avoid misunderstandings and difficulties with your cooperating teacher is to come prepared with a number of short activities that could be called "one-day wonders." What do you do really well? Do you enjoy art?

A simple lesson, appropriate for fall, might be to come to class with the following materials for each child: a two-inch ball of clay (carefully wrapped in plastic so the clay won't dry out), paper plates to define work space, and lunch bags for gathering leaves and seeds lying on the ground. (This lesson has been successfully used with preschoolers and primary age children.) During free play or recess, the children can be directed to pick up and place in the bags items from the play yard that remind them of Fall. Typically, students will gather all kinds of leaves, twigs, seed pods, dry weeds, and even stones and pebbles.

Upon return to the classroom, the following directions can be given:

"At the science (or discovery) center, you will find a stack of paper plates and a large plastic bag with balls of clay. You may choose the science center as one of your options to explore this afternoon. Place one of the paper plates on the table; carefully take one of the balls of clay from the plastic bag and place it on your plate. Shape the ball of clay into any form you wish and use any of the materials you brought in from the play yard as decorations. When you finish, leave your sculpture on its paper plate and place on the window sill."

What you *can* do is make better use of the time you do have through planning and organizing your workdays.

First, analyze the way you spend your work hours over a three-day period. Keep a log and record what you did, how much time you took doing it and whether or not the time was spent productively. Your log should help you get a better grip on your workday and boost your efficiency.

Some other potentially useful time tips are:

- *Start the day with at least 10 minutes of an activity you really enjoy.* Exercise, read the newspaper, linger over a second cup of coffee. This should give you the positive attitude you need to face the day.

- *Set priorities.* Determine what you must accomplish today. Follow up with a list of tasks you might get to if things go well, put the others on hold.

- *Set time limits.* Be realistic, wary of tasks that take up more time than they are worth.

- *Speed up decision-making.* Define the problem, generate a reasonable number of alternatives with relevant staff and reach a decision. Don't waste time mulling over an infinite number of alternatives.

- *Beware of perfectionism.* It causes defeatism and stress. Count your imperfections and mistakes as learning experiences. Try to do better next time.

- *Keep your desk clear.* Don't handle papers more than once. Read a paper through the first time and, if possible, take action then. If you have to put it in your in-box, dispose of it next time around. Do it, delegate it, file it, or throw it away.

- *Periodically re-evaluate goals*, both short and long term. Keep a handle on deadlines and objectives that must be met within specific amounts of time.

Figure 9-5 Avoid the time crunch [By Bettye W. McDonald in *Keys to Early Childhood Education*, Vol. 2, No. 2 (Feb. 1981), Washington, D.C.: Capitol Publications, Inc.]

(You will want to demonstrate the process as you give the directions, especially with preschoolers. With primary age children, drawings of each numbered step placed at the science/discovery center may be sufficient.)

Do you enjoy stories? Another example of a successful "one-day wonder" is the following first grade language art lesson:

Introduce as follows:

"I've brought you one of my favorite stories to share during storytime today. It's called *Rosie's Walk*, by Pat Hutchins."

After you finish the reading, you might tell the children, "Those children choosing to go to the writing center during our center activities may dictate to me or Mrs. Nguyen (or write) your own versions of *Rosie's Walk*. When you have finished, you may illustrate your story. Since only four students can come at once, remember that the rest of you will have a chance later in the week."

Other possibilities for "one-day wonders" are limited only by your imagination. Many cooperating teachers who may be reluctant to turn over large segments of time to a student teacher are willing to do so with "one-day wonders" that fit smoothly into the curriculum. Any area of the curriculum can work, but it is always best if you can agree with your cooperating teacher on one specific area, perhaps one that she does not particularly enjoy.

One-day wonders that set up for on-the-spur-of-the-moment will most usually be used. One can fit a number of them (stored separately) in a large tote bag or cardboard file that can be stowed somewhere in the classroom. These preplanned activities are a sort of insurance policy and relieve the panic of possibly being asked to do a last-minute activity. Other one-day wonders designed by former student teachers follow:

- Colored gummed paper worker hats (precut chef, cowboy, fire fighter, police officer, nurse, sailor, farmer, doorman, cab driver, etc.), art paper, crayons. Children lick and stick, add a face if they wish, and possibly share a story about their hat or give their created person a name.

- Tongs, tweezers (blunt), chop sticks, colored (three colors or more) cotton balls, (shake powdered tempera and balls *in closed* plastic zipped bags), containers. Children sort colors by picking up with tools.

- Mounted photos of children snapped in action in the classroom. Lots of discussion and excitement. "Tell me about the photograph you've chosen." Works well if child stands in front of group giving all a good look first.

- Small plastic cars and roads drawn on shelf paper. The road is drawn by the student teacher beforehand with other features such as houses, stop signs, trees, dead ends, railroad tracks, parking spots, etc. Use your imagination. A roll of masking tape secures the road to table tops or floor. Good for outside as well as inside. Shelf paper can be rolled and ready. Many children will want to talk about what they are doing and where they are going.

Site Politics

One of the most difficult placement situations is one that is consumed with conflicts. Power struggles between teachers, the director or principal, parents, community, or any other group makes the student feel as if he is being pressured to take sides. The student teacher is usually afraid to join either faction and tries to be a friend to all. This situation should be discussed with your supervisor quickly. Make sure to convey to the supervisor that you are willing to work through any difficult situation but that you want her to be aware of your perception of your placement site's political tensions.

● THE ROLE OF COMMUNICATION

Communication is a broad term, defined as giving and/or receiving information, signals, or messages. Human interactions and contacts are full of nonverbal signals accounting for 60 percent to 80 percent of most human encounters. De Spelder and Prettyman (1980) have identified some of the more easily recognized nonverbal communications:

- facial expression, figure 9-6
- body position, figure 9-7
- muscle tone
- breathing tempo
- pitch of voice

A two-way process of sending and receiving (input and output) information occurs in true communication. Communication skills can be learned; however, it is not easy (Sciarra and Dorsey, 1979). It is imperative that all participants in the student teaching experience have good communication skills. This idea cannot be overemphasized. The

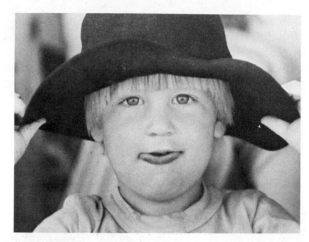

Figure 9-6 Reading the expressions in children's eyes and faces is a nonverbal communication skill. (Courtesy of Nancy Martin)

whole climate of interpersonal relationships in an education center can be affected by an individual's ability to communicate. As Sciarra and Dorsey point out:

> The director (principal) has the major responsibility for creating a climate of care, trust, and respect. This climate can best be achieved by demonstrating caring behaviors, by taking steps to build feelings of community, and by developing good communication skills among and between all members of the center (school) community.

Student teacher growth and self-realization can depend on the communication skills of the student teacher and others. According to Rogers and Freiberg (1994) it is through a mutually supporting, helping relationship that each individual can become better integrated and more able to function effectively. Student teachers can model appropriate communication behaviors, increasing effectiveness for other adults and children. Since every family encounters differences in opinion and values at times, a child center or school can expect disagreements between adults, between children, and between children and adults. This is why good, effective communication skills are essential.

No doubt your student teaching group contains people with diverse opinions and backgrounds. Your placement site may also reflect our multi-ethnic and multicultural society. Communication between individuals is enhanced by feelings of trust and openness. In some discussions and verbal exchanges you are bound to gain insights into your beliefs and those of others. Jones (1986) believes:

> I am unlikely to recognize the distinctive elements of my culture unless I have opportunities to compare it with other cultures—other ways of being human. Living in a multicultural society and world, I must learn to make the comparison—to become aware that any culture represents only one set of many possible choices, all of them valid ways of being human.

Communication: Reacting to Bias

With the multicultural representations in many early childhood classrooms and early childhood staff members present in society today, a teacher is bound to encounter bias. What one adult deems appropriate and worthwhile another may see as inappropriate. Carter and Curtis (1994) point out teachers have a set of seven choices in how to respond when adults express bias:

1. attacking,
2. defending,
3. empathizing,
4. investigating,
5. reframing,
6. excusing, and
7. ignoring.

Some of a teacher's responding communication choices can be assaultive or defensive while others may foster awareness and sensitivity (Carter and Curtis, 1994). Analyze the following teacher responses, and decide which promote the early childhood goal of working as a supportive partner with parents.

> Situation: Alfredo's mom tells you most of the activities planned at school and lots of the equipment don't allow Alfredo to be a real boy and is more suited for attending girls.

Could you finish please so I could talk?

Enough, let's move on this.

I'm at my wit's end!

This is becoming painful to me.

Confidence

Honesty

Figure 9-7 Silent Messages: The above positions or gestures are some of the most common means of nonverbal communication.

Teacher's seven choices:

1. "Alfredo chooses his own activities Mrs. Santos. You don't want us to force him to play more vigorous games, do you?"

2. "We're an accredited school, we've been approved by experts."

3. "You're distressed over Alfredo's behavior at school."

4. "You're concerned that Alfredo will not fit in with the other boys?"

5. "Alfredo chooses many sedentary activities over more vigorous play right now. He's really enjoying books and exploring writing tools. Your feeling is that this might not allow him to develop physical skill. Our program offers outdoor vigorous play but at the moment Alfredo is following his own interests."

6. "Well Alfredo is just being Alfredo."

7. "Mrs. Santos, has this been a good day for you?"

Which choices would identify the above problems appropriately? What bias is present? Could it be the parent's cultural expectations?

Caring and Sharing: A First Step in Communicating

What makes a person interesting or easy to talk with? Why do we discuss problems with some individuals and not with others? Perhaps it is because that person with whom we can talk freely loves and accepts us as we are at that moment. Love and acceptance can be demonstrated a number of ways. Saying it may be the easiest way; showing it through actions may be the toughest. With children, giving attention and not interfering with their freedom of choice helps develop their feelings of self-worth and value. Touching also usually reinforces rapport; a pat, hug, or open lap for young children expresses love and acceptance. A wink, a notice of accomplishment, or a sincere recognition of a special uniqueness in an individual helps feelings of caring and sharing grow. Setting the stage for easy approaching and interacting also helps. Respecting an individual's needs, feelings, and desires and building a support system based on love and respect may, as Selye

(1974) suggests, promote security and freedom from distress that hinders the attainment of potential.

Student teachers work and plan ways to establish rapport with children and adults on their first working days, figure 9-8. Communications depend on first contacts and interactions. Weir and Eggleston (1975) suggest there are definite skills, based on perseverance and know-how, beginning teachers can acquire to establish an easy flow of daily conversations with children.

- Offer a personal greeting to each child.
- Take time to listen and respond to the child who is bursting to tell a story.
- Make a point of giving a special greeting to the shy child; verbalize the child's actions.
- Introduce new vocabulary.
- Help children plan for the day, building on prior experiences and introducing new ones.
- Permit children to solve their own problems through language.
- Find time to talk personally with each child during the day about important events or experiences in their lives.

Figure 9-8 Being together and enjoying a brief walk can enhance communication.

- Find opportunities to elaborate and expand children's language, figure 9-9.

- Explain requests or demands to children so that they will understand. Avoid repeating what children already know.

- Avoid expressing shock or punishing children for asking questions about physical functions.

- Talk to the children more than to classroom adults.

Children's communication skill and degree of cooperation may affect how a student teacher relates to and views particular children. Student teachers tend to gravitate toward conversation with children who respond, use their names, and establish eye contact and to those children who are most like themselves, making them feel "at home." They also interact with the child who gains their attention. Popular, well-liked children usually fit this description. Seeing the challenge in developing trust and open communication with each attending child, student teachers observe children who ignore the teacher's conversational overtures, change the subject, say something

Figure 9-9 Elaborate and expand children's language.

irrelevant, or otherwise reject them. They sometimes find approaching a small group of children or a child in solitary play works best.

Children who feel good about themselves and experience caring teachers usually find greater success in communication with newcomers.

Armstrong (1994) offers additional guidelines:

1. Build solid, trusting relationships before seeking information from children.

2. Keep conversation related to action that is strongly relevant to children's interests or is part of their everyday experience.

3. Try role playing with manipulative toys that allow the relationship between early language and activity to flourish.

4. Use words and styles that "belong" to the children and that take into consideration their competence level.

5. Be empathetic; try to see situations from the child's point of view.

6. Probe for responses by asking questions a new way, but avoid suggesting answers.

7. Select times to talk that don't interfere with children's favorite activities.

Authenticity

Much has been written about being *real* with children and adults. This means sharing honestly your feelings without putting down or destroying feelings of competency and self-worth. The term *congruent-sending* was coined by Gordon (1972), well known for his work in human communication. His definition follows:

> Congruence refers to the similarity of what a person (the sender) is thinking or feeling inside, and what he communicates to the outside. When a person is being congruent, we experience him as "open," "direct," or "genuine." When we sense that a person's communication is incongruent, we judge him as "not ringing true," "insincere," "affected," or just plain "phony."

The resulting risk in sending real messages without skill is that we may experience rejection.

Student teachers can learn to express a wide range of real feelings in a skillful way. Anger is perhaps the hardest to handle skillfully. Ginott (1972) has advice for dealing with anger:

> The realities of teaching make anger inevitable. Teachers need not apologize for their angry feelings. An effective teacher is neither a masochist nor a martyr. He does not play the role of a saint or act the part of an angel. He is aware of his human feelings and respects them. Though he cannot be patient, he is always authentic. His response is genuine. His words fit his feeling. He does not hide his annoyance. He does not pretend patience. He does not demonstrate hypocrisy by acting nice when feeling nasty.
>
> An enlightened teacher is not afraid of his anger because he has learned to express it without doing damage. He has mastered the secret of expressing anger without insult.
>
> . . . When angry, an enlightened teacher remains real. He describes what he sees, what he feels, and what he expects. He attacks the problem, not the person. He protects himself and safeguards his students by using "I" messages.

A student teacher's idea of the perfect teacher as being always calm and cool may inhibit communicating and produce feelings of guilt. A multitude of emotions will be present during student teaching days; a daily diary or journal helps students pinpoint feelings in early stages, and written expression is often easier than oral sharing with a supervisor. Usually, pleasant feelings are the ones most easily described and orally transmitted. Recognizing the build-up of bad feelings may take a special tuning into the self. Common tension signals include:

- Shrill, harsh, or louder voice tone.
- Inability to see humor in a situation.
- Withdrawal and/or silence.
- Continual mental rehashing of an emotionally trying encounter.

Abidin (1982) states that sharing feelings, including those you consider negative, can help develop a closeness to others.

"Sharing yourself" is a method of building a better relationship and we know that people with close relationships will take into consideration the feelings, ideas, values and expectations of people they love and feel close to. "Sharing yourself" is a way in which close families influence the behavior of each other, but the object of the method is developing closeness, understanding, and love, not power, over one another.

"I" Messages

Message sending takes practice, and is only one part of a communication sequence—input or sending. A series of teacher-sent "I" messages follow. You will probably be able to picture the incident which evoked them.

> "I'm very sad that these pages in our book about horses are torn and crumpled. Book pages need to be turned with care, like this."
>
> "I get so upset when materials I planned to use with the children disappear."
>
> "Wait a minute. If all the student teachers take a break together, there will be only one adult in the classroom. I'm frustrated; I thought there was a clear statement about taking separate breaks."
>
> "I'm confused about this assignment. I feel like I missed an explanation. Can we talk about it sometime today?"
>
> "I'm feeling very insecure right now. I thought I sensed your disapproval when you asked the children to stop the activity planned for them."

Abidin suggests one should guard against "I" messages that are destructive; they sometimes send solutions or involve blaming and judgmental phrases. These are false "I" messages:

> "I feel frustrated when you behave so stupidly."
>
> "I am angry when you don't keep your promises. Nobody will be able to trust you."

The ability to send "I" messages is a communication skill that follows recognition of feelings and an effort to communicate directly with the individuals concerned. At times we provoke strong feelings within ourselves, and an "inner" dialogue ensures.

"I" messages do not tend to build defensiveness as do "you" messages. The communication starts on the right foot.

● LISTENING: THE ABILITY TO RECEIVE

> We listen with our ears, of course,
> But surely it is true
> That eyes, and lips, and hands, and feet
> can help us listen, too.

Though commonly used with children, this poem may aid student teachers' communicative listening skills. The poem is describing "active listening," a term also attributed to Gordon (1972):

> In recent years psychotherapists have called our attention to a new kind of listening, "active listening." More than passively attending to the message of the sender, it is a process of putting your understanding of that message to its severest of tests—namely, forcing yourself to put into your own words to the sender for verification or for subsequent correction.

One encounters four basic types of verbal communication (from other adults):

Communication, for *building relationships*;

Cathartic communication, for releasing emotions and relating our troubles;

Informational communication, for sharing ideas, information, and data; and

Persuasive communication, for reinforcing and changing attitudes or producing a desired action (Cavanaugh, 1985).

Burley-Allen (1982), author of *Listening: The Forgotten Skill*, believes people who listen will interact with others more effectively and make fewer mistakes, and that saves time.

To practice good listening try the following nine tips:

- Focus on content and ideas.
- Don't prejudge or second-guess.
- Listen for feelings.
- Jot down facts when appropriate.

- Make eye contact, watch nonverbal cues.
- Avoid emotional rebuttals by keeping an open mind. Realize there are emotionally laden words.
- Give signs you're actively receiving.
- Try to identify main ideas and supportive ideas. Store key words for they'll make messages easier to remember.
- Respond, rephrase, ask and/or answer questions whether explicit or implied.

Cavanaugh (1985) points out that after 48 hours, the average listener only retains 25 percent of material he hears in a 10-minute presentation. The rest is gone forever.

The active listening process is probably more difficult to learn than that of "I"-message sending. Most individuals have developed listening habits that block true listening. Lundsteen (1976) has labeled four chief listening distortions:

1. *Attitude cutoff* blocks the reception of information at the spoken source because expectation acts on selection. For example, if a student has a strong negative reaction every time he hears the word *test*, he might not hear the rest of this message: "The test of any man lies in action."

2. *Motive attributing* is illustrated by the person who says of a speaker, "He is just selling me a public relations line for the establishment," and by the child who thinks, "Teachers just like to talk; they don't really expect me to listen the first time because they are going to repeat directions 10 times anyway."

3. *Organizational mix-up* happens while one is trying to put someone else's message together—"Did he say 'turn left, then right, then right, then left,' or . . . ?" or "Did he say 'tired' or 'tried'?"

4. *Self-preoccupation* causes distortion because the "listener" is busy formulating his reply and never hears the message: "I'll get him for that; as soon as he stops talking, I'll make a crack about how short he is, then . . ."

Preoccupation with one's own message is a frequent distortion for young listeners. Hanging onto their own thoughts during communications takes a great deal of their attention and energy. Some teachers help out by suggesting that young listeners make small, quick pictures to help cue their ideas when their turn to speak arrives. That way they can get back to listening. Older children may jot down "shorthand" notes to help them hold onto ideas and return to the line of communication.

New active listening habits can change lives and communicating styles, giving individuals a chance to develop closeness, insight, and empathy.

> To understand accurately how another person thinks or feels from his point of view, to put yourself momentarily into his shoes, to see the world as he is seeing it—you as a listener run the risk of having your own opinions and attitudes changed. (Gordon, 1972)

Peters (1990), well-known co-author of *In Search of Excellence*, suggests listening is much more than hearing:

> Listen naively. But don't just listen! Most of us are lousy listeners—with friends, spouses, co-workers. Hearing is about empathy.

To develop new listening habits, it is necessary to make a strong effort. The effort will pay off dramatically, as it provides an opportunity to know others at a deeper level. It is a chance to open a small inner door and catch a glimpse of the "authentic" self. By listening closely, a new perception of an individual can be revealed; our own thoughts about how we are going to answer are secondary.

> Before that, when I went to a party I would think anxiously "Now try hard. Be lively. Say bright things. Don't let them down." And when tired, I would drink a lot of coffee to keep this up. But now before going to a party, I just tell myself to listen with affection to anyone who talked to me, to be in their shoes when they talk; to try to know them without my mind pressing against theirs, or arguing, or changing the subject. No! My attitude is: "Tell me more. This person is showing me his soul. It is a little dry and meager and

full of grinding talk just now, but presently he will begin to think, not just automatically talk. He will show his true self. Then he will be wonderfully alive . . ." (Ueland, 1941/1966)

The student teacher hopes others will recognize his or her teaching competencies. Being anxious to please and display what one knows, one can focus communication on sending messages and convincing others of one's value. New listening skills will take conscious practicing. To gain skill in active, reflective listening, an exercise called "mirroring" is often used. The examples below (Abidin, 1982) mirror back to the child the feeling the listener has received.

1. Child, pleading: "I don't want to eat these baked potatoes. I hate them."

   Listener: "You don't like baked potatoes."

2. Child, pleading and forlorn: "I don't have anything to do today. What can I do? I wish there was something to do!"

   Listener: "You're bored and lonely."

3. Child, angry and confused: "I hate Julie. She always cries and tries to get her way. If I don't do what she wants, she goes home."

   Listener: "You're angry and confused," figure 9-10.

4. Child, stubborn and indignant: "I don't want to take a bath. I'm not even dirty. I hate baths anyway. Why do I have to take a bath every day?"

   Listener: "You don't want to take a bath."

5. Child, crying: "Fran won't let me play with her dolls. She's mean. Make her give me some of them to play with."

   Listener: "You're angry with Fran."

6. Child, crying because of hurt finger: "Ow! Ow! It hurts! Ow!"

   Listener: "It sure hurts."

Adults find mirroring and reflecting back feeling statements easier with children than adults. With use, mirroring statements feel more comfortable and the sender, whether a child or an adult,

Figure 9-10 Physical comforting is one way to establish bonds of acceptance between children and adults. (Courtesy of Nancy Martin)

feels he or she has been heard. With adults, clarifying mirroring-type questions seem more natural and are conducted in the following fashion:

"Am I hearing you say you're really angry right now?"

"Is frustration what you're feeling?"

"You're saying you don't want to be told what to do?"

Asking Questions

Part of the student teaching experience involves your asking questions to get information. The dilemma here may be that you are afraid to have others feel you are uninformed or lack intelligence. Do not believe you are supposed to know all the answers during student teaching just because you've succeeded in making it to one of the last classes. Do not worry about asking what you perceive to be stupid questions. Probably many of the other students in the class are wondering the same thing. Asking questions can be a determining factor contributing to your success as a student teacher.

Remember student teaching is an emotion-packed human endeavor. As Peters (1990) notes: zest, joy, pride and fun are near to the heart of any successful enterprise.

Staff Communication

Harris (1995) suggests the following tips to improve staff communication:

- Beware of kicking and stroking at the same time. When we tell someone something positive, then reprimand, then end with a positive, we call that *sandwiching*. Some workshops teach this as a *soft* technique, but it does send conflicting messages.
- Whenever possible, plan the message. Think of what the message is and how, where, and when you want to send it.
- In order for communication to be effective, spend as much time listening as talking. Be attentive.
- Don't imply a choice if there is not a choice. Tentative language and manner are fine in some circumstances, but they often suggest an option that may not exist.
- Tape record an hour or so of routine, day-to-day conversations. Look for hidden agendas, soft or padded language, and other indicators that you are not sending clear messages.
- Say what you mean, mean what you say.
- Feedback is a continuous process, not just a one-time action. Learn to give and elicit feedback on a regular basis.
- Look at the person you are talking to and establish eye contact throughout the conversation.
- Sometimes it is better to deliver a message to a group of people at once. It is, however, still important to allow for feedback and to follow other rules such as eye contact.
- If it appears that no one is listening, the problem may be exactly that. No one including us—is listening.

Cultural Variety

Attending children may come from widely diverse cultures and countries. They may belong to newly arrived groups or well established ethnic populations. You can expect cultural conflicts to occur in values, goals, and parental child-handling techniques. A teacher may have to do immediate, quick research to learn about the culture of a particular attending family.

Communicating will require tact and patience. It takes time to develop both mutual understanding and trust. Teachers need to know what parents want for their children, and what concerns they experience when leaving their child in group care or at school.

Some parents will be slow to open up and will need encouragement to speak their minds or ask questions. Teachers purposefully make classrooms comfortable. Classrooms accept and value diversity. Many teachers design special parent areas if classroom space permits.

A teacher's own personal values, goals, and priorities need to be clarified and identified if dialogue is to be effective. Pinpointing the teacher's areas of discomfort or annoyance as well as knowing a parent's areas of concern or dissatisfaction is a first step in the problem solving-dialogue-conflict negotiation and resolution process. Chapter 3 helps a student teacher identify her personal values.

SUMMARY

Student teaching is a miniature slice of life and living. Problems arise and are common to all. Some situations change with time, others need extended communication to be resolved.

Growth and change are experienced sometimes easily, sometimes painfully. It is helpful to maintain a caring and sharing feeling, open communication, and a sense of humor. Time and successful experience take care of most initial difficulties. The supervisor's and cooperating teacher's roles are to provide supportive assistance. Team status may evolve slowly and depend on student effort.

Skill in sending and receiving oral and written messages is a necessary skill for student teachers. The whole sharing and caring climate of the student teaching experience depends in part on communication know-how. Developing rapport with adults and children during early days helps people become relaxed and comfortable, promoting student teacher attempts to display emerging competencies.

Love and acceptance are established in a variety of ways, figure 9-10. Authenticity in communication is deemed highly desirable and effective to earn acceptance during student teaching. "I" messages are an integral part of effective communication skills. Skill in sending "I" messages and active, reflective listening increase with practice and become a natural part of the student teaching experience.

SUGGESTED ACTIVITIES

A. Interview three practicing teachers about their joys and problems in student teaching.

B. Rate the following situations as M (major problem) or m (minor concern). Discuss the results in small groups.

1. A student teacher is placed in a class where the child of a best friend is attending. The best friend asks for daily reports.

2. Little Johnny tells a cooperating teacher that he is afraid of the student teacher.

3. Bonnie, a student teacher, finds she is susceptible to colds and infections.

4. Children do not respond to the student teacher's rule statements.

5. The student teacher has had no background experience with children of the ethnic group where placed.

6. The student teacher is used as an aide in the classroom.

7. A child's mother tells the cooperating teacher she does not like the idea of a student teacher taking over the classroom.

8. The supervisor rarely visits the classroom.

9. One of the student teacher's planned activities ends in pandemonium. Paint is all over

the walls and floor, and the children are uncontrolled.

10. A student teacher has difficulty planning activities that suit the children's age and interest level.

C. List briefly three possible courses of action for the following student teacher situations. Of the three, what do you feel is the best course of action?

1. Amy, a fellow student teacher, confides in you that she objects to the way her cooperating teacher punishes children.

2. Joey, a four-year-old, says, "You're not the teacher. I don't have to do that" when you ask him to return blocks he has played with to the bookcase.

3. You have a great idea about rearranging the room and do so in the morning before the children or cooperating teacher arrive. The cooperating teacher is obviously upset upon entering the room.

4. You tried very hard to encourage Qwan to complete a task, and the cooperating teacher quickly finishes the task for him to make sure he is not late for snack.

5. You cannot seem to get any feedback on your abilities as a student teacher from either the cooperating teacher or the supervisor.

6. You notice you are spending an increasing amount of time straightening, table wiping, sink cleaning, and with block area maintenance.

7. You realize you do not know any parents' first names, and half of the semester is over.

8. Manuela and Colleen are student teaching in the same classroom. Manuela feels Colleen is insensitive to Mexican culture and rarely builds a sense of ethnic pride in the children.

9. Carol, a student teacher, plays the guitar and is a talented folksinger. She has not planned a classroom activity to share her talent.

10. Your supervisor gives you credit for setting up a new activity area that the children are exploring with enthusiasm; however, the cooperating teacher was the one who set up this activity. Since your supervisor has encouraged you to add new activities, you did not correct the mistake. The next day you feel badly about taking credit but are reticent to approach your supervisor with the truth.

D. Answer the following questions: If you don't know an answer right away, observe yourself for awhile or ask someone close to you.

- How do I behave when I'm feeling overstressed? (Some people get angry, others withdraw, some cry more easily, others become forgetful, etc.)

- What are some of the warning signs that tell I am about to go over the amount of stress I can handle?

- What do I do that helps relax me and release my stress:

- Are my ways of relaxing healthy for me?

- Do I have time in my life that is just for me? If yes, how often during the week?

- Do I take my own need for relaxation and time out seriously enough?

- Do I know any relaxation techniques that I can practice?

- Am I aware of how I talk to myself inside my own mind? Am I telling myself negative or hopeless things that contribute to increasing my stress level?

- Am I aware that I have a choice about how I want to deal with my own stress?

  Analyzing your reactions to stress can be eye opening.

E. Identify the following statements as either true or false. Note the statements that you felt were controversial. Share your opinions with the class.

Being Real (Adapted from Greenberg, 1969)

1. I should behave calmly and coolly at all times.
2. I never feel helpless or angry with children in my care.
3. In classroom interaction, children's feelings are more important than teacher's feelings.
4. A competent teacher keeps emotions under control at all times.
5. I love all the children in my care equally.
6. I treat all children alike.
7. Children are handled individually and differently by most teachers.
8. A continuous, positive, warm, affectionate adult/child relationship is easily maintained on a day-to-day basis.
9. A teacher's emotions are easy to hide from children and other teachers.
10. A teacher should try always to be positive rather than negative even if feelings toward a child are negative.
11. Continuous positive comments are not real and sincere, and children know it.
12. Children appreciate being treated honestly and are encouraged to deal more honestly with their own feelings, thereby being able to control them.
13. Each teacher has certain personality traits they favor in children.
14. Some teachers favor boys over girls.
15. I have no prejudices.
16. As we get to know adults and children, our prejudices often disappear.
17. A good teacher knows all about new methods and teaching techniques.
18. Teachers often live with confusion and uncertainty about what exactly the children in their care are learning.
19. Learning rarely involves struggle and conflict.
20. A well-adjusted teacher is always in balance, with little stress, struggle, conflict, or anxiety because that teacher has figured out the right way to handle children.
21. A child's physical appearance and mannerisms can influence whether the teacher likes or dislikes that child.
22. Almost all teachers lose their temper at one time or another while in the classroom.
23. Teacher anger often occurs as the result of accumulated irritation, annoyance, and stress.
24. A child usually responds to anger with anger.
25. A teacher who faces his or her own anger and expresses it without hurting the children can help the children learn to face and accept their own anger.
26. Children should know that adults can get angry and still like them.

F. Form groups of six for the following role-playing activity. Select two members to role play; others will be observers. Switch role playing until all group members have had two turns.

"Role Playing in Reflecting Listening"

Directions: Analyze each of the following role-played statements or situations. Offer suggestions for active listening responses.

1. Student teacher to cooperating teacher: "Your room needs more organization."
2. Cooperating teacher to student teacher: "Mary, have you been having problems at home lately?"
3. Irritated cooperating teacher to student teacher: "John, you've been ill too often. We must be able to rely on our student teachers to be here every day."
4. Critical parent to student teacher: "My daughter needs her sweater on when she goes out of doors."
5. One student teacher to another: "Mrs. Brown, the director, only sees what I do wrong, not what I do right."

6. One student teacher to another: "You always leave the sink a mess."

7. John, a preschooler, is dumping paint on the floor.

8. Student teacher to child who is not going to the wash area: "It's time to wash hands."

9. Mary, a four-year-old, hit you because you insisted that she share a toy.

10. College supervisor to student teacher: "Filomena, I'm confused. Your assignments are always late. Weren't my directions clear?"

11. Cooperating teacher to student teacher: "When you were doing your activity, I had a difficult time not stepping in. The boys were destroying the girls' work."

G. In three conversations during the coming week, inhibit your responses and focus on listening. What happened? Share your experiences with the group.

H. With a classmate, describe incidences during student teaching when "listening with affection" would be most difficult.

I. Using Carter and Curtis's (1994) seven choices discussed in this chapter, react to the following situations with teacher statements that fit each of the seven types mentioned.

Situation 1. Tran and Luc are parents of attending children and also serve as center volunteers. Their English is limited. Another parent volunteer tells you it's a poor idea to let Tran and Luc volunteer at the center because the children will learn Vietnamese instead of English.

Situation 2. Bill's father is angry because you've stopped Bill from bringing his prized six-guns to school.

Situation 3. "I don't want my child forced to help himself at lunch time. Don't you people know he won't eat properly?"

REVIEW

A. List common student teacher problems.

B. Briefly describe what you feel are prime areas or issues of conflict in student teaching.

C. Write a student teacher "I" message for each of the following situations:

1. Fred, your cooperating teacher, does not have his usual warm greeting and has barely spoken to you all morning.

2. Your supervisor has given you a failing grade on an assignment. You spent many hours on that assignment, and you feel like dropping the class.

3. You cried during the staff meeting when other adults suggested one of your activities with the children was a flop.

4. Another student teacher in your classroom is not living up to assigned duties, making it twice as difficult for you.

5. A child says to you, "I wish you were my mommy."

6. Your cooperating teacher has asked you not to pick up and hold a particular child. You feel the child needs special attention.

7. An irate parent says to you, "This school policy about bringing toys from home is ridiculous."

8. Your neighbor says to you, "I hear you're going to college to become a babysitter. How wasteful of your talents."

D. Define the following terms:
   authentic communication
   nonverbal messages
   rapport
   congruent sending
   active listening
   motive attributing
   self-preoccupation listening

E. Give an example of an appropriate student teacher verbalization for each of the following:

   1. Offer a personal greeting to a new child.

   2. Avoid expressing shock when a child asks about genitalia seen on another child.

F. Choose the best answer to complete each statement.

   1. Your cooperating teacher has informed your supervisor that you were not prepared for class on the preceding day. This is not the first time it has happened. Your supervisor seems upset since you two have already discussed this problem. In talking to your supervisor, you want to use active listening techniques in communicating. You say,

      a. "You need to explain assignment dates again, please."

      b. "She's always criticizing me; I'm really upset."

      c. "But I was prepared. I brought in two flannel-board stories and a music game!"

      d. "I can see you're disappointed and perhaps a bit angry, too."

      e. "Isn't there any way I can please the two of you?"

   2. Your cooperating teacher is always stepping in and taking over in guidance situations. You have pleaded to be allowed to follow through so children will know you mean what you say. You decide to send a congruent feeling statement at a staff meeting. You say,

      a. "I'm really frustrated. You always take over."

      b. "I've had it. Can't you let me finish what I start?"

      c. "I'm confused. I want the children to know I mean what I say, but it's just not happening."

      d. "You need to step back and let me follow through with the children."

      e. "I know you're trying to help me, but I don't need your help."

   3. You feel you can easily handle the whole day's program, but you haven't been given the opportunity. You say to your supervisor,

      a. "Please help me. The cooperating teacher doesn't give me enough to do."

      b. "I feel I'm competent enough to handle a whole day's program."

      c. "I'm just doing clean-up and housekeeping most of the time."

      d. "You could ask my cooperating teacher to give me more responsibility."

      e. "I'll sure be happy when I finish and have my own class."

   4. Mrs. Schultz is angry and yells, "Janita wet her pants again. I don't think any of you remembered to remind her!" You respond by saying,

      a. "You're upset because you don't think we reminded Janita."

      b. "They all wet sometimes, Mrs. Schultz!"

      c. "I didn't see her wet today."

      d. "We remind all the children right before snacks."

      e. "My child wets at school also!"

   5. Congruent sending and authentic sending are

      a. very different.

      b. easy skills for most adults.

      c. similar to active listening.

      d. very similar.

      e. similar to parcel post sending.

G. Create a one-day wonder.

REFERENCES

Abidin, R. R. (1982). *Parenting skills: Trainers' manual* (2nd ed.). New York: Human Sciences Press.

Armstrong, J. L. (January 1994). Mad, sad, or glad: Children speak out about child care. *Young Children, 49*(2), 22–23.

Brooks, D. M. (1978). *Common sense in teaching and supervising*. Washington, DC: University Press of America.

Burley-Allen, M. (1982). *Listening: The forgotten skill*. New York: Wiley.

Burnett, J. K. (1967). *A student teacher speaks*. From Kraft, L. E., & Casey, J. P. *Roles in Off-Campus Student teaching*. Champaign, IL: Stipes Publishing Co.

Carter, M., & Curtis, D. (1994). *Training teachers: A harvest of theory and practice*. St. Paul, Redleaf Press.

Cavanaugh, W. (May 19, 1985). You aren't listening! *San Jose Mercury News*, p. 1PC.

Danoff, J., Breitbart, V., & Barr, E. (1977). *Open for children*. New York: McGraw-Hill Book Co.

De Spelder, L. A., & Prettyman, N. (1980). *A guidebook for teaching family living*. Boston: Allyn and Bacon, Inc.

Fuller, F. (March 1969). Concerns of teachers: A developmental conceptualization. *American Educational Research Journal, 6*, 207–226.

Ginott, H. (1972). I'm angry! I'm appalled! I am furious! *Teacher and Child*. New York: Macmillan Publishing Co., Inc. Reprinted in *Today's Education Magazine*, NEA Journal (Nov. 19, 1972).

Gordon, T., Ph.D. (1972). The risks of effective communication. *Parent Notebook*, a publication of Effectiveness Training Associates.

Gordon-Nourok, E. (1979). *You're a student teacher!* Sierra Madre, CA: SCAEYC.

Green, E. (1994). State-of-the-art professional development. J. Johnson & J. McCracken (Eds.), in *The Early Childhood Career Lattice: Perspectives of Professional Development*. Washington, DC: National Association for the Education of Young Children.

Greenberg, H. M. (1969). *Teaching with feeling*. New York: Macmillan Publishing Co., Inc.

Harris, J. (July/August 1995). Is anybody out there listening? *Child Care Information Exchange*, #104, 82–84.

Hendrick, J., Ph.D. (1975). *The whole child: New trends in early education*. St. Louis: C. V. Mosby Co.

Jones, E. (1986). *Teaching adults*. Washington, DC: NAEYC.

Katz, L. (1972). Developmental stages of preschool teachers. *Elementary School Journal*, pp. 50–54.

Keirsey, D., & Bates, M. (1984). *Please understand me* (5th ed.). Del Mar, CA: Gnosology Books Ltd.

Lewis, C., & Winsor, C. B. (1968). Supervising the beginning teacher. *Educational Leadership, XVII*, 3.

Lundsteen, S. W. (1976). *Children learn to communicate*. Englewood Cliffs, NJ: Prentice-Hall, Inc.

Meyer, D. E. (1981). *The student teacher on the firing line*. Saratoga, CA: Century Twenty-One Publishing.

Oberg, K. (1992). Reaching child care teachers: When experience precedes education. Occasional Paper. Pasadena, CA: Pacific Oaks College.

Peters, T. (February 12, 1990). To fail well, go out and do something stupid. *San Jose Mercury News*, p. 20.

Read, K., & Patterson, J. (1980). *The nursery school and kindergarten*. (*1980*) (7th ed.). New York: Holt, Rinehart & Winston Inc.

Rogers, C., & Freiberg, H. (1994). Freedom to learn (3rd ed.). New York: Merrill/Macmillan.

Sciarra, D. J., & Dorsey, A. G. (1979). *Developing and administering a child care center*. Boston: Houghton Mifflin Co.

Selye, H. (1974). *Stress without distress*. New York: The New American Library.

Stevens, J. H., Jr., & King, E. W. (1976). *Administering early education programs*. Boston: Little, Brown and Co.

Tittle, C. K. (1974). *Student teaching*. Metuchen, NJ: The Scarecrow Press, Inc.

Ueland, B. (November 1941). Tell me more. *Ladies Home Journal*, 58:51, as quoted by Clark Moustakas in *The Authentic Teacher*. Cambridge: Howard A. Doyle Printing Co., 1966.

Weir, M. K. & Eggleston, P. J. (November/December 1975). Teacher's first words. *Day Care and Early Education*.

RESOURCES

Rogers, C. (1961). *On becoming a person*. Boston: Houghton Mifflin Co.

Problem Solving

After studying this chapter, the student will be able to:

- Identify a sequential approach to problem solving.
- Describe three alternatives when faced with problems.
- Use alternative solutions.
- State both sides of a problem.

After being there eight weeks, the children call me to help. They hug me sometimes, and it helps me feel good about myself.

Maria Martinez

Something that threw me was the fact that the playground rules were different from the school where I work. When I saw a child standing on the big cement tunnel my first thought was "Oh my goodness he'll fall and kill himself!" Fortunately my cooperating teacher moved over to the tunnel and calmly asked the child how to safely get up and down. This was a good lesson for the technique facilitated problem solving and used child ideas. My first day went faster than greased lightening, and I survived.

Lois Akers

All the suggestions about getting on eye level when communicating with children so you can look them in the eye are proving correct and important. I feel like I spend the majority of my time with bent knees or sitting on tiny chairs.

Nathalia Ozernoy

I'm working up the courage to tell a fellow student teacher she's not doing her share. My supervisor suggested I tell her how frustrated and angry I am before I explode. It's so easy to say "you" but I plan to stick to "I'm feeling . . . , I'm expecting . . ."

Glo Hopkings

Conflicts are part of life. Resolving these conflicts depends largely on individuals' reactions to them. You have already developed a style of reacting; it varies according to the age, sex, dependency, and love you have for the other persons involved. Problem solving becomes easier when an established, trusting relationship exists between people.

Moustakas (1966) has identified two ways teachers and children establish relationships.

179

Two ways in which teachers may establish significant bonds in their relationships with children are the confrontation and the encounter. The confrontation is a meeting between persons who are involved in a conflict or controversy and who remain together, face-to-face, until feelings of divisiveness and alienation are resolved and replaced by genuine acceptance and respect, even though differences in belief and attitude may continue to exist. The encounter is a sudden spontaneous, intuitive meeting between teacher and child in which there is an immediate sense of relatedness and feeling of harmony and communication.

● THEORIES IN PROBLEM SOLVING

Glickman (1981) has pinpointed three distinct styles that school administrators or directors, who often face staff conflicts, use in human interactions, figure 10-1. At one end of Glickman's continuum is a nondirective style of relating; collaborative or joint problem solving is seen in the middle; directive style at the other extreme. You may function according to each of these styles when faced with conflicts, figure 10-2.

In your attempts to solve problems, you will want to adopt a planned approach rather than a random one. Glickman's planned and thoughtful responses (1981) are as follows:

- *Listening*: saying nothing, perhaps nodding, being attentive, waiting for the speaker to finish.
- *Clarifying*: replying with questions intended to give a fuller understanding of the problem.
- *Encouraging*: talking at great lengths about other problem factors.
- *Presenting*: offering your thoughts on the situation or behavior.
- *Problem solving*: initiating the discussion with statements aimed at exploring solutions.
- *Negotiating*: attempting to reach a settlement quickly.
- *Demonstrating*: physically showing how to act, what to do, or what to say.
- *Directing*: detailing what one must do.
- *Reinforcing*: delineating the conditions and consequences of the solution.

Freire (1993) has identified three aspects of problem solving: naming the problem; analyzing the causes; and acting to solve the problem. In addition, Freire has identified three stages of consciousness in problem solving: magical problem solving; naive problem solving; and critical problem solving. Personalizing this theory, figure 10-3, for student teachers as it relates to problem-solving styles involves answering the following:

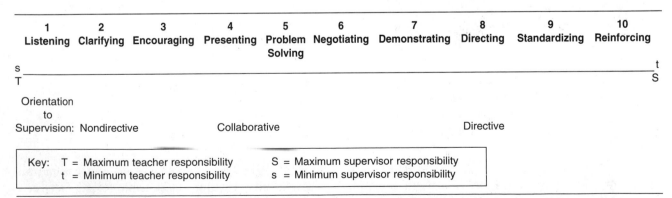

Figure 10-1 The supervisory behavior continuum. (Reprinted with permission of the Association for Supervision and Curriculum Development and Carl D. Glickman. Copyright © 1981 by the Association for Supervision and Curriculum Development. All rights reserved.)

Nondirective	Collaborative	Directive
Help another by Listening Asking clarifying questions Encouraging to find one's own solution **Help yourself by** Self-analysis Self-assessment Finding your own solution	**With one or more individuals** Talk it out Name and describe conflicts Give and take Mediate and show ideas Negotiate Form a pact Come to agreement Contract with one another	**Help another by** Telling them what to do Showing them what to do Making a rule to follow Commanding that it be done in a certain way **Help yourself by** Making a clear rule about your own conduct

Figure 10-2 Problem solving.

	Magical problem solving	Naive problem solving	Critical problem solving
Naming the problem	No problem seen, or accepted as facts of existence	Individual's behavior deviates from ideal roles or rules	Unjust or conflict-producing rules and roles of the system
Analysis of causes	External, inevitable: God, fate, luck, chance	Individual inadequacies in self or others	Historical causes; vested interests of groups; internalization of roles and rules by others
Acting to solve the problem	Passive acceptance conformity	Reform individuals	Transform one's internalized roles and rules and change the system's roles and rules.

Figure 10-3 Aspects of problem solving. (Reprinted from "Education for What?" by A. Alschuler, et al., in Human Growth Games, J. Fletcher [ed.], 1978, with permission of the publisher, Sage Publications, Beverly Hills, CA.)

- Do you passively accept problems as just your luck without trying to change them? (*Magical*: "That's just the way it is; I'm unlucky.")

- Do you realize problems exist, putting the cause on your own shoulders? (*Naive*: "If I did this or that, it would have been okay.")

- Do you tend to blame the system, the process, or the situation rather than yourself or others? (*Critical*: "No one can pass student teaching; it's just too hard.")

Examining problem-solving theories may help you understand yourself and your problem-solving style, figure 10-4.

● A PROBLEM-SOLVING PROCESS

Most problems can be faced in a sequential manner. This text suggests problem solving in a rational manner when emotions are under control. Take some time alone to cool down or physically burn off excessive tension before you try to use it. Substituting new behaviors into your problem-solving style takes time and effort. Practice is necessary.

Sending "I" messages and active listening will avert problem build-up. However, you do have the choice of living with a problem and not working on it. This can work for short periods but usually erodes the quality of your relationship with others or with yourself. Alienation occurs in most

Figure 10-4 Group problem solving occurs in student teacher classes.

instances, but you may prefer this course of action and be prepared for its consequences. Most often you will choose to confront others or yourself and work toward solutions that eliminate the problem. Familiarize yourself with the following. It suits many different situations.

Step 1. Recognition of tensions, emotions, or the problem.

Step 2. Analysis. (Who and what is involved? When and where does it occur? Whose problem is it?)

Step 3. Sending "I" messages. (Active listening and reflecting messages.)

Step 4. Discussion. (Probing; getting more data. Who owns the problem?)

Step 5. Stating both sides of the problem clearly.

Step 6. Proposing and finding possible solutions.

Step 7. Agreement to try one of these solutions. Agreement to meet again if the solution does not work.

Step 8. Consideration of willingness, time, and effort to solve the problem.

This process can be attempted but will not work if one party refuses to talk, mediate, or look for courses of action that will satisfy everyone involved.

Refusing to act on solutions also hinders the process. Problem solving is two-sided even when you are the only one involved. At step 2, one sometimes realizes the problem belongs to another, and the best course of action is to help that person communicate with someone else. Often a problem may disappear at step 3.

The discussion, step 4, can include "I'm really interested in talking about it" or "Let's talk; we'll examine just what's happening to us." However, there is a tendency to blame rather than identify contributing causes. Getting stuck and not moving past step 4 hampers resolution of the problem. Statements like "You're right; I really avoid cleaning that sink," or "I'm really bothered by interruptions during planned group times," all involve owning the problem.

Before possible solutions are mentioned, a clear statement of conflicting views, step 5, adds clarification.

With a child: "You'd like to paint next, and I told Carlos it's his turn."

With a fellow student teacher: "You feel the way I handle Peter is increasing his shyness, and I feel it's helping him."

With a cooperating teacher: "I think my activity was suitable for the group, but you think it didn't challenge them."

With a supervisor: "You feel I tend to avoid planning outdoor activities; I think I've planned quite a few."

Your confrontation might start at step 6. ("Let's figure out some way to make the noisy time right before nap a little calmer and quieter.") Finding alternate solutions admits there are probably a number of possibilities. "Together we'll figure a way" or "That's one way; here's another idea." A do-it-my-way attitude inhibits joint agreement. Thinking alternatives over and getting back together is helpful at times. Seeking a consultant who offers ideas can aid solving problems that participants see as hopeless.

When all parties decide to try one solution, step 7, consideration should be given to meeting again if that particular alternative does not work. ("We'll try it this week and discuss whether it's working next Monday.")

Step 8 reinforces both sides. "We figured it out." "Thanks for taking the time to solve this." "I appreciated your efforts in effecting a solution." This process is not to be used as a panacea; rather, it contains helpful guidelines.

Classroom problems can involve any aspect of the student teaching situation, figure 10-5. Interpersonal conflicts will take both courage and consideration of the proper time and place to confront.

> The teacher is sometimes afraid to confront a child who is hostile, caustic, or vengeful. Such a teacher avoids and avoids until the accumulation of feelings becomes so unbearable an explosion occurs, and the teacher loses control. Once the self is out of control, there is no possibility to bring about a positive resolution of the problem. But when the hateful, rejection emotions subside, there is always hope that the teacher can come to terms with the child and reach a depth of relatedness and mutuality (Moustakas, 1966).

Arrange to problem solve when participants have no classroom responsibilities and where there will not be any interruptions or noninvolved observers.

Figure 10-5 Feeling that you are always stuck with snack preparation is a problem.

Can teachers promote child problem solving and discovery? Britz (1993) encourages teachers to articulate problems they face and discuss solutions with children. She feels children then become more aware of the significance of the problem-solving process.

Problem-solving conversations can involve individual children and small and large groups.

Resistance

Resistance to rules and not conforming to what is expected can be seen in both children and adults. It is usually viewed as negative behavior. Moustakas believes it is healthy:

> Resistance is a way for the child to maintain his own sense of self in the light of external pressures to manipulate and change him. It is a healthy response, an effort of the individual to sustain the integrity of the self.

Resistance and controversy can become challenges that develop our understanding and let us know others at a deeper level, figure 10-6. Though

Figure 10-6 Through problem solving, we can actually understand a child at a deeper level.

confrontations may frighten student teachers in early days, later they are seen as opportunities to know more about the children and adults.

> The anxiety in facing an embittered, destructive child can be eliminated only in actual confrontation with the dread child because until we actually meet him, we cannot know him (Moustakas, 1966).

SUMMARY

Problem-solving skills are important for student teachers, figure 10-7. There seem to be definite styles of relating to others during problem-solving situations. Students are urged to practice new techniques in problem solving. Early fears of confronting tend to disappear as communicative problem solving becomes a way to know and understand others. In problem solving, teachers model the skills for children; therefore, the children may also learn to use them, figure 10-8.

SUGGESTED ACTIVITIES

A. Choose a partner and discuss your style of solving problems or getting your own way with your family. List techniques that you believe

Figure 10-7 Woodworking is often a favorite activity, but it may require problem-solving conversation. (Courtesy of Jim Clay)

help individual solutions but are destructive to joint solutions. After five minutes, discuss this with another partner. Report back to the total group.

B. In the following situations, state as clearly as possible what you think are both sides of the problem. Then describe two alternatives that you feel might satisfy both parties of each conflict.

1. Cecelia has been assigned to student teach from 9:00 to 2:30 on Tuesdays. Her cooperating teacher, Mr. Kifer, notices she has been leaving early. Cecelia has been arriving 10 to 15 minutes early each day. Her cooperating teacher confronts Cecelia one day before she departs. "Leaving early, Cecelia?"

2. Henri, a four-year-old, has been told repeatedly by the student teacher that he must put the blocks he used back on the shelf. Henri has ignored the request continually. The student teacher requests the cooperating teacher

Figure 10-8 Will these children solve the problem of wanting the same book?

ask Henri to replace the blocks since he does not respond to the student teacher.

3. The cooperating teacher has been silent most of the morning. The student teacher can feel tension mounting and says, "I'm really feeling uncomfortable because I sense there is something wrong." The cooperating teacher ignores the remark. At the end of work, the student discusses the situation with the supervisor.

4. Christopher, a student teacher, is fuming. "After all the work I put into the activity, she didn't even mention it," he says to Charlotte, another student teacher.

5. "I'd really like to present this new song to the children," says Robin, a student teacher. "You didn't put it in the plan book, Robin, and I have a full day planned," the cooperating teacher says. "Let's talk about it; I can see the disappointment on your face." Robin replies, "It's not disappointment. I can't see why the schedule is so inflexible." "Let's talk about that after the morning session, Robin."

6. "I sure needed your help at circle today," the cooperating teacher said. "I was in the bath-room with Anthony; he's got those pants that button at the shoulders," the student teacher answers.

7. "I'm really tired today, Mrs. Cuffaro," the student teacher answers when asked why she stayed in the housekeeping area most of the morning. Mrs. Cuffaro says, "There were lots of other children who could have used your assistance, Annette. Will you have time to talk when the children are napping?" "Sure," Annette replies.

8. Miriam, an attractive student teacher, is assigned to an on-campus laboratory school. Male friends often hang around the lobby or ask the secretary to give her messages and notes. The secretary has told Miriam this is bothersome. Miriam tells the secretary the notes often concern getting a ride home since she does not have a car.

C. Read each statement. Of the two courses of action, select the one you feel is appropriate. In small groups, discuss your choices.

1. Some of your money has been missing from a locker you share with another student teacher.

   A. You should consult with your supervisor.

   B. You should ask the other student about it.

2. You have spoken sharply to one of the children.

   A. You ask your cooperating teacher if you can step out of the room for a minute.

   B. You ask your cooperating teacher to move the child into the cooperating teacher's group.

3. You do not feel comfortable singing; you feel your voice is "toad-like."

   A. You should use a record to teach the song.

   B. You should say, "I'm a real toad at singing."

4. Your supervisor expected you at a meeting, and you forgot to attend.

A. You suggest you pick the next meeting time.

B. You confess to forgetting.

5. An aide in the classroom seems very competent to you. You feel she has more skills than the cooperating teacher. She makes a remark about the cooperating teacher's lack of patience with a particular child.

A. You agree with her.

B. You ask, "Have you and Miss Tashima ever discussed child-handling techniques?"

6. Vicki, a student teacher, is friendly, attractive, and charming. She has barely passed her previous classes, and has used her personal charm more than study skills. In student teaching, she's sliding, doing only the minimum amount of work. She feels both her supervisor and resident teacher are aware that she is "trying only to slide by."

A. Vicki should drop out.

B. Vicki should admit her past actions have caught up with her.

7. Leticia works in a community preschool. She feels that the theory in classes has focused on the ideal rather than the practical. Her supervisor has warned that her methods produce child behaviors that are negative and growth limiting.

A. Leticia says, "You know what is in the books isn't real; that's not the way it is in preschool."

B. Leticia asks, "Exactly which of my behaviors produce those child behaviors?"

8. Although Gloria knows spanking children is against the law, she is reluctant to tell her co operating teacher in the community-affiliated preschool. Everyone who works at the school accepts it as appropriate. Gloria can see the children's behavior changing.

A. Gloria should keep silent.

B. Gloria should consult with her supervisor.

9. Sydney has been placed in a preschool where the cooperating teacher often leaves the room, leaving her in full charge of 20 preschoolers. Sydney handles it well and has planned many interesting, exciting activities for the children.

A. She should talk to her cooperating teacher about her responsibility.

B. She should consult with her supervisor.

10. Connie has been placed in a school that handles children of an ethnic group different from her own. She feels excluded and out of step, even though her cooperating teacher has been friendly.

A. She should discuss the problem with the cooperating teacher.

B. She should wait and see if the feeling subsides. If not, she should talk to her supervisor.

11. The cook at the center where Teresa has been placed is never happy about the way Teresa cleans the tables after lunch.

A. She should ask the cook to show her how it should be done.

B. She should ask her cooperating teacher about the cook.

12. A parent compliments Peter, a student teacher, about activities he has planned that are multicultural. "You offer the children so many activities that Mrs. Bridgeman, the cooperating teacher, would never have thought of! I'm glad you're a student teacher in her classroom!"

A. Peter should smile and discuss the remark with the cooperating teacher.

B. Peter should defend the cooperating teacher because he knows the classroom is full of multicultural materials.

REVIEW

A. Arrange the following problem-solving steps in order, based on the eight-step sequence. You may find that more than one applies to the same step.

1. Cooperating teacher: "We'll put paintings without names in this box this week and see what happens." Student teacher: "Okay."

2. Student teacher: "You feel children's art work should always have the child's name printed in the upper left corner."

3. Cooperating teacher: "You could put names on the art work when you're the adult in the art area."

4. Student teacher: "I feel the child's name should be put on the art work only when the child gives permission to do so. If the children don't ask to have their names put on, they will learn the consequences when it's time to take the art home."

5. Student teacher: "I could tell each child what will happen if there is no name on his or her painting."

6. Cooperating teacher: "There's been quite a bottleneck when parents try to find their child's art work at departure time. Sometimes there are no names printed in the upper left corner."

7. Student teacher: "You would like to put each child's name on his or her art work, and I think each child can learn something if I don't print his or her name when he or she does not give me permission to do so."

8. Student teacher: "I appreciate your understanding my point of view."

9. Cooperating teacher: "You could write the child's name lightly if that child said no."

10. Cooperating teacher: "I think the lesson to be learned isn't worth the commotion at closing."

11. Student teacher: "This is the way I feel about names on art work."

B. Using Glickman's "planful" responses, identify the following statements. (Example: "Tell me more about it." *Encouraging.*)

1. "Do you mean you're feeling angry?"

2. "Just stop helping the child."

3. "The way I look at it, you've been asking for a lot of direction from the cooperating teacher."

4. "I'll put the chairs up on Tuesdays; you can do it on Thursdays."

5. "Tell her it's her turn."

6. "If you straighten the closet every day, he'll get the message and do it too."

7. "I think I hear anxiety in your voice."

8. "Look the speaker in the eyes."

9. "There's more, isn't there?"

C. Briefly answer the following questions.

1. How can facing a defiant child be considered a challenge?

2. What is positive about a child resisting expectations and doing something his or her own way and in his or her own time?

D. Match items in column 1 with their *opposites* in column II.

I	II.
1. Silence and withdrawal	a. Scaring your opponent
2. Problem solving	b. Focusing on your verbal defense
3. Listening	c. Blowing up
4. Self-solution	d. Out of control, irrational
5. Early "I" message	e. Avoiding confrontations
6. "Planful"	f. Alienation, and living with the problem
7. Encounter	g. Being given a command
8. Using tears	h. Talking too much
9. Ignoring child behavior	i. Confronting a child for hitting another

E. Complete the following statements.

1. If a person refuses to talk about a problem . . .

2. One can resign oneself to alienation when . . .

3. The hardest part of problem solving for me is . . .

4. Some techniques for problem solving which were not encouraged in this chapter are . . .

5. One problem that is probably going to occur in student teaching that was not mentioned in this chapter is . . .

F. List as many possible alternative solutions as you can for the following problem.

Winona has been placed with a cooperating teacher who, in her opinion, has created a classroom environment that offers the children few play choices. She has communicated this idea to her cooperating teacher, who then asks Winona for suggestions. Winona's suggestions might include . . .

REFERENCES

Britz, J. (1993). Problem solving in early childhood classrooms. *ERIC Digest*, EDO-PS-93-1.

Friere, P. (1993). *Pedagogy of the oppressed* (20th anniversary ed.). New York: Continuum.

_____. (1970). *Education for critical consciousness*. New York: Seabury Press, Inc.

Glickman, C. D. (1981). *Developmental supervision*. Alexandria, VA: Association for Supervision and Curriculum Development.

Moustakas, C. (1966). *The authentic teacher*. Cambridge: Howard A. Doyle Printing Co.

RESOURCES

Chiarelott, L., Davidman, L., & Ryan, K. (1990). Interpreting metaphors of schooling from *Lenses on Teaching*. Ft. Worth, TX: Holt, Rinehart, & Winston.

CHAPTER

11

Case Studies, Analysis, and Applications

OBJECTIVES

After studying this chapter, the student will be able to:

- Use at least three different types of observation forms: narrative (anecdotal), event sampling, and fixed interval (time sampling).
- Analyze a child's behavior from information gathered through observation and develop an individual learning plan for the child.
- Describe the difference between observation and conjecture.
- Discuss the role of the school and parents in working with a child.

Guillermo was my most fascinating child. He was bilingual. His family from Guatemala was trying so hard to adjust to the United States.

Forrest Graham

I'll be looking for a part-time job so I can go on in school. The more children I encounter the more I realize I need to know more.

Mukema Oblatela

CASE STUDIES

As a student teacher you may be asked to complete a child case study. The assignment requires in-depth analysis and recording of the child's achievements, development, and learning processes.

A collection of data can involve:

- systematic observations
- work samples
- assessments and testing
- reviewing creative artwork
- videos, photographs, or tape recordings
- dictations
- anecdotal records (factual notes recording spontaneous events and happenings)
- checklists, inventories, or rating scales
- interviews with child and others
- home visits and other activities

What's collected may depend on both your college instructor's assignment criteria and the purpose of the study undertaking.

Materials and data are arranged in chronological order so assessments can compare earlier with later work and happenings. If student teacher evaluation is required, records document child progress and student teacher hypothesis. Case studies development can often provide a basis for planning parent-teacher conferences.

A strict code of confidentiality and anonymity concerning the child's identity is observed when student teachers collect data or share evaluations. Parents' presence in the school or classroom make confidentiality extremely important. The temptation students face in wanting to discuss their case study child with other adults has led to a few unfortunate and emotionally charged parent-school discussions.

Assignments may require a "whole child" view or narrower aspects of the child's development and/or behavior.

Most training programs assign in-depth case studies so student teachers begin to realize the benefits accrued from watching one child intently and attempting to satisfy curiosity about the hows and whys of that one child's actions and speech. Student teachers therefore become researchers who reserve fast judgments, interpret carefully, hypothesize, explore many possible reasons for behavior, and begin to see child development "in the flesh."

OBSERVATION FORMS

In this chapter, we are going to go beyond our earlier description of behavior and observation in order to help you understand how to use different types of observation forms and, more importantly, how to use the information learned to develop learning plans for the observed child.

Narrative

This is one of the simplest forms to use when observing children. A narrative describes the child's behavior as it occurs. As the observer, you can sit to one side of the room or yard with a small notebook, figure 11-1. Pick a child to observe, and simply record what you see. Your narrative might look something like this:

Stevie, one of the new children in the room of five-year-olds at the ABC School, enters the room and hangs onto his mother's coat, with his finger in his mouth. He looks unhappy as his mother says impatiently, "Let go, Stevie; you're too big to act like a

Figure 11-1 Observation can take place inside the classroom.

baby. You know I'm in a hurry to get to work this morning." Stevie looks at another child, Hiroku, who is playing with the blocks. "Look at how nicely Hiroku is playing! Why don't you go over and play with him."

Stevie begins to cry as his mother attempts to drag him over to the block area. He whines, "Don't wanta stay today, Mama. Wanta go home!"

Mrs. Thomas, the teacher, intervenes. "Mrs. Conway, could you stay awhile today? I know Stevie would like to show you the dinosaur he made yesterday. It's drying on the shelf over by the window. Stevie, why don't you show the dinosaur to your Mom?"

(Mrs. Thomas really knows how to handle Stevie's reluctance to separate from his mother, doesn't she? Look at how happy he is now, showing his dinosaur to his Mom! I remember how much time he took yesterday when he made it; I didn't think he'd ever finish! But Mrs. Thomas let him take as much time as he needed to feel satisfied. I guess she knew that if he got started describing the dinosaur to his mother, he'd forget about her having to leave. I wonder why Mrs. Conway doesn't give Stevie a little extra time each day when she brings him instead of hurrying him so. She knows he hates to be left in a hurry!)

After a minute or two of describing the dinosaur and its ferocity, Stevie goes to the door with his mother. "Bye, Mom. See you this afternoon." Stevie runs off. "Hiroku, let me play with some of the blocks!" "OK, Stevie. Wanta help me build a garage for the big trucks?"

"Sure."

Stevie and Hiroku work quickly and build a garage for three of the big trucks.

Juan and Mike come in together with Mike's older brother Pat.

"I'll be back at 3:30 when school gets out. Be ready, you two."

"Teacher will see we're ready, Pat; you know we'll be ready," says Mike.

Juan goes over to the garage Stevie and Hiroku have built. "I want the red truck," he demands. "Can't have it. We need it," protests Stevie. Juan grabs the truck. Stevie gets to his feet and shouts, "Gimme it back!" Stevie tries to grab the truck from Juan. A tug-of-war begins as both boys shake the truck between

them. Hiroku says to Stevie, "Aw, let him have it. We got enough trucks anyway." Stevie lets go of the truck, sits back down on the floor, puts his finger in his mouth, and sulks.

How might this same interaction appear if you were using a different observation form? (However easy the narrative is to read, it does remove you from the classroom action while you are writing.) The narrative can be abbreviated somewhat through the use of the anecdotal record form. Figure 11-2 illustrates this narrative in anecdotal form.

Event Sampling Form

In contrast to the narrative and anecdotal forms, an event sampling form, figure 11-3, might be used. In this form Stevie's play behaviors are being observed. In addition, the times of each observation are indicated to provide additional information. Two theorists lend themselves to a consideration of children's play behaviors in terms of an observation model. They are Parten (1932), whose play categories have been useful for many years, and Piaget (1962).

Parten divided play behaviors into the following categories: *onlooking* (observing, talking, but not participating), *solitary* (play without reference to another child), *parallel* (play in which two or more children may be using similar materials without personal interaction), *associative* (play in which two or more children may be using the same materials but each child is doing a separate activity; for example, each child may be using blocks, building separate towers), and *cooperative* (play in which there is a common goal toward which two or more children are working; for example, the children are using blocks to build one house (p. 244).

Piaget suggested that there are three types of play common among preschoolers; *symbolic* (play in which the objects with which the child is playing become something else; for example, blocks become a garage or a house), *practice* (play in which the child continuously repeats an activity as though to master it; for example, in block play, trying over and over to build an ever taller structure without calling it a tower), and *games* (play in which the children follow a set of agreed-upon rules).

		Student Teacher: MB
Name of School: ABC School, Day-Care Center		Date: 16 September

Identity Key (DO NOT use real name)	Description of What Child Is Doing	Time	Comments
S. — Stevie	S. enters, clings to M.'s coat. Finger in mouth.	8:03	S. looks unhappy.
M. — S.'s Mom	M., "Let go, S. You're too big to act like a baby. I'm in a hurry; you know it!"		I wish S.'s M. wouldn't do that!
T. — Teacher	Lk how nice H. plays by self!		
H. — Hiroku	Why not play w/him		
J. — Juan	S. cries.	8:05	
Mi. — Mike	T. suggests S. show M. dinosaur fr yesterday.		I wish I'd thought of that; S. is really proud of his dinosaur.
P. — Pat, Mike's brother	S. and M. to see dino.		
	S. says "Bye" to M.; goes to H., "Lemme play w/you."	8:08	
	H. says, "Let's build a garage for the trucks."		Good for H.; he always has good ideas!
* * *	* * * * * * * *	* *	* * * *
	J., Mi., & P. come in.	8:47	
	J. says, "I want the red truck."		
	S., "No; we need it." J. grabs the truck.	8:55	Oh oh, I better watch & see what happens.
	H. says, "Let him have it. We have enough trucks."		I love kids like H. He is so mature!

Figure 11-2 An anecdotal record form.

In looking at the anecdotal record and narrative account of Stevie's early-morning activities, it would be noted on the event sampling form that he was involved in cooperative-symbolic play with Hiroku. If, however, Stevie was followed throughout the day, observations might look more like the rest of the event sampling form in figure 11-3.

Fixed Interval Model

Many student teachers do not have the time to sit and observe; they are, instead, actively involved in what is happening in the classroom, often teaching or supervising small groups of students. The *fixed-interval* or *time sampling* model may be the observation form to use, figure 11-4.

● ANALYSIS OF OBSERVATION

As you look at your fixed-interval observations and comments on Maya in figure 11-4, what hypotheses might you generate? Has Maya resolved the Erikson tasks appropriate for her age? Does she appear field sensitive or independent? What may be the indications of whether she is concrete operational or not?

Certainly given the speed with which Maya finished the math "sponge" problems and her subsequent absorption in the tangram activities, it is easy to hypothesize that Maya is positively resolving the task of industry. Also, her assertion that she would like to be at the writing center and asking if she could design her own tangrams suggests successful

Child: Stevie			Date: 16 September
	Symbolic	Practice	Games
Onlooking:	Watching H. & J. in playhouse (9:45 am)		
Solitary:	Pretending to be Superman on jungle gym (10:23 am)	Putting puzzles together (8:35 am) On swg. Trying to pump self (10:40 am)	
Parallel:	Bldg rd for car in sandbox (3:20 pm)	Dumping H_2O fr 1 container to another at H_2O table (2:57 pm)	
Associative:		Bldg towers w/sm blks next to H. (8:30 am)	
Cooperative:	Bldg garage w/lrg blks w/H. (8:12 am)		Following H.'s directions for card game, "War" (2:10 pm)

Figure 11-3 A two-dimensional play model, combining event and time sampling.

resolution of initiative. Her ignoring of the "sponge" problems until the last minute may indicate that the problems are too simple for her and that she needs an extra challenge in math or, assuming that she rushed through them unsuccessfully, an indication of some unresolved autonomy. Checking to see how well she has completed the problems will allow you to accept or reject that particular hypothesis.

Maya's desire to work alone and carefully with the tangrams, plus her wanting to create her own designs, could be indications of a field-independent learning style. Observing her step-by-step analysis of the tangram puzzles might also suggest a logical sequential learning style. And, her enjoyment of math challenges, as you have seen before, suggests that she may be concrete operational.

As mentioned in the observations of Stevie, the best method is to combine forms, using different ones for different purposes. Although they take the most time, the narrative and anecdotal forms provide the most information. Forms such as the two-dimensional play model are handy to use when time is limited. They also supplement the narrative forms well and provide much information relevant to their single purpose. We have used the example of play behaviors, but you might want to use social behaviors or attending behaviors.

When working with a child who is asocial, anti-social, or overly social, social behaviors become more important to observe. One such form, figure 11-5, was developed by Goodwin and Meyerson for use in the classroom and is called the Teacher/Pupil Interaction Scale (TPIS). The scale measures four types of teacher behavior and four types of student behavior on another two-dimension form. The teacher behaviors are as follows: (1) instruction, (2) reinforcing, (3) nonattending; and (4) disapproving. The student behaviors are: (1) attending; (2) scanning; (3) social; and (4) disruptive. Both teacher and student behaviors are defined as follows:

Teacher Behavior

Instruction: Makes explanation, talks to pupil, gives directions, asks questions, etc.

Reinforcing: Dispenses appreciation, smiles, nods; makes physical contact by patting, touching; dispenses material rewards.

Nonattending or neutrals: Withholds attention, sits passively, attends to personal notes, works with other pupils, attends to activities that do not include the pupil being observed.

Child: Maya
T = teacher
St = Student; Ss = students

Grade: 3rd
Date: 12 October

8:30 am: Enters classroom, place lunch box & jacket in cubby
8:30 am: Sits at desk, talks to J. (a student in her group), ignores math "sponge" activity on board
8:40 am: Still talks to J.
8:45 am: (Bell rings.)
            (I was busy taking roll & lunch count; didn't note what M. was doing)
8:50 am: Talks to G. (another St. in her group)
            (Should be saying pledge and completing math "sponge" activity on chalkboard)
8:55 am: (T. reminds children that 1st activity of the a.m. will begin at 9:00 & that "sponge" problems are to be placed in her "in-basket")
            Maya quickly completes problems & turns in paper
9:00 am: All Ss sitting quietly on carpet squares, choosing centers; Maya waves hand excitedly; "Writing center! Writing center!"
            T reminds her that she has been in the writing center for the past 2 days and that others like the writing center too;
            "Why not try the math center, Maya?" T. suggests
9:05 am: Maya pouts, "But, I want to go to the writing center."
9:10 am: Still pouting but goes to math center where tangram puzzles and pieces are arranged to stimulate problem solving.
9:15 am: M. complains, "These tangrams are too easy! Can I make some of my own?" T. says "Of course, Maya; maybe you'd like to
            have B. work with you?" "No!" . . . emphatically said
9:25 am: M. working very carefully
9:30 am: M. still working carefully
9:45 am: (I'm too busy; unable to check on M.)
9:50 am: M. looks intent on creating a new design
9:55 am: T. rings a bell & warns Ss they have 5 min to finish their center work. Reminds those who haven't that they can finish after recess.
10:00 am: M. says, "I'm nearly finished with my design; may I stay in for recess and work on it?" T. suggests to M. that she should get
            some fresh air and exercise too. M. groans but agrees.
(I have yard duty this am recess and I notice that Maya is off by herself drawing in the dirt. I wonder if she's still working on her new tangram design or dreaming up a new one. As I approach her, she quickly erases what she's been working on.)

Figure 11-4 Fixed-interval or time sampling model.

Disapproving: Criticizes, corrects, admonishes, re-proves, expresses generally negative feelings, statements, etc.

Pupil Behavior

Attending: When receiving direction or instructions, maintains eye contact or heeds direction. When performing desk work, attends to work (turns pages, uses pencil, looks at paper), figure 11-6. When addressed by teacher, child attends.

Scanning: Looks about room; watches other children; daydreams; makes no verbal or physical contact with other children.

Social contacts: Teaches other children; talks to others; walks about room interacting with others but does not attract the general attention of the class with noise or disturbances.

Disruptive: Calls attention to self by behaviors that are audible/visible throughout the room, e.g. tapping with pencil, throwing objects, shouting.

It is difficult to think that all teacher/pupil interactions could be reduced to only four actions by each. If you use the scale, you will discover that many actions can be comfortably placed in one of the four categories.

The real advantage of the TPIS is that the observer records interactions for only one minute at a

Pupil: Maya	Date: 14 October
Observer: Student Teacher	Times: 8:37 am
Teacher: Cooperating teacher	8:57 am
	9:28 am
	10:09 am
	10:38 am

8:37 am: Children wating for bell

	1	2	3	4	
A			3		Activity: T. arranging papers
B			3		at her desk; most Ss working
C			3		on math "sponge" activity.
D			3		
E		3			Maya has been talking to J.;
F		3			now is looking out the window.
G		3			
H		3			
I			3		Talking to G. and J.;
J			3		G. shushes her.
K			3		
L			3		

8:57 am: "Sponge" time

	1	2	3	4	
A			3		
B			3		
C			3		
D			3		
E		4			Tchr reminds
F		4			M. to finish
G		4			math "sponge"
H		3			paper.
I		3			
J		3			Maya really
K		3			works fast! I
L		3			am surprised she
					does as well as
					she does.

9:28 am: 1st Center Activity Time

	1	2	3	4	
A	3				Maya wrkg on
B	3				tangrams (her choice).
C	3				
D	3				
F	3				Interesting, Maya seems
G		3			to be day-dreaming.
H	3				
I	3				
J	3				I'm really pleased to
K	3				see how well Maya can
L	3				work.

10:09 am: Recess

	1	2	3	4	
A		3			
B		3			
C	3				Maya is truly
E	3				engrossed—
F	3				wonder what
G	3				she's doing?
H	3				
I		3			
J		3			
K	3				I bet she's
L	3				drawing another
					tangram design!

10:38 am: 2nd Center Activity Time

	1	2	3	4	(Maya is working on map of neighborhood w/J., G., & W.)
A	3				
B	3				
C	3				
D	3				
E	2				T. compliments group
F	2				on how well the map
G	2				is progressing
H	2				
I	3				
J	3				
K			3		Maya's angry because G. wants to use different map symbol
L			3		than she; T. waits to see if Ss can resolve own conflict.

Figure 11-5 Teacher/Pupil Interaction Scale (TPIS).

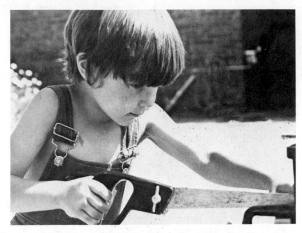

Figure 11-6 This child is attending to a chosen task.

time. Thus, it lends itself to the busy teacher who does not have the leisure to complete a narrative, anecdotal, or play model form. TPIS rating procedures are as follows:

1. The observer makes a judgment each five seconds for a one-minute sample of teacher/pupil interaction. Three five-minute blocks taken during an hour over a three-day period provide a reliable basis for judging the typical behavior of a pupil. A five-minute block consists of five one-minute samples, with a one-minute pause between each sample.
2. Pupil behavior is designated by the column in which the rating is made.
3. Each row indicates a single five-second sample.
4. The teacher behavior is designated by a number (1 through 4), and is entered in the column that describes what the pupil is doing.

Please note in figure 11-5 that the example does not include a five-minute block of time but rather includes five one-minute samplings of behavior taken at times when the student teacher found a minute in which to record. You may find for your own purposes that taking one-minute samplings throughout the day gives you as much information as you need in order to develop a picture of what the child you are observing is like. Also, please note that we in-

cluded a brief description of the action in order to help clarify the coding. Remember that the horizontal numbers at the top refer to pupil behavior; the numbers entered by the observer refer to teaching behavior.

Analyzing Observations

One reason, perhaps the main reason, for observing children is to help you, as the observer, better understand the child. This is why we used two children to illustrate the observation techniques covered in the unit.

Stevie: What have we learned about Stevie just from observing him in action? What questions have we raised? Let us start with our opening narrative observation.

Stevie has difficulty separating from his mother when she brings him to school. The narrative describes typical behavior, not exceptional. If we caught Stevie on an exceptional day, we would have noted that this was not his usual behavior. We can also surmise that Stevie's mother almost seems to encourage his desire not to have her leave; in spite of reminding him that she has to leave quickly, she takes time to listen to Stevie describe his dinosaur. Stevie then seems quite happy to let his mother leave, especially since his friend Hiroku is playing with the large blocks, which Stevie enjoys. In the later interchange between Stevie and Juan, we might guess that Juan is the more aggressive since he simply tells Stevie that he wants the red truck and takes it. We might also guess that Stevie does not know how to solve his problem as smoothly as Hiroku, as he enters into a tug-of-war with Juan over the truck. Hiroku, in contrast, recognizes that even if Juan takes the red truck, he and Stevie still have two trucks with which to play; arguing over the third truck is not worth it. A later indication of Hiroku's social maturity (and leadership ability) occurs in the incident of the card game. Hiroku knows how to play "War" and patiently explains the rules to Stevie. Even when Stevie loses his temper and throws the cards because he thinks Hiroku will win, Hiroku does not lose his temper but, instead, quietly picks up the cards.

An analysis of Stevie's play behaviors tends to show that, except for his play with Hiroku, Stevie prefers solitary or parallel play to cooperative or associative play. He also appears to use symbolic and practice play more than play involving rules, such as the card game. We might surmise that Stevie, intellectually, is not at the stage where he can understand or internalize what rules mean. Perhaps giving him some of the Piagetian tasks, measuring his ability to classify and conserve, would be of value in understanding Stevie more fully. This idea may be pursued later.

Other observations of Stevie have noted the following behaviors: During music times in the large group, Stevie typically sings loudly and off-key. The cooperating teacher has asked us to ignore him because she feels he's doing it for the attention. "Shushing" him, she feels, will only reinforce the behavior. Some of the other children are already beginning to ask him to be quiet; others are laughing at him. When this happens, Stevie giggles and sings even more loudly and more off-key. At times, the cooperating teacher cannot totally ignore Stevie and has told him to leave the group if he is unable to behave, a move that usually quiets the boy.

A second observed behavior causing concern occurred on the afternoon of the morning Stevie and Juan had argued over the red truck. During outdoors free play after rest time, Stevie was playing with Hiroku in the sand box. They had been smoothing the sand and building a road for some of the small cars from the outside toy box. Juan had climbed into the sand box and joined them when Stevie picked up a fistful of sand and threw it at Juan. Shaking his head and rubbing his eyes, Juan complained about sand in his eyes. At this point, the cooperating teacher sent Juan to the school nurse to have his eyes washed out, asked Stevie to come out of the sand box, and took him aside to re-explain the school rules about playing in the sand box. Indirect attempts to discover if Stevie deliberately had thrown the sand at Juan because he was still angry about the incident with the truck may prove fruitless. When asked point blank, however, if he had thrown the sand at Juan because he was angry, Stevie is likely to answer yes. He may not understand that his anger is related to the incident of the truck, though, since that had happened a while before.

In a conference with Stevie's mother, the cooperating teacher has learned that since she and her husband are renting a small house with only two bedrooms, Stevie and his two brothers sleep in the same room and go to bed at the same time. "After all," she says, "the boys are only four years apart in age. They go to bed between 8:00 p.m. and 9:00 p.m., depending on what's on television. Their father and I let them watch one show each evening if they've been good and if Tommy, the eight-year-old, has done his homework." When asked when the boys are awakened, she replies, "We have to be up at 6:00 a.m. so we can get breakfast and still get to work on time. And you might know that Stevie knows every trick in the world to make us get a late start!" The mother states that she believes the boys get enough sleep, especially with the nap the two younger ones receive at the after school day care center each day. (The middle boy, a first grader, comes to the center after school each day as does the older boy.)

Stevie's father works at a local foundry; his mother is a clerk-typist in a county office. Although Mr. Conway works 8:00 a.m. to 4:00 p.m. and could pick up his sons at approximately 4:45 p.m., he firmly believes that their care is his wife's responsibility. Thus, the three boys have to wait until about 5:45 p.m. when their mother can pick them up. Efforts on the part of the center staff, director, and teachers to persuade the father to attend parent/teacher/staff conferences have met with flat refusals and the statement that "raising kids is a woman's responsibility, not a man's; you speak to my wife."

The effect of the father's attitude is apparent in the behavior of the three boys, Stevie in particular. Smaller than most of the other five-year-olds at the center, Stevie tends to be slyly aggressive rather than overtly. He seems to know that in a one-to-one argument with any of the other boys in the room, he would lose. So, he throws sand or blocks, trips another, or knocks over another child's block tower. "But, teacher, it was an accident," he will insist when confronted. Another effect of his father's attitude is seen in Stevie's choices for play—large blocks, trucks and cars, swings and jungle gym, tricycles, wagons, puzzles, and clay. But, go in the playhouse? Paint at the easel? Stevie calls these activities "sissy," and refuses to play.

His attachment to Hiroku seems to be related to the fact that Hiroku is the tallest and best coordinated boy in the room. Hiroku appears to understand Stevie's need to be associated with him and cheerfully accepts Stevie's company. It is difficult for Stevie when Hiroku is absent. On those days, Stevie stays by the teacher's side or stands along the wall with his finger in mouth and just watches what is going on.

Stevie's mother has been asked about his playmates at home. "Why, with two older brothers to play with, he doesn't need anybody else!" she replies. The teacher gently points out that Stevie seems "lost" when Hiroku is absent and suggests that maybe Stevie could invite a child home to visit him on the weekend. The mother's reaction to this suggestion is as though the teacher has taken leave of her senses. "With three young ones already, you're telling me I should have another one over? What's wrong with Stevie playing with his brothers? They play real nice together, hardly ever any arguing!" The teacher realizes that one of Stevie's problems socially is the fact that he does not need to make friends in order to have someone with whom to play. The teacher also realizes that Stevie's friendship with Hiroku may be related more to the fact that Hiroku is bigger and more mature and may remind Stevie of his next older brother. The teacher also realizes, after talking with Stevie's mother, that his parents do not share her concern with Stevie's lack of sociableness.

Finally, the teacher decides to have you, her student teacher, make several observations of Stevie. In this way she hopes to develop a learning plan for Stevie through which she can encourage him to greater sociability.

Maya: As a result of the time sampling of Maya's behavior, we have already discussed some of the possible hypotheses. You have noted Maya's behavior on the TPIS two days later than your original observation with the time sampling. What new information have you learned? First of all, you have checked Maya's math "sponge" activities and discovered that not only has she completed the set correctly but that she has also lined up each problem neatly and sequentially. On the second day of free-choice center activities (a three-days-per-week morning option in your cooperating teacher's classroom), it was interesting to note that Maya chose to work in the math manipulatives center to design another tangram. (You had tried to solve the one she worked on so industriously two days before and had found it difficult.) You formulate an hypothesis that Maya appears to be an advanced thinker, Perhaps a potential candidate for the school's gifted-and-talented (GATE) program. As you were observing with the TPIS while supervising the map activity, you also have noticed Maya's spatial abilities. She has had no difficulty placing her home on the map in geographic relation to the school; her argument with Graciela was based, in part, upon the latter's insistence that her home was located in closer proximity to the school than Maya felt it was and, in part, on Graciela's insistence that houses should be indicated on the map by a square with a roof and Maya's equal insistence that the representation did not have to look like a little house, that a square would do as well. Graciela eventually agrees with Maya and the two girls place squares on the map indicating where their respective homes are located. Later, in checking with the cooperating teacher, you discover that Maya is correct in her placement of where Graciela lives, not Graciela. You wonder if Maya will bring up the misplacement with Graciela the next day the girls choose to work on the map.

In the meantime you ask your cooperating teacher if you may administer some of the Piagetian tasks to Maya to test your hypothesis regarding her being in the concrete operational stage. The teacher suggests that you should ask Maya's parents for permission, so you write a short letter for Maya to take home with a tear-off slip at the bottom for Mr. or Mrs. Wiesniewski to sign. The next day, permission granted, you take Maya to the nurse's office and present some of the Piagetian tasks. She finds it easy to conserve mass, length, liquid quantity, and area and complains, "These games are kind of dumb, don't you think? Haven't you anything harder?" At age eight, you don't think she'll be able to solve the concept of displacement of water but you set out the necessary glasses and weighted, small plastic pill containers in front of her. She confidently predicts that the heavier object will displace more water and is surprised when it doesn't. She asks if she can put both objects back in the water herself and you say, "Of course." She picks up both (the pill containers are weighted unequally with heavy screws and bolts), manipulates them, looks at them, places one and then the other back in the jars of water. Much to your surprise (as she takes the objects out of the water again), she then announces, "I think this is kinda like the balls of clay. It doesn't make any difference whether they were round or sausage-shaped; they still had the same amount of clay. I think that it may not make any difference how much the pill bottles weigh; it may just be how big they are." In your mind there is no doubt that Maya is likely gifted. You try one more task, asking Maya to project what life may be like for her when she's an adult. Here her fertile imagination and her enjoyment of science fiction color her response.

A conference with the cooperating teacher, Mr. and Mrs. Wiesniewski, and you has resulted in the parents' decision to allow you to develop an individual learning plan for Maya at the math center to stimulate her problem-solving abilities and challenge her advanced mathematical reasoning abilities.

Mr. and Mrs. Wiesniewski also agree to allow Maya to be tested for possible placement in the school's GATE program the following year. (In the school district where you are student teaching, the GATE program is only for fourth and fifth graders. Prior to fourth grade, classroom teachers are expected to provide extra stimulation for gifted and talented students within the regular classroom.)

Applications: Developing a Learning Plan for Stevie

Since the goal or objective for Stevie is to increase his sociability, what social behaviors have been observed? There is his social behavior toward his mother as he shows her his dinosaur, describes it, and acts out its ferocity. Next, there is his accepting Hiroku's invitation to build a garage with the large blocks and his cooperative play with Hiroku in building towers of small blocks as well as a garage of large ones. Later, there is his cooperative play with Hiroku as they play the card game. In every case of positive social interaction recorded, Stevie was interacting only with Hiroku. In terms of other social behaviors, Stevie interacted with the class, Juan, and Hiroku in negative ways.

Also noted through the observations is the pride with which Stevie talks to his mother about his dinosaur and the care with which he paints it. The teacher thinks that perhaps having the children who made dinosaurs talk about them would be a way in which Stevie could make a positive impression upon the other children.

How will the learning plan look? As with any lesson plan, a learning plan for even one child should contain five elements: (1) the name of the child for whom the plan is being developed; (2) the objective for the plan; (3) any materials or equipment necessary; (4) teacher and student activities; and (5) a time estimate and an evaluation of the plan's effectiveness, figure 11-7.

Since Hiroku is one of the "stars" in the room of five-year-olds, you might also plan to ask another child or two to join Stevie and Hiroku as they play with the blocks. Stevie may not want to share but the chances are that Hiroku will. In this way, Stevie will be playing with two more children other than Hiroku. Why two more? It is easier to exclude one child from play than two children. Also, if Stevie does not want to play with anyone but Hiroku, the other two can play together *parallel* to Stevie and Hiroku.

Another ploy might be to ask Stevie to introduce a new child, assuming a new child enters the center. In this way, Stevie could learn to feel important to

---

Name: Stevie   Date: 25 September

Objective: Stevie will show off his dinosaur to the other children. He will name it, describe it, describe its appearance, and pretend to be a dinosaur.

Materials and Equipment: The dinosaurs the children have made.

Procedures:

Teacher Activities	Student Activities	Time
1. During morning circle time, ask the children who made dinosaurs if they would like to share them with the others.		
2. Wait for answers.	Most children will enthusiastically say "Me, I want to show mine!"	5 min.
3. If Stevie doesn't respond, ask him directly.		
4. Compliment Stevie on what a good dinosaur he made.		
5. Compliment another child or two.		
6. Have children get their dinosaurs.	Children go to shelf where dinosaurs are drying. (Make sure they're dry first.)	2 min.
7. Ask who wants to go first.		
8. Unless Stevie volunteers, pick a more outgoing child to start.	After one or maybe two children share, have Stevie share.	5 min. for each child
9. If Stevie forgets, remind him that he knows the name of his dinosaur, its size, what it eats, and so on.		
10. Thank the children who shared. Remind the rest that they'll have time tomorrow.		

Evaluation:

Figure 11-7 An individual learning plan.

another child in much the same way Hiroku feels important in his relationship with Stevie.

Still another idea might be to ask Stevie to bring one of his favorite books from home to share during storytime. The teacher would have determined, of course, that Stevie has some books at home. She may also have asked his mother if Stevie has one favorite book. Similar to this idea is the sharing of a favorite toy. However, this is not always an appropriate idea, especially if one of the children has no toy to share; a teacher should be careful about encouraging children to bring toys from home. In addition, some children are possessive about their toys and become upset if another child plays with them. Some centers encourage the sharing of toys; but, once the toy has been displayed and explained, it is put away until the child leaves for home. At other centers, if a child brings a toy, then that child is expected to share it. A breakable toy might be shown but it would not be shared.

Let us now assume that our interventions regarding the development of Stevie's sociability have met with some success. What are the next steps? Perhaps we will no longer need to develop an individual learning plan for Stevie. It is quite possible that he will continue to make progress without any special attention. It is also possible that, having made progress in social development, we would want to turn our attention to his emotional or physical development. In order to get a clearer picture of Stevie's development, we might want to use a developmental checklist or a standard test or inventory. (A checklist can be found in the Appendix.)

Developing a Learning Plan for Maya

The easiest, least objectionable way to provide challenging math learning exercises for Maya is to devise a set of new activities for the math learning center. You will, of course, provide activities that the others in the class can succeed in and enjoy, but you will also prepare several advanced activities designed for Maya's special ability, figure 11-8.

OBSERVATION AND CONJECTURE

At the beginning of this chapter we listed, as an objective, the ability to describe the difference between observation and conjecture. We deliberately used both throughout the various observations.

Study the narrative in the first pages of this chapter. The observation starts with a simple description of Stevie entering the day care center one morning. As soon as we state, "He really looks unhappy," however, we are no longer simply describing; we are making an inference about how Stevie must feel based upon how he looks. We are giving an opinion about the child. Opinions based on evidence are conjectures.

On the anecdotal record form (figure 11-2), the column labeled "Comments" is for your conjectures or hypotheses as to why a child or another person may have done something. The column labeled "Description of What Child is Doing" is for description only. Notice that there are no value terms used; any value words are saved for the "Comments" column.

In the fixed-interval or time sampling model (figure 11-4), notice that the student teacher made several value judgments, "*ignores* math 'sponge'," "*quickly completes*," "waves hand *excitedly*," "working *very carefully*" in her use of qualifying words. Her "hypothesis" is that Maya is ignoring the math sponge exercise and so is her assumption that Maya quickly completed it. How did she know Maya had completed the activity? It might have been better for the student teacher to have simply described Maya's behavior and written her conjectures or hypotheses at the bottom. The same mistake is made on the TPIS observation form. How does the student teacher know Maya is "*engrossed*"? Obviously, she is again making an hypothesis or conjecture.

Applications: More about Individual Learning Plans

Although not specifically covered earlier, in preparing an individual learning plan, you must always remember the child's total environment. Let

Child: Maya	Date: 17–28 October
Objective:	Maya will explore addition and subtraction of fractions using fraction tiles. After practice, she will design her own algorithms. (It is possible that Brent, Akiko, Jaynese, Tomas, and Richie are also ready for this exploration in fractions. If so, perhaps Maya can be paired with one of them and work cooperatively on designing problems for the others.)
Materials and equipment:	At least four sets of fraction tiles; simple problems for student practice; direction cards.
Procedures: Anticipatory Set:	Announce to students that there is a new activity involving something called fractions in the Math center for anyone interested to try. Ask the class as a whole if anyone knows what a fraction is. Anticipate several answers. Ask students to explain their reasoning behind any answer they might give.
Instruction:	Ask students who are willing to come to the chalkboard and write their fractions, presenting them in some pictorial way. Have other students ask any questions they may wish to ask regarding what the volunteers have drawn on the board. Readiness to learn fractions will become apparent in the answers.
Guided Practice:	Since the activities are placed at a learning center, guided practice almost becomes a form of independent practice. Students typically work in groups of 2–5 at the math center and assist each other in the learning process. You will also have left the tangram exercises and exercises in addition, subtraction, and multiplication with manipulatives for those students not ready for fractions.
Closure:	At the end of the 2-week trial period with fractions in the math center, you will meet in a small group with those students who have been using the experiences with fractions and ask them what they think they've learned. Depending on answers, you plan to leave the center as is to allow for more independent practice for some and add some new challenges for those who are ready for them.

Figure 11-8 Individual learning plan for Maya.

us take a look at Maria, figure 11-9. Is her behavior a cause of concern? It is important to consider what is normal. Assuming that it is early in September and that Maria is a new student in the center, her behavior of watching others from a distance and playing

| | | Student Teacher: _____ | |
| | | | |

Name of School: _____   Date: _____

Identity Key (do NOT use real name)	Description of What Child is Doing	Time	Comments
M. — Maria T. — Teacher ST. — Student Teacher S. — Susie J. — Janine B. — Bobby Sv. — Stevie	M. arrives at school. Clings to mother's hand, hides behind her skirt. Thumb in mouth.	9:05	Ask T. how long M. has been coming. I bet she's new.
	M. goes over to puzzle rack, chooses a puzzle, goes to table. Dumps out, and works puzzle quickly and quietly. B. & Sv. come over to work puzzles they've chosen. M. looks at them, says nothing, goes to easels, watches S. paint. S. asks M. if she wants to paint. M. doesn't answer.	9:22 9:30	Her eye/hand coordination seems good. I wonder why M. doesn't respond. Ask T. if M. has hearing problem.
	M. comes to snack table, sits down where T. indicates she should. Does not interact with other children at table.	10:15	Is M. ever a quiet child.
	M. stands outside of playhouse, watches S. & J. They don't ask her to join them.	10:47	She looks like she'd like to play.
	M. goes right to swings, knows how to pump.	10:55	Nothing wrong with her coordination.
	During Hap Palmer record M. watches others, does not follow directions.	11:17	Hearing? Maybe limited English? (She looks of Spanish background.)

Figure 11-9 Anecdotal record on Maria.

by herself, figure 11-10, may not be unusual for a marginally bilingual child from a culture in which females are expected to be quiet and nonassertive. Observing quietly at first is normal behavior for many young children. If Maria had been in school for seven or eight months, she might have become more social and acquired a greater knowledge of English. (We are assuming Maria is attending a preschool in which competence in speaking English is encouraged. Some preschools attempt to preserve the child's original language rather than to encourage the use of English.)

What does our observation of Maria suggest in regard to planning for her education? First, it suggests that we want to answer our questions: Is she hard of hearing? Is Spanish her dominant language?

Is she encouraged to be obedient and well-behaved at home? Let us assume that she is not hard of hearing; Spanish is her dominant language; and she is encouraged to be quiet and obedient at home. Now, what are our goals for Maria?

We might want to encourage Maria's interaction with Susie and Janine, two of the more outgoing children in the center, figure 11-11. Because Susie can easily think of something to play with another child, we might suggest that Susie ask Maria to join her in an activity. We should, however, be more cautious with Janine. We know we can pair Maria with Janine at the easels or at the puzzle table, but it might not be a good idea to pair them together at activities such as sociodramatic play unless Susie is present. Janine might be less tolerant of a child who is not fa-

Figure 11-10 When Maria is not watching others play from a distance, she is playing by herself.

Figure 11-11 These two children are good friends and will accept Maria and play with her.

miliar with the English language. In contrast, Susie might even know some Spanish, if there are a number of Spanish-speaking children at the center. You might speak to Maria in Spanish yourself. Undoubtedly your cooperating teacher does.

The Student Teacher's Role

One of the roles of a student teacher is that of an observer. During the first days of placement, the student teacher will often be given time to observe. This is an especially valuable time for both the student teacher and the cooperating teacher. Take advantage of this period. Observe several children carefully; confer with your cooperating teacher and college supervisor regarding which children to observe. After you have completed your observations, discuss them with your cooperating teacher, supervisor, and peers. It is fascinating to listen to someone else's perceptions of your observations. Often we become emotionally involved with the children whom we observe; thus, we can receive a different perspective from those who do not know them as well, or who know them as well as does our cooperating teacher. This situation can be reversed. Many

cooperating teachers know that their judgment of children can be obscured by knowledge of the children's backgrounds. A student teacher's judgment, in contrast, is not affected by this factor.

We are reminded of a time when we were new to a community and had, as one of our students in a kindergarten, a five-year-old named Tony. Not knowing Tony's background, we evaluated his behaviors based on our expectations of and experiences with five-year-olds. Tony was quite ordinary and average. His intellectual, linguistic (language), physical, social, and emotional development were appropriate for his age. He was, in many ways, typical in comparison to other five-year-olds. Later, during our first parent conference, we discovered that Tony's father was the president of a local college. If we had known that fact, it is likely we would have treated Tony as if he was an exceptional child. His physical development was perhaps more advanced; at five, he could skip well, pump himself on a swing, and was beginning to learn how to jump rope. He also had good ball handling skills and could catch and throw competently. (Tony had ample opportunity to swing, jump rope, throw and catch a ball, and learn how to skip because he had an older brother who encouraged him to learn these skills.) We might have expected Tony's language development to be advanced; he was exposed to a sophisticated level of language every day through contact with his father and mother. Regarding social and emotional development, Tony again seemed to be average for his age; he had several friends among the boys of his own age group; he seemed to have the usual amount of curiosity and competence for boys of his age.

If we had known that Tony's father was a college president, we could have expected more from Tony than what he could deliver. What are the results of expecting more than a child can deliver? The child may stop trying to succeed. Another result is that the child may become aggressive and frustrated when asked to accomplish more than the child is able to do.

Assume that Tony is a current student of ours. Should an individual learning plan be developed for Tony? The activities offered to the other children would most likely be appropriate for Tony. Let us also assume we had a conference with his parents. From this meeting, we discovered that they have high hopes for Tony's success in school. In fact, they had placed him in a preschool to increase his "readiness" for kindergarten. They state that since Tony already knows the alphabet letters and sounds, they expect him to begin to learn how to read and want him placed in a preprimer. Since they insist that Tony also knows his numerals to 100, they also expect him to begin to learn addition and subtraction. Furthermore, they expect Tony to become more attentive, to increase his attention span. Tony's parents expressed no interest in Tony's physical learning experiences. They feel that he does not need any specific teaching in terms of physical ability; that, since he has a climbing structure at home, he receives all the physical exercise he needs.

In this hypothetical situation, some of Tony's parents' goals will be met through the regular curriculum. We might honestly feel that some of their other goals are more appropriate for first grade.

Should we tell his parents this? Will they listen?

We can reassure Tony's parents that we share many of the same goals. We can remind them to attend the upcoming Back-to-School Night, at which time the goals and expectations of our program will be explained. We can stress to Tony's parents that helping Tony feel good about himself is as worthwhile a goal as is allowing him time to explore the different activities available in our classroom.

What is the student teacher's role in working with Tony? It could be to give him a one-to-one learning opportunity. The cooperating teacher might ask you to confirm whether or not Tony (and other children as well) recognizes the alphabet letters and sounds and whether he understands the concept of numbers or has simply memorized his numerals from 1 to 100. As a result of your checking how much Tony and any of the other children know and remember from preschool, the cooperating teacher might decide that the parents' expectations are not appropriate. In the meantime, however, in order to let the parents feel more confident about the kindergarten program, the cooperating teacher might assign you to work with Tony on a one-to-one basis. The cooperating teacher may feel that in time Tony's parents will realize that their expectations are unrealistic.

We have suggested thus far that the student teacher has a role in observing children who are chosen by the cooperating teacher, the supervisor, or the student teacher him- or herself. A second role is that of working on a one-to-one basis with an individual child, figure 11-12. The student teacher is also a participant in parent conferences and in-school and out-of-school activities.

Student teachers quite naturally are invited (and urged) to attend functions such as parent education meetings, staff conferences, parent or school-sponsored dinners, and fund-raising events. The student teacher should become a part of the life of the school or day care center.

Conferencing

The student teacher is often included in parent conferences; but, you will want to defer to your co-

Figure 11-12 Working on a one-to-one basis.

operating teacher for the most part. Naturally, if you are asked a direct question by either the parent or teacher, you should answer. Primarily, however, your role will be that of observer rather than participant. You should remember that statements made at a parent conference are confidential. The privacy of parents and children should be respected. Do not repeat anything that was said with others except when appropriate. For example, if your cooperating teacher asks you for your opinions after a conference, you would naturally discuss them. Also, the cooperating teacher might assign you the task of reporting on the conference.

One exception to this rule of confidentiality occurs in student teaching seminars. It is appropriate to discuss your student teaching assignment with your peers and supervisor but not outside the seminar.

Referral Resources

Many schools and early childhood care centers have a list of local resources a student teacher may examine. Most also require parents to list their family doctor and other pertinent emergency information at the time of registration. Frequently, low-cost clinics are used for referrals. The same is true for

dental care. Under PL 99-457, most preschools and centers are expected to refer suspected special needs children for testing to their local elementary school districts, and many also refer, on the request of parents, to private counseling services, educational psychologists, or psychiatrists.

Two other frequently used resources are county child care referral services and child abuse agencies. Your local telephone book will have county office listings. In California, for example, most counties have a Child Care Coordinating Council, or Four C's as it is widely known. Four C's is a resource for all parents and schools, centers, and day care homes. They maintain up-to-date lists of licensed schools, centers, and family day care homes, among other resources listed. Four C's will also assist the newcomer who wants to inquire about licensing a new family day care home. They can provide information on local resources that is not available from other sources. For example, a newcomer with a health handicapped child may know of a national organization but not a local one. Other parents may not know of local chapters because they do not know about the national organization itself. Currently, one of the growing needs of families is after-school child care. Fortunately, many school districts operate on-site after-school care programs. Others contract with their local parks and recreation departments or with local nonprofit organizations such as the YMCA or parent-sponsored groups. Bussing is frequently supplied for children who have to be transported from their school to another facility. Student teachers occasionally are encouraged to become after-school care workers in order to supplement their incomes.

Other referral sources are public and private social services. These services can offer a wide variety of help ranging from food stamps to foster home care to financial aid to Alcoholics Anonymous.

More Examples of Developing Individual Learning Plans

At this point, we would like to present a few other models of individual learning plans so that you can try out different forms to see which works best.

Study figure 11-13. It is a lesson plan for second grade science and focuses on the topic of pets. The classroom contains several pets: a rabbit, a mouse, an aquarium with tropical fish, and a terrarium with a turtle. The cooperating teacher has brought her pet parakeet for the children to observe; and at the end of the week, she is planning a "Pets' Day." Parents have been duly notified; children who wish will bring their pets into the courtyard outside the classroom. Those without pets at home have been provided with several options—using one of the classroom pets and studying it during the week of "Pets'

Day" and reporting on that pet as their own; designing their own special pet and making a clay or papier-maché model of it, specifying what it eats, when it sleeps, and so on; choosing one of the many books about pets, ordinary and unusual, and presenting an oral informational report about the pet they've chosen from the book; and so forth. Extra supervision has been elicited from among the parents who have volunteered for occasional help. And, as the student teacher assigned to the classroom, you have been asked by your cooperating teacher to design an individual plan for Joelle.

Name: Mrs. Gomes
Room: 11   Grade: 2
Subject: Integration of science, literature, language arts, reading, & math

Week: 27
Date: 2–6 May
Theme: Pets

Morning Block:

8:30 am: "Sponge" activity: Writing and drawing in journals.
Sentence starts: "My pet . . ." and "If I had a pet, it would be a . . ." and "If I were a pet, I'd want to be a . . ."

8:45 am: Read: first five pages of *The Biggest Bear* by Lynd Ward.
Ask children to predict what they think will happen next.
In cooperative learning groups, have children write and illustrate what they predict will happen on the next two pages.

9:15 am: Have reporters in each group read what group has predicted. After proofreading, post completed stories on bulletin board.

9:50 am: Recess.

10:00 am: Brainstorming: Have children state what their pets are.
In order to include students with no pets, ask them to say what pet they would like to have or which classroom pet they like best. After the first few pets have been listed, ask children to predict which one seems to be the most popular pet among the students in classroom #11. Write down the prediction at the top of the chalkboard for future reference. As additional pets in any one category are named, keep a tally of them. Have children graph results. Ask children to look at their graphs and see how accurate their prediction of what the most popular pet was.

10:45 am: Snack time. (Lunch at 12:30 pm seems too late for many of the children; so, during "snack time," your cooperating teacher allows students to eat a part of their lunch or to bring a snack if they're having the school-provided lunch. [A unit on nutrition has taught them to bring nutritious snacks].)

11:00 am: Physical Education with PE resource teacher.

11:40 am: If not completed earlier, each cooperative group will proofread and copy their story pages for posting on the bulletin board. Then groups are to choose one pet for further study. Each group should choose a different pet from any other group. Any two groups choosing the same pet will decide cooperatively which one should change. (The class has studied conflict resolution.) After choices are made, group leaders are to go to the in-class library and look for books about their pet. This is an activity that will be carried throughout the week as groups focus on the history of their pet, its foods, its size, its popularity, how it lives in the wild and how it lives in a home, and how it is raised. Students may bring in photographs of their own pets to illustrate the final reports.

(While children are working, my cooperating teacher plays soft classical music in the background. I've noticed that the children seem to enjoy it.)

Figure 11-13 Second grade lesson plan.

Let us assume that Joelle's mother had been suspected of child abuse when Joelle was in first grade and that the teacher had even reported one incident of suspicious bruises to Child Protective Services (CPS). After an investigation, CPS did not feel removal from the home was justified but did recommend counseling for the mother. (The father had deserted the family upon the birth of Joelle's youngest sibling, and your cooperating teacher has told you that Joelle comes from a large family of five children of whom she is the oldest.) In second grade you have noted the following behaviors: Joelle frequently engages in aggressive hitting and kicking on the play yard both before school and during recesses; in the classroom, you have seen her destroy a seatmate's creative writing paper, throw books on the floor, and use foul language. More than once you or your cooperating teacher have had to remind Joelle to handle the classroom pets more gently; you both know that one of the fish died because Joelle removed it from the aquarium "to see what would happen," she said.

Learning Plans. Note in looking at figure 11-14 that the student teacher's individual learning plan is not totally separate from her cooperating teacher's; in-

---

Morning Block: 8:45 am – 12:30 pm

8:30 am: Greet Joelle with a smile when she enters, stay near her desk as students begin journal assignment to help her if she seems to have difficulty getting started and to ask her questions to stimulate her thinking, if this seems necessary. Perhaps ask her if she has a pet and what it is. (I've noticed that Joelle usually arrives at school between 8:30 and 8:35 am and generally settles down initially to write or draw in her journal, so my job here will be to help her with her thoughts and spelling, if she asks, which she has done in the past.)

8:45 am: I'll be reading *The Biggest Bear*; when students are asked for ideas about what they think will happen next, I'll look to see if Joelle has her hand raised and be sure to call on her and, I hope, compliment her response.

Work with Joelle's cooperative learning group. Look for signs of frustration on her part; remind other students in the group that there are no bad ideas. (I've noted that sometimes the others in her group don't listen to Joelle or ignore her input because they sometimes think what she says isn't of value in their eyes. A gentle reminder usually helps.)

If I sense that Joelle is getting ready to explode, I'll urge her to come with me to the back of the room where I've set up a special lesson, related to the topics of pets, she can work on. (I've brought in 25 pounds of clay for students to use in various art projects and I'll urge Joelle to punch and pound the clay to smooth out the air bubbles and make a model of her pet or an imaginary one. The punching and pounding is needed to remove the air bubbles anyway and it should help relieve some of the anger I've seen Joelle display.)

9:50 am: I'll be going out with Joelle to the play yard to try to observe what sets her off. If possible, I hope to be able to intervene before any arguments. I'm going to work with her using some of the ideas from the conflict resolution lessons or other simple ideas like counting to 10 before acting; taking a deep breath; going to another part of the play yard; talking to me; and so on. (I don't know how successful any of these may be, and I'm hopeful too that a reminder of some of the conflict resolution ideas she learned earlier this year may be enough to get Joelle to think before she strikes.)

10:00 am: During this part of the morning, I'll be busy asking the children what kinds of pets they have and writing the categories on the chalkboard. I'll be especially alert to Joelle's participation at this point. If she does not participate and, especially if she makes any negative remarks or looks angry, my cooperative teacher is prepared to take over for me and I'll take Joelle to the art room. (We are fortunate at our school that we have a separate room for art activities that we can not do in the regular classroom. I'm fortunate in that few classes use the art room during the mornings. But, I'll check the schedule when I come to school. If necessary, I'll switch plans and take Joelle to the art room initially and to the back of our room now.) Since I will have already determined what kind of pet Joelle either has or hasn't or what kind of pet she would really like to have, what we'll be doing in the art room is constructing a "home" for her pet with the wood scraps available there. This activity will allow Joelle to pound nails with the hammer and, again, provide her with a way to vent her anger.

10:45 am: If we are still in the art room, I'll ask Joelle if she wants to return to the classroom or stay here for snack time.

11:00 am: PE—Joelle rarely has difficulty during PE because she likes the activities and Mrs. Okahara.

11:40 am: If necessary, accompany Joelle to counselor; otherwise repeat other steps.

Figure 11-14 Learning plan for Joelle—Topic: Pets.

stead, it dovetails with hers. Mrs. Gomes has asked the student teacher to design the integrated unit on pets and added her own suggestions where she has thought it necessary. Notice that although the student teacher is to conduct the brainstorming session, Mrs. Gomes is prepared to take over should Joelle become unruly. This is a cooperative effort on the part of the two; Mrs. Gomes has assigned Joelle to the student teacher in the hope that working on a one-to-one with a new person and being given a choice of narrowly defined activities will demonstrate to Joelle that there are acceptable ways to show anger that do not hurt anyone.

How has Mrs. Gomes arrived at this course of action? First, she has taken into account that many children who are abused are angry and aggressive and that schools see this aggression in fighting behavior on the play yard and destructive behaviors in the classroom. Together with the school counselor, Mrs. Gomes, the student teacher, and the principal have designed the plan for Joelle. (Not every elementary school has a counselor, but this district has made an effort to reduce aggressive acts in schools with a high incidence of vandalism and acts of violence against pupils. One of the reasons behind the district's problem has been the closing of a large manufacturing plant that had employed a majority of the town's workers. Recently there have been a rise in the divorce rate, more cases of alcoholism, and an increasing number of reported child abuse incidents.) This cooperative action works well with students like Joelle who have special needs but who are not, under federal definitions, "children with disabilities."

There will be times when a student teacher is asked to work one-to-one with a "special needs" or "at risk" child. We will cover this in greater detail in our next chapter.

Parent Involvement. We have not discussed in detail the parents' role in the development of an individual learning plan. The best plans are those made with the parents' approval and support. Certainly in the case of Stevie, the mother seems to care and be concerned. Although she may not see any reason to worry about Stevie's social behavior at home, she may be easily persuaded that he could be more social at school.

In Maria's case, her mother might want Maria to learn both English and Spanish. That could be her reason for placing Maria in a "bilingual" center. In writing an individual learning plan for Maria, then, the mother's concern that Maria retain her knowledge of Spanish while learning English must be respected.

In the example of Tony, the problem is possibly that the parents' goals are different than those of the school, at least initially. Assigning the student teacher to work with Tony on a one-to-one basis might be all that is necessary, especially since he is typical for his age.

We have provided a model of an individual plan for a possibly abused second grader, Joelle. As the oldest child of five in a dysfunctional family, she appears to need clear limits, suggestions for alternative actions, and, very likely, more attention from a CARE-ing adult. The clear limits are based upon an analysis (using the Dreiker model) of her aggressive actions as revenge against her mother's suspected abuse that is generalized against all adults in an position of authority. Offering Joelle a choice between two alternatives helps her resolve her need to exert autonomy and recognizes her need for power or control over at least one part of her life. (We would suspect that she has very little power at home.) Not mentioned, but applicable in this example, are the logical consequences that have been arranged for antisocial behavior at this particular school—*isolation* or removal from the class by segregation at the front or back of the room under supervision of a student teacher, aide, or parent volunteer; removal to the art room; removal to talk to the counselor. In each example, the removal does not exclude the student from an assignment as alternatives related to the primary assignment are offered.

You should note in all of our examples that the goal of the school is parent education, as well as child education. Especially in Stevie's and Tony's cases, where the parents' perceptions of the children differ with those of the school, it is important for the teacher and/or director to enable the parent to see more clearly what the child's needs are at school. This is not always easy to accomplish. Sometimes compromises must be made. One such compromise is suggested in the example of Joelle by having the student teacher work with her on a one-to-one basis to establish rapport and provide alternative actions to channel her aggressive tendencies.

SUMMARY

In this chapter we presented several examples of observation techniques. The simplest is the narrative but it also requires the most time. Although it is more complicated, the Teacher/Pupil Interaction Scale (TPIS) takes little time, can be put onto a 3×5 index card, is inconspicuous, and can be supplemented with comments to the side describing the action being noted. Also introduced were the two-dimensional play model and a time sampling model; an anecdotal record form was reviewed. No one form is any better than any other, and student teachers are urged to use their own creativity to devise forms for their own specific uses.

We discussed the development of an individual learning plan for a child. Examples of how an individual plan dovetails with the cooperating teacher's plan were presented. In addition, we discussed the roles of the parent, school, and student teacher in developing and implementing such a plan.

SUGGESTED ACTIVITIES

A. Read *The Children We See* by B. Rowen. Try out some of the observation forms presented. Again, discuss the results of data gathered in terms of effective information received.

B. Select a child, with your cooperating teacher's approval, for whom you will develop an individual learning plan. Implement the plan, and evaluate its effectiveness. Use the form in figure 11-2 or 11-9 or look at the example in figure 12-8.

C. For an overview of how the exceptional student is defined and for activity ideas, read Chapters 1 through 4 in Gearheart, Weishahn, & Gearheart's *The Exceptional Student in the Regular Classroom*, 4th ed. Discuss "special" students with your peers, cooperating teacher, and supervisor. Do you think you have some "special" students in your school or center?

REVIEW

A. List examples of observation techniques, and state at least one reason why each technique is effective.

B. Read the following descriptions of behavior. For each child, analyze and develop a learning plan that contains at least one general behavioral objective.

1. Denise, a five-year-old kindergartner, is sitting on the swing. "Teacher, come push me," she demands. "Try to pump, Denise," responds the teacher. "Don't know how," Denise whines. "Push me, Susan," Denise says to a child going by on a tricycle. "Can't now. Push yourself," answers Susan. Pete comes up to the swing. "Get off and let me swing," he states. "No! My swing!" Denise cries. (Denise looks like she is going to cry.) The teacher's aide comes over and asks, "Do you want me to show you how to make the swing go?" Denise answers, "Please."

2. The following chart was developed by Greg, a student teacher in a first-grade classroom. He was interested in Brian's attending behavior. Starting with the TPIS, he adapted it into a simpler form on which he could check off observations as he noticed them throughout the 9:00 a.m. to 10:00 a.m. activity hour. On a 3×5-inch card which he could hold in the palm, Greg drew a vertical line, dividing the card in half lengthwise. He then wrote "Attending" on the one side, "Nonattending" on

the other. (Question: How much attending behavior should the teacher expect of a six-year-old during a free-choice center activity period? Do Greg's observations appear to provide sufficient information to develop any conjectures about Brian's behavior? What hypotheses might you suggest regarding Brian's sitting under the desk behavior? Discuss the possibilities with your student teacher peers and instructor.) (See figure 11-15.)

3. Johnny, a three-and-a-half-year-old in a morning preschool, is the subject of the third observation. The two-dimensional play model, combining event and time sampling, was used to gather data. (Question: Do three-year-olds do as much onlooking and solitary play as Johnny? Should you be concerned?) (See figure 11-16.)

		Attending		Nonattending
Mon.	9:05	yes (t.i.)*		
	9:16		no	(sitting
	9:27		no	under desk)
	9:40		no	
	9:48	yes (t.i.)		
Tues.	9:07		no	
	9:18		no	
	9:25	yes (t.i.)		
	9:34	yes		
	9:40		no	(sitting
	9:47		no	under the
	9:55		no	desk again)
Wed.	9:02		no	
	9:12	yes (t.i.)		
	9:20	yes (t.i.)		
	9:35		no	
	9:42		no	
	9:58		no	
Thurs.	9:05		no	
	9:15	yes (t.i.)		
	0:00	yoo		
	9:48		no	(back under
	9:55		no	the desk again)
Fri.	Brian was absent			

*t.i. = teacher initiated

Figure 11-15 Attending/Nonattending chart.

4. Jimmy is a four-year-old at a private day care center/nursery school. Figure 11-17 is a time sample of his behavior during outside free play. (Question: Is Jimmy's poor gross motor coordination something about which the teacher should be concerned?)

C. Identify each of the following statements as either inferences or observations.

1. Juan likes to read.
2. Susette has a new dress.
3. Sammy is a mean boy.
4. Kimberly has emotional problems.
5. Janine has a smile on her face.
6. Mikel hit Sandel on the playground.
7. Maria had a frown on her face.
8. Mark looks unhappy.
9. Kathy likes to play with clay.
10. Lupe is an affectionate little girl.

D. Think of one child you are currently trying to help. With a group of classmates discuss what learning outcomes would be visible (seen in the child's behavior or performance) if you succeeded beyond your wildest dreams. List attempts (teaching strategies) that might produce the observable learning and observable changes in the child. Think about environmental factors, scheduling, teacher words or behaviors, planned child activities, and conferences with others as possible teaching strategies.

E. Read the following situations. Then read the statement made by a parent. What would you consider to be an appropriate response? Discuss your responses with your peers, cooperating teacher, and supervisor.

1. One day Tony gets into a fight with Alfredo. As you know, Tony's father is a college president, and his mother a well-educated CPA; however, Alfredo is from a single-parent family. He also belongs to an ethnic and religious minority. The fight was provoked by Alfredo

Child: Johnny			Date: 17 Nov.
	Symbolic	Practice	Games
Onlooking:	Watches 3 girls in playhouse, when asked to join, shakes head No. (9:35 am)	Watches children go up & down slide. (10:22 am)	
	Watches J. & A. at easels. T. asks, "Do you want to paint, J.?" "No." (11:05 am)	Watches children in sandbox, filling cups & pails over & over. (10:35 am)	
		Watches children on swing. (10:45 am)	
Solitary:	"See my cracker? It's a plane!" Zooms cracker thru air; makes plane sounds. (10:03 am)	Sits on swing while teacher's aide pushes. (10:50 am)	
Parallel:	Picks up egg beater at H$_2$O table. Beats H$_2$O. Says, "I'm making eggs for breakfast." (11:12 am)	Picks up paint brush at easel; lets paint drip. Picks up next brush. Repeats with remaining brushes. (11:35 am)	

Figure 11-16 Observation Sample.

who perceives Tony as stuck up. Your cooperating teacher calls both of Tony's parents and asks for a conference. Tony's mother responds immediately and says, "What's going on in your school? How come Tony got assaulted? What are you going to do about it?"

2. Joelle Farmer arrives at school one morning with bruises on her arm. (As mentioned previously, abuse had been reported when Joelle was in first grade.) You suspect that Mrs. Farmer has abused the child again and, with your cooperating teacher's permission, walk with Joelle to the nurse's office. After her examination, the nurse confirms your suspicions and suggests that the police should be notified. "Why don't we call Child Protective Services?" you ask. The school nurse replies, "Since Joelle has been abused before and the investigation by Child Protective Services was inconclusive and, frankly, I think nothing was done, I think we might accomplish more if we call the police. You do know that only the police can remove Joelle from the custody of her mother, don't you?" Returning to Mrs. Gomes's room, you tell her what the nurse has suggested: you are not sure that you should be the person making the phone call to the police. Mrs. Gomes reassures you that she will make the call during the first recess.

10:05 am:	J. runs stiffly toward two of his friends on tricycles. "Let me ride!" he shouts.
10:10 am:	J. is happily riding on the back of E.'s tricycle. E. has to stop to let J. climb on. J. first placed his left foot on, lifted it off, placed the same foot on again, took it off; finally he put his right foot on and then successfully put his left foot on.
10:15 am:	J. is still riding on the back of E.'s tricycle.
10:20 am:	J. and E. have switched places. J. had difficulty pedaling up the slight grade. E. pushed from behind.
10:25 am:	E. has suggested that he, J., and S. go to the work bench. J. picks up the hammer and a nail. He hits the nail awkwardly into a block of wood. E. says, "Hey, watch me! Hold the nail like this!"
10:30 am:	E. is holding J.'s hands with his, showing him how to drive the nail into the block of wood.
10:35 am:	J. is sitting in the sandbox, shoveling sand into a bucket. E. is still at the work bench.
10:40 am:	J. is putting sand into another bucket. He looks surprised when the bucket overflows. He reaches for the first bucket. S. says, "I'm using it now," and pushes a third pail toward J.
10:45 am:	J. and S. are smoothing down the sand, calling it a road. They go and get a couple of cars to run on their road. E. joins them, having completed his project at the work bench.
10:50 am:	When called to clean up for activity time, J. climbs out of the sandbox. As he does this, his foot catches on the edge and he falls down. He gives the sandbox a kick and joins the others to come inside.

Figure 11-17 Observation Time Sample.

Later that morning, Mrs. Farmer storms into the classroom and screams, "Who do you think you are calling the police on me? Are you telling me I beat up my own kid?"

3. You are concerned about Mark's apparent neglect. He arrives at preschool in dirty, torn clothing. His hair would never be combed if it were not done at school; he often smells of stale urine and fecal matter. You discover that his underpants look like they have been worn for a month without having been washed. You ask the cooperating teacher if you and she can make a home visit. The mother says, "No. The mister don't want no one to come when he ain't home." You finally persuade her that it is important to talk about Mark. She reluctantly agrees. After the usual opening remarks, you ask, "Do you have a washing machine at home?" Mark's mother responds negatively, eyes you suspiciously, and asks, "What business is it of yours whether the mister and me has a washing machine?"

4. Kathy Mumford caught your attention for two reasons. First, she is always cocking her head to one side and holding it close to the paper when she draws or writes. You notice she frequently squints when she tries to read material on the chalkboard and has, more than once, copied a math "sponge" problem incorrectly. One day, she even asked you if she could switch seats with Alicia so she could see the side chalkboard more easily. You also have had to repeat directions for Kathy and have noticed that she sometimes asks her seat-mate to re-explain directions to her. You do not have the services of a school nurse, so you call Kathy's mother and ask if she can come to the school for a short conference. In the meantime, you look at Kathy's registration form and doctor's statement. The doctor has noted a slight nearsightedness but no apparent hearing problem. You suspect that Kathy has deficiencies in both, yet you hesitate to contradict Kathy's pediatrician. When Mrs. Mumford arrives, you decide to ask about Kathy's behavior at home. Mrs. Mumford admits that Kathy does sit close to the television and seems inattentive at times. "I thought Kathy might have a problem hearing but Mr. Mumford, he put an end to Kathy's not hearing. You know what he did? He sat in the kitchen while she was in the family room and whispered, 'Kathy, do you want some ice cream, honey?' Well, Kathy answered right away! Mr. Mumford and I both think Kathy just gets too involved in things. She's not deaf!"

5. Josip is one of those students who never sits still for a minute. He moves around constantly from the moment he enters the child care center until naptime, when he must be urged strongly to lie down. Naptime is agony for Josip; he twists and turns, grumbles, sighs to himself, and disturbs everyone around him. Yet, when he does fall asleep, you have difficulty awakening him. Sometimes, in fact, your cooperating teacher has allowed him to continue to sleep. You think Josip may not get enough sleep at night and decide, with your cooperating teacher's approval, to ask his mother about it. "Mrs. Milutin, when does Josip go to bed?" you ask. "Sometimes he really takes a long nap at school."

Mrs. Milutin responds, "Well, of course he sleeps at school! That is why his father and I cannot get him to sleep at home! Maybe if you do not allow Josip to sleep at school, he will sleep better at home!"

F. For each of the five children in the preceding review activity, write an appropriate behavioral objective for an individual learning plan in the curriculum area indicated.

1. Tony will be able to . . .

(An objective related to learning the letters in his name)

2. Joelle will be able to . . .

(An objective related to writing a short paragraph about her pet)

3. Maya will be able to . . .

    (An objective related to her creating at least 2 original tangrams)

4. Kathy will be able to . . .

    (An objective related to classifying at least five common fruits and vegetables in the proper class)

5. Josip will be able to . . .

    (An objective related to trying at least two or three foods which are new to him)

REFERENCES

Gearheart, B. R., Weishahn, M. W., & Gearheart, C. J. (1996). *The exceptional student in the regular classroom* (6th ed.). New York: Merrill/Macmillan.

Parten, M. B. (1932). Social participation among preschool children. *Journal of Abnormal and Social Psychology, 33,* 243–269.

Piaget, J. (1962). *Play, dreams and imitation in childhood.* New York: W. W. Norton & Co., Inc.

RESOURCES

Almy, M., & Genishi, C. (1979). *Ways of studying children* (rev. ed.) New York: Teachers College Press.

Barrett, D. E. (1979). A naturalistic study of sex differences in children's aggression. *Merrill-Palmer Quarterly, 25,* 192–203.

Barrett, D. E., & Yarrow, M. R. (1977). Prosocial behavior, social inferential ability, and assertiveness in children. *Child Development, 48,* 475–481.

Benjamin, A. C. (September 1994). Observations in early childhood classrooms: Advice from the field. *Young Children, 49*(6), 14–20.

Bentzen, W. R. (1997). *Seeing young children: A guide to observing and recording behavior* (3rd ed.). Albany, NY: Delmar.

Brandt, R. M. (1972). *Studying behavior in natural settings.* New York: Holt, Rinehart, & Winston.

Cartwright, D., & Cartwright, G. (1974). *Developing observational skills.* New York: McGraw-Hill.

Cohen, D., & Stern, V. (1970). *Observing and recording the behavior of young children.* New York: Teachers College Press.

Cohen, D. H., & Stern, V. (1978). *Observing and recording the behavior of young children* (2nd ed.). New York: Teachers College Press.

Cummings, E. M., Iannotti, R. J., & Zahn-Waxler, C. (1985). Influence of conflict between adults on the emotions and aggression of young children. *Developmental Psychology, 21,* 495–507.

Irwin, D. M., & Bushnell, M. M. (1980). *Observational strategies for child study.* New York: Holt, Rinehart, & Winston.

Phinney, J. S. (1982). Observing young children: Ideas for teachers. *Young Children, 37,* 16–24.

Richarz, A. S. (1980). *Understanding children through observation.* New York: West Publishing.

Weaver, S. J. (1984). *Testing children.* Kansas City, MO: Test Corporation of America.

12

Working with Children with Disabilities

After completing this chapter, the student will be able to:

- Define "special."
- List at least five characteristics of "special" children.
- State the categories of "special need" according to the Individuals with Disabilities Education Act, PL 101-476.
- Discuss the concept of "least restrictive environment."
- Discuss the implications of "least restrictive environment" to the teacher of an early childhood program.
- Discuss the implications of recent special education laws for preschools, child care centers, and elementary schools.

Just when I thought I knew the characteristics of two-year-olds well, along came Gregory! He taught me to look for new ways to reach individual children.

Danielle Tracy

I was asked to work with one of the children who had a learning disability. I really got involved in what was happening in the child's home. I became interested in the child's life.

Deanna Miller

I need a lot more course work and training in handling children. What I try is to wait until a shy child gets used to me before starting an individual conversation. I purposely plan quiet times to balance active, vigorous classroom activities.

Kim Pailsey

● LAWS RELATING TO THE EDUCATION OF YOUNG CHILDREN WITH "SPECIAL NEEDS"

We know that most of you think that all children are special; we do also. However, it is important to recognize that some children have needs beyond those of the average child; some have needs that can be met only by a team of specialists working together for the welfare of the children. To meet the needs of "special" children, the federal government passed into law the Education for All Handicapped

Children Act, Public Law 94-142, in 1975. Every state was given a deadline of fall 1977 to implement this law with legislation of its own.

The Education of All Handicapped Children Act, PL 94-142

According to PL 94-142, handicapped children are defined as follows:

> Sec 121a.5 Handicapped children.
>
> (a) As used in this part, the term "handicapped children" means those children evaluated in accordance with sections 121.a530-121.a.534 as being mentally retarded, hard of hearing, deaf, speech impaired, visually handicapped, seriously emotionally disturbed, orthopedically impaired, other health impaired, deaf-blind, multi-handicapped, or as having specific learning disabilities, who because of those impairments need special education and related services.

Public Law 94-142 provides a "free, public education" for all handicapped children between the ages of five and 21. The law further guarantees the right of every citizen to have available a "full educational opportunity" (Section 613).

What are the mandates of PL 94-142?

- A free and appropriate public education, including special education and related services, for all handicapped children ages five to 21; programs for children ages three to five if mandated by state law.

    Special education is defined as instruction specially designed to meet the unique needs of handicapped children. It may include classroom instruction, physical education, home and hospital instruction, and institutional instruction. (Physical education was often omitted from the curriculum in special classes, especially those for children with orthopedic handicaps. It was felt that the physical and/or occupational therapy they received was equivalent to physical education. According to the intent, it is not.)

    Related services are those commonly referred to as support services: speech therapy, psychological counseling, vocational counseling, transportation, etc.

- The law makes a distinction between *first priority* and *second priority* children. First priority children are those with severe handicaps within any disability who are not receiving an adequate education. For example, local public education districts traditionally did not educate the severely emotionally disturbed, the severely mentally retarded, or even the deaf, blind, or deaf-blind. These children were normally educated, if at all, in state or private institutions.

- Parents must be informed about the projected evaluation of their children. This must be done in writing and in the parents' native language. The parents must be involved and give permission at every step of the process of identification, evaluation, educational placement, and evaluation of that placement. They have the right to see all files, observations, tests, etc., administered to their children. They may question an evaluation and ask for a second opinion. (The law is unclear about who is responsible for a second evaluation, the district or the parent.)

- Each child identified as needing special education or related services must have an Individual Education Program (IEP) approved by the parents. This program includes short- and long-range objectives for the child, specific materials that will be used, the time in which the objective is to be accomplished, and the name of the individual responsible for its implementation and evaluation. The IEP must be evaluated at least once each year.

- Each child is to be placed in the "least restrictive environment," figures 12-1, 12-2, and 12-3. What is "least restrictive" for one child may not be for another. For example, a child with severe cerebral palsy of the athetoid type (limp, twitchy muscles) who is strapped into a wheelchair and cannot communicate may not belong in a regular classroom until that child acquires the ability to communicate. At this point, assuming the child *can* communicate with peers, the child might properly be placed in the regular class and receive the related services of speech therapy, physical therapy, occupational therapy, and adapted physical

Figure 12-1 The "least restrictive environment" may be having the child sit in a special chair . . . (Courtesy of Jody Boyd)

dominant language, if he or she has a limited knowledge of English or is non-English speaking.

• Provisions are included for the appointment of a *surrogate* or substitute in cases when a parent refuses to participate or is unable to participate in the process.

Implications of Public Law 94-142

It is clear that PL 94-142 includes early childhood education. For this reason, you may find some "special" or handicapped children at your school or center. If you are in a Head Start class, or any publicly funded program, for example, it is important to remember that they must serve identified handicapped children. The preschool, kindergarten, and primary classrooms are appropriate for many "special" children. Children with orthopedic problems can fit quite comfortably into a regular classroom as long as the classroom is accessible. (Accessibility is

education. Assuming no mental defect, the regular classroom teacher may need no special materials in the classroom other than a book holder and a raised desk that would fit over the child's wheelchair, with a clasp to hold the child's papers.

• Due process is guaranteed for every child and family. The parents have the right to sue the district if they feel that the best interests of their child are not being served. For example, a mentally retarded child could be recommended for placement in a special day class. The parents may feel that the child can remain in the regular class for many activities such as art, music, physical education, lunch, and recess; the district may feel otherwise. The parent then may sue the district for what they perceive to be the inappropriate placement of the child.

• Evaluation of the child must be done with instruments that are nondiscriminatory in terms of race and ethnicity. Testing must also be in the child's

Figure 12-2 . . . or it may be having the physical therapist position the child's head while the child uses his/her arms . . . (Courtesy of Jody Boyd)

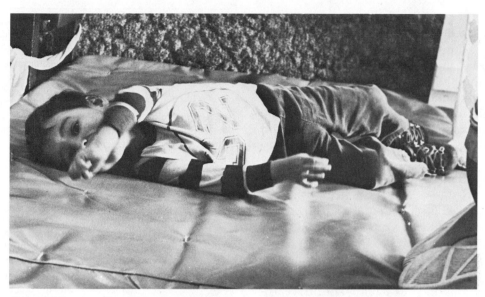

Figure 12-3 . . . or it may be letting the child roll free on a mat. (Courtesy of Jody Boyd)

covered by PL 93-380, Section 504.) A lack of wheelchair ramps is not considered to be a valid excuse for not admitting a child in a wheelchair. Children with partial sight, children who are hard of hearing, and children with mild retardation and emotional problems can be placed in "normal" preschool, kindergarten, or primary classrooms. They can overcome their limitations, figure 12-4.

Both the "special" and "normal" child profit from association with each other. In one case involving a child who was hard of hearing, all of the children learned sign language in order to communicate better with that child. In fact, the children learned sign language faster than the teacher! In another example, a behavior-disordered (depressive) child was placed in a regular preschool. The children quickly learned to tolerate temper tantrums and screaming. To a visiting stranger, they would explain, "Don't worry about Richie. He just needs to be alone now." In many ways the children were more tolerant than some of the parents.

Special children are no different than any other child; if you meet them with kindness and CARE, they will reciprocate. Mildly mentally retarded chil-

Figure 12-4 Children can overcome physical limitations. (Courtesy of Jody Boyd)

dren often integrate well into the preschool setting. They often have good social development, and their physical development may be almost normal. Their language may be simpler than that of peers, but they often make their needs known through body language. They may not be able to do some of the cognitive tasks well, but they can derive as much pleasure from painting, role playing, and playing with clay, blocks, and trucks as any other child. Knowing that this child is less able cognitively than some of the other children, you can work with activities the child *can* do successfully and reduce the amount of stress associated with goals that are too high. One private preschool has a policy to integrate "special" and "normal" children. The director allow four identified "special" children in a class of 24. Over the period of 20 years since this policy has been in effect, the school has taught mentally retarded children, children with orthopedic problems, and partially sighted, hard of hearing, emotionally disturbed, speech-impaired, and health-impaired children, as well as other children who were not as yet identified as having specific learning disabilities. With parental permission, other children can learn to help orthopedically impaired children with bathroom visits and other activities—both children profit.

Other Public Laws

PL 94-142 was just one of many laws pertaining to the education of young children with "special needs" (a preferable term to "handicapped" and one you will find used throughout this chapter). In fact, special education for preschool children with special needs is more than 30 years old. Figure 12-5 summarizes the laws, related to special education services for young children, passed since 1965.

Implications of Public Law 99-457

PL 99-457 contains some of the same features found in PL 94-142: the provision that school districts must provide a free, appropriate, public education for all identified three- to five-year-olds; an individualized education plan (IEP) for each identified handicapped child, placement in the "least restrictive environment"; due process protection; and nondiscriminatory testing and confidentiality.

The principal difference is the recognition of the need for family involvement if a preschooler is to be helped to achieve his or her full developmental po-

PL 89-313 (1965)	Provided federal funds to establish early intervention programs for "children with disabilities," birth to age five. (Voluntary.)
PL 90-538 (1968)	Established the Handicapped Children's Early Education Program (HCEEP), now the Early Education Program for Children with Disabilities (EEPCD). (Voluntary initially.)
PL 91-230 (1969)	Provided funds to states for the education of "young children with disabilities." (Voluntary.)
PL 93-644 (1974)	Amended Head Start legislation and required that 10 percent of children served must be those with disabilities.
PL 94-142 (1975)	The Education for All Handicapped Children Act; discussed in detail in this chapter.
PL 98-199 (1983)	Provided grants to states to plan, develop, and implement a service delivery system for handicapped children, birth through age five. (Mandatory for states receiving federal funds.)
PL 99-457 (1986)	Again provided funds to states to plan services for children, birth through age five, as a condition to receiving further federal funds. (Essentially, then, became mandatory.) Also discussed in this chapter.
PL 101-336 (1990)	Americans with Disabilities Act: Required that individuals with disabilities, including children, have equal access to public and private services.
PL 101-476 (1990)	The Individuals with Disabilities Act (IDEA); discussed in this chapter.
PL 102-119 (1991)	Allowed states up to two years to implement PL 101-476 (IDEA), because of differences between fiscal years of some states and federal government.

Figure 12-5 Public laws related to special education for young children.

tential. Under PL 99-457 the IEP is changed to an Individual Family Service Plan (IFSP) in recognition that programs for the very young require parent involvement as much as, if not more so, than that of the multidisciplinary team. A second difference is the provision of state grant programs for infants and toddlers with assistance to be given "in planning, developing, and implementing a statewide system of comprehensive, coordinated, multidisciplinary, interagency programs" (Bauer and Shea, 1990, p. 10). A third difference, recognizing the difficulty of being able to pinpoint specific diagnoses with the very young, is the release from the requirement to label categorically. Thus, the very young child being serviced under PL 99-457 does not have to be specifically labeled, as under PL 94-142, to receive services.

The implications for preschools and children's centers are obvious. Early diagnosis is encouraged and enhanced, and public school districts are to provide services to preschools and children's centers. One word of caution: school districts have found special education to be almost prohibitively expensive and the federal government has never completely funded it. States, then, under the threat of losing all of their federal monies, have had to make up the difference. The result has been the *encroachment* into monies for regular education to fund special education. Directors and teachers of preschool and children's centers need to recognize a school district's reluctance to provide services, then, for any but the severely handicapped. They need also understand that school districts will only provide services to children who are residents of their specific districts. Since many children are placed in day care centers, and to a lesser extent in preschools, located in communities other than the one where they live, the school district near the center may refuse to provide services and inform the center that they must contact the district where the child's family resides.

The preschool mentioned before began to allow "special needs" students to enroll soon after the implementation of PL 94-142. The preschool itself was located in a school district that provided services to three- to five-year-olds resident in the district. Of four "special needs" children admitted one year, the parents of a child with mild cerebral palsy informed the director that they had been paying for all of their child's special needs—specifically, speech therapy, occupational therapy, and physical therapy. The director was surprised and suggested that the school district should be responsible now that the child was four. The director had already made arrangements for two children in the preschool to receive the services of a speech therapist from the local district, so she informed the district's director of special services that there would now be three children to ser-

vice. However, when the child's address was checked, the preschool director was informed that the child lived, by one block, in another district. When the second district was contacted, the preschool director was told that they had no services for preschoolers; thus, even though a speech therapist from the first school district was already servicing children at the preschool, the needs of this particular child were not being met. Under PL 99-457 this could not happen as the child's home district now has to provide the services.

Individuals with Disabilities Education Act, PL 101-476

With the passage in 1990 of IDEA, not only were the provisions of PL 94-142 and its amendments incorporated into the new law, but the term *handicapped* became *children with disabilities.* Added to the law was a provision for children whose first language or mode of communication might not be English. Two more categories of special needs were defined by PL 101-576, children with autism and children with traumatic brain injuries. Three additional services were also included: rehabilitation counseling, social work services, and spoken descriptions of on-screen video productions (DVS) that are provided over the second of two audio channels on stereo television sets.

Prior to the passage of PL 101-476, PL 101-336 (1990), known as the Americans with Disabilities Act, became law. The Americans with Disabilities Act is "major civil rights legislation that extends beyond educational issues. Specifically, it requires that individuals with disabilities have equal access and reasonable accommodations to public and private services, including equal access to enrollment in early childhood facilities" (Wolery and Wilbers, 1994, p. 19).

In 1991, amendments to IDEA were passed. PL 102-119 allows states extra time, sometimes as long as two years, to implement their programs. These amendments became necessary because the federal fiscal year differs from that of most states; thus, for states with a fiscal year ending on June 30, planning to implement a federally funded program that was not budgeted until October was difficult. In addition to allowing states extended time for implementation of programs, PL 102-119 stipulated that states were to seek to serve traditionally underserved special needs populations—"particularly minority, low-income, inner city, and rural populations" (Bowe, 1995, p. 434). Another thrust has been the trend toward "full inclusion," that is, the inclusion of special needs children into classes and environments with their non-disabled peers.

A Final Word on the Implications of the Public Laws

It is clear that the public laws include early childhood education. For this reason, you are likely to find some special needs children in your school or center.

"Special" Children

"Special" children are as different from each other as are "normal" children, but not all "special" children are easily recognizable, figure 12-6. There are signs that can help you identify a "special" child. Does "Johnny" hold his head to one side constantly? Does he squint? (He may need glasses.) Does he ignore directions unless you are close to him and facing him? Is his speech unclear? (He may have a hearing problem.) Does the child have frequent bouts with *otitis media*, a middle ear infection?

Is the child not learning to talk at the same rate as his peers? (He may have a problem of language delay.) Is she still using baby talk when most of her peers have outgrown it? (She may have a speech problem.) Is he frequently out of breath? Does he sneeze often? (He may have an allergy that should be properly diagnosed by a doctor. Fortunately, most health problems are diagnosed by family doctors; your role might simply be to monitor the child's medication if the doctor asks you. Children taking medication often have to be observed to decide if the dosage is appropriate; doctors must know if the child's behavior changes in any way, such as increased drowsiness or irritability.)

Figure 12-6 Not all "special" children are easily recognizable.

Is the child extremely aggressive or withdrawn? (She may be emotionally disturbed.) Is the child extremely active? Does he have a short attention span? Is he easily distracted? Does he have problems with cause and effect relationships? Does he have difficulty in putting his thoughts into words? (He may have a learning disability.) Is the child much slower than her peers in talking and completing cognitive work such as classifying objects? (She may be mildly mentally retarded.) It is important to note that these characteristics are only indications of the problem, not solid evidence that the problem does exist. Only a qualified person can make the actual determination.

Do you have a child at your center who is talking in sentences at age two or two-and-a-half? Is this child larger, taller, and heavier than other children of the same age? Does this child enjoy excellent health? Does he or she already know the names of the primary and secondary colors? Does the child already know the letters in his or her name? Does this child see relationships between seemingly unrelated objects? This child may be special in the sense of being gifted or talented.

Working with the "Special" Child

In general, working with the "special" child is not much different than working with the "normal" child. Your cooperating teacher will, in most instances, give you clues for teaching a "special" child.

The child with a speech or language impairment may need one-to-one tutoring, figure 12-7. An early indication of a hearing impairment is lack of language skills or unclear speech. If you suspect a child has a hearing loss, you should discuss your perceptions with your cooperating teacher. She may suggest to the parent that the hearing be checked. If the child is experiencing language delay, it may be because the parent has not spent much time talking to the child. Indeed, some children speak in what sounds like "television language." You should provide these children with opportunities to use verbal language. You may need to name objects for them and provide them with descriptive adjectives. You may play several language activities with these chil-

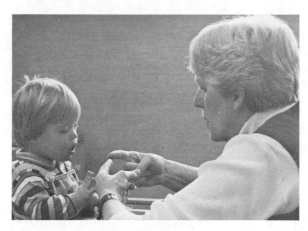

Figure 12-7 It is common to work one-to-one with a "special" child. (Courtesy of Jody Boyd)

dren such as feelie-box games and guessing games in which they describe and use language.

The mentally retarded child may need no special attention beyond your being attuned to activities that may be frustrating. Your teacher may ask you to assist the child in certain activities known to be more difficult. For example, during a fingerplay, you may be asked to hold the child on your lap and to manipulate the child's fingers. The mentally retarded child might also need some extra help in language; slow language development is often a characteristic of a mentally retarded child.

You may experience greater difficulty in working with the behavior disordered and the learning disabled child. This is because it is sometimes difficult to identify a child who has behavior problems or a learning disability.

Non-English-Proficient Children

Children of immigrant and refugee families are increasingly represented in classrooms. Their numbers are expected to grow dramatically during the next decade. Often termed "children of color," they include Hispanics, Asians, Pacific Islanders, and others.

Student teachers may face the immediate task of communicating acceptance and respect to children with varying degrees of standard English proficiency. No single description fits these children. They are widely diverse. Teachers strive to decrease children's feelings of alienation and isolation, if it exists (Thonis, 1990). Many of these children have backgrounds and cultural understandings that can be tapped as classroom resources.

Student teachers need to become familiar with the specific planning and program(s) for students who do not understand and/or speak English. Planning is based upon the following assessments:

- How proficient is the child in the language of the home?
- Can the child understand and speak English?
- Is the child's language and speech appropriate for his or her age?
- What degree of comfort or discomfort is present at school?
- What experiences are developmentally appropriate for this child?

Commonly Used Tests

Retardation is easily measured with any well-known standard intelligence test. Despite the fact that intelligence testing (often called IQ testing for Intelligence Quotient, a figure based upon the standard deviation of the norm group and 100 as the mean or average) has come under fire over the past 15 to 20 years, its use is still widespread. As a tool in understanding the child's intellectual development in regard to predicting possible success in school, the IQ test provides valuable information. Combined with other measures of a child's development (such as the checklist previously referred to and found in the Appendix), the IQ test can provide a differential picture of the child's school-related abilities. One major drawback to the Stanford-Binet is its verbal emphasis. The Wechsler Intelligence Scale for Children and the Wechsler Preschool/Primary Intelligence Scale attempt to provide both verbal and performance measures of intelligence. However, both of these tests may discriminate against a child from a racial and/or cultural minority. Even though both have been translated into other languages, there is still the question of appropriateness. For most preschools, a developmental checklist provides as good or better information than an IQ test. The major advantage to the IQ test, of course, is in its use in diagnosing mental retardation. It seldom, however, provides clues regarding how to work with the child who is diagnosed as retarded.

If we use a developmental checklist (see Appendix), which relies upon our observation of the child, we can develop a learning plan based upon what we see. Noting that a three-year-old child can walk upstairs alternating the feet, but walks downstairs one foot at a time, we might have the child hold our hand at first. Then we can have the child hold onto a railing. Finally, we can urge the child to try without any support. If we note that a child is still speaking two-word sentences, we can provide for more language experiences on a one-to-one basis. In every case we should not urge the child to accomplish tasks that are not appropriate to his or her developmental level. The child who cannot gallop will not learn to skip; but perhaps the child is ready to learn how to slide one foot after the other sideways.

There is probably no area more controversial than that involving behavioral difficulties. Many teachers may think a child is emotionally disturbed but do not know how to approach a parent. The term "behavior disorders" is more commonly used now to indicate children who have problems of behavior but who may not, in terms of a psychiatric definition, be truly "emotionally disturbed." Often, when you see a young child with behavior problems, you are likely to see a family with problems. The term dysfunctional is sometimes used to describe families with problems that affect their children. To many parents, even the suggestion of a behavior problem with their child brings about a defensive reaction, such as, "Are you telling me I'm a bad parent? That I don't know how to raise my own child?" Teachers and administrators attempt to avoid value-laden terms that may arouse a defensive reaction in parents and, instead, will substitute terminology such as "acts out," "has no friends," "daydreams," or "fights" or "tries to hide in the back of the room." We have to understand how difficult it is for a parent to accept the possibility that something may be wrong with the child. If the parents have no idea that the child is not perfectly "normal," it becomes extremely difficult to convince them that there may be a problem.

Facing the possibility that their child may not be perfect, some parents actually grieve for the lost image of what their child was to have been. They grieve in much the same way they would grieve if the child had died. They become angry and accuse us of prejudice, of not really knowing their child. Some parents verbally attack our skills and suggested diagnosis; others deny that anything is wrong. Most go through a period in which they blame themselves for causing the child's problems. In some instances, we may feel that they are indeed responsible for the problems of the child, and we must be careful not to prejudge.

The child with a behavior disorder may or may not present a problem in the classroom. Certainly the aggressive child presents a challenge and must be watched closely. For this reason, it is not uncommon for the teacher to assign an aide or student teacher to work on a one-to-one basis with the child to try to control the child's outbursts. Holding the child on your lap, allowing the child to hit a weighted clown doll instead of a child or adult, removing a child to the back of a classroom or "benching" on the play yard, allowing the child to punch clay or pound nails into scrap wood instead of hurting another person, having the child bite on a leather strap or chew a wad of sugarless bubblegum when he or she feels like biting, having the child run around the playground when he or she feels like exploding are all good techniques. Remember that behavior modification works well with children who are behavior disordered.

You should be aware that as the withdrawn, depressed child becomes better, he or she is likely to become aggressive. This is known as the pendulum effect. When a depressed child reaches this stage and begins to act out, some parents become angry and fearful; they stop therapy, not understanding that the child must release the pent-up anger. They do not understand that it will take time for the child to learn how to deal with anger in socially accept-able ways. We can reassure the parent that this phase is normal for the child. We can also be alert for signs that the child needs to be alone to stomp, yell, throw, and hit without hurting anyone. In some schools, the child may be directed to go to another room where the child can throw nerf balls, pound on clay, or hit a weighted clown doll. In others, there may be a "time out" corner in which the child will be told to sit until he or she feels ready to rejoin the group. Whatever the technique used, you may be asked to remain with the child for safety purposes. At the same time, you can acknowledge the child's anger and suggest ways in which the child can channel it in a positive direction.

The child suspected of having learning disabilities presents a challenge. While some parents are willing to accept a diagnosis of possible learning disabilities, others are not. What is a learning disability? According to PL 94-142 a "specific learning disability"

> . . . means a disorder in one or more of the basic psychological processes involved in understanding or in using language, spoken or written, which may manifest itself in an imperfect ability to listen, think, speak, read, write, spell, or do mathematical calculations. The term includes such conditions as perceptual handicaps, brain injury, minimal brain dysfunction, dyslexia, and developmental aphasia. The term does not include children who have learning problems which are primarily the result of visual, hearing, or motor handicaps, or mental retardation, of emotional disturbance, or of environmental, cultural, or economic disadvantage. (Federal Register, 1977, 300.5)

School districts commonly define a learning disability in terms of a child's actual achievement in relation to what the achievement is of his or her age peers. The unfortunate result of this practice has been postponing the identification of a student until he or she is two or more years behind age peers, a practice that has meant, in too many cases, three and even four years of failure for the child. The damage to the child's self-esteem can be almost irreparable. Another commonly used definition is that a learning disability is reflected as a significant discrepancy between the child's potential ability and his or her actual achievement in learning to read, write, or figure. The curriculum areas of reading, language arts, and mathematics are most typically involved.

Does this mean that a preschooler does not have a learning disability? Many preschool teachers, parents, and educational psychologists who are capable diagnosticians would disagree. Cruikshank (1986) has attempted to develop a definition that is not dependent upon school achievement:

> Specific learning disabilities is a chronic condition of presumed neurological origin which selectively interferes with the development, integration, and/or demonstration of verbal and/or nonverbal abilities. Specific learning disabilities exist as a distinct handicapping condition in the presence of average to superior intelligence, adequate sensory and motor systems, and adequate learning opportunities. The condition varies in its manifestations and in degree of severity. Throughout life the condition can affect self-esteem, education, socialization, and/or daily living activities. (1986, p. 2)

What are some of the characteristics you might see in a preschooler that could signal the possibility of a learning disability? Typically, you see a child who appears immature; who frequently has difficulties with language, both receptive and expressive; who acts impulsively; and who may seem to be "hyperactive." (Be careful about calling a child hyperactive, though; be aware that being a high-energy child does not necessarily mean hyperactive.) Look at Cruikshank's definition: does the child in your preschool have difficulty using language? Does he use unreferenced pronouns because he can't remember what the object's name is? Is this the child who can't think of more than one word to describe an object in a "feelie" box or repeats a word a playmate has just used instead of coming up with her own? Does this child display poor coordination for her age? Does the child have difficulty following simple requests? Does he dislike changes in the routines of the preschool? Does the four-year-old child prefer interacting with the three-year-olds more

than with the children her own age? Is the four-year-old child unable to tell what letter you've drawn on his back, indicating difficulty transferring from a tactile to a visual image? Do you have to remind this child constantly of the rules from day to day? None of these characteristics by itself would be symptomatic of a possible learning disability; taken together and being seen daily might be cause for suggesting a more formal evaluation by a qualified expert in learning disabilities. In the meantime, the child's parents may ask your cooperating teacher if she can arrange for some one-on-one learning for their child. In turn, the cooperating teacher may ask them to attend a conference involving everyone who works with the child to develop an individual learning plan that will involve them all, figure 12-8. (See Appendix for checklists to use to determine modality strengths and weaknesses.)

Other investigators and researchers, notably Kirk (1972), Cruikshank (1977), and Kephart (1967) strongly believe that learning disabilities are a true category. Kirk even defined them as a disturbance in the perceptual processes of the child; the child's vision is fine but what the child sees is distorted in relation to what others see. Likewise, another child might hear perfectly well but does not process or attend to auditory stimuli. Still another child might not have good coordination; thus the child's kinesthetic sense seems disturbed. There is some evidence to suggest that the learning disabled child may have perceptual deficits, but there is also evidence to suggest that diet (Feingold, 1975), disorders of input and/or output, disorders of verbal and nonverbal learning (Meyen, 1978), and even brain functioning may be at fault (Strauss & Lehtinen, 1947).

Attention Deficit Disorder (ADD)

One category in special education often seen in child care and schools today is attention deficit disorder (ADD) and attention deficit with hyperactivity disorder (ADHD). The Diagnostic and Statistical Manual of Mental Disorders, 4th edition (DSM-IV, 1994), recognizes three kinds of attention disorders: the previously mentioned ADD and ADHD plus a third, an unspecified attention disorder. As with

SCHOOL: ABC Preschool   STUDENT'S NAME: Tommy   C.A.: 43   DATE: 14 Oct

LONG-RANGE GOAL: Tommy will expand his vocabulary both at school and at home.

FUNCTIONAL DESCRIPTION OF THE PROBLEM: Tommy speaks in telegraphic sentences; his language is frequently unintelligible, which has led to interpersonal problems with peers. Assessments by School District DEF shows that Tommy is developmentally normal on all criteria except language. His pediatrician's report shows no difficulty with hearing but a severe case of pneumonia when Tommy was 8 mo., followed by a relapse at 9 mo. Tommy's mother admits overprotecting him and worrying about his frequent bouts with upper respiratory infections. Tommy's attention span appears short relative to peers at ABC Preschool.

BEHAVIORAL STRENGTHS: Tommy is agile and well coordinated.

SHORT-TERM OBJECTIVES	INTERVENTION ACTIVITIES AND MATERIALS	PERSON(S) RESPONSIBLE
(Section 3153, Title V Regulations) (Specify time, specific behavior, evaluation conditions & criteria)		
1. Tommy will use 3–4 word sentences when talking in the classroom. (6 mo.)	ST or aide will model speaking in complete sentences & ask child to repeat model; "Feelie Box" will be used on 1:1	Teacher, with assistance of ST or aide
4. Tommy will retell stories using complete sentences of 3–4 words (8 mo.)	Mother or father will read to boy each evening before bed, model complete sentence construction & have him repeat or construct his own sentences	Parents
6. Tommy will practice using sentences under guidance of District DEF's speech therapist. Word lotto games, etc., will also be used. (6 mo.)	Peabody Early Experiences Kit	Speech & language therapist
9. Mr. & Mrs. Fabian will be offered an opportunity to participate in LDA (Learning Disabilities Association) support group & to receive counseling. (on-going)	District DEF psychologist gives parents information regarding County LDA support group; may ask LDA to call parents	DEF School Dist. psychologist

CRITERION MEASURE without modeling or prompting. Tommy will be speaking in 3–4 word complete sentences.

Reviewed: _____
_____
                                                        Speech Therapist

_____
                                                        Teacher

Revision(s) Recommended:
                                                        School Psychologist
_____
                                                        Date: _____

_____
(Parent 1)   (Parent 2)

Figure 12-8 Part of an individual family services plan.

learning disabilities, there are some who believe ADD and ADHD are simply labels for children whose temperament runs at a faster rate than "normal" (Bee, 1989; Reid, Maag, & Vasa, 1994).

Children with ADD typically have difficulty concentrating for prolonged periods of time, some even for five or 10 minutes. For some of these children taking a stimulant drug such as ritalin, dexadrine, or cylert appears to help. For others, especially those allergic to drug therapy, specifically designed computer games appear to help.

If you have children with ADD in your center or classroom, one proven way to work with them is to keep them busy. Allowing them the freedom to move from one center to another is another way. However, a room with many choices may be difficult for ADD children; in many ways they need less stimulation rather than more. You may have to suggest gently to the child that he or she choose one of two options. "I notice no one is painting at one of the easels and I also notice that your friend Jean Pierre is the only child playing with the blocks. Why don't you paint a picture or join Jean Pierre?" Your room may have a sheltered corner or area where these children may go when overstimulated.

Children Born to Mothers Who Were Substance Abusers

Children born to mothers who were or are substance abusers are often born addicted to the drugs the mother was abusing and may appear to be hyperactive, learning disabled, or to have an attention deficit. Caretakers working with these children have noted that they often overreact to stimuli; thus, they need environments that contain fewer, rather than more, curriculum possibilities and fewer children with whom to interact.

As infants, these children may need constant care. They are frequently born prematurely and have to spend their first weeks, and even months, in pediatric intensive care units in a hospital. After release from the hospital, caretakers may still need to use pediatric monitors with these infants when they're asleep as sudden infant death syndrome (SIDS) has more frequently been observed with

them. These infants have also been difficult to console when crying. They appear to overreact to stimuli and have difficulty in adjusting themselves to changes. Swaddling the infants has been shown effective.

Upon entry into preschool and school, these children still become overstimulated. They may strike out at anyone, child or adult, physically near them and their behavior may be unpredictable. Obviously, this leads to difficulties in establishing friendships with the other children. If you have children born to substance abusing mothers in your child care center, preschool, or school, they have been shown to work better in small groups and in rooms with minimal stimuli. For more information, you may want to contact your local children's hospital or large city school district. School districts in many cities such as Los Angeles, New York, and Chicago have suggestions for how to work more effectively with these children. Don't be afraid to contact them.

Given the many theories as to what causes learning disabilities, what is the teacher to do? Among the several techniques proven effective with the learning disabled are:

- Structure. A well-planned classroom. Classroom rules are posted for older children and repeated often to younger ones so they understand the limits.

- Consistency of discipline by the teacher.

- Behavior modification.

- CARE. Be congruent; acceptant; reliable; and empathetic. It works with all children, especially the learning disabled child.

- Alternate quiet and active activities. Provide for enough physical exercise to tire the active child; allow the child enough freedom to move around often. Do not expect the child to sit still unless you are there.

- Love. A family medicine specialist, Lendon Smith, M.D., made the following statement (1981) to an audience of early childhood educators. "We have 5,000 children on stimulants to calm them down. All that 4,995 of them need is a little love." Smith was decrying the tendency of parents and teachers to ask medical doctors to place the seemingly overactive child on stimulants or drug therapy. He advocates instead that we use diet, physical exercise, relaxation exercises, and proven educational techniques such as those previously mentioned. We urge you to do the same.

Working with Parents of Special Needs Children

Research (Chinn, Winn, & Walters, 1985) has shown that parents of "special needs" children go through a process similar to the grief reactions described by Kubler-Ross in *On Death and Dying* (1969). It is as though parents must allow the image they had held prior to the child's birth or prior to the onset of his or her handicapping condition to die, and grieve for the child-that-cannot-be because of his or her "special needs." In interactions with parents, then, you may see a father denying that his son or daughter has a problem while the mother is blaming herself and is wracked with guilt. Also, parents often project feelings of blame upon the preschool, center, or elementary school. One reason for the high divorce rate among parents of "special needs" children is that two parents are seldom at the same step in the grief process at the same time, a fact that obviously leads to dissension at home.

In cases where the child has a clear disability, diagnosed by a medical doctor at an early age, parents have to adjust and do learn to accept the child and any concomitant problems earlier than parents of a child who has what are often called "invisible handicaps"—learning disabilities, mild retardation, and behavior disorders. What this means to teachers of both preschools and elementary schools is that they may have to be especially sensitive to what stage of grieving the parents may be in. Working with these parents may require all of a teacher's communication skills and he or she still may not be successful in persuading parents that their child needs "special" attention. (This is one reason why elementary schools may assign a child, whose family is "income eligible," to work with the Chapter 1 teacher or another child to receive help from a reading specialist,

student teacher, aide, or volunteer. [Chapter 1 of PL 95-581, the Education Consolidation Act of 1981, provides federal funds for compensatory education of children from low-income families.])

The Individual Family Services Plan

You should note that figure 12-8 represents only selected items that might be listed on Tommy Fabian's IFSP. As stipulated in PL 99-457, a multidisciplinary approach is taken, one that involves the preschool, the local school district, and a local community resource group. The student teacher, under the direction of the cooperating teacher, has an important role in modeling language and in listening to responses; the school district speech therapist and psychologist each have their roles in working both with Tommy and with the family. Finally, a community organization, the local county chapter of the LDA, has been enlisted for family support. (It is important to remember that having a "special needs" child may mean that the child's parents will often experience feelings of disbelief, anger, and helplessness; a support group can be invaluable in alleviating these feelings.)

SUMMARY

In this brief introduction to the "special" child, we presented an overview of current thinking regarding the integration of the "special" child into the regular classroom. We attempted to show that, in many instances, the "special" child can do very well in the regular room. Such integration has almost always been successful. Of course, there can be awkward moments initially, but other children often prove more tolerant than adults in accepting the "special" child.

We presented an overview of the public laws and listed some of their major provisions. We discussed the term "least restrictive environment," and emphasized that what is least restrictive for one child may not be for another.

We have presented a sample of short-term objectives from an Individual Family Services Plan for a family with a preschool child who may have a possible learning disability. We have also explained why working with families who have "special needs" children can present difficulties.

Finally, we offered some practical suggestions for working with the "special" child. We tend to agree that these techniques seem appropriate for all children. Methods that work well with one population are often applicable to another. For more specific ideas, you may wish to refer to the Suggested Readings list in the Appendix.

SUGGESTED ACTIVITIES

A. Visit a preschool or elementary school that has "special" children in attendance. Spend at least one morning watching the "special" children, taking notes as you observe. What similarities and/or differences do you find between the "special" children and the "normal" children? Discuss your answers with your peers and supervisor.

B. Visit a preschool for "special" children or a special education class in an elementary school. Again, take notes on your observations. In what ways is this "special" class different from or similar to the regular classroom? Discuss your answers with your peers and supervisor.

C. Visit a residential center for the "special" child. Discuss your observations with your peers and supervisor.

REVIEW

A. Write your own definition of "special."

B. What are five characteristics of a "special" child?

C. According to the public laws, what are the different categories of "children with disabilities"?

D. Read the following descriptions of behavior. Identify the child in each situation as "special" or "normal." Discuss your answers with your peers and supervisor.

1. Ladan is a new child in your room of four-year-olds. Her mother says that the family speaks English in the home; however, you have doubts. In the classroom Ladan seems to be more of a spectator than a participant. You note that when playing "Simon Says" Ladan does not appear to know what to do but copies her neighbor.

2. Richie is an abused two-year-old who has recently been placed in a foster home. He enters preschool every morning like a small whirlwind, running around the room, kicking at block structures other children have built, knocking over puzzles others are making, and screaming at the top of his lungs.

3. Even though Kosuke has been in your kindergarten class for nearly the entire year, his behavior has not changed noticeably from the first day. He still clings to his mother's hand when she brings him to school, and cries for three to five minutes after she leaves. He has only one friend in the room, and efforts to persuade him to play or work with another child are met with tears.

4. Elena, a pretty, dark-haired seven-year-old in your after-school day care center, complains every day she comes in about her headaches and her queasy stomach. You have wondered if she were coming down with the flu (it had been going around), but Elena has no fever and the complaints are a chronic occurrence.

5. Jorge is a student in a bilingual first grade but seldom talks in either Spanish or in English. When he does speak, he usually speaks so softly that only the students next to him can hear. When you urge him to speak up, Jorge often lowers his head and says nothing. He does appear to understand when given directions but you are concerned about his noncommunicative behavior. When his mother is questioned, she's not concerned because Jorge's older brother Carlos had displayed similar behavior when he had first entered school.

REFERENCES

Bauer, A. M., & Shea, T. M. (1990). *Teaching exceptional students in your classroom.* Boston: Allyn & Bacon.

Bee, H. (1989). *The developing child.* New York: Harper & Row.

Berk, L. E. (1994). *Child development* (3rd ed.). Boston: Allyn & Bacon.

Bowe, F. G. (1995). *Birth to five: Early childhood special education.* Albany, NY: Delmar.

Chinn, P. C., Winn, J., & Walters, R. H. (1985). *Two-way talking with parents of special children: A process of positive communication.* St. Louis: C. V. Mosby.

Cruikshank, W. M. (1977). *Learning disabilities in home, school, and community.* Syracuse, NY: Syracuse University Press.

Cruikshank, W. M. (1986). *Disputable decisions in special education.* Ann Arbor, MI: University of Michigan Press.

Federal Register (1977) PL 94-142, 300.5.

Feingold, B. F. (1975). *Why your child is hyperactive.* New York: Random House.

Kephart, N. C. (1967). Teaching the child with a perceptual handicap. In M. Bortner (Ed.), *Evaluation and education of children with brain damage.* Springfield, IL: Charles C. Thomas Publisher, pp. 147–192.

Kirk, S. A. (1972). *Educating exceptional children.* Boston: Houghton Mifflin.

Kubler-Ross, E. (1969). *On death and dying.* New York: Macmillan.

Meyen, E. L. (Ed.). (1978). *Exceptional children and youth: An introduction.* Denver: Love.

Reid, R., Maag, J., & Vasa, S. (1994). Attention deficit hyperactivity disorder as a disability category: A critique. *Exceptional children, 60*(3), 198–214.

Smith, L. (1981). The uses of stimulant drugs with "hyperactive" children: Right or wrong? Address presented at the annual conference of the National Association for the Education of Young Children in Anaheim, CA. November 6, 1981.

Strauss, A. A., & Lehtinen, L. E. (1947). *Psychopathology of the brain-injured child.* New York: Grane & Stratton.

Thonis, E. W. (February/March 1990). Teaching English as a second language. *Reading Today*, IRA, 7(4), p. 8.

Wolery, M., & Wilbers, J. S. (Eds.). (1994). *Including children with special needs in early childhood programs.* Washington, DC: National Association for the Education of Young Children.

RESOURCES

Barkely, R. (1981). *Hyperactive children: A handbook of diagnosis and treatment.* New York: Guilford.

Bayley, N. (1969). *The Bayley scales of infant development* (2nd ed.). New York: The Psychological Corporation.

Berk, L. E. (1989). *Child development.* Boston: Allyn & Bacon.

Bernstein, D. K., & Tiegerman, E. (1985). *Language and communication disorders in children.* Columbus, OH: Merrill.

Chandler, P. A. (1994). *A place for me: Including children with special needs in early care and education settings.* Washington, DC: National Association for the Education of Young Children.

Dehouske, E. (1982). Story writing as a problem-solving vehicle. *Teaching Exceptional Children, 1* (1), 11–17.

Gearheart, B. R. (1992). *Learning disabilities: Educational strategies* (5th ed.). Columbus, OH: Merrill.

Gearheart, B. R., Weishahn, M. W., & Gearheart, C. J. (1996). *The exceptional student in the regular classroom* (6th ed.). New York: Merrill/Macmillan.

Heward, W. L., & Orlansky, M. D. (1992). *Exceptional children: An introductory survey of special education* (4th ed.). New York: Merrill/Macmillan.

Kroth, R. L. (1985). *Communicating with parents of exceptional children.* Denver, CO: Love Publishing.

Landau, S., & McAninch, C. (May 1993). Research in review: Young children with attention deficits. *Young Children, 48*(4), 49–58.

Levy, L., & Gottlieb, J. (1984). Learning disabled and non-LD children at play. *Remedial and Special Education, 5*(6), 43–50.

Long, N., Morse, W., & Neuman, R. (Eds.). (1982). *Conflict in the classroom* (2nd ed.). Belmont, CA: Wadsworth.

Quigley, S., & Paul, P. (1984). *Language and deafness.* San Diego, CA: College-Hill.

Safford, P. L. (1989). *Integrated teaching in early childhood: Starting in the mainstream.* New York: Longman.

Shea, T., & Bauer, A. (1987). *Teaching children and youth with behavior disorders.* Englewood Cliffs, NJ: Prentice-Hall.

Siegel, E., & Gold, R. (1982). *Educating the learning disabled.* New York: Macmillan.

Smith, D. D. (1981) *Teaching the learning disabled.* Englewood Cliffs, NJ: Prentice-Hall.

Turnbull, A. P., & Turnbull, H. R. III. (1981). *Parents speak out.* Columbus, OH: Merrill.

"Understanding the Americans with Disabilities Act: Information for Early Childhood Programs." (No Date).

Brochure published by the National Association for the Education of Young Children.

U.S. Department of Education. (1987). *Eighth annual report to Congress on the implementation of PL 94-142.* Washington, DC.

Wolery, M., Holcombe, A., Venn, M. L., Brookfield, J., Huffman, K., Schroeder, C., Martin, C. G., & Fleming, L. A. (November 1993). Research report: Mainstreaming in early childhood programs: Current status and relevant issues. *Young Children, 49* (1), 79–84.

CHAPTER

13

The Changing American Family

OBJECTIVES

After completing this chapter, the student will be able to:

- List a minimum of five factors influencing families in the United States today.
- Discuss five or six of the major changes seen in families today.
- List at least five ways in which parents can serve as volunteers.
- State a minimum of five precautions to remember when working with parents.
- Design a plan for parent participation in any school or center in which the student hopes to be employed.

At my first PTA meeting, I remember being apprehensive and then astounded at the tremendous diversity of parents and other relatives in attendance. We looked like a mini-UN conference!

Karen Sarafian

Many young children lead complicated lives. When they talk about their dad, their stepdad, their mother's boyfriend, their father's girlfriend, etc., they don't bat an eye. And Mondays, after some children have been with their weekend parent, some have adjustment problems or are overly tired.

Clarisa Ho

THE AMERICAN FAMILY IN THE '90S

There is no doubt that the family in the United States has been undergoing major changes over the past 20 years. Among these are the rise in the numbers of women with young children who work (estimated at more than 60 percent of those with children under six); the growing divorce rate (fully 50 percent of all first marriages end in divorce in some urban areas); the rise in the number of "blended" families (one divorced parent marrying another divorced parent); the problem of homelessness; single-parent families, some by choice; the "feminization" of poverty and the concomitant rise in the number of children living in poverty (estimated in 1995 by the Children's Defense Fund [CDF] as one child out of every four and among infants and toddlers, at 27 percent of all infants and toddlers (pp. 17–18)); the rise in the number of illegitimate births; the number of "children raising children" (Raspberry, 1986); the number of older women having children; the rise in the numbers of nonwhite births; the rise in the numbers of non-English-proficient children; mobility; and the breakdown of the infrastructure in many of our cities. There are also increases in the number of children born to mothers who are substance abusers and HIV-positive carriers.

Not only are changes seen in families: one only has to read such publications as Toffler's *Third Wave* (1980), Naisbett's *Megatrends* (1981), and Naisbett and Auburdene's current *Megatrends 2000* (1990) to see the changes occurring in our society. Toffler claims that a fourth wave of change has already occurred. First-wave societies were based on hunting, gathering, fishing, or herding; the second wave saw the shift to agriculture; the third, the shift to manufacturing; the fourth is commonly seen as the shift to an information age.

With each of these changes has come the demand for different social and educational skills and thus the need for schools to change their goals also. Where it was possible a generation ago to find a job that required little skill, the 1990s demand a broad technological knowledge base and a worker who is adaptable, is able to relate well to others, has good problem-solving skills, and is able to be retrained as technology makes obsolete initially acquired skills (Berns, 1993).

If California is any example of changes occurring throughout the United States, we have only to look at the following: In the 1989–1990 school year minorities became the majority; one out of every five students is limited-English proficient and one in four lives in poverty (Butler, 1990). At least two major school districts have become insolvent and have had to be rescued by the state. A state trustee, with power to abrogate any decisions made by the local school boards, has been appointed to manage the districts (San Francisco *Chronicle*, 1990). In addition, there are the environmental concerns of poor air quality, traffic gridlock, natural disasters (earthquakes, hurricanes, fires, floods, and so on). As the Cold War has ended, and defense industries have closed, and as the Armed Forces have "downsized," there has been increased unemployment. One other factor should be mentioned: With the move toward a balanced federal budget and the implementation of the "Contract with America," funds for families and children have dwindled. Many states have reduced Aid to Families with Dependent Children (AFDC) payments to income-eligible families. In 1995, statistics revealed that "the child poverty rate was higher in 1993 than in any year since 1964" (Children's Defense Fund, 1995, p. 19).

Changes such as these stress many families, and we, as teachers and caregivers, must be sensitive to the stress that the families of the children in our care and classrooms feel. We also need to be aware of our own stress levels; we are not going to be effective in conferencing with a stressed parent if we cannot manage effectively our own stress. And, to help the children in our care achieve their full potential, we must keep lines of communication with parents open; we must try to establish some kind of rapport so that we, as teachers, form a partnership with the parents to better help the children. We need always to remember that the parents are their children's first teachers and, in many ways, their best teachers.

Lickona (1993) identifies his concern about the American society's influence on families:

Increasing numbers of people across the ideological spectrum believe that our society is in deep moral trouble. The disheartening signs are everywhere: the breakdown of the family; the deterioration of civility in everyday life; rampant greed at a time when one in five children is poor; an omnipresent sexual culture that fills our television and movie screens with sleaze, beckoning the young toward sexual activity at ever earlier ages; the enormous betrayal of children through sexual abuse; and the 1992 report of the National Research Council that says the United States is now *the* most violent of all industrialized nations.

● HISTORY OF EARLY CHILDHOOD EDUCATION

In 1856 the first kindergarten was established by Margarethe Schurz and her husband, Carl, in Wisconsin. Elizabeth Palmer Peabody, a wealthy woman dedicated to bettering society and education, was so impressed with the Schurzes that she became a self-appointed spokesperson for kindergartens. Her interest and sponsorship coincided with several factors: the first compulsory attendance laws, opposition to child labor, a sharp rise in the number of children in relation to the total population, and a growing number of immigrant children of working parents. Many educators viewed the kindergarten movement as a vehicle to aid in the acculturation of the immigrant child (Osborn, 1975).

By 1900 John Dewey had convinced the administration at the University of Chicago to open a laboratory school, containing a class for four- and five-year-olds that he called the "Sub-Primary." In 1907 Maria Montessori opened the *Casa dei Bambini* in Rome. In 1909 the first White House Conference on Children was held; its concerns were child care and development (Osborn, 1975).

In 1912 the Children's Bureau (now a part of the Office of Child Development) was established, and the first cooperative nursery school was opened in 1916 by a group of faculty wives at the University of Chicago. Soon many major universities had child development laboratories, and private parent-cooperative nursery schools were established in most large cities (Osborn, 1975).

During these early years, some nursery classes were sponsored by settlement houses, church groups, and other organizations in many of the big cities. Educating the young child had been seen as a vehicle for reaching and influencing immigrant families isolated by language and cultural barriers who were clustering in what were rapidly becoming big-city ghettos. Hull House in Chicago and Henry Street Settlement in New York were typical (Goodlad, 1984).

For the most part, though, the education of young children was an opportunity available only to those who could afford it, primarily the middle and upper-middle classes. It was also available in college communities and suburban cities. During World War II, one exception to this pattern emerged. Child care centers, such as the Kaiser Centers, located near war-related industries, operated 24 hours each day, provided medical care for the sick child, gave a hot meal that could be taken home with the parent after a long day at the shipyard, and offered other services such as counseling. After the war, the centers closed.

With the advent of Head Start and the concept of compensatory education, the federal government entered the field of early childhood education; that influence is still felt today. Legislators passed the Economic Opportunity Act of 1964 and the Elementary and Secondary Education Act of 1965, which funded "early intervention" programs; many still exist today (Goodlad, 1984). Written into these acts were provisos for active parent participation. Parents from poverty backgrounds with little or no education were presumed to be knowledgeable. In particular, they were knowledgeable about their children and community. No longer would an upper-middle class "do-gooder," usually white, come into a minority neighborhood and tell parents how to raise and educate their children. It was a major step forward to where we are today, with Parent Advisory Committees and parent volunteers.

Where are we today? Throughout the 1970s, 1980s and early 1990s there was a growing trend to full-time day care. As inflation problems hit more families, more mothers joined the work force. This created a need for extended day care, which led many former nursery schools to offer after-school care. It has also led to franchised operations, such as Kindercare and Merry Moppets. The number of children being cared for in licensed care has grown steadily. Currently, approximately 32 percent of the children in day care are cared for in a center; nearly 33 percent are cared for by relatives; 25 percent are cared for in family day care homes, 7.5 percent are cared for by an unrelated caregiver in the child's home, and the remaining two percent are cared for in a variety of other ways. (See chapter 20, figure 20-1.) Parent priorities in selecting child care are shown in figure 13-1.

The 1980s saw a gradual increase in the number of employers providing or sponsoring day care services, particularly those who employ a large number of women. Some employers have established their own day care centers. Others have provided vouchers for employees with children, which are redeemable at certain day care centers in the community.

Children of Despair

Daily crime and violence, and the less than adequate health care which exists in some inner cities, can sap a family's hope of ever attaining economic security. Young children touched by despair and anger display the resultant behaviors in school settings.

Working with these children, who are often called "at risk," may mean interacting frequently with their parents. Screening children's day-to-day health has become a very important concern.

Sensitive teaching techniques and program activities that help children and families adapt, cope, problem solve, and survive, and that aid upward mobility, need staff discussion and attention.

Are the Children You Teach Hungry?

It is estimated that almost 14 million children under 18 lived in economically disadvantaged families in 1991. The poverty rate is climbing more rapidly than at any time in U.S. history. Poor diets produce behavioral results, and teachers during the '90s will need to be aware of causes of some chil-

---

MOTHERS' TOP 10 PRIORITIES

Safety is the top priority for mothers looking for family day care; only 29% cited a licensed or registered provider. The top 10 criteria:

Rank		Percent saying "extremely important"
1	Attention to children's safety	83%
2	Provider's communication with parents about their children	73%
3	Cleanliness	72%
4	Attention children receive	69%
5	Provider's warmth toward children	68%
6	Provider's style of discipline	61%
7	Provider's experience in taking care of children	60%
8	Provider's openness to parents' dropping in	58%
9	Attention to nutrition	58%
10	Number of children per adult	56%

Figure 13-1 (Source: Families and Work Institute; survey of 804 mothers. From *USA Today*, April 1, 1993, p. 8D)

dren's inattentiveness, lower energy levels, increased absence due to illness, and the hopelessness that poverty breeds. A center's nutrition program, then, and cleanliness have become very important to many low-income parents.

The Importance of Fathers

Another sobering statistic comes from a *U.S. News and World Report* study of why fathers are important, titled "Honor Thy Children." Shapiro and Schrof (1995) state that two of every five children in the United States do not live with their biological father. They and their associates raised several issues, such as whether or not marriage and parenting skills can be taught, how children can reconnect to noncustodial fathers, whether divorces should be more difficult to obtain, and in what ways fathers can be supported. The study pointed out the part that fathers play in the raising of their children. Shapiro and Schrof open with the sentence, "Dad is destiny," and continue with "More than virtually any other factor, a biological father's presence in the family will determine a child's success and happiness. Rich or poor, white or black, the children of divorce and those born outside marriage, struggle through life at a measurable disadvantage, according to a growing chorus of social thinkers" (p. 39). Material from research in the field then is presented to reinforce their claim of disadvantage. The opening article in the *U.S. News* study concludes with a quote from David Blankenhorn, author of *Fatherless America: Confronting Our Most Urgent Social Problem*, and founder of the New York-based Institute for American Values, "being a loving father and a good husband is the best part of being a man" (p. 49).

● PARENTS AS VOLUNTEERS

In many ways, the well-educated, middle- or upper-middle class parent has often been involved at the preschool level, in cooperative schools, and child development centers associated with universities. These same parents often carried their interest and involvement in their children's education into the elementary school as volunteers. Prior to World War II, few married women worked, and there were few single parents. Because of the Depression during the 1930s, there were no paid aides in most elementary schools. Teachers who wanted to individualize programs often asked parents for help. Others felt parents did not belong in the classroom, although they were welcome at PTA/PTO meetings and at school fund-raising events.

The compensatory education programs brought a new focus on the parent (Brewer, 1992). The findings of many studies on class size and the effects of the teacher: pupil ratio on learning are in favor of smaller classes. A review of 59 studies revealed that lowering the teacher:pupil ratio led to better results on cognitive measures and favorable effects on both teachers and students in terms of higher morale, more positive attitudes, self concepts, etc. (Smith & Glass, 1990). One of the easiest ways to lower the teacher:pupil ratio is through the use of parent volunteers, figure 13-2.

With young children, many states limit class size for preschool to 15:1 for four-year-olds, 12:1 for

Figure 13-2 Parent volunteers lower adult:child classroom ratios.

three-year-olds, and as low as 3:1 for infants. Unfortunately, in public elementary schools, classes in the primary grades (grades 1 through 3) are often as large as 31:1 or even higher and are dependent on the teachers' contract with the local school board. One kindergarten where we placed a student teacher had 33 students in the classroom with only one teacher and one part-time aide. On the other hand, most professionals believe smaller class size in both preschools and elementary schools promotes a higher quality of education. It is presumed that the younger the child, the more the child needs adult attention. While the concept of using parent volunteers works in theory, in practice there are many limitations. Many mothers are currently working and do not have the time to volunteer; others, particularly low-income and/or minority parents, may not feel welcome or needed, or feel that they have no skills or knowledge of value to share.

What is a teacher to do when federal and state mandates require parent participation? As always, there is less of a problem with the nonworking parent. There may be many reasons why the parent does not work, and you need to be sensitive to them.

One parent may not work because there is a baby at home and no one with whom the baby can be left. Another may be disabled or have problems with mobility.

In most communities in past years the administration of school programs was left to the professionals—the principal and teachers in a public school, the director in a preschool. Most of these professionals were middle class, often white. They perceived their role as one of informing parents about their children's behaviors, especially learning behaviors. Thus, parent-teacher conferences were held at regular intervals. During these conferences, teachers told parents what their children had been doing on various measures of learning and classroom behavior. The professionals sometimes felt that the parent did not know how to parent; they sometimes looked down on the parent whose English was different and whose clothing was old, torn, and unstylish. Parent-teacher organizations were usually led by middle-class, nonworking mothers. Lower-class parents tended to be ignored if they attended. Soon they stopped coming, and unkind teachers and other parents would say, "Well, what can you expect of parents with no background in school who speak broken English? They just don't care." Fortunately, federal compensatory education programs demanded parent participation. It is recognized that almost all parents love and care for their children and want what is best for them. Of course, there are those to whom children are a nuisance, but this is a phenomenon found across all social classes. There are neglectful upper-class parents, as well as uncaring middle- and lower-class families.

It is time in the 1990s to change our definition of parent volunteer work. Traditionally, teachers, both in preschool and elementary school settings, have looked at parent volunteers as extra hands in the classroom. But with 53 percent of all women with children under six working (and that figure jumps to over 70 percent when mothers of five- to 18-year-olds are included), we need to look at parent volunteerism in a different way. Are we realistic, then, when we expect parents to be able to assist in the classroom? In what other ways can we involve par-

ents? How can we attract the busy career-oriented parent, the overworked single parent, the homemaker with three small children, or the undereducated teen parent? What expectations should we have regarding their possible involvement?

In what ways can parents in different early childhood programs involve themselves or live up to a center's expectation? They:

- provide insights, background and material, and perspectives that help facilitate individualized learning and program planning
- serve as supportive users of child care services by attending meetings, participating in projects, and receiving school information pertinent to their child's growth and development or the school's viability
- teach their children and reinforce school learning and experiences
- volunteer and provide classroom assistance and materials
- consult with teachers (centers) serving as collaborators and advisors
- work as paid classroom aides providing unique talents, and social and cultural continuity for attending children
- participate in the center's decision-making process
- financially support the center's continued operation and existence therefore providing jobs for workers
- vote for measures that provide support and upgrade early childhood education for America's children and families

● HOW TO MOTIVATE PARENTS TO VOLUNTEER

One might say that anything a parent does of his or her own free will to be of some service to the teacher is being a volunteer, figures 13-3 and 13-4. Parents have been baking cookies for classroom parties for years. They have also sewn beanbags, mixed homemade clay, and brought in old toys for a toy share-in. Parents have built climbing structures and house equipment, put up fences, installed swings, and cleaned yards and rooms. Many of these activi-

Figure 13-3 Parent volunteers often help with instruction. (Courtesy of Jody Boyd)

ties have been done at home or on the parents' free time, figure 13-5. These are volunteer activities.

The 21st annual Gallup poll of the public's attitude toward the public schools (Elam, 1989) provides us with four key ideas: (1) improve lines of communication, (2) hold more conferences, (3) remember to ask parents for help, and (4) plan more special functions. Preschools tend to maintain closer contact with parents than do elementary schools; and, to a certain extent, the same procedures are used. Both send newsletters home to parents; typically, both hold parent conferences (generally scheduled at least twice during the year); teachers in both settings regularly telephone parents (too often, unfortunately, to report a problem with the child rather than to report a successful incident); both frequently have fundraisers planned and implemented by a PTA/PTO/Parent Advisory Committee. Why do parents feel that communication is a problem? Perhaps one answer lies in the formal nature of many of these forms of communication.

One elementary school principal we know insists that all teachers, including student teachers assigned to her school, telephone the parents of every student in their respective classes at least once a month. During the opening week of school, teachers send home a notice with their students that lists times when they will be free to make or receive calls and asks parents to indicate what times will best suit their busy schedules. These hours generally include at least one lunch hour and one after school period of two hours.

Some teachers who live locally also may indicate hours available in the early evening. The result has been overwhelmingly positive. One parent states, "I used to dread hearing from Robert's teacher; I knew it had to be about something bad he'd done. Now, I hear about the good things he's done and it makes the not-so-good things seem a lot better!" (A thank you to Suzon Kornblum, principal at Walters School, Fremont, CA, for sharing this anecdote.)

Why do parents want more conferences? The answer here is also probably related to communication. Regardless of how we may feel they do not want to be bothered, parents do want to keep in close touch with their children's teachers and do not look upon a phone call or a short conference as a "bother." No parent likes to be called only when something goes wrong; and regularly scheduled conferences, other than when they are formally required for biannual reporting, help build rapport and a sense of teamwork between parent and teacher.

Working parents often can help more than teachers assume they can; many wait to be called and are disappointed when they are not. One reason

Figure 13-4 There are so many classroom tasks for volunteers.

parents stated that they would like to be *invited* to volunteer is that they may not feel like they can make a regular commitment to the classroom but that they can and would like to be invited to help out occasionally. Other parents are simply more reserved or may feel that they have little to offer and are, therefore, reluctant to volunteer unless asked. Teachers may mistake reticence as a "no" when the parent may be expecting the teacher to say, "Would you be able to . . . ?"

Special events, as we might remember from our own school days, are a sure winner and draw a large number of parents into the school. When the weather permits, one family day care home provider plans Saturday family picnics for the parents of the children in her care; she also plans birthday and holiday parties. As a result, she has a waiting list of neighborhood working parents who would like to have their infants, toddlers, or preschoolers in her home day care.

One elementary school principal starts the year with a barbecue for the families of all the children attending his school and underwrites the cost of the hot dogs himself; the PTA provides the buns, condiments, baked beans, soft drinks, and ice cream bars. Parents are asked only to bring themselves and all of their

children, regardless of age. This principal has managed to turn around a school with many dissatisfied parents, much dissension among the different ethnic groups in attendance, and too much vandalism.

Other highlights of the school year include Saturday morning as well as evening PTA meetings to accommodate the schools' parent population, composed largely of two working parents or working single parents. Child care is always provided and there is a potluck lunch on Saturdays. A major highlight (and fund-raiser) of the year in the spring is the annual International Day festival, when parents from the different ethnic groups provide foods and there are folk singing and dancing performances by their children.

Throughout the year, different classrooms sponsor programs for the parents; a bulletin board in the entry hall of the school is reserved for the "Student of the Week," with an appropriate certificate being awarded every Friday. The parents of the child are invited to attend the award ceremony, and many parents arrange their work hours so they can. The student of the week plans his or her bulletin board; the child's school and family pictures may be displayed; there are drawings of favorite toys, TV shows, foods, posting of best papers, and so on.

Before the end of the school year, every child in attendance receives a school-wide award of some kind for creative writing effort, top math grade in her classroom, best drawing or painting, best craft project, grade-level science fair awards, and so forth. Knowing that not every student can be a school-wide student of the week, several teachers have a classroom student of the week. One kindergarten teacher has the other children draw a picture of their student of the week classmate; the pictures are then posted on the bulletin board together with the student of the week's own picture and school picture. Teachers of older students often have classmates write an essay about their "student of the week" peer.

Some of the special occasions include a school-wide science fair with grade-level prizes being awarded (incidentally, every participant receives at least an "honorable mention" ribbon); a school-wide arts and crafts fair, again with grade-level awards and the added benefit to the children of an opportunity to sell their creations should they choose; the publication of a school creative writing book, in which every child has a self-chosen best effort (drawing, painting, essay, poem, myth, and so on) bound and placed on display in the school library. Books from previous years are fitted with pockets and check out cards and are among the more popular items carried in the library. Special occasions are limited only by the imagination of the teachers, parents, directors, and/or principals planning them.

The question remains, though, how do you persuade nonparticipating parents that they are needed? Most, if not all, preschools, centers, and elementary schools have parent handbooks that provide basic information about the school or center for parents; many also have staff handbooks available for teachers and student teachers that provide helpful hints. They often include communication strategies and specific techniques and activities useful in working with parents.

One way to encourage a parent to participate is to speak to the parent about your expectations for his or her involvement at the time the child is registered. Some centers and schools provide parents

Figure 13-5 This father enjoys volunteering at the school on his day off. (Courtesy of Jody Boyd)

with a list of activities in which they may participate; the parent is asked to check those activities he or she feels comfortable doing. The teacher then calls on the parent when needed and invites the parent to help out.

The home visit can lead to better rapport between the parent and school. It is possible for a discerning teacher to note special talents on a home visit (hand-sewn curtains or drapes; potted plants; newly painted walls that the parents did themselves; cooking abilities). The teacher can follow up by requesting the parent to use that talent on a school project, figure 13-6. Parents who protest that they have no skills may think the teacher means teaching skills and may not realize that wielding a paintbrush can sometimes be of more value. Gardening skills are also frequently overlooked. Parents may not realize how much care goes into maintaining the landscape of a center and may be delighted to spend an afternoon digging the ground for a garden the children will be planting during the next week. A teacher might want to sprout beans and

Figure 13-6 A creative parent volunteer designed and posted this bulletin board.

peas and then transfer them into a vegetable garden, allowing the children to weed and water the beans and peas, watch them grow, and finally pick, cook, and eat the fruits of their labor.

McCracken (1995) recommends the following:

- People's names are pronounced and spelled correctly (ask if you're not sure).

- Family members are welcome as active participants in the group's activities (taking children's dictation; sharing family stories, treasures, or recipes).

- Continuity between home and group is valued (staff communicate in children's home languages, information is exchanged regularly).

- Differences with family members or among staff are resolved gracefully (using the same conflict-resolution techniques we facilitate with children).

- We bring the community into our classroom (volunteers, hands-on demonstrations, acknowledgment of donations of materials such as lumber or books).

- Children reach out into the community (frequent field trips; walks around the neighborhood; getting to know people, buildings).

Studies of Parent Participation

A friend who is a kindergarten teacher in a private church-sponsored school visits the home of every incoming child during the late summer. She always brings a simple toy to entertain the child and to make the child feel important. With the child busily occupied, the parents then feel more relaxed, rapport is easily established, and requests for help are met with a more positive frame of mind. This teacher usually has between one-fourth and one-third of her parents unable to help out during the school day due to work or school commitments. The remaining parents are expected to donate at least one morning or afternoon each week to the program. Even knowing that they are expected to assist once each week, many parents are relatively inactive. Of 20 parents, this teacher knows she will be fortunate if four or five assist regularly. More likely than not, assistance will be limited to out-of-school kinds of assistance (baking cookies, making bean bags) rather than in-school assistance (Hessler, 1995).

Studies have indicated that teachers who work with parent volunteers place much value in the parents and in their labor, figure 13-7. In her research, Buchanan (1978) found that teachers who made regular use of parent volunteers were more apt to have positive attitudes about the value of the parents in the classroom. Teachers in districts where volunteers received some training were also more favorable in their attitudes. Teachers who did not feel threatened by the presence of volunteers tended to use them more in instructional activities. Teachers with negative perceptions of the value of volunteers were more likely to use them less and to use them in activities such as running a copy machine and yard supervision.

A teacher of an ungraded primary class in a suburban school district knows that her classroom cannot function without the assistance of parent volunteers. Since her class is an optional one within the structure of a traditional elementary school, one expectation of all parents, choosing this setting for their children, is active parent involvement in the classroom. In the same district there is one entire elementary school operating without standard age-level grades. Again, the expectation of parents who choose this school is their active classroom involvement (Peters, 1988, personal communication).

Comer (1988) relates the story of how one school in New Haven, Connecticut, went from having children scoring at the bottom of the achievement tests every year to one with the top scores in the district. How was this accomplished? One key was the active involvement of parents in making curriculum decisions cooperatively with teachers. Another key was providing these basically low-income, often dysfunctional families with an array of social services and empowering them as knowledgeable teachers of their own children. A third key was the retraining of the teaching staff, including the transfer of teachers unable to accept change.

The success of parent involvement in shared decision making with the schools was also highlighted in three television offerings, the CBS news special,

Figure 13-7 Harder School's appreciation lunch for parent volunteers.

"American's Toughest Assignment: Solving the Education Crisis" (September 6, 1990); the PBS program, "Learning in America: Schools That Work" (September 5, 1990); and KQED's locally broadcast show, "Why Do These Kids Love School?" (September 5, 1990).

Generally, there are advantages for everyone involved in parent participation programs. Teachers have the additional resource of the volunteer's time, energy, and talent; parents have the satisfaction of knowing that they are making an active contribution to their children's learning; and children feel that their parents care more, so they achieve more in school.

Tom Kerr, editor of *Early Childhood News*, suggests the following strategies for promoting parent involvement in Head Start:

1. Inform parents about Performance Standards . . . guide and review with them throughout the planning and participation stages to ensure that standards are being met.

2. Reinforce the shared decision-making responsibilities of staff, administrators, board members, and parents through substantive training of staff and parents on their roles and responsibilities.

3. Emphasize and demonstrate the Head Start program's philosophy about parent involvement, including the importance of the partnership

concept in pre-service and in-service staff training. (1993, p. 14)

Teacher Attributes

Comer and Poussaint (1992) note the following teacher attributes positively influence teacher-parent relationships:

- warmth
- openness
- sensitivity
- flexibility
- reliability
- accessibility

From the parent's perspective, these teacher characteristics are desirable: trust, warmth, closeness, positive self-image, effective classroom management, child-centeredness, positive discipline, nurturance, and effective teaching skills (Swick, 1992).

Strategies

Swick (1992) describes strategies he believes have proven valuable in the promotion of strong parent-school partnerships:

> The degree to which strategies are related to the needs and interests of parents and to the unique situations of schools and teachers influences the level of success. Home visits, conferences, parent centers, telecommunication, involvement in the classroom, participatory decision-making, parent and adult education programs, home learning activities, and family-school networking are some of the many strategies that have effectively engaged parents and teachers in supportive and collaborative roles.

Caring and Compassion

Teachers may work with parents who are stressed, troubled, economically strapped, and faced with other stresses. As Stone (1987) points out:

> It is not always other people who suffer from accident, catastrophic illness, robberies or rapes, loss of jobs, drug or alcohol abuse, abandonment. It's people we meet and know, even in children's centers.
> and

If we, as teachers, extended compassion to everyone, not just to children, parent-teacher relationships will have a chance.

Family Support Structure

As NAEYC (1994) points out:

Social indicators clearly point to a shift in the traditional support structure for children and families.

Child centers are becoming increasingly important as supportive parent partners in young children's care and education, figure 13-8. Student teachers can expect to become teachers who will be more involved in parent's needs and lives than past generations of care providers.

Parent Outreach

Prekindergarten centers with the funds necessary to support such activities are expanding parent services and supportive assistance programs.

A number of activities and questions should be considered in developing an early childhood parent outreach plan.

1. Gather information about families in the community.

   What are their needs?

   Are parents willing to attend meetings?

2. Collect the following data:

   Is parental discipline strict, too easy, or moderate?

   How is (are) guidance technique(s) affecting young children?

   What are family communication styles?

   Do children with antisocial behaviors exist?

   Is substance abuse prevalent in the community?

   What is causing parent stress? Poverty? Isolation? Crime? Unemployment? Lack of resources? Other factors?

SUMMARY

Parent participation is a many-faceted phenomenon. Volunteering includes assisting in the classroom, as well as baking cookies for snack time, helping build climbing structures, attending parent

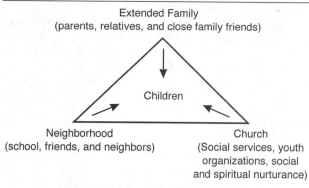

TRADITIONAL SUPPORT STRUCTURE

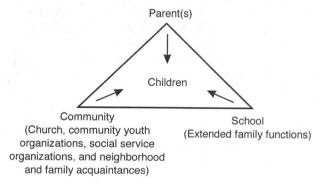

EVOLVING SUPPORT STRUCTURE

Figure 13-8 Changing support structures for children and families. [Reprinted with permission from the National Association for the Education of Young Children. *The Early Childhood Career Lattice: Perspectives on Professional Development*, (1994) J. Johnson and J. McCracken, (Eds.), Washington, DC: National Association for the Education of Young Children. Copyright ©1994.]

good lines of communication; shared decision making, together with cooperative planning of curriculum; and acceptance of the parent.

SUGGESTED ACTIVITIES

A. Visit three or four different types of preschools or elementary schools. These might include a publicly supported day care center, a proprietary preschool and/or child center, an adult education-sponsored nursery school, the early childhood center associated with your college or university, a public elementary school, and a private and/or parochial elementary school. Talk with the teachers, directors, or principals about how they involve parents. Discuss your findings with your peers and supervisor.

B. With your cooperating teacher, develop a list of activities for volunteers for use in your own classroom.

C. Role play the following situations:
   1. Parent feels parents of children "caught" in doctor play with suggestive overtones should be asked to terminate their child's enrollment.
   2. Parent group asks teacher to increase academic instruction with children.
   3. Father requests teachers to encourage a child bitten by another to bite the attacker.
   4. Parent requests "nail biting" child be punished at school.

education meetings, sewing beanbags, and many more activities.

The historical use of parents as volunteers was discussed and some studies on the use of parents as volunteers were reviewed. Remember: Do not be discouraged if parent participation in the classroom is low. It takes time to establish rapport with parents, especially those from different cultures. Remember the keys to success, as demonstrated by Comer and the CBS and PBS television offerings:

REVIEW

A. What are five different ways in which parents can serve as volunteers?

B. Name five precautions to keep in mind when working with parents.

C. Design a plan for a parent education meeting. What are your objectives? What materials or equipment will you need? Describe the procedures. Discuss your plan with your cooperating teacher, peers, and supervisor. Implement the plan, and evaluate its effectiveness.

REFERENCES

Berns, R. M. (1993). *Child, family, community: Socialization and support.* (3rd ed.). Ft. Worth, TX: Harcourt Brace Jovanovich College Publishers.

Blankenhorn, D. (1995). *Fatherless America: Confronting our most urgent social problem.* New York: Basic Books.

Brewer, J. A. (1992). *Early childhood education: Preschool through primary grades.* Boston: Allyn & Bacon.

Buchanan, E. C. (1978). *Parent volunteers in California's early childhood education schools.* Master's Thesis, California State University, Hayward.

Butler, L. H. (1990). The changing face of California. Address presented at the Stanford University Conference on Diversity, May 22, 1990.

CBS News Special. (September 6, 1990). *America's toughest assignment: Solving the education crisis.*

Children's Defense Fund. (1995). *The state of America's children yearbook 1995.* Washington, DC: Author.

Comer, J. (November 1988). Educating poor minority children. *Scientific American, 259*, 11, pp. 88–95.

Comer, J. P., & Poussaint, A. F. (1992). *Raising black children: Questions and answers for parents and teachers.* New York: NAL–Dutton.

Elam, S. M. (September 1989). The 21st annual Phi Delta Kappa/Gallup poll of the public's attitudes toward the public schools. *Phi Delta Kappan, 77*(1), 41–54.

Goodlad, J. (1984). *A place called school: Prospects for the future.* New York: McGraw-Hill.

Hessler, D. (1995). Personal communication.

Kerr, T. (Ed.). (November/December 1993). Promoting parent involvement in Head Start. *Early Childhood News*, p. 14.

KQED Special. (September 5, 1990). *Why do these kids love school?*

Lickona, T. (November 1993). The return of character education. *Educational Leadership, 51*(3), pp. 6–11.

McCracken, J. (July/August 1995). Image-building: A hands-on developmental process. *Child Care Information Exchange, 104*, pp. 48–55.

Naisbett, J. (1988). *Megatrends.* New York: Warner Books.

Naisbett, J., & Auburdene, P. (1990). *Megatrends 2000.* New York: William Morrow.

National Association for the Education of Young Children. (July 1994). Public policy report. Starting points: Executive summary of the report of the Carnegie Corporation of New York task force on meeting the needs of young children. *Young Children, 49*(5), 58–61.

Osborn, D. K. (1975). *Early childhood education in historical perspective.* Athens, GA: Early Childhood Education Center, University of Georgia.

PBS Special. (September 5, 1990). *Learning in America: Schools that work.*

Peters, G. A. (1988). Personal communication.

Raspberry, W. (9 November 1986). Children having children. Keynote address presented at the annual conference of the National Association for the Education of Young Children, Washington, DC.

Shapiro, J. P., & Schrof, J. M., with Tharp, M., & Friedman, D. (February 27, 1995). Honor thy children. *U.S. News & World Report, 118*(8), pp. 38–49.

Smith, M. L., & Glass, G. V. (Winter 1990). Meta-analysis of research on class size and its relationship to attitudes and instruction. *American Educational Research Journal, 27*, 419–433.

State takes over Richmond and Oakland school districts. San Francisco *Chronicle*, May 12, 1990, p. A19.

Stone, J. G. (1987). *Teacher-parent relationships.* Washington, DC: National Association for the Education of Young Children.

Swick, K. J. (1992). Teacher-parent partnerships. *ERIC Digest*, EDO-PS-92-12.

Toffler, A. (Ed.). (1980). *Third wave.* New York: Morrow.

RESOURCES

Berger, E. H. (1994). *Parents as partners in education: The school and home working together* (4th ed.). New York: Merrill/Macmillan.

Cataldo, C. Z. (1987). *Parent education for early childhood: Child rearing concepts and program content for the student and practicing professional.* New York: Teachers College Press.

Chase, S. (1989). *Who killed Ozzie and Harriet?* KNBR, San Francisco, News Special.

Comer, J. P. (1993). *School power: Implications for an intervention project.* New York: Free Press.

Croft, D. J. (1979). *Parents and teachers: A resource book for home, school, and community.* Belmont, CA: Wadsworth.

Elam, S. M., & Rose, L. C. (September 1995). The 27th annual Phi Delta Kappa/Gallup Poll of the public's attitude, toward the public schools. *Phi Delta Kappan, 77*(1), 41–56.

Elkind, D. (1995). School and family in the postmodern world. *Phi Delta Kappan, 77*(1), 8–14.

Frymier, J. (1992). *Growing up is risky business, and schools are not to blame.* Bloomington, IN: Phi Delta Kappa.

Galinsky, E. (1987). *The six stages of parenthood.* Reading, MA: Addison-Wesley.

Gestwicki, C. (1996). *Home, school, community relations.* (3rd ed.) Albany, NY: Delmar.

Glick, P. C. (January 1989). Remarried families, step-families, and step children: A brief demographic profile. *Family Relations, 38,* 1, 24–27.

Hallissy, E. (December 7, 1990). Richmond schools chief ousted—fiscal crisis. *San Francisco Chronicle,* p. A1.

Kagan, S. (Ed.). (1987). *America's family support programs: Perspectives and prospects.* New Haven: Yale University Press.

Kroth, R. L., & Simpson, R. L. (1977). *Parent conferences as a teaching strategy.* Denver, CO: Love Publishing.

Lay-Dopyera, M., & Dopyera, J. (1990). *Becoming a teacher of young children* (4th ed.). New York: McGraw-Hill.

Mindel, C. H., Haberstein, R. W., & Wright, R., Jr. (Eds.). (1988). *Ethnic families in America* (3rd ed.). New York: Elsevier.

Nedler, S., & McAfee, O. (1979). *Working with parents: Guidelines for early education and elementary teachers.* Belmont, CA: Wadsworth.

Nickel, P. S., & Delany, H. (1985). *Working with teen parents.* Chicago, IL: The Family Resource Coalition.

Oyemade, U. J., & Washington, V. (July 1989). Drug abuse prevention begins in early childhood (And is much more than a matter of instructing young children about drugs!). *Young Children, 44*(4), 6–12.

Quisenberry, J. D. (Ed.). (1982). *Changing family life-styles.* Wheaton, MD: Association for Childhood Education International.

Seefeldt, C. (November/December 1985). Parent involvement: Support or stress? *Childhood Education,* pp. 99–102.

Seefeldt, C., & Barbour, N. (1990). *Early childhood education: An introduction* (2nd ed.). Columbus, OH: Merrill.

Tiedt, P. L., & Tiedt, I. M. (1989). *Multicultural teaching* (3rd ed.). Boston: Allyn & Bacon.

Washington, V., & Oyemade, U. J. (September 1985). Changing family trends—Head Start must respond. *Young children, 40*(5), 12–20.

14

Parents and Student Teachers

OBJECTIVES

After studying this chapter, the student will be able to:

- Name at least five techniques to use when interacting with parents.
- Watch a videotape, or listen to an audiotape, of a parent-teacher conference and analyze the interaction according to a theory of communication such as the Johari model.
- Participate in a mock parent-teacher conference, role playing both parent and teacher.
- Make a home visit with the cooperating teacher, write a report on the results of the home visit, and discuss it with peers, cooperating teacher, and supervisor.

What an education! It was impossible to ignore how individual parents separated from their children each day. Some kids got a farewell kiss and hug, others seemed shoved into the room.

Bing Anza Bohtua

I'll never forget the time my cooperating teacher told a parent about finding lice in her child's hair.

Friedel Huber

Deliver me from parent conferences! It's like walking on eggs blindfolded, and talking with someone who expects you to be an expert on a subject (their child) that they know a hundred times better than you do.

Shyree Torsham

I was placed at a parent cooperative preschool for student teaching. The play yard had the most creative and innovative play materials and structures. I learned what compulsory father involvement could achieve, and marveled at the Saturday father work crew's hard work. It was a terrifically maintained facility.

Nana Ghukar

The politics of some parent advisory group members confused many issues. My cooperating teacher and the school's director were models of professionalism. They seemed to be able to soothe differing factions with ease. This part of student teaching reminded me of something I remembered from previous classes. The school really was a microcosm of our diverse American society.

Rae Jean Wittsby

● INTERACTING WITH PARENTS

Most interactions with parents are informal, figure 14-1. The most frequent interaction occurs when parents bring and pick up their children from the center or school. The parents will say something to the teacher or smile and nod. These constitute interactions. Often when we have noted that children have done something commendable during the day, we will mention it briefly to the parents when the children are picked up. Likewise, if we think there has been a problem, we often take a few minutes to explain what has happened. Communications such as these are typical of the informal kind.

More formal communications consist of scheduled parent-teacher conferences and home visits. During a parent-teacher conference, a teacher might discuss the developing friendship between two children, figure 14-2. In each case the parents will have prior notice about the conference or home visit. They can then plan ahead. If the meeting is to take place at school, the parents can anticipate questions they may need to ask. Some parents may tell what they think we want to hear rather than the truth.

Honig (1979) has outlined some of the goals of parent-teacher interaction, they follow:
to increase
- parent self-assurance
- responsibility for parenting
- competence in learning-facilitation, interaction with the young child, and
- knowledge of how to use community resources and agencies.

Student teachers can observe their cooperating teacher's care of teacher-parent relationships noting the effectiveness of communications and actions.

First impressions of a child care facility form as parents park, enter, and observe lobby areas. The upkeep and maintenance of the school, grounds,

Figure 14-1 Most interactions with parents are informal.

Figure 14-2 The development of friendships may be discussed at parent-teacher conferences.

and equipment catch parent's eyes. Sounds and smells are noted. The people and conversations encountered, and staff manner and demeanor create distinct impressions. Parent phone inquiries also allow callers to assess the warmth, knowledge, and careful attention to detail provided by the answering staff member. Each center is felt to have a unique personality as judged by each new parent.

New student teachers are encouraged to observe staff and parent exchanges and introduce themselves as student teachers when parents approach. As the student teacher becomes acquainted and skilled, some cooperating teachers may feel parent contact can be handled by the student. It is wise to discuss this point with your cooperating teacher and college supervisor. Stone (1987) states that helping parents feel at ease is an art.

Children's Separation from Parents

Student teachers will observe daily how individual children enter and separate from their parents or adult caretaker at arrival. Separating from parents can be painful even though preschool is exciting and challenging (Stone, 1987). Some children need time to adjust and readjust to group care. Student teachers are often asked to aid entering children by providing attentive, patient support and comfort.

If the child permits, holding the child is suggested. Words that help could be, "You want your mom, but she needs to go to work. After nap time she'll come to get you. Let's go see what Lorie and Ebert are making at the center table."

Be prepared to stay near, hold, or comfort a crying child when a parent needs to leave after staying for an additional time to help the child with the transition. Short periods of parent absence are lengthened and, with teacher coaching, assurance, and parent firmness, most children adjust.

Stone (1987) mentions a teacher technique which aids some distressed children. "You're having a pretty hard time. Would it help if I wrote a note from you to your father? Tell me what to write in your note."

Problems with Reunion at Pickup Time

Many systems and ideas have been used to make parent pickup time easier for children, teachers, and parents. Teacher messages and the relating of anecdotes to individual parents often quickly take place at this time. Since cooperating teachers have the ultimate responsibility in a classroom, student teachers may respond to parent inquiries but also should refer the parent to the regular teaching staff. Children's belongings, including projects and artwork, are collected beforehand. Children are made ready to be picked up and, at times, are partially or fully dressed for outdoors. Teachers usually step in to help parents with dawdling or obstinate child behavior. Stone (1987) suggests friendly casual teacher actions, looks, and good-byes, and conveying limited "child concerned" information in a brief conversation. If more detailed information about the child is necessary for a parent, a note or follow-up phone call to arrange a conference is in order. The teacher's goal is to have a smooth transition with established routines. Schools adopt a variety of procedures to make departure times successful and as stress-free as possible.

MODELS OF COMMUNICATION

One communication model compares the process of communication to a telephone call in which there is a caller who is sending a message through a specific channel—the telephone—to a receiver, who has to decode the message (Berlo, 1960). Whether the message is understood depends upon five variables: the communication skills and the attitudes of both the receiver and sender, their knowledge, the social system to which each belongs, and their cultures, figure 14-3. Any differences between the sender and receiver on any of the variables can lead to misunderstandings.

Let us study a hypothetical situation involving Hernán, a student in your full-day, bilingual kindergarten; his mother, Mrs. Camacho; and Mrs. Garcia, the teacher. Mrs. Garcia thinks that Hernán is not getting enough sleep and telephones Mrs. Camacho to ask if she can come for a brief conference when she comes to pick up her children. Mrs. Camacho reluctantly agrees. Before the teacher and mother meet, they may already be processing information. Mrs. Garcia's inner thoughts are as follows:

Sender	Message	Channel	Receiver
Communication skills Attitudes Knowledge Social system Culture	Content Structure	Eyes (seeing) Ears (hearing) Hands (touching) Nose (smelling) Mouth (tasting) Body in space (kinesthesia)	Communication skills Attitudes Knowledge Social system Culture

Figure 14-3 Variables in a communication model.

Hernán always looks tired when his mother brings him to school every morning. During our rest time, he often falls asleep. Not many of the other five-year-olds do. For most of them, in fact, rest time is "squirm" time. It seems that we hardly even begin to turn on the music on the tape recorder before Hernán falls sound asleep. I've also noticed that Hernán is hard to awaken when rest time is over; I think he'd like to sleep for a longer period of time than we give him. I bet he doesn't get enough sleep at home. I think I'll talk to his mother about it.

After making an appointment with Mrs. Camacho for that evening, Mrs. Garcia may begin plans on how to approach the subject of Hernán's sleep schedule. Her ideas may be as follows:

I've always believed that the best approach in working with parents is first to let them know that I have the welfare of their child on my mind. I think I'll start by stating how much I enjoy having Hernán attend school. Then, let me see, should I come right out and ask how much sleep he gets? Maybe it would sound better if I ask when he goes to bed and when he gets up. If I don't think he's getting enough sleep, I can ask Hernán's mother how much sleep she thinks Hernán should get. Wait a minute, maybe I can ask her how much sleep her other children, Tomás and Roberto, used to get when they were five. No, I think asking when Hernán goes to bed and gets up is a better approach. Mrs. Camacho seems like a knowledgeable and caring mother. Certainly, Hernán arrives clean and well dressed every day.

In the meantime, Hernán's mother may be thinking along these lines:

Now why would Hernán's teacher want to talk about Hernán? I thought I filled her in on everything she needed to know when I enrolled him. Maybe he's been acting up at school. Maybe he got into a fight with Dave. Goodness knows he talks about beating up Dave if he keeps teasing him. Maybe it's finally happened. Carlos (Hernán's father) would surely be proud of Hernán for a change. He's always telling the boy to stop being such a sissy and letting Roberto or Tomás stick up for him! Maybe she wants me to bake something for school or take a day off work to help out. She knows I can't afford to take any more time off.

Perhaps a different approach would have been to ask the question over the telephone. Indeed, many teachers would do exactly this. Why bother a busy parent with a conference if the information can be handled on the telephone? Other teachers, however, prefer to ask any sensitive questions face-to-face in order to watch reactions. (Since many schools ask parents to fill out extensive questionnaires, some parents could feel that, through questioning of this type, their word is being doubted.)

Let us now proceed with the actual interaction between the two parties.

Teacher: Mrs. Camacho, please come into my office where it'll be quieter. Boys, why don't you find something to play with? Hernán, why don't you show Tomás where things are around the room? Roberto, I bet you remember where to find toys, don't you? (The boys go off to play, and Mrs. Camacho and Mrs. Garcia go into the office. Mrs. Garcia asks Mrs. Camacho if she would like a cup of coffee. Mrs. Camacho accepts.)

Mrs. Camacho, as you know, we are always concerned about the children and want what's best for them (She really looks tired this evening.)

Mother: (What's Mrs. Garcia mean? I know she has always been concerned about the children in her class. I remember how worried she was when Roberto had the flu two years ago, and I've told her more than once how happy I was that Hernán was placed in her class.) Yes, I remember how you called me when Roberto was so ill.

Teacher: Well, I've noticed that Hernán seems to sleep heavily during rest. Does he take rest on weekends? (That's as good a start as I can think of. Start with an observation; ask the parent if they've noted similar behavior at home. That's worked before.)

Mother: (I wonder what she's angling for?) Let's see. I think Hernán always takes a rest on the weekend. I like the boys to keep pretty much the same schedules as during the week, you know.

Teacher: What time does Hernán go to bed? Is it the same time as on weekdays? (I might as well simply ask her.)

Mother: We put the boys to bed between 8:00 p.m. and 9:00 p.m. weekdays, and we like to do the same on weekends so Mr. Camacho and I can get to a late movie or dinner once in a while. (What does she want? She *knows* what time the boys go to bed.)

Teacher: Do the boys get up at the same time on the weekend? (There, maybe that will get at what I'm trying to say. I'd lay odds that they sleep longer in the morning on the weekends.)

Mother: Tomás is usually up before Mr. Camacho and me. He likes to go into the living room and watch television Saturday mornings. When Mr. Camacho and I get up, all three boys are usually glued to the television.

Teacher: What time would that be?

Mother: About 9:00 a.m. usually. You see, Saturdays are the only days we get to sleep in, and we know the boys will be fine watching television. Also, their grandmother is usually up around 8:00 a.m., and she keeps an eye on the boys, especially if they go in the yard to play.

Teacher: Is Hernán ever asleep when you get up?

Mother: Once in a while but not usually. If we let the boys watch television Friday evening until 9:00, Hernán is usually still asleep after Mr. Camacho and I get up Saturday. Why are you asking me these ques-

tions about sleep and bedtimes? (I wonder what she wants to know.)

Teacher: I've wondered whether Hernán slept more on the weekend than during the week. You see, as I said before, I've noticed that he really falls sound asleep during resttime. You know, some children need more sleep than others. Have you noticed any difference with the three boys? (Maybe this will give her an idea that Hernán may need more sleep than the others. I hope so.)

Mother: Let me think. When Tomás was little, he didn't used to sleep too much. I remember it really annoyed me when I was carrying Roberto that Tomás didn't want to take a nap! And he wasn't even two yet! Roberto, though, was taking a nap even when after he came home from kindergarten. I remember being glad kindergarten was just a half-day program then. (Mrs. Garcia nods.) Roberto always needed more sleep than Tomás. That Tomás is like a live wire, always sparking!

Teacher: What about Hernán?

Mother: Hernán always seemed more like Tomás when he was little. But lately he seems more like Roberto. He and Roberto are real close, you know, always playing together. Tomás has his own friends now, especially since he's on the soccer team. Say, why don't you ask Tomás when Hernán gets up Saturday mornings? (Mrs. Camacho's voice trails off.) I think you're wondering if having all three boys go to bed at the same time is right for Hernán. Is Hernán getting enough rest?

Teacher: Exactly. What do you think?

At this point we are going to analyze the interaction according to the model in figure 14-3. Let us look first at our sender, Mrs. Garcia. What do her communication skills seem like? What appears to be her attitude toward Mrs. Camacho? Upon what is she basing her knowledge of the situation? From what kind of social system does Mrs. Garcia come? What is her cultural background? What about Hernán's mother? What is her cultural background? First, we might suggest that Mrs. Garcia's communication skills are reasonably sharp. She starts with an observation of Hernán and asks Mrs. Camacho to confirm or deny similar behavior on weekends.

Then Mrs. Garcia attempts to bring Mrs. Camacho to the same conclusion by asking if she had noted any differences between one boy and another. Eventually, because her communication skills are reasonably sharp, Mrs. Camacho realizes what Mrs. Garcia is asking and asks the question herself.

Second, in studying the interaction, we might surmise that Mrs. Garcia and Mrs. Camacho have smooth lines of communication between them. (You will note your cooperating teacher easily deals with parents who are known from previous experiences. You will also note, as a general rule, that the more a teacher deals with parents, the greater that teacher's skill.)

Next what can we guess about Mrs. Garcia's social system and culture? Her social system is her school and her family; her culture may be seen as Hispanic-American middle class. Mrs. Camacho's social system appears to be bureaucratic at work (she is a clerk-typist at a county office). Given Mr. Camacho's occupation at a foundry and his views of raising children as "women's work," we might surmise that the Camachos are from the Hispanic-American working class. Although Mrs. Garcia and Mrs. Camacho are both Hispanic, we do not know if they are from the same Hispanic cultural group. It is possible that one is from a Puerto Rican background and the other from a Mexican one. The differences in their social class may contribute to their differing views. A home visit might confirm many of our surmises. If we make further inquiries, we might discover that Mrs. Camacho has had some advanced secretarial training at a local junior college and that she attended a communications workshop for county employees who deal with the public.

Let us now look at the message. What was its content? How was it treated? What structure did it take? Simply, the content involved describing Hernán's rest time behavior at school to his mother. Mrs. Garcia was reporting to Mrs. Camacho. The structure involved verbal input, watching nonverbal input closely. It also involved asking questions in order to persuade Mrs. Camacho to see that Hernán might need more sleep. Part of the structure was also concerned with arranging the factors in a par-

ticular order. First, Mrs. Garcia directed the boys to entertain themselves and suggested to Hernán that he show his oldest brother the location of toys and equipment. In this way, Mrs. Garcia gave Hernán a job to do that would make him feel more competent and give him the opportunity to direct his bossy, oldest brother. Then Mrs. Garcia spoke directly to the second-oldest boy, telling him that he would know where things were and, indirectly, rewarding him for his good memory.

Next Mrs. Garcia arranged for a quiet and private conference. (In a case such as this, Mrs. Garcia probably would have asked her aide to take charge in the room.) Knowing that Mrs. Camacho would enjoy a cup of coffee, Mrs. Garcia offered her some. (Having something to drink and/or eat helps establish rapport. It also helps a tired parent relax.) In addition, Mrs. Garcia did not sit behind her desk but, instead, sat on a chair next to Mrs. Camacho.

What channels of communication were used during the interaction? Most obviously were the ears for hearing and the eyes for seeing. Since Mrs. Garcia offered a cup of coffee or tea to Mrs. Camacho, the mouth or sense of taste would have been involved also. It is difficult not to involve the sense of touch and the kinesthetic sense. Shaking hands involves touch; walking, sitting down, and holding a mug of coffee or tea all involve the kinesthetic sense. It is through these messages from our senses that we interpret the stimuli that form our world. Under many circumstances, each person involved may have separate interpretations of the same set of stimuli; this is where misunderstandings develop. In our multicultural, multiracial culture we are, perhaps, prone to misunderstandings that can arise from different interpretations of the same data.

Look at figure 14-3. Let us assume that Mrs. Garcia is a well-educated (master's degree in early childhood education), articulate, middle-class Hispanic woman. Let us further assume that she was raised by educated religious parents. Mrs. Garcia's values will reflect her upbringing. Strict but warm-hearted, she believes in practicing her religion every day. She attempts to see the good in everyone. Even when she disagrees with someone, she tries to see their point. A believer in God and family, Mrs. Garcia also defers to Mr. Garcia in personal family matters.

What would happen if Hernán's mother was a poorly educated single parent who had just arrived in this country? Her reaction to Mrs. Garcia might be very different than that which was previously described. First, using figure 14-3, there would be a difference on each of the variables or characteristics listed under Sender and Receiver. These differences in communication skills, knowledge, social system, and culture could make it extremely difficult for Mrs. Garcia to communicate with Mrs. Camacho.

Even less obvious differences can block understanding. One such block was suggested in the first description of Hernán's parents. Mr. Camacho was described as a foundry worker who thought raising children was women's work. As a result, the boys had to remain at the school an hour longer than necessary because he would not pick them up. It was further suggested that Mr. Camacho was proud of his oldest boy, Tomás, because of his size and athletic ability and less proud of Hernán who was small for his age. We might also assume a difference in the way in which Mrs. Garcia and Mrs. Camacho view Hernán. For example, Mrs. Garcia might see a sensitive, quiet little boy who needs a lot of loving care. Mrs. Camacho might see Hernán as a "sissy" who was afraid to stand up for his own rights. Mrs. Garcia might try to educate the parents to make them change their attitude about what characteristics a boy or man should have. In doing so, it is likely that she might fail. This is because attitudes are resistant to change. Mrs. Garcia might have more success helping Hernán feel better about himself in terms of activities at school. Mrs. Garcia should interfere in the family matter only if she perceives that Mrs. Camacho has some doubts about her husband's views. Even then, Mrs. Garcia should proceed carefully. Changing family attitudes is risky. Regardless of how we might feel about how a father treats his son, it is important to remember that the child has to learn to live with the parent's attitude.

The Johari Model

Let us now consider a second model of communication: the Johari model, which was named after its two originators, Joseph Luft and Harry Ingham. The Johari model is presented in figure 14-4. In the model there are four "windows." The upper left corner window is "open"; in other words, what is presented to another person is known both to the other person and to the self. The upper right corner is the "blind" window. This window represents those aspects of ourselves that are evident to others but not to ourselves. The lower left corner is the "hidden" window. In any interpersonal exchange, there may be aspects of ourselves that we may want to hide from another person. The last window, on the bottom right side, is "unknown." There are aspects about a person both unknown to that person as well as to any observer.

Let us use the example of the interaction between Mrs. Garcia and Mrs. Camacho to illustrate how the Johari window might look. Before the conference Mrs. Camacho might keep the "open" part of her window fairly small. Mrs. Garcia, in contrast, may have a larger "open" window and keep her "hidden" window larger, at least initially. As the two women begin to feel more comfortable the "open" windows of each will widen, and Mrs. Garcia's "hidden" window will become smaller. Mrs. Camacho's "blind" window may become smaller as she begins to realize that Hernán may need more sleep, something that she had not thought about before.

The Johari model can be adjusted to increase or decrease various parts according to the situation. For example, as a person grows older, he or she will often learn more about the self; that person's "blind" and "unknown" windows may grow smaller. In a new

	Known to self	Not known to self
Known to others	Open	Blind
Not known to others	Hidden	Unknown

Figure 14-4 The Johari model of communication. (From *Of Human Interaction* by Joseph Luft. Palo Alto, CA: National Press Books, 1969.)

social situation in which one feels uncomfortable, one's "open" window might be quite small. With a best friend, however, this "open" window might be very large.

Nonverbal Communication

We have suggested that nonverbal communication often tells more than verbal communication about how someone feels. In the previous example, the teacher noted that Mrs. Camacho seemed tired. Was there any evidence for this? Most likely, it was based upon nonverbal communication. Study figure 14-5. You will note that nonverbal communication involves body talk, such as gestures, facial expression, eye expression, stance, and large body muscles. Motions such as a wave of the hand, a shrug of the shoulders, a smile, standing erect or slumping all send messages. Actions like pushing one's chair closer or away from another and leaning forward or back also seem to send messages.

Just as nonverbal communications give clues, so does verbal communication. The tone, pitch, rate, and loudness of a person's voice send messages. When a person is excited, the pitch of the voice will rise and the rate of speech will increase. Excitement causes a person to speak more loudly. Anger often makes a person speak more loudly and quickly, but the pitch may become lower and the tone hard. As mentioned by Gordon (1974), we should strive to be "active listeners." We should listen to hidden messages, not just to words.

The observation that Mrs. Camacho looks tired is based upon her knit eyebrows, turned-down corners of the mouth, slumping shoulders, quiet voice, and slow rate of speech. She may use no words to indicate her fatigue. In fact, listening only to her words does not give us any clue as to how she feels. This is based totally upon nonverbal clues and our active listening.

Conferencing: Communication Techniques

In order to grasp fully the different methods of communication, it is a good idea to act out situations. You should take turns with your peers role playing parents and teachers. Try this: On a three-by-five card, write a communication problem you have observed at your center or school. Place all the cards in a box. Pair off with another student teacher and pick a problem from the box. Discuss and decide how you both would resolve the problem. Present your results to the class. Your peers should use the models of

Message sent through body talk	Specific Physical Expression					
	Gesture	Facial expression	Eye expression	Large Body muscles	Stance or posture	Comments

Message sent vocally	Specific Vocal Expression				
	Tone	Pitch	Rate	Loudness	Comments

Figure 14-5 Nonverbal interaction sheet.

communication to analyze the action of the conference being role played. You and your partner should use the same form so that you can discuss how you both see the action. You will find this exercise interesting. It will be helpful to be aware of some specific communication techniques that work in conjunction with the models of communication.

The following are suggestions for planning and conducting teacher-parent conferences:

- In working with parents, the first rule is to put them at ease. Seat the parents comfortably. Offer something to eat or drink, especially if the conference is at the end of a workday.

- Try to begin the conference in a positive manner. Even if you need to report a child's negative behavior or ask the parent a difficult question, always start on a positive note. Comment on the child's good behaviors or actions before stating what the child does incorrectly.

- Try to elicit from the parent a description of the child's behavior in school. (This is especially appropriate in a setting such as a parent-cooperative or child development center.) If the parent has not seen the child in action at school, ask about the child's observed behavior at home or in other social settings such as church, if appropriate. This will enable you to study the degree of parental perceptivity regarding the child's behavior.

- Be specific when describing the child's behavior, figure 14-6. Avoid generalities. Use descriptive, preferably written, accounts taken over a period of at least three consecutive days, with several samplings per day.

- Keep samples of the child's work in a folder with the child's name and with the date indicating when the sampling was taken. Actual samples of work can speak more loudly and eloquently than words.

- Avoid comparisons with other children. Each child is unique. Most develop in idiosyncratic ways that make comparisons unfair. (If the comparison must be done for a valid reason, do this carefully and only with your cooperating teacher's permission.)

- When you have to present some negative behavior, *avoid*, as much as possible, making any evaluation about the goodness or badness of the child and/or the parent.

- Remember your attitude is important. You can choose to CARE.

- Keep any conference "on focus." Remember that most parents are busy; their time is valuable. Do not waste it. Discuss whatever is supposed to be discussed. Do not stray off course.

- Be cheerful, friendly, and tactful.

- Act cordially; remember your manners even if the parents forget theirs. Remember that it takes two to argue.

- Be honest; avoid euphemisms. Do not say "Tony is certainly a creative child!" when you really mean "Boy! Can Tony ever find ways to bother me!"

- Be businesslike, even with a parent who may be a friend. In this situation, you are the professional, not the friend.

- Know your facts and the program so well that you never feel defensive discussing it.

Figure 14-6 Monica frequently helps classmates.

- Be enthusiastic, even if you are tired and feeling down.
- Do not discuss another child unless it is appropriate.
- Do not make judgments before you have had the opportunity to see all the evidence.
- Do not betray confidences. A child will often tell you something that should not be repeated or something about the parents, which is best overlooked. If, however, you think the disclosure is important to the child's welfare, discuss with your cooperating teacher and/or college supervisor. Rely upon their recommendations.
- Observe the parents' body language. It will often tell you more about how they are really feeling than the words they say.

In the rest of this chapter, we will present some ground rules for home visits as well as some ideas for parent involvement in the school.

☛ PLANNING THE HOME VISIT

Some schools have a policy that the family of each enrolled child must be visited at least once during the school year. Other schools, both public and private, have a policy that teachers should visit the families of every enrolled child during the latter part of the summer prior to the opening of school. If you are student teaching in a school where home visits are an accepted feature, planning a home visit usually involves no more than choosing, with your cooperating teacher, which home to visit. Many times the cooperating teacher may ask you to visit the home of a child with whom you are having difficulty establishing rapport. Other times you may be asked to visit the home of a child with whom you have had little interaction. You may be asked to visit the home of a child who needs more attention than another.

Your first step is to contact the parents and let them know you would like to make a home visit. Since most parents will ask why, it is a good idea to discuss the reason for the visit with your cooperating teacher prior to telephoning or speaking to the parents. In many cases your response may be simply

that you would like to get to know the child better. Other times the cooperating teacher will suggest you tell the parents that your cooperating teacher recommended your visiting the home. If the school requires home visits, the parents may be more hospitable than those from a center without such a policy.

Another point that should be made concerns planning home visits at homes of parents from different ethnic or social groups. Parents may be suspicious of your motive in wanting to visit, especially at a school or center without a home visitation policy. In this situation, you should defer to the wishes of your cooperating teacher and allow the cooperating teacher to make the choice and the initial contact with the parents. In some cases you will accompany the cooperating teacher rather than make a solo visit.

Regarding the question of home visits, in most cases it is best to ask the parents when they bring or pick up their child. It helps to watch nonverbal cues in planning how you will ask. (Obviously, if the parents seem tired, cross, and/or hurried, you should wait. It is better to ask when the parents are in a good mood and when they have the time to talk for a few minutes.) Naturally, the longer you are at a center, the better some parents will begin to know you. With one of these parents, you may feel quite comfortable about planning the home visit over the telephone. Your cooperating teacher may even encourage a telephone contact so that you can gain experience making such calls.

Let us assume that you and your cooperating teacher have discussed which child's home that you and your cooperating teacher are to visit. *Your cooperating teacher will speak to the parents, preferably in person.* She waits until the parent comes to pick up the child and seems unrushed. At this point, she could ask if there is a convenient time for the two of you to visit the child at home. The mother will most likely ask why; your cooperating teacher may say, "We'd like to get to know Sandy better."

Mrs. Campbell, Sandy's mother, may or may not bring up some obstacles. She may work in a 9:00 a.m. to 5:00 p.m. job so that, unless you could plan the visit on the weekend, it would not be convenient for her. (Of course, home visits can be planned at any time, including weekends, evenings, and even holidays.) Your cooperating teacher may suggest an evening or a coming holiday. Naturally, some parents do not work; therefore, they may have more time during the day in which to plan a visit. (Sandy Campbell comes from an economically disadvantaged family and receives a free lunch. She often arrives at school in clean, but too large clothing, and appears wan and undersized. You feel a home visit might provide you with an opportunity to know the child's background, and thus the child, better.)

After setting the time and day for the home visit, you may want to talk again with your cooperating teacher. What is the purpose of the home visit? Most commonly, it provides you with the opportunity to become better acquainted with the child. What should you look for? In addition to seeing how the child behaves at home, you are interested in watching the interactions that take place between the child and others in the home—parents, siblings, other relatives, and/or friends. Logically, too, you will want to note what kind of a home it is. (A child may live in a very poor section of town yet have a home that is clean and warm in atmosphere. Another may live in a mansion that is well-kept and beautifully furnished; yet, the atmosphere may be cold and sterile, without love.)

Now the two of you are ready for the home visit. You both have talked to Mrs. Campbell, and she has suggested that a week from Saturday at 2:00 p.m. would be best for her. Since you live in a large, urban community, you have to plan on a trip across town. You both estimate that it will take about one-half hour to make the trip and allow an extra 15 minutes in case you get lost.

● THE HOME VISIT

You arrive at the Campbells' apartment a few minutes early. You both decide to look around before you go into the apartment. The Campbells live in a lower-income area. The streets are dirty and littered with paper, broken bottles, and empty soda and beer cans. There is little grass in front of the apartment house; the yard is generally unkempt and weedy. The apartment house, like the others on the street, is built in motel fashion. It is badly in need of paint, and you easily can see that local teenagers have used the walls for graffiti. There are at least two abandoned cars on the street. One has no tires, and its windows are smashed; the other is resting on its rims and is severely dented as though it had been hit in an accident and never repaired. Further down the street, a group of youths are playing soccer in the street. Some of them appear to belong to an ethnic minority. A radio or record player is blaring from one of the apartments; a baby is heard crying.

You get out of the car, lock it, and look at the mailboxes to see which apartment is the Campbells'. They live in apartment 2E. You begin to make your way through the cluttered hallway and almost trip over a small, grubby child riding a rickety, old tricycle. "Who ya lookin' for?" she demands. You tell her you are going to visit the Campbells. The little girl responds negatively. "Oh them! They're sure stuck up. Why dya want to see them?" You walk past the child, who keeps pestering you with questions. When she sees that you have no intention of answering, she rides off.

You walk up the stairs to the second floor, noting the chipped paint and shaky railings. You go past the apartments with the blaring radio and the crying child, arriving finally at 2E. You ring the bell. Sandy answers. She is spotlessly clean and wearing what appears to be her Sunday dress. She greets you shyly, ducking her head. You enter a sparsely furnished but immaculate apartment. The television is on; Sandy goes into the kitchen and announces your arrival. Mrs. Campbell enters and asks you to sit. She has just made some tea and offers you some. You thank her and accept. She leaves and returns quickly with four steaming mugs, one each for you and your cooperating teacher, one for herself, and a small one for Sandy.

Before your cooperating teacher can ask anything, Mrs. Campbell hesitantly and nervously says, "I want to apologize for making you come all this way on a Saturday, but I dare not ask for time off from work. And I did think your wanting to visit us was such a nice thing. It's good for Sandy to see you're interested in her like that." Your cooperating teacher murmurs something about wanting to get to know Mrs. Campbell better as well, figure 14-7. Mrs. Campbell suggests to Sandy that she show you some of her books. "I think books are so important. Sandy and I go to the library every two weeks, and she picks out six books to bring home to read. You know I read to her every night, don't you?"

You wonder if Sandy and Mrs. Campbell live by themselves or if there are any others who share the apartment. You then remember that Mrs. Campbell listed two parents on Sandy's school enrollment form. "Is Mr. Campbell at work?" your cooperating teacher asks. Mrs. Campbell sighs. "I only wish he were!" she says. Sandy announces, "Daddy's at the races. He thinks Sandy's Dream is going to win today. He told me my name would bring him good luck." Mrs. Campbell admonishes Sandy. "Now, you be quiet, Sandy. Miss Julie doesn't care about what Daddy's doing." Mrs. Campbell smiles slightly and shrugs her shoulders. "Mr. Campbell has been out of work lately and has been going to the races to pass the time." Without thinking, the teacher asks what Mr. Campbell does for a living. "He's a heavy equipment operator; you know, he

Figure 14-7 Home visits enable the child, parent, and teacher to get to know each other better.

operates those big road-grading machines they use to build highways. Only, there hasn't been much work lately, and Mr. Campbell doesn't like to take jobs away from home. It makes it real hard on Sandy and me, though, because there's only my salary to live on. You know, we used to have our own home in suburbia but we had to give it up in order to pay our bills after John lost his last job."

You remember that Mrs. Campbell listed her job as billing clerk for a large corporation with headquarters in your area. You get the impression that Mrs. Campbell is trying very hard to maintain her small apartment the same way she kept her former home.

A shout from the apartment from next door can be heard. "You'll have to ignore the Browns," Mrs. Campbell says. "They always fight when he's had too much to drink." Angry voices can be heard screaming at each other.

Sandy has disappeared and returns with a dilapidated rag doll in her arms. "Want to see Andrea?" (Sandy pronounces it like An-Dray-a) she asks, thrusting the doll under your nose. "Sandy, don't bother Miss Julie when we're talking," admonishes Mrs. Campbell. "That's okay, Mrs. Campbell." You pick up the doll and look closely at it, smiling at Sandy. "Sandy, I think you love your doll very much, don't you?" Sandy enthusiastically nods her head. Mrs. Campbell gives her a quick look and shake of her head. Sandy goes over to her mother, sits down on the rug, and plays with her doll.

The cooperating teacher and Mrs. Campbell continue the conversation for another 15 or 20 minutes. You wonder if Mr. Campbell will come home from the racetrack before you leave, and you decide that Mrs. Campbell chose this time for you to come knowing that Mr. Campbell would not be there. It makes you wonder about their relationship. Mrs. Campbell has offered no information about Mr. Campbell other than to answer the teacher's question about his work. You sense some underlying feelings of anger and despair but also feel that it is none of your business.

You both soon rise to leave and thank Mrs. Campbell and Sandy for their hospitality. You and your teacher hand Sandy your mugs. She turns to her mother and asks if she can walk you to your car. Mrs. Campbell replies, "Okay, Sandy, but come right back upstairs. I don't want you playing with those no-good riffraff downstairs." She turns to your co-operating teacher and explains that the children who live below are "real rough and use language I don't approve of so I don't let Sandy play with them." "They swear," Sandy volunteers, "and use words my Momma and Daddy won't let me repeat." Mrs. Campbell glances quickly at the teacher.

"It's not so bad now, but I worry about when Sandy grows a little older. It won't be easy keeping her away from them when they all get into school together." Her face brightens a little. "But maybe we'll be able to move from here by then. We're trying to save so we can move across Main Street." You understand what she means. The houses and apartments across Main Street are cleaner and better kept; most people own their own homes.

Reflections on the Home Visit

After returning to your own home, you jot down your impressions of the visit with Mrs. Campbell and Sandy. Your first impression is that they seem out of place in the neighborhood. Mrs. Campbell obviously attempts to keep the apartment clean. Sandy is always clean and wears clean clothes to school. At the age of four, she already knows to wash her hands when she goes to the bathroom; you have not had to remind her as you have the other children. You also noted that Sandy eats slowly and uses good manners, reflecting good training at home.

Your second impression is that Mrs. Campbell is under great strain where Mr. Campbell is concerned. You understand why Sandy is such a quiet child. Mrs. Campbell is a quiet woman who is training Sandy to be a quiet child at home. You also understand why Sandy rarely mentions her father. It is obvious that Mrs. Campbell disapproves of her husband spending time at the races. You suspect that Mr. and Mrs. Campbell have probably had many arguments about this matter, especially since their finances seem somewhat precarious. You may have also surmised that the couple has had many arguments about Mr. Campbell's unemployment. These disagreements

may be another reason why Sandy is quiet and subdued. Sandy may blame herself for the difficulties her parents express between themselves. You begin to realize why Sandy needs emotional support before trying something new and much praise when accomplishing something that is fairly simple. In addition, Sandy's desire to please her mother is carried into her relationship with adults at school; she is always seeking adult approval. "Is this the way you want it done?" or "Do you want me to help you?"

As you relate your impressions to your cooperating teacher, you have another thought. Not only did the Campbells seem out of place in the neighborhood, but you suspect that Mrs. Campbell has no friends among her neighbors. You wonder to whom she would turn when and if she ever needed help. The cooperating teacher suggests that Mrs. Campbell might receive support from the pastor at her church. She had listed a church affiliation on the questionnaire that she completed when she enrolled Sandy. You and your cooperating teacher agree that Mrs. Campbell probably attends church regularly. Certainly, Sandy has talked enough about Sunday school to confirm this possibility. You are slightly relieved to think that Mrs. Campbell is not quite as isolated as you had thought.

● OTHER HOME-SCHOOL INTERACTIONS

At this point we have talked only about two types of home and school interactions: the parent conference (formal and informal) and the home visit. There are many other types of interactions as well, figure 14-8. Many preschools, day care centers, and elementary schools have parent advisory boards that develop policy and procedures, plan parent education programs and fund-raising events, and even interview prospective teachers, aides, or parents who wish to enroll their children in the center.

Even if a school or center has no parent advisory board, it may hold regular parent education programs. Some preschools, especially those associated with adult education classes on child development, include parent education as a mandatory part of their program. Other preschools send home checklists of possible topics for parents in planning parent education meetings. Topics may range from discipline and related problems to specific areas of the curriculum to planning for emergencies.

Most elementary schools have regularly scheduled PTA/PTO meetings. Typically, the September meeting is called Back-to-School night and offers an explanation by each teacher of the class curriculum. Generally, teachers arrange displays of the children's work on bulletin boards and explain curriculum goals for the year. Many teachers have parent sign-up sheets posted for parent volunteer help, and all teachers attempt to establish rapport with their respective parent groups. Student teachers are traditionally introduced at this time also.

Another form of home-school interaction consists of formal and informal written communications.

Figure 14-8 Sample of a center's event bulletin.

Most public school districts and private schools send newsletters home to parents. These typically include a calendar of upcoming district and school events and articles for parents on specific parts of the curriculum, ideas for parents to implement at home, and so on. These may be written by the superintendent and/or headmaster/director or by curriculum specialists and consultants. Sometimes individual teachers prepare newsletters to send to parents or for students to take home to their parents. They frequently include news about topics that will be taught in the class that month, articles written and illustrated by the children themselves, requests for toys and/or books, requests for volunteers for an upcoming field trip, and so on. Newsletters frequently include curriculum items for parents to try at home (especially arts and crafts), recipes for snacks, and a question/answer column for parents. They may also contain a swap column or notices of toys to exchange. There may even be a column written by the parents. Some centers and most school newsletters advertise parent education/PTA/PTO meetings.

Polls of Parent Attitudes

In response to what activities people would include for parents if they were a school principal, the top three answers were parent-teacher conferences, parent education, and newsletters. A PTA or PTO (Parent/Teacher Association and Parent/Teacher Organization) and parent volunteers were fourth and fifth respectively. Child care during conferences was listed sixth; after-school programs for working parents was seventh. Special support groups for parents were listed eighth (reflecting the growing number of families with single parents) and Parents Anonymous (a telephone hot line for potential and actual child abusers) came in eighteenth. Interestingly enough, home visits were listed sixteenth; however, this may be because the questionnaire addressed itself to public schools rather than to parents with preschool youngsters (Elam, 1990).

In the latest poll of the attitudes of the public toward the public schools, there are some major changes to note. Forty-one percent of the people surveyed rated schools in their own communities highly (grades of A and B), and this figure has been remarkably consistent over the past 10 years (not varying, with one exception of seven percent, more than one to three percent). However, the perception of the schools in the nation as a whole was quite different; only 20 percent of the respondents graded them with an A or a B. Again, this figure has been reasonably consistent over the past 10 years, dropping from the highs of 27 and 28 percent in 1985 and 1986. Still, a drop of seven or eight percentage points is not too dramatic.

New concerns were voiced in this year's poll: lack of discipline, lack of parental control, and violence. Inclusion came under attack also: Respondents were asked, "In your opinion, should children with learning problems be put in the same classes with other students, or should they be put in special classes?" Responses indicated that only 26 percent felt special needs students should be placed in regular classes while two-thirds (66 percent) felt special students should be in special classes. Eight percent said they didn't know. These figures are, perhaps, an indication that the general public has a long way to go before full inclusion becomes widely accepted. They also may sound an alarm for educators that the public is not well informed about inclusion (Elam & Rose, 1995).

Precautions

Obviously a survey of parents whose children are enrolled in your center or school will be of more value than a national survey. You will never truly know what activities the parents perceive as being important unless you ask.

If you belong to a racial or ethnic group that is different from that of the parents, you will need to be especially sensitive to the cultural differences, figure 14-9. Even social class differences among people of the same racial and ethnic group can lead to communication blocks. Differences in education promote problems also. You need to know whether the parents can read and understand English well enough to answer the survey.

If you have several non- or limited-English-speaking (NES or LES) parents, you may want to have another person translate the survey, either orally or in writing, so that the NES or LES parents

Figure 14-9 Children's cultural backgrounds may be both similar and different.

active in school activities because they do not believe they are wanted or educated enough. This can result in the parents feeling that they are not respected by the teacher, director, or student teacher. This feeling can become more bitter if the teacher belongs to a different race or ethnic group. As you begin to work with minority families, you will need to develop insight into the problems that may be unique to them.

Single-parent families are also prone to stress, some created by the myths surrounding the stereotype of the minority or single parent. It is a myth, for example, that the child from a single-parent family will have emotional problems. The truth may be that had the parent remained married to an abusive other parent, the child might have been disturbed. Likewise, it is a myth that the single parent lacks interest in the school's activities. Since most single parents are women, and women tend to have lower-paying jobs with less personal freedom, they may not be able to participate in the school program. Be very careful not to interpret this as a lack of interest. The truth may be that single parents cannot take time off from work in order to be more active. The single parent may compensate by talking with the child every evening and sending notes when questions arise. The single parent may not have time to bake cookies for a party but may be willing to buy napkins. Another single parent may not have time to be a classroom volunteer but may be able to arrange her or his work time to chaperone a field trip.

Be aware that single parents may need a support group, especially if they have no family members living close by. If you have several children from single-parent families, you might even want to plan a parent education meeting devoted to their needs. At one Head Start center, the number one request by parents who were asked about preferences for the program's parent education meeting was the topic of "stress and the single parent" (Cutteridge, 1990, personal communication).

Be sensitive, especially if you are in an infant/toddler center; understand that the mother may feel guilty leaving her child every day to go to work. Even parents of older children can feel this way, as can parents from families in which both par-

can provide input. If you know of even one parent who has difficulty reading English, you can discuss the questions on your survey in an informal interview, asking the questions orally. With LES and NES parents, it is sometimes of value to ask the parents to spend some time in the room with their child. Then you can ask the child to explain to the parents what is happening in the room. Children, especially preschoolers, acquire a second language much more easily than adults, and they make good teachers for their parents. This is particularly true in centers where there is warmth and respect for everyone.

When there are obvious social class differences, it is important to realize that some parents may not be

ents work. Remember that most mothers work not because they want to, but because they have to. Many of them might be happier to be home with their child. Some mothers, mostly professionals, choose to work because they enjoy their jobs.

Unfortunately, many families cannot exist without the income from two working parents. Be sensitive to ways in which they can involve themselves in the life of the center without taking away from their limited time. Parent education meetings are fine, but not if a parent of limited income has to hire a babysitter. Knowing this, your cooperating teacher or director may make arrangements for children to be cared for on site. Many families may not have a car and must rely on public transportation. Find out when buses travel and what routes are available. Make sure the meetings end on time so a parent does not miss the bus.

Remember that parent education, however important it may seem to you, may not be as valuable to every parent. Many will choose to attend when the topic presented meets their needs and be absent when it does not. Others may find it too hectic to try to attend a meeting held in the evening. They may reason that there is not enough time after getting out of work, picking up the children, arriving home, fixing dinner, and eating.

There will always be one parent upon whom you can rely regardless of the circumstances. Do not take advantage of this. Some parents cannot say no.

A Parent-Teacher Dilemma

At a time when early childhood experts are urging teachers to implement more informal, open-ended, child-initiated curriculums, teachers face an increased demand for basic skill, academic instruction for preschool children. Stipek, Rosenblatt, and Di Rocco (1994) believe teachers have two choices for dealing with parental pressure: they can give in, or they try to educate parents. They recommend the second choice. Because parents and teachers have fundamentally the same goals for young children, the task of educating parents about developmentally appropriate practice may be easier than it would seem.

SUMMARY

In this chapter we discussed interactions between parents and student teachers and between parents and teachers. We have presented you with three models of communication, both verbal and nonverbal. Finally, we presented a list of some specific techniques to use when interacting with parents.

Always remember: Most parent-teacher communication is informal in nature. Therefore, it is important to remember that the impression you make in informal interactions may often set the stage for how a parent views and accepts you.

We have detailed a home visit as seen from the student teacher's perspective. We included illustrations not only of the physical description of the parents' home but also of the feelings experienced by the student teacher. We also discussed other home and school interactions—from the informal and formal interview to the newsletter and parent education meeting. Finally, we have cautioned you to be aware of cultural, familial differences, pointing out that these exist even within what appears to be a single culture.

Awareness of the parents' communities can be obtained through procedures as simple as a drive through the neighborhood or as complex as a formal written survey for parents to answer. Such knowledge will make you more sensitive to the parents and help you communicate with them. The parents will then be more interested in what is going on at the school and will be more willing to become active in its support.

SUGGESTED ACTIVITIES

A. If your school has videotape equipment, role play a difficult parent conference in which you play the teacher attempting to talk to a mother about her physically aggressive child and she refuses to believe you. Observe yourself during playback. Using figure 14-5, notice your nonverbal communications. Analyze your verbal communication, using either figure 14-3 or 14-4. Discuss your analysis with your peers, supervisor, and/or cooperating teacher.

B. Read Fast's *Body Language in the Work Place*. Replay your videotaped role play and analyze the body language you and the "parent" used.

C. Observe the arrival of children and parents at a local preschool program. Who greets them? How are separation difficulties managed? How are teachers building school-home relationships? Would you change any school procedures? If so, why?

D. With your cooperating teacher's permission, interview some of the parents at your center. What kinds of support systems do they appear to have? In what type of activity at the center do they enjoy participating or do they prefer not to participate? Why?

E. Check the mode of transportation used by the parents at your center. Do most of them have their own cars? Do many of them use public transportation? Do some of them walk? What are the implications for parent education meetings regarding the most common mode of transportation? Discuss this with your peers, cooperating teacher, and supervisor.

F. How are local schools in your community helping to assimilate newly arrived immigrants into the system? What kinds of specialized materials are being used, if any? What kinds of specialized services are offered? Discuss your findings with your peers and supervisor.

G. Interview a single parent. Find out some of the advantages and the disadvantages of raising a child alone. What support system does the parent need? What are some of the resources they use? Have they been satisfied with the services?

H. Take a poll of your fellow student teachers. What kinds of life-styles are represented? Discuss your findings.

I. With a group of four classmates, discuss how a teacher might demonstrate sensitivity toward the following parents.

- single parent who had child while in high school
- low-income parent
- grandparent raising daughter's child
- foreign-born parent
- parent whose child wears designer clothes to school
- nonliterate parent
- newly divorced parent
- non–English-speaking parent
- parent employed as school's cook
- Asian parent who works as a classroom volunteer
- Hispanic parent who is a migrant worker
- out-of-work, welfare parent

REVIEW

A. Using the Johari model, draw how you might appear in the following:

1. How you appear to your best friend.
2. How a young child might appear to his or her parent.
3. Anyone in a new environment.
4. An older person facing a new situation.
5. A student on the first day of class.
6. Someone who is unsure of herself.
7. A teacher who unexpectedly is asked by the principal to come into her or his office.
8. Your reaction when the director of your placement center comes into your room unexpectedly.
9. How you may appear to your students on the last day of class.
10. How you may appear to a group of peers whom you know well and respect.

B. Read the following dialogue. Then complete the activity which follows.

Setting: It is early in the year. This is Susie's first experience in preschool. An only child of older parents, Susie always comes to school in clean dresses with ruffles and lace trim. Susie is average in size for her four years. She is attractive and has dark hair and dark eyes. A rather dominant child, Susie has excellent language skills which she uses to boss other children. Because of this behavior, Susie has come into conflict with Janice, a small, wiry child who has been attending the preschool since she was three. Janice is very assertive and clearly resents Susie. Susie does not like Janice. Their mutual dislike has led to a clothes-pulling incident. As a result, the ruffle on Susie's dress was partially torn off and Janice's shirt collar was ripped. As the student teacher, you became involved because the incident erupted on the playground when you were in charge. Mrs. Brown, your cooperating teacher, has contacted both mothers and arranged to see each parent separately. She has asked you to talk to Mrs. Smith, Janice's mother, while she talks to Mrs. Jones, Susie's mother. She explains further that Mrs. Smith is rather proud of Janice's assertiveness and understands that it sometimes leads Janice into altercations with the other children. You have met Mrs. Smith before and have sat in on at least one parent conference with her. You feel comfortable explaining what happened. (Some training programs advise cooperating teachers that student teachers are not qualified to hold individual conferences with parents.)

Student teacher (*ST*): Mrs. Smith, it is good to see you again. Wouldn't you like to come into the office? I think there may be a cup of coffee left in the pot. (You greet Mrs. Smith with a smile. You remember that she likes a cup of coffee after work and had two cups during the last conference. You pour a cup of coffee for Mrs. Smith and a cup of tea for yourself. You sit in the chair at a right angle to her.)

Mrs. Smith (*MS*): Thank you. You know how much I enjoy my coffee, don't you? Now, what's happened? I know you wouldn't ask me here without a reason.

ST: Well, today, when the children were outside for free play, Janice and Susie had an argument. (You say this with a shrug of your shoulders and a slightly nervous smile.)

MS: I've been wondering when that would happen. You know, Janice often tells me how much she hates Susie! (She says this looking directly at you.

You begin to feel uncomfortable and look away.) What happened exactly?

ST: Well, Janice and Susie got into a clothes-pulling fight before I knew what had happened. Unfortunately, Janice's shirt collar was torn, and the ruffle on Susie's dress was ripped. (You look at the floor as you say this, feeling uncomfortable about not having intervened before the fight erupted.)

MS: You know, Janice's shirt was new. I should have known better than to let her first wear it to school. (She laughs.) You know, I sometimes think Janice is more like a boy than a girl! That's why I let her wear pants all the time. Fortunately, a torn shirt is easy to mend, but I hate mending! I never did figure why Susie always has a dress on; it must really hamper her play. (She looks sharply at you.) Hey, it's okay. These things happen from time to time. I know Janice well enough to know that she's bound to get into a fight once in a while. She's just like her older brother. In fact, I think he's the one she admires most!

Identify the following statements as either *true* or *false*. If the validity of any statement cannot be determined due to lack of information, identify it as such.

1. Mrs. Smith seems to be more comfortable than the student teacher.

2. The student teacher's approach to the conference was effective.

3. The student teacher watched Mrs. Smith's body language.

4. Mrs. Smith understands the situation well.

5. This was probably one of the student teacher's first conferences alone without the support of the cooperating teacher.

6. Using the model in figure 14-3, both Mrs. Smith and the student teacher appear to have equally refined communication skills.

7. According to the model in figure 14-3, the student teacher and Mrs. Smith are most likely from the same culture.

8. Using the model in figure 14-4, Mrs. Smith reveals a larger "open" window than the student teacher.

9. Based on the model in figure 14-4, the student teacher most likely has a larger "blind" window than Mrs. Smith.

10. The student teacher appears to have a larger "hidden" window than Mrs. Smith.

C. Name five suggestions for planning a parent-teacher conference.

D. Using one of the communication models presented, analyze the home visit reported in this unit. Ask the following questions of yourself.

1. Were the communication skills of the student teacher and Mrs. Campbell equally sharp?

2. Did the student teacher and Mrs. Campbell seem to have similar attitudes? Did they have similar values? Is it likely that they came from similar cultural backgrounds?

3. Using the Johari model, describe the communication skills of the student teacher and Mrs. Campbell.

E. Read the following statements. Determine whether they are effective communication statements or blocks to effective communication. If any statement is neither, identify it as such.

1. To parent who picks up child late: "Mrs. Jones, you know you're supposed to pick up Susan before 6:00 p.m."

2. Quietly, and on a one-to-one with a parent about an upcoming parent education meeting: "We've followed up on your request and, at Tuesday's meeting, one of the county social workers will talk about applying for food stamps and AFDC. We hope you'll be able to attend."

3. To parent bringing child to center in the morning: "Why don't you go with Randy to the science corner? He has something to show you. Randy, show your Dad what you found yesterday."

4. To parent with limited skills in English: "Mrs. Paliwal, we hope you'll be able to stay today so you can see the kinds of things we do here at ABC School. You know, we think it's important for the parent to become involved in the school's activities, and Anil seems so shy. I think he might feel better if you could stay with him for a few minutes. How about it?"

5. On the telephone to parent whose child has been involved in a fight at school: "Mr. Smith, we're hoping you might stop by early this evening to pick Steve up. We know how busy you are, but we're busy too and Steve needs you."

6. To a mother who is berating a child other than hers: "You know we never raise our voices to the children, Pat."

7. To parent reading story to own child during free play: "Mrs. Smith, would you please watch the children at the waterplay table? Johnny, why don't you play with Sammy over at the puzzle table?"

8. To harried parent who arrives with crying child later than usual; mother is late for work and is blaming the child: To child: "Jimmy, I know you like to play with clay; why don't you go over to the clay table and ask Miss Susan what she is doing?"

9. On the telephone to parent whose daughter wet her pants and has no dry ones at school: "Mrs. Carter, Kathy wet her pants this morning. I hope you won't mind that we put her into a spare pair we had on hand. Tomorrow you can bring an extra pair so if Kathy has another accident, she'll have her own clothes to wear."

10. Across the playground to parent pushing own child on a swing: "Mrs. Koster, come over here please. Mary knows how to pump herself. Don't baby her."

REFERENCES

Berlo, D. K. (1960). *The process of communication.* New York: Holt, Rinehart & Winston, Inc.

Cutteridge, A. (1990). Personal communication.

Elam, S. M. (September 1990). The 22nd annual Phi Delta Kappa/Gallup poll of the public's attitudes toward the public schools. *Phi Delta Kappan, 78*(1), 43–56.

Elam, S. M., & Rose, L. C. (September 1995). The 27th annual Phi Delta Kappa/Gallup poll of the public's attitudes toward the public schools. *Phi Delta Kappan, 77*(1), 41–56.

Fast, J. (1994). *Body language in the work place.* New York: Viking Penguin.

Gordon, T. (1974). *T.E.T.: Teacher effectiveness training.* New York: David McKay Co., Inc.

Honig, A. S. (1979). *Parent involvement in early childhood education.* Washington, DC: National Association for the Education of Young Children.

Stipek, D., Rosenblatt, L., & Di Rocco, L. (March 1994). Making parents your allies. *Young Children, 49*(3), 4–9.

Stone, J. G. (1987). *Teacher-parent relationships.* Washington, DC: National Association for the Education of Young Children.

RESOURCES

Berger, E. H. (1994). *Parent as partners in education.* (4th ed.). New York: Merrill-Macmillan.

Gage, J., & Workman, S. (November 1994). Creating family support systems: In Head Start and beyond. *Young Children, 50*(1), 74–77.

Gallup, A. M. (September 1988). The twentieth annual Gallup Poll of the public's attitudes toward the public schools. *Phi Delta Kappan,* 31–46.

Gallup, G. H. (September 1979). The eleventh annual Gallup Poll of the public's attitudes toward the public schools. *Phi Delta Kappan,* 31–45.

Foster, S. M. (November 1994). Successful parent meetings. *Young Children, 50*(1), 78–80.

Luft, J. (1969). *Of human interaction.* Palo Alto, CA: National Press Books.

Phi Delta Kappan (May 1995). Special issue on the American family. Bloomington, IN: Phi Delta Kappa.

Rich, D., & Mattox, B. (1977). *101 activities for building more effective school-community involvement.* Washington, DC: Home and School Institute.

Seefeldt, C. (November/December 1985). Parent involvement: Support or stress. *Childhood Education,* pp. 98–102.

Stone, J. (May 1993). Caregiver and teacher language—Responsive or restrictive? *Young Children, 48*(4), 12–18.

U. S. Department of Education. (1987). *Schools that work: Educating disadvantaged children.* Washington, DC: U. S. Government Printing Office.

Wood, C. (November 1994). Responsive teaching: Creating partnerships for systematic change. *Young Children, 50*(1), 21–28.

CHAPTER

15

Being Observed

OBJECTIVES

After studying this chapter, the student will be able to:

- List important goals of observation, evaluation, and discussion.
- Describe five observation techniques.
- Identify five possible student teacher observers.

I treasure the videotape made during my last day of student teaching. I'm a real teacher! It's undeniable!

Lacey Medieros

I could have kissed my college supervisor! She noticed my cooperating teacher really wasn't letting me teach. So she asked her to join her in the teacher's lounge for a mid-morning cup of coffee. Finally I was teaching!

Legretta Banks

Why is it I do poorly when I'm watched? Things ran smoothly as long as I didn't know I was being observed. Fortunately both my strong points and growth areas were talked about in daily evaluations. The problem finally disappeared except for the tiny knot I get now. Maybe I'll always have it.

Casey Morgan

Although the primary focus of student teaching is on the student teacher, all adults involved experience change and growth. A process combining observation, feedback, and discussion is often necessary to acquire new skills or expand existing skills. Methods of observation vary with each training program, but they all are basically a record of what was seen and heard. An analysis of this record is called an assessment or evaluation. Observation, analysis, evaluation, and discussion can be described as a continuous and ever-present cycle. It starts during student teaching and ends at retirement.

Professional teaching involves lifelong learning and continuous efforts to improve. As more discoveries are made about the process of human learning and as our society changes, teachers assess existing teaching methods, try new ones, and sometimes combine elements of both new and old methods. Observation is important to this process. The student teacher begins by being watched and ends up watching himself as a practicing teacher!

Teaching competency can be viewed as a continuum—you can have a little of it, some of it, or a lot of it—and there's always room for more competency growth (Albrecht, 1989).

It's important to realize you'll probably doubt your ability at times, especially on "bad days," which are bound to happen:

> It is human to have bad days—days when I just don't like putting a lot of effort into my school plans, days when I seem short-tempered and nothing seems to go right, days when I feel discouraged and question my effectiveness as a teacher, and even days when I feel overwhelmed rather than excited by all there is to learn about teaching, and children. (Humphrey, 1989)

● GOALS OF OBSERVATION, EVALUATION, AND DISCUSSION

Important goals of the observation/evaluation/discussion process for student teachers follow:

- To give student teachers valid assessments of their level of performance through specific, descriptive feedback

- To allow suggestions and helpful ideas, which aid students' acquisition of skills, to flow between participants

- To create a positive attitude toward self-improvement and self-knowledge

- To establish the habit of assessing performance

- To maintain the standards of the teaching profession

Through observation and evaluative feedback, the student teacher receives objective data that by herself she cannot collect, figure 15-1. Levin and Long (1981) describe the developments that follow:

> Students receive evidence about whether they have reached the set standard, what they have learned successfully, and what they still need to learn. As a result, students begin to develop a positive view of their own learning abilities.
>
> Students who have more self-confidence and a greater desire to learn become more involved as they progress in their learning. Gradually, they need less external help to reach a defined standard and may even take over the corrective procedures themselves. Effec-

Figure 15-1 You will be observed working with your own group of children.

tive use of feedback corrective systems helps teachers develop more confident students who not only achieve at a higher level but who also learn how to learn.

Evaluation may sound ominous to the student teacher because it is usually connected to a grade or passing a class or training program. A breakdown in trust may occur. Actually, evaluation is a chance for improvement, a time to realize that all teachers are a combination of strengths and weaknesses. Adopting a new view of evaluation will allow trust to remain intact:

> While in the past, evaluation has been conceived mainly as a process of passing judgment, nowadays it is seen as a continuous process of collecting information and supplying feedback for improvement. (Levin & Long, 1981)

The quality of the feedback given to a student teacher is an important factor.

> Feedback information can be effective if and only if it is followed by corrective procedures which correct weaknesses of learning and instruction. (Levin & Long, 1981)

Feedback needs to be consistent and constructive throughout a student teacher's placement.

> In most teacher-training programs, great importance is attached to the practicum's end-of-the-day conference. These conferences generally include how the day went, how particular children behave, and what plans should be made for the next day. It is also the time for the master teacher to evaluate the student teacher's abilities and recommend improvement.
>
> Feedback as a teaching procedure has received considerable attention in the brief literature of research on teaching. In general, feedback does change or influence an individual's performance *if* given meaningful interpretation, and *if* delivered consistently and constructively. (Thompson, Holmberg, & Baer, 1978)

Observational feedback may pinpoint behavior the student can then examine while teaching, figure 15-2. Feedback is information, which the reporter believes to be true and accurate, on an individual happening or interaction. Discussions following observations include identifying what went well, praise, descriptive analysis, examination of situational factors, the creation of action plans, further analysis of written records, child behavior particulars, action/reaction relationships, and any other feature of the observation that is important.

Ideally when supervisors build trust, student teachers can be:

- clear about the supervisor-student teacher evaluation relationship;
- supervised by people who listen well, clarify ideas, encourage specificity, and take time to understand what the student is trying to present to the children;
- free to request value judgments; and
- convinced their supervisor is an advocate for their success in the classroom.

METHODS OF OBSERVATION

Training programs collect data on student teachers' performances in many different ways. Among the most common collection techniques are:

Figure 15-2 Another student teacher can observe a peer and give valuable feedback.

Direct Observation

Direct observation is usually accomplished via a recorded specimen description, time sampling, and/or event sampling. This can be either obtrusive (the observed individual is aware of the process) or unobtrusive (collecting data without the subject's knowledge, perhaps from an observation room), figure 15-3.

- Time sampling: An observer watches and codes a set of specific behaviors within a certain time frame.
- Specimen description or narrative: A "stream of consciousness" report that attempts to record all that occurs.
- Specimen description involves recording everything that the individual does or says with as much information about the context (people involved, circumstances that might be influencing the behavior, and so on) as possible.
- Event sampling: A detailed record of significant incidents or events.

Criterion-referenced Instrument

An analysis of whether the subject can perform a given task or set of tasks. (An example can be found in the Appendix.)

Figure 15-3 Observation rooms usually have one-way windows and counter-top writing desks.

Interview

Usually a specific set of questions asked in a standard manner, figure 15-4.

Rating Scale

The observer sets a point value on a continuum in order to evaluate a characteristic or skill, figure 15-5.

Videotaping

A video camera records a student teaching sequence.

Tape Recording

Only sound is recorded.

Filming

A sound or silent record.

Combinations of these methods are frequently used. Some cooperating teachers work alongside their student teachers and take mental notes rather than written ones.

● CLINICAL SUPERVISION

Clinical supervision was initially promoted as a method to improve instructional practices by providing supervisors with a structured and cooperative approach to teacher supervision and accountability (Sullivan, 1980). Developed by Cogan and his associates in the 1950s while working with student teachers in Harvard University's Master of Arts in Teaching program, clinical supervision, "in contrast to other supervisory efforts, [was] designed as a professional response to a specific problem . . . . Cogan and his colleagues decided that their supervisory practices of observing a lesson and then conferring with the [student] teacher were inadequate" (Sullivan, 1980, p. 5). Clinical supervision was quickly adopted by other universities in their teacher education programs and by school district personnel in supervising experienced teachers.

Underlying clinical supervision is the assumption that if the student teacher and his or her supervisor cooperatively define the focus of each supervision visit, the student teacher has the opportunity to address specific problems rather than global ones. A supervisory visit might focus, for example, on the stu-

Area	Percentage				
	Almost always	Usually	Undecided	Sometimes	Seldom
1. Does the student teacher plan adequately for classroom experience?					
2. Does your student teacher utilize modern teaching methods effectively?					
3. Does your present student teacher provide adequately for individual differences?					
4. Is your student teacher able to control the behavior (discipline) of students?					
5. Does your student teacher meet class responsibilities on time?					
6. Is your student teacher able to evaluate students adequately?					
7. Does your student teacher cooperate with you?					
8. Is your student teacher willing to do more than minimum requirements?					
9. Does your student teacher attend extra classroom related social and professional functions? (Clubs, sports, PTA, faculty meetings, etc.)					
10. Does your student teacher seem ethical in his relationships with faculty and students?					
11. Is your student teacher able to motivate students to a high level of performance in a desirable manner?					
12. Does your student teacher demonstrate facility in oral communication?					
13. Is your student teacher able to organize?					
14. Does the student teacher seem to possess an adequate subject matter (content) background?					
15. Does your student teacher demonstrate that she has received an adequate, liberal (well rounded) education?					

Figure 15-4 Sample of interview instrument used for cooperating teacher's evaluation of student teacher. (From *The Student Teacher's Reader*, by Alex Perrodin. Chicago: Rand McNally & Co., 1966.)

dent teacher's questioning strategies or upon the responses the teacher makes to student questions. It might also focus on interactions among specific students in the class or upon management techniques used by the student teacher. The advantage of using clinical supervision was thought to lie in the reduction of stress for the student teacher and increased ability to address specific, mutually agreed upon problems.

NAME _____

The professional qualities of each student teacher
will be evaluated on the following criteria:

A four-point scale is used:
(1) needs improvement
(2) satisfactory
(3) above average
(4) outstanding

	1	2	3	4
PERSONAL QUALITIES				
1. Attendance and punctuality	___	___	___	___
2. Dependability	___	___	___	___
3. Flexibility	___	___	___	___
4. Resourcefulness	___	___	___	___
5. Self-direction, sees what needs to be done	___	___	___	___
6. Sensitive to other people's needs and feelings	___	___	___	___
7. Tact, patience, and cooperation with others	___	___	___	___
8. Sense of humor	___	___	___	___
9. Attitude toward children	___	___	___	___
10. Attitude toward adults	___	___	___	___
11. Attitude toward administrators	___	___	___	___
12. Well-modulated voice, use of language	___	___	___	___
13. Ability to evaluate self and benefit from experiences	___	___	___	___
14. Dressed appropriately	___	___	___	___

Comments: _____
_____

	1	2	3	4
WORKING WITH CHILDREN				
1. Aware of safety factors	___	___	___	___
2. Understands children at their own levels	___	___	___	___
3. Finds ways to give individual help without sacrificing group needs	___	___	___	___
4. Skill in group guidance	___	___	___	___
5. Skill in individual guidance	___	___	___	___
6. Listens to children and answers their questions	___	___	___	___
7. Consistent and effective in setting and maintaining limits	___	___	___	___
8. Encourages self-help and independence in children	___	___	___	___
9. Sensitive to children's cues in terms of adding to their knowledge or encouraging verbal skills	___	___	___	___
10. Aware of total situation, even when working with one child	___	___	___	___
11. Sensitivity to a developing situation in terms of prevention rather than cure	___	___	___	___

Comments: _____
_____

	1	2	3	4
WORKING WITH OTHER TEACHERS, PARENTS, AND VOLUNTEERS				
1. Willingness to accept direction and suggestions	___	___	___	___
2. Is friendly and cooperative with staff members	___	___	___	___
3. Observes appropriate channels when reporting on school matters	___	___	___	___
4. Respects confidential information	___	___	___	___
5. Establishes good working relationships	___	___	___	___
6. Does not interfere in a situation another teacher is handling	___	___	___	___
7. Shows good judgment in terms of knowing when to step into a situation	___	___	___	___

Comments: _____
_____

Figure 15-5 Student teacher responsibilities and evaluation form (rating scale).

PROGRAMMING

1. Provides for teacher-directed and child-initiated activities
2. Plans in advance and prepares adequately
3. Makes routines and transitions valuable and interesting
4. Plans and implements age-appropriate, attractive activities
   and materials in the following areas:
   Self-Esteem/Self-Help
   Music/Movement
   Health/Safety
   Science/Discovery
   Cooking/Nutrition
   Art/Creative
   Outside Environment/Play
   Cultural Awareness/Antibias
   Language/Literature
   Dramatic Play
   Math/Measurement
   Other Areas
5. Creative and problem solving activities are interesting and appropriate.
   Comments: _____
   _____

Figure 15-5 Continued.

The steps in clinical supervision are as follows:

1. the pre-observation conference where the focus for the upcoming observation is decided;

2. the observation itself;

3. analysis by the supervisor with consideration of possible strategies for improvement;

4. the post-observation conference; and

5. the post-conference analysis by the student teacher and the supervisor, at which time strategies for improvement are elicited from the student teacher and confirmed or counseled for change by the supervisor.

In reality clinical supervision has been reported to have had varying degrees of success. Goldhammer (1969) saw extensive possibilities in the use of clinical supervision. On the other hand, Mattaliano (1977) cited three specific reasons why clinical supervision was not more widely used: (1) the complexity of the process, (2) the lack of clearly identified competencies for performance, and (3) the lack of research (Sullivan, 1980, p. 38). Another reason is the need for training and practice in the process and the pressures of time on many supervisors.

Training programs have been developed (Boyan & Copeland, 1978), but the fact remains that "training, administration, and development needs still exist" (Sullivan, 1980, p. 39).

Clinical supervision has its strong proponents (Della-Dora, 1987; Tenenberg, 1988, personal communications). In supervising student teachers, Tenenberg cites the change made by one of his student supervisees when the agreed-upon focus for his observation was on student teacher responses to pupil input in her first grade class. Initially, Tenenberg noted the overuse of negative feedback by the student teacher: "No, that's not right; does someone else know what the answer is?" "You don't seem to have studied your assignment." "Sit still and listen; you're not in this classroom to play!" After providing constructive feedback and asking the student teacher to analyze her own responses (carefully videotaped for that purpose), the student teacher began to focus on using positive feedback. A later observation showed responses, such as, "Roger, you're thinking about alternatives; have you considered . . . "; "Ayesha, you're on the right track; can you add to what you're suggesting?" and "Let's see how many possible answers we can think of to this question" (a way of allowing every response to be the "right" one). In this example, the student teacher, who previously had had difficulty with classroom management, established a better working relationship with her pupils and her management problems diminished accordingly.

Nolan, Hawkes, and Francis (1993), using case study analysis, have identified factors of the clinical supervision process that seemed to facilitate changes in teacher thinking and behavior:

1. the development of a collegial relationship where the teacher feels safe and supported;

2. teacher control over the products of supervision;

3. continuity in the supervisory process over time;

4. focused, descriptive records of actual teaching and learning events as the basis for reflection; and

5. reflection by both the teacher and supervisor as the heart of the process of post-conferencing.

Cognitive Coaching

Cognitive coaching is a process involving (student) teachers exploring the thinking behind their practices (Garmston, Linder, & Whitaker, 1993). This type of evaluation process helps student teachers talk about their thinking and also become aware of teaching decisions. It doesn't require following a specific model of instruction but instead supports the student teacher's acquired skills and strengths while also promoting growth in unexpected teaching areas. A cognitive coach, in this case a student teacher's supervisor, asks questions about skills to be honed and improved and possible new ventures in growth areas.

Cognitive coaching is similar to clinical supervision in its use of the pre-conference, observation, and post-conference format. It emphasizes to a greater degree teacher improvement of instructional effectiveness by becoming more reflective about teaching and informed teacher decision making. (Garmston, Linder, & Whitaker, 1993).

The ultimate goal of using this evaluatory process is enhancing the student teacher's ability to self-monitor, self-analyze, and self-evaluate.

Pre-conference discussion concentrates on four basic questions:

1. What are your objectives?

2. How will you know when you've reached them?

3. What is your plan? and

4. On what other aspects of your teaching do you want information? (Garmston, Linder, & Whitaker, 1993)

A supervisor skilled in cognitive coaching asks probing questions. Student teachers may feel uncomfortable working out questions for themselves rather than being given immediate answers. When faced with self-analysis, teachers, experiencing a cognitive coaching evaluation, search their own minds, unlocking ideas that might not have presented themselves. Garmston, Linder, and Whitaker (1993) believe the reflection learned through this method of evaluation helps develop problem-solving skills as teachers examine experience, generate alternatives, and evaluate actions.

● RELIABILITY

Observations must serve as a reliable and accurate source of information. In student teaching, the participants understand that each observation record covers only a short space of time compared to the length of the student teacher's placement. Each individual will have a slightly different perception of what was seen and heard. Areas of competence that receive similar interpretations from different observers over a period of time should be of special interest to student teachers.

Reliability refers to the extent to which observations are consistent over time and "the extent to which a test is consistent in measuring over time what it is designed to measure" (Wortham, 1995, p. 250). The similarity of information in data gathered in different observations confirms the reliability of the measurement. For example, if both a videotaped observation and a time sampling seem to point to the same measurement of skill or teaching behavior, the reliability of the data will increase.

The degree of obviousness of the collection method also merits consideration. Videotaping may produce unnatural behavior. Hidden cameras and tape recorders raise ethical questions. Observation rooms and one-way screens are familiar and unobtrusive methods commonly used in laboratory training centers. Objective recording of teaching behavior is a difficult task. Observations can be subjective and reflect the observer's special point of view.

Supervisors and cooperating teachers try to keep all observations objective during student teaching. Discussions between the observed and observer can add additional factors for consideration before analyses and evaluations occur.

To remove subjective comments from teacher observation, Oliver (1981) advocates the use of "ethnographic methods." He suggests observers should attempt to describe precise teaching episodes, using extensive note-taking that leaves little doubt and allows "others less knowledgeable to see qualities and aspects of the classroom that are not readily discernible." Oliver suggests that observers use the following steps as observation guidelines.

1. *Casing the Room:* The initial minutes of the observation revolve around "casing the room" or "shagging around." This involves mapping the physical layout of the class, noting such items as the arrangement of tables, learning aides (bulletin boards, resource centers, etc.), and storage areas for student materials.

2. *Entering Interactions:* The second stage emphasizes the cordiality of verbal greetings between teacher and student. How teacher and students enter the room, exchange greetings, and prepare for the instructional process is a valuable source of information for supervisors and teachers. Additional data on the number of students in the class, sex of the students, and ethnicity of students add further value in clarifying entering interactions.

3. *Trafficking:* Once the instructional episode has started, noting the patterns of action in the classroom (e.g., how students move about the room getting water, etc.) provides critical information regarding the organization and management of instruction.

4. *Communication:* The verbal and nonverbal interactions between teacher-student and student-student are a crucial part of this supervision-observation process. How does the teacher call on or make contact with students? What tone of voice and choice of words does the teacher use? What is the reaction of the students? Noting student ethnicity and sex and the manner of teacher-directed comments provides additional information that highlights the ecology of the classroom.

5. *Rule Structure:* How is the rule structure established and adhered to? How does the teacher respond to disruptive behavior? What preceded the behavior? How do students respond to the teacher's actions? This recounting of events aids in clarifying and discovering the underlying scheme of social judgments.

6. *Beginnings, Ends, Transitions:* One important aspect of classroom life that appears crucial to teacher performance is that of tracking time and the sequencing of activities. In addition to noting time devoted to activities, off-task and on-task behavior of pupils helps to provide a clearer picture of what happens in the classroom. What do teachers do during transitions? What is the frequency and duration of transitions? How much time is allotted for the activity? Clearly, the importance of time is a salient variable in the observation of the instructional process.

7. *Post-observation Conference:* As in most supervisory settings, the importance of the post-observation conference cannot be overstated. The teacher should present his personal impressions of the lesson prior to discussing the ethnographic observation. This facilitates self-evaluation and recall of the salient aspects of the lesson. The additional information provided by the ethnographic narrative aids the teacher in clarifying and understanding the antecedents and the consequences of classroom events. This multimodality of ethnographic narratives provides

the teacher and supervisor with an excellent tool for increasing teacher effectiveness.

Ongoing and cumulative evaluations of students' performances are designed to verify students' competencies. In student teaching they allow students to discover, plan, and ponder. Without outside assessment and evaluation, assessment is limited to self-assessment.

Observers and Evaluators

It is possible to be observed and assessed by many people during your student teaching experience. Some students prefer only the supervisor's and cooperating teacher's assessments. Others actively seek feedback from all possible sources. A wide base of observational data on competency seems best. Other possible observers in most student teaching placements are:

- self, figures 15-6, 15-7, and 15-8
- classroom assistants, aides, and volunteers
- other student teachers
- the center's or school's support staff (cooks, nurse, secretary, etc.)
- children
- parents
- community liaison staff
- administrative staff or consulting specialists, figure 15-9

Student teachers can develop their own rating systems based on teaching characteristics that are important to them. Simple tallies are helpful in recording changes in behavior.

Discussion

Discussions held after data are collected are keys to growth. The meeting's feeling tone, its format, location, time of day, and degree of comfort can be critical. The communication skills of both participants contribute to success in promoting student teacher skill development.

Two types of discussions, formative and summative, occur during student teaching. An initial formative discussion sets the stage for later discussions. Goals, time lines, and evaluative procedures are explained. Additional formative discussions will follow placement observations. A summative conference finalizes your total placement experience and scrutinizes both the placement site and your competencies.

During discussions, you will examine the collected data, add comments about extenuating circumstances, form plans to collect additional information, and consider initiating new actions that could strengthen your existing skills through change or modification. Suggestions for improvement are self-discovered and formed jointly with the cooperating teacher or supervisor.

Child behavior resulting from student teacher behavior is a focal point for discussions, figure 15-10. Influencing factors such as room settings, routines, child uniqueness, and the student teacher's technique, method, and behaviors are examined closely.

Discussions that are descriptive and interpretative and involve value judgments about child education and professional teaching are common.

Pre- and Post-Conferences—Supervisor Evaluations. More and more supervisors are conducting pre-observation conferences so student teachers can brief them about classroom details and the activities or lesson plan the supervisor will observe. Post-conferences after supervisor observation are a standard procedure, and the review of observation notes helps student teachers reflect on their skills. Tips, resource ideas, and possible areas for growth are discussed. Sometimes post-conference discussions lead naturally to pre-conference ones. "What happens next week?"

Dealing with Evaluations

Student teachers should try to develop a positive attitude about what may appear to be an emphasis on their weaknesses. However, this attitude may come slowly for some student teachers. Conferencing covers student teachers' strengths but sometimes promotes a "report card" feeling that is hard to shake. Nelson and McDonald (1952) have the following advice for student teachers.

The student teacher should:

INSTRUCTIONS

1. As you study the grid, circle each description you feel makes a fairly accurate statement of an attitude, skill, or preference of yours.
2. From the choices you make, write a paragraph or two describing yourself.

If you follow these instructions thoughtfully and honestly, you will have a relatively clear idea of how you see yourself in relation to your effectiveness as a teacher of young children.

Plans ahead, wants to know schedule	Versatile, spur-of-the-moment okay	Prefers to work out own problems	Good under supervision
Trusts own judgment	Often seeks advice	Friendly, open personal life	Friendly but personally reserved
Good at delegating and organizing responsibility	Prefers to let others do the organizing	Best with older children and adults	Best with young and very young
Works well with parents	Prefers to work without help	Liberal, likes new ideas	Conservative and slow to change
Skilled in many areas	About average in abilities	Remembers names, dates — uses her knowledge	Not particular about details — takes what comes
Prefers to share responsibility	More efficient when working alone	Patient, does not rush others or self	Impatient, prefers to get things done fast
Likes to take risks	Cautious, prefers proven methods	Efficient, likes order	Casual, can muddle through
Hates to be late	Relaxed about time and schedule	Active in many outside interests	Prefers audience/bystander role
Often relates physically	Usually relates with words only	Friends with everyone	Prefers a few close friends
Has many ideas	Initiates little but will join in	Positive, optimistic	Somewhat negative, cynical
Works best when job roles well-defined	Prefers flexible job roles	Prefers to be boss	Prefers to be subordinate
Keeps things neat and clean	Messiness no problem	Prefers to work with things	Prefers to work with people
Feelings hurt easily	Pretty thick-skinned	Stable, consistent background	Diverse background
Determined, persistent, stubborn	Easy going, will give up fairly easily	Likes to be in on everything	Prefers to mind own business and not get involved
Likes routine and willing to do same things over and over	Likes variety	Likes working on many projects at same time	Likes to work on one thing at a time
Relaxes by doing something active	Relaxes by resting, sleeping	Needs very little sleep	Feels best with plenty of sleep
Easily satisfied	Somewhat particular	Likes competition and challenge	Prefers noncompetitive work
Introversive, introspective	Outgoing, extrovert	Nonconforming	Adaptive, complaisant

Figure 15-6 Student teacher self-rating sheet. (From *Be Honest With Yourself*, by Doreen Croft. © 1976 by Wadsworth Publishing Company, Inc. Reprinted by permission of Wadsworth Publishing Company, Belmont, CA)

1. Anticipate criticism and welcome its contribution; take a positive attitude toward any advice which is offered by the principal, college supervisor, training teacher, and even from the pupils; expect to have efforts improved; accept all criticism without permitting feelings to be upset.

2. Develop a feeling of security in the things which one knows to be correct, but never to be so confident that one cannot see the other person's point of view.

STUDENT TEACHER SELF-EVALUATION FORM

Instructions: Evaluate your own performance on this form. To the left of each characteristic listed below, write a *W* if you are working on it, *M* if it happens most of the time, or an *A* if it happens always.

Relationships
_____ 1.   I share my positive feelings by arriving with an appropriate attitude.
_____ 2.   I greet children, parents, and staff in a friendly and pleasant manner.
_____ 3.   I accept suggestions and criticism gracefully from my co-workers.
_____ 4.   I can handle tense situations and retain my composure.
_____ 5.   I make an effort to be sensitive to the needs of the children and their parents.
_____ 6.   I am willing to share my ideas and plans so that I can contribute to the total program.

Goals
_____ 1.   The classroom is organized to promote a quality child development program.
_____ 2.   I constantly review the developmental stage of each child so that my expectations are reasonable.
_____ 3.   I set classroom and individual goals and then evaluate regularly.
_____ 4.   I have fostered independence and responsibility in children.

Classroom skills
_____ 1.   I arrive on time.
_____ 2.   I face each day as a new experience.
_____ 3.   I can plan a balanced program for the children in all skill areas.
_____ 4.   I am organized and have a plan for the day.
_____ 5.   I help each child recognize the role of being part of a group.
_____ 6.   I help children develop friendships.
_____ 7.   I maintain a child-oriented classroom and the bulletin boards enhance the room.

Professionalism
_____ 1.   I understand the school philosophy.
_____ 2.   I maintain professional attitudes in my demeanor and in my personal relationships while on the job.
_____ 3.   I assume my share of joint responsibility.

Personal Qualities
_____ 1.   I have basic emotional stability.
_____ 2.   My general health is good and does not interfere with my responsibilities.
_____ 3.   My personal appearance is suitable for my job.
_____ 4.   I evaluate my effectiveness as a member of my teaching team in the following manner:
$$-\ \ 0\ \ 1\ \ 2\ \ 3\ \ 4\ \ 5\ \ +$$
(Low)   (High)

My teaching team
_____ 1.   I've earned the respect and acceptance of team members

---

Figure 15-7 Student teacher self-evaluation form.

3. Evaluate and criticize one's own efforts. Often one can soften necessary criticism by anticipating one's own weaknesses and discussing them with a supervising teacher.

4. Be consistent in acting on suggestions which are made. One should not make the same mistake day after day.

5. Do not alibi or defend mistakes which were made. One's greatest improvement will be made by overcoming deficiencies, not by defending them.

STUDENT SELF-EVALUATION

Put a check in one box in each line choosing which best describes your performance.

1	2	3	4	5	
I often think critically about how my behavior affects children and other adults.	Sometimes I try to analyze classroom interactions.	From time to time I think about how I affect others in the classroom.	I rarely rehash what happened during the day in the classroom.	I give little thought to classroom interactions.	REFLECTION
I have a clear idea of important goals with children and work daily to accomplish them.	Some of my goals are clear, others are still being formed.	My goals are not always clear, but at times I think about them.	I use my center's goals for planning and have a few of my own.	I mainly handle each day by providing activities that teach specific concepts and making sure children behave.	CLARITY OF GOALS
I'm always responsible for what I do and say.	Most of the time I take responsibility for what happens.	At times I feel responsible for my actions.	I can't control all that happens—that's my attitude.	What goes wrong is mostly others' fault.	RESPONSIBILITY
I do what's assigned and needed before deadlines, and check to see it's completed on time.	I usually complete jobs in a timely manner.	I finish jobs that I choose to finish mostly on time.	I start but often something happens before I finish assignments.	I'm late, and often don't finish what's expected of me.	DEPENDABILITY
I always find what I need and create when necessary in activity planning.	I'm pretty good at getting what needs to be secured.	I sometimes can find or create what's necessary.	I rarely know how to go about getting things I need for the classroom.	I expend little effort at locating hard to find items or materials for child instruction.	RESOURCEFULNESS
I rarely need others to direct my work.	Most of the time I don't need the help of my supervisor.	I ask for help when the going gets rough and that's not often.	I need advice frequently and depend on others to solve my problem.	Lots of help and supervision is necessary.	INDEPENDENCE
I'm active in teacher associations and attend nearby conferences.	Sometimes I attend professional association meetings and training opportunities.	I go to the library occasionally to consult the experts.	Haven't the time now to join or attend professional group doings but plan to in the near future.	I don't wish to become a member of a professional group.	PROFESSIONAL GROWTH
I change and create new happenings in my classroom and try new ways joyfully.	I will try some new ways and strategies.	If it's suggested I try new ways to do things.	I'm pretty stressed about trying something I've not done before.	The old routines and ways are comfortable. Why change them?	CREATIVITY
I respect and enjoy being a helpful team player.	I do help others on my team.	I will share ideas and give time to other team members.	I don't really function well with others, I'd rather do it myself.	Teams don't accomplish much and waste time. Not helpful at all.	TEAM MEMBERSHIP

Figure 15-8 Rate yourself.

Emotionally mature and well-adjusted personality
Alert and enthusiastic
Professional competency
Genuine interest in people, children, teaching
Professional attitude
Good appearance and grooming
Above-average scholastically
Wide interests and cultural backgrounds
Leadership qualities
Sense of humor
Willingness to learn and desire to grow professionally
Success in directed teaching
Creativeness
Understanding of children
Interest in community participation
Moral character
Cooperative
Good health
Ability to communicate effectively
Good penmanship
Interest in curriculum development
Flexibility
Sincerity
Appropriate humility
Ability to organize

Figure 15-9 Administrators' responses to the question, "What would you like to know about student teachers?"

6. Do not argue the point when one feels that a criticism has been unjustly made; rather one should govern further actions and the injustice will usually automatically vanish.

7. Use judgment in interpreting criticisms. Whenever criticisms seem to conflict, it is necessary that the student use a great deal of common sense in interpreting their application.

8. Keep one's poise and sense of humor; one should not become so emotionally disturbed that one cannot act intelligently on the problem at hand.

9. Assume that the teachers are friends; one should understand that they are trying to help one to learn correct procedures and techniques. They are not merely trying to make one miserable.

One strategy a student teacher will find useful when handling evaluator comments is saying, "Yes, I understand your concern. I had concern as well. Let me tell you about the circumstances that occurred. I doubt you were aware of them. Tell me what you would have suggested in that case."

Discussions can describe a wide range of student and teacher behaviors. Clarification of terms can be helpful to student teachers. Keeping records of discussions will aid your planning. They can be reviewed prior to follow-up conferences. Action plans resulting from previous discussions are usually the primary focus of later ones.

College supervisors have the ultimate and final burden of approving a candidate for graduation from training programs. If one questions a gathering of supervisors, one hears both anguish and elation— elation that they have had a small part in an individual teacher's development; anguish because they are forced to make decisions. Their goal as supervisors is to assure that each candidate possesses the knowledge, skill, and competency necessary to interact sensitively, creatively, and successfully with both children and adults. The task of assessing individual students involves observing human relations. Some student teachers of diverse cultural and language backgrounds may be tremendously talented and insightful with children but may find readings and academic testing in student teaching classes particularly difficult.

PEER EVALUATIONS

Many graduated student teachers feel peer evaluations were tremendously helpful for a number of reasons. (1) They are nonthreatening because a "grade" is not at issue. (2) A peer may have greater empathy or understanding because they are experiencing many of the same or similar problems. (3) Peers know how it feels to be observed and evaluated, so "tread softly." (4) Suggestions offered may have recently been field tested. A student teacher's successes are passed on to another student teacher for consideration. (5) When one becomes the evaluator, one experiences increased insight into the role of the college supervisor and cooperating teacher.

Figure 15–10 Whether a student teacher's planned activity will capture and hold child interest is the focus of this training class discussion.

(6) Seeing a peer's assigned classroom and cooperating teacher offers new data, new techniques. (7) Additional teaching methods, activities, and so on, are observed and possibly considered and tried in their own classroom, and (8) There's something in assuming the role of an observer-evaluator that makes one feel competent and professional. All the positive aspects of peer evaluations have not been mentioned in this discussion, and there have been unfortunate instances of friction between peers.

It is wise to follow college instructor guidelines closely. Often peer evaluators are asked to stick to the positive aspects of a peer's behavior and carefully suggest growth areas. One of the rating forms found in this chapter or elsewhere completed by a peer can be used to be sure the observer focuses on a variety of teaching skills. Post-evaluation discussions center on the observed explaining to the observer what was happening during the observation and what student teacher intentions were present. The assignment may involve turning in both peers'

notes of the evaluation discussion, rather than observational particulars.

Increasingly peer evaluations are seen as aiding student teachers' reflective thinking and their analysis of skills. Student teachers observing others often ask themselves important questions about their own teaching styles. Costa and Kallick (1993) believe every educator needs a trusted person who will ask provocative questions and offer helpful critiques.

Constructive Evaluation

Evaluation should be viewed as a critique promoting positive change. The following are suggestions designed to provide maximum evaluating benefits:

- Start your debriefing by asking the evaluator (cooperating teacher, college/university supervisor, director/principal) to identify what she thought were the best parts of the lesson/activity and what parts needed improvement.

- Ask for specific examples to clarify what the evaluator means.
- An "I hear what you're saying" response is better than a defense or argument.
- Separate specific comments from other teaching areas where you are functioning well; try to remember that it is the lesson being critiqued, not you as a person.
- Think of suggestions as being constructive, not as being negative criticisms.

SUMMARY

Observation, evaluation, and discussion are integral parts of student teaching. Different methods are used to observe the student's progress. The realization of professional growth through the use of an evaluative method and subsequent discussion depends on a number of different factors, including the process and method of measurement and the people involved. It is important for the student teacher to maintain a positive attitude and consider self-evaluation a vehicle for improvement. Both formative and summative discussions are part of an analysis of the student teacher and the placement experience. Planning to enhance strengths and overcome weaknesses takes place during discussions and is a growth-promoting part of student teaching.

SUGGESTED ACTIVITIES

A. Form groups of four. On slips of paper, write down your fears about being observed and evaluated. Put the slips in a container. Each student takes a turn drawing a slip of paper and describing the fear and the possible cause.

B. Develop your own rating sheet for assessing student teacher performance.

C. Identify for the class some important questions that you would like your cooperating teacher to answer during your summative discussion.

D. As a class, vote on the validity of the following statements. Use a "thumbs up" signal if the statement is true; remain still if you believe the statement is false. When voting on the more controversial statements, ask your instructor to turn from the class, elect a student to count the votes, and record the final tally.

1. It is unfair to compare one student teacher with another.
2. It is a good idea to have one student teacher tutor another.
3. Peer evaluations should be part of everyone's student teaching experience.
4. Confidentiality in rating student teachers is imperative.
5. Sharing discussion notes with other student teachers may be helpful to both students.
6. Evaluations by supervisors or cooperating teachers should never be shown to employers of student teachers.
7. A student teacher's placement could inhibit the growth of professional teaching competencies.
8. One can experience considerable growth without evaluative feedback.
9. Criticism is threatening.
10. Being observed and evaluated is really a game. Self-discovery and being motivated to do your best is more important.
11. An individual's manner of dress, hair style, etc. should not be included in an evaluation because this has nothing to do with effective teaching.
12. Observation and evaluation can increase professional excellence.
13. Every student should receive a copy of all written evaluations of his or her performance.
14. There is no such thing as constructive criticism!
15. Evaluators tend to see their own teaching weaknesses and inadequacies in the student teachers they observe.

E. As a class, discuss peer observations. Answer the following questions.

   1. Is peer observation, evaluation, and discussion valuable? Would peer observation be desirable and practical for your training group?

   2. Are there any guidelines that should be established for peer observation?

F. Identify the conflicting views of professional image that are shown in the following student teacher recommendation. Can you detect any racial/ethnic stereotypes?

5 June

To: Whom It May Concern

From: May J. York, PhD
        Professor of Education

Subject: Recommendation for Shu-Wei (Sheila) Ly

I was Ms. Ly's university supervisor during the final phase of her student teaching. She had entered Cal State, Hayward's program as a transfer from our sister university in Fresno. She had completed two semesters of Fresno's program leading to their Multiple Subjects credential with an authorization in Early Childhood Education. Prior to entry at Hayward, Ms. Ly had completed two previous student teaching assignments—one in preschool, one in fourth grade.

After acceptance in Hayward's program, Ms. Ly requested a placement in a class for the gifted, and initially I had placed her at Gomes School in Fremont, but the 45 mile one-way commute was difficult for her (she lives in San Francisco). She asked, then, if she could be placed at the Nueva Learning Center in Hillsborough (approximately 10 miles from her home). Since Cal State, Hayward is a public institution, we rarely place a student teacher in a private school. However, since her previous placements had been in public programs, I reluctantly agreed to the placement for Ms. Ly.

As you may know, Nueva is specifically designed as a school for gifted and talented (GATE) students. The computer lab, to which Ms. Ly was assigned as a student teacher to Ms. Patience Yang, afforded a unique setting with unique challenges for Ms. Ly. Stu-

dents from all grade levels at Nueva come to the computer lab on a regularly scheduled basis, sometimes with assignments from their respective classroom teachers, sometimes only with suggestions for Ms. Yang and, subsequently, Ms. Ly, to supplement classroom activities.

At Cal State, Hayward, we evaluate student teachers in five areas of achievement: 1) assessment of student needs and interests; 2) instructional planning (based upon the assessment of needs and interests); 3) implementation of the plans; evaluation of the same and student learning; 4) classroom management; 5) and professional development and self-growth, including relationships with other professionals and parents, and professional ethics and development.

Since I always ask my student teachers to complete a self-evaluation, Ms. Ly stressed the personal and professional growth she had experienced during this placement. Ms. Ly now recognizes that while she truly had thought she preferred working with gifted and talented students, she now realizes that, in many ways, the GATE student is no different from any other student. Since she was teaching students in kindergarten through grade six, Ms. Ly also gained another insight—she recognizes that she relates more comfortably with younger students than with the older ones. In fact, she told me that kindergarten, and even preschool, were her preferred grade levels.

As mentioned before, Nueva offered unique challenges for Ms. Ly. One was her ability to do any long-range planning for her students. The regular classroom teachers often did not provide much information about what lessons, extensions of lessons, and so on, they wanted her to offer in the computer lab. For example, to support and complement the kindergarten teacher's unit on the rain forest, Ms. Ly completed a computer-based unit using KidPix software. She used the sentence stem "I went to the rain forest and I wondered . . . " to stimulate the children's imaginations. Students then were able to bring up pictures to illustrate such things as what kinds of plants and animals might be found in the rain forest.

She correctly identified one young second grader's interest in math but his reluctance to learn how to spell. Ms. Ly used that interest to develop the boy's vocabulary and improve his spelling by having him learn, and spell correctly, several mathematical terms. This encouraged him to learn more about spelling other words unrelated to math but related to some of his other interests. The Learning Company's Spellbound software proved to be the perfect tool for these sets of individualized lessons. And with an unmotivated third grader, whose interests lay in the theater, Ms. Ly grouped him with two peers to develop a script based on "The Three Stooges." Subsequently, the three boys practiced their respective roles and presented their skit to the rest of the students at Nueva and parents at the Spring Open House.

The computer lab presented some challenges in management, especially with the older students. The lab is located in a rather long, narrow room with computers arranged in two rows facing each other, 12 to each side of the long tables on which they sit. It becomes easy for children essentially to hide behind the computer at which they are presumably working. Thus, there were times when I observed her that some students (fifth graders) were playing Jeopardy instead of working on lessons related to the 1940s that they were to complete for their various classroom projects. It is possible that Ms. Ly's preference in teaching the younger students related to the fact that the younger students listened and followed directions better than did the older ones, who had more individualistic interests.

Certainly, assessing student learning was not difficult. The children's various completed computer-generated projects revealed how well each lesson met its goals. Planning, however, was more difficult, due to the individualistic nature of the students' projects. With the exception of the rain forest unit for the kindergarten children, every other lesson had to be tailored to the individual student, as were the math and spelling and "Three Stooges" units mentioned above. As you can well imagine, this created much extra work for Ms. Ly.

In terms of any position for which she might apply in the San Francisco Bay area, I feel that Ms. Ly might be a good candidate for a kindergarten or first grade. In her earlier student teaching assignments at Cal State, Fresno, she appears again to have been more successful teaching the younger students, especially in terms of the guidance function. She plans well; she relates to individual students warmly. Although basically a quiet, soft-spoken person, who does not relate immediately to adults, Ms. Ly did establish warm relationships with Ms. Yang and with some of the parents of the students in attendance at the computer lab. In conclusion, I would recommend Ms. Ly without hesitation and with no further qualification for any preschool, kindergarten or lower primary grade classes.

G. Write a description of children's observable behaviors in your future classroom at the end of a six-month period of child attendance. Cover one morning's hypothetical work-play time. In other words, if your goals were reached, what would the children be doing, saying, observing, and so on. Examine your list and star any descriptions that you could attribute to your individual teaching efforts and style. Go back to your list. In your present student teaching classroom is it possible to promote any or all of the children's observable behaviors you mentioned above? Discuss with small group then the total student teaching class.

REVIEW

A. Name three methods of observational data collection. Give examples.

B. Select the answer that best completes each statement.

1. The process of observation, evaluation, and discussion

   a. includes observations from supervisors and employers.

   b. usually ends when the student teaching experience ends.

   c. continues after the student teacher graduates and is valued by teachers and employers.

d. ends when improvement occurs.

e. can be best performed by the student teacher alone.

2. One of the primary goals of observation, evaluation, and discussion is to

a. stress the student teacher's weaknesses through peer evaluation.

b. increase control.

c. judge how quickly a student can respond to suggestions.

d. criticize student teachers.

e. None of these

f. All of these

3. Feedback can be defined as data that

a. are collected through observations and are to be evaluated and communicated to the one being observed.

b. are recorded by a student teacher during discussion.

c. include a free lunch.

d. are withheld from a student teacher.

e. None of these

4. If interviews are used to collect data on student teaching, each interviewee should

a. answer only the questions he or she wishes to answer.

b. always be asked the same questions in the same manner.

c. be asked for factual data only.

d. be asked for opinions only.

e. be given a specified length of time to answer each question.

5. One benefit of videotaping for the purpose of observation is

a. the student teacher and supervisor can evaluate the tape together.

b. it is less frightening than other methods.

c. a camera captures a more natural view of a student teacher.

d. it saves time.

e. All of these

6. If a student teaching skill is evaluated using three different observational methods and each confirms the same level of competency, the three tests would probably be

a. rated as reliable.

b. rated as highly valid.

c. rated as accurate.

d. standardized.

7. The collection technique that records a series of significant incidents is called a(n)

a. time sampling.

b. rating sheet.

c. specimen description.

d. event sampling.

e. questionnaire.

8. An unobtrusive method of observation might involve

a. hidden microphones.

b. an observer with a tape recorder.

c. an observer viewing from a loft.

d. an observer in an observation room.

e. All of these

9. If one was trying to assess the rapport that a student teacher developed with a group of children, one could

a. observe how many children initiated conversation with the student during a given time period.

b. record and analyze what the children say.

c. count how many times a child touched the student teacher during a given time period.

d. observe how many times a child shares an interest or concern with a student teacher.

e. All of these

10. A final discussion that informs the student teacher about his teaching skills is a(n)

a. formative discussion.

b. initial discussion.

c. summative discussion.

d. incidental discussion.

e. alternate discussion.

C. Complete the following statement.

The five individuals who could probably provide the most reliable and valid data concerning my teaching competency are . . .

D. Using another source of reference, write a definition of reliability or validity of assessment methods or instruments. Cite the author and publication date of your reference material.

E. Five individuals observed the same traffic accident. Match the person in Column 1 to the feature in Column II that he or she would be most likely to observe.

I	II
1. Car salesman	a. driver's license and/or license plate numbers
2. Police officer	
3. Doctor	b. children involved in the accident
4. Teacher	
5. Insurance adjuster	c. damage to the automobiles
	d. make and model of the automobiles involved
	e. injuries to those involved

F. What five skills would most cooperating teachers observe before a summative discussion?

G. Write three pieces of advice to student teachers to help them accept constructive criticism.

REFERENCES

Albrecht, K. (December 1989) Momentum. *Child Care Information Exchange*, Issue No. 70, p. 37.

Boyan, N. J., & Copeland, W. D. (1978). *Instructional supervision training program.* Columbus, OH: Merrill.

Costa, A., & Kallick, B. (October 1993). Through the lens of a critical friend. *Educational Leadership, 51*(2), 49–51.

Della-Dora, D. (1987) Personal communication.

Garmston, R., Linder, C., & Whitaker, J. (October 1993).

Reflections on cognitive coaching. *Educational Leadership, 51*(2), pp. 57–61.

Goldhammer, R. (1969). *Clinical supervision: Special methods for the supervision of teachers.* New York: Holt, Rinehart, & Winston.

Humphrey, S. (November 1989). The case of myself. *Young Children, 45*, 1, 17–22.

Levin, T., & Long, R. (1981). *Effective instruction.* Alexandria, VA: The Association for Supervision and Curriculum Development.

Mattaliano, A. P. (1977). Clinical supervision: The key competencies required for effective practice. Doctoral dissertation, University of Massachusetts. Dissertation Abstracts International, 38, 2060A.

Nelson, L., & McDonald, B. (1952). *Guide to student teaching.* Dubuque, IA: William C. Brown & Co.

Nolan, J., Hawkes, B., & Francis, P. (October 1993). Case studies: Windows into clinical supervision. *Educational Leadership, 51*(2), pp. 52–56.

Oliver, B. (Spring 1981). Evaluating teachers and teaching. *California Journal of Teacher Education*, VIII.

Sullivan, C. G. (1980). *Clinical supervision: A state of the art review.* Washington, DC: Association for Supervision and Curriculum Development.

Tenenberg, M. (1988). Personal communication.

Thompson, C. L., Holmberg, M. C., and Baer, D. M. (1981). *An experimental analysis of some procedures to teach priming and reinforcement skills to preschool teachers.* Monographs of the Society of Research in Child Development. Chicago: University of Chicago Press.

Wortham, S. C. (1995). *Measurement and Evaluation in Early Childhood Education*, 2nd ed. Englewood Cliffs, NJ: Prentice-Hall.

RESOURCES

Cogan, M. L. (1973). *Clinical supervision.* Boston: Houghton Mifflin.

Cogan, M. L. (1976). Rationale for clinical supervision. *Journal of Research and Development in Education, 9*(2), pp. 3–19.

Glickman, C. D. (Ed.). (1992). *Supervision in transition.* Washington, DC: Association for Supervision and Curriculum Development.

Kasindorf, M. E. (1989). *Competencies: A self-study guide to teaching competencies in early childhood education.* Atlanta: Humanics.

Kowalski, T. J., Weaver, R. A., & Henson, K. T. (1994). *Case studies of beginning teachers.* New York: Longman.

Teaching Styles and Techniques

After studying this chapter, the student will be able to:

- Identify at least three different teaching styles.
- Define and describe his or her own teaching style.
- Discuss the relationship between a philosophy of education and a teaching style.

My supervisor has been fooled! This is not a good classroom for a student teacher. The cooperating teacher is a fraud, everything is done for show or to impress. Sure the room looks great and the children are well behaved, but there's no enthusiasm for learning, and the bright children are just plain bored.

Name Withheld

I was intimidated watching my cooperating teacher. She was so professional. After a while I realized I had teaching strengths she admired and appreciated. We made a great team. She "zigged," I "zagged" but we pulled together. Our different approaches to the same goals made the classroom livelier. Oh what discussions we had!

Maeve Critchfield

I'll never throw away my supervisor's first written evaluation comments, which made me feel like a "real teacher." She noticed so many good things I was doing unconsciously. Yes, she pointed out things to work on too.

Dee Silvia-Bahoon

● TEACHING MODELS

What is meant by teaching style? It is the vehicle through which a teacher contributes his unique quality to the curriculum. Much has been written about teaching style—in particular, the phenomenon of teachers modeling themselves after the teachers who influenced them in the past.

Placing a student teacher with a "master" or cooperating teacher has its disadvantages as well as advantages. Most college supervisors try to place student teachers with those cooperating teachers who will provide a positive model and are willing to allow the student teacher to practice. However, there are many excellent teachers who are unwilling to work with student teachers. This is because it takes much energy and time to work with student teachers; they have to be watched, referred to resources, conferenced, and encouraged. In addition, most colleges and universities do not compensate

287

cooperating teachers in any tangible form for their time and energy. As a result, some student teaching placements are less than desirable.

Of course, this situation sometimes works out well. A student teacher with experience as a teacher aide may do quite well in a classroom where the cooperating teacher is less than an excellent model and provides little supervision or guidance. In some cases, the student teacher may even act as a *positive role model* for the mediocre cooperating teacher.

Good cooperating teachers will offer suggestions about different lessons to try. They will introduce the student teachers to all areas of the curriculum, usually one area at a time. Most cooperating teachers will allow a certain amount of time for student teachers to observe and become acquainted with the children. Before the end of the student teaching experience, however, most strong cooperating teachers will expect a student teacher to handle the whole day and all parts of the curriculum, figure 16-1. All student teachers will inevitably "borrow" or copy their cooperating teachers' styles; this results from having worked so closely together.

Figure 16-1 At first, student teachers will work in areas where they are most comfortable. Later, they will be expected to handle all parts of the curriculum. (Courtesy of Steve Howard)

Sometimes, though, a cooperating teacher's style is so unique, so much a part of her self, that it is too difficult to copy. We are reminded of a male cooperating teacher who stood six feet, four inches tall and weighed around 240 pounds. Female student teachers had problems using his behavior control techniques; the difference in their sizes precluded the use of physical presence as a discipline technique. One complaint the college supervisor heard regularly was, "Of course Mr. Smith has no problems of control! Look at him!" What many student teachers failed to recognize initially was that Mr. Smith used other techniques as well—close observation of the classroom; moving toward the source of potential trouble before it erupted; quietly removing a child from a frustrating activity; and firm and consistent application of classroom rules.

A cooperating teacher may be so gifted that a student teacher feels overwhelmed. In this situation, the student teacher needs to look at only one facet of the cooperating teacher's expertise at a time. For example, in focusing on how the teacher begins each day, the student teacher may find a model that is not quite so difficult as the total model appears. It may be the cooperating teacher takes time each morning to greet each child with a smile and a personal comment.

There are also situations where the cooperating teacher is unable to explain how something is done, like the mathematician who can solve a complex problem without knowing how. Intuitive teachers and those who are very involved have this difficulty; they are unable to explain why they do one thing and not another.

Teaching styles are also an extension of the teacher's self. Rogers and Freiberg (1994) contend that the teacher must know the self before effectively teaching another. This means that you have enough self-knowledge to judge from observing your cooperating teacher what activities and techniques will work for you, which ones you may have to modify, and which ones are best not used. Techniques with which you are truly uncomfortable are best put aside until you can become comfortable with them.

Specific Models

Mr. Smith is a true master teacher. After having taught every grade in elementary school and because he believes there are too few male teachers in the lower primary grades, he has chosen to teach kindergarten. Choosing kindergarten also reflects Mr. Smith's beliefs in the importance of having children begin elementary school with a positive step and in the importance of the family. He plans to involve the parents in the learning processes of their children and extends an open invitation to parents to visit in his room any time they wish. At Back-to-School Night, Mr. Smith is prepared with a Parent Handbook he has developed and elicits from his parents promises to assist at classroom learning centers, to be available as chaperones on field trips, to bake cookies or cupcakes for classroom celebrations, and to help in other appropriate ways—sharing on "International Day," teaching the children a folk song in their native language, demonstrating a special art technique typical of their respective culture, and so on.

Upon entering Mr. Smith's room, a visitor can immediately see that it is arranged into several areas. An entrance area is formed by a desk to the left of the door and the children's cubbies on the right. A parent bulletin board is mounted on the wall by the desk. A large area with shelves housing large blocks, trucks, cars, etc., is found behind the cubbies. An inside climbing structure, built by the parents, is located in the corner. Underneath, there is a housekeeping area complete with stove, sink, cupboards, table, and chairs. In the opposite corner is a quiet area protected by a large, comfortable couch. This area is further defined by its carpet, floor pillows, and bookshelves. On the shelves, there are many picture and story books which Mr. Smith periodically changes for added interest. Three tables with chairs are to the left of the quiet area and straight ahead from the door. Shelves and cupboards along the wall can easily be reached by the children and contain art materials and small manipulatives—puzzles, legos, unifix cubes, Cuisinaire rods, geoboards, and so on. The window wall opposite the door is the math and science center. In addition, a waterplay area is found here as well as a terrarium and a large magnifying glass with objects to investigate in a nearby box.

The first impression most visitors have is how busy and happy everyone appears to be. A parent may be found supervising at the language center, writing down a story dictated by one of the chilren (to be illustrated later); another parent, may be supervising at the workbench outside the door, watching as four or five children saw, hammer, and nail a wood sculpture. Mrs. Smith may be located at the science center directing two children's attention to their bean plants.

One way of studying Mr. Smith's classroom is to look at his teaching style. It seems very student-centered, which it is. It is highly flexible, changing as student interests change. For example, one day a child brought a chrysalis to school. Mr. Smith immediately asked the children to guess what they thought it might be. He listened intently to every guess, even the wild ones. He asked the child who brought it if she knew what she had found. When the child indicated that she did not, Mr. Smith proceeded to tell the students that they should watch the chrysalis every day to see what was going to happen. He resisted the urge to tell them anything more other than they would receive a big surprise. He placed the chrysalis in a large jar, placed cheesecloth over the opening, and secured it with a rubber band. Fortunately, the butterfly emerged from the chrysalis on a school day, and the children had the excitement of watching it. Mr. Smith allowed the children to watch despite the fact that science had not been scheduled for that particular time. Indeed, the children were so interested that no one wanted to go out to recess when the bell rang!

One might ask whether Mr. Smith's teaching style is congruent with one's perception of him as a person. In talking to him and becoming better acquainted with him, one might find that Mr. Smith sees himself more as a learner than as a teacher. He attends teacher conferences regularly to learn new techniques and presents workshops himself in his areas of expertise—how to plan and implement a "developmentally appropriate" kindergarten curriculum; using science to stimulate the kindergarten child's interest; managing the center-based kindergarten; and so forth. He was one of the first teachers in his school to ask that "special needs" children be placed in his classroom, even before PL 94-142 was enacted. His bias that all students are special and his student-centered classroom make it easy to integrate children with special problems.

Further exploration reveals that he is an avid gardener, likes to fish, enjoys woodwork, and would like to enroll in a workshop on stained glass. Mr. Smith appears as gifted outside of the classroom as he is within it.

It is easy to see that Mr. Smith values all the children in his class, figure 16-2. It is one of the reasons he is so effective, especially in regard to working with "special" children. It also is apparent that Mr. Smith is able to empathize with his children. He is gentle with those who have experienced a serious loss; he refuses to allow an angry child to bait him, and quietly speaks to the child one-to-one; he shares

in the excitement of a child who has taken a first train trip and may urge this child to share the experience with the others. The only times anyone has seen him angry involved a suspected case of child abuse and some of the money-saving policies of the board of education.

If a student teacher were to ask Mr. Smith about his teaching style, he would answer that it is based on his philosophy of education. This, he would continue, is the belief in the inherent goodness of all children and in their innate need to explore the world. He would be able to provide a written statement of his beliefs and curriculum goals for the year.

Mr. Smith's teaching is very much a part of himself—steady and imaginative with a desire to create a total learning environment for his students. In looking at Rogers's criteria, it is clear that Mr. Smith is congruent, acceptant, reliable, and empathetic, and that his students perceive these characteristics in him as well. One can tell that each child is as important as the next. He uses many nonverbal responses, touching one child on the shoulder as a reminder to settle down and get to work, giving another a sympathetic hug, getting down on his knees to speak directly and firmly to an angry child. From all of his words and actions, it is obvious that Mr. Smith teaches children much more than subject matter.

Let us now look at another teacher, Mrs. Lehrer, a teacher of an alternative "school within a school," an ungraded primary class of 33 children in grades one through three. Mrs. Lehrer starts each day by having the children line up outside the door, walk quietly into the classroom and form a semicircle around her by the chalkboard. The children sit down, and Mrs. Lehrer takes the roll. Next, a child announces the day of the week and the date and places the date on a cardboard calendar beside the chalkboard. Children frequently share the books they have written and illustrated at the writing center. Mrs. Lehrer teaches the children bookbinding so that all of the children's own books may become a part of the class library. Checking out and reading each other's books is one of the children's favorite activities during Sustained Silent Reading (SSR).

Figure 16-2 This teacher values each child and takes advantage of every learning opportunity.

After sharing, the children are then assigned to different tasks. One group of four may be assigned to the writing center where a parent eagerly awaits to assist. Another group of three may be asked to work at the art center, illustrating the stories they have written the day before. Two children may be assigned to paint at the easels and to design pictures for the next bulletin board. A group of six may be assigned to work with the bilingual aide on a social studies report they will present later to the class. Six more may go to one of the shelves containing the pattern blocks and wait for Mrs. Lehrer to give them directions on what to do with the Math Their Way task they are to complete. Six of the remaining children may go to the science center to record the results of an experiment begun the day before that involves the diffusion of food coloring in water. Once finished with their recording, they look in the folder placed in the center for the next experiment to complete. A parent oversees the center to help when needed. Of the remaining six, Mrs. Lehrer has arranged them in cross-age pairs; three third graders are helping first and second grade "buddies," one who is possibly learning disabled and two others who seem to be "slow learners," with their reading.

A strict disciplinarian, Mrs. Lehrer does not allow any aggressive acting-out behavior. If a child becomes involved in a fight, that child is quickly reminded that such behavior is not allowed and is sent to the principal. Mrs. Lehrer does not allow a child to interrupt when someone is speaking. Mrs. Lehrer has the classroom rules posted prominently in the front of the room beside one of the chalkboards. If asked, she will explain that the class cooperatively decided on the rules. Interestingly, there are only three: "I have the right to express myself in my classroom" (a picture illustrates a raised hand and is placed next to the words); "I have the right to be heard in my classroom" (the picture illustrates several children's heads listening to a child standing and speaking); and "I have the right to feel safe in my classroom" (the picture with the international sign for "No" illustrates two children fighting).

Upon entering Mrs. Lehrer's classroom, the visitor is impressed by how noisy it is. All of the children seem to be busy at the assignments they have been given. Two parents are busy assisting, one at the writing center, the other at the art center where children are busy constructing papier-mâché figures for a puppet show they will present that will introduce their peers to a story one of them has written. The bilingual aide is assisting two Hispanic children with their Spanish reading, and Mrs. Lehrer is circulating throughout the room checking on the progress of the others. Two "special needs" children are in the Resource Center at the time of observation and four soon-to-be-identified Gifted and Talented third graders are engrossed in practicing a play to be presented initially to the class and then at the upcoming PTA meeting.

What kind of teacher does Mrs. Lehrer appear to be? Is she congruent, acceptant, and empathetic? In talking with Mrs. Lehrer, it is obvious that she sees herself as a good teacher. After all, her children do well on the end-of-year tests. Many of them, in particular, are above grade level in reading and math. Her children also obey class rules and respect each other. As one listens to Mrs. Lehrer and observes more closely what is happening in her classroom, it becomes more apparent that, in spite of the seeming freedom and flexibility of the centers and the learning assistance of parents and aide, Mrs. Lehrer's classroom is more teacher-oriented than student-oriented. Children are assigned to centers; they do not have any choice. While most of them appear contented and actively involved, during the time of observation, an incident has occurred that has made the visitor uncomfortable—one of the first grade boys argued with his third grade "buddy" and called him a name. Mrs. Lehrer's face became angry-looking and she said sharply, "We work cooperatively in our classroom. If you can't cooperate with Justin, David, go to the 'time out' chair until I tell you you may return." David replied that he thought the 'time out' chair was 'stupid' and Mrs. Lehrer immediately sent the boy, accompanied by the "buddy," to the principal's office. Later, she explains to the visitor, "I simply won't tolerate that talking back from any of my children, especially from those 'fresh-mouthed' boys!"

Is Mrs. Lehrer a congruent teacher? Is her teaching a reflection of herself? If we become friends with Mrs. Lehrer, we would discover that her small house is immaculate, with everything in its place. She is a person of habit; rising, eating, and going to bed at the same time every day whether it is a school day or not. When meeting for an evening out, her friends know she will be punctual, almost to the minute. They know that she will have only one cocktail before dinner, order a fish special from the menu, and fall asleep at a musical performance because she usually goes to bed at 10:00 p.m. Because her schedule is just as rigid and exact as her teaching, Mrs. Lehrer is a congruent teacher.

Mrs. Lehrer is respected by many parents, especially those who have chosen to have their children placed in her room. They are pleased that many of the children are reading above grade level; they like the cross-age "buddy" system; however, they are somewhat in awe of Mrs. Lehrer because of her reputation as a strict, although "good," teacher.

If one inquired about Mrs. Lehrer's philosophy of education and curriculum goals, she would most likely answer, "It's simply to direct each of the children, to teach them to behave, read, write, and learn their mathematics." In terms of curriculum goals, Mrs. Lehrer would state, "I always follow district goals. In fact, I served on the curriculum committee the year the goals were revised." If questioned further, Mrs. Lehrer would again talk about the importance of reading, writing, and mathematics. Most likely, she will point out that some parents approve of her emphasis upon the basics. (One, of course, will wonder why Mrs. Lehrer has said nothing about the children!)

Another way of studying these two teachers is to look beyond their teaching styles to their leadership styles. As we know, Mr. Smith runs a student-centered classroom and has a flexible curriculum that changes with student interest and enthusiasm. We also know that the students' needs come first. What is his leadership style? One might say that it is democratic. The students all have a say as to what

will happen from day to day. Mr. Smith respects all opinions and ideas, and he teaches this to his students.

Mrs. Lehrer, in contrast, runs a teacher-centered classroom and has a fixed, somewhat rigid curriculum. In terms of her leadership style, one would have to admit that it is authoritarian. She is the final authority in her room.

OTHER TEACHING STYLES

We presented extreme examples of two teaching and two leadership styles. With most teachers, however, you will find variants of these extremes. Between these two contrasting styles, student centered and teacher centered or democratic and autocratic, lie others. The style of most teachers lies somewhere between Mr. Smith's and Mrs. Lehrer's, and a few may even lie at a further extreme. Many teachers follow a more or less set schedule from day to day. Free play usually starts the day in preschool; a "sponge" activity, such as journal writing or a few simple math problems, frequently starts the day in grade school. Sharing activities and attendance follow. Outdoor play and recess follow indoor activities. Quiet play alternates with active, noisy play. Rest follows lunch. Free play and less structured activities such as art, music, or physical education occur before dismissal time.

Many teachers follow a more or less rigid schedule with such curricula as reading and math. These disciplines are sequential; children must know A before they can proceed to B. Many teachers allow more flexibility with activities such as the fine arts. Thus, many curriculum choices may be a reflection of student and/or teacher interest, figure 16-3. A teacher who is proficient in art will provide many art activities; a teacher with interests in music will provide many musical experiences for the students, figure 16-4.

While observing as a student teacher, you will find there are almost as many different teaching styles as there are teachers. Teachers tend to emphasize those areas of the curriculum that they feel are more important; they also tend to emphasize those areas in which they have greater expertise. The

Figure 16-3 This area was developed as a result of the teacher's and children's interests.

major characteristic of all truly great teachers, though, is their ability to empathize with their students. Look closely; does the teacher show evidence of really liking the students? Does that teacher CARE? CAREing is the secret to good teaching.

Stereotyping Good and Bad

In order to understand fully a teacher's style, one has to understand the teacher's philosophy and underlying attitude toward the students. Does this teacher accept the children? Does this teacher feel that children are inherently good? Some teachers believe that all children are essentially bad and have to be taught to be good. Their teaching style reflects this attitude. Usually autocratic, they have rigid classroom rules. Children are told that they will behave in a particular way; any infringement upon the rules usually will bring swift punishment.

Does the teacher feel that children can be trusted? The teacher's style will reflect this belief. Classroom rules will be elicited from the children, with the teacher reminding them of a rule they may have overlooked. Children who misbehave are not considered bad but as needing more socialization time in which to learn. Punishment often takes the

form of physical removal from the situation and isolation until the child feels ready to rejoin the class.

Does Mr. Smith believe children are good or bad? Does Mrs. Lehrer? From the information presented so far, you only can guess that Mr. Smith believes children are inherently good and that Mrs. Lehrer may not.

A teacher may believe that most children are good and then have an experience with a psychologically damaged child who challenges this belief. At this point, the teacher may accept the fact that most, but not all, children are good. The danger is that the experience with the psychologically damaged child can lead the teacher to formulate a stereotype about all children who look like this child, who come from the same socioeconomic background, who belong to the same racial or ethnic group, or who are of the same sex. Of Mr. Smith and Mrs. Lehrer, which is most likely to use stereotypic thinking? Stereotypic thinking occurs more often in rigid people than in flexible people.

Flexibility

Let us also look at another factor—curriculum planning. The amount of planning needed is often overlooked in a classroom like Mr. Smith's. The vis-

Figure 16-4 Cooperating teachers and student teachers often use similar teaching techniques.

itor does not realize how much work goes into the arrangement of the learning centers. The classroom looks open, free, and flexible. Indeed, it is all of these. None of it is possible, however, without a great deal of careful planning. Ask Mr. Smith how many years it has taken to develop his classroom and how much work he still does during free time to maintain the atmosphere. You will find that Mr. Smith is continually revising, updating, and trying out new things. Much careful planning goes into any successful open and free environment.

In contrast, observe Mrs. Lehrer. During questioning, you will discover that she is still using many of the materials she developed during her student teaching years and first years of teaching. If she makes a change, it is usually at the request of her principal or at the suggestion of the parent of a child she likes. She seldom makes changes on her own and is quite comfortable with what she has always done. Some of her critics have suggested, "Mrs. Lehrer claims to have 12 years of experience; I maintain she has one year of experience repeated eleven times!" There is, unfortunately, much truth to the statement.

● TWO NEGATIVE MODELS

For further contrast, let us look at a third teacher, Ms. Young. A visitor to Ms. Young's room is immediately impressed by the noise level. All the children seem to be talking at once. Confusion appears to reign, with children constantly moving from one area to another. Ms. Young prides herself on her love for preschool children. Her room is arranged so that table activities are possible on one side of a large, almost square, room. She usually has clay at one table, cut-and-paste activities at the second, changing activities at the third. One day the visitor might find materials for tissue paper collages; another day the activity might be fingerpainting, on another day, there might be macaroni of various colors to string. Along one wall are shelves with puzzle racks, boxes of crayons and paper, and books the children may take to a carpeted area. Along another wall, there are blocks of different sizes and wheeled toys, such as trucks and cars, with a clear

space for play. In the far corner opposite the door is a playhouse. The window wall has low shelves containing some articles that might be science-oriented—shells, a large magnifying glass, rocks, some wispy plants in a neglected terrarium (Ms. Young confesses that she really does not know much about plants). Along the last wall is a sink with a water-play area. Two easels are found nearby. Cubbies for children's sweaters and share items are near the door. These cubbies serve to mark off the entrance area from the carpet area.

After becoming accustomed to the noise level and confusion, the observer notes that some children appear to be dominant. One large boy is ordering a group of boys at the block area to build a garage for his truck. A girl is ordering children around in the playhouse. One or two children seem to be confused by the noise; they are sitting rather unhappily on the sidelines. One boy catches your eye because he moves from one activity to another, staying only five seconds at each place. It seems there must be more than the 12 children in the room because of the mass confusion.

If asked about her philosophy of teaching, Ms. Young would answer, "Why, love, of course. I just love my children!" If asked about a schedule, she may answer, "Why, I don't need a schedule. I let the children decide for themselves what they want to do." If you were to point out that some of the children appear unhappy, Ms. Young is likely to reply, "Oh, they'll get used to it after a while."

How would one categorize Ms. Young's teaching style? Does she have one? The organized chaos of her classroom appears to fulfill the needs of some children, especially those from homes that have taught and encouraged self-sufficiency. But in looking at Ms. Young's classroom and her laissez-faire attitude toward the children, one will conclude that she does not have a teaching style. She does not have a philosophy of education; what she does in the room is haphazard.

The consequences of this aimless approach to curriculum is that some of the activities Ms. Young introduces are good, many are mediocre, and some are poor for the ability levels and interests of the children. Because of the lack of adequate supervision, there are occasional accidents and some of the more timid children's self-concepts are hurt. The more aggressive children are not helped either; they learn to be bullies and feel that "might makes right." They are not taught how to channel their aggressiveness into socially accepted actions. They are allowed to become leaders by default rather than learning how to lead and follow. To the trained observer, Ms. Young's classroom does not provide for the maximum growth of all the children.

Let us visit a private Christian school for our next example. Mr. Adams is the first grade teacher. Upon entering his room, the visitor's first impression is how quiet it is. Every child is sitting each at his or her own separate desk and seems busily engaged in the ditto they have been given. Questions would not arise until one might notice that few children look happy or engrossed. Mr. Adams rings a bell every 20 or 30 minutes and hands the children another worksheet to complete.

When asked about his philosophy of education, Mr. Adams responds that since children are born in sin, they must be taught to be good. He starts each day with a reading from the Bible, followed by a recitation of Bible verses by four or five children. He explains that each child is expected to memorize a Bible verse every day so that when they are called upon to recite, they can. He will tell a visitor that he calls upon the children in a random pattern, because "some children will always be prepared; others are seldom prepared." The children who are not prepared are called upon to recite more frequently and are punished.

Mr. Adams follows a rigid schedule; each child is assigned to a task and is expected to complete it before the bell rings. Every child is expected to complete reading and math worksheets within a specified time. There are no blocks, no easels, no dramatic play area, no arts and crafts materials, no interest corners. In fact, Mr. Adams's classroom is reminiscent of a high school classroom and seems rather sterile. Even the bulletin board, containing a few examples of "our best work," lacks color. The posted schedule of the day on the front chalkboard never varies.

If asked about the harshness of the schedule, Mr. Adams would insist the children are learning discipline; that it is fair for everyone to have the same opportunity to play with materials. Questioned about the apparent joylessness of his charges, Mr. Adams might reply, "Children are born in sin and should obey their elders. While they are in my care, they will obey me just as they would obey their parents at home. It's what the parents expect of us."

Is Mr. Adams a congruent teacher? Given his fundamentalist Christian background, the answer would be yes. Is he acceptant? Obviously, the answer is no, unless the child is good. What are the characteristics of a good child? Mr. Adams will tell you that it is a child who obeys rules, who memorizes a Bible verse every day, and who completes all of the assigned work without complaint. Is Mr. Adams empathetic? Again, the answer is no. In fact, Mr. Adams is highly suspicious of terms like *empathy* and believes that humanistic education is the work of the devil. Is he acceptant of the children? He believes *they* need to accept *him*.

SUMMARY

We observed Mr. Smith, a model master teacher with a clearly stated (and written) curriculum philosophy and goals of education. We have also looked at what is perhaps a typical teacher, Mrs. Lehrer. Although more authoritarian than Mr. Smith and less acceptant of all children, Mrs. Lehrer's teaching style with its emphasis on the basics is admired by many parents. We presented Ms. Young, a teacher with no real philosophy of education or stated curriculum goals other than to let the children play. Finally, we described Mr. Adams's classroom, and explained his philosophy to show the relationship between stated beliefs and teaching style. We also suggested that there is a relationship between a teacher's ability to CARE and their philosophy of education, which leads them to establish clear curriculum goals for their students.

Of the four teachers described, Mr. Smith obviously CAREs; Ms. Young may CARE but makes the critical error of mistaking freedom in the classroom with lack of structure and limits. Mrs. Lehrer would protest that she does CARE, but in reality she lacks empathy for the more assertive boys in her room. Mr. Adams does not even see the need to be acceptant or empathetic. A rigid set of rules and expectations are all that is necessary. He would most certainly see himself as a congruent person as well as a reliable one.

What should you, as a student teacher, do? Perhaps of greatest importance is to discover your own teaching style. What areas of the curriculum are you most comfortable with? Why? Do you see yourself as a CAREing person? Do you have a philosophy of education? In our four examples, do you see the relationship between each teacher's beliefs and curriculum practices? Think about your curriculum goals; consider how your feelings about working with young children influence these goals. Remember, especially, the positive model of Mr. Smith. Think of how he looks upon himself as a learner, how he looks at each child, how he listens to them, how flexible his curriculum is, how student-centered his curriculum style, and how democratic his leadership style.

SUGGESTED ACTIVITIES

A. Read Chapters 1 and 2 of *In Search of Teaching Style* by Abraham Shumsky. How do the descriptions of Teachers A and B compare to those of Mr. Smith, Mrs. Lehrer, Ms. Young, and Mr. Adams? Discuss the similarities and differences with your peers and college supervisor.

B. Write your philosophy of education. Describe it in relation to your curriculum style. Discuss this with your peers and supervisor.

C. Picture yourself the teacher of a group of culturally diverse four-year-old preschoolers. You are asked to create an activity attempting to have each child learn his address. Outline (write) the activity you've planned in a sequential fashion to share with a group of fellow students. Then have the group turn to the Appendix.

REVIEW

A. List two basic extremes of teaching styles and curriculums.

B. Read each question. Of the choices given, select the most appropriate answer.

1. Of Mr. Smith, Mrs. Lehrer, Ms. Young, and Mr. Adams, who is most likely to use stereotypic thinking?
   a. Mr. Smith
   b. Mrs. Lehrer
   c. Ms. Young
   d. Mr. Adams

2. Of the four teachers described, who is the most CAREing?
   a. Mr. Smith
   b. Mrs. Lehrer
   c. Ms. Young
   d. Mr. Adams

3. Who exhibits congruence?
   a. Mr. Smith
   b. Mrs. Lehrer
   c. Ms. Young
   d. Mr. Adams
   e. Both a and b

4. Of the four, who exhibits unconditional acceptance of their students?
   a. Mr. Smith
   b. Mrs. Lehrer
   c. Ms. Young
   d. Mr. Adams
   e. Both a and c

5. Of the four, who is consistent in his or her actions?
   a. Mr. Smith
   b. Mrs. Lehrer
   c. Ms. Young
   d. Mr. Adams
   e. Both b and a

C. Read the following descriptions of classroom interaction. Identify each teaching behavior as student centered or teacher centered. If a behavior is neither, identify it as such.

1. Teacher A is standing to one side of the playground during outdoor free play. She is busy talking to her aide. One child approaches another who is riding a tricycle. The first child wants to ride the tricycle and attempts to push the rider off. "How many times do I have to tell you you have to wait until I blow the whistle? You won't get your turn until you learn to wait!"

2. Teacher B is busy assisting four children on a cooking project. The bilingual aide is working with six children on a reading ditto. A parent volunteer is working with five others on an art project, and the student teacher is overseeing the remaining children with their unfinished reading assignments. A child with the student teacher complains in a loud voice, "This is a dumb assignment! I want to cook! Why can't I?" Teacher B looks at and signals the student teacher to try and resolve the problem alone.

3. Two boys are arguing loudly as they enter the preschool. Teacher C, who is standing by the door greeting each child, quickly takes a boy in each hand. She quietly asks, "What's the matter with you two today?" After listening to each boy and insisting that each listen to the other, she suggests a separate active play, based upon the knowledge of what each enjoys doing. They comply, and minutes later they and another child are spotted playing cooperatively with the large blocks.

4. Teacher D is standing in front of her class. The children are watching as she explains the activity; making pumpkins out of orange and black paper. After the children go to their assigned tables, it is apparent that at least two children do not know what to do. They sit glumly with their hands in their laps. Teacher D comes over and says, "Don't you two ever listen to directions?"

5. During roll, one of the boys in Teacher E's room begins to cry. Another child yells, "Cry-baby." Teacher E quietly speaks, "Sean, remember that we agreed we wouldn't call each other by names that can hurt. Stevie, come up here by me so we can talk. The rest of you can choose what activities you want to do. Mrs. Castilla, will you take over so I can talk to Stevie?"

6. Several children are busy playing in the sandbox. Jui-I begins to throw sand at Nohad. Nohad retaliates in the same manner. Soon others join in. Jimmie gets some sand in his eyes and cries. Jui-I stops throwing sand and is hit in the face by Nohad. Teacher F watches and wonders when the children will restore order.

7. Michael runs excitedly into his room at preschool only to have Teacher G say, "Michael, you know we don't run in school. Now, go back out and come in again like a gentleman."

8. The children are all sitting on the floor in a semi-circle facing Teacher H. Teacher H asks, "Who has something they want to share today?" Several hands go up. "Let's have George, Ana, Mike, and Jan share today." Noting a look of disappointment on Mary's face, he says, "Mary, I know you're disappointed but remember, you shared something with us yesterday. Don't you think we ought to give someone else a chance today?" Mary nods in agreement, and George begins to speak.

9. Deerat is standing at the front of the class reading a story from the basic reader. The other children are following along, reading silently. It is obvious that Deerat is a good reader and tries to vary her tone of voice. The child fluently reads the paragraph, but something is wrong. Teacher I interrupts her. "You are reading carelessly. It's not 'the coat,' it's 'a coat.' Now, start over again, and read every word correctly."

10. Ron is a new child in preschool. After greeting him and walking with him to the table

with crayons and paper, Teacher J goes back to the door to greet more children. When Teacher J thinks to look back at Ron, he notices Ron is busy drawing all over the top of the table. He goes quickly over to Ron, hands him another piece of paper, and says quietly, "Ron, use paper for drawing." He later comes back with a wet sponge and shows the child how to clean up the marks.

D. Identify whether the following statements are stereotypic or factual.

1. Women are more emotional than men.

2. Women are more nurturing than men.

3. Men think more logically than women.

4. Men are usually taller than women.

5. Asian children are better students than non-Asians.

6. Children from poor families do not do as well in school as children from middle-class families.

7. Boys from minority families fight more than other boys.

8. Attractive children are spoiled.

9. Children who are highly verbal are often gifted.

10. Homely children are not as bright as attractive ones.

11. Children who have no siblings are spoiled.

12. Oldest children in a family are not as social as youngest ones.

REFERENCES

Rogers, C. R., & Freiberg, H. J. (1994). *Freedom to learn* (3rd ed.). New York: Merrill/Macmillan.

Shumsky, A. (1968). *In search of teaching style.* New York: Appleton-Century-Crofts.

RESOURCES

Kowalski, T. J., Weaver, R. A., & Henson, K. T. (1994). *Case studies of beginning teachers.* New York: Longman.

Mosston, M., & Ashworth, S. (1990). *The spectrum of teaching styles: From command to discovery.* New York: Longman.

The Whole Teacher— Knowing Your Competencies

After studying this chapter, the student will be able to:

- Describe the major areas of teacher competency.
- Complete a self-assessment process.
- List desirable personal characteristics and abilities of teachers.
- Develop a plan that arranges, in order of priority, the student's future competency development.

Peer evaluations were valuable and eye-opening. The skills fellow student teachers displayed and the way the room looked and the on-going activities gave me lots of ideas. I think I obtained more insight into the role of a supervisor.

Joan Chang

I never did get used to being watched!

B. K. Sutton

Things really piled up and got out of hand during the final days of the semester. I let everything else in life slide. The class was the most demanding one I've taken.

Tina Roney

Student teaching is both rewarding and demanding. The nature of the work requires a wide range of job skills and competencies. Gaining a clearer picture of teaching competencies will help you plan for your own professional growth. This chapter pinpoints personal skills, abilities, and characteristics you may already possess and which serve as the basis for teaching competency.

Student teachers vary in the ways they accept responsibility for the act of teaching. Some students shift from assistant to full teacher easily while others experience self-doubt and question their motives for teaching.

Your life experiences and work with children have probably led you to pursue teaching as a career; you have "selected yourself" into the profession.

COMPETENCY-BASED TRAINING

Teacher education has experienced a movement toward competency-based training (sometimes called

299

I. To establish and maintain a safe, healthy environment
 1. Safe: Candidate provides a safe environment to prevent and reduce injuries.
 2. Health: Candidate promotes good health and nutrition and provides an environment that contributes to the prevention of illness.
 3. Learning environment: Candidate uses space, relationships, materials, and routines as resources for constructing an interesting, secure, and enjoyable environment that encourages play, exploration, and learning.

II. To advance physical and intellectual competence
 4. Physical: Candidate provides a variety of equipment, activities, and opportunities to promote the physical development of children.
 5. Cognitive: Candidate provides activities and opportunities that encourage curiosity, exploration, and problem solving appropriate to the developmental levels and learning styles of children.
 6. Communication: Candidate actively communicates with children and provides opportunities and support for children to understand, acquire, and use, verbal and nonverbal means of communicating thoughts and feelings.
 7. Creative: Candidate provides opportunities that stimulate children to play with sound, rhythm, language, materials, space, and ideas in individual ways to express their creative abilities.

III. To support social and emotional development and provide positive guidance
 8. Self: Candidate provides physical and emotional development and emotional security for each child and helps each child to know, accept, and take pride in himself or herself and to develop a sense of independence.
 9. Social: Candidate helps each child feel accepted in the group, helps children learn to communicate and get along with others, and encourages feelings of empathy and mutual respect among children and adults.
 10. Guidance: Candidate provides a supportive environment in which children can begin to learn and practice appropriate and acceptable behaviors as individuals and as a group.

IV. To establish positive and productive relationships with families.
 11. Families: Candidate maintains an open, friendly, and cooperative relationship with each child's family, encourages their involvement in the program, and supports the child's relationship with his or her family.

V. To ensure a well-run, purposeful program responsive to participant needs
 12. Program management: Candidate is a manager who uses all available resources to ensure an effective operation. The candidate is a competent organizer, planner, recordkeeper, communicator, and a cooperative co-worker.

VI. To maintain a commitment to professionalism
 13. Professionalism: Candidate makes decisions based on knowledge of early childhood theories and practices, promotes quality in child care services, and takes advantage of opportunities to improve competence, both for personal and professional growth and for the benefit of children and families.

Figure 17-1 CDA competency goals and functional areas. [From Phillips, C. (Ed.). (1991). *Essentials for child development associates working with young children*. Washington, DC: Council for Early Childhood Professional Recognition.]

performance-based) as an outgrowth of the application of behavioristic psychology, economic conditions, and major teacher education evaluation studies (Tittle, 1974). Federal funds promoted the identification of the Child Development Associate (CDA) competencies. A CDA is a person who is able to meet the physical, social, emotional, and intellectual growth needs of a group of children in a child development setting. These needs are met by establishing and maintaining a proper child care environment and by promoting good relations between parents and the center. In 1988, the Council of Early Childhood Professional Recognition surveyed CDAs and reported the following results:

- 80 percent of CDAs work in Head Start programs.
- 43 percent of those working in Head Start had been Head Start parents.
- 28 percent had some college education (76 percent of this group had attained a two-year or higher degree)
- 53 percent worked with young children for more than five years.

CDA competencies are a widely distributed and accepted listing of early childhood teacher competency goals, figure 17-1. Figure 17-2 offers definitions.

The Child Development Associate or CDA is a person who is able to meet the specific needs of children and who, with parents and other adults, works to nurture children's physical, social, emotional and intellectual growth in a child development framework. The CDA conducts herself or himself in an ethical manner.

The CDA has demonstrated competence in the goals listed below through her or his work in one of the following *settings*.

1. In a center-based program (CDA-CB).
2. In a home visitor program (CDA-HV).
3. In a family day care program (CDA-FDC).

Within a center-based setting, a person who demonstrates competence working with children from birth to three is a Child Development Associate with an *Infant/Toddler Endorsement*; or,

A person who demonstrates competence working with children aged three through five is a Child Development Associate with a *Preschool Endorsement*.

Within any of the above settings, a person who works in a bilingual program and has demonstrated bilingual competence is a Child Development Associate with a *Bilingual Specialization*.

Figure 17-2 Official definition of the CDA.

CDA training phases follow:

Phase I: Fieldwork
Student participates daily in child care program(s).

Phase II: Instructional Course Work
Attendance at a series of group seminars provided by a college, university, or other post-secondary educational institution.

Phase III: Integration and Evaluation
Integration of fieldwork, course work, then final evaluation.

● THE WHOLE TEACHER

Teaching competency growth can be compared to child growth. Teachers develop intellectually, socially-emotionally, physically, and creatively as do children. Skills often omitted on competency listings, yet which are becoming more and more important to early childhood teachers in our society, are stress reduction and stress management techniques, holistic health awareness and practice, moral and ethical strength, researching skill, parenting education and family guidance counseling, public relations, and political "know-how." Job situations can create the need for skills not covered in your teacher training. As society changes, the early childhood teacher's role as a partner to parents in child education changes.

Personal Abilities and Characteristics

What personal characteristics, traits, abilities, or "gifts" are described in early childhood teachers? Gage (1971) describes teacher behaviors on the basis of experimental evidence of their relationship with desirable outcomes or aspects of teaching:

Warmth. By warmth we mean the tendency of the teacher to be approving, to provide emotional support, to express a sympathetic attitude, and accept the feelings of pupils.

Teaching behaviors include:

• accepting child feelings.
• praising or encouraging.
• joking in ways that release tension.
• possessing an inveterate incapacity to think poorly of other persons, especially children.
• relating in a nonauthoritarian manner.
• displaying low or non-existent jealousy of others.
• causing pupils to feel their goals, sensibilities, abilities, and interests are taken into account.

Cognitive Organization. Early childhood teachers carry with them a set of "organizers" for subject matter that provide them, and so their pupils, with "relevant ideational scaffolding" that discriminates new material from what has been learned previously and integrates it at a level of abstraction, generality, and inclusiveness that is much higher than that of the learning material itself.

Teaching behaviors include:

• presenting information so that clear, stable, and unambiguous meanings emerge and are retained.

Orderliness. By "orderliness" we mean the teacher's tendency to be systematic and methodical in his or her self-management.

Teaching behaviors include:

- being responsible and businesslike rather than evasive, unplanned, slipshod.

Indirectness. A tendency toward indirect methods of teaching consists in giving pupils opportunities to engage in overt behavior, such as talking and problem solving, relevant to the learning objectives rather than merely listening to their teacher, and to discover ideas and solutions to problems rather than merely receiving them for the teacher.

Teaching behaviors include:

- accepting or using student ideas.
- questioning.
- stimulating, imaginative conversation.
- encouraging pupil participation and initiative, figure 17-3.
- permitting pupils to discover.
- displaying willingness to forbear furnishing every answer the pupil needs to know in an activity but not abandoning the pupil.
- guiding with verbal explanation.

Instructional Problem Solving. By ability to solve instructional problems we mean the teacher's ability to solve problems unique to his or her work in a particular subdivision of the profession.

Teaching behaviors include:

- pinpointing significant problem aspects.
- finding successful solutions somewhat easily.

According to Hamachek (1992), effective teachers who have few discipline problems possess a sense of humor; are fair, empathetic, more democratic than autocratic; and are able to relate easily and naturally to pupils on any basis—group or one-to-one, figure 17-4. Teacher behaviors that exemplify the "effective teacher" include:

- Willingness to be *flexible*, to be direct or indirect as the situation demands.
- *Ability to perceive* the world from the student's point of view.
- Ability to *personalize* their teaching.
- Willingness to *experiment*, to try new things.
- Skill in *asking questions* (as opposed to seeing self as a kind of answering service).
- *Knowledge* of subject matter and related areas.
- Provision of *well-established* assessment procedures.
- Provision of definite study helps.
- Reflection of an *appreciative* attitude (evidenced by nods, comments, smiles, etc.).

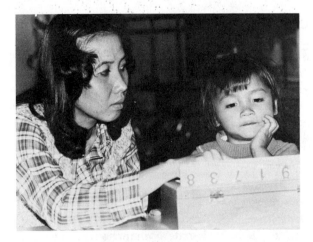

Figure 17-3 Encouraging responses is a teaching competence.

Figure 17-4 Effective teachers can relate easily to the children on a one-to-one basis or as a group.

- Use of *conversational manner* in teaching—informal, easy styles.

CDA training materials specify the following personal capacities as essential for Child Development Associates:

- To be sensitive to children's feelings and the qualities of their thinking.
- To be ready to listen to children in order to understand them.
- To use nonverbal forms and adapt adult verbal language and style to maximize communication with the children.
- To be able to protect orderliness without sacrificing spontaneity and childlike exuberance.
- To be perceptive to individuality and make positive use of individual differences within the group.
- To be able to exercise control without being threatening.
- To be emotionally responsive, taking pleasure in children's successes and being supportive in their troubles and failures.
- To bring humor and imagination into the group situation.
- To feel committed to maximizing the child's and family's strengths and potentials.

Dispositions

A relatively new term is used by Katz (1993) to describe desirable teaching behaviors: *dispositions.* Various attempts to define dispositions include the words inclinations, traits, tendencies, propensities, proclivities, and predilections. Katz believes usage of the term *dispositions* is ambiguous and inconsistent. Katz's definition follows:

> A disposition is a pattern of behavior exhibited frequently and in the absence of coercion and constituting a habit of mind under some conscious and voluntary control, and that is intentional and oriented to broad goals.

A student teacher can have as a goal to strengthen certain desirable teaching dispositions and weaken undesirable ones. Having a skill and knowledge of professional practices may not mean one actually uses them. Katz (1993) uses the example of a children's curriculum that presents early formal instruction in reading skills during preschool that may undermine children's dispositions to be readers.

What teaching dispositions do you as a teacher wish to strengthen? Probably:

- a curiosity and wonderment about classroom happenings and experiences;
- an enthusiasm concerning the challenges of teaching;
- a desire to observe and uncover children's needs and interests;
- a realization that one can continually learn, develop, and sharpen teaching skills and abilities; and
- working to gain children's trust and confidence and promote each child's self-realization.

Perhaps you can think of many others.

CAN EARLY CHILDHOOD STUDENTS SHARPEN CRITICAL THINKING SKILLS?

Kress (1992) designed a course of study and subsequent class activities to help early childhood college majors become aware of and use critical thinking skills. Kress' study concluded that critical thinking skills or use of them could be increased through training exercises. Ennis (1985) identified 13 dispositions (defined as attitudes and motivations) of critical thinkers; they follow.

The ability to:

1. Be open-minded.
2. Take a position (and change a position when the evidence and reasons are sufficient to do so).
3. Take into account the total situation.
4. Try to be well informed.
5. Seek as much precision as the subject permits.
6. Deal in an orderly manner with the parts of a complex whole.

7. Look for alternatives.

8. Seek reasons.

9. Seek a clear statement of the issue.

10. Keep in mind the original and/or basic concern.

11. Use credible sources and mention them.

12. Remain relevant to the main point.

13. Be sensitive to the feelings, level of knowledge, and degree of sophistication of others.

Let's look at a couple of classroom situations and decide what critical thinking skills could be modeled by this teacher.

Situation 1. A posted chart keeps slipping off the wall. Children bring it to the teacher's attention and Jamie asks "Why won't it stay? What can we do to fix it?"

Situation 2. Large wooden blocks are being carried outside for play on a cement patio. Children are busily making structures. Teacher knows these blocks were donated by the parent group and now are being scratched and damaged. She decides to discuss the problem with the class.

Situation 3. Everyone wants a turn looking at a new book read at story time. The waiting list is long and some children are anxious that they won't have a turn before having to leave for home.

Manley-Casimer and Wasserman (1989) point out that many classroom environments encourage teacher action "without thinking" or taking the time to process a decision. They feel teacher preparation often ignores the decision-making responsibilities of teachers. As a student teacher you will take on an increasing amount of daily decisions. Would you use the thoughtful, reflective approach of a critical thinker in situations 1, 2, and 3 above?

In situation 1, a critical thinking approach to the wall chart problem would begin with teacher recognizing the alertness and helpfulness of the children. Jamie might be answered with "Let's find that out, Jamie. Why might the chart keep slipping?" If nothing is offered by the child, the teacher could think out loud giving a few possible reasons, #8, and also might involve #3, #5, #12 above.

The teacher's behavior suggests he/she enjoys the quest for answers. If children do offer ideas such as "The tacks fell out," "The glue came off" or "Johnny did it," each idea is accepted and investigated. Analyze situations 2 and 3 to determine how many critical thinking skills might be modeled by the teacher or promoted in children.

How does a student teacher become proficient in critical thinking skills? By participating in a training program, Carter and Jones (1990) point out, adults learn complex teaching tasks in much the same way as young children learn: through experimenting, problem solving, talking with peers, asking questions, and making mistakes and reflecting on them.

National Association for the Education of Young Children's Accreditation Criteria

Staff skills as outlined in NAEYC's accreditation criteria serve as a listing of teacher behaviors found in high-quality programs. Student teachers can use this listing as competency goals and a standard of excellence. See the Appendix.

● SELF-PERCEPTION

Researchers have attempted to probe how "effective" or "good" teachers view their abilities and the abilities of others. If a teacher likes and trusts himself, that teacher is more likely to perceive others the same way. According to Hamachek (1992),

> They seem to have generally more positive views of others—students, colleagues, and administrators. They do not seem to be as prone to view others as critical, attacking people with ulterior motives: rather they are seen as potentially friendly and worthy in their own right. They have a more favorable view of democratic classroom procedures. They seem to have the ability to see things as they seem to others—from the other's point of view. They do not seem to see students as children "you do things to" but rather as individuals capable of doing for themselves once they feel trusted, respected, and valued.

Combs (1965) cites the results of several studies dealing with the way "good" teachers typically see themselves:

- Good teachers see themselves as identified with people rather than withdrawn, removed, apart from, or alienated from others.
- Good teachers feel basically adequate rather than inadequate. They do not see themselves as generally unable to cope with problems.
- Good teachers feel trustworthy rather than untrustworthy. They see themselves as reliable, dependable individuals with the potential for coping with events as they happen.
- Good teachers see themselves as wanted rather than unwanted. They see themselves as likable and attractive (in a personal, not a physical sense) as opposed to feeling ignored and rejected.
- Good teachers see themselves as worthy rather than unworthy. They see themselves as people of consequence, dignity, and integrity as opposed to feeling they matter little, can be overlooked and discounted.

Students entering the field of teaching have their own ideas regarding qualities important for success. They include being able to communicate ideas; having interest in people; having a thorough knowledge of teaching skills; having a pleasing manner and creative ability; being able to get along well with colleagues (*New Patterns of Teacher Education and Tasks*, 1974).

You have received feedback from your cooperating teacher, your supervisor, and perhaps others. This input is the basis of your understanding of how your competencies are viewed by others. Your perception of your teaching competencies is formed based on your own self-analysis and others' feedback.

● SELF-ANALYSIS

Self-analysis will increase your awareness of discrepancies and inconsistencies between your competency goals and your present teaching behavior. As you become more accurate in self-perception, your professional identity and confidence will grow. You may even be able to predict how others will react to your teaching behaviors. You will resolve the tendency to center on yourself (a common tendency of beginning teachers), and develop the abil-

ity to focus more on children's learning and teacher/child interactions.

Numerous self-rating scales exist; figures 17-5, 17-6, and 17-7 are examples. Other examples can be found in the Appendix.

---

1. Do I work within the policies and procedures established by the placement site.
2. Do I makes use of knowledge and understanding of child development and curriculum in early childhood education?
3. What are my relationships with each child?
4. How do I manage small and large groups?
5. Do I use good judgment in situations?
6. Do I plan for appropriate blocks of time indoors and outdoors?
7. Do I make good use of indoor and outdoor space?
8. Do I provide for transitions and routines?
9. Do I add to the attractiveness of the playroom?
10. Do I take care of equipment?
11. Do I consider health and safety factors in planning my activities?
12. Do I offer a wide range of experiences so that children can make choices according to their interests and needs?
13. Do I allow for various levels of ability among children?
14. Do I know how and when to ask questions?
15. Do I talk too much?
16. Do I make adequate provisions for variety in planned activities?
17. Do I see myself as a member of a team?
18. Do I coordinate my efforts with those of my co-workers?
19. Am I able to assume full responsibility in the absence of co-workers?
20. Do I participate in staff meetings?
21. Am I able to transfer concepts from theoretical discussions at staff meetings and workshops to action in my own programs?
22. Do I find ways to help children understand the roles of other adults at school?
23. Do I maintain good professional relationships with parents?
24. Do I recognize the importance of seeing the child as a member of the family?
25. Do I share a child's experiences with the parents?
26. Do I know when to refer parents' or a child's problems to an appropriate person?
27. Do I experiment with note-taking systems to assist in planning, to evaluate growth, and to form the basis for written records?
28. Do I use the information in records appropriately?
29. Am I a member of at least one professional organization in the field?
30. Do I attend meetings conducted by professional groups?

Figure 17-5 Student teacher's self-evaluation guide.

Using a 1–5 rating scale—1 meaning possesses much skill in this area to 5 meaning little skill displayed. Rate both yourself and how you feel others would rate you.

	Self	Others
1. Clear explanations	_____	_____
2. Leads children to self-conclusions and discoveries	_____	_____
3. Verbal interaction	_____	_____
4. Gives reasons	_____	_____
5. Motivates children's desire to find out	_____	_____
6. Demonstrations	_____	_____
7. Promotes comparisons	_____	_____
8. Enthusiastic encounters	_____	_____
9. Accepts children's limitations	_____	_____
10. Plans effectively	_____	_____
11. Guidance techniques	_____	_____
12. Organizes time	_____	_____
13. Developmentally appropriate activities offered	_____	_____
14. Parent interactions	_____	_____
15. Directing work of others	_____	_____
16. Keeping records	_____	_____
17. Observing children	_____	_____
18. Awareness of child needs	_____	_____
19. Awareness of adult needs	_____	_____
20. Cultural sensitivity	_____	_____
21. Accepts responsibility	_____	_____
22. Knows routines	_____	_____
23. Builds effective relationships with children	_____	_____
24. Attracts children's interest	_____	_____
25. Liked by children	_____	_____
26. Liked by adults	_____	_____

Figure 17-6 Rate yourself.

If you were judged on your personal characteristics, how would you rate yourself? How would others rate you? Place your rating in front of each characteristic, and then how others might perceive you. Use a rating scale of 1–5 with 1 representing "I've got a small amount of this" and 5 representing a generous amount.

Self		Others
_____	warmth	_____
_____	enthusiasm	_____
_____	businesslike attitude	_____
_____	patience	_____
_____	maturity	_____
_____	energy	_____
_____	encouragement of individual responsibility	_____
_____	ingenuity in planning for young children	_____
_____	flexibility	_____
_____	enjoyment of young children	_____
_____	encouragement of young children	_____
_____	reflective	_____
_____	open minded	_____
_____	organized	_____
_____	tolerance	_____
_____	abler to face ambiguity	_____
_____	ability to make inferences	_____
_____	ability to provide and plan teaching material	_____
_____	knowledge of early childhood education practices	_____
_____	clear educational philosophy	_____
_____	cultural sensitivity	_____
_____	understanging of child development	_____

Figure 17-7 Self-analysis.

After assessment, you can decide what additional skills you would like to acquire, figure 17-8. Put these skills in order of their importance to you. You are the director of your learning and the designer of your plan for future accomplishment.

When trying to assess your progress it may be difficult to isolate how you feel about yourself from how you feel about how others view you.

Recognize that a large part of the life-space of a new teacher involves human interaction. 'Others' enter the teacher's life-space, interact with teacher, and contribute to the teacher's perception of the relationship. Many view these interactions as crucial to the beginning teacher's feelings of success or failure—because it is through a teacher's interaction with others that he/she tests expectations and constructs a concept of self-as-a-teacher (Ryan et al. 1977).

Figure 17-8 Working with other adults may be a skill you feel is important.

SUMMARY

"The whole teacher" is made of a vast array of possible teaching skills and abilities. Teaching competencies (performance objectives) have been identified by individuals and groups based on value judgments concerning appropriate or desirable teaching behaviors. There are many teaching competency lists in circulation; the CDA list is widely accepted.

Each student teacher gathers feedback on teaching skills from others and from self-analysis. Examples of self-rating scales were presented to aid the student's development of a plan of priorities for future competency growth.

SUGGESTED ACTIVITIES

A. Write a self-analysis.

B. Develop a plan that lists, in order of priority, competencies you would like to acquire.

C. Invite a CDA representative to discuss the CDA professional preparation program.

D. Work in groups of three or four to draw a comical figure, a "perfect teacher" on a large paper or poster or chalkboard. Translate your drawing to the rest of the class. (Example: Roller skates on feet to get around the classroom quickly.)

E. Read the following and briefly describe your reactions and comments. Share your ideas with the class.

There is no perfect early childhood teacher, rather only individual teachers with varying degrees of competence exist. Teacher training should magnify strengths and produce teachers who differ greatly.

F. Complete the following statements.

1. My present strengths (teaching competencies) include . . .

2. My plan for developing more competencies includes working on . . .

G. Where do you belong on the line between each extreme? Draw a stick person at that spot.

Talkative_____Quiet

Eager to please_____Self-assured

Outgoing_____Shy

Punctual_____Late

Accepting_____Rejecting

Leader_____Follower

Flexible_____Rigid

Sense of humor_____Serious

Organized_____Disorganized

Academic_____Nonstudious

Patient_____Impatient

Warm_____Cool

Enthusiastic_____Apathetic

Active_____Passive

Open_____Secretive

Direct_____Indirect

Good communicator_____Poor communicator

Autonomous_____Conformist

Creative_____Noncreative

Animated_____Reserved

Talented_____Average

Sexist_____Nonsexist

Specialist_____Generalist

H. *Guidelines for Early Childhood Professionals: Associate, Baccalaureate, and Advanced Levels* (1994) suggests your training program (classes) should include the following. How well prepared do you feel in the areas listed below? Use W = well prepared, A = adequately prepared, N = need additional background.

- child growth and development _____
- historic and social foundations of early childhood education _____
- awareness of value issues _____
- ethical issues _____
- legal issues _____
- salary and status issues _____
- staff relations _____
- the importance of becoming an advocate for upgrading the profession and improving the quality of services for children _____
- child guidance and group management _____
- curriculum planning _____
- developmentally appropriate activities _____
- special needs children _____
- observing and recording child behavior _____
- family and community relations _____
- parent involvement _____
- child health, safety, and nutrition _____
- establishing child environments _____
- cultural pluralism _____

I. Read and comment on the following:

1. "Most books I've read about teaching indicate that the prime requisite for a teacher is a 'love of children.' Hogwash! What you must love is the vision of the well-informed, responsible adult you can help the child become." (Calisch, 1969)

2. "In every good classroom personality (teacher) there is some of P.T. Barnum (circus owner), John Barrymore (actor), Ringo Starr (per-

former) and Houdini (magician)." (Calisch, 1969)

3. "Your job as a teacher is to help the child realize who he is, what his potential is, what his strengths are. You can help him learn to love himself." (Calisch, 1969)

REVIEW

A. Choose the answer that best completes each statement.

1. A student teacher
   a. needs to develop all the competencies which experts recognize.
   b. should strive to display all competencies.
   c. should develop an individualized plan for competency development.
   d. should rely completely on feedback gained through the comments of others when developing a professional growth plan.
   e. can ignore competencies others consider important.

2. Lists of teacher competencies are based on
   a. research studies that correlate teacher behaviors and child accomplishment.
   b. value judgments of individuals and/or groups.
   c. recognized teacher abilities and skills.
   d. the qualities parents feel are desirable in teachers.
   e. what teacher training programs produce in student teachers.

3. The most widely accepted list of teacher competencies for teachers of children under age five is
   a. Head Start teacher competencies.
   b. graduating level competencies.
   c. NAEYC competencies.
   d. ECE competencies.
   e. CDA competencies.

4. A student teacher's view of competency best forms when

   a. others comment on student teaching episodes.

   b. children are watched for growth through the student teacher's planned activities or behavior.

   c. self-evaluation and feedback are combined.

   d. parents assess the student teacher's effectiveness.

   e. feedback includes comments from the entire staff.

5. The main purpose of developing plans to acquire other teaching skills is to

   a. facilitate growth.

   b. have student teachers learn all listed competencies.

   c. make student teachers realize their limitations.

   d. make student teachers realize their strengths.

   e. make sure the profession maintains quality performance.

B. Are there CDA competencies that you feel are not important or applicable in your present placement classroom? What are they and why?

REFERENCES

Calisch, R. W. (1969). So you want to be a real teacher? *Today's Education, 58*, NEA.

Carter, M., & Jones, E. (October 1990). The teacher as observer: The director as role model. *Child Care Information Exchange, 100*, pp. 27–30.

Combs, A. W. (1965). *The professional education of teachers.* Boston: Allyn and Bacon, Inc.

Competence, 7, 1. 1988 National CDA Survey Results Are In (March 1990, pp. 2–3). Washington, DC: Council for Early Childhood Professional Recognition.

Ennis, R. H. (1985). A logical basis for measuring critical thinking skills. *Educational Leadership, 43*(2), 44–48.

Essentials for child development associates working with young children. (1991). Washington, DC: Council for Early Childhood Professional Recognition.

Gage, N. L. (1971). Desirable behaviors of teachers. *Studying Teaching.* (2nd ed.). J. Raths, J. Poncella, and J. Van Ness (Eds.). Englewood Cliffs, NJ: Prentice-Hall, Inc.

Guidelines for early childhood professionals: Associate, baccalaureate, and advanced levels. (1994). Washington, DC: National Association for the Education of Young Children.

Hamachek, D. (1992). *Encounters with the self.* (4th ed.). New York: Harcourt Brace.

Katz, L. G. (September 1993). Dispositions as educational goals. *ERIC Digest*, EPO-PS-93-10.

Kress, A. (1992). Infusing thinking skills in early childhood education: Coursework to facilitate decision making by community college students. *Practicum Report*, Nova University, ED 350078.

Manley-Casimir, N., & Wasserman, S. (1989). The teacher as decision maker: Connecting self with the practice of teaching. *Childhood Education*, Annual Theme Issue, *65*(5), pp. 288–293.

New Patterns of teacher education and tasks. (1974). Paris: Organization for Economic Cooperation and Development.

Ryan, K., et al. (1977). *The first year teacher study.* Ohio: Ohio State University.

Tittle, C. K. (1974). *Student teaching.* Metuchen, NJ: The Scarecrow Press, Inc.

RESOURCES

Accreditation Criteria and Procedures. (October 1991). Washington, DC: National Association for the Education of Young Children.

Byers, L., & Iristi, E. (1961). *Success in student teaching.* Lexington, MA: D.C. Health and Company.

Essentials for child development associates working with young children. (1991). Washington, DC: Council for Early Childhood Professional Recognition.

Levin, T., & Long, R. (1981). *Effective instruction.* Alexandria, VA: The Association for Supervision and Curriculum Development.

Phillips, C. (Ed.). (1991). *Essentials for child development associates working with young children.* Washington, DC: Council for Early Childhood Professional Recognition.

Rogers, C. R., & Freiberg, H. J. (1994). *Freedom to learn.* (3rd ed.). New York: Merrill/Macmillan.

CHAPTER

18

Quality Programs

OBJECTIVES

After studying this chapter, the student will be able to:

- List 10 factors of a quality program.
- Describe the different types of quality programs.
- Discuss the relationship between a program's philosophy and its quality.
- Discuss the importance of the teacher and director in a quality program.
- List six of the areas evaluated under NAEYC accreditation criteria.
- Discuss the process of self-evaluation and its relationship to the accreditation process.

I'll never forget the time I watched my cooperating teacher's enthusiasm at reading group time. She looked as if she enjoyed the story as much as the group of children.

At recess I asked if it was a new reading series. She told me the book had been used for three years at her grade level. I marveled at her ability to make reading the story new, alive, and interesting to yet another group of children.

Marie Ota

My cooperating teacher and I became good friends. We still see one another at district meetings. I was privileged to have apprenticed under such an excellent model.

Rich Bacon

In looking at the concept of quality, what comes to your mind? High quality always suggests something that goes beyond the ordinary. In a program for young children, then, quality suggests that it exceeds minimal standards. Doherty-Derkowski (1995) states,

- A high quality early childhood program is one that:
- supports and assists the child's physical, emotional, social, language, and intellectual development; and
- supports and complements the family in its child-rearing role. (p. 4)

We might also want to include the fact that a high-quality program, in general, seeks to employ well-trained teachers who more than meet minimal education requirements of their respective states and usually pays a higher salary and offers more benefits than programs of lesser quality.

MEETING CHILDREN'S NEEDS

Among the factors to consider regarding the quality of an early childhood program is whether the program meets each child's developmental needs. There must be an awareness of and attention to the needs of the children.

What are the needs of children during their early years? Accepting the validity of theories discussed in previous units, their needs are to self-actualize, to know and understand, and to develop aesthetically. Children need to trust the significant people in their environment, resolve the questions of autonomy and initiative, and learn to become industrious.

Implications according to Maslow's and Erikson's Theories

Let us briefly return to the theories of Maslow and Erikson. What are the implications for a quality program in regard to these theories? The first factor would be an environment in which the child's physical safety was considered. Quality programs have the physical environment arranged so that the children can explore without encountering physical dangers such as electric cords, tables with sharp edges,

unprotected electric outlets that children could poke at, and so on. In a quality program, the physical environment has been childproofed, figure 18-1.

The second factor is attention to the child's need for psychological safety. Essentially, a quality program should provide for predictability, decision opportunities, and reasonable limits. Predictability teaches the rudiments to learning about time and safety. With predictability comes the safety of knowing that certain activities will happen at certain times, such as snacktime, group time, indoor and outdoor play, etc.

Children have little control over their lives, and, in our modern industrial society, they have little opportunity to contribute to the family welfare. If, however, they have freedom of choice within the limits set, they can and do exert control over this part of their lives and thus learn how to make decisions. They also learn to accept the consequences of their decisions. Limits allow the child the safety of knowing what behaviors are acceptable and not acceptable. Limits teach the child the concept of right versus wrong and help the child develop inner control over behavior, figure 18-2.

A third factor is attention to belongingness and love needs. A quality program will provide for these. All children need to feel that they are a part of a social group; a preschool, day care center, classroom, and family can provide the sense of group

Figure 18-1 Preschool classrooms are busy; therefore, all possible hazards should be carefully considered.

Figure 18-2 It takes time for some children to learn to work cooperatively.

identity that is so important for the young child's positive growth.

Esteem needs are met in a quality program. Care is taken by all staff members to ensure that the children's self-concepts are enhanced. Look to see how the workers in a program relate to the children. Do they CARE? Do they take time to listen to the children? Do they compliment children when they have accomplished some goal? Do they make a conscious effort to bolster the children's self-esteem?

Are self-actualization needs met? Quality programs have enough equipment and materials with which the children can interact. Are there enough art materials, books, and cut-and-paste opportunities? Is there a climbing apparatus? Are there tricycles and swings enough so that no child has to wait too long? Are there enough puzzles? Are they challenging? Is the playhouse corner well furnished? Are there enough props to stimulate sociodramatic play? Are there both large and small blocks? Is there a water table, a sand area, a terrarium, an aquarium, a magnifying glass? Are there enough small manipulatives? Are the play areas and yard clean and well-kept? Do the children look happy?

Balanced Program

A quality program will have a balanced curriculum: language, motor activities, arts and crafts, storytime, music, creative movement, counting oppor-

tunities, matching pictures, colors, shapes, science opportunities; none of these is neglected in a quality program. Because of its importance, language will be emphasized in curricular areas in a quality program. Look at and listen how language is used and encouraged. It is during the preschool years of two and one-half to five that the child makes the most progress in language. Having a vocabulary of maybe only three hundred words at two and one-half years, the preschool child will expand this to perhaps 3,000 by age five. In receptive vocabulary, the 800 known by the two and one-half-year-old will grow to nearly 10,000 by age five. At the same time, the child is learning the syntactic rules of the language: present, past, and future tenses; the use of the negative form, the interrogatory form, and the conditional. All of this language ability is, for the most part, acquired without formal teaching. A quality program, however, recognizes this growth of language in the young child and provides opportunities for the child to hear language being used in proper context, to listen to models of language, and to practice growing language competencies. In addition, a quality program affords many opportunities for language enrichment, figure 18-3.

A quality program will have a quiet corner or private space for the children so that any child can be alone when necessary or desired. Children, espe-

Figure 18-3 A quality program provides many opportunities to explore literature.

cially those who spend long hours in a center every day, need time and space to be alone. Some children live in homes that afford them little or no privacy.

Personnel and Philosophies

Perhaps the most important factor in quality programs is the personality of the teacher and director, essentially the physical, mental, emotional, and social characteristics. Is this a person who really *likes* children? Does this person appear to be upbeat? Are there "laugh lines" in the corners of the eyes? Does this person smile when talking? Does there appear to be a mutual respect between this person and the children? When talking to the children, does this person stoop in order to be at their level? Is this person *with* the children or *over* the children? Is this a person trained in child development? A warm, loving, knowledgeable teacher and director can make almost any program—public or private—a quality one, given the space and materials with which to work.

The second most important factor is the underlying philosophy of the program, the basic principles by which the program is guided. Are there stated objectives? Is there a written statement of philosophy? Is the curriculum based upon a knowledge of child development principles? Are there printed materials describing the program in terms of what the teacher and director want for the children? Or is this a program with no statement of purpose, no written goals, no clear curriculum? Worse yet, is this a program that assumes that you know all you need to know about the program on the basis of its label, for example, Montessori, Christian?

Beware of any program which uses a name and has no written philosophy or goals. Beware, also, of a program whose stated goals are not congruent with child development principles. Watch out for the program whose philosophy does not stress respect and love for each child. Beware of any program in which helping children acquire strong self-concepts is not listed as a goal. Be wary of a program in which one part of the curriculum is overemphasized at the expense of the others. A cognitive curriculum is fine *if* attention also is given to the child's social, emotional, and physical growth needs as well.

Be wary of a program with teachers who stress boys' activities as different from girls' activities. Be wary of teachers who seem to have different expectations of boys and girls.

STANDARDS OF QUALITY PROGRAMS

To assist you as a student teacher, there are many published source materials available. The National Association for the Education of Young Children (NAEYC), for example, publishes a leaflet "Some Ways of Distinguishing a Good Early Childhood Program." The factors discussed are:

1. There is ample *indoor and outdoor space*: about 35 square feet of free space per child indoors and 100 square feet of space per child outdoors.
2. *Safe, sanitary, and healthy conditions* must be maintained.
3. The *child's health* is protected and promoted.
4. A good center helps children to develop *wholesome attitudes toward their own bodies* and bodily functions.
5. The importance of *continuity in the lives of young children* is recognized *without over-stressing routines or rigid programming*.
6. A good center provides appropriate and sufficient *equipment and play materials* and makes them readily available for each child's enjoyment and development (figure 18-4).
7. Children are encouraged to use materials and gradually increase their skills for *constructive and creative processes*.
8. Children are helped to increase their use of *language* and to *expand their concepts*.
9. Opportunities for the child's *social and emotional development are provided*.
10. Because young children are so closely linked to their fathers and mothers, a good center considers the *needs of both parents and children*.
11. Consideration is given to the *entire family's varying needs*, along with special recognition for the growth and protection of the child enrolled.

Figure 18-4 Quality programs have innovative and inviting outdoor climbing structures.

12. There are *enough adults* both to work with the group and to care for the needs of individual children.

13. A good center does more than meet the minimum standards set for *licensing* by the state and/or federal regulating agency.

14. Staff members have a positive outlook on life. They realize that *human feelings* are most important.

15. The adults in a good center *enjoy and understand children* and the process by which they learn.

16. Because the entire staff has a direct or indirect influence on each child, all members try to work with one another.

17. In a good center, staff are alert to *observing* and recording each child's progress and development.

18. The good center uses all available *community resources* and participates in joint community efforts (figure 18-5).

(Reprinted by permission from NAEYC. Copyright © 1981, National Association for the Education of Young Children, 1834 Connecticut Avenue N.W., Washington, D.C. 20009.)

In studying this list, it is easy to see that, although not specifically stated, Maslow's hierarchy of needs is considered. Erikson's developmental tasks have been considered as well. NAEYC's list, however, goes beyond simply relating conditions to developmental theory. It also introduces the importance of looking at minimum standards as set by governmental authorities, suggesting that a good program exceeds such minimal standards. For example, federal or state standards may suggest that a ratio of 12 children (two- and three-year-olds) to one adult is sufficient. A quality program may have eight to 10 children for every adult.

Although a school cannot become licensed without meeting minimum standards regarding indoor and outdoor space, there are programs which *average* the number of children throughout the day and exceed the minimum recommended number during hours of prime use. For example, a center may be licensed for 28 children and have as few as 10 present at 8:00 a.m. and eight at 5:45 p.m.; yet, they may have as many as 34 present between 10:00 a.m. and 3:00 p.m. The total number of children present throughout the day may be averaged so that a par-

Figure 18-5 Quality programs often encourage parent participation.

ent may never be aware of the overcrowding at mid-day. Some centers will employ a nutrition aide at lunchtime to assist in meal preparation. Although this person may never work with the children, he or she may be counted as an adult when figuring the ratio of children to adults. Many parents are unaware of these types of practices, none of which would be present in a quality program.

● TYPES OF QUALITY PROGRAMS

It is important to recognize that there are many different types of early childhood programs; each one may be of quality. There are, for example, day care centers; state-funded child care programs; Head Start and Montessori programs; parent-cooperatives; and private, nonprofit and profit-making preschools and primary schools. In each of these, a student teacher or parent can find good programs, mediocre programs, and, unfortunately, poor programs.

Programs reflect the underlying philosophy of their director, head teacher, or proprietor. It takes time to interview and observe carefully to determine quality. One may discover, upon close observation, that children have no freedom of choice as to what toys they will play with, that they are, instead, assigned toys. It is also easy to be deceived by a glib promotional director, head teacher, or proprietor. Smooth talk and right answers do not make a quality program. Look carefully when presented with a persuasive director. Is this person putting into action policies that are in the interest of the children?

We are reminded of a private center in which there are many toys and materials for the children to play with. There is also a lot of space both indoors and outdoors. Yet, it is not a quality center and does not run a quality program. Why? Unfortunately, the owner has little or no background in early childhood education and, in an effort to keep down costs, employs two teachers who only meet minimum state standards for licensing. These teachers are underpaid; consequently, there is a high rate of turnover. The owner also brings her own child to the center and has difficulty relating to any child who does not play well with hers.

There is no easy answer to "policing" poor or mediocre programs. The center in the preceding example is the only one in a lower-middle-class neighborhood. There are many single parents in this neighborhood. In families with two parents, usually both parents work. Due to transportation difficulties and a lack of room in and eligibility for the community's well-known quality centers, this center is the only one available for many children.

● WHO DECIDES THE QUALITY OF A PROGRAM?

As we suggested, the director has a responsibility regarding the quality of a program. Indirectly, parents also have a say in a program's quality. Obviously, there would be no program without clients (parents). Thus, if a client buys an inferior service (education), he or she has the choice to stop using it. The solution is, however, not always so simple. Parents may not have many options in terms of the immediate neighborhood. This may be compounded by the parents' lack of knowledge; they may judge a program by its external appearance, e.g., its cleanliness, personal perceptions of the director's competence.

Quality is also dependent upon the type of program. For example, in a program sponsored by a public school district, quality is determined not only by a director or teacher but also by government regulations, by the principal in whose school the program is located, and, ultimately, by the local board of education and its policies.

A public program must adhere to prescribed standards. However, in most public schools, ultimate quality depends upon the teacher and the supervising principal. In a private program, quality may depend upon several people. In a proprietary preschool, quality is related to the personality and training of the proprietor. Is this person a loving, caring human being? Does this person have formal training in early childhood education, or does she hire people who are loving and caring and have formal training? In any proprietary school, you will find the same range of quality as in a public program.

Who determines quality in a Montessori program, for example? Does the name, Montessori, promise that all its programs will have the same standards, the same quality? In the United States, there are two main approaches to Montessori education, both of which are called Montessori schools. One branch is the schools that are under the sponsorship of the Associatione Montessori Internationale (AMI), with headquarters in Switzerland and headed by Maria Montessori's son. AMI schools adhere very closely to Maria Montessori's original curriculum. Its teachers are trained in the philosophy, with the didactic (teaching) materials designed by Dr. Montessori herself. In AMI schools, you will generally find the same materials being used regardless of where the school is located. You will also find that the teachers have basically the same training in philosophy and methodology. Still, there will be differences in quality. Just as in the public schools or in the proprietary centers, quality will depend, to a large extent, upon the teacher's personality. Does the teacher really *like* children? Does that person CARE? Are the children happy? Look carefully.

The other type of Montessori program is sponsored by the American Montessori Society (AMS), whose headquarters are in New York State. AMS schools are less like the original Montessori schools in that, although they use the didactic materials developed by Dr. Montessori, they make use of modern trends toward a greater emphasis on gross motor and social development. AMS programs vary widely; the personalities of the directors and teachers are the important factors.

Another determining factor is who or what organization sponsors the school. Many churches sponsor schools and day care programs. In this case, quality depends not only on the personality of the director and teachers but upon the philosophy of the sponsoring church. Church-sponsored schools can also be excellent, mediocre, and poor. The teachers or day care workers always make the difference.

Studies of Quality

The Cost, Quality and Child Outcomes in Child Care Centers Study (1995) is described as a landmark study linking data on program costs and quality to child outcomes. Fig. 18-6 displays study results. Four hundred randomly selected centers in

California, Colorado, Connecticut, and North Carolina were assessed. Half the centers were nonprofit and half profit making.

The following study conclusions were highlighted by researchers:

- Child care at most centers in the United States is poor to mediocre.

- Children's cognitive and social development are positively related to the quality of their child care experience across all levels of maternal education, child gender, and ethnicity.

- Consistent with previous research, the quality of child care is related to specific variables:
  - higher staff-child ratios
  - staff education
  - administrators' prior experience
  - teacher wages
  - teacher education, and
  - specialized training.

- States with more stringent licensing standards have fewer poor-quality centers. Centers that

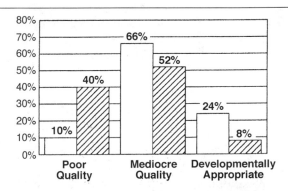

☐ Preschool classroom quality   ☒ Infant classroom quality

Note: Data are based on the *Early Childhood Environment Rating Scale* (Harms & Clifford, 1980) and the *Infant/Toddler Environment Rating Scale* (Harms & Clifford, 1989).

Figure 18-6 Quality ratings in preschool and infant classrooms. Reprinted with permission from the National Association for the Education of Young Children. From Cost, Quality and Child Outcomes in Child Care Centers. (May 1995). *Young Children, 50*(4).

comply with additional standards beyond those required for licensing provide higher quality services.

- Centers provide higher-than-average overall quality when they have access to extra resources that are used to improve quality.
- Center child care, even mediocre-quality care, is costly to provide.
- Good-quality services cost more than those of mediocre quality but not a lot more.
- Center enrollment affects costs.

Most professionals agree with NAEYC's National Institute for Early Childhood Professional Development that "the most important determinant of the quality of children's experiences are the adults who are responsible for children's care and education" (NAEYC, 1994).

Cost, Quality and Child Outcomes in Child Care Centers (1995) reinforces what was found in the "National Child Care Study" in that overall quality of care in center-based child care programs is poor to mediocre (Whitebook, Phillips, & Howes, 1993).

Many factors contribute to poor quality, including strong price competition in the marketplace, lack of consumer demand for quality, poor licensing standards, staff-child ratios, staff education, administrator experience, and center revenue and resources, to name but a few.

Most experts and researchers believe high-quality programs have a high adult-child ratio, a relatively small group size, age-appropriate activities, a safe environment, and access to comprehensive services as needed, such as health and nutrition and parent involvement.

Pre-kindergarten teachers with the highest levels of education are found in public school pre-kindergartens. Those with lowest levels are teaching in for-profit centers. (Morgan, et al., 1993).

ACCREDITATION AND ITS RELATIONSHIP TO QUALITY

For many years schools (usually high schools, although both elementary and middle schools or junior highs have been involved), colleges, and uni-

versities have undergone periodic accreditation procedures by the Accrediting Commission for Schools, hereafter referred to as the Commission. The Commission divides the United States into several regions that each have their separate commissioners who use the same criteria to evaluate programs. The purpose of accreditation, stated on the first page of the Visiting Committee Handbook (1994), is:

Fostering excellence in elementary and secondary education; Encouraging school improvement through a process of continuous self-study and evaluation; and Assuring a school and its public that the school has clearly defined and appropriate educational goals and objectives, has established conditions under which their achievement can reasonably be expected, appears to be accomplishing them substantially, and can be expected to continue to do so. (p. 1)

The criteria the Visiting Committee is expected to use are that the school will have:

1. A statement of philosophy;
2. A clearly defined organizational structure;
3. A plan for student support services;
4. A curricular program with written course descriptions and objectives;
5. Co-curricular programs that supplement the formal instruction of the school;
6. A well-qualified staff;
7. A safe and adequate school plant; and
8. Continuing financial support to provide a quality program.

Visiting committee members undergo training each year to ensure that they are up-to-date on any changes involved in the accreditation process and to provide members with additional practice regarding the application of the criteria prior to the visitation. Committee members include teachers, administrators, college/university faculty, students (if appropriate), and community representatives, such as school board members and/or representatives of business and industry. There are generally five or six members on any one Visiting Committee. After the visitation, a written report is forwarded to the Commission with the accreditation recommendation. The commissioners meet, usually in the late spring, read all of the Visiting Committee reports, and vote either to approve or amend the Visiting Committee's recommendations. Accreditation terms are generally for six years (maximum), three, one, or to deny.

Since many elementary and middle schools do not go through regional accreditation by the Commission, several states have instituted their own version of accreditation, commonly referred to as program quality review (PQR). In California and some other states, for example, the state board of education requires that all schools in the state undergo periodic PQRs. These involve a self-study, as does accreditation by the Commission, and review by a team of evaluators. Included on the review team are teachers, administrators, and state board of education representatives who have all received training in how to conduct a PQR. The reviewers prepare a report for the state superintendent of instruction and the state board of education members who have the final authority to accept the report, ask that the school undergo further review, or reject the report. Reviews are conducted every three years, so it is a continuing process.

The National Association for the Education of Young Children, concerned with how to ensure quality programs for young children, especially as they relate to developmentally appropriate practices, established the National Academy of Early Childhood Programs to administer accreditation procedures in 1985. These involved some of the same steps used by the Accrediting Commission for Schools. Any program wishing to be accredited writes NAEYC and requests that it be placed on the calendar for an accreditation visit. Once the date of the visit is confirmed, the program conducts a self-study, involving formal reports by the administrator, the staff, and parents. The result is a program description that includes a center or school profile, the results of classroom observations (both the teacher and the director complete this), and the results of the administrator report that ties together the results of the ratings of the program by staff and parents.

Areas evaluated are:

1. Interactions among staff and children
2. Curriculum
3. Staff-parent interaction
4. Staff qualification and development
5. Administration
6. Staffing
7. Physical environment
8. Health and safety
9. Nutrition and food service
10. Evaluation (Bredekamp, 1987)

After completion of the self-study and its subsequent reception at NAEYC, a trained validator visits the center or school to verify the self-study much in the same manner as the Visiting Committee or the PQR reviewers. The validator's report is then read by at least three commissioners who make the final accreditation decision. Since its institution in 1985, close to 1,800 programs have been accredited. Figure 18-7 illustrates accredited programs and those in the process of self-study. As the process becomes better known, as more and more programs implement developmentally appropriate practices, and especially as parents begin to demand accredited programs for their children, the number of approved programs should rise.

Does accreditation assure quality? In many ways, yes. The self-study alerts teachers, directors, principals, and others involved in the process to any areas of needed improvement, especially those impinging directly on standards required for accreditation. Often, then, when visiting committees, reviewers, or validators arrive, changes have already been instituted to improve an area likely to cause concern. One principal difference, though, between the accreditation by the Accrediting Commission and that of the program quality review or National Academy is the point on philosophy. Where the Commission accredits on how closely, among other factors listed, the curriculum goals match school philosophy, PQR reviewers are interested in how closely elementary

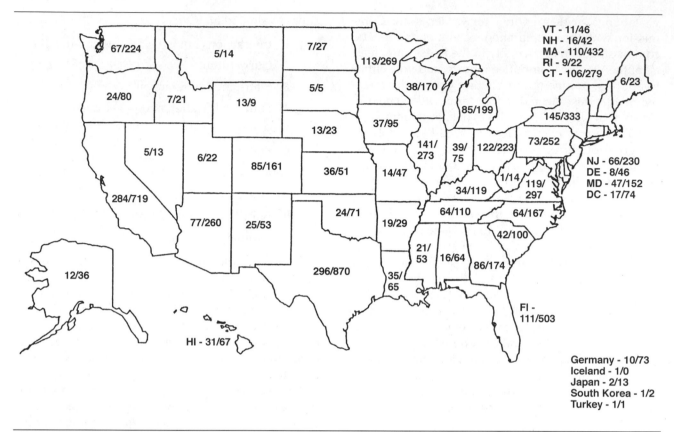

Figure 18-7 Number of accredited programs/programs in self-study (as of August 1993). Reprinted with permission from the National Association for the Education of Young Children. NAEYC Annual Report (November 1993). *Young Children, 49*(1).

school curriculum goals and objectives match those set forth in state curriculum guides, and National Academy validators observe to see how closely preschool/day care centers/preschool-primary school goals and objectives match the standards of the National Academy. Thus, emphasis shifts from school to state to national standards.

Does Accreditation Make a Difference?

In a recent study of 877 preschools/day care centers and 645 family day care homes, the *San José Mercury-News* (Johnson, 1995) found that accreditation did indeed make a difference. One aspect of quality studied was the number of Type A complaints filed against the center or family day care home. (Type A violations include the use of physical

punishment, spanking, yelling, humiliating the child, and so forth; not enough indoor and/or outdoor space for the number of children in care; facility problems, such as cleanliness, proper storage of poisons, fencing of pools, and so on; not enough safety seats and/or belts in cars and vans used to transport children; insufficient supervision of children; and others.) In the study not only did accredited preschools and centers have fewer Type A violations (7 percent), 58 percent had no violations of any kind. In comparison, 31 percent of the nonaccredited preschools and centers were cited with Type A violations and only 23 percent were found with no violations. The most common Type A violations related to teacher qualifications and/or the teacher-child ratio; insufficient care and supervision; violation of the child's personal rights (spanking, for example); child activities and storage space, including enough space for the children's activities and proper storage of poisonous materials; buildings and grounds; fixtures and furniture; food services; and staff criminal background checks. (September 10, 1995, p. 25A).

In looking at nonprofit preschools and centers compared to those that operate for profit, the *Mercury-News* found another interesting fact related to quality. Of the 275 for-profit centers investigated, 43 percent were found to have had Type A violations; of the nonprofit centers, only 25 percent had had Type A violations filed. (According to State of California definitions, profit-making centers include ownership by an individual, a for-profit corporation, and a partnership; nonprofit centers include those operated by a nonprofit group, county, and other public agency [p. 25A]). In other words, a proprietary center owned by an individual or by a partnership is considered a for-profit center. Nationally operated corporate centers such as KinderCare and La Petite Academy are examples of for-profit centers.

MENTORING PROGRAMS

The more experienced worker tutoring and serving as an example to the new worker has always been a way of training. Mentoring programs have emerged as one of the most promising ways to stabilize and support the child care work force in order to guarantee more reliable and high-quality care for young children (National Center for the Early Childhood Work Force, 1995).

The National Center for the Early Childhood Work Force (1995) describes the mentoring effort:

> Throughout the country, mentoring programs have emerged as one of the most promising strategies to retain experienced teachers and providers and thereby guarantee more reliable, high quality care for young children. Experienced teachers and providers participate in programs designed to give them the skills necessary to teach other adults how to care for and educate infants and young children. Upon taking on the role of mentor teacher, most teachers and providers re-

ceive additional compensation for training protégés; gain new respect from their co-workers and parents and renew their own commitment to working with children in the classroom or home. As dozens of programs develop, the need to share information grows.

The Early Childhood Mentoring Alliance, a newly emerging group, intends to provide a forum for sharing information and providing technical assistance. The Alliance is supported by a consortium of foundations.

DEFINING AN OPTIMAL EDUCATION AND CARE SYSTEM

Hawaii's Governor's Office of Children and Youth, (O'Donnell, 1994) has described what is felt by many educators to be an outstanding system:

> An optimal early childhood education and care system will enable all children to reach their full potential, prepare them for a life of successful learning and enable them to become productive community members. Comprehensive and coordinated services with appropriate cognitive, physical, and social development in a consistent, healthy, and safe environment offered by competent and nurturing adults, from birth throughout the early years, in a variety of settings are all quality elements. The optimal early childhood system will provide all children in Hawaii with equal access to quality educational care resources which are appropriate to families' life circumstances and preferences.

SUMMARY

In this chapter, we attempted to provide guidelines by which you can evaluate the quality of an early childhood education program. We have suggested that a quality program is one that takes into consideration the developmental needs of the children and that exceeds, rather than meets, minimum standards for state licensing. We have also suggested that quality programs may be found in many different settings ranging from federally funded programs to parent-cooperatives and proprietary profit-making centers, figures 18-8 and 18-9.

Figure 18-8 How would you evaluate this classroom's use of display areas?

We also presented a review of the accreditation processes, sponsored by the Accrediting Commission for Schools and by the California State Board of Education's Program Quality Review, as these apply to the provision of quality elementary school programs. NAEYC's National Academy of Early Childhood Programs and its accreditation process was briefly explained as was its impact on quality programs for children from birth through age eight. (Most accredited programs are for children from birth through age five, the public schools not applying for accreditation through NAEYC but, instead, undergoing program quality review or some other form of state accreditation.)

Quality programs depend upon you as student teachers. You need to strive to preserve and improve upon these programs when you enter the field. Quality programs can exist only if quality people fight for them.

SUGGESTED ACTIVITIES

A. Visit at least three of these different types of early childhood programs: a Montessori school, a Head Start program, an NAEYC accredited program, a proprietary day care center, and/or a public school kindergarten, first, second, or third grade classroom. Evaluate them on the 18 factors of a good program from NAEYC or look at the Accrediting Commission for Schools criteria and interview the teachers and/or principal of the school you visit and ask them about their self-study. Are the programs of equally good quality? Why or why not?

B. Summarize your evaluations of the programs you choose to observe. Discuss your ideas with your peers and supervisor.

Figure 18-9 How would you evaluate this classroom's use of display areas?

C. Read Maria Montessori's *The Montessori Method.* Discuss your comments with your peers and supervisor. Compare the program you visited with the ideas found in this book.

REVIEW

A. List 10 features of a quality early childhood program.

B. Read each of the following descriptions of different early childhood programs. Decide whether each paragraph is describing a quality program, a mediocre program, or a poor program. If you do not have sufficient data to make a decision, indicate this. Discuss your answers and opinions with peers and college supervisor.

1. This private preschool/day care center is located in a former public school. Each morn-

ing the director greets every child as they enter. Each child has a wide choice of activities. Clay containers are placed on one table; crayon boxes and paper on another; scissors, old magazines, and scraps of construction paper are on a third, with sheets of blank paper and glue sticks. Some children prefer to go to the block area, the book corner, or housekeeping corner. The outside play area beckons those who wish to climb, ride, swing, or play at the water table or in the sand box.

The director has a degree in early childhood education, as does the only paid aide. Parents are seen often; both fathers and mothers stay with their children for a few minutes. The director speaks to each parent and sends home a monthly newsletter to inform parents of special activities and to solicit help for special projects. (For example, both the indoor and outdoor climbing structures were built by parents.)

The director carefully interviews every prospective family who wishes to place their children in the center. The director insists upon at least one visit by both parents and the child before final acceptance. Prospective parents receive a written statement of philosophy and curriculum. During these meetings, the director has been known to state, "I expect parents to interview me as carefully as I interview them."

2. This after-school program is sponsored by a franchised nonprofit organization. The director of the program has an AA degree in early childhood education. Certified teachers or CDA holders work with the children (ages five to nine). In addition, there are many volunteers recruited from a local community college and high school. The program is located in empty classrooms in four elementary schools and in the nonprofit organization's main facility.

Because the latter facility does not meet state standards, children are asked to join the organization. As a result, the organization is exempt from having to meet standards. For example, although there is ample outside play area at the school sites, there is none at the main facility site. This after-school program has a written statement of purpose and goals, a conceptual outline covering such items as safety, self-image, adult role models, a stimulating environment, etc.; a parent advisory group; and a daily schedule listing curriculum factors. The adult to child ratio is listed as 15:1 but has been known to exceed 25:1 when volunteers have been absent.

The program schedules free time for the first 30 minutes so that the children can unwind from their school day. This is followed by snack time, activity time (arts and crafts, gymnastics, swimming, field trips, etc.), clean-up time, and free time during which quiet activities such as games, reading, homework, and drawing can be done.

3. This Montessori program (AMS) is located in the parish hall of a church. The director is a breezy, enthusiastic woman whose wealthy father sponsored her investment in the school. She received some training at the American Montessori Schools Center in New York, but she does not hold any degree. Her school has the usual Montessori equipment, and children can be seen quietly engaged in a variety of the typical self-directed activities—fitting shapes into a board, placing cylinders of various sizes into the appropriate holes, washing dolls' clothes on the washboard, sweeping the walk, etc. One boy intrigues the observer; he is busy peeling carrots with a peeler and is very intent.

The director spends much time talking on the phone with friends; most of the instruction is left to the aides. She recently attended a self-improvement seminar and is anxious for her employees to do the same. She is not willing, however to pay their way. The turnover among her employees is high; she pays an aide only minimum wage.

The children in the program appear subdued and do not display much spontaneity. At least one parent has removed a child from the program because the director ridiculed the child's obesity.

4. This first grade program is located in a large public elementary school of approximately 900 students in kindergarten through fifth grade. Having been opened only four years ago the school is almost new. The primary wing contains 12 classrooms. Each room is carpeted and has regular and clerestory windows that allow for a maximum of natural light to be suffused throughout the room. Each room also has a side area, with linoleum floor, that contains a sink, water fountain, storage closets, a small refrigerator, and a round table suitable for six to eight students and an aide or parent volunteer. This area also contains a two-sided easel. Children sit in groups of two to four at individual desks arranged in small groups.

The first grade teacher has a guinea pig in a cage on a shelf labeled "Discovery Center." Located on the shelf are books containing pictures of guinea pigs, some requiring little or no reading, others requiring more. A chart depicting the amount of food and water used by Rafael (the name voted on by the class) each day is maintained by the children assigned on a rotating basis to Rafael's care. A bulletin board by the entry door has a graph completed by the children of drawings of their favorite foods. Another graph posted on the wall contains pictures drawn by the children illustrating the different ways they come to school.

On your visit, some children are busy working with a parent volunteer at the side table on a story she is assisting them in writing. Two other children are taking care of Rafael. A student teacher has grouped six more children in a small circle at the back of the room near the teacher's desk and is doing some one-to-one correspondence exercises with them. The cooperating teacher has assigned different groups math exercises using the Math Their Way manipulatives and is circulating around the room responding to questions and posing her own questions to check on student understanding.

C. Discuss mentoring as it relates to a program's possible quality.

D. How would you describe the quality of our nation's day care? Cite sources.

REFERENCES

Accrediting Commission for Schools, Western Association for Schools and Colleges (WASC). (1994). *Visiting Committee Handbook.* Burlingame CA: Accrediting Commission for Schools.

Bredekamp, S. (Ed.). (1987). *Guide to accreditation by the national academy of early childhood programs.* Washington, DC: National Association for the Education of Young Children.

Cost, quality and child outcomes in child care centers. (1995). Washington, DC: National Center for the Early Childhood Work Force.

Doherty-Derkowski. (1995). *Quality matters.* Don Mills, Ontario: Addison-Wesley Publishers Limited.

Harms, T., & Clifford, R. (1980). *Early childhood environment rating scale.* New York: Teachers College Press.

Harms, T., & Clifford, R. (1989). *Infant/toddler environment rating scale.* New York: Teachers College Press.

Johnson, S. (September 10–12, 1995). The dangers of day care. San José, CA: *San José Mercury News.*

Morgan, G., Azer, S., Costley, J., Genser, A., Goodman, I., Lombardi, J., & McGrimsey, B. (1993). *Making a career of it: The state of the states report on career development in early care and education.* Boston: The Center for Career Development in Early Care and Education at Wheelock College.

National Association for the Education of Young Children. (March 1994). Professional development. *Young Children, 49*(3), 68–77.

National Center for the Early Childhood Work Force. (January 1995). Mentoring programs: An emerging child care career path. *Compensation Initiatives Bulletin, 1*(3).

National Center for the Early Childhood Work Force. (1995). *Cost, quality, and child outcomes in child care centers.* Washington, DC: Author.

O'Donnell, N. S. (1994). *Highlights of early childhood education and care in Hawaii.* Honolulu, HI: Hawaii Governor's Office of Children and Youth.

Whitebook, M., Phillips, D., & Howes, C. (1993). *The national child care staffing study revisited.* Oakland, CA: Child Care Employee Project.

RESOURCES

Bredekamp, S. (undated.) *Regulating child care quality: Evidence from NAEYC's accreditation system.* Washington, DC: National Association for the Education of Young Children.

Cost, Quality and Outcomes Study Team. (May 1995). Cost, quality, and child outcomes in child care centers: Key findings and recommendations. *Young Children, 50*(4), pp. 40–44.

Endsley, R. E., Minish, P. A., & Zhou, Q. (Spring/Summer 1993). Parent involvement and quality day care in proprietary centers. *Journal of Research in Childhood Education, 7*(2), 53–61.

Howes, C. (1986). *Quality indicators for infant-toddler care.* Paper presented at the annual meeting of the American Educational Research Association. San Francisco, CA. ED 273 385.

Join the early childhood mentoring alliance. (March 1995). *Mentoring News, 1*(1), National Center for the Early Childhood Work Force.

Jorde-Bloom, P. (May 1993). Full cost of quality report: "But I'm worth more than that!" *Young Children, 48*(4), 67–72.

Kontos, S. (1991). Child care quality, family background, and children's development. *Early Childhood Research Quarterly, 6*(2), pp. 249–262.

Mentoring programs: An emerging child care career path. (January 1995). *Compensation Initiatives Bulletin, 1*(3), National Center for the Early Childhood Work Force.

National Association for the Education of Young Children Annual Report. (November 1993). *Young Children, 49*(1).

National Center for the Early Childhood Work Force. (March 1995). The early childhood mentoring alliance. *Mentoring News, 1*(1).

National Center for the Early Childhood Work Force. (March 1995). Join the early childhood mentoring alliance. *Mentoring News, 1*(1).

National Head Start Association. (1993). *Investing in quality: The impact of the Head Start Expansion and Improvement Act of 1990 in its first year of implementation.* Alexandria, VA: National Head Start Association.

Phillips, D. A. (Ed.). (1987). *Quality in child care: What does the research tell us?* Washington, DC: National Association for the Education of Young Children.

Quality, compensation, and affordability. (September 1994). *Young Children, 49*(2), 65.

Reinsberg, J. (September 1995). Reflections on quality infant care. *Young Children, 50*(6), 23–25.

Willer, B. (Ed.). (1990). *Reaching the full cost of quality in early childhood programs.* Washington, DC: National Association for the Education of Young Children.

Professional Commitment and Growth

After studying this chapter, the student will be able to:

- Define professionalism and what being a professional means to him.
- Explain the importance of acquiring a sense of professional commitment.
- List four different activities that promote individual professional growth.
- Name two early childhood professional associations and describe the benefits of membership in each.

My family and friends complained that I didn't have time for them when I was in student teaching practicum. And I didn't! I barely kept up and turned assignments in late at times.

Bill Jackson

My most memorable experience in student teaching has been the kindness, help, and cooperation that I received. So much praise and encouragement made it easier.

Carole Mehors

My dream is to have a school of my own among evergreen trees in a small mountain town. I'll call the school "Tiny Piney" or "Evergreen Academy" or such.

Nomsa Ncube

I was convinced my cooperating teacher didn't like me! Our teaching styles seemed so different. Her attitude toward teaching made me wonder why she'd kept at it so long. Things got better. She had big problems in her personal life which she struggled to keep out of her classroom manner. It was then that I caught glimpses of her teaching strengths.

Carrie Lee Foulkes

As a student teacher, you are already considered a professional. Professionals are those individuals whose work is predominantly nonroutine and intellectual in character. They make constant decisions that call for a substantial degree of discretion and judgment. Professional status is gained through a display and application of professionally recognized teaching skills and techniques. Admittedly, some of your skills are new, emerging, and wobbly, while others are definitely observable. You are currently being measured against standards established by those in the same profession.

DEFINITIONS

Professionalism is the ability to plan knowledgeably and competently to make a sustained difference: To diagnose and analyze situations, to select the most appropriate interventions, to apply them skillfully, and to describe why they were selected (VanderVen, 1988). As early as 1925, in attempting to define professionalism for the business community, Follet stated, "Profession connotes for most people a foundation of science and a motive of service [that must] rest on the basis of a proved body of knowledge [and be] . . . used in the service of others" (Fox & Urwick, 1982, p. 88). While there is no question that early childhood educators are involved in the service of others, there are questions about education and the "body of knowledge." Most would agree that child development is one block of the proven body of knowledge; however, when states allow the licensing of child care workers with no more than six semester units of coursework or less, does this constitute a "foundation of science"? One answer to this question has been the National Association for the Education of Young Children's development of an early childhood "career lattice." The key elements listed in "A Conceptual Framework for Early Childhood Professional Development" are those, which, if achieved, are all a part of what professionalism encompasses. But more of this later, when we discuss professional development. One mark of the professional being that professionals are always learning, always seeking to be better at what they do, always growing in knowledge and ability to perform their job.

CONCERNS IN THE PROFESSION

Your teaching day includes tasks that, on the surface, appear custodial in nature, such as helping at clean-up time, supervising the children as they wash their hands, serving snacks, and encouraging them to rest. Each is a learning time for children, and your professional skill is at work. Helping a child who is struggling to slip on a sweater is done in a professional way and is an opportunity to help the child become more independent.

Professional status, everyone agrees, is a problem for this career field. Societies award status to trained, educated individuals who provide valuable services to society. People can easily tick off on one hand high-status professions and possibly what they consider middle-status professions. Early childhood workers will not be among them.

What are the possible reasons this career field has not obtained the recognition and status it deserves? There are no simple answers but rather many conjectures by many writers. Included among those frequently cited reasons are the following:

- A blurred image between parenting and paid child care providers in the public's mind

- Public attitudes that almost anyone can watch children

- Public perceptions including child care as requiring little or no specific knowledge, education, or skill

- Caregivers' attitudes toward themselves, particularly feelings of personal or collective lack of power

- Lack of early childhood teacher self-esteem or assertiveness

- A public perception of child care workers providing a dedicated service rather than a service for personal gain

- A lack of societal concern for children by the clients of the early childhood professional

- The turnover rate of pre-kindergarten teachers as opposed to the life-long careers of other recognized professionals

- Lack of a professional culture that includes values, norms, terminology, agreement, and symbols common to members of the profession

- An unclear or controversial body of theoretical knowledge and specialized technique(s) that serve as the basis for work actions, advice giving, or planned child activities

- Less than well known and publicly recognized professional associations, societies, and standard monitoring groups

- A body of recognized professional child care teacher attributes or common standards by which individuals could be measured or licensed
- Lack of the career groups' collective political clout
- Lack of employee bargaining power in work situations
- Low or minimal entry level requirements or qualifications
- The historical origins of child care work
- General public attitudes concerning the failure of educational systems
- Lack of state uniformity in educational requirements for beginning early childhood teachers

Primary level professionals may find the last two items applicable to their situation also, and

- A general concern about the quality of primary school education and the lack of uniformity from one state to another

In addition, primary level professionals may discover:

- A lack of respect for public education and the feeling that public education has failed
- A feeling that the teacher unions (the National Education Association and the American Federation of Teachers) are too powerful politically and protect teachers who should be fired
- A lack of understanding by parents, and often by principals, regarding what constitutes "developmentally appropriate practice"

As Kraybill (1989) notes:

> As recently as 1985 the Department of Labor gave day care workers and nursery school attendants a low skill-level rating on a par with kennel keepers.

Most of early childhood teachers agree with Kelley (1990):

> It is essential that we view ourselves as professionals, that we present ourselves to the world as professionals, and that we expect to be accepted as equals in a world of professionals. In order to accomplish this, we must first learn to value ourselves.

Many early childhood staffers' reticence to accept themselves as professionals may be partly responsible for low salaries and job classifications that equate pre-kindergarten teacher's work with attendants, custodians, and domestics. The "baby sitter" image in the public's view has been difficult to escape. Advocacy training is now a recommended part of pre-service training.

A teacher's pride in the profession is justified. Stevens and King (1976) describe the importance of a teacher's respect for the job.

> The teacher of young children should see himself or herself as indispensable in the pivotal aspects of early childhood learning. Pride in one's profession and the attitude that it is one of the most vital jobs in our contemporary society cannot be over-stressed.

After student teaching, you will know that the job of an early childhood teacher is demanding, challenging, complex, necessitates constant decisions, and can be physically and emotionally taxing as well as being highly satisfying and rewarding.

The early childhood teaching profession should attract and hold the best candidates our society has to offer—"dedicated, conscientious, highly qualified, and highly trained men and women"—who work with our society's most prized resource and hope for the future—children and families (Stevens and King, 1976, p. 146).

PROFESSIONAL BEHAVIOR AND COMMITMENT

Professionalism, Sawyers (1971) states, entails understanding both children and yourself plus "plain old hard work." She has identified some of the demands that "pros" make on themselves and their behavior.

1. Being a professional requires that you give full measure of devotion to the job.
2. Being a professional means you don't need rules to make you act like a professional.
3. Professionals accept responsibilities assigned to them with as much grace as they can muster up and then work in a positive way to change those duties that deter their teaching.

4. A professional joins with others in professional organizations that exchange research and ideas on how children learn and institute action to benefit all children.

5. A professional understands herself, is aware of her prejudices, and makes a concerted effort to get rid of them.

6. A professional treats children as people with feelings.

7. A real professional speaks up for the child when he needs somebody to speak out for him.

8. A professional is an educator who is informed about modern trends in education.

Other behaviors that mark you as a professional range from those that seems obvious to those that are subtle. As a professional, you will

- be punctual;
- notify your center or school, in advance if possible, when you must be absent;
- be prepared;
- dress appropriately;
- maintain confidentiality and avoid gossiping about either the children or your peers;
- maintain positive health habits (e.g., cleanliness in personal hygiene, modeling positive eating habits, demonstrating ways to deal with stressful situations positively, and so on); and possibly
- become an advocate for children and early childhood workers.

Each teacher's commitment to teaching could be placed on a continuum, figure 19-1. Where would

you place yourself? Probably at the high end; student teachers spend long hours both in and out of their classrooms and may feel that they are barely hanging on. This feeling can continue through the first year on the job. Katz (1972) describes a new teacher's inner thoughts as being preoccupied with survival.

> Can I get through the day in one piece? Without losing a child? Can I make it until the end of the week—the next vacation? Can I really do this kind of work day after day? Will I be accepted by my colleagues?

Anxieties stem from a desire to become a professional while at the same time questioning one's stamina, endurance, and capability to do so. Your commitment to the profession will be nourished by the supportive adults that surround you in your student teaching experience.

Severe tests to a student teacher's professional commitment may happen if a placement site models attitudes that downgrade the value and worth of the profession. A good grasp on professional conduct and commitment helps the student teacher sort out less than professional behavior. Improved and continued high standards in the profession depend upon the newly trained professionals' enthusiasm, idealism, knowledge, and skills and the experienced professionals' leadership. Newly trained professionals can strengthen the field through their identification with practicing, committed professionals.

Advocacy

Advocacy takes time, energy, and knowledge. It involves everyday contact with people. Student teachers may have a desire to become involved but lack the knowledge of how to begin.

Low	High
• Little concern for students.	• High concern for students and other teachers.
• Little time or energy expended.	• Extra time or energy expended.
• Primary concern with keeping one's job.	• Primary concern with doing more for others.

Figure 19-1 Commitment continuum. (Reprinted with permission of the Association for Supervision and Curriculum Development and Carl D. Glickman. Copyright © 1981 by the Association for Supervision and Curriculum Development. All rights reserved.)

ADVOCACY GROUPS

ABC (Alliance for Better Child Care), 122 C St. N.W. Suite 400, Washington, DC 20001. Focuses upon increased support for child care.

ACT (Action for Children's Television), 20 University Rd., Cambridge, MA 02138. Focuses upon children's improved television programming.

American Bar Association, 1800 M St., N.W., Suite 200, South, Washington, DC 20036. Focuses upon child protection and child welfare issues.

Association of Child Advocates, P.O. Box 5873, Cleveland, OH 44101-0873. Focuses upon a national association of state advocacy groups, information, and technical assistance resources; offers a national conference.

Center for Public Advocacy Research, 12 W. 37th St., New York, NY 10018. Focuses upon research and policy.

Children's Defense Fund, 25 E Street, N.W., Washington, DC 20001. Monitors federal legislation and policy.

Child Care Employee Project, 6536 Telegraph Ave., Suite A-201, Oakland, CA 94609. Focuses on employee (worker) advocacy.

National Center for the Early Childhood Work Force, 733 15th Street, N.W., Suite 1037, Washington, DC 20005. Focuses on collation of facts and figures related to child care workers and advocates for improved salaries and working conditions.

Figure 19–2 Advocacy groups.

One way to involve yourself in advocacy is to list 10 issues you feel are the most pressing. Then select the one issue that moves you most strongly. Student teaching commitments may make advocacy at this time near to impossible! These paragraphs strive to make you aware of the need for future advocacy. In your daily contacts with other adults, particularly family and friends, you will be instrumental in their developing opinions of child care and early childhood education. You are, right now, a representative of the profession. What you say and do may influence others' priorities and voting behavior. See figure 19-2.

Since advocacy means being aware of legislation, the legislative process, and individuals and groups who support child care issues, a first step is identifying groups or individuals who monitor and help author legislation.

● PROFESSIONAL GROWTH AND DEVELOPMENT

Early childhood teaching offers each professional a lifelong learning challenge. The goal of professional growth includes the unfolding of potentials and achieving greater self-actualization. True self-actualization leads to an increasing sense of responsibility and a deepening desire to serve humanity (Vargiu, 1978).

Maslow has described the conflict individuals face as they struggle toward increasing excellence.

> Every human being has both sets of forces within him. One set clings to safety and defensiveness out of fear, tending to regress backward, hanging on to the past . . . afraid to grow away from primitive communication with mother uterus and breast, afraid to take chances, afraid to jeopardize what he already has, afraid of independence, freedom and separateness. The other set of forces impels him forward toward wholeness of Self and uniqueness of Self, toward full functioning of all his capacities, toward confidence in the face of the external world at the same time he can accept his deepest, real, unconscious Self. (From Anderson and Shane's *As the Twig is Bent*, 1971)

Your management of professional growth planning is dependent upon you. When your future job includes promotional, material, or rewarding incentives, it may add impetus. Your attitude toward your professionalism will give a high priority to activities that contribute to your skill development.

As a professional, you will actively pursue growth. Maslow describes the struggle and possible outcomes of your pursuit.

> Therefore we can consider the process of healthy growth to be a never ending series of free choice situations, confronting each individual at every point throughout his life, in which he must choose between the delights of safety and growth, dependence and independence, regression and progression, immaturity and maturity, (From Anderson and Shane's *As the Twig is Bent*, 1971)

Your efforts to grow professionally will become part of your life's pattern. You will experience the "tugs and pulls" of finding the time and energy to follow your commitment.

Individual Learning Cycles

Just as you have watched children take enormous steps in learning one day and just mark time another, your professional growth may not be constant and steady. Harrison (1978) observed the phenomenon of "risk and retreat" in self-directed learning.

> The learning cycle is our name for the natural process of advance and retreat in learning. We observed early in our experiments with self-directed learning that individuals would move out and take personal risks and then would move back to reflect and integrate the experience.

Such "risk and retreat" relates to what Piaget described as the process of equilibration. You as a learner assimilate new material first as an accommodation with past learning (the risk); then, the assimilation becomes "play" (the retreat). But such a retreat is important to the process of equilibration as you seek to establish an equilibrium between old and new learning.

Reflection or standing still at times may give ideas time to hatch. Being aware of your own creative "idea hatching" can make you more aware of this creative process in children (Alexander, 1978).

Many other factors will influence the ebb and flow of your future growth as a teacher. The energy draining nature of teaching's demanding work can sometimes dampen enthusiasm for future growth, as can the attitudes of those with whom you work. You may periodically need contacts with other professionals to rekindle your commitment.

NAEYC's Professional Development Position Statement

In an effort to gain public support for the importance of high-quality early childhood programs and facilitate the professional development of child care workers, the National Association for the Education of Young Children (1994) published a position statement, "A Conceptual Framework for Early Childhood Professional Development." National Association for the Education of Young Children recognized the following key elements in planning efforts to improve early childhood care and education systems:

1. a holistic approach to the needs of children and their families that stresses collaborative planning and service integration across traditional boundaries of child care, education, health, and social services;

2. systems that promote and recognize quality through licensing, regulation, and accreditation;

3. an effective system of early childhood *professional development* that provides meaningful opportunities for career advancement to ensure a well-qualified and stable work force;

4. equitable financing that ensures access for all children and families to high-quality services; and

5. active involvement of all players—providers, practitioners, parents, and community leaders from both public and private sectors—in all aspects of program planning and delivery.

Working with a number of other groups National Association for the Education of Young Children's National Institute for Early Childhood Professional Development fosters the development of a comprehensive, articulated system of professional development for *all* individuals in *all* early childhood settings. The National Association for the Education of Young Children framework includes various components, and uses the symbol lattice to communicate combining diversity and uniqueness (Bredekamp and Willer, 1992). Both vertical and horizontal strands of the lattice system are interconnected in the model, which connects additional preparation and training to increased responsibility and compensation.

Defining characteristics of early childhood professionals, a specialized body of knowledge and competencies were identified that set them apart from other professionals. They:

- demonstrate an understanding of **child development** and apply this knowledge in practice;

- **observe and assess children's behavior** in planning and individualized teaching practices and curriculum;

- establish and maintain a **safe and healthy environment** for children;

- **plan and implement [a] developmentally appropriate curriculum** that advances all areas of children's learning and development, including social, emotional, intellectual, and physical competence;

- establish supportive relationships with children and implement developmentally appropriate techniques of **guidance and group management**;

- establish and maintain positive and productive **relationships with families**;

- support the development and learning of individual children, recognizing that children are best understood in the context of **family, culture, and society**; and

- demonstrate an understanding of the early childhood profession and make a commitment to **professionalism**. (National Association for the Education of Young Children, 1994)

Professional early childhood workers must incorporate these ideas into the daily responsibility to establish and maintain productive relationships with colleagues, work effectively as a member of an instructional team, communicate effectively with parents and other family members, and communicate effectively with other professionals and agencies concerned with children and families in the larger community to support children's development, learning, and well-being (National Association for the Education of Young Children, 1994).

Levels of Training

Figure 19-3 displays National Association for the Education of Young Children's identified levels of professional development.

The following principles of the professional development process were gathered from National Association for the Education of Young Children's review of available research:

This is designed to reflect a continuum of professional development. The levels identify levels of preparation programs for which standards have been established nationally.

Early Childhood Professional Level VI

Successful completion of a Ph.D. or Ed.D. in a program conforming to NAEYC guidelines; OR

Successful demonstration of the knowledge, performance, and dispositions expected as outcomes of a doctoral degree program conforming to NAEYC guidelines.

Early Childhood Professional Level V

Successful completion of a master's degree in a program conforming to NAEYC guidelines; OR

Successful demonstration of the knowledge, performance, and dispositions expected as outcomes of a master's degree program conforming to NAEYC guidelines.

Early Childhood Professional Level VI

Successful completion of a baccalaureate degree from a program conforming to NAEYC guidelines; OR

State certification meeting NAEYC/ATE certification guidelines; OR

Successful completion of a baccalaureate degree in another field with more than 30 professional units in early childhood development/education including 300 hours of supervised teaching experience, including 150 hours each for two of the following three age groups: infants and toddlers, 3- to 5-year-olds, or the primary grades; OR

Successful demonstration of the knowledge, performance, and dispositions expected as outcomes of a baccalaureate degree program conforming to NAEYC guidelines.

Early Childhood Professional Level III

Successful completion of an associate degree from a program conforming to NAEYC guidelines; OR

Successful completion of an associate degree in a related field, plus 30 units of professional studies in early childhood development/education including 300 hours of supervised teaching experience in an early childhood program; OR

Successful demonstration of the knowledge, performance, and dispositions expected as outcomes of an associate degree program conforming to NAEYC guidelines.

Early Childhood Professional Level II

II. B. Successful completion of a one-year early childhood certification program.

II. A. Successful completion of the CDA Professional Preparation Program OR completion of a systematic, comprehensive training program that prepares an individual to successfully acquire the CDA Credential through direct assessment.

Early Childhood Professional Level I

Individuals who are employed in an early childhood professional role working under supervision or with support (e.g., linkages with provider association or network or enrollment in supervised practicum) and participating in training designed to lead to the assessment of individual competencies or acquisition of a degree.

Figure 19-3 Definitions of early childhood professional categories. [From Professional Development. *Young Children*, *49*(3), March 1994, pp. 68–77.]

1. Professional development is an ongoing process.

2. Professional development experiences are most effective when grounded in a sound theoretical and philosophical base and structured as a coherent and systematic program.

3. Professional development experiences are most successful when they respond to an individual's background, experiences, and current context of their role.

4. Effective professional development opportunities are structured to promote clear linkages between theory and practice.

5. Providers of effective professional development experiences have an appropriate knowledge and experience base.

6. Effective professional development experiences use an active, hands-on approach and stress an interactive approach that encourages students to learn from one another.

7. Effective professional development experiences contribute to positive self-esteem by acknowledging the skills and resources brought to the training process as opposed to creating feelings of self-doubt or inadequacy by immediately calling into question an individual's current practice.

8. Effective professional development experiences provide opportunities for application and reflection and allow for individuals to be observed and receive feedback upon what has been learned.

9. Students and professionals should be involved in the planning and design of their professional development program. (National Association for the Education of Young Children, 1994)

Professional Growth and Compensation

Along with designing a professional development model, National Association for the Education of Young Children (1994) has also pinpointed growth and compensation recommendations. The following are National Association for the Education of Young Children's guidelines:

- Early childhood professionals with comparable qualifications, experience, and job responsibilities should receive comparable compensation regardless of the setting of their job. This means that a teacher working in a community child care center, a family child care provider, and an elementary school teacher who each hold comparable professional qualifications and carry out comparable functions or responsibilities should also receive comparable compensation for their work.

- Compensation for early childhood professionals should be equivalent to that of other professionals with comparable preparation requirements, experience, and job responsibilities.

- The provision of an adequate benefits package is a crucial component of compensation for early childhood staff.

- Compensation should not be differentiated on the basis of the ages of children served.

- Early childhood professionals should be encouraged to seek additional professional preparation and should be rewarded accordingly.

- Career ladders should be established, providing additional increments in salary based on performance and participation in professional development opportunities. (National Association for the Education of Young Children, 1994)

Figure 19-4 reports on the different career levels suggested by the draft matrix for California's Child Development Permit.

PROFESSIONAL GROWTH OPPORTUNITIES

At times when the enthusiasm for teaching seems to dwindle, teachers need to pursue other courses of action to refresh their excitement and eagerness to learn and grow. Early childhood teachers have a wide range of alternative routes to professional growth. For example:

- Additional credit coursework, advanced degrees, figure 19-4
- Apprenticing and exchanging teachers
- Independent study
- Visitation and travel
- Professional group membership

Level	Units/Degree	Experience	Supervision	Renewal	Equivalences
Aide	High school diploma	None	Supervised by Teacher I or II		
Assistant	6 ECE units	None	Supervised by Assoc. Teacher, Teacher I or Teacher II	None	Accredited HERO programs (includes ROP)
Associate Teacher	ECE-12 units core courses: CD Child family Comm. Curriculum	50 days of 3+ hrs./day within 2 consecutive yrs.	May supervise assistant, but not aide	Every 5 yrs. 80 clock hrs. (average 1 sem. unit) educ./training toward addt'l. permit req. within 5 yr. period	CDA
Teacher I	24 ECE + 16 GED } 40 units	200 days of 3+ hrs./day within 4 consecutive yrs.	May supervise all of the above	Every 5 yrs. 160 clock hrs. (average 2 sem. units)	BA or higher degree in CD/ECE or specific related field w/ supervised student teaching exp. in EC setting
Teacher II	24 ECE + 16 GE units + 2 adult super-vision units + 6 specialization units	200 days of 3+ hrs./day within 4 consecutive yrs. (incl. 100 days of supervising adults)	May supervise all of the above	Every 5 yrs. 240 hours (average 3 sem. units)	BA or higher + 12 units CD/ECE incl. 3 units (50 days) supervised field wk. in ECE setting. (Renewal hrs. must be in ECE)
Site Supervisor	AA with 24 ECE + 6 admin. + 2 adult super-vision skills units	Teacher II status and experience	Single site supervision	Every 5 yrs. 240 hours in professional devel. (avg. 3 unit semester)	
Director	BA with 24 ECE + 6 units admin. + 2 units adult supervision skills course	Site Supervisor status + 1 program yr. of site super-visor experience	Multiple sites	Every 5 yrs. 240 clock hours professional devel. (avg. 3 sem. units)	

Figure 19-4 Child development permit matrix (draft 1/94).

- Workshops, meetings, and skill and study sessions, figure 19-5
- In-service training
- Conference attendance

Additional Coursework

Credit and noncredit college coursework leads to advanced skill and degrees. Coursework frequently results in on-the-job application of ideas, spreading enthusiasm throughout a preschool center. Local college career placement centers and/or counseling centers provide a review of college catalogs and bulletins. Coursework descriptions and particulars can be examined for all colleges.

Child Development Associate (CDA) Training

One nationally developed training program, CDA, a community-based training program, leads to a CDA credential. CDA training outlines and evaluates teaching competencies. Some CDA training programs are linked to community colleges,

Figure 19-5 Study sessions promote teacher growth.

other training programs cannot be used toward a degree (Morgan, et al., 1993). See figures 19-3 and 19-4. Other performance-based evaluation and licensing systems are being considered and used in cities and states to assure teaching competencies and alleviate teacher shortages. These may or may not lead to college credit.

Teacher Certification

Each state has developed some state policy concerning teacher certification and credentialing. There is a definite lack of commonality. As McCarthy (1988) states, "the use of the same term does not reflect the commonality among the states that one might assume." The most prevalent pattern of certification (six states) authorizes certificate holders to teach children from three to eight years of age.

The best place to consult when trying to determine what credentials, certificates, permits, and licenses exist for workers in early childhood programs in a particular state is that state's Department of Education. It's best to secure requirements in writing. Often teacher qualification requirements change depending on funding sources. Publicly supported centers usually have higher and stricter standards requiring the completion of additional education and experience.

Unfortunately many states do not require beginning early childhood teachers to have successfully completed college-level coursework before entering the career field. This is changing rapidly as parents demand trained caregivers and quality programs.

Apprenticing, Demonstrating, and Exchanging Teaching

You may know a teacher with whom you would like to study and whose direction and tutelage could be growth producing. Volunteering in this teacher's classroom offers opportunities for closer examination of techniques. It may be possible to earn college credit through enrolling in a cooperative work experience program or independent study course; check your local college.

In a demonstration-teaching arrangement, you watch and discuss methods with practicing teachers. Hearing explanations and asking questions gives insight into different ways to accomplish teaching goals. Most professionals will provide this type of short-term arrangement.

Exchanging teachers within a school is sometimes considered growth producing. New partnerships stimulate new blends of techniques. Many schools permit a shifting of staff members, enabling gifted and talented teachers to share their ideas. Cross-matching and lively discussions act as healthy catalysts.

Independent Study

Self-planned study allows one to choose the subject, sequence, depth, and breadth of professional growth. Your home library will grow yearly, funds permitting! You will spend much time reading books and other material. These resources will be a tribute to your professional commitment. Professional journals and magazines provide research articles and practical suggestions. A brief list of periodicals follows:

- *Young Children* (bimonthly publication of National Association for the Education of Young Children. See professional organization list, figure 19-6.)
- *Day Care and Early Education*
- *Child Care Quarterly*
- *Child Health Talk* (quarterly publication)
- *Learning 90*
- *Child Study Journal*

- *Childhood Education*
- *American Education Research Journal*
- *The Black Child Advocate* (quarterly newsletter), figure 19-6

Organization and association newsletters carry timely information of interest.

A starting point for independent study may be the bibliographies and book titles you collected during your training.

Visitation and Travel

Other teachers' classrooms will always be a valuable resource and study possibility. Observing other classrooms offers good ideas, clever solutions, and provocative discoveries. Conferences often schedule tours of local outstanding programs.

Almost every country has group child care, and you have probably developed a list of programs in your own community you would like to observe. The professional courtesy of allowing observers is widespread. Directors and staff members frequently provide guided tours that include explanations and discussions of goals, program components, and teaching philosophies.

Professional Group Membership

You will find professional early childhood group membership to be one of the best ways to locate skill development opportunities. A common goal of professional associations and organizations is to provide educational services and resources to members, figure 19-6.

Association publications are generally reasonably priced and current. Publication listings are available upon request from main office headquarters.

There are special student membership rates, and joining a local affiliate or branch group during student teaching is highly recommended. Association newsletters will keep you informed of activities and developments of interest to professionals.

The advantages of local professional membership are numerous. Workshops, study sessions, and conferences provide favorable circumstances for professional development, figure 19-7. There are opportunities to meet other professionals, discuss views

ACEI (Association for Childhood Education International) 11501 Georgia Ave., Suite 315, Wheaton, MD 20902. Interested in high standards and professional practices. Journal, book and informational materials publisher.

AMS (American Montessori Society, Inc.), 175 Fifth Ave., New York, NY 10010. An organization that focuses on Maria Montessori's approach to early learning, which emphasizes providing children with purposeful work in an environment prepared with self-educative, manipulative learning devices for language, math, science, practical life, etc.

CDA (Council for Early Childhood Professional Recognition), 1718 Connecticut Ave., N.W., Suite 500, Washington DC 20009. Offers a national credential to successful candidates after assessment of competencies. A newsletter and educational resources also available.

CEC (Council for Exceptional Children), 1920 Association Dr., Reston, VA 20091. An organization of teachers, school administrators, and teacher educators focusing on the concerns of children who are gifted; retarded; visually, auditorily, or physically handicapped; or who have behavioral disorders, learning disabilities, or speech defects.

CWLA (Child Welfare League of America), 440 First St., N.W., Suite 310, Washington, DC 20001. Devoted to assisting deprived, neglected, and abused children. Publishes informational material.

NAEYC (National Association for the Education of Young Children), 1509 16th St., N.W., Washington, DC 20036. Association of early childhood professionals interested in quality education. Publishes books, journal, and a wide range of teacher and parent materials.

National Black Child Development Institute, 1023 15th Street, N.W., Suite 600, Washington, DC 20005. Publishes *The Black Child Advocate* and *Child Health Talk*.

Society for Research in Child Development, 100 N. Carolina Ave., S.E., Suite 1, Washington, DC 20063.

OCD (Office of Child Development, U.S. Department of Health and Human Services), PO Box 1182, Washington, DC 20013. Responsible for long-range planning and development of concepts in children's and parent's programs and legislation affecting children.

PCPI (Parent Cooperative Preschools International), 9111 Alton Pkwy., Silver Spring, MD 20910. An organization of individuals and groups interested in promoting the exchange of resources and information among persons involved in cooperative nursery schools, kindergartens and other parent-sponsored preschool groups.

ERIC/ECE (Educational Resources Information Center, Early Childhood Education), 805 West Pennsylvania Ave., Urbana, IL 61801. Collects and catalogs material of interest to early childhood educators.

Figure 19-6 Professional groups, resources, organizations, and associations.

and concerns, and jointly solve problems. The talents of early childhood experts are tapped for the benefit of all the members.

A fascinating and exhilarating experience awaits the student teacher upon first attending a national conference. There will be so much to see and sample, so many inspiring ideas, materials, and equipment to examine—a virtual overdose of stimuli that wholesomely feeds your attempt to grow.

Workshops, Meetings, Skill and Study Sessions

Workshops, skill sessions, and meetings are smaller versions of state and national conferences. Diverse and varied, they cover topics related to early childhood. Practical how-to's, theoretical presentations, and advocacy meetings are popular.

Identification with the spirit of professionalism, which can be defined as striving for excellence, motivates many of the attending participants. Most communities schedule many professional growth meetings each year and encourage student teacher attendance.

In-Service Training

In-service training sessions are designed to suit the training needs of a particular group of teachers and/or caregivers. They are arranged by sponsoring

Figure 19-7 Updating and exposure to new ideas never end for teachers.

agencies or employers. Typically, consultants and specialists lead, guide, plan, and present skill development sessions and/or assessments of program components. There is usually no fee, and attendance is mandatory. Often staffs decided the nature and scope of the in-service training, and paid substitutes free staff members from child supervision duties.

● PARENTS' ATTITUDES TOWARD PROFESSIONALISM

Early childhood teachers may make many assumptions concerning how attending children's parents view their work. It is important to assess parents' attitudes and perceptions and plan strategies that encourage acceptance of early childhood educators as professionals.

SUMMARY

Student teachers strive for recognition of their professional skills and try to achieve standards established by those in the same profession. Pride in the early childhood profession grows as student teachers realize the dedication and skills of others already teaching. The important contribution the profession makes to children, families, and society cannot be overrated. The commitment to update continually and gain additional skills begins in training and continues for a lifetime. Each professional teacher is responsible for his or her own unique growth planning schedule.

Many activity choices leading to advanced skills are available, and most professionals engage in a wide variety. Additional coursework and training, professional group membership, conference and workshop attendance, in-service training, visitation, and exchange teaching lead to the learning and discovering of new techniques. Social interactions in educative settings reinforce individual teachers' commitment to professionalism

SUGGESTED ACTIVITIES

A. Name three books related to early childhood teaching that you plan to read.

B. Get on the mailing list for early childhood education publications.

C. In groups of four to six, develop a wallchart that lists factors that promote professionalism and those that impede professionalism in early childhood teachers.

D. Rate each statement based on the following scale. Discuss your results with the class.

strongly agree	mildly agree	cannot decide	mildly disagree	strongly disagree
1	2	3	4	5

1. Being professional includes proper make-up and clothing at work.

2. It is unprofessional to keep using the same techniques over and over.

3. Professional commitment is more important than professional growth.

4. Professional growth can involve coursework that does not pertain to children and/or families.

5. A teacher can grow professionally by studying children in the classroom.

6. Professional association fees are so expensive that student teachers can rarely afford to join.

7. One of the real causes for the lack of status of early childhood teachers is their own attitudes toward professional growth.

8. It is difficult to feel like a professional when salaries are so low.

9. Most teachers who pursue professional skills receive little recognition for their efforts.

10. You can learn all you need to know about handling children's behavior by watching a master teacher.

E. Invite a panel of practicing teachers to discuss the topic, "Best Ways to Grow Professionally."

F. Investigate groups in your community that schedule skill sessions, workshops, or meetings offering growth opportunities to early childhood teachers. Report your findings to the class.

G. Attend and/or volunteer at a professional in-service meeting (PTA, NAEYC, ACEI, local, state, national early childhood related workshop or training gathering). Write a brief summary. Include how you will be able to implement information into your present student teaching experience or your future work with children.

H. Read the following quote, then discuss with a small group. Report your agreement or disagreement to the total class.

Most individuals enter the field (ECE) in roles that require little or no professional preparation. Many eventually complete certificate and degree programs and advance their careers by taking on greater and more varied responsibilities. But not all. Low salaries and the lack of perceived potential for career advancement cause many practitioners to drop out before they pursue a CDA or enroll in a college certificate or degree program. (Morgan, et al., 1994)

What other factors may inhibit a teacher's desire to become more skilled or assume greater responsibility?

REVIEW

A. Name four benefits of professional group membership.

B. Match items in Column I with those in Column II.

I	II
1. rate of teacher growth	a. pulling ideas together
2. commitment	b. code of ethics
3. standards	c. advances and retreats
4. consolidation	d. depends on individual's activities
5. learning cycle	e. ranges from high to low
6. professionals	f. constant intellectual decisions
7. apprenticing	g. expert advice
8. visitation	h. on-site training
9. workshops	i. studying with another
10. in-service training	j. professional courtesy

C. Select the answer that best completes each statement.

1. The person most responsible for a particular teacher's professional growth is

   a. the employer.

   b. the parent.

   c. the child.

   d. the teacher.

   e. None of these

2. Of the following entries, one that is a well-known early childhood professional magazine is

   a. *The Whole Child.*

   b. *Child and Learning.*

   c. *Young Children.*

   d. *Helping the Child.*

   e. *The Professional Growth Journal.*

D. Describe attitudes that motivate teachers to spend time at weekend workshops.

E. Complete the following statement. Lifelong learning is typical of the professional teacher who . . .

F. In the following paragraphs, make note of all statements that indicate questionable professionalism.

I made an appointment to observe a class in a community school. As I arrived, the director nodded and indicated that I was to enter a classroom labeled "The Three's Room." The teacher and aide looked at me, then quickly looked away. I sat quietly near the wall. The teacher approached, demanding, "Who sent you in here?" "The director," I answered. She went back to the aide and whispered to him briefly. The teacher began a conversation with Mrs. Brown, who just arrived. She mentioned that her daughter, Molly, refused to eat lunch and kicked a hole in a cot at naptime. "I told you I'd tell your mother," the teacher said to Molly, who was standing at her mother's side.

Time for outside play was announced. The teacher and aide left the room for the play area. One or two children failed to follow the group outside. I wasn't sure if I could leave them inside so I stood in the doorway and looked out. The children must have headed out the other door to the director's office while I took note of the play equipment.

The aide approached. "Looking for a job?" he asked. "I could work afternoons," I answered. "Well, the person who teaches four-year-olds is quitting," he offered. "It's an easy job. You just watch them after naptime till their parents come." "Thanks for telling me about it," I said.

I left the yard to return to the director's office. She was on the phone with a parent and motioned me to sit in a chair opposite her desk. She was describing the school's academic program to the parent, and winked at me when she told the parent every child learned the alphabet, shapes, and colors besides reading a number of words. She hung up the phone and said to me, "Sometimes they're hard to sell." I thanked the director for allowing me to observe. She acknowledged this and asked, "Did you notice the teacher or aide leaving the children unsupervised? I've been too busy to watch them, but we've had a couple of complaints." "No," I lied, not wanting to become involved. Hoping to change the subject, I asked, "Do you have any openings for a teacher in the afternoon hours?" Since I needed money badly, a part-time job would be welcome. "We will have a position available starting the first week of October," she answered. The director then proceeded to describe job duties. They ranged from planning the program to mopping the floors at the end of the day. I told her I needed time to think over the offer. The director insisted she needed to know immediately, so I accepted.

REFERENCES

Alexander, R. (1978). Life, death, and creativity. *Human Growth Games.* Beverly Hills, CA: Sage Publications.

Bredekamp, S., & Willer, B. (March 1992). National Institute. Of ladders and lattices, cores, and cones: Conceptualizing an early childhood professional development system. *Young Children, 47*(3), 47–50.

Fox, E. M., & Urwick, L. (1982). *Dynamic administration: The collected papers of Mary Parker Follet.* New York: Hippocrene Books, Inc.

Harrison, R. (1978). Self-directed learning. *Human Growth Games.* Beverly Hills, CA: Sage Publications.

Katz, L. (February 1972). Developmental stages of preschool teachers. *The Elementary School Journal.*

Kelley, K. G. (1990). Awareness of your needs as a caregiver. Position paper, California State University, Hayward, p. 32.

Kraybill, B. K. (1989). Professionalism in child care: a comparison between parent and staff perceptions. Thesis, California State University, Hayward, p. 40.

Maslow, A. (1971). Defense and growth. From Anderson, R. H., & Shane, H. G., *As the Twig is Bent.* Boston: Houghton Mifflin Co.

McCarthy, J. (1988). *State certification of early childhood teachers: An analysis of the 50 states and the District of Columbia.* Washington, DC: NAEYC.

Morgan, G., Azer, S., Costley, J., Elliott, K., Genser, A., Goodman, I., & McGimsey, B. (March 1994). Future pursuits: Building early care and education careers. *Young Children, 49*(3), 80–83.

Morgan, G., Azer, S. L., Costley, J. B., Genser, A., Goodman, I. F., Lombardi, J., & McGimsey, B. (1993). *Making a career of it. The state of the states report on career development in early care and education.* Boston: Center for Career Development in Early Care and Education, Wheelock College.

National Association for the Education of Young Children. (March 1994). NAEYC position statement: A conceptual framework for early childhood professional development. *Young Children, 49*(3), 68–77.

Sawyers, B. J. (1971). On becoming a pro. *For New Teachers.* New York: Macmillan

Stevens, J. H., Jr., & King, E. W. (1976). *Administering early childhood education programs.* Boston: Little, Brown and Co.

VanderVen, K. (1988). Pathways to professionalism. In B. Spodek, O. Saracho, and D. Peters (Eds.), *Professionalism and the Early Childhood Educator.* New York: Columbia University Press, pp. 137–160.

Vargiu, J. G. (1978). Education and psychosynthesis. *Human Growth Games.* Beverly Hills, CA: Sage Publications.

RESOURCES

Bents, M., & Gardner, W. (Summer 1992). Good teaching: Some views and prototypes. *Action in Teacher Education, XIV*(2), pp. 38–42.

Bredekamp, S. (January 1995). National Institute: What do early childhood professionals need to know and be able to do? *Young Children, 50*(2), 67–69.

Brooke, G. E. (September 1994). My personal journey toward professionalism. *Young Children, 49*(6), 69–71.

Burke, P. (Summer 1994). Licensing and career-long teacher education. *Action in Teacher Education, XVI*(2), pp. 14–18.

Duff, R. E., Brown, M. H., & VanScoy, I. J. (May 1995). Reflection and self-evaluation: Keys to professional development. *Young Children, 50*(4), 81–88.

Greene, E. (1994). State-of-the-art professional development. In J. Johnson & J. McCracken (Eds.), *The Early Childhood Career Lattice.* Washington, DC: National Association for the Education of Young Children, pp. 91–95.

Johnson, J., & McCracken, J. B. (Eds.). (1994). *The early childhood career lattice: Perspectives on professional development.* Washington, DC: National Association for the Education of Young Children.

Jorde-Bloom, P. (1988). *A great place to work: Improving conditions for staff in young children's programs.* Washington, DC: National Association for the Education of Young Children.

Katz, L. (May 1984). The professional early childhood teacher. *Young Children, 38*(5), pp. 3–11.

Koll, P. J., Herzog, B. J., & Burke, P. J. (Winter 1988–89). Continuing professional development. *Action in Teacher Education, X*(4), pp. 24–31.

Lieberman, A. (April 1995). Practices that support teacher development: Transforming conceptions of professional learning. *Phi Delta Kappan, 76*(8), pp. 591–596.

Mann, D. (September 1995). Can teachers be trusted to improve teaching? *Phi Delta Kappan, 77*(1), pp. 86–88.

Morgan, G. (1994). A new century/a new system for professional development. In *The early childhood career lattice.* J. Johnson, & J. B. McCracken, (Eds.). Washington, DC: National Association for the Education of Young Children.

National Association for the Education of Young Children. (1984). Position statement of nomenclature, salaries, benefits, and the status of the early childhood profession. *Young children, 40*, pp. 52–53.

Pacific Oaks College and Children's Center. (Winter 1994). *Advancing careers in child development: California's plan.* Pasadena, CA: Pacific Oaks College.

Swanson, J. (September 1995). Systematic reform in the professionalism of educators. *Phi Delta Kappan, 77*(1), pp. 36–39.

Wadlington, P. (May 1995). Basing early childhood teacher education on adult education principles. *Young Children, 50*(4), pp. 76–80.

Wear, S. B., & Harris, J. C. (Summer 1994). Becoming a reflective teacher: The role of stimulated recall. *Action in Teacher Education, XVI*(2), pp. 45–51.

Willer, B., & Bredekamp, S. (May 1993). National Institute. A "new" paradigm of early childhood education professional development. *Young Chldren, 48*(4), pp. 63–66.

Willer, B., & Bredekamp, S. (May 1995). A "new" paradigm of early childhood professional development. *Young Chldren, 50*(4), pp. 63–72.

Wise, A., & Liebrand, J. (October 1993). Accreditation and the creation of a profession of teaching. *Phi Delta Kappan, 75*(2), pp. 133–136.

20

Trends and Issues

After studying this chapter, the student will be able to:

● Discuss one trend and its influence on planning children's programs.

● Write a brief statement describing the nation's current public policy decisions and young children's care.

● Choose an issue and with a peer present the salient facts concerning the issue.

I'll be advocating for children and myself as long as I teach. I couldn't believe my cooperating teacher was so concerned about children's rights, laws, and working conditions. I was just trying to become a really good teacher. She's so aware of factors influencing quality care and works in her free time with professional groups and projects. That's dedication!

Dale Wildeagle

I think I can say I'm an eclectic student teacher. I grab the best of what I see and it's incorporated into my teaching style. There's also some original, unique, me included.

Ann Ng

My cooperating teacher is a baseball buff. You wouldn't believe how he uses baseball-related material to teach children math and science.

Shirley Booker-Maddux

Any consideration of the trends and issues existing in our field must be selective. It is probable that a trend in which you are deeply interested has been mentioned briefly or even been omitted and that an issue about which you feel strongly also has been neglected. Included in this chapter are the trends and issues we think have primacy. As a consequence, then, you may wish to focus on those that are important to you.

● **TRENDS**

Trends constitute one area of interest in early childhood. We have attempted to include a few of the major trends we see today. Among these are:

• The growing number of women in the work force, especially those with very young children

- Children living in poverty, together with a consideration of homelessness among families with young children
- Child abuse and neglect, including children left to care for themselves
- State and local funding
- Standards in teacher preparation
- Growing private investment
- The increasing popularity of the Reggio Emilia program
- The antibias curriculum and the need for multicultural curricular experiences
- Public school sponsorship of preschool programs
- School-age programs
- Parent education
- Using computers with young children
- Incorporating authentic assessment in both teacher education programs and in programs for young children

We will not discuss all of these trends; we have chosen to expand only on those which are more salient. The shortage of qualified teachers, for example, is covered more fully under the issue of adequate compensation rather than here as a trend. Likewise, while teenage pregnancies have increased dramatically over the past 10 years (and have contributed to the number of children living in poverty, as has homelessness), we have chosen to leave it to you as individual researchers to delve more deeply into the question. The same approach has been taken with the trend toward the involvement of private business in running the public schools. Our problem is that entire books have been written on some of these topics; we wish only to whet your interests.

Few specialists argue with facts indicating the ever-increasing need for child care for working parents.

- In the 1990s, the number of children younger than six needing child care will grow by more than 50 percent (Children's Defense Fund).
- Between 1986 and 2000, 25 million women and 24 million men will join the labor force, while 12 million women and 16 million men will leave the labor force (Bureau of Labor Statistics).
- One half of preschool children have mothers employed outside the home. By the year 2000 that figure will rise to nearly seven in ten (Children's Defense Fund, 1990).
- There has been a dramatic increase over the past two decades in the number of children spending time in out-of-home arrangements that supplement the care provided by their parents (Willer, 1992), figure 20-1.
- Nearly half (43 percent) of preschool children with employed mothers and 30 percent of those with nonemployed mothers are enrolled in a center (Willer, 1992).
- In 1992 an estimated 1.6 million children younger than six years of age were living in a home maintained by grandparents. It is further reported that 64 percent of these children had only their mother present, and 12 percent had neither parent present in the grandparents' home.
- Of the 100 million women 16 and older in the United States, 58 million were labor force participants (working or looking for work) during 1992. Women experienced their highest labor force participation rate of all time in 1992—57.8 percent. They also accounted for 60 percent of total labor force growth between 1982 and 1992. (U.S. Department of Labor, 1993).
- Labor force participation for women continues to be highest among those in the 35–44 age group: 77 percent of women in this age group were in the labor force in 1992; 74 percent, for those 25–34 years old. (U.S. Department of Labor, 1993).
- In March 1992, 74 percent of divorced women were labor force participants; likewise for 65 percent of single, never-married women; 62 percent of separated women; 59 percent of married women with spouses present. (U.S. Department of Labor, 1993).
- The more education a woman has, the greater the likelihood she will seek employment. Among women 25 to 54 years of age with less

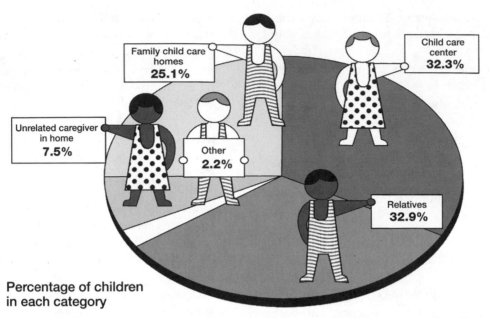

Family child care homes
25.1%

Child care center
32.3%

Unrelated caregiver in home
7.5%

Other
2.2%

Relatives
32.9%

Percentage of children in each category

Figure 20-1 Child care arrangements. More than 57 percent of children younger than five whose mothers were employed and who were not cared for by a parent during working hours were either in family child care homes or child care centers in 1991. (Source: Census Bureau, "Who's Minding the Kids? Child Care Arrangements: Fall 1991," Current Population Reports: May 1994. Calculations from Table B, Series P70-36.)

than four years of high school, only 51 percent were labor force participants. For female high school graduates with no college, 74 percent were in the labor force. Among women of the same age group with four or more years of college, 84 percent were in the labor force. (U.S. Department of Labor, 1993).

- The 34 million women with children under age 18 had a labor force participation rate of 67 percent in March 1992. Fifty-eight percent (9.6 million) of mothers with preschoolers (children under age of six) and 55 percent (5.3 million) of mothers with children under age three were labor force participants in March 1992. (U.S. Department of Labor, 1993).

- In 1991 women represented 63 percent of all persons 18 years old and over who were living below the poverty level (U.S. Department of Labor, 1993).

- In 1991, 53 percent of women with an infant younger than one were in the labor force (Morgan, Azer, Costley, Genser, Goodman, Lombardi, & McGrimsey, 1993).

- The demand for care has already outstripped the supply of practitioners with relevant, specialized training in early childhood (Morgan, et al., 1993).

- In 1991, 73 percent of black mothers were in the labor force. African-American children are at greater risk because families are less able to afford the cost of enrolling their children in high-quality centers (Moore, 1995).

- The lowest-paid child care workers in this country average less than $9,000 a year; the highest paid average less than $16,000 (Whitebook, Phillips, & Howes, 1993).

Mothers continue to enter the work force in greater numbers than in past decades. The Bureau of the Census figures from 1977 to 1991 show that more than twice as many mothers with children under five sought child care. Parent choices (as seen in percentages) for child care situations also seem to have changed: Care in the homes of others has decreased while care in facilities, such as centers and schools, has increased; care in the child's own home has remained relatively stable, figure 20-1.

By 1990 it is estimated that two-thirds of the projected population of preschoolers will have working mothers. The number of relatives (including fathers) providing child care has continually declined since 1965 while child care center enrollment has steadily increased.

The following situations, promoted by present national child care policies, are attracting public attention:

- The lack of quality care for infants and toddlers within the financial reach of single-parent workers.

- Middle-income (and higher) parents are supporting child care for low-income parents through taxes. Public programs have higher teacher qualifications and lower teacher-child ratios. Parents desire quality for their own children and find few private centers with ratios and teacher qualifications equal to publicly funded centers.

- Many parents want a center with a strong education component. Most state licensing laws for private centers only mandate child custodial safety. Publicly funded centers have developmental child programs, but most taxpaying parents find their children ineligible for services.

These issues of national or family responsibility, child and family rights, and existing inequity will affect every early childhood educator.

There is hope, for our country is moving closer to establishing a national policy regarding early childhood education and child care. Expanded federal funding for programs and services is expected during the 1990s. Indeed, Project Head Start received notice of additional funding in 1992. Efforts to improve quality and affordability have become political issues, as are child care administrative entities, training of staff

and providers, standards, and standard enforcement. More and more action groups and politicians are voicing their opinions and positions. Two-parent and single-parent working families are no longer viewed as the exception but rather the norm. Proposed solutions to concerns over our children's educational achievements compared to children in other industrialized nations, and housing, school dropout rates, teen pregnancy, poverty, and other national problems urge the provision of quality education.

Consider the following:

- Every 47 seconds, an American child is abused or neglected (675,000 a year) (Children's Defense Fund, 1990).

- Every 67 seconds, an American teenager has a baby (472,623 in 1987) (Children's Defense Fund, 1990).

- Every 53 minutes, an American child dies because of poverty (10,000 a year) (Children's Defense Fund, 1990).

- 1,000,000 children in California are in unlicensed care or are left alone for all or part of the day (League of Women Voters, 1990).

- Only 1 percent of all U.S. households consists of a father raising his children alone (U.S. Bureau of the Census).

- Every night an estimated 100,000 children go to sleep homeless (Children's Defense Fund, 1990).

- Only 29 states and the District of Columbia have infant-to-worker staffing requirements that meet the four-to-one ratio recommended by the National Association for the Education of Young Children (Children's Defense Fund, 1990).

- It is predicted that 60 percent of all children will live in a single-parent home during the 1990s (Galinsky, 1990).

- The median income of college-educated women is about the same as that of high school-educated men (U.S. Bureau of the Census).

Child Poverty

The following figures concerning child poverty are gleaned from U.S. General Accounting Office

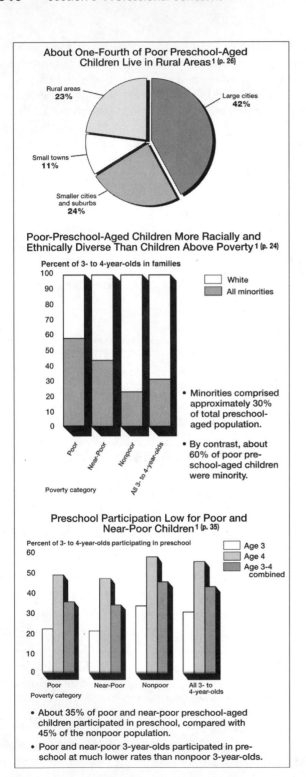

About One-Fourth of Poor Preschool-Aged Children Live in Rural Areas[1] (p. 26)

Rural areas 23%
Large cities 42%
Small towns 11%
Smaller cities and suburbs 24%

Poor-Preschool-Aged Children More Racially and Ethnically Diverse Than Children Above Poverty[1] (p. 24)

Percent of 3- to 4-year-olds in families

White
All minorities

Poverty category

- Minorities comprised approximately 30% of total preschool-aged population.
- By contrast, about 60% of poor preschool-aged children were minority.

Preschool Participation Low for Poor and Near-Poor Children[1] (p. 35)

Percent of 3- to 4-year-olds participating in preschool

Age 3
Age 4
Age 3-4 combined

Poor   Near-Poor   Nonpoor   All 3- to 4-year-olds
Poverty category

- About 35% of poor and near-poor preschool-aged children participated in preschool, compared with 45% of the nonpoor population.
- Poor and near-poor 3-year-olds participated in preschool at much lower rates than nonpoor 3-year-olds.

(1993) and U.S. Department of Commerce (1993) statistics:

Not only were preschool children poorer than the rest of the population in 1990, they also became poorer between 1980 and 1990.

- From 1980 to 1990 the number of poorer children increased by 28 percent, while the total preschool-age population increased by only 16 percent.

  — The number of preschoolers in poverty increased in all but four states between 1980 and 1990.

  — Poorer preschoolers are more likely to live in cities and suburbs, but about one-fourth live in rural areas, figure 20-2.

  — While members of all minority groups comprise approximately 30 percent of the total preschool population, 60 percent of preschoolers living in poverty are members of a minority group, figure 20-2.

  — The number of preschoolers living in single-parent families increased for all categories. However, 60 percent of poor and 30 percent of near-poor children of preschool age live in single-parent families as compared to the less than 10 percent of the nonpoor preschool population who live in single-parent families.

- About 35 percent of poor and near-poor three- and four-year-old children participated in preschool, compared with 45 percent of the nonpoor population.

Figure 20-2 Child Poverty

Sources
[1]U.S. General Accounting Office. (1993). *Poor preschool-aged children: Numbers increase but most not in preschool.* (GAO/HRD-93-111BR).
[2]U.S. Department of Commerce, Bureau of the Census. (1993). *Poverty in the United States: 1992.* (**Current Population Reports**, Series P60-185).

Child Abuse

While not directly related to poverty, child abuse can be one of the consequences. Other causes are thought to be the current loss of jobs due to "downsizing," as it has been called; the concomitant problem of new jobs being in the service sector and, consequently, less well paying than the job downsized; the need for two incomes to support families financially and the often related stress placed on these families; and substance abuse in families, such as alcoholism. Most likely there are other causes for child abuse; we have simply listed some of the more obvious.

All states require teachers to report suspected cases of child abuse. Berliner (1993) explains:

Each state's child abuse reporting law defines child abuse, designates mandated reporters, describes standards and procedures for making a report, and establishes the consequences for failure to report.

Abuse law entails:

- sexual abuse (adult-child sexual contact);
- physical abuse (intentional injury);
- failure to provide a child's basic needs (neglect); and
- emotional abuse.

Teachers and day care providers are specified as mandated reporters in state law; consequently, penalties exist for non-reporters. Most states provide immunity from liability to all "good-faith child abuse reporters," not only mandated reporters. Approximately 12 states have enacted provisions for civil or criminal penalties for malicious reports of child abuse. A reasonable suspicion of child abuse is a valid reason for reporting.

To whom do you report? Child protective services and law enforcement agencies are the two most common agencies receiving reports and investigating them. Generally, if the suspicion of abuse is not life threatening, child protective services is the agency called. If, however, the child seems in immediate danger, a law enforcement agency is usually notified as only they can legally remove a child from the custody of the parent(s).

One caveat here: Child care professionals and teachers need to be aware of the cultural values and ethnic differences in families of attending children. Newly arrived immigrant families may not be aware of abuse law and may continue to use corporal punishment or other harsh disciplinary practices or even health practices deemed appropriate in their country of origin.

On a warm, sunny day in mid-October, Eugenia, a newly enrolled Filipina child in the first grade classroom where you are student teaching, comes to school one morning with a heavy wool scarf wrapped around her neck. During the morning, you note that she appears uncomfortable, but all efforts to persuade her to remove the scarf are unsuccessful. After lunch, as the classroom becomes even warmer and Eugenia is sweating visibly, she finally takes off the heavy wool scarf. Immediately you notice large round welts on her neck and suspect child abuse. Your cooperating teacher also notices the welts, goes to the office, and notifies child protective services (CPS).

Before the end of the school day, a social worker from CPS arrives and removes Eugenia from the classroom to talk to her. Unfortunately, the child's English is not well developed. When the mother arrives at school to pick up Eugenia and walk home with her, the social worker informs her that she is reluctant to allow the child to go. The mother, who only speaks Tagalog, cannot understand what is happening; Eugenia is unable to explain what is happening either. A police officer is called; but she also cannot speak Tagalog. At this point, the school secretary intervenes and suggests calling in a classroom aide who speaks both Tagalog and English fluently.

When the aide speaks to the mother and questions her about the welts on Eugenia's neck, she translates, "Eugenia's mother simply was doing what she has always done in the Philippines when one of her children has awakened with a complaint about a sore throat. She took a large coin, probably a quarter, judging from the size of the welts, heated it, and rubbed Eugenia's neck with it, producing the welts you see. Then the scarf is wrapped around the neck to hold in the heat. The practice is common among rural, relatively uneducated people in certain parts of the Philippines."

State and Local Funding Decisions

As federal taxes are returned to states, decisions concerning amounts to be allocated to young children's programs and services will be made at state and local levels. Young children's needs will compete with other social and welfare needs. Professionals are fearful, and they worry about cutbacks in existing publicly funded operations. As taxpayers, they may support decreasing federal administrative costs while they also support increased federal funding for ensuring and expanding child program quality.

Standards in Teacher Preparation

Increasingly stringent standards regulating all facets of child care, including teacher preparation, are a reality. Present federal legislation mandates higher state standards for some states in an attempt to increase the overall quality of prekindergarten child care.

Child care teaching staffs with training when compared to other women in the labor force have attained higher levels of formal education. Most teachers view learning as a lifelong pursuit. Saturday, summer, and evening study is commonplace, and many colleges offer a continuous array of growth opportunities and updating opportunities.

As Whitebook, Howes, and Phillips (1989) point out:

> The education and work environment of child care teachers are essential determinants of the quality of care. Teaching staff provide more *sensitive* and *appropriate care giving* if they completed more years of formal education, received early childhood training at the college level . . . .

Shortage of Trained Teachers

Many states are experiencing a shortage of trained early childhood workers. Costley (1988) calculates that all of the graduates of the 1,650 four-year colleges and two-year associate programs in the United States offering degrees in early childhood education would constitute barely enough staff for existing early childhood centers in Massachusetts and New York (Morgan, Azer, Costley, et al., 1993).

On the other hand, in a study conducted by the Association for School, College, and University Staffing (ASCUS) Inc., Marshall (1996) reports the results from a survey of 584 colleges and universities with teacher preparation programs. Respondents from 11 geographic areas were asked what their perceptions were on the supply of and demand for teachers in a variety of fields. In elementary–pre-K, elementary-kindergarten, and elementary-primary, there were reported surpluses or a balance between supply and demand in every region of the United States except Hawaii. The only other exceptions were in the fields of bilingual and special education. Marshall urges teacher education candidates not to be discouraged and suggests "[c]onsider the wisdom of adding an area of certification in which the demand is great. Perhaps most importantly, be as flexible as possible in your thinking about where you want to teach" (p. 46). Marshall writes that the problem for many graduating teacher candidates is lack of mobility and/or reluctance to leave one geographic area with few jobs for new teachers for another with a shortage. He suggests:

> Check with your career services office about the availability of ASCUS job-search publications. *The 1996 Job Search Handbook for Educators* presents articles on every phase of a job search—from writing your resumé to relocation issues. . . .

Growing Private Investment and Public Support

Americans place child care among the top five services the federal government should provide.

Private enterprise has scrutinized child care as a potentially lucrative industry. Chains of preschools grow ever larger. KinderCare Learning Centers, Inc., the nation's largest child care chain, was included in *Business Week's* "Top 1000—America's Most Valuable Companies," an annual ranking of public corporations based on their market value (Child Care Information Exchange, 1989). KinderCare's market value was reportedly $789 million, with 1986 sales of $265 million and profits of $35 million (an increase of 33 percent over 1985 profits).

A number of child care businesses in the United States are expanding and testing the waters outside U.S. borders. KinderCare has opened a center in England and plans an additional 40–50 centers there (Neugebauer, 1995). La Petite Academy, the nation's second largest child care chain, operates four centers in Tokyo. Bright Horizons Children's Centers, one of the nation's largest operator of centers for employees, has also been involved in Japanese child care development. Asian and South American countries are seen as future sites for the child care business investment.

Interactions between child care communities and businesses are increasing. Neugebauer (1995) points out that doing business in foreign lands sounds exotic and exciting; and, increasingly, systems, products, and support will flow freely across national boundaries.

In the public school sector, again, private business has intervened. Witness the success of Channel One (Johnson, 1995), sponsored by Whittle Communications in several high schools throughout the United States. At the elementary level has come the development of charter schools which, although tax supported, are free to follow the goals and curricular choices of their governing boards. These generally consist of parents, teachers, students, and, frequently, a sponsoring business that provides technological hardware and support. This sometimes involves personnel from the business going to the school and teaching children (and teachers) how to use the technology (*San Jose Mercury-News*, March 16, 1995).

Consider also the challenge presented by Edison Project schools, sponsored and financed in part by Christopher Whittle. Whittle put together a team of seven people, four who were specialists in management or the media; one who was a Chicago principal; one, a former Brookings Institution fellow; and the seventh, a former professor and president of Yale University, Benno Schmidt. (Whittle is also the sponsor of the above-mentioned Channel One.) Under the Edison Project:

> Each student will have a computer, a monitor, a printer. . . . Student workstations will be hooked up to electronic central libraries. . . .

> . . .

> Teachers will visit students at their workstations and students will visit the teacher and other students at will. . . . There will be little homework . . . because students will be at work from eight in the morning to six in the evening. (Brodinsky, 1993, p. 546)

One of the more controversial aspects of the Edison Project schools is that they are to be privately operated on a for-profit basis. The first schools were projected to open in 1995 for 150,000 students from the grades one through six. Whittle's plan eventually calls for "each school to have its own day-care center and offer elementary, middle school, and high school courses" (Brodinsky, 1993, p. 542).

Parents and Children with Special Needs

Early childhood teachers and directors are handling many "at risk" children and stressed families. Early childhood centers hopefully will be staffed by well-trained caregivers able to help special-need and/or disruptive children while offering supportive assistance to parents. The need for center consultant assistance or special therapy provisions is growing as family economic pressures increase, teenage births continue, and the divorce rate increases.

Reggio Emilia

Anyone keeping up on their reading in the last few years has come across Reggio Emilia's approach and fundamental principles. Gandini (1993), New (1990), Katz (1990), and others have attempted to inform American educators about the specifics and philosophical base of Reggio Emilia's programs. Reggio Emilia, a city in northern Italy of roughly 130,000 inhabitants, has hosted more than 10,000 international educators. For 25 years the city has committed 12 percent of the town's budget to the provision of high quality child care (New, 1990).

Services provided to families and children (infant to age six) are free and combine social services with education (Gandini, 1993). Gandini describes the basic principles or fundamental ideas of the Reggio Emilia approach as follows:

- All children have preparedness, potential, curiosity, and interest in constructing their learning, in engaging in social interaction, and negotiating with everything the environment brings to them.

- Education has to focus on each child—not each child in isolation but each child seen in relation with other children, with the family, with the teachers, with the environment of the school, with the community, and with wider society.

- For children to learn, their well-being has to be guaranteed; the well-being of children is connected with well-being of parents and teachers.

- Children's rights should be recognized, not only children's needs.

- Parent participation is considered essential and takes many forms including:
  - work in schools
  - discussions of education and psychological issues
  - special events, celebrations
  - excursions

- Physical school layout encourages encounters, communication, relationships, choices, problem solving, and discoveries.

- Children's own sense of time and their personal rhythms are considered in planning and implementing activities and projects.

- Cooperation makes possible the achievement of complex goals.

- Teachers working in pairs see themselves as researchers, preparing documentation of their work with children.

- The curriculum is not established in advance, although teachers have goals and make hypotheses about what direction activities and projects might take.

- Teachers facilitate children's exploration of themes and work on short- and long-term projects.

- A special teacher with a well equipped workshop (studio) monitors and records children's artistic expression in a great variety of media. Reggio Emilia educators use "100 languages" of expression to describe children's work rather than art.

- Transcripts of child remarks, discussions, photographs of activities, and representations of their thinking and learning are kept by the special teacher to document learning. This serves as the basis for:
  - parent involvement
  - teacher understanding
  - evaluation of teacher efforts
  - facilitation of conferencing and consultation between teacher and staff
  - making children aware their effort is valued, and
  - creating an archival record and history of the school

Gandini (1993) notes many basic ideas originated in the United States and inspired the work of educators at Reggio Emilia.

Other features of the Reggio Emilia's approach to early education include the concept of teachers as learners, the importance attributed to the role of the environment, the use of long-term projects with small groups of children as the major curriculum strategy, and the emphasis on children's many symbolic languages (art, sculpture, painting, writing, and others) (New, 1990).

School-age Programs

Before- and after-school child care programs are a growing phenomenon. They developed during the mid- and late 1970s and blossomed in the 1980s and 1990s. The demand has grown in proportion to the number of employed mothers from both two-parent and one-parent households. It has also grown in proportion to the numbers of mothers of preschool children in some kind of day care. For example, the Bureau of Labor Statistics (U.S. Department of Labor, 1993) reported that approximately 29 percent of mothers with children between three and five were in the work force in 1970. By 1980, this figure had risen to 42 percent and by 1993 to close to 50 percent. If we look at the numbers of employed mothers with children between the ages of six and 17 in 1970, the Bureau of Labor Statistics reported only 42 percent of mothers working. By 1980 this figure jumped to nearly 68 percent and by 1993 had risen to 70 percent. Who should take care of these school-age children while the mother or parents work? Some parents, accustomed to day care provisions for their preschoolers, often asked their former preschool or day care center to accept their school-agers. Other parents demanded that schools or city-sponsored parks and recreation departments develop programs for their school-agers.

The phenomenon is also related to economics. While in 1970 many two-parent families could exist on one wage-earner's salary, by 1993 we find that it often takes two working adults to provide for a family's food and housing needs. This is compounded by the rise in single-parent households, the majority of which are headed by females. Single-parent males, however, also need after-school child care for their children. Again, the question has been raised, who should be responsible for this care? Schools, parks and recreation departments, private preschool centers, the YMCA/YWCA, 4H clubs, relatives? All of these and others now do provide school-age child care.

School-age child care is seen as a regular program designed for children ages five to 12 during the times when school is not in session and parents are at their employment *before school, after school*, and *on school holidays.*

Bussing is frequently supplied for children who have to be transported from their elementary school to another facility. Student teachers occasionally are given student teaching placements in school-age care programs.

After-school programs are specifically designed for kindergartners through fifth graders after they have completed their academic day. Many children who are older than fifth graders are involved in extra-curricular activities that finish later in the day, closer to the time a parent would return home from work, or are seen as able to fend for themselves. Many primary children who are not enrolled in school-age programs return to empty houses with their keys around their necks to do chores and homework. These "latch key" children, as they are called, may also care for younger siblings. An estimated two to six million school-age children are left at home without adult supervision before and after school, and there seems no end to the pressing and increasing need for quality school-age programs.

Quality in School-Age Programs

Since there are many organizations caring for school-aged children, there are issues related to quality. The principal issue is whether or not the program meets state licensing standards. Your college supervisor may want to apprise you of your own state's regulations and recommendations for quality school-age child care. Some programs encourage and even demand that children in their care join their organization. The organization may be exempt from meeting state standards. It may only have to meet the organization's own standards. One program, for example, did not have child-sized toilets in its bathrooms at its main building. Parents did not complain because they were happy to have their children cared for by an organization they trusted. In another example, a high school student, enrolled in a California Regional Occupations Program (ROP) designed to prepare her to meet state requirements as an assistant in a day care center, discovered that she was going to be responsible for *her own* after-school child care class. Her mother, who had a master's degree in early childhood education and was teaching at a local community college, was appalled and questioned the legality of the placement. The school in question insisted that the placement was legal because the cooperating teacher was next door and could supervise easily.

If you are placed as a student teacher in a school-age day care facility, you may note similar abrogations of the law. The question then arises, what should you do? First of all, you should report the problem to your college supervisor. Secondly, you might talk to your on-site cooperating teacher. If indeed state laws are being overlooked, your college supervisor must know, and your placement should be changed.

● ISSUES

There are many issues we could have chosen to present. Some have already been covered. We have, therefore, chosen to introduce only a few of the major issues here:

- Articulation of two-year programs with four-year ones
- The antibias curriculum
- Parent education
- The "back to basics" movement
- Public school sponsorship of preschool programs
- Computer use with young children
- Family day care
- Language and literature with young children
- Authentic assessment
- Portfolios
- Security concerns
- Adequate compensation, including the Worthy Wage Campaign

Articulation Efforts between Associate Degree and Baccalaureate Degree Training Programs

There is renewed interest in college-level efforts to aid student transfer of college units in early child-hood education/child development from lower to higher degree institutions. Only seven states guarantee acceptance of transfer credits among public institutions statewide. Morgan, et al. (1993) point out that more agreement in this area needs to take place. Some private institutions, with more flexibility, have agreed to the transfer of units from lower degree institutions. Another move has been the assessment of experiential background and acquired skills as substitutes for college credit. The Child Development Associate (CDA) has laid the groundwork for this.

Antibias Curriculum

As lifestyles change and demographers point out projected higher birth rates for some culturally diverse and newly arrived populations, increased interest in bias-free child activity planning for all children has occurred in early childhood programs, figure 20-3. A nonsexist and nonracist child curriculum continues to be important along with increased sensitivity to possible biased opinions or visual models presented in instruction and instructional media.

Single-parent families, seniors, children of color, children and adults with handicapping conditions,

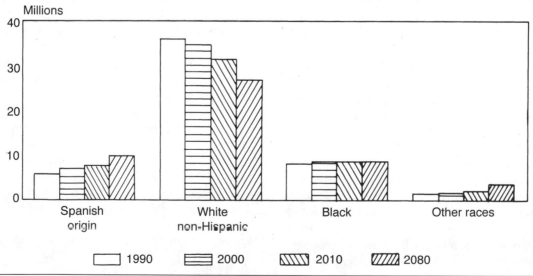

Figure 20-3 U.S. Population Projections of Children by Race, 1990–2080. (Bureau of the Census, 1986, "Projections of the Hispanic Population: 1983 to 2080," Current Population Reports, Series P-25, No. 995; and Kellogg, J.B. "Forces of Change," Phi Delta Kappan, November 1988.)

one-child families, and minority ethnic families appear with increasing frequency in children's books and commercial instructional materials as publishers have become responsive to early childhood educators.

Carter and Curtis (1994), influenced by the antibias curriculum work of Derman-Sparks and the ABC Task Force (1989), have identified current assumptions that serve as the basis for decision making in their early childhood teacher training. They feel, as they continue their growth as teacher trainers, these assumptions could change or be modified. Carter and Curtis (1994) assume the following:

1. Everybody has a culture; culture is learned and includes, but goes beyond, ethnicity.

2. The dominant culture of power in this country has been shaped by European American male perspectives and interests.

3. Bias comes in many forms; invisibility and lack of cultural relevancy are as detrimental as stereotyping.

4. Antibias practices require that we recognize European American cultural dominance and learn how its assumptions become a bias when applied universally. We must learn new attitudes, information, and behaviors as we unlearn acquired biases.

5. To be inclusive and genuinely multicultural requires that we make a place for those historically left out, misrepresented, or disenfranchised. Given the stakes, this will likely stir up emotions and conflict that we must learn to work with.

6. Adults come to programs and workshops with a complex web of influences from backgrounds that must be untangled as they learn and unlearn across diversity.

7. As adults come to deeper understandings about themselves and working with diversity, these understandings will influence their work with children, going beyond tokenism to counter biases and be culturally sensitive.

Which of these assumptions are new to you and may change your values? Did any assumption reinforce a value you already had? Could these assump-

tions affect your work with adults and children of varied backgrounds? How?

Unfortunately, we have seen a backlash from the emphasis on multiculturalism in the United States. Especially in those states with large immigrant populations who speak languages other than English, we currently see an effort to rescind affirmative action policies and to declare an "English only" policy for voting pamphlets sent by state and local agencies, for teaching in the public schools, and in other public venues. At the University of California and at the urging of the governor, affirmative action is no longer supposed to be used as a criterion for admission (*San Francisco Chronicle*, 1995). Such an outcry has occurred, however, that the regents have not implemented the policy—but who knows what may happen in the future?

This backlash has also led to moves in California to deny schooling, welfare, and medical/hospital care to illegal immigrants. Although the courts have stated that this cannot be done, there still are many voters who support such actions. The need for an antibias, multicultural emphasis in our curricula has never been more urgent!

Parent Education

Increasing the parents' awareness of the technical and skilled nature of raising children is an issue of great interest to early childhood educators. Parents seem to be searching for materials and techniques that will help them raise competent, capable, successful children. Most professionals support parent access to information and assistance and see it as a component of a center's operation. With funding cutbacks, this service is usually the first to disappear. The goal of most parent education efforts is to strengthen and promote existing child-rearing practices rather than teach parenting. The issue involves early childhood professionals' abilities to pinpoint parenting skills accurately, teach them effectively, and give honest feedback to parents who do not see their teaching methods as affecting their child's progress. Another issue concerns hard-to-reach parents whose children have a need for change in order to cope with school life and society as a whole.

Back to Basics

The "back to basics" pressure is very apparent to early childhood teachers, and the issue of creating a balance between child exploring, choosing, and doing, and structured teacher-guided academics seems to be a real problem. How do teachers promote a love of learning and preserve children's confidence in themselves as learners, while offering a "back to basics" preschool curriculum?

Teachers worry about preschool programs that concentrate on the rote memorization of the alphabet, phonics instruction, reading, and advanced number concepts. Parents may feel this type of program is desirable, and directors respond by pressuring teachers to provide it. This conflicts with what many teachers feel to be best. When the bulk of instruction is based on uninteresting, highly symbolic, and abstract material, young children's own interests, curiosity, and self-concepts are in jeopardy.

Katz (1981) attempts to clarify this issue; she defines a basic skill as:

- *transcurricular* in nature. It is useful in most curricular areas. (Example: Child being able to ask for clarification.)
- *having dynamic consequences.* This skill leads to acquiring greater skill. (Example: Highly verbal child interacts with adults, making skill grow.)
- *recursive*: it feeds on itself.
- a relatively *discreet unit of action*, observable in a short period of time, fairly visible. (Example: writing, counting.)
- something that can be learned in a lesson; *learned by direct instruction.*
- getting *better with practice.*
- something that can be learned in small steps.

One issue in Katz's discussion is that some early childhood teachers may be instructing basic skills at the expense of children's dispositions to use them. Katz does not endorse a particular curricular model but suggests programs should engage children's minds, encourage choices, promote child concentration, and have "return to" activities that sustain child interest over a period of time.

Philosophies dealing with children's natural curiosity and programs that are intellectually focused seem to have positive "sleeper effects" (skills appear in children's later years). There are many related issues in the "back to basics" instructional model as opposed to self-guided instruction. These issues will be subject to much study and research in the future.

Public School Sponsorship

The issue of increased public school sponsorship of preschools continues. One side argues that increasing public school involvement is cost effective, ensures overall quality, fills empty classrooms, uses existing fiscal and operational management systems, and employs retrained elementary teachers. Others claim that private program sponsors and/or community sponsors are more responsive to parents, better located, and cheaper. In some states kindergartens have become full-day programs (Granucci, 1990).

Mitchell and Modigliani's (1989) research, looking at prekindergarten and existing public kindergartens, confirmed fears about quality and lack of developmentally appropriate child activities:

> Even when prekindergarten classrooms were good, the kindergartens in the same building were usually highly academic, teacher-directed, tightly scheduled, and heavily reliant on work books (78% of the observed kindergartens had workbooks).

A number of early childhood educators worry about adding four-year-olds to the domain of public school systems.

> I see a clear danger in adding four-year-olds to a school system if the trend to downward extension of grade school subject matter and methodology continues. (Curry, 1990)

The debate will continue as more and more states gradually increase their involvement in and funding of prekindergarten programs operated under the auspices of public school systems.

Computers and Young Children

In recent years, there has been much interest in computers and packaged software development. More and more, children are actually using computers rather than merely observing them. Companies are scrambling to create effects on color television screens with voice prompts, musical sounds, and clever picture forms and have developed simple keyboards. As screen happenings are shared and discussed, child interest and motivation increase.

Contrary to popular beliefs about the danger of computers with young children that predicted children would become isolated, sitting in their separate cubicles, working at a keyboard, this has not been the case. Walk into any center with computers and observe. You frequently will find two or even three children playing and/or working with any given program, as the following observes:

> On a recent visit to a private kindergarten program with computers both in the classroom and in a computer lab, we observed Kimberly, sitting with her friend Christina at the classroom computer, excitedly telling her friend about the program they were exploring, "Grandma and Me."
>
> "My grandma and I went to the beach, too," Christina interjected, "but there weren't many other people there that day because it was foggy and cold."
>
> "That's not part of the story, Christina," admonished Kimberly, "Look at what happens next."
>
> The two girls sat at the computer for about 25 minutes, Kimberly "reading" the story to Christina who had not used this particular program before. Christina kept interrupting with her own story of her visit to the beach with her own grandma. Eventually Kimberly seemed to realize Christina's need to tell about her trip to the beach and ignored the fact that it was different than the program they were using. She even suggested that perhaps Christina could "write" about her trip to the beach with her grandma when they went to the computer lab.
>
> On a later visit to the computer lab, both girls were absorbed in using the "KidPix" program. Christina kept telling Kimberly how she used the "Flying Colors" program when she visited her grandma and how it differed from what they were trying to do with "KidPix."

Should we worry that the future will be a single child working at a single computer? The answer is a resounding no! In most elementary school primary grades, children work in twos and even threes at the computer. Children accept correction from the computer more easily than they do from the teacher; thus, the computer becomes a tool for reinforcing mathematics concepts, for example, and for science problem solving as well as for word processing and classroom desktop publishing (Kearsley, Hunger, Furlong, 1992).

Family Day Care Licensing

A merger of interests is evolving between in-home and in-center staffers. Networking has provided additional contacts. Professional early childhood conferences now offer sections specifically designed to attract day home operators and to probe mutual concerns. Another factor that has helped is the number of early childhood graduates with AA degrees who have opted to establish day homes of their own. Often, rewards for day home operators surpass those of private proprietary in-center teachers.

Some states are adding education and training requirements for family day care providers. California, for example, requires that all day care providers must have training in health, safety, and nutrition; first aid; and cardiopulmonary resuscitation (including CPR for infants and young children). Family day care providers are also expected to obtain 15 hours of in-service training each year. Typically, these hours are met by attendance at local conferences sponsored by such groups as National Association for the Education of Young Children (NAEYC) and Association for Childhood Education International (ACEI) affiliates. Local Resource and Referral agencies also arrange for training as does the Red Cross. Kontos (1992) stated that there "are many fine examples of family day care training programs across the country," but she chose to review 20 programs that had been published in monographs, journals, or accessible databases (p. 121) and two that were unpublished. Most of the training consisted of group sessions such as workshops and "rap" groups, and, less frequently, home visits (only three programs). Toy lending libraries were provided by eight of the programs, and radio/television broadcasts were utilized by four of the studies reviewed. Formal classes at colleges and/or vocational schools were used in four of the studies.

Kontos reported that the most unique program format was one sponsored by the Texas Agricultural Extension Service. It was an independent study program that utilized videotapes with an accompanying study manual.

> In this program 75% to 90% of the caregivers completed each chapter of the study manual, and 89% watched all of the videotapes. . . . The study manual was more likely to be rated "very helpful" (94%) than were the videotapes (53%). The reports of the caregivers seemed to confirm that they used the self-study materials, and more than 75% reported that they liked the self-study format and not having to go to meetings. (p. 129)

With the shortage of and need for infant and toddler day care as more and more mothers of very young children enter or remain in the work force, the need for family day care will increase. Since most family day care home providers have only a high school education, the trend appears to be toward regulation by states and the stipulation for some kind of training. The National Association of Family Child Care and the National Association for the Education of Young Children do accredit family day care homes of those providers choosing to undergo the process. Perhaps as more providers choose to become accredited, parents will be more comfortable in their choice of a family day care home for their infants and toddlers as well as for their older children.

In the *San Jose Mercury-News* study, the researcher looked at 645 licensed family day care homes. Were these homes any safer than centers? Unfortunately, the answer was no. Family day care homes were cited with slightly more Type A violations than were centers (35 percent of the homes compared to 31 percent for all centers as a whole). Does accreditation by the National Association of Family Child Care make a difference? We really don't know: The *Mercury-News* article did not include any comparison figures. We might assume that accredited family day care homes would be safer than those that are nonaccredited. However, cost could be a factor in a provider choosing not to go through the accreditation process. Ultimately, the family day care provider who does choose accreditation does so for personal satisfaction. In an interview with Rose Shea, who runs the first family day care home to be accredited in San Jose, she stated,

> "I could have kept my business going without becoming accredited . . . but it's a validation of what I do, like a pat on the back for doing a good job" (Johnson, 1995).

If you are interested in the criteria and process involved in accrediting family day care providers, you should contact the National Association of Family Child Care in Washington, DC. Their telephone numbers are 1-800-359-3817 (for information) and 1-817-831-5095 (to become accredited).

Language and Literacy

Language development techniques have been influenced by an increased focus on national literacy. Studies seem to show children's literary knowledge slipping when today's young children are compared to former generations. Consequently, early childhood programs concentrate on introducing quality books and helping young children realize the functional use of the language arts (speaking, listening, writing, and reading) in their daily lives.

Young children are currently viewed as developing understandings along many lines. Differing degrees of knowledge and attitudes evolve as they attempt to sort their experiences. Readiness as a term is passé—children are now seen as always ready to encounter and categorize life's daily events based on recognized features.

Language is intertwined with most all human endeavor and is learned during all preschool activities. One cannot divorce language learning from art, science, numbers, or any other curriculum area, figure 20-4.

The whole language movement has influenced elementary school and early childhood programming. Its developmentally appropriate, child-centered instructional outlook meshes well with current early childhood theory and practice. Children's reading test scores have indicated phonics instruction should not be ignored and may be a necessary supplement to whole language program planning.

Authentic Assessment (Elementary School Children)

As more focus is placed on the concept of developmentally appropriate practice at the kindergarten and primary grade levels, questions have been raised as to the value of traditional assessment techniques that rely on standardized testing at the end of the school year. Perrone (1991) differentiates between testing and assessment by stating that the latter is a process of gathering information to meet a variety of evaluation needs. As a process, then, assessment, depends upon many indicators and sources of evidence. The development of portfolios has been one suggestion as a better measure of students' progress. It would contain samplings of each student's work plus an assessment procedure that might involve observation notes, anecdotal records, and possibly an interview with the student.

Work samplings, selected daily and/or weekly, might include examples of math papers, creative writing assignments, a book report or two, drawings from each of the four quarters in the school year, a snapshot of the student working in her or his cooperative learning group, another snapshot or even a videotape of the student participating in a physical education lesson.

Authentic assessment may involve the teacher and/or the school psychologist interviewing a student and arranging tasks for the student to explain as he completes them. For example, a student might be asked to explain how she is solving a word problem in math or she might be given a problem situation and asked to explain how she might resolve it. Another task might focus on having the student write and illustrate a short story for the examiner. States that have been experimenting with authentic assessment have discovered that the greatest drawback is the time element involved in conducting a thorough assessment (Guidarini, 1992; Lipton and McTighe, 1992; McAfee and Leon, 1991; Perrone, 1991).

Portfolio Development

Increasingly, teacher preparation programs are urging and/or requiring their student teachers to develop a professional portfolio. The portfolio should include a statement of personal teaching philosophy; representative lesson plans, together with samples of student work; photographs of the classroom, especially of bulletin board displays designed during the student teaching assignment(s); and any other pertinent material, such as case studies of children. The aspiring teacher may wish to include a videotape of a particularly successful lesson involving a science center activity or a language activity. The videotape will allow a prospective principal and interviewing teachers to see the applicant in action.

Figure 20-4 Language is part of almost all activities.

In some districts applicants will discover that there are several steps involved in the hiring process. An initial screening, looking only at applications and resumés, may be done at the district office. Then there may be an interview by a principal or by a team composed of the principal and other teachers at the school. A third step may involve the applicant being asked to present a lesson to one of the classes at the grade level for which the hiring is being done. If you've survived all of these steps and the agony of wondering whether or not you will ever get the job, all we can say is, "Good luck!"

Security Concerns

After the terrible tragedy in Oklahoma City's child care center April 19, 1995, security has become a real concern. The Child Care Information Exchange (1995) encourages centers to conduct security audits. The following questions are suggested for audits:

1. Do you have specific procedures in place for responding to all likely emergencies (natural disasters, fires, accidents)?

2. Do you have a written procedure for evacuating your center that staff and children can implement on "autopilot"?

3. Do you have an off-site location where children can be kept until parents can pick them up if your building cannot be reinhabited after an evacuation? Are parents aware of this arrangement?

4. Do you have a plan for notifying parents when you have to evacuate your building and leave all records behind?

5. Do you have supplies readily available to provide for staff and children's needs when you evacuate your building on short notice or when you must remain with children in your building for an indefinite time in an emergency?

6. If you had to account for every child in your center, what would you do to determine that 100 percent were present? If you used this procedure today, would you be able to account for each child? Would this procedure be effective if you had to evacuate under stressful conditions?

7. Do you have sound procedures in place for continually accounting for all children on field trips?

8. Do you have regular maintenance procedures established and followed for center vehicles? Are vehicle drivers carefully screened? Are they trained to handle emergency situations?

9. Is access to the center controlled in a consistent and sensible way?

10. What procedures do you have to limit visitor access to child-occupied areas of the center? Are there facility features which help secure the perimeter of the building and which notify personnel when security has been breached?

11. Are parents dropping off and picking up children in any possible danger? Are staff coming to and leaving work in any danger? What are your strategies for ensuring their safety?

12. Do you have procedures for dealing with an adult who is under the influence of drugs or alcohol when he/she arrives to pick up a child?

13. Do you have procedures to ensure that children are released only to adults specifically authorized to pick them up? (Some programs are requiring photo IDs of anyone authorized to pick up the child.)

14. Do you have procedures to provide assurance that incidents of abuse cannot occur at your center?

15. Do you have rigorous screening practices to assure that only qualified staff are employed by the center?

16. Do you have procedures for immediately responding to accusations of abuse?

17. Before undertaking a corporate/government management contract, are you adequately evaluating the risks per the location of the facility, the type of business being conducted by the corporate sponsor, and other uses of the building?

18. Does your program have an aggressive policy to ensure that children wear seat belts?

19. Are parents or staff smoking around children? How does your program inform adults about the risks secondhand smoke poses to young children and about the negative role modeling smokers provide?

20. Does your center have routines established for preventing the spread of communicable disease? More importantly, are these rigidly adhered to?

21. Does your area have child care for sick children? Parents should be given the name(s) of any facility or day care home that specializes in caring for sick children, including infants and toddlers. As more and more mothers of young children enter the work force, centers or homes specializing in sick child care are on the increase. These are frequently staffed with licensed vocational/practical nurses (LVNs/LPNs) or registered nurses (RNs) and usually have a pediatrician on call for emergencies.

Although these suggestions are aimed at preschool and day care center directors and teachers, they are, in many ways, applicable to elementary schools, public and private. In these days of child abduction by noncustodial parents and strangers, many schools have implemented controlled access to children, requiring visitors to sign in and out at the office, community aides questioning those in the halls whom they do not recognize. In some schools that have experienced violence, requiring students, teachers, and visitors to pass through a metal detector is not uncommon.

Adequate Compensation

Over the years, much as been said about the low salaries paid to child care workers and teachers (Bellm, Gnezda, Whitebook, & Breunig, 1994; Carter & Curtis, 1995; Draude, 1995; Katz, 1995; Pelo, 1995; Whitebook, 1995).

Dating back to the earliest days of the NAEYC, a concern about salaries and working conditions existed. This organization, now 90,000 members strong, launched its quality, compensation, and affordability

activities in 1987. In 1990, NAEYC's Full Cost of Quality Campaign attempted to inform both the profession and the public concerning the real and true cost of quality programs. Real and true costs reflect compensation with staff professional preparation.

Updated results of the 1993 National Child Care Staffing indicate that the consistency and quality of care is not improving (Whitebook, Phillips, & Howes, 1993). Fewer than 20 percent of centers offer full health benefits to all staff and salaries for teachers and providers hover at approximately $10,000 per year (Bellm, Gnezda, Whitebook, & Breunig, 1994).

A few bright lights in possible salary increases for early childhood workers are seen in military child care projects and in the Child Care and Development Block Grant legislation of 1990. The Head Start Reauthorization Act of 1994 was thought to affect salaries positively. The law encouraged Head Start agencies to adopt salaries based on training and experience (Bellm, Gnezda, Whitebook, & Breunig, 1994). States leading the way in finding ways to increase monetary rewards to teachers in accredited quality centers are Alaska, California, Connecticut, Hawaii, New York, North Carolina, Oregon, Pennsylvania, Texas, and Wisconsin.

Worthy Wage Campaign. Many early childhood professionals and leaders have urged advocacy for worthy wages. Consider the following:

- [W]e must take action, we must come together to acknowledge each other's work and pain and stress and love of the field and desire to stay (Pelo, 1995).

- New mechanisms of financing must be found that will bridge the gap between the full costs of quality that include a well-compensated staff and, at the same time, a service at a price families can afford (Katz, 1995).

- Our field desperately needs the activism and energy of discontent to establish an urgency that can move child care reform closer to the top of our national goals (Morin, 1995).

- School teachers didn't get better wages and benefits because parents of the country said, "You're doing great work, so we're going to pay you better" (Draude, 1995).

- Teachers in the Worthy Wage Movement have come to understand that doing what's right for children means pressuring to make this situation understood and mobilizing a demand for change (Carter & Curtis, 1995).

- Parents and teachers should also seek (advocate for) centers that have access to extra resources beyond parent fees that are used to improve quality. In the Cost, Quality, and Child Outcomes Study sponsored by the Child Care Center, those centers were operated by a variety of public agencies (public schools, state colleges and universities, or operated by municipal agencies), work-site centers, and centers with public funding tied to higher standards (Whitebook, 1995).

Morgan, Azer, Costley, Elliott, Genser, Goodman, and McGrimsey (1994) reflect the feeling of most workers in the following: "Increased knowledge and skills in early care and education should be rewarded with increased responsibility, compensation, and status," [and] "License individuals as well as child care centers."

The National Center for the Early Childhood Work Force (NCECW), a policy, advocacy, and research organization, initiated the Worthy Wage Campaign in 1991. Any child care worker or interested individual can become a campaign member by asking for a membership brochure from:

NCECW (National Center for the Early Childhood Work Force)
733 15th Street, NW, Suite 1037
Washington, DC 20005-2112
Telephone: 1-800-U-R-WORTHY

In the 1980s Massachusetts became the first state to allocate funds exclusively to raise the salaries of early child care and education providers. The Massachusetts early care and education community is currently lobbying the state legislature for additional funds. A new effort by an impressive array of organizations entitled "Fair Rates for Fair Wages Campaign," if successful, will increase worker salaries in publicly subsidized programs. Private center employees hope

for campaign success that could produce a ripple effect for workers in for-profit and not-for-profit centers.

But Carter and Curtis (1994) invoke a word of caution:

> Current economic priorities and conditions, along with societal attitudes, create difficult circumstances for those who choose early childhood education as a profession. In many cases teachers have internalized attitudes about "women's work" and have become self-sacrificing and passive when expected to work with less than adequate ratios, materials, wages, benefits, and working conditions.

And Wishon (1994) reminds us that early childhood educators must carry on the work of past generations in becoming advocates for improving conditions for early childhood workers. He sees today's advocates as "gatekeepers of promises for young children" with their fate and destinies entrusted to our care dependent on present advocacy efforts. But advocacy cannot be done alone; increased education and training must also take place for improved wages and benefits and working conditions.

SUMMARY

Most of society's economic, social, political, and technological trends affect families and young children. Knowledge of trends is crucial to effective teaching, program planning, and supportive relationships with parents. Changes occur that can enhance children's opportunities and potentials, have neutral effects, or create inequities or unfavorable development. Some of the issues discussed in this unit include quality, public policy, arising special needs, nonsexist program planning, parenting education, "back to basics" approach, public school preschool sponsorship, computer use, preschools as investments, family day care liaisons, and assessment.

As you already know, books have been written on many of the above trends and issues; our intent was to whet your interests and present brief overviews, together with a few examples, of the differing trends and issues as we see them.

SUGGESTED ACTIVITIES

A. Read the following example of what happened to one of our student teachers. In small groups of three or four, discuss the example. What should the student teacher do? Who is liable?

As a student teacher in Ms. Ng's second grade classroom, you remain late one afternoon to read the children's journals. At approximately 5:30 PM you leave to return to your apartment and notice an older child (fourth or fifth grade?) whom you do not know sitting on the front steps of the school and crying.

"What's wrong?" you inquire.

"I missed the school bus and no one's come to pick me up," responds the child.

"Did you ask the secretary to call your parents?" you ask.

"She said no one answered at home, and my dad's work phone was answered on his voice mail so she left a message that I needed to be picked up but he hasn't come!" the child wailed.

"Do you want me to wait with you?" the student teacher questioned.

"Please . . . I'd feel so much better . . . it's beginning to get dark and I'm afraid," she cried.

You ask the girl what her name is and where she lives. She tells you her name is Julie and mentions her address (an area across town from the school). Then, after waiting more than an hour, you suggest that you could drive Julie home as it appears the father never received the message.

You wonder why Julie's mother wasn't called, so you ask, "Could your mother pick you up?"

"My Mom and Dad are divorced; I live with my Dad; we don't know where my mom is," the child responds.

"Maybe I could take you home," you suggest.

"Would you? Please?" asks Julie.

You and Julie walk to your car in the parking lot and start toward her home. On the way, as you are crossing a very busy, major road with no traffic light to control your access, a car without lights hits into your car as you are making the crossing. You and Julie are shaken up, and the driver's side of your car is damaged.

B. Make a list of current issues in early childhood teaching. In groups of three to five, arrange them in order of their importance for young children's education and welfare in the United States. Share and compare results with the whole group.

C. Read an article on a trend or issue in early childhood education (ECE), ECE teaching, or ECE programs. Use the *Current Index to Journals in Education* or some other resource to locate one. On a separate sheet, provide the following information to review the article.

- Title of article
- Author(s)
- Journal or publication's name
- Date of publication
- Pagination
- General findings of the study or article (number of subjects, ages, testing device or procedure, results); key ideas, points, or conclusions
- Your reactions

D. Read the information in figure 20-5. Identify libraries in your area that provide ERIC materials. Find and read an article in your area of interest and report your findings to the group.

E. With a peer, list at least five hobbies or collections elementary school children might find interesting.

F. What people in a community might be asked to demonstrate a skill or craft to a group of children attending a school-age after-school program?

G. In a small group, discuss the following quote and report key points to the total group.

Teachers do need to present positive images of ethnic groups to counteract the negative ones prevalent in society. Young children, especially, need to see models of people of color who have accomplished great things. Teachers should help students develop more positive attitudes toward minority groups during the early years. . . . (Willis, 1993)

What is ERIC?

ERIC is a nationwide system funded by the National Institute of Education. ERIC is designed to make information on all aspects of education readily available. ERIC covers such subjects as child development, classrooom techniques, reading, science, social studies, counseling, career education, adult education, rural and urban education, teacher education, higher education, testing, educational administration, and special education.

Who can use ERIC?

You can — whether you are a teacher, researcher, librarian, student, legislator, parent, tinker or tailor. ERIC is for anyone who wants information related to education.

Where is ERIC?

More than 668 libraries and other institutions in the United States and other countries have the ERIC document collection on microfiche. Write to ERIC/EECE for a list of the ERIC collections in your state. Many more institutions subscribe to the printed indexes for the ERIC collection.

What is in ERIC?

When you use ERIC, you can find citations to:

ERIC Documents — primarily unpublished or "fugitive" materials, including more than 160,000 research studies, program descriptions and evaluations, conference proceedings, curriculum materials, bibliographies, and other documents.

ERIC Journals — articles in more than 700 education-related journals.

How do I use ERIC to find citations?

ERIC Documents — Use ERIC's monthly abstract journal *Resources in Education* (*RIE*). *RIE* includes subject, author, and institution indexes and gives you an abstract of each cited document.

ERIC Journals — Use ERIC's other monthly publication *Current Index to Journals in Education* (*CIJE*). *CIJE* lists about 1,800 new journal citations each month and includes a short annotation for most articles cited.

What if I want to read a document or journal article cited in RIE or CIJE?

ERIC Documents — The complete text of most ERIC documents is available on microfiche (a 4×6 inch card of microfilm) which must be read on a microfiche reader. Libraries and other institutions which have the ERIC collection have microfiche readers. Many institutions also have microfiche reader printers that can make paper copies from the microfiche.

ERIC Journal — To read the article from a *CIJE* citation, you look up the journal in your library or ask your librarian to borrow it for you. (Articles cited in *CIJE* are not available on microfiche.)

How can ERIC materials be ordered?

ERIC Documents — Most ERIC documents can be ordered from the ERIC Document Reproduction Service (EDRS) in Alexandria, Virginia. You can write ERIC/EECE for an order form or use the one in each *RIE* issue.

ERIC journals — About 75 percent of the journal articles cited in *CIJE* can be ordered from University Microfilm in Ann Arbor, Michigan. Write ERIC/EECE for an order form or use the order information in *CIJE*.

How can I search ERIC by computer?

One of the most effective ways to use ERIC is to order a computer search of the ERIC database on a particular topic. There are computer search services in many libraries and other institutions.

How does information get into ERIC?

Sixteen ERIC Clearinghouses, in various locations across the United States, collect and process ERIC documents for *RIE* and prepare citations for *CIJE*. Each Clearinghouse is responsible for a different subject area, such as elementary and early childhood education or teacher education.

Do the Clearinghouses offer any other services?

The ERIC Clearinghouses offer various services including answering questions, searching ERIC by computer, and distributing mini-bibliographies, newsletters, and other publications. Check with individual Clearinghouses for details.

How do I find out more about ERIC?

Contact the ERIC Clearinghouse on Elementary and Early Childhood Education or any other ERIC Clearinghouse. We will be happy to send you additional information on ERIC, *RIE*, *CIJE*, other ERIC Clearinghouses, computer searches, or document ordering. We can also send you a list of ERIC collections and institutions offering computer searches of ERIC in your geographical area.

ERIC Clearinghouse on Elementary and
Early Childhood Education
College of Education
University of Illinois
Urbana, Illinois 61801
(217) 333 1386

Figure 20-5 The ERIC system. (Prepared by the ERIC Clearinghouse on Elementary and Early Childhood Education [ERIC/EECE].)

REVIEW

A. List five current debatable trends and/or issues in early childhood education.

B. Describe briefly what you feel is public policy on day care in the United States.

C. Elaborate on both sides of the nonsexist curriculum issue or the "back to basics" issue.

D. Choose the answer that best completes each statement.

1. The real issue in increasing public schools' sponsorship of preschool programs is
   a. the mediocrity of public education.
   b. our private enterprise system.
   c. lack of parent pressure for programs.
   d. quality care as a public priority.
   e. All of these

2. Based on studies of public attitudes toward a nonsexist preschool program for children, it is evident that
   a. all parents want this type of curriculum.
   b. some parents want this type of curriculum.
   c. most parents do not care.
   d. only parents with strong religious affiliations want this type of curriculum.
   e. only females think this type of curriculum is important.

3. Parent education components at early childhood centers are
   a. growing and viable.
   b. shrinking due to lack of parent interest.
   c. shrinking because of economics.
   d. growing within the public school system.
   e. remaining about the same in number.

4. Public monies for child care operations are now in jeopardy because
   a. the public wants to choose its own type of child care.
   b. volunteers are plentiful and are flocking to empty church buildings to care for children.
   c. parents prefer family day care.
   d. they compete with other kinds of welfare and social services for funding.
   e. All of these

5. Parenting skills are
   a. easy to teach.
   b. seen as being technical in nature by a growing number of parents.
   c. best taught in junior high school because of the growing number of teenage pregnancies.
   d. so diverse they cannot be taught.
   e. understood by most parents because of mass media's interest in them.

6. The "back to basics" movement has influenced early childhood programs by
   a. ruining children's opinion of themselves as learners.
   b. alerting teachers to solve the balance between "structure" and discovery.
   c. increasing the number of abstract rote memorization activities in many schools.
   d. Both a and b
   e. Both b and c

E. List four subjects on which much research is currently focused.

REFERENCES

Bellm, D., Gnezda, T., Whitebook, M., & Breunig, G. S. (1994). Policy initiatives to enhance child care staff compensation. In *The early childhood career lattice: Perspectives on professional development*. Washington, DC: National Association for the Education of Young Children.

Berliner, L. (August 1993). Identifying and reporting suspected child abuse and neglect. *Topics in Language Disorders, 13*(4), pp. 15–24.

Brodinsky, B. (March 1993). How "new" will the "new" Whittle American school be? A case study in privatization. *Phi Delta Kappan, 74*(7), 540–547.

Carter, M., & Curtis, D. (1994). *Training teachers: A harvest of theory and practice.* St. Paul: Redleaf Press.

Carter, M., & Curtis, D. (January 1995). From our readers. *Young Children, 50*(2), 3, 83.

Child Care Information Exchange, 67, June 1989.

Child Care Information Exchange, (July/August 1995). Is your center secure? *104*, pp. 38–39.

Children's Defense Fund. (1990). *Children 1990.* Washington, DC: Children's Defense Fund.

Costley, J. (1988). Testimony before the early childhood task force of the National Association of State School Boards.

Curry, N. E. (March 1990). Presentation to the Pennsylvania State Board of Education. *Young Children, 45*(3), 17–23.

Derman-Sparks, L., & The ABC Task Force. (1989). *Antibias curriculum: Tools for empowering young children.* Washington, DC: National Association for the Education of Young Children.

Draude, W. (January 1995). From our readers. *Young Children, 50*(2), 4, 82.

Galinsky, E. (January 1990). Raising children in the 1990s. *Young Children, 45*, 2, 26.

Gandini, L. (November 1993). Fundamentals of the Reggio Emilia approach to early childhood education. *Young Children, 49*(1), 4–8.

Granucci, P. (March 1990). Kindergarten teachers: working through our identity crisis. *Young Children, 45*, 3, 6–11.

Guidarini, A. (1992). Alternate procedures to use in assessing the progress of kindergarten students. Unpublished master's degree thesis, California State University, Hayward.

Johnson, S. (September 10–12, 1995). The dangers of day care. San Jose, CA: *San Jose Mercury News.*

Katz, L. (1981). Salient research on learning in early childhood education and implications for action. Alexandria, VA: Association for Supervision and Curriculum Development.

Katz, L. (November 1990). Impressions of the Reggio Emilia preschools. *Young Children, 45*(1), 11–14.

Katz, L. (January 1995). From our readers. *Young Children, 50*(2), 4–5.

Kearsley, G., Hunter, B., & Furlong, M. (1992). *We teach with technology: New visions for education.* Wilsonville, OR: Franklin, Beedle & Associates.

Kontos, S. (1992). *Family day care: Out of the shadows and into the limelight.* Washington, DC: National Association for the Education of Young Children.

Lipton, L., & McTighe, J. (February 1992). Authentic assessment. Training institute sponsored by Phi Delta Kappa, Tampa, FL.

Marshall, C. A. (Winter 1996). Teacher supply and demand: Let the research guide your plan. *Kappa Delta Pi Record, 32*(2), 44–46.

McAfee, O., & Leong, D. (November 1991). Linking assessment and planning: How to collect, interpret, and use assessment information to promote development. Presentation made at the Annual Conference of the National Association for the Education of Young Children, Denver, CO.

Mitchell, A., & Modgliani, K. (September 1989). Young children in public schools? *Young Children, 44*, 6, 56–61.

Moore, E. (May 1995). Mediocre care: Double jeopardy for black children. *Young Children, 50*(4), 47.

Morgan, G., Azer, S. L., Costley, J. B., Elliott, K., Genser, A., Goodman, I. F., & McGrimsey, B. (March 1994). Mediocre care: Double jeopardy for black children. *Young Children, 49*(3), 80–83.

Morgan, G., Azer, S., Costley, J., Genser, A., Goodman, L., Lombardi, J., & McGrimsey, B. (1993). *Making a career of it: The state of the states report on career development in early care and education.* Boston: The Center for Career Development in Early Care and Education at Wheelock College.

Morin, J. (January 1995). From our readers. *Young Children, 50*(2), 82.

Neugebauer, R. (July/August 1995). Child care and the global economy, *Child Care Information Exchange, 104*, 9–16.

New, R. (November 1990). Excellent early education: A city in Italy has it. *Young Children, 45*(1), 4–10.

Pelo, A. (January 1995). From our readers. *Young Children, 50*(2), 3, 82.

Perrone, V. (1991). *Expanding student assessment.* Alexandria, VA: Association for Supervision and Curriculum Development.

Roe, M., & Vukilich, C. (Fall/Winter 1994). Portfolio implementation: How about R for realistic? *Journal of Research in Childhood Education, 9*(1), 5–14.

U.S. Department of Commerce, Bureau of the Census. (1993). *Poverty in the United States: 1992.* Current population reports, series P60-185.

U.S. General Accounting Office. (1993). Poor preschool-aged children: Numbers increase but most not in preschool. GAO/HRD-93-111BR.

Whitebook, M. (May 1995). What's good for child care teachers is good for our country's children. *Young Children, 50*(4), 49–50.

Whitebook, M., Howes, C., & Phillips, D. (1989). *Who cares? Child care teachers and quality of care in America.* Berkeley, CA: CCEP.

Whitebook, M., Phillips, D., & Howes, C. (1993). *The national child care staffing study revisited.* Oakland, CA: Child Care Employee Project.

Willer, B. (January 1992). An overview of the demand and supply of child care in 1990. *Young Children, 47*(2), 19–22.

Willis, S. (September 1993). Multicultural teaching: Meeting the challenges that arise in practice. Association for Supervision and Curriculum Development Update, p. 1.

Wishon, P. M. (January 1994). On our watch: Connecting across generations of early childhood advocates. *Young Children, 49*(2), 42–43.

RESOURCES

Bergen, J. R., & Feld, J. K. (July 1993). Developmental assessment: New directions. *Young Children, 48*(5), 41–47.

Celano, D., & Neuman, S. B. (February 1995). Channel One: Time for a TV break. *Phi Delta Kappan, 76*(6), 444–446.

Child care in California. League of Womens Voters of California, 926 J St., Suite 100, Sacramento, CA 95814.

Cohen, D. (June 1995). What standards for national standards? *Phi Delta Kappan, 76*(10), 751–757.

Eisner, E. W. (June 1995). Standards for American schools: Help or hindrance? *Phi Delta Kappan, 76*(10), 758–764.

Galinsky, E. (August 1989). Is there really a crisis in child care? If so, does anybody out there care? *Young Children, 44*, 5, 3.

Hills, T. W. (July 1993). Assessment in context–teachers and children at work. *Young Children, 48*(5), 20–28.

Jennings, J. F. (June 1995). School reform based on what is taught and learned. *Phi Delta Kappan, 76*(10), 765–769.

Johnson, J. (February 1995). Channel One: The dilemma of teaching and selling. *Phi Delta Kappan, 76*(6), 437–442.

Kane, M. B., & Khattri, N. (September 1995). Assessment reform: A work in progress. *Phi Delta Kappan, 77*(1), 30–32.

Kinder Care on Business Week Top 1000 List. (July 1987). *Child Care Information Exchange, 56*, p. 9.

Kraybill, B. (1992). Director Afterschool Programs, Livermore Valley Recreation and Park Department, Interview.

League of Women Voters of California, 926 J St., Suite 1000, Sacramento, CA 95814.

Lewis, A. C. (June 1995). An overview of the standards movement. *Phi Delta Kappan, 76*(10), 744–750.

Meisels, S. J. (July 1993). Remaking classroom assessment with the work sampling system. *Young Children, 48*(5), 34–40.

No author. (March 16, 1995). Some San Jose schools may be privatized. *San Jose Mercury-News*, p. B-1.

No author. (December 10, 1995). Is this the end for affirmative action? *San Francisco Chronicle*, p. A-1.

Puckett, M. B., & Black, J. K. (1994). *Authentic assessment of the young child: Celebrating development and learning.* New York: Merrill/Macmillan.

Research in brief: Child care workers salaries. (1989). Washington, DC: Institute for Women's Policy Research, pp. 3–4.

Roe, M., & Vukilich, C. (Fall/Winter 1994). Portfolio implementation: How about R for realistic? *Journal of Research in Childhood Education, 9*(1), 5–14.

Schweinhart, L. J. (July 1993). Observing young children in action: The key to early childhood assessment. *Young Children, 48*(5), 29–33.

Schweinhart, L. J. (January 1995). The United States needs better child care. *Young Children, 50*(2), 48.

Seefeldt, C. (Ed.). (1990). *Continuing issues in early childhood education.* New York: Merrill/Maxwell/Macmillan.

Steglin, D. A. (1992). *Early childhood education: Policy issues for the 1990s.* Norwood, NJ: Ablex.

Trawick-Smith, J., & Lambert, L. (March 1995). The unique challenges of the family day care provider: Implications for professional development. *Young Children, 50*(3), 25–32.

U.S. Department of Labor, Bureau of Labor Statistics. (1986). *Current Population Survey*, Bulletin 2251, Washington, DC: U.S. Government Printing Office.

Warger, C. (Ed.). (1988). *A resource guide to public school early childhood programs.* Washington, DC: Association for Supervision and Curriculum Development.

Wartella, E. (February 1995). The commercialization of youth: Channel One in context. *Phi Delta Kappan, 76*(6), 448–451.

Weis, L., Altbach, P. G., Kelly, G. P., & Petrie, H. G. (Eds.). (1991). *Critical perspectives on early childhood education.* Albany, NY: State University of New York Press.

Wortham, S. C. (1995). *Measurement and evaluation in early childhood education.* (2nd ed.). Englewood Cliffs, NJ: Prentice Hall.

Wright, J. L., & Shade, D. D. (Eds.). (1994). *Young children: Active learners in a technological age.* Washington, DC: National Association for the Education of Young Children.

CHAPTER

21

Student Teaching with Infants and Toddlers

OBJECTIVES

After studying this chapter, the student will be able to:

- List at least three characteristics of a quality infant/toddler center.
- Discuss some of the research on day care for infants and toddlers.
- Describe the general regulations of an infant center (including health concerns).
- Cite techniques for approaching and working with children.
- Describe caregiving as a teaching activity.
- Identify activities for infants and toddlers.

I asked to be placed in an infant/toddler center. Student teaching there pointed out caregiver skills I hadn't dreamed of. Thank heavens I've a strong back. That's really necessary!

Michaela Grossman

Wash your hands, wash your hands, then, do it again. I think the staff said that hundreds of times!

Pat Booth

One of my friends said I'd never want children of my own if I worked at a toddler program. Wrong! It made me want children of my own even more.

Briana DeLong

● STANDARDS

Most infants and toddlers today are cared for by relatives or in family day care homes. Many parents feel, rightly or wrongly, that the infant thrives better in an environment most like the home. Family day care homes are popular. State licensing in California mandates low adult-infant and adult-toddler ratios. The National Association for the Education of Young Children has been urging a ratio of 1:4 as a national standard. A quality center may deliberately choose to keep its ratio 1:3.

One of the reasons for the lack of national standards lies in the belief that all young children, especially infants and toddlers, belong at home with their mothers. This attitude, however, does not recognize what is happening in the workplace. The fastest growing group of new workers is women with children under six.

● CHARACTERISTICS OF A QUALITY INFANT/TODDLER CENTER

The 18 characteristics of quality programs, as discussed earlier, are applicable to infant and toddler centers. However, perhaps physical and psychological safety should come first. Because of their helplessness, babies require a lot of warm, loving care. Erikson would say they need to know that the adults in their lives can be trusted. According to Maslow, they need to have their deficiency needs met—satisfying biological and physical safety needs, psychological safety needs, belongingness and love needs, and esteem needs. By meeting deficiency needs, the center can help guide the infant and toddler toward self-actualization.

What is most important, perhaps, in the infant center is a genuine affection for babies. Parents looking for day care for their infants should look for this quality and choose very carefully. However common it may be for a child to cry every morning when getting ready to leave or clinging to the parent when being left, these may be signs that something may not be right. If these behaviors persist and are accompanied by the infant's failure to gain weight appropri-ately, they likely signal a problem with the setting and/or the provider(s).

Variety in Infant/Toddler Programs

There is probably as much variety in infant/toddler programs as there is in preschool programs. Each program will be, for the most part, a reflection of the person in charge. A loving professional who truly CAREs will provide a warm, loving environment for the infants and toddlers, figure 21-1. The staff will care enough to ensure that the rooms and fenced outdoor areas used by infants and toddlers are safe.

One interesting program model is called the Resources for Infant Educators (RIE) model. Its spokeswoman in the United States is Magda Gerber, and its philosophy is based upon the work of Dr. Emmi Pikler of Hungary. Pikler has stated, "I have to stress that by no means do we believe it is advantageous to rear infants away from their families . . . Only if this is not possible should the infant spend time in group care." (Gerber, 1971, p. 1)

In particular Pikler believes that infants should receive *individualized care* in a group setting. Some infant centers have interpreted this to mean that the same caretaker should always, inasmuch as is possible, care for the same infant day after day. In this way,

Figure 21-1 Encouraging motor activities is an essential part of a curriculum for toddlers. (Courtesy of Jody Boyd)

the infant can form a bond with the caretaker the same way a bond is formed with the infant's mother and/or father.

Some of the specific techniques endorsed by Pikler have become widely accepted in infant/toddler care centers in the United States. Some of the techniques are: assigning the same adult to the same infant; speaking softly and gently to the infant; and taking time to explain carefully the purpose of changing a diaper, figure 21-2. Due to the efforts of Gerber and university sponsorship, Pikler's philosophy and techniques have become well known.

Other exemplary infant programs have been associated with major universities as a part of the training programs for students in child development. One such program is associated with the University of North Carolina at Greensboro. The infant/toddler program provides what Keister calls "individual care in a group setting." (1977, p. 11) Because the center trains students, its caretakers are highly qualified, loving people. With the availability of student assistants, the adult-infant ratio is often as low as 1:2.

Playing with Infants

Adults aim for adult-infant play that keeps the infant involved and active but neither bored nor overly agitated. Play episodes facilitate bonding/

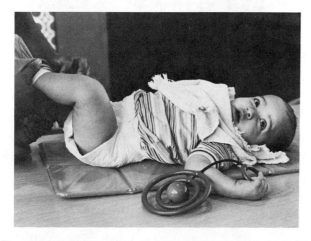

Figure 21-2 The curriculum in an infant center includes changing diapers. (Courtesy of Jody Boyd)

attachment and encourage infant attention to social interaction.

Adult recognition of babies' moods and interests is necessary when attempting a play sequence. Knowing when to calm the infant and when to introduce a new play feature that extends play is a skill in infant care giving. Knowing when the infant is best left alone is also important.

Adults enjoy infant play; it's a natural activity that promotes optimum development. By six months of age simple child-adult cooperative play begins to become more elaborate. Almost all playing situations couple play with language, and infants learn to expect a "your turn, my turn" sequence.

Quality

Unfortunately the quality of care provided in many infant and toddler centers is questionable. The Cost, Quality, and Outcomes Study Team (1995), after visiting 400 randomly selected centers in 1993, found:

> Child care at most centers in the United States is poor to mediocre, with 49% of infants and toddlers in rooms having less-than-minimal quality.

● HOME VERSUS DAY CARE CENTER

Keister's original study compared infants who attended the center with infants reared at home. On a series of measures evaluating physical, social, emotional, and cognitive growth, the differences were not significant. In a follow-up study of the infants after their entry in school, no negative results were reported. Positive results pointed to the greater sociability of the infants who attended the center and their quicker assimilation into school routines, figure 21-3. The important point about infant/toddler centers is that group care seems not detrimental as long as it is individualized, consistent, and nurturing.

● A CURRICULUM FOR INFANTS AND TODDLERS

Another question often raised by people who are unfamiliar with infants and toddlers is "What do you mean when you say you 'teach' infants and tod-

Figure 21-3 Self-help, when encouraged during the infant/toddler period, promotes further self-help in preschoolers.

dlers?" Many people, including parents, misunderstand just how much their children learn during their first years of life. Even those who do know may feel that all the child does is play.

A curriculum for infants and toddlers should be tailored to the developmental age of the child, figure 21-4. Noticing that an infant has just begun to reach and grasp, the curriculum should provide this infant with opportunities to do so by arranging attractive objects within sight and reach. Another infant may be starting to coo; speaking and cooing with the youngster can stimulate imitation. For the infant beginning to crawl, a safe area is essential.

Some good sources for activities to implement in an infant/toddler center can be found in Gonzalez-Meña's and Eyer's *Infancy and Caregiving* (1980), Bailey's and Burton's *The Dynamic Self* (1982), Fowler's *Infant and Child Care* (1980), Weiser's *Infant/Toddler Care and Education*, 2nd edition, (1991).

For a thorough treatment of what can be considered a developmentally appropriate curriculum for infants and toddlers, see Bredekamp's (1987) *Developmentally Appropriate Practice.* (Lally, Provence, Szanton, and Weissbourd designed the original "De-

velopmental Milestones of Children from Birth to Age 3.") Educators and student teachers may find Lally's developmental stages helpful. He considers children from birth through eight months as being in the stage of "the early months," eight- to 18-month-olds as "crawlers and walkers," 18-month-olds to three-year-olds as "toddlers and 2-year-olds."

● STUDENT TEACHING WITH INFANTS AND TODDLERS

An infant/toddler center is an entirely new world, one that is completely different from the preschool environment. Every infant/toddler center is operated a little differently. However, most centers have similar regulations regarding children's health, caregivers' health, and diaper-changing procedures. A student teacher should request a staff handbook. Read it *before* you go to the center. Be prepared to ask questions about anything you do not understand. Babies need consistency, and it is important that you are able to fit into the center routines as quickly as possible. Most important—relax and enjoy the children!

Figure 21-4 This child's experiences are tailored to her developmental age.

● GENERAL RULES AND REGULATIONS

The physical setting and philosophy of a center will determine how various routines are carried out, figure 21-5. Centers usually have specific rules and routines regarding health and safety, medications, emergencies, feeding, diapering, and naps.

Health and Safety

- Smoking is not allowed in infant/toddler centers.
- Coffee, tea, etc., should be consumed in staff areas only.
- Never leave a child unattended on a changing table or in a high chair.
- Do not leave children unattended inside or outside. They can easily injure themselves.
- Ill infants should not be in the center. Infants who have bad colds, fevers, or contagious diseases are usually cared for at home.
- If you are ill, you should not be in the center. You will not be efficient if you are not feeling well. In addition, your illness may spread to the children.

Figure 21-5 Bathing routines require safe surroundings. (Courtesy of Irene Sterling)

If you contract a contagious illness, notify the center immediately.

- Wash your hands. The most important health measure you can take is to wash your hands before and after diapering or cleaning noses and before feeding a child.
- Watch for signs that a child may not feel well. Some symptoms are digging at or pulling ears, listlessness, glassy eyes, diarrhea, limping, etc.
- Parents should be given the name(s) of any facility or day care home that specializes in caring for sick children, including infants and toddlers. As stated in chapter 20, these are frequently staffed with licensed professionals.

Medication

Normally, only a regular staff person will be allowed to give medication. You should be aware of medication schedules for the children. You might need to remind the staff when medications are due.

You also need to be aware of the effects medications may have on the children. They may become sleepy, agitated, or show allergic symptoms. You must be alert to changes that occur when medicine is given and be able to communicate these to the staff.

Emergencies

- *Stay calm.*
- Speak calmly and quietly to the child.
- Alert the staff that an emergency has occurred. They should be able to administer the appropriate first aid measures until the child can see a physician.
- Help calm the other children. They will respond to the situation the same way you do. If you are agitated and upset, they will respond to your feelings; likewise, if you remain calm, they usually will also.

Feeding

- Wash your hands.
- Read the child's chart to see what kind of food

and/or formula to give and how much. (*Remember*: Do not feed a child from a baby food jar; use a dish, figure 21-6. Saliva, which contains bacteria, will get in the jar and spoil the remaining food.

- Gather all the things you need for feeding: bib, washcloth, spoons, sponges, etc. It may be helpful to bring one spoon for you to feed the child and a spoon for the infant to "help."

- Tell the infant what you are going to do. Let the infant anticipate being fed.

- Settle the child comfortably. (You may want to make sure the child has a clean, dry diaper before feeding, so she will be more comfortable and attentive.)

- The child will let you know when more food is desired. When the child opens the mouth, respond by feeding.

- Talk to the child. Eating is a time to enjoy pleasant conversation and socialization, and young children like being talked to. You can talk about the food, its texture, color, temperature, taste, etc. Eye contact is important.

Figure 21-6 Children at this infant/toddler center are fed from dishes, not from jars. (Courtesy of Irene Sterling)

- Encourage the child to help feed him or herself. It is a little messier, but it means more independence later.

- If they refuse to take the last ounce of a bottle or the last little bit of solid food, do not push it. The child knows when he or she is not hungry.

- Be sure to burp bottle-fed children when they need it. You may want to check with the child's caregiver for any special instructions.

- When the baby is finished, wash the face and hands. Again, tell the baby you are going to do this. Encourage the child to take part in this activity. Be gentle with the washcloth.

- Take off the bib and put the baby down to play.

- Clean up. Be sure to wipe off the high chair, the tray, the table, and the floor. Put dishes and bottles in the sink.

- *Record* what and how the child ate.

Diapering

- Gather everything you need to change the baby: diapers, clean clothes, baby wipes, medicated ointment (if needed) and anything else that may be required.

- Tell the child what you are going to do. Set the child on the diaper table.

- Keep one hand on the child at all times.

- Take off the wet diaper and clean the child thoroughly with a warm, wet cloth. Apply any ointment according to the parent's instructions.

- Talk to the child about the process. Talk about being wet, dry, and clean. Describe the process of dressing and undressing; you can talk about the baby's clothes and body parts. Involve the baby in the process. Ask the child to lift the legs or give you an arm to put through the sleeve. (*Note*: How diapers are changed also gives children messages about their sexuality. If you are relaxed and casual about changing them and washing their genital area, children get the message that they are "okay.")

- Put the child in a safe place. Dispose of the diaper

and soiled clothes according to the directions you are given.

- Clean the changing table. Use germicidal solution.
- Wash your hands. Clean changing tables and clean hands will help prevent the spread of disease.
- Record the diaper change. Be sure to note bowel movements. Make note of anything unusual: diarrhea, constipation, diaper rash, unusually strong urine odor, or anything else that seems out of the ordinary.

Toilet Learning

Toilet learning is too frequently treated with embarrassment in parenting books and meager research has been done on the topic. Many parents and caretakers do not understand that although bladder and bowel control is a skill, it may not be taught; it is learned.

Infants begin life with automatic emptying of the bladder and bowel. Bladder capacity is so small that wetting may occur every hour or so. Automatic emptying is triggered by the filling of the bladder or bowel that sets off rhythmic contractions over which the infant has no control.

It is not until the nervous system matures during the first year or two that infants and toddlers show awareness of the sensations of a full bladder or bowel. What behaviors would alert you to this?

- a look of concentration while all activity stops
- crossing the legs
- fidgeting
- holding onto the crotch with one or both hands
- less frequent wetting
- regularity you can count on
- a keener awareness of body functions
- a sudden dislike of things messy
- a more sensitive sniffer
- use of the appropriate vocabulary
- improving communication abilities
- some self-dressing skills

- an interest in the habits of others (Eisenberg and Murkoff, 1995, pp. 27–28)

Conscious holding of urine is helped by a gradually increasing bladder capacity. By the second year, capacity has usually doubled and the frequency of wetting is about every two or three hours. Emptying is still automatic and dependent upon a full bladder or bowel. When parents or caretakers boast that toddlers at 14, 18, or 21 months are toilet trained, be aware that this is more often an indication that the parents/caretakers recognize the signs of the impending need and place the child on a potty chair than it is an indication that the child is toilet trained.

By three years most children have learned to resist the emptying of their bowels until it suits them. At this age also, most children have learned to hold urine for a considerable time when the bladder is full. This holding ability requires conscious control of the perineal muscles, used in the same way as is the bowel sphincter. At this age, however, accidents often occur as children do not have total control over urine release. This becomes so obvious when the child who has just been taken to the toilet and not urinated goes back to play and immediately wets.

During the fourth year most children have acquired conscious control over both bowel and bladder muscles. But it is important to remember that full control is not completely accomplished until about six years of age when starting the urine stream from a partially full bladder becomes possible.

Learning bladder and bowel control is far from simple. Think of what children must learn:

- to remove and replace pants;
- eventually to flush the toilet;
- to use toilet tissue; and
- to wash their hands upon completion.

In spite of these complexities, most children acquire toileting skills with a minimum of help.

When Should Toilet Learning Begin?

The answer to this is to recognize that toilet learning will be most successful when the children show clear signs of recognizing bladder or bowel tension. These signs vary from child to child; you will be able to recognize them after they have occurred several times just before the child has wet or had a bowel movement. Look for any of the following signs mentioned earlier: stopping what she is doing and looking as if she is concentrating; crossing his legs as if trying to prevent himself from wetting; beginning to fidget, pulling at you; making sounds or using baby words such as "wee-wee"; and/or putting her hands on her crotch as if she could feel she is about to empty her bladder.

How Do You Handle Accidents?

Number one rule is to remember that accidents are inevitable. Treat accidents matter-of-factly. Wash your hands. Change the child's pants and clean up without irritation. Wash your hands again; if used, disinfect the changing table. If you have missed the child's cue and not moved fast enough to help the child urinate or defecate, compliment the child on his ability to try to get your attention. Recognize that some accidents may be your fault, not the child's.

Many people will give you advice about toilet learning. Your cooperating teacher may follow a routine of taking toddlers to a potty chair at regular intervals. Even if you know that most toddlers do not acquire complete control until four to six years of age, you can go along with the center's policy; regular toileting helps those toddlers with regular rhythmicity acquire control at an earlier age than those with an irregular rhythmicity, figure 21-7. If a parent complains that her child was toilet "trained" before she placed him in the day care center and is angry because your cooperating teacher has asked her to bring in diapers, let the cooperating teacher handle the problem. If the parent tries to involve you, defer to center policy. Be patient with those parents who keep their child in diapers at age three. Perhaps, as busy, working parents, they find it easier than to try to learn the subtle cues the child may be providing. Or, they may not know what cues to look for.

One Final Word

Most children learn by example. As one two-year-old learns to use the toilet independently, he or she becomes a role model for other children. In a family-type center with a mixture of ages, older children provide the role models for the younger ones. Parents also become role models for their children at home. Treat toilet learning like the natural process it is and don't worry about the three-year-old who still is having daily accidents.

Check for problems such as constipation, diarrhea, painful urination, and so on. Check for any dietary-related difficulties—a diet low in fluids and fiber will often provide cues to problems with constipation. Above all, relax and don't make a big deal about toileting; all children will learn eventually with or without formal teaching!

Naptime

Young children may vary considerably in their naptimes. You must be alert to signs of sleepiness in order to prevent a young child from becoming overtired. Toddlers usually learn very quickly to adjust to the nap schedule of the program. Watch for yawning, rubbing of eyes, pulling of hair, thumbsucking, and disinterest in toys or people.

All these are signs that a young child may be ready for a nap. Before putting the child down,

Figure 21-7 Learning to use the toilet is a part of the curriculum. (Courtesy of Judy Boyd)

quickly check his or her schedule. Make sure the child is dry and is not due to be fed soon. You may want to feed a child a little ahead of schedule if they are sleepy. Make sure you have a clean crib and blanket. Also, check to see if the child has any special toy to sleep with.

If you are helping a child who is new to the center, the child may be reluctant to take a nap. This is because the child is in a strange place, full of strangers.

Check to see if the child prefers to sleep on the back, side, or stomach. Most infants are placed on their backs or sides to sleep as a precaution against SIDS (sudden infant death syndrome). If the parent assures you that the infant prefers sleeping on his stomach, be sure that no pillow is used nor too soft a cover or stuffed toy with which the infant accidentally could be smothered. Many older infants and toddlers enjoy sleeping on their stomachs.

You may find it helpful to sing softly, rub the back gently, or rock in order to help the child settle down to sleep. Dimming the center's lights may help calm the child. Many times all the excitement of the center and the other children make it difficult for babies to sleep. Be patient, but firm.

Do not feel you failed if you do not get instant success. Ask the staff for suggestions. Infant center staffs are usually more than willing to answer questions, listen to concerns, or offer suggestions.

● APPROACHING AND WORKING WITH CHILDREN

When working with infants and toddlers, remember that every child is an individual. Even tiny infants have preferences. They may like to sleep on their backs or sides rather than stomachs; they may like to be burped on the shoulder rather than on your knees. When you are caring for a child, take a minute to try and find out what some of their preferences may be.

When working with children of this age remember:

- Your size may be frightening to a child.
- Keep confidential material to yourself. Medical, financial, personal, and family information is

privileged information that helps you understand the child more completely.

Working with Infants

Children need to hear your voice, so *talk to them.* They need the social contact that only another person can provide. Hearing language is also the way children learn to talk. Be sure you use clear, simple language. *Speak softly.* Voice tone and volume greatly affect the children. If you speak in a loud, excited voice, the children are very likely to become loud and excited in response.

Encourage anticipation by telling the children what you are going to do. Say "Now we are going to change your diaper." They will respond and cooperate when you let them know what to expect.

Try to be at *eye level to the children.* Sitting or kneeling on the floor brings you closer to their line of vision. *Make eye contact.* When bottle feeding, playing, diapering, etc., look directly at the children. Meet and hold their gaze when talking to them. You like to have people look at you; babies undoubtedly feel the same way.

Move slowly around infants. Young children do everything in slow motion. They often get upset and overstimulated when adults run around them excitedly. Young infants need time to understand the changes that are happening. Be affectionate and warm but *do not hover.* Be ready to hug, hold, and comfort when they need it, but let them be free to explore. Young children need to be able to move around and experience their environment, figure 21-8. They need to find their own solutions to problems whenever they can. Let the children experiment with toys and invent uses. Intervene only when they are likely to get hurt, are obviously in distress, or are too frustrated to cope. Becoming independent, competent, and self-sufficient is hard work; children need loving, secure adults and a safe place to begin the process.

Encourage the babies to help you in caregiving. You need to dress them, change them, and feed them. However, they will help if you let them. Recognize their attempts to participate and encourage them. It does not take much longer, and the rewards are many times greater.

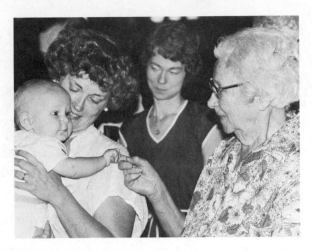

Figure 21-8 Infants can meet new people as they experience their environment. (Courtesy of Nancy Martin)

Working with Toddlers

Toddlers are a very special group. They are just beginning to understand that they *are* people. They are seeing themselves as separate from their parents for the first time. They are compelled to explore and understand their environment. They must assert themselves as individuals. If you can recognize their need to be an individual without feeling personal insecurity, you will have made a giant step in dealing effectively with them.

Toddlers, more so than infants, will challenge your authority. They may test you, until they can feel secure in your response. You will need to call on all your reserves of strength, firmness, patience, and love to deal with them. They are loving, affectionate, giving, sharing, joyful, spontaneous people; take pleasure in them.

You may find some of the following ideas helpful when you are working with toddlers. Read the suggestions, and think about them. Try to put them into practice.

Make *positive statements.* Say "Feet belong on the floor." When children hear the words "don't" and "no" constantly, they begin to ignore them.

Give choices only when you intend to honor them. If Johnny's mother said that her son must wear his jacket when playing outside, do not ask John, "Do you want your jacket?" Instead, say "Your Mom wants you to wear a jacket today." If you give a choice and the toddler says "no," you are already in a conflict you could have avoided.

Avoid problems by *being alert.* Watch for signs that a child may be getting too frustrated to handle a situation or that a fight over a toy is about to start.

Use distraction whenever possible. If you see two children insisting on the same toy, see if the children can work it out themselves. If not, try to interest one of them in something else. You might point out a toy just like it or remind them of another enjoyable activity.

If an argument does erupt, *avoid taking sides.* Help both children understand how the other child feels. *Encourage the use of words* to handle situations. Encourage the children to name things, to express happiness, sorrow, excitement, and other emotions. *Let the children talk.* Correct grammar and pronunciation will come later. Practicing verbal expression is the most important thing.

Act on your own suggestions. If you say, "Time to clean up. Start putting the toys away," the children are more likely to follow your suggestions if they are accompanied by actions.

Make *alternative suggestions* if some children continually ignore safety rules or disturb others: suggest an alternate activity the child likes; suggest taking turns; suggest cooperation; or remove the child from the activity. Be firm but calm. *Do not take the children's reaction personally.* You may hear "I don't like you!" Say, "I know you are angry. It's okay to be angry." Toddlers respect fairness and desperately want limits they can depend on.

Do not make promises you cannot keep. Just say you will have to ask if you do not know. Toddlers understand that.

CAREGIVING AS A TEACHING ACTIVITY

Consider the following curriculum areas, usually included in the preschool program: motor; cognitive; language; social; sensory; self-esteem; mathematics. All these areas are encountered during routine caregiving activities.

Think about the routines when you change a diaper:

- You talk to the child, telling what is going to happen. The child is developing a sense of sequential events.

  SOCIAL
  LANGUAGE
  MATHEMATICS

- You take off the child's diaper and let the legs move freely. The child feels the air on the body.

  MOTOR
  SENSORY

- You tell the child that the diaper is wet or has bowel movement.

  COGNITIVE
  SENSORY

- You wash the child with a wash cloth or wipe. You apply diaper rash medication if necessary. You talk about how this feels.

  SENSORY
  LANGUAGE
  COGNITIVE

- You put a new diaper on the child and then, possibly, clothes. The new diaper is dry and feels more comfortable.

  SENSORY
  LANGUAGE
  COGNITIVE

- You talk about what is happening, encouraging the infant to help you by lifting the legs, putting out an arm, etc.

  LANGUAGE
  MOTOR
  SOCIAL

- The infant is now more comfortable and probably happier. You have had an opportunity for a special one-to-one experience with the child. For a few minutes of a busy morning, the infant has your complete attention.

  SELF-ESTEEM
  SENSORY
  SOCIAL

What about feeding?

- You know it is time to give a bottle or feed a child. You tell the child you are going to prepare the food. You are again helping the child develop a sense of sequence of time.

  MATHEMATICS
  LANGUAGE
  SOCIAL

- The young infant may be just starting to eat and learning to eat from a spoon; the older infant may be using fingers

  MOTOR
  LANGUAGE
  SELF-ESTEEM

or learning to use a spoon. How special you feel when you succeed.

- You sit with the child or a small group of children while they eat lunch. You talk about what they are eating, about how it tastes, its texture, and color. A child who does not like peas may be encouraged to try three peas or two pieces of carrots.

  SOCIAL
  LANGUAGE
  COGNITIVE
  SENSORY
  MATHEMATICS

- The bottle-fed child or slightly older infant has your total attention. You talk to the child. You make eye contact while feeding the infant, holding the child close and safe.

  SELF-ESTEEM
  LANGUAGE
  SENSORY

- After eating, you wash the face and hands with a warm, wet cloth. First, the right hand; then, left. The older child may be able to help you.

  SENSORY
  LANGUAGE
  COGNITIVE
  MOTOR

These are just two examples of the many routines that happen in an infant center. Think of how many things are happening to a child during these routines. Think about what else is happening. What other messages is the infant receiving? Think about bathing and dressing to go outside. What about naptime? What kinds of things could you do that would make naptime go more smoothly and be a more complete experience for each child?

● ACTIVITIES IN THE INFANT/TODDLER CENTER

Play can usually be divided into two types: social play, in which a child interacts with an adult or another child, and object play, in which the child interacts with an object or toy, figure 21-9. Children of all ages engage in both types of play, and the following guidelines are true for any child.

Effective Social Play

- Activities for infants are not preschool activities "geared down." Infants are a specific age group that need specific activities.

Figure 21-9 Interactions between children and adults enhance learning. (Courtesy of Irene Sterling)

- Play *with* the children, not *to* them. Try to interact, not entertain. The adult can initiate the activity but should wait for the child to respond.

- Involve different ways of communicating in your social interactions: looking, touching, holding, laughing, talking, rocking, singing, and laughing. Give infants a lot of different social responses to learn.

- Be sensitive to infants' signals. If they are interested, they will laugh, coo, look, smile, and reach. If tired or disinterested, they may fuss, turn away, or fall asleep.

- *Talk* to the infant. Children learn talk from the moment they are born. The more language they hear, the more they will learn. Name actions, objects, and people.

- Offer new ways of doing things. Demonstrate how something works. Encourage persistence. Do not direct children as to the "right" way to use a toy; let them explore and experiment. (Obviously, if some danger is involved, use your judgment and intervene when necessary.)

- Be sensitive to variations initiated by the child and be ready to respond to them.

A child can use play materials either alone or with an adult. Adults should use judgment in the choice of materials presented to each age group. A toy that a two-month-old might enjoy might not be appropriate for a nine-month-old. When offering materials to the children, remember:

- Toys and materials should encourage action. Materials should not just entertain but elicit some action.

- Toys should respond to the child's action. When the child pushes or pulls a toy, the toy should react. The ability to control parts of one's world, to learn cause and effect, is an important part of learning at this early age.

- Materials should be versatile. The more ways a toy can be used, the better it is.

- Whenever possible, toys should provide more than one kind of sensory output. For example, a clear rattle lets the child see, as well as hear, the action.

Play and playthings are an important part of the environment. You should not be led to believe that constant stimulation is the aim. Even very young infants need time to be alone and to get away from it all. It is important to be sensitive to the infant's cues about feelings to help avoid overstimulation and distress.

The following are some activity ideas for infants (one to 12 months old). Remember that some activities are appropriate for many ages.

- Change the infant's position for a different view.

- Use bells, rattles, and spoons to make noise.

- Exercise the infant's arms and legs.

- Rub the infant's body with different textured materials.

- Put large, clear pictures at eye level for the infant to look at.

- Imitate the sounds the infant makes.

- Record the children's sounds, and play them back.

- Put toys slightly out of reach to encourage rolling over and reaching.
- Take the babies outside on warm days. Let them feel the grass and see trees and plants.
- Call the children by name.
- Play "Peek-a-boo" with the children.
- Hide toys and encourage the children to look for them.
- Attach a string to toys, and show the children how to pull them. (*Caution*: do not leave the child unattended with the string; they may get entangled.)
- Make puppets for the children to look at and hold.
- Let the children play with mirrors.
- Play games and sing, using parts of the body. Make up songs about feet, hands, noses, etc.
- Show children how to bang two toys together.
- Let the child feed him or herself. Give peas, diced cooked carrots, or small pieces of fruit to practice with.
- Play "pat-a-cake," "row-row-row your boat." Encourage the children to finish the songs for you.
- Listen for airplanes, trucks, cars, dogs, etc., outside, and call the children's attention to them.
- Roll a ball to the child and encourage the child to roll it back.
- Play "hide and seek."
- Play music for the children; encourage them to clap along.
- Have hats for the children to wear. Let them see themselves in the mirror.
- Read to the children. Point out the pictures; encourage the child to point to them.
- Let the children play with different textures.
- Put toys upside down and sideways. See how the children respond to the changes.
- Play pretending games.
- Show the children how to stack blocks.
- Make obstacle courses for the children to crawl over, around, and through.

- Let them play with measuring cups and spoons in water, sand, or cornmeal.
- Play "follow the leader."
- Make an incline for the children to roll objects down.
- Have the children set the table with plastic cups and dishes.
- Hide a clock or toy under a towel and see if one of the children can find it.
- Have purses and bags for the children to carry things in.
- Give the children puppets to play with. Watch how they use them.
- Let the children fingerpaint with nontoxic paint.
- Let them go barefoot in the sand and grass so they can feel the textures.
- Use old-fashioned clothespins for the children to put around the rim of a coffee can or plastic container. (Make sure that any sharp edges are filed down.)
- Encourage the children to help put their toys away.
- Let them practice opening containers, e.g., plastic margarine bowls. Put a toy in the container to encourage them to open it.
- Make toys for the children; be inventive! Let your imagination go. Remember that the toys should have no sharp edges and should be too large to fit in the mouth.

Infant activities grow gradually more and more complex as the children mature. Usually by 12 to 14 months, the child is walking and beginning to talk. An infant of this age is quite accomplished mentally. The infant understands that objects are separate and detached. The infant rotates, reverses, and stacks things, places them in and removes them from containers in order to further consider their separateness.

Projects for toddlers can be more complex in response to their increased mental and physical abilities. Small group activities can usually be tried with some success. When planning activities for and working with toddlers, remember that the activities should be kept as simple as possible. In addition, plan ahead. Anything that can go wrong will. Bring everything needed to start and finish the project.

Below are some ideas you might want to try with the toddlers. Watch the children, and see what you can think they might enjoy.

- Easel painting (one-color paint, use soap to help it come out of clothes).
- Have waterplay. Use measuring cups for pouring.
- Coloring. Use a limited number of large size crayons and a large sheet of paper. For a change, try covering the whole table with paper.
- Collage. Try using starch and tissue paper with paintbrushes.
- Fingerpainting. For a change, try yogurt or pudding. (Be sensitive to the feelings of those parents who don't want their children to "play" with food.)
- Paint on cloth pinned to the easel. It makes a great gift for parents.
- Music. Use drums, rhythm sticks, clapping games, simple exercises to music.
- Flannelboard stories. Keep them short and graphic.
- Bubble blowing. This should be done sitting down. Emphasize blowing through a straw. Use a cup with water and soap. Collect *all* straws; they can be dangerous if a child falls on them. *Note:* A small slit cut near the top of the straw prevents child's sucking up soapy water.
- Gluing. Use torn paper, tissue, magazine pictures, etc. Avoid small beans, peas, etc. that could be swallowed or put up noses.
- Play dough, made with salt, flour, and nontoxic color.
- Hand and foot prints.
- Body tracings.
- Paint a large cardboard box; cut shapes in the sides. Children can climb through the sides after they paint it.
- Go on a sock walk. Plant the seeds collected on a wet sponge. (More suitable for older toddlers.)

- Do simple shape rubbings. (More suitable for older toddlers.)
- Make simple roll-out cookies or use frozen dough for the children to roll out and cut with cookie cutters.

● CHILD'S PHYSICAL ENVIRONMENT*

As a student teacher, the new adult at your placement site, you will need to study both indoor and outdoor space. Try to answer the following:

- Are there as many play spaces at any one time as there are children enrolled in the program?
- Are the outdoor spaces safe?
- Are climbing structures high enough to challenge the children but low enough and cushioned underneath so falls will not hurt or injure any child?
- Are there enough wheeled vehicles for the number of children who want to ride them?
- Is there a "road" for the wheeled vehicles to follow?
  Are traffic rules made clear and enforced?
- If there is a sandbox, is there a cover?
- Are water tables set away from major play areas but close to the water supply?
- If a splashing pool is used, is it located near the water supply and sufficiently far from the rest of the play area to prevent children from being splashed who do not want to be wet? Is the pool drained at night and stored?
- Are there outside and inside water fountains? Are these at child height?
- If cups or plastic glasses are used, are they disposable or personalized to minimize the spread of germs?
- Are there child-sized toilets or potty chairs? Are they easily accessible to children learning to use the toilet? Are they out of the way of crawlers?

---

*This part of chapter 21 was contributed by Kathy Kelley, Director, Campus Child Care Center and Instructor in Early Childhood Education, Chabot College, Hayward, CA.

Are they disinfected frequently and always after bowel movements?

- If there a sink for washing hands by the diaper changing table? Is there a sink in the staff bathroom area for washing hands after toileting?

- Do staff wash their hands before preparing food?

- Are children directed to wash their hands before eating?

Infant and Toddler Language Development

It is never too early to read to children. Just the sound of the voice, the lilting quality of speech, and the caregiver's proximity aids ultimately in language acquisition. Initially, one may just point to pictures and name objects for the child(ren). Later, explanations can be expanded and feedback requested from the children. Although it is never too early to read, it IS important to gauge reading level and length of time spent on one activity, according to how the children respond. Ability to concentrate varies dramatically among children. However, it is true that very young children generally have very short attention spans. The ability to focus on a given object or activity increases dramatically in the first three years. Studies show that the "observing" child is participating and learning even while not actively involved in the current activity.

Heavy cardboard books, designed for small hands, are easily handled, excellent manipulatives, and a wonderful way for children to have their first experiences with "reading."

One surefire activity of interest to children of any age is music. Simply singing can create great excitement and provides tremendous opportunities for learning. Whereas speech is unpredictable, music uses words that are the same with every repetition (even with possible minor variations). Children more easily learn the words to songs within the pattern of melody, rhythm, and rhyme—thereby enhancing their language development. Kurkjian (1990) uses a broad musical repertoire to facilitate English language learning in her (mostly) limited English-proficient kindergarten class. According to Kurkjian, a daily ritual use of children's songs, with substitution of words, accomplishes the English teaching in this setting.

The use of concrete "props" at music time reinforces learning. There are hundreds of songs incorporating body parts and including movement components that bring forth peals of delight from the children. In the context of music, even the shy child is more readily drawn out and more willingly participates.

AWARENESS OF YOUR OWN NEEDS AS A CAREGIVER

We have taken the preponderance of this chapter to discuss elements of caregiving essential to the optimal development of very young children. Doubtless, in reading of and thinking about all these elements, you have wondered if and why children ever turn out all right. How can any caregiver provide enough, yet not too much, essential nurturance for good outcomes? Amidst wondering all this, you might wonder "what about me as the provider? How can I take care of myself?"

The childcare profession is notorious for low wages, long hours, and difficult assignments. Historically, providers have received little respect, few benefits, and not much money.

Although everyone talks about children representing the future, children can be the first losers in times of economic hardship. Although the importance of the early years are (by 1995, almost universally) acknowledged, we see poor allocation of resources to early childhood endeavors.

Fortunately, in recent years, more effort has gone into the area of early childhood development, the provision of child care, and the education of our children in the early years. Also fortunately, the profession of early childhood education is increasingly espoused by informed, educated, and intelligent providers. It is essential that we view ourselves as professionals, that we present ourselves to the world as professionals, and that we expect to be accepted as equals in a world of professionals. In order to accomplish this, we must first learn to value ourselves.

In your relationships with parents and co-workers, believe in your professional status and behave accordingly. Making yourself knowledgeable, keeping yourself interested, treating your infant charges and their parents as well as your co-workers sensitively and ethically will reap great rewards for you in how all these people respond to you in turn. Continue to educate yourself not only by participating in classes and reading but by remaining open to the different experiences of the different families in your center, the individual children, and the other staff members. A willingness to be aware of different needs and different capabilities in those around you is a hallmark of professionalism.

In the course of each day, as well as in a global sense, we as caregivers must learn also to take care of ourselves. Just as the infants must be given opportunities to balance activity with periods of rest, the providers must have opportunities to make choices in their activities, locations, and levels of stimulation. There are countless activities that potentially enhance any given domain of development. As the caregiver, select the one you can enjoy for that day. Children understand that the needs of their caregivers vary. They can (to a limited extent) moderate their levels of noise, activity, and curiosity if they understand that these conflict with the needs of their caregiver.

Perhaps most importantly, take your responsibilities seriously, but do not take responsibility for those elements of your job that you cannot change. Most every child care center has had dysfunctional families in attendance. Every center has its own challenges internally. Part of being a professional is the recognition of these challenges, the willingness to work to resolve what is in your power to change, and the ability to accept those aspects that are not changeable.

Parents

Approximately 50 percent of mothers of very young children now participate in the labor force. This means they have two jobs. As workers, they have responsibilities not only to their families but to their employers. This forces them to be highly dependent on "care" situations for their children. Care must be regular and dependable. When providers can be reliable and flexible, it is easier for parents to perform *both* their jobs well. In this sense, the child care is responsive to the needs of parents. Being there when parents expect and providing the program as represented makes for consistency.

Consistent Care

For the babies themselves, consistent and responsive care is more complicated. If possible, infants should have the same caregiver for most of their time in child care. If it is absolutely necessary to have multiple caretakers, the child should be well acquainted with any secondary caregivers before her primary caregiver leaves. Any person(s) involved with a group of children should have a thorough familiarity with the facility, its policies, and any program components.

Regular, routine care is essential for infants. Routines provide comfort and security for children, especially the very young. Learning and positive growth experiences are only possible when stress is at a minimum, and routine reduces stress for children. This does not mean that we should avoid novelty entirely! However, novel situations should occur in a context of predictability.

One of the most essential predictable elements must be that caregivers respond to the needs of the infants. Most early childhood experts agree that it is impossible to "spoil" a child before six months to a year of age (Spock & Rothenburg, 1992; Bowlby, 1982; Elkind and Weiner, 1978; White, 1975). White does "not believe you can spoil a baby in the first seven months of life." In fact, he strongly suggests, "you respond to your baby's crying in a natural way" (p. 11). Elkind and Weiner (1978) cite research studies indicating "that parents who respond to their infants' cries are likely to provide conditions of warmth and nurturance that will stop the crying, enable their children to feel secure, and make them less likely to cry or demand unreasonable attention in the future" (pp. 135–136). They go on to contrast the children of unresponsive parents, who tend to fuss and cry a great deal later on. "Babies whose cries are heard and responded to promptly and with loving care tend to become relatively undemanding, easily satisfied, and well-behaved infants" (p. 136). Bowlby (1982) talks about spoiling in relation to attachment. He states,

. . . no harm comes to [the child] when [the mother] gives him as much of her presence and attention as he seems to want. Thus, in regard to mothering—as to food—a young child seems to be so made that, if from the first he is permitted to decide, he can satisfactorily regulate his own "intake." (p. 357)

To echo these experts, a caregiver should respond promptly to calls for attention, attempt to discover the cause of discomfort or need; and, if there is no serious problem, comfort the child. Only if she clearly cannot make an effective intervention, after trying the above, should she allow a young infant to "cry it out" (White, 1975).

For older children, too, responsiveness can only assist in nurturing a positive developmental outcome. The basic sense of trust comes out of having one's needs taken seriously and having them responded to appropriately. Not only will responsive care create trust for the caregiver, but the child will feel valued and validated, resulting in a positive sense of self-esteem. Elkind, in a 1989 conference in Sacramento on "The Hurried Child," pointed out that the best way to prepare a child to face hardship is to provide a loving, nurturing environment in which she can develop self-esteem and trust in her caretakers.

Positive nurturance has even been found to affect physical growth. Caplan and Caplan (1979) note:

> All children need the security of knowing that they are satisfactory, that they are loved and valued (without any reservations). Interest, attention, praise, comfort, assurance—none of these slows down the growth process, and of themselves, none will spoil a child. (p. 105)

Responsive care applies not only to the crying infant. It is equally important for the exploring, curious, learning child. Thus, responsiveness also applies to awareness of developmental level, current level of functioning, and knowledge of appropriate tasks, objects, and expectations for given ages.

SAFETY

Probably the first element parents look for in a care situation is safety. Every parent and provider has heard countless times of the importance of "child-proofing" their space. Gerber (1971) advocates total noninterference with infants' exploration whenever possible—and this is possible, she says, only by providing a totally safe, child-proof environment geared to the developmental levels of the children.

Among the essential considerations in child-proofing are:

- Dangerous objects are not present or are locked up; these objects include

  sharp or breakable items;

  chemicals—drugs, cleansers, cosmetics;

  plastic bags, balloons, or other items that can cause suffocation

  Furniture is sturdy, and bookcases are fastened to the wall, so that the children learning to walk will not pull them down on themselves when using them for support, or attempting to climb them.

- Electrical sockets are plugged with child-proof inserts; electrical appliances cannot be pulled down or turned on by children.

- Heaters are safe to walk on or touch or are covered with a safety grate.

- Windows and doors are latched with child-proof latches.

- The facility is clean and well maintained; rugs are fastened down and regularly vacuumed.

- Staff do not drink coffee or other hot liquids which can spill on children or which children can consume.

- Staff are vigilant about activities of children, rather than conversing among themselves.

- Caregivers are aware of health hazards and infectious diseases and take routine steps to minimize the spread of illness. It is an undervalued health fact that merely washing hands each time a diaper is changed or a nose wiped can cut illness (or exposure to illness) by over 75 percent. Regularly wiping door knobs, washing toys, and minimizing the use of baby bottles in the play area, can likewise cut illness for both providers and children.

- Awareness of contagious illnesses and their symptoms must also be exercised by staff—with rigid guidelines for attendance by children exhibiting those symptoms.

- Lists of toxic plants should be readily available, particularly if the center has either indoor or outdoor plants within children's reach.

- Lists of parent emergency numbers, paramedics, and poison control centers should be posted in locations readily available and known to staff. Emergency treatment consent forms must be on file for each child, with guidelines about parental preferences.

- Lists of child allergies (if any) and medical conditions should also be readily available and visible to staff.

- Food service should take into consideration potential spoilage of dairy products if left unrefrigerated or if mixed with even miniscule amounts of saliva.

SUMMARY

In this chapter, we discussed why there is a need for quality infant and toddler day care. We also mentioned some of the programs about which there is evidence indicating there are no long-term detrimental effects. In fact, some of the research tends to reveal more positive outcomes of early care, especially regarding later social adjustment, and cognitive and language development.

Infant and toddler center routines and procedures depend on the philosophy and physical setting. Every center has guidelines for the caregivers' behaviors. Knowing guidelines and fitting quickly into center practice is a prime student teacher goal.

Learning takes place during each child's encounter with a caregiver. Caregivers can develop many skills for the child's benefit. Many action activities and experiences planned for this age group incorporate reciprocal responses from adults and play objects. The roots of independence and verbal ability develop as do individual preferences.

SUGGESTED ACTIVITIES

A. Read Burton L. White's *The First Three Years of Life*. Discuss the seven phases of development with your peers and college supervisor. Does the infant/toddler center where you are student teaching use some of the White's suggestions in its curriculum?

B. Read Magda Gerber's *Resources for Infant Educators*. Discuss Pikler's and RIE's philosophies. Does the center at which you are student teaching employ any of Pikler's and RIE's techniques?

C. If you have not worked in or done student teaching in an infant/toddler center, visit one for one hour. List all staff behaviors which protect children's health or safety. Report your findings to the group.

D. Research, through local licensing agencies, the number of infant/toddler programs that were licensed in the past year in your community.

E. In groups of three to four, discuss infant/toddler care for teenage parents. Decide what type of care would best suit the teenage parents in your community. Report your ideas to the class.

F. Obtain a job description for an infant/toddler teacher.

REVIEW

A. List three characteristics of a quality infant/toddler center.

B. Describe expected student teacher behavior during emergencies.

C. List ways a caregiver could promote learning when bathing a 15-month-old child.

D. List possible signals that indicate a child is tired.

E. Select the answer that best completes each statement.

   1. The factor that may best limit the spread of infection is

a. periodic caregiver screening.

b. change of room temperature.

c. handwashing.

d. the use of clean sponges.

e. the use of spray disinfectants.

2. When feeding a young child,

a. watch for signals that indicate the child is full.

b. make sure the child finishes a small serving.

c. he or she is expected to try a little of everything.

d. eat along with the child.

e. All of these

3. Telling infants that it is time to change their diapers is

a. ridiculous and silly.

b. difficult.

c. not important.

d. important.

e. important, but you should use baby talk.

4. An important part of student teachers' work in an infant and toddler center is

a. recording care specifics and asking when in doubt.

b. watching first, rather than pitching right in.

c. to let the regular staff do most of the talking.

d. to move quickly and efficiently.

e. telling parents how their children are acting.

5. If an infant or toddler is using a toy incorrectly,

a. show the proper usage.

b. show *you* can do it correctly.

c. leave the child alone if it is not dangerous.

d. talk about the right way to use it.

e. All of these

REFERENCES

Bowlby, J. (1982). *Attachment and loss, 1.* (2nd ed.). New York: Basic Books, Inc., Publishers.

Bredekamp, S. (Ed.). (1987). *Developmentally appropriate practice in early childhood programs serving children from birth through age 8.* (1987). Washington, DC: National Association for the Education of Young Children.

Caplan, F., & Caplan, T. (1979). *Second twelve months of life.* New York: Putnam.

Cost, quality, and child outcomes in child care centers. (1995). Washington, DC: National Center for Early Childhood Work Force.

Eisenberg, A., & Murkoff, H. E. (March 1995). What to expect: Is it potty time? *Parenting,* pp. 27–28.

Gerber, M. (1971). *Resources for infant educators.* Los Angeles: Resources for Infant Educators.

Keister, M. E. (1977). *The good life for infants and toddlers.* (2nd ed.). Washington, DC: National Association for the Education of Young Children.

Kurkjiian, J. Music for the Young Child. California Music Educators Association Conference, March 17, 1990, Oakland, California.

Spock, B., & Rothenburg, M. (1992). *Baby and child care.* New York: Dutton.

Weiser, M. G. (1991). *Infant/toddler care and education.* (2nd ed.). New York: Merrill/Macmillan.

RESOURCES

Ainsworth, M. D., Blehar, M. C., Waters, E., & Wall, S. *Patterns of attachment: Assessed in the strange situation and at home.* Hillsdale, NJ: Lawrence Erlbaum, 1978.

Barclay, K., Benelli, C., & Curtis, A. (May 1995). Literacy begins at birth: What caregivers can learn from parents of children who read early. *Young Children, 50*(4), 24–28.

Bronfenbrenner. (1979). *The ecology of human development: Experiments by nature and design.* Cambridge, MA: Harvard University Press.

Daniel, J. E. (September 1993). Infants to toddlers: Qualities of effective transitions. *Young Children, 48*(6), 16–21.

Elkind, D., & Weiner, B. (1978). *Development of the child.* New York: John Wiley.

Gelnow, A. (September 1994). Caregivers' corner: Shaving cream: Foamy fun for toddlers. *Young Children, 49*(6), 39.

Harlow, H. F. (1959). Love in infant monkeys. *Scientific American, 200,* 6, pp. 68–74.

Harlow, H. F., & Harlow, M. K. (1962). Social deprivation in monkeys. *Scientific American, 207,* 5, pp. 136–146.

Honig, A. S., & Lally, J. R. (1981). *Infant caregiving: A design for training.* Syracuse, NY: Syracuse University Press.

Honig, A. S. (March 1993). Mental health for babies: What do theory and research teach us? *Young Children, 48*(3), 69–76.

Hughes, F. P., Elicker, J., & Veen, L. C. (January 1995). A program of play for infants and their caregivers. *Young Children, 50*(2), 52–58.

Morris, S. L. (January 1995). Supporting the breastfeeding relationship during child care: Why is it important? *Young Children, 50*(2), 59–69.

Myers, J. (March 1994). Caregivers' corner: Keeping children's clothing dry at potty time. *Young Children, 49*(1), 15.

Spitz, R. A. (1945). Hospitalism: An inquiry to the genesis of psychiatric conditions in early childhood. *The Psychoanalytic Study of the Child,* 1, 53–74. New York: International Universities Press.

Spitz, R. A. (1945). Hospitalism: A follow-up report. *The Psychoanalytic Study of the Child,* 2, 113–117. New York: International Universities Press.

White, B. L. (Fall 1980). Should you stay home with your baby? *Educational Horizons, 59,* 1, p. 26.

White, B. (1975). *The first three years of life.* Englewood Cliffs, NJ: Prentice-Hall.

Wilson, L. C. (1995). *Infants & toddlers curriculum and teaching.* (3rd ed.). Albany, NY: Delmar Publishers.

APPENDIX

Chapter 3

NAEYC CODE OF ETHICAL CONDUCT AND STATEMENT OF COMMITMENT

Preamble

NAEYC recognizes that many daily decisions required of those who work with young children are of a moral and ethical nature. The NAEYC Code of Ethical Conduct offers guidelines for responsible behavior and sets forth a common basis for resolving the principal ethical dilemmas encountered in early childhood education. The primary focus is on daily practice with children and their families in programs for children from birth to 8 years of age: preschools, child care centers, family child care homes, kindergartens, and primary classrooms. Many of the provisions also apply to specialists who do not work directly with children, including program administrators, parent educators, college professors, and child care licensing specialists.

Standards of ethical behavior in early childhood education are based on commitment to core values that are deeply rooted in the history of our field. We have committed ourselves to

- Appreciating childhood as a unique and valuable stage of the human life cycle
- Basing our work with children on knowledge of child development
- Appreciating and supporting the close ties between the child and family
- Recognizing that children are best understood in the context of family, culture, and society
- Respecting the dignity, worth, and uniqueness of each individual (child, family member, and colleague)

- Helping children and adults achieve their full potential in the context of relationships that are based on trust, respect, and positive regard

The Code sets forth a conception of our professional responsibilities in four sections, each addressing an arena of professional relationships: (1) children, (2) families, (3) colleagues, and (4) community and society. Each section includes an introduction to the primary responsibilities of the early childhood practitioner in that arena, a set of ideals pointing in the direction of exemplary professional practice, and a set of principles defining practices that are required, prohibited, and permitted.

The ideals reflect the aspirations of practitioners. The principles are intended to guide conduct and assist practitioners in resolving ethical dilemmas encountered in the field. There is not necessarily a corresponding principle for each ideal. Both ideals and principles are intended to direct practitioners to those questions which, when responsibly answered, will provide the basis for conscientious decision making. While the Code provides specific direction for addressing some ethical dilemmas, many others will require the practitioner to combine the guidance of the Code with sound professional judgment.

The ideals and principles in this Code present a shared conception of professional responsibility that affirms our commitment to the core values of our field. The Code publicly acknowledges the responsibilities that we in the field have assumed and in so doing supports ethical behavior in our work. Practitioners who face ethical dilemmas are urged to seek guidance in the applicable parts of this Code and in the spirit that informs the whole.

NATIONAL ASSOCIATION FOR THE EDUCATION OF YOUNG CHILDREN'S CODE OF ETHICAL CONDUCT

Section I: Ethical responsibilities to children

Childhood is a unique and valuable stage in the life cycle. Our paramount responsibility is to provide safe, healthy, nurturing, and responsive settings for children. We are committed to supporting children's development by cherishing individual differences, by helping them learn to live and work cooperatively, and by promoting their self-esteem.

Ideals

I-1.1—To be familiar with the knowledge base of early childhood education and to keep current through continuing education and in-service training.

I-1.2—To base program practices upon current knowledge in the field of child development and related disciplines and upon particular knowledge of each child.

I-1.3—To recognize and respect the uniqueness and the potential of each child.

I-1.4—To appreciate the special vulnerability of children.

I-1.5—To create and maintain safe and healthy settings that foster children's social, emotional, intellectual, and physical development and that respect their dignity and their contributions.

I-1.6—To support the right of children with special needs to participate, consistent with their ability, in regular early childhood programs.

Principles

P-1.1—Above all, we shall not harm children. We shall not participate in practices that are disrespectful, degrading, dangerous, exploitative, intimidating, psychologically damaging, or physically harmful to children. *This principle has precedence over all others in this Code.*

P-1.2—We shall not participate in practices that discriminate against children by denying benefits, giving special advantages or excluding them from programs or activities on the basis of their race, religion, sex, national origin, or the status, behavior, or beliefs of their parents. (This principle does not apply to programs which have a lawful mandate to provide services to a particular population of children.)

P-1.3—We shall involve all of those with relevant knowledge (including staff and parents) in decisions concerning a child.

P-1.4—When, after appropriate efforts have been made with a child and the family, the child still does not appear to be benefiting from a program, we shall communicate our concern to the family in a positive way and offer them assistance in finding a more suitable setting.

P-1.5—We shall be familiar with the symptoms of child abuse and neglect, and know and follow community procedures and state laws that protect children against abuse and neglect.

P-1.6—When we have evidence of child abuse or neglect, we shall report the evidence to the appropriate community agency and follow up to ensure that appropriate action has been taken. When possible, parents will be informed that the referral has been made.

P-1.7—When another person tells us of their suspicion that a child is being abused or neglected but we lack evidence, we shall assist that person in taking appropriate action to protect the child.

P-1.8—When a child protective agency fails to provide adequate protection for abused or neglected children, we acknowledge a collective clinical responsibility to work toward improvement of these services.

P-1.9—When we become aware of a practice or situation that endangers the health or safety of children, but has not been previously known to do so, we have an ethical responsibility to inform those who can remedy the situation and who can keep other children from being similarly endangered.

Section II: Ethical responsibilities to families

Families are of primary importance in children's development. (The term "family" may include others, besides parents, who are responsibly involved with the child.) Because the family and the early childhood educator have a common interest in the child's welfare, we acknowledge a primary responsibility to bring about collaboration between the home and school in ways that enhance the child's development.

Ideals

I-2.1—To develop relationships of mutual trust with the families we serve.

I-2.2—To acknowledge and build upon strengths and competencies as we support families in their task of nurturing children.

I-2.3—To respect the dignity of each family and its culture, customs, and beliefs.

I-2.4—To respect families' childrearing values and their right to make decisions for their children.

I-2.5—To interpret each child's progress to parents within the framework of a developmental perspective and to help families understand and appreciate the value of developmentally appropriate early childhood programs.

I-2.6—To help family members improve their understanding of their children and to enhance their skills as parents.

I-2.7—To participate in building support networks for families by providing them with opportunities to interact with program staff and families.

Principles

P-2.1—We shall not deny family members access to their child's classroom or program setting.

P-2.2—We shall inform families of program philosophy, policies, and personnel qualifications, and explain why we teach as we do.

P-2.3—We shall inform families of, and, when appropriate, involve them in policy decisions.

P-2.4—We shall inform families of, and, when appropriate, involve them in significant decisions affecting their child.

P-2.5—We shall inform the family of accidents involving their child, of risks such as exposures to contagious disease that may result in infection, and of events that might result in psychological damage.

P-2.6—We shall not permit or participate in research that could in any way hinder the education or development of the children in our programs. Families shall be fully informed of any proposed research projects involving their children and shall have the opportunity to give or withhold consent.

P-2.7—We shall not engage in or support exploitation of families. We shall not use our relationship with a family for private advantage or personal gain, or enter into relationships with family members that might impair our effectiveness in working with children.

P-2.8—We shall develop written policies for the protection of confidentiality and the disclosure of children's records. The policy documents shall be made available to all program personnel and families. Disclosure of children's records beyond family members, program personnel, and consultants having an obligation of confidentiality shall require familial consent (except in cases of abuse or neglect).

P-2.9—We shall maintain confidentiality and shall respect the family's right to privacy, refraining from disclosure of confidential information and intrusion into family life. However, when we are concerned about a child's welfare, it is permissible to reveal confidential information to agencies and individuals who may be able to act in the child's interest.

P-2.10—In cases where family members are in conflict, we shall work openly, sharing our observations of the child, to help all parties involved make informed decisions. We shall refrain from becoming an advocate for one party.

P-2.11—We shall be familiar with and appropriately use community resources and professional services that support families. After a referral has been made, we shall follow up to ensure that services have been adequately provided.

Section III: Ethical responsibilities to colleagues

In a caring, cooperative work place human dignity is respected, professional satisfaction is promoted, and positive relationships are modeled. Our primary responsibility in this arena is to establish and maintain settings and relationships that support productive work and meet professional needs.

A—Responsibilities to co-workers

Ideals

I-3A.1—To establish and maintain relationships of trust and cooperation with co-workers.

I-3A.2—To share resources and information with co-workers.

I-3A.3—To support co-workers in meeting their professional needs and in their professional development.

I-3A.4—To accord co-workers due recognition of professional achievement.

Principles

P-3A.1—When we have concern about the professional behavior of a co-worker, we shall first let that person know of our concern and attempt to resolve the matter collegially.

P-3A.3—We shall exercise care in expressing views regarding the personal attributes or professional conduct of co-workers. Statements should be based on firsthand knowledge and relevant to the interests of children and programs.

B—Responsibilities to employers

Ideals

I-3B.1—To assist the program in providing the highest quality of service.

I-3B.2—To maintain loyalty to the program and uphold its reputation.

Principles

P-3B.1—When we do not agree with program policies, we shall first attempt to effect change through constructive action within the organization.

P-3B.2—We shall speak or act on behalf of an organization only when authorized. We shall take care to note when we are speaking for the organization and when we are expressing a personal judgment.

C—Responsibilities to employees

Ideals

I-3C.1—To promote policies and working conditions that foster competence, well-being, and self-esteem in staff members.

I-3C.2—To create a climate of trust and candor that will enable staff to speak and act in the best interests of children, families, and the field of early childhood education.

I-3C.3—To strive to secure an adequate livelihood for those who work with or on behalf of young children.

Principles

P-3C.1—In decisions concerning children and programs, we shall appropriately utilize the training, experience, and expertise of staff members.

P-3C.2—We shall provide staff members with working conditions that permit them to carry out their responsibilities, timely and non-threatening evaluation procedures, written grievance procedures, constructive feedback, and opportunities for continuing professional development and advancement.

P-3C.3—We shall develop and maintain comprehensive written personnel policies that define program standards and, when applicable, that specify the extent to which employees are accountable for their conduct outside the work place. These policies shall be given to new staff members and shall be available for review by all staff members.

P-3C.4—Employees who do not meet program standards shall be informed of areas of concern and, when possible, assisted in improving their performance.

P-3C.5—Employees who are dismissed shall be informed of the reasons for their termination. When a dismissal is for cause, justification must be based on evidence of inadequate or inappropriate behavior that is accurately documented, current, and available for the employee to review.

P-3C.6—In making evaluations and recommendations, judgments shall be based on fact and relevant to the interests of children and programs.

P-3C.7—Hiring and promotion shall be based solely on a person's record of accomplishment and ability to carry out the responsibilities of the position.

P-3C.8—In hiring, promotion, and provision of training, we shall not participate in any form of discrimination based on race, religion, sex, national origin, handicap, age, or sexual preference. We shall be familiar with laws and regulations that pertain to employment discrimination.

Section IV: Ethical responsibilities to community and society

Early childhood programs operate within a context of an immediate community made up of families and other institutions concerned with children's welfare. Our responsibilities to the community are to provide programs that meet its needs and to cooperate with agencies and professions that share responsibility for children. Because the larger society has a measure of responsibility for the welfare and protection of children, and because of our specialized expertise in child development, we acknowledge an obligation to serve as a voice for children everywhere.

Ideals

I-4.1—To provide the community with high-quality, culturally sensitive programs and services.

I-4.2—To promote cooperation among agencies and professions concerned with the welfare of young children, their families, and their teachers.

I-4.3—To work, through education, research, and advocacy, toward an environmentally safe world in which all children are adequately fed, sheltered, and nurtured.

I-4.4—To work, through education, research, and advocacy, toward a society in which all young children have access to quality programs.

I-4.5—To promote knowledge and understanding of young children and their needs. To work toward greater social acknowledgment of children's rights and greater social acceptance of responsibility for their well-being.

I-4.6—To support policies and laws that promote the well-being of children and families. To oppose those that impair their well-being. To cooperate with other individuals and groups in these efforts.

I-4.7—To further the professional development of the field of early childhood education and to strengthen its commitment to realizing its core values as reflected in this Code.

Principles

P-4.1—We shall communicate openly and truthfully about the nature and extent of services that we provide.

P-4.2—We shall not accept or continue to work in positions for which we are personally unsuited or professionally unqualified. We shall not offer services that we do not have the competence, qualifications, or resources to provide.

P-4.3—We shall be objective and accurate in reporting the knowledge upon which we base our program practices.

P-4.4—We shall cooperate with other professionals who work with children and their families.

P-4.5—We shall not hire or recommend for employment any person who is unsuited for a position with respect to competence, qualifications, or character.

P-4.6—We shall report the unethical or incompetent behavior of a colleague to a supervisor when informal resolution is not effective.

P-4.7—We shall be familiar with laws and regulations that serve to protect the children in our programs.

P-4.8—We shall not participate in practices which are in violation of laws and regulations that protect the children in our programs.

P-4.9—When we have evidence that an early childhood program is violating laws or regulations protecting children, we shall report it to persons responsible for the program. If compliance is not accomplished within a reasonable time, we will report the violation to appropriate authorities who can be expected to remedy the situation.

P-4.10—When we have evidence that an agency or a professional charged with providing services to children, families, or teachers is failing to meet its obligations, we acknowledge a collective ethical responsibility to report the problem to appropriate authorities or to the public.

P-4.11—When a program violates or requires its employees to violate this Code, it is permissible, after fair assessment of the evidence, to disclose the identity of that program.

Copyright © 1989 by the National Association for the Education of Young Children.

This Code of Ethical Conduct and Statement of Commitment was prepared under the auspices of the Ethics Commission of the National Association for the Education of Young Children. The Commission members were Stephanie Feeney (Chairperson), Bettye Caldwell, Sally Cartwright, Carrie Cheek, Josué Cruz, Jr., Anne G. Dorsey, Dorothy M. Hill, Lilian G. Katz, Pamm Mattick, Shirley A. Norris, and Sue Spayth Riley. Financial assistance for this project was provided by NAEYC, the Wallace Alexander Gerbode Foundation, and the University of Hawaii.

Reprinted with permission from the National Association for the Education of Young Children, *Accreditation criteria & procedures, 1991, revised edition.* Washington DC: NAEYC, copyright 1989.

National Association for the Education of Young Children

Statement of Commitment

As an individual who works with young children, I commit myself to furthering the values of early childhood education as they are reflected in the NAEYC Code of Ethical Conduct. To the best of my ability I will

Ensure that programs for young children are based on current knowledge of child development and early childhood education.

Respect and support families in their task of nurturing children.

Respect colleagues in the field of early childhood education and support them in maintaining the NAEYC Code of Ethical Conduct.

Serve as an advocate for children, their families, and their teachers in community and society.

Maintain high standards of professional conduct.

Recognize how personal values, opinions, and biases can affect professional judgment.

Be open to new ideas and be willing to learn from the suggestions of others.

Continue to learn, grow, and contribute as a professional.

Honor the ideals and principles of the NAEYC Code of Ethical Conduct.

EVALUATION OF STUDENT TEACHER COMPETENCIES

Student Teacher's Name: _____

Date: _____

Major classes yet to be completed. _____

_____

5= Extraordinary performance
4= Surpassed competency expectations
3= Displayed competency
2= Needs improvement
1= Unable to determine
0= not observed

Working with Children's Development of Cognitive, Intellectual, and Critical Thinking Skills

Student:

1. Stimulates children's open-mindedness by asking guiding questions which promote child thoughtfulness and discussion.
2. Helps child seek reasons, causes and effects, and relevant features of situation.
3. Has a "Let's-find-out" manner.
4. Accepts wild answers and promotes guessing.
5. Exhibits enthusiasm for experimentation and inventiveness.
6. Sees child interests and provides expanding experiences.
7. Plans activities involving sequencing, ordering, comparing, predicting measuring, similarities and differences, and other thought-provoking experiences.
8. Helps children express their discoveries and share them with others.
9. Can live with child misconceptions and provides additional child experience so child may change idea due to new evidence.
10. Models a thoughtful, critical thinking analysis approach in child-teacher interactions.
11. Provides hands-on materials when possible but uses photos or representations.
12. Additional competencies (list and rate).

Working toward Child Self-Control and Self-Valuing

1. States rules clearly and firmly.
2. Promotes conflict resolution.
3. Monitors all classroom areas.
4. Accepts anger and helps child express it in socially acceptable ways.
5. Preserves child dignity in guidance situations.
6. Gives child choice when choices exist.
7. Rearranges or restructures the environment to promote child success.
8. Issues abundant encouragement in a genuine way.
9. Helps children work out ways to solve their disagreements.
10. Observes constantly children removed or isolated to gain self-control.
11. Keeps own voice and emotions under control.
    Comments:

Working toward Children's Language and Literacy

1. Offers standard English usage.
2. Listens closely and responds with interest.
3. Promotes child expression of ideas and imagination.
4. Encourages child talk during child focus and discovery.
5. Skilled at offering a broad-based language arts program.
6. Can be described as a "subtle opportunist" in teacher-child discussions.
7. Uses open-ended questioning techniques.
8. Offers quality literary activities.
9. Notes child interest in alphabet letter writing, decoding, and reading words and provides appropriate expansion activities.
10. Plans a wide variety of activities to stimulate child expression.
11. Activities planned are full of child-talk.
12. Provides room settings and inviting materials where children explore language arts.
13. Understands child's home language background.

14. Offers culturally relevant activities.
    Comments:

Working toward Children's Socio-Emotional Development

1. Works to establish friendships between children and adults.
2. Reflects in actions and speech a valuing of individuality and diversity.
3. Promotes empathy.
4. Recognizes child accomplishments and verbalizes positive specific comments.
5. Names children and gives each status in the group.
6. Creates an atmosphere of caring and trust.
7. Creates an affectionate bond with group.
8. Accepts strong child feelings and sensitivities.
9. Displays ethnic diversity in planned activities.
10. Offers nonsexist curriculum.
    Comments:

Working toward Children's Creative Expression

1. Offers open-ended, nonstructured creative activities.
2. Is interested in child's process over product.
3. Displays child work or showcases children's creative expression.
4. Is creative in planning activities with imaginative as well as standard art, drama, music, and manipulative materials.
5. Plans well for child-adult clean-up of messy activities.
   Comments:

Working toward Child-Centered Environments

1. Creates aesthetic room areas.
2. Monitors prudent child use of equipment.

3. Works with children in room maintenance.
4. Plans inviting room centers.
5. Designs new room features coinciding with child interests and current themes.
6. Notices child comfort.
   Comments:

Working for Child Safety and Health

1. Offers activities promoting child health and safety.
2. Monitors children's whereabouts at all times.
3. Promotes health habits in bathroom areas.
4. Promotes hand washing when appropriate.
5. Strictly follows training guidelines for protection against bloodborne pathogens. Obeys disposal procedures.
6. Monitors for symptoms or signs of child illness.
7. Prevents child accidents.
8. Recognizes unsafe conditions.
9. Is familiar with room evacuation plan.
10. Reports all child injuries.
11. Knows medical conditions of attending children.
    Comments:

Professionalism

1. Keeps confidences.
2. Has appropriate professional image.
3. Has gained team member status.
4. Shares ideas, techniques, concerns at staff meetings.
5. Understands parent-teacher relationships.
6. Possesses a code of ethical conduct.
7. Is a responsible, dependable worker.
8. Completes tasks in a timely manner.
   Comments:

Overall Rating (using 1–5 scale) _____

Comments: _____

_____

_____

_____

Date: _____

Evaluator: _____

Circle One: student, peer, cooperating teacher, supervising instructor, other. _____

If you were to write a letter of recommendation for this student teacher for a prospective employer, it would state the following: _____

_____

_____

_____

SELF-EVALUATION QUESTIONS
(Primary Grade Teachers)

(From "Let's Be Specific." ACEI Primary Education Committee, 3615 Wisconsin Avenue, Washington, DC 20016.)

Do you really believe—

- in the great worth and dignity of human beings?
- that each individual is unique?
- that there is a natural push for growth?
- that a strong, positive self-image is essential to learning?
- that nearly every child is above average in something, that each child has a strength or talent?
- that every human being can change, and change for the better, as long as he lives?
- that education should produce self-actualizing, independent thinkers?
- that no one of any age does anything with determination and verve without being involved in it?
- that any piece of information will have its effect upon behavior to the degree to which an individual discovers its personal meaning?
- that whatever derogates the self—whatever causes a person to feel that he is less liked, wanted, acceptable, able, dignified or worthy—that thing undermines both mental health and learning?
- that the purpose of the school system is to eliminate failure?
- that each child must experience success most of the time?

If a teacher gives only lip service to the above statements, there needs to be an honest self-assessment of values and behaviors.

What can I do in a specific way to help children develop adequate self-concepts?

Do I make it apparent that I really like children—

- by showing joy at being with them?
- by accepting their ideas as worthy of serious investigation?
- by using a positive way of asking, inviting, receiving, and answering questions?

Do I talk so much that there is no time for children to express ideas?

Do I feel easy about taking time to capitalize upon children's ideas and knowledge—

- in open discussion?
- as recorded on experience charts (composite, individual plans, reports, evaluation of trips, science experiments, maps, graphs, and charts)?
- in practical and imaginative writing?

Do I ascertain what children already know about a particular interest or subject?

Do I differentiate instruction to meet individual needs—

- by flexible and interchanging group patterns and as much individualization as is possible?
- by using various procedures and materials?

Do I make assignments for all children from the same book or duplicated sheet?

Do I stimulate individual thinking by asking—

- What do you think and why?
- How would you solve the problem?
- What is your opinion?
- What do you think is going to happen in this story as you look at the pictures? The title? The chapter headings?
- How do you feel about the story?
- How would you end the story?

Do I provide a healthy environment with a reasonable amount of guidance, direction, and support so that there is intrinsic motivation to learn?

Do the children and I organize activities in which there is learning in cooperative endeavors?

Do I try to keep competitive activities to a minimum?

Do I help the child to be proud of any improvement, even if his work does not reach a standard?

Do I find ways to have a child indicate his own progress or improvement?

Do I show that I like or dislike a child by non-verbal communication (gestures, frowns, winks, reassuring pats)?

Do I show that I dislike a child by using sarcasm, negative criticism or labeling?

Do I set realistic goals for the age level of my group of children?

Do I help children set realistic goals for themselves?

Do I see that each child has a chance to display his work at some given time?

Do I arrange a parent-teacher conference for reporting progress and for finding out strengths and weaknesses of the child?

Do I write the parents notes or make telephone calls asking for information about the child, or expressing commendation?

Does a conference take place at times other than when the child has a problem or is in trouble?

Do I develop a child's diversified talents?

Do I make best uses of the child's resources?

Do I arrange an environment and activities so that each child can show where he can excel?

Do I ask parents to tell me about special aptitudes?

Do I let each pupil face up to his best and worst personal characteristics and come to accept his strengths and weaknesses?

Do I pigeonhole children as slow, bright, average, troublesome, show-off?

Do I evaluate skills and behaviors other than academic achievement?

- Creative talents, skills of communication, planning, decision making, leadership abilities, the making of wise choices, abilities having to do with mechanical and physical performance, giftedness in art, music, and social relationships.

Do I help children recognize talents and abilities of others?

Do I invite custodians, cooks, clerks, and other personnel of the school and community to tell about their work so that there can be appreciation of the value and dignity of all kinds of work?

Do we discuss occupations of fathers and mothers and how each person's work helps in the lives of others?

Do I encourage children to write thank-you notes to parents and school personnel expressing appreciation for taking time to talk or be with us?

Do I arrange for choice of activities and self-selection of materials and experiences?

- science corner
- library corner
- art at easels or murals
- modeling with clay, papier-mâché, dough
- listening post for music and poetry

- dramatic play—puppetry, role-playing, dress-up corners

Do I involve the children in planning and putting plans into effect? In evaluating programs?

Do I impose a teacher-planned list of activities to be neatly checked off one by one?

Do I keep those in at recess who have not finished the list of teacher-planned activities?

Do I take advantage of an individual's personal experiences and feelings with—

- a discussion of a current bit of news having to do with local, state or national events?
- a discussion of personal experiences of members of the class?
- questions sparked by looking at collections of rocks, plants, insects, animals, shells, nests?

Do I take time to relate children's personal experiences to book or story content?

Do I welcome to the classroom as resource persons parents and others in the community?

Do I relate all skill training to total learning so that a child recognizes his need for learning such skills?

Do I have a "show and tell" period, when some children may be placed at a disadvantage; a period that might encourage materialistic values?

Do I include time in the day's program during which children may have opportunity to tell of unique experiences, good books read, TV shows seen, records heard, of special incidents and trips, for showing prized possessions?

Do I teach understanding of cultural differences by showing strengths, talents, contribution of each culture represented?

Do I show favoritism in arrangement of groups in the classroom (ethnic, slow, fast, deprived)?

Do I like some of my pupils and only "tolerate" others?

Do I know that my observed behavior may determine attitudes of children toward each other?

Do I make rejecting comments to the children: "Isn't it nice that Bobby (troublemaker) isn't here today?"

Do I set up a situation in which a child is diminished before the group because of poor oral reading?

Do I display only the best work of the group?

Do I help children acquire general American English without making them ashamed because of dialects or grammar used in the home?

Do I embarrass a child by calling attention to mistakes of speech and writing before the group?

Do I make comparisons by giving gold stars and other rewards for accomplishments to the disparagement of some children?

Do I discourage children's efforts by changing their work myself?

Do I help each child attain success in his expected level of behavior and performance?

Do I show pleasure with a child's success because of what it does for him?

Does a child's success please me because it adds to my self-aggrandizement?

Do I help each child to become self-directed by looking at myself as a facilitator of learning rather than as a dispenser of information?

Chapter 4

Developmental Theory	Stimulus-Response (S–R)	Cognitive-Interactionist	Psychosexual: Interactionist	Maturationist
Theorists and researchers	Skinner Bushell Baer Resnick Englemann Karnes Miller & Camp	Piaget Kamii Weikart Lavatelli Nimnicht Hughes	Erikson Biber	Gesell Ilg Ames

Type of program exemplars	Preacademic/academic
	Behavior analysis
	  DISTAR
	  DARCEE
	  Ameliorative
		Cognitive-discovery
		  Montessori
		  Weikart cognitively
		    oriented curriculum
		  Nimnicht responsive
		  Tuscon (TEEM)
		  British primary/open
		    models
			Discovery
			  Bank Street
			  Educational Develop-
			    ment Center
				Discovery
				  Traditional nursery
				    schools
				  Play schools

Nature of content	Preacademic/academic
	  skills
	Skills/attitudes neces-
	  sary for cultural com-
	  petence
		Development of logical
		  thinking skills
		Development of internal
		  cognitive structures,
		  schemes, typical ways
		  of thinking, acting on
		  environment
			Social-emotional devel-
			  opment — of basic
			  attitudes/values and
			  ways of interacting
			  with others
				Development of whole
				  child

Expected outcomes	Child who is competent
	  to perform specific
	  operations that are
	  culturally requisite
		Child who confidently
		  acts on environment
		  and organizes experi-
		  ence; exhibits flexibility
			Autonomous, mastery-
			  oriented, powerful
			  child
				Child who has developed
				  his unique abilities

Nature of learning process	An observable, measur-
	  able change in behav-
	  ior directly transmitted
	  through teaching
		Learning through spon-
		  taneous active play
		Active construction of
		  reality, internalization
		  of external reality
			Active, reflective resolu-
			  tion of problems and
			  difficulties given social
			  constraints through ef-
			  fective ego functioning
				Nonoppressive, en-
				  riched environment
				  that is supportive of
				  natural development
				  and learning

Sequence of content	Nonstage
	  Simple → complex
	  Concrete → abstract
	  Logical analysis/task
	    analysis
	  Prerequisite skills
	  Component skills
	  Empirical skills
		Developmental stages
		  Sensorimotor
		  Preoperational
		  Concrete operations
		  Formal operations
			Erikson's Developmen-
			  tal stages
			  Trust
			  Autonomy
			  Initiative
			  Industry
				Following genetic given

Figure Ap-1 Theoretical framework for early childhood education curriculum models. (From Joseph H. Stevens, Jr. and Edith W. King, *Administering Early Childhood Education Programs.* Copyright © 1976 by Little, Brown and Company, [Inc.]. Reprinted by permission.)

Resolution of Hunt's problem of the match	Match by teacher of each learning task to child's level of skill development	Match by child of skill to learning task within environment structuring by teacher (At times match provided by teacher)	Match by child of skill to learning task within some structuring by teacher	Match by child alone of skill to learning task
Role of teacher	Assesses/diagnoses Prescribes objectives and task Structures favorable environment Teaches directly Reassesses Models Selectively reinforces	Observes Assesses child's interest and skill Structures environment in line with child's interests and skill Questions Extends Redirects	Observes Helps child to recognize problem situations Helps to resolve problems in socially appropriate ways Supports development of mastery and autonomy Structures environment	Observes Structures environment
Role of child	Respondent role—operates on environment in response to cues, discriminative stimuli	Active experimentation, exploration, selection	Active exploration and self-directed activity	Self-directed activity
Purpose of early schooling	Acceleration of child's development	Enhancing child's breadth and depth of total development	Assist child in resolving developmentally appropriate personal-social problems	Allow child to grow and develop at own rate
Scope of content	Basic skills Reading, Arithmetic, Science, etc. Attitudes Achievement motivation Persistence Delay of gratification	Physical knowledge Social knowledge Logical knowledge Development of symbolic function	Development of healthy attitudes and modes of interacting	Development of whole child Social, emotional, physical, intellectual development

Figure Ap-1 Continued.

WHAT ARE THE PREFERRED LEARNING MODALITIES OF YOUR STUDENTS? (Appropriate for use in elementary grades)

Test for Three Types of Learners

How do you determine whether a student is a   visual auditory kinesthetic learner?

To give the test you need:

1. A group of not more than 15 students as it is difficult to observe more than that number of students at one time.

2. A list of the student's names which you can mark as you observe their reactions.

> V–Visual learner
> A–Auditory learner
> K–Kinesthetic learner

Reactions to watch for:

VISUAL LEARNERS will usually close their eyes or look at the ceiling as they try to recall a visual picture.

AUDITORY LEARNERS will move their lips or whisper as they try to memorize.

KINESTHETIC LEARNERS will use their fingers to count off items or write in the air.

The student with a photographic mind will repeat things exactly in the order they are given and will be disturbed if someone changes the order.

GIVING THE TEST

Start by telling your students that you are going to see what kind of learners they are: visual, auditory or kinesthetic.

This test consists of pretending that the students are going to the store to get some items for you. First you will WRITE the list on the board, allowing students to watch you, but *they must not copy it*. Next, you will give them the list orally, you will not write it *and neither must they*. Then you will dictate the list ORALLY to them and *they will write it down*.

NOTE: Most predominant characteristic used as a symptom. One specific test or tests where student has the highest recall is a reinforcement of his native way of learning. However, the symptoms are the prime indication.

FIRST PRESENTATION

1. Write the list on the board while the students are watching. Do not let them write

   LIST

TOOTHPASTE	SOAP
KLEENEX	COMB
STATIONERY	

2. Allow students to view the list for approximately one minute while you observe their reactions and mark the symptoms after the students' names.

3. ERASE the list.

4. Ask, "Who would *like* to repeat the items for me?"

5. Observe that the visual learners will wave their hands enthusiastically.

6. Call on them to recite ORALLY, one at a time. Note that after a few students have recited, a few more timid hands will go up. These usually are auditory learners who have learned the list, *not from seeing* it but from hearing the list from other students.

7. As you notice a student's symptoms, make V, A, or K after his name.

Note: For younger students use list of

PENCIL	ICE CREAM	STAMPS
TOY	PAPER	

SECOND-PRESENTATION

1. Dictate the list ORALLY (no writing by either teacher or students). Repeat the dictation a second time, pausing for a moment after each item.

   LIST

FOLDER PAPER		RUBBER BANDS
TALCUM POWDER		NAIL FILE
NAIL FILE	or	POP CORN
COUGH DROPS		ERASER
SHAVING CREAM		BANDAIDS

2. OBSERVE that the visual learners will close their eyes to try to see the items. The auditory learners will whisper each item as you dictate it. The kinesthetic learners will use their hands to mark off the number of items or will write the words in the air.

3. Ask, "Who would like to repeat the list?"

4. The auditory learners will be the most eager to respond, although other students will try to repeat the items you have dictated.

5. Make the appropriate notations of V, A, or K after the students' names as you observe their reactions.

THIRD PRESENTATION

1. Tell the students to have pencil and paper ready to write the list as you dictate it orally. Tell them you will not count spelling. In fact, spell any words as you dictate if you see the spelling creates a problem.

2. After you have finished dictating the list, tell the students to rewrite the list, and to look at the one they have written from your dictation.

3. When they have finished rewriting the list, tell them to turn the paper over and WRITE THE LIST FROM MEMORY.

4. After they have finished, check to see which students have been able to repeat the list wholly or in part.

5. Notice that students who were unsuccessful in either the first or second presentation of the test are frequently the first ones to finish.

LIST

LIPSTICK		PEN
BANDAIDS		SOAP
RAZOR BLADES	or	CANDY
COUGH SYRUP		COMB
FOUNTAIN PEN		STRING

The test may be repeated, using numbers. Most students have a different form of recall for numbers than they have for words.

EVALUATION OF THE TEST

1. A teacher will have a better understanding of the individual differences of the students.

2. The teacher can encourage the students to find their natural way of learning. "Join it—don't fight it."

3. While all three types of learning should be developed a student should use his natural way to learn when he is under pressure of studying for tests, etc.

THE VISUAL LEARNER should realize that while he learns fast, he can forget equally fast. To strengthen his recall, it is good to develop the practice of writing and outlining the subject.

THE AUDITORY LEARNER will be benefitted by use of a tape recorder. The more he hears a subject, the more recall is possible.

THE KINESTHETIC LEARNER must *write* to recall material learned. Outlining material is a very effective method of strengthening recall.

A PHOTOGRAPHIC MIND is like a polaroid camera; the picture develops fast and can fade equally fast unless the emulsion is placed on the picture. In the learning process, the emulsion is to WRITE as well as LOOK. The photographic mind will often have a real problem in abstract thinking, especially in math. Seeing the picture in association with the abstraction often assists a student of this type.

Usually a person has more than one way to learn. He may be, perhaps highly visual, fairly kinesthetic, not auditory, or any other combination. However, all three types of learning should be developed as far as possible in each student. An audio learner should try to visualize what he hears. A visual learner should try to be more attentive in lecture programs or language laboratory work. A kinesthetic learner should try to listen and to visualize, but all three need to *WRITE*.

How can a teacher cover all three types of learners in one group? By presenting material in the three ways of learning.

VISUAL: Ability to *hear* and *write* what is *seen*.

AUDITORY: Ability to *recognize visually* and *write* what is *heard*.

KINESTHETIC: Ability to *hear* and *visualize* what is *written*.

Chapter 5

BIBLIOGRAPHY FOR UNDERSTANDING DIVERSITY

A caregiver's guide to culturally sensitive care for infant and toddlers. Sacramento, CA: State Dept. of Ed., P.O. Box 271, Sacramento, CA 95802-0271.

Jones, E., & Dermon-Sparks, L. (January 1992). Meeting the challenge of diversity. *Sparks, Young Children, 47,* 2, Washington, DC: National Association for the Education of Young Children. pp. 12–22.

Klein, T., Bittel, C., & Milnar, J. (September 1993). No place to call home: Supporting the needs of homeless children in the early childhood classroom. *Young Children, 48*(6), pp. 22–31.

Kotloff, L. J. (March 1993). Fostering cooperative group spirit and individuality: Examples from a Japanese preschool. *Young Children, 48*(3), pp. 17–23.

Mensher, G. B. (November 1994). A Harriet Tubman celebration: Here's how we do this annual mixed-age project. *Young Children, 50*(1), pp. 64–69.

Moore, E. K. (May 1995). Mediocre care: Double jeopardy for black children. *Young Children, 50*(4), p. 47.

No author. (March 1993). Educate yourself about diverse groups in our country by reading. *Young Children, 48*(3), pp. 13–16.

No author. (March 1993). Enriching classroom diversity with books for children, in-depth discussion of them, and story-extension activities. *Young Children, 48*(3), pp. 10–12.

Whiting, B., & Edwards, C. (1988). *Children of different worlds.* Cambridge, MA: Harvard University Press.

Wickens, E. (March 1993). Penny's question: "I will have a child in my class with two moms—what do you know about this?" *Young Children, 48*(3), pp. 25–28.

Chapter 6

To illustrate how the curriculum web expands into an integrative unit on Japan, Sharon Ridge, third grade teacher at Flood School, wrote the following general goals to guide her planning. She then included the introduction for the unit and listed some of the activities, field trips, and classroom books she would use.

Please note that these are NOT lesson plans but instead are used as guidelines by Ms. Ridge as she develops her specific daily lessons.

GENERAL GOALS

LITERATURE:	Identify and explain the theme of *The Big Wave.*
	Describe and illustrate the setting from *The Big Wave.*
LANGUAGE:	Recognize and use nouns and adjectives correctly.
POETRY:	Write a haiku and Japanese lantern.
MATH:	Demonstrate knowledge of liquid measurement (standard and metric).
	Use \$, ¢, and ¥ in problem solving and mathematical operations.
SCIENCE:	Demonstrate understanding of cause and effect: tidal waves and volcanoes.
	Demonstrate understanding of the water cycle.
	Recognize a variety of fish from the ocean life zones.
	Complete experiments using water: buoyancy, desalinization, evaporation, etc.

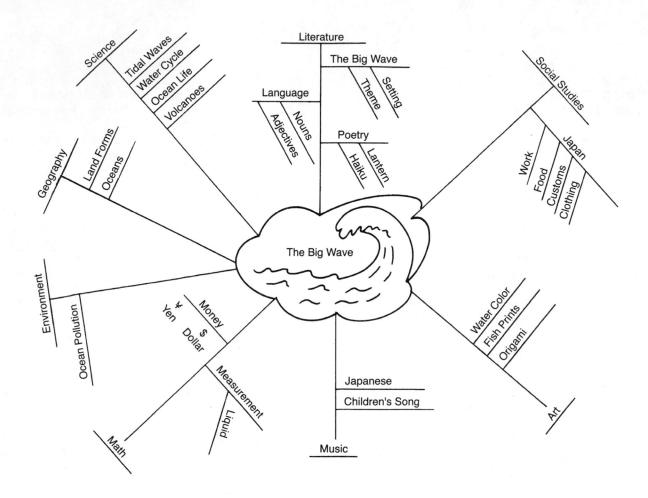

GEOGRAPHY: Locate Japan on a map; identify the ocean, islands, major cities.

Define landforms: island, volcano.

SOCIAL STUDIES: Demonstrate knowledge of Japanese customs, work, food, and clothing.

ENVIRONMENTAL: Discuss the causes of ocean pollution and environmental consequences.

ART: Paint a Japanese scene using water colors.

MUSIC: Learn three Japanese children's songs.

INTRODUCTION: Have students brainstorm (in small groups or with a partner) things that they already know about Japan and things that they would like to find out. Have groups or partners report and compile a whole class list.

INQUIRIES: Using Bloom's Taxonomy (these are just a few):

KNOWLEDGE

1. Label five oceans on a world map.

2. Define island and volcano.

3. Locate Japan on a map; identify the ocean, islands, major cities.

4. Name three ocean life zones or habitats and describe characteristics of each.

5. Memorize a poem about the ocean or ocean life.

COMPREHENSION

1. Report on an ocean habitat.

2. Prepare and deliver a television documentary which discusses disposal of waste in the oceans.

3. Express your feelings about whale hunting.

4. Explain the differences between two ocean life zones.

5. Identify animals and plants living in one of the ocean habitats.

APPLICATION

1. Draw and label your favorite ocean habitat.

2. Interpret the effects of pollution on ocean life.

3. Build a model of a volcano.

4. Dramatize a situation defending ocean life's right to a clean environment.

5. Interview an adult about what she knows about ocean life, tidal waves, volcanoes, Japan.

ANALYSIS

1. Examine the effects of oil spills on ocean life and birds.

2. Compare or contrast two ocean life zones.

3. Analyze the relationship between the density of human population along the shoreline and polluted waters.

4. Investigate the causes for tidal waves and volcanic eruptions.

5. Analyze problems caused by tidal waves and volcanic eruptions.

EVALUATION

1. Predict the potential ecological disaster resulting from continued ocean pollution.

2. Recommend ways to guard against ocean pollution.

3. Evaluate the decision to return to the fishing village (*The Big Wave*).

4. Explain and evaluate a Japanese custom.

5. Decide which Japanese custom you would like to practice.

SYNTHESIS

1. Write a science fiction story about exploring the dark zone.

2. Invent a machine to explore the dark zone or clean up ocean pollution.

3. Design an underwater community.

4. Explore the possibility of humans living under the ocean.

5. Create a haiku or Japanese lantern.

CLOSURE: Build a diorama depicting something you learned from this unit. Show and tell about your diorama to the first grade.
Field Trips: Moss Beach, 7 miles north of Half Moon Bay; Japanese Tea Garden, San Mateo or San Francisco

BOOKS:
The Big Wave, Pearl S. Buck
Sadako and the Thousand Paper Cranes, Eleanor Coerr
Crow Boy, Taro Yashima
Count Your Way Through Japan, Jim Haskins
Secrets of the Samurai, Carol Gaskin
Volcanoes, Seymour Simon
Earthquakes, Franklin M. Branley
Tidal Waves and Other Wonders, Q. L. Pearce
The Magic School Bus at the Waterworks, Joanna Cole
Water Precious Water, Project Aims.
Overhead and Underfoot, Project Aims

Chapter 7

BEHAVIOR MODIFICATION

In terms of behavior modification, it is important to be objective. The term has acquired a negative connotation that is unfounded. Everyone uses behavior modification, whether it is recognized or not, from turning off the lights when children are to be quiet to planning and implementing a behavior modification plan. In any plan, there are seven steps:

1. Keep a log of observations on the child. Really look at what the child is doing. Do this at least five times a day, for at least three days in a row, figure AP-2.

2. Read your observations; look for patterns. Is this child predictable? Does he or she usually have a temper tantrum around 9:30 a.m.? Does the child often fight with another in late afternoon?

3. Look for the reinforcers of the behavior noted in your observations. Does the child misbehave in order to get attention from the adults in the room? Do friends admire the behavior?

4. Decide on a schedule of reinforcement after finding the current reinforcer.

5. Implement the new reinforcement schedule. Give it time. Many teachers fail to use a reinforcement plan for a long enough period of time. Try a minimum of two weeks to two or three months. (Behavior that has taken two or three years to develop will not change in one or two days.)

6. Keep a second log of observations. On the basis of your study of the initial observations, analyze this second series and note whether your reinforcement schedule has worked.

7. Stop your planned reinforcement schedule. See if the child goes back to the former pattern of behavior. If so, go back to the second step and start over.

Look at the second and third steps. You have completed your observations and now you need to find the reinforcers of the observed behavior. The behavior must bring some kind of reward to the child. As the teacher, your job is to discover what the reward is.

Many student teachers fail to understand the nature of the child's reward system. You look at what an adult perceives as negative behavior (hitting another child, for example), and may decide to institute a schedule of reinforcement or a behavior modification plan without taking that first step, understanding why the child hits.

Study step 4; planning a reinforcement schedule. Look at the child in the sample log (figure AP-2). Assume that the description of behavior is typical of Maria's everyday behavior.

In your analysis of the log, what do you see? Three questions have been raised: Is Maria fairly new to the school? Does she have a hearing problem? Is she bilingual or does she have limited understanding of English? The answers to these questions come during the discussion of observations. Yes, Maria is new to the school. This is only her second week. No, she does not have a hearing problem, but she is bilingual. In fact, the cooperating teacher suspects that Maria may be less bilingual than her mother claims. What has reinforced Maria's behavior? First, she is unfamiliar with English. Second, her cultural background is different. Girls of Spanish background are often expected to be quiet, helpful around the house, and obedient to their elders. Certainly, this explains Maria's behavior, for she willingly helps with clean-up. What are appropriate goals for Maria? Assume that you and your cooperating teacher decide that the most appropriate goal is to help Maria feel more comfortable in the room and that adult approval is the most logical reinforcer to use. Your reinforcement schedule might start by greeting Maria at the door every day when she arrives. Smile at her and say, "Buenas dias Maria. It's nice to see you today." Take her by the hand and go with her to a different activity each day. (If Maria seems uncomfortable changing activities so often,

| Name of School: _____ | | Student Teacher: _____ Date: _____ | |

Identity Key (do NOT use real name)	Description of What Child is Doing	Time	Comments
M. – Maria T. – Teacher ST. – Student Teacher S. – Susie J. – Janine B. – Bobby Sv. – Stevie	M. arrives at school. Clings to mother's hand, hides behind her skirt. Thumb in mouth.	9:05	Ask T. how long M. has been coming. I bet she's new.
	M. goes over to puzzle rack, chooses a puzzle, goes to table. Dumps out, and works puzzle quickly and quietly. B. & Sv. come over to work puzzles they've chosen. M. looks at them, says nothing, goes to easels, watches S. paint. S. asks M. if she wants to paint. M. doesn't answer.	9:22 9:30	Her eye/hand coordination seems good. I wonder why M. doesn't respond. Ask T. if M. has hearing problem.
	M. comes to snack table, sits down where T. indicates she should. Does not interact with other children at table.	10:15	Is M. ever a quiet child!
	M. stands outside of playhouse, watches S. & J. They don't ask her to join them.	10:47	She looks like she'd like to play.
	M. goes to swings, knows how to pump.	10:55	Nothing wrong with her coordination.
	During Hap Palmer record M. watches others, does not follow directions.	11:17	Hearing? Maybe limited English? (She looks of Spanish background.)

Figure AP-2 Anecdotal record form.

stay with the activities she enjoys at first.) Introduce her to the other children at the activity she chooses. Take advantage of the fact that Susie is one of the more mature, self-confident children in the room, and quietly ask her to include Maria in some of her activities. Instead of allowing Maria to watch Susie paint, go to Maria with her painting smock, put it on her, and suggest that she try the activity. When she does pick up the brush and experiment with painting, compliment her action.

Do not worry about Maria's lack of knowledge of the English language. When Maria hesitates, use pointing and naming to help her. Accept the fact that Maria may always be a shy child; do not push her to be outgoing if that is not her nature.

Continue these activities each day. After a few weeks, make another set of observations. (You may not need this step; you may already see the difference.) Still, it is good practice to do the second observation just to check on your feelings. It is more than likely that Maria is already greeting you with a smile as she enters, and that she is beginning to play with Susie and some of the other more outgoing children.

Do you believe that changing Maria's behavior was easy? A more difficult example could have been chosen. However, cases like Maria's are common and many children enjoy a period of watching and listening before joining in activities. You should become aware of these common problems in order to become sensitive about your potential power in the classroom. The word *power* is deliberately being used because, next to the parents or primary caretaker, you, as teacher, are the second most important person in the child's life. You have a tremendous potential for influencing the child.

Aggression is defined here as any intentional behavior that results in physical or mental injury to any person or animal, or in damage to or destruction of property. Aggressive actions can be accidental actions, in which there is no intentionality; instrumental actions, in which the child deliberately employs aggression in pursuit of a goal; or hostile actions, in which the child acts to cause harm to another person.

Assertion is defined here as behavior through which a child maintains and defends his or her own rights and concerns. Assertive behavior reflects the child's developing competence and autonomous functioning and represents an important form of developmental progress. Assertiveness also affords the young child a healthy form of self-defense against becoming the victim of the aggressions of others.

Cooperation is defined here as any activity that involves the willing interdependence of two or more children. It should be distinguished from compliance, which may represent obedience to rules or authority, rather than intentional cooperation. When children willingly collaborate in using materials, for example, their interactions are usually quite different than when they are told to "share."

From Jewett, J. (1992). Aggression and Cooperation: Helping Young Children Develop Constructive Strategies. *ERIC Digest*, EDO-PS-92-10.

Chapter 11

EMERGENCY SHELTER PROGRAM, INC.
PARENT-CHILD EDUCATION CENTER

Developmental Checklist

Name: _____   Birth date: _____

	Present	Date Observed
I. Infants		
3 mo. Motor development		
Neck muscles support head steadily		
Moves arms/legs vigorously		
May move arm/leg on one side together		
On stomach, holds chest/head erect 10 seconds		
When picked up, brings body up compactly		
May bat at objects		
Reaches with both arms		
Perceptual development		
Follows slowly moving object w/eyes and head from one side of body to other		
Looks at fingers individually		
Stops sucking to listen		
Visually seeks source of sound by turning head and neck		
Hands usually held open		
Social development		
Smiles easily and spontaneously		
Gurgles and coos in response to being spoken to		
Responds to familiar faces with smile		

	Present	Date Observed
3 mo. Social development (continued)		
Protests when left by mother		
Cries differentially when hungry, wet, cross, etc.		
Cognitive development		
Begins to show memory; waits for expected reward like feeding		
Begins to recognize family members and others close to him/her		
Explores own face, eyes, mouth with hand		
Responds to stimulation with whole body		
6 mo. Motor development		
Rolls from back to stomach		
Turns and twists in all directions		
Gets up on hands and knees, rocks		
Creeps on stomach; may go forward and backward		
Balances well when sitting, leans forward		
Sits in chair and bounces		
Grasps dangling object		
May sit unsupported 1/2 hour		
Rolls from back to stomach		
Perceptual development		
Holds one block, reaches for 2nd, looks at a 3rd		
Reaches to grab dropped object		
Coos, hums, stops crying in response to music		
Likes to play with food		
Displays interest in finger-feeding self		
Has strong taste preferences		
Rotates wrist to turn and manipulate objects		
Often reaches with one arm instead of both		
Sleeps through the night		
Social development		
Prefers play with people		
Babbles and becomes excited during active play		
Babbles more in response to female voices		
Vocalizes pleasure/displeasure		
Gurgles when spoken to		
Tries to imitate facial expressions		
Turns in response to name		
Smiles at mirror image		
Disturbed by strangers		
Cognitive development		
Remains alert 2 hours at a time		
Inspects objects for a long time		

	Present	Date Observed
6 mo. Cognitive development (continued)		
Eyes direct hand for reaching		
Likes to look at objects upside down and create change of perspective		
May compare 2 objects		
Has abrupt mood changes; primary emotions: pleasure, complaint, temper		
9 mo. Motor development		
Crawls with one hand full		
Turns while crawling		
May crawl upstairs		
Sits well		
Gets self into sitting position easily		
Pulls to standing		
May "cruise" along furniture		
Social development		
Eager for approval		
Begins to evaluate people's moods		
Imitates play		
Enjoys "peek-a-boo"		
Chooses toy for play		
Sensitive to other children; may cry if they cry		
May fight for disputed toy		
Imitates cough, tongue clicks		
Cognitive development		
Uncovers toy he has seen hidden		
Anticipates reward		
Follows simple directions		
Shows symbolic thinking/role play		
May say "dada" and/or "mama"		
Grows bored with same stimuli		
II. Toddlers		
12 mo. Motor development		
Can stand, cruise, may walk		
Pivots body 90 degrees when standing		
If walking, probably prefers crawling		
May add stopping, waving, backing, carrying toys to walking		
Climbs up and down stairs, holding hand		
May climb out of crib or playpen		
Gets to standing by flexing knees, pushing from squat position		
Lowers self to sitting position with ease		
Makes swimming motions in bath		

	Present	Date Observed
12 mo. Motor development (continued)		
Wants to self-feed		
May undress self		
Perceptual development		
Reaches accurately for object as (s)he looks away		
Puts things back together as well as takes them apart		
Builds tower of 2–3 blocks after demonstration		
Uses hammer and pegboard		
Likely to put 1–2 objects in mouth and grasp a 3rd		
Cares for doll, teddy bear—feeding, cuddling, bathing		
Enjoys water play in bath or sink		
Social development		
Expresses many emotions		
Recognizes emotions in others		
Gives affection to people		
Shows interest in what adults do		
May demand more help than needed because it's easier		
May refuse new foods		
Resists napping, may have tantrums		
Fears strange people, places		
Reacts sharply to separation from mother		
Distinguishes self from others		
Cognitive development		
Perceives objects as detached and separate to be used in play		
Unwraps toys		
Finds hidden object, remembers where it last was		
Remembers events		
Groups a few objects by shape and color		
Identifies animals in picture books		
Responds to directions		
Understands much of what is said to him		
Experiments with spatial relationships: heights, distances		
Stops when "no" is said		
Points to named body part		
18 mo. Motor development		
Walks well, seldom falls		
Sits self in small chair		
Walks up/down stairs one step at time holding hand of adult or rail		
Enjoys push toys		
Likes to push furniture		
Enjoys pull toys		

	Present	Date Observed
18 mo. Motor development (continued)		
Enjoys riding toys to propel with feet on ground		
Strings large beads with shoelace		
Takes off shoes and socks		
Swings rhythmically in time to music		
Follows one/two step directions		
Perceptual development		
Demonstrates good eye-hand coordination with small manipulatives		
Will look at picture book briefly, turns pages but NOT one at a time		
Enjoys small objects (s)he can manipulate		
Social development		
Makes distinction between "mine" and "yours"		
Makes social contact with other children		
Smiles and looks at others		
May begin to indicate what (s)he wants by talking, pointing, grunting, body language		
Cognitive development		
Plays with blocks, can build tower of 2–3 blocks without model		
Can sort by colors, shapes (if exposed)		
Remembers where (s)he put a toy even if the next day		
III. Two-year-olds		
Gross motor:		
2.0 yrs. Runs well without falling		
Kicks ball without overbalancing		
Stairs: goes up/down alone 2 feet per step		
Jumps from first step, one foot leading		
Stops when running to change direction		
Propels self on wheeled toy with feet on floor		
Catches large ball by body trapping		
Jumps 8″ to 14″		
2.6 yrs. Walks several steps tiptoe		
Walks several steps backwards		
Walks upstairs alternating feet		
Stands on balance beam without assistance		
Throws objects and tracks visually		
Bounces ball, catches with both hands		
Bends at waist to pick up object from floor		
Jumps over string 2″–8″ high		
Fine Motor:		
2.0 yrs. Turns knob on TV, toys, etc.		

	Present	Date Observed
Fine Motor (continued)		
Turns door knobs, opens door		
Builds 3–5 block tower		
Holds pencil in fist		
Scribbles, stays on paper		
Puts ring on stick		
Strings 1″ beads		
Puts small objects into container		
Paints with whole arm movement		
Folds paper in half		
Removes jar lids		
Builds 7–9 block tower		
Completes simple inset puzzle		
Traces circle		
Paints with wrist action		
Uses spoon without spilling		
Holds glass, cup with one hand		
Makes small cuts in paper with scissors		
Places 6 pegs in pegboard		
Language and speech:		
Receptive:		
Understands most commonly used nouns and verbs		
Responds to 2-part command		
Enjoys simple story books		
Points to common objects when they are named		
Understands functions of objects, e.g. cup-drink		
Understands 200–400 words		
Expressive:		
Verbalizes own actions		
Uses 2–3 word phrases		
Asks what and where questions		
Makes negative statements		
Labels action in pictures		
Approx. 50-word vocabulary (2 yrs.)		
Answers questions		
Speech sounds:		
Substitutes some consonant sounds, e.g., w for r, d for th		
Articulates all vowels with few deviations, P, B, M, W, H, K, G, N, T, D		
Psychosocial skills:		
Sees self as separate person		
Conscious of possessions—"mine"		

2.6 yrs. (aligned with "Removes jar lids")

	Present	Date Observed
Speech sounds (continued)		
Psychosocial skills (continued)		
Shy with strangers		
Knows gender identity		
Watches others, may join in play		
Begins to use dramatic play		
Helps put things away		
Participates in small-group activity (sings, claps, dances, etc.)		
Says "no" frequently, obeys when asked		
Understands and stays away from common dangers		
Cognitive skills:		
Responds to 3-part command		
Selects and looks at picture books		
Given 3 items, can associate which 2 go together		
Recognizes self in mirror		
Uses toys symbolically		
Imitates adult actions in dramatic play		
Self-help skills:		
Can undress self		
Can partially dress self		
Gains mastery over toilet needs		
Can drink from fountain		
Washes/dries hands with assistance		
IV. Three-year-olds		
Gross motor:		
3.0 yrs. Runs smoothly		
Stairs: walks down, alternating feet		
Climbs ladder on play equipment		
Throws tennis ball 3 feet		
Pedals tricycle		
1 or 2 hops on dominant foot		
Can make sharp turns while running		
Balances briefly on dominant foot		
3.6 yrs. Stands on either foot briefly		
Hops on either foot		
Jumps over objects—6 inches		
Pedals tricycle around corners		
Walks forward on balance beam several steps		
Fine motor:		
3.0 yrs. Uses one hand consistently in most activities		

	Present	Date Observed
Fine motor (continued)		
Strings 1/2″ beads		
Traces horizontal/vertical lines		
Copies/imitates circles		
Cuts 6″ paper into 2 pieces		
Makes cakes/ropes of clay		
3.6 yrs. Winds up toy		
Completes 5–7 piece inset puzzle		
Sorts dissimilar objects		
Makes ball with clay		
Language and speech:		
Receptive:		
Understands size and time concepts		
Enjoys being read to		
Understands IF, THEN, and BECAUSE concepts		
Carries out 2–4 related directions		
Understands 800 words		
Responds to or questions		
Expressive:		
Gives full name		
Knows sex and can state girl or boy		
Uses 3–4 word phrases		
Uses /s/ on nouns to indicate plurals		
Uses /ed/ on verbs to indicate past tense		
Repeats simple songs, fingerplays, etc.		
Speech is 70%–80% intelligible		
Vocabulary of over 500 words		
Language and speech: (continued)		
Speech sounds:		
F, Y, Z, NG, WH		
Psychosocial skills:		
Joins in interactive games		
Shares toys		
Takes turns (with assistance)		
Enjoys sociodramatic play		
Cognitive skills:		
Matches six colors		
Names one color		
Counts two blocks		
Counts by rote to 10		
Matches pictures		

	Present	Date Observed
Cognitive skills (continued)		
Classifies objects by physical attributes, one class at a time (e.g., color, shape, size, etc.)		
Stacks blocks or rings in order of size		
Knows age		
Asks questions for information (WHY and HOW)		
Can "picture read" a story book		
Self-help skills:		
Pours well from small pitcher		
Spreads soft butter with knife		
Buttons and unbuttons large buttons		
Blows nose when reminded		
Uses toilet independently		
V. Four-year-olds		
Gross motor:		
4.0 yrs. Stairs: walks down, alternating feet, holding rail		
Stands on dominant foot 5 seconds		
Gallops		
Jumps 10 consecutive times		
Walks sideways on balance beam		
Catches beanbag thrown from a distance of 3 ft.		
Throws 2 beanbags into wastebasket, underhand, from distance of 3 feet		
Hops on preferred foot distance of 1 yard		
4.6 yrs. Walks forward on line, heel-toe, 2 yards		
Stands on either foot for 5 seconds		
Walks upstairs holding object in one hand without holding the rail		
Walks to rhythm		
Attempts to keep time to simple music with hand instruments		
Turns somersault (forward roll)		
Fine motor:		
4.0 yrs. Builds 10–12 block tower		
Completes 3–5 piece puzzle, not inset		
Draws person with arms, legs, eyes, nose, mouth		
Copies a cross		
Imitates a square		
Cuts a triangle		
Creases paper with fingers		
Cuts on continuous line		
4.6 yrs. Completes 6–10 piece puzzle, not inset		
Grasps pencil correctly		

	Present	Date Observed
Fine motor (continued)		
Copies a few capital letters		
Copies triangle		
May copy square		
Cuts curved lines and circles with 1/4 inch accuracy		
Language and speech:		
Receptive:		
Follows 3 unrelated commands		
Understands sequencing		
Understands comparatives: big, bigger, biggest		
Understands approximately 1,500 words		
Expressive:		
Has mastery of inflection (can change volume and rate)		
Uses 5+ word sentences		
Uses adjectives, adverbs, conjunctions in complex sentences		
Speech about 90%–95% intelligible		
Speech sounds:		
S, SH, R, CH		
Psychosocial skills:		
Plays and interacts with others		
Dramatic play is closer to reality with attention paid to time and space		
Plays dress-up		
Shows interest in sex differences		
Plays cooperatively		
May have imaginary playmates		
Shows humor by silly words and rhymes		
Tells stories, fabricates, rationalizes		
Goes on errands outside home		
Cognitive skills:		
Points to and names 4 colors		
Draws, names, and describes picture		
Counts 3 or 4 objects with correct pointing		
Distinguishes between day and night		
Can finish opposite analogies (Brother = boy; sister =)		
Names a penny in response to "What is this?"		
Tells which of 2 is bigger, slower, heavier etc.		
Increased concepts of time; can talk about yesterday, last week, today, and tomorrow		
Self-help skills:		
Cuts easy food with knife		
Laces shoes (does not tie)		

	Present	Date Observed
Language and speech (continued)		
Self-help skills (continued)		
Buttons front buttons		
Washes and dries face without help		
Brushes teeth without help		
Toilets, self, manages clothes by self		

VI. Five-year-olds

Gross motor:

		Present	Date Observed
5.0 yrs.	Stands on dominant foot 10 seconds		
	Walks backward toe to heel 6 steps		
	Walks downstairs carrying object without holding rail		
	Skips		
	Jumps 3 feet		
	Hops on dominant foot 2 yards		
	Walks backward on balance beam		
	Catches ball with 2 hands		
	Rides small bike with training wheels		
5.6 yrs.	Stands on either foot 10 seconds		
	Walks backward 2 yards		
	Jumps rope		
	Gallops, jumps, runs in rhythm to music		
	Roller skates		
	Rides bicycle without training wheels		

Fine motor:

		Present	Date Observed
5.0 yrs.	Opens and closes large safety pin		
	Sews through holes in sewing card		
	Opens lock with key		
	Completes 12–25 piece puzzle, not inset		
	Draws person with head, trunk, legs, arms, hands, eyes, nose, mouth, hair, ears, fingers		
	Colors within lines		
	Cuts cardboard and cloth		
5.6 yrs.	Builds tinker toy structure		
	Copies first name		
	Copies rectangle		
	Copies triangle		
	Prints numerals 1–5		
	Handedness well-established		
	Pastes and glues appropriately		
	Cuts out paper dolls, pictures from magazine		

	Present	Date Observed
Language and speech skills:		
Receptive:		
Demonstrates preacademic skills such as following directions and listening		
Expressive:		
Few differences between child's use of language and adults'		
Can take turns in conversation		
May have some difficulty with noun-verb agreement and irregular past tenses		
Communicates well with family, friends, and strangers		
Speech sounds:		
Can correctly articulate most simple consonants and many digraphs		
Psychosocial skills:		
Chooses own friends		
Plays simple table games		
Plays competitive games		
Engages in sociodramatic play with peers, involving group decisions, role assignment, fair play		
Respects others' property		
Respects others' feelings		
Cognitive skills:		
Retells story from book with reasonable accuracy		
Names some letters and numbers		
Uses time concepts of yesterday and tomorrow accurately		
Begins to relate clock time to daily schedule		
Uses classroom tools, such as scissors and paints, meaningfully		
Draws recognizable pictures		
Orders a set of objects from smallest to largest		
Understands why things happen		
Classifies objects according to major characteristics, e.g., apples and bananas can both be eaten		
Self-help skills:		
Dresses self completely		
Ties bow		
Brushes teeth unassisted		
Crosses street safely		
Dries self after bathing		
Brushes hair		
Ties shoes without assistance		
VII. Six-year-olds		
Walks with ease		
Runs easily, turns corners smoothly		
Gallops		

	Present	Date Observed
VII. Six-year-olds (continued)		
Skips		
Jumps rope well		
Throws overhand, shifts weight from back to front foot		
Walks length of balance beam:		
forward		
backward		
sideways		
Rides bicycle		
Uses all playground equipment:		
swings self		
uses merry-go-round		
climbs dinosaur		
swings by arms across ladder		
Writes name, address, phone number		
Reads "I Can Read" books		
Can count to 100		
Can retell story after having read it		
Understands concept of numbers 1–10		
Understands concept of 1 more, 1 less		
Can complete simple arithmetic problems (addition and subtraction)		
Can write simple story		
Can illustrate story appropriately		
Plays cooperatively with others		
Stands up for self		
VIII. Seven-year-olds		
Performs all gross motor skills well except for mature overhand ball throwing		
Knows when to lead and follow		
Knows what (s)he does well		
Knows when to ask for help		
Can draw diamond		
Draws house with straight chimney		
Enjoys card games such as Rummy, Crazy 8's, Hearts, Old Maid, etc.		
Enjoys organized sports activities such as kickball, soccer, baseball, track, swimming, etc.		
Enjoys reading		
Enjoys games such as checkers, parcheesi, etc.		
Willing to tackle new problems		
Eats well-balanced diet		
Solid peer relations		
Is responsible		
Writes legibly		
Can articulate most speech sounds without distortion or substitution		

	Present	Date Observed
IX. Eight-year-olds		
Able to use mature overhand ball throw		
If given opportunity for practice, can perform all gross motor skills well, including the mature overhand ball throw		
Enjoys organized sports activities, may want to play on a team		
Is developing a sense of industry, an "I can do" attitude		
Knows what s/he can do well and when s/he needs help		
Enjoys reading		
Enjoys games with rules		
Is able to master pronunciation of all phonemes and most graphemes of the English language		
Enjoys word play games such as puns and double entendre		
Has solid peer relationships		
Is able to assume responsibility for own actions		
Willing to try out new activities		
X. Nine-year-olds		
In addition to characteristics of 8-year-olds listed above, 9-year-olds are usually solidly in the Piagetian stage of concrete operations. As such they:		
Can master all arithmetic operations		
Understand concepts of reversibility		
Can think logically if provided with concrete situations and/or manipulatives		
Are able to conserve mass, length, area, weight, among other operations		
Can form classification hierarchies		
Are able to transfer learning from one situation to another		
Physically, some 9-year-olds, especially girls, may be entering a growth spurt characterized by rapid long-bone growth		
Some early development of secondary sex characteristics also possible		
Language development sees:		
Understanding of negatively worded questions, such as "The only factor NOT in the sequence of events . . ." "Which one of the following is NOT . . ."		
and double pronoun referrents such as "She baked her the birthday cake." "He accidentally hit him with the ball."		
Socially, 9-year-olds:		
Enjoys the company of their peers		
Often group into informal "clubs"		

INDIVIDUAL LEARNING PLAN FOR ALAN

1. Activity title: Watching a Live Bird
2. Curriculum area: Science and language arts (vocabulary)
3. Materials needed: Live bird in cage. Table or counter for cage.
4. Location and set-up of activity: Bird cage with parakeet will be set up in corner of room where two counters come together. This will keep cage safer than if placed on a table and counter is at eye level for children so they can see easily.
5. Number of children and adults: Alan and student teacher.
6. Preparation: Talk about pets with Alan. (Ask him what pet he has. I know he has a dog and two cats.) Ask him if he knows what a bird is. Tell him I am going to have a surprise for him.
7. Specific behavioral objective: Alan will watch the parakeet for at least three minutes. He will be able to call the bird a parakeet and say its name, Ernie. (Long-range objective could be to have Alan feed the bird and give him water.)
8. Developmental skills necessary for success: Willingness to watch and listen quietly.
9. Procedure: When Alan comes to school Tuesday, greet him at door; remind him about the surprise you promised. Take his hand; lead him to corner where bird cage is sitting. Ask Alan if he knows what is in the cage. Anticipate that he will know "bird." Tell him that this bird is called a parakeet and that the bird's name is Ernie. Ask him to repeat "parakeet" and "Ernie." Ask him what color Ernie is. Anticipate that he knows the color green. If he doesn't say green, remind him that Ernie is green. See what else is green and remind Alan that he knows what color green is—green like the grass, for example, or green like Tony's shirt, etc.
10. Discussion: Covered under procedure, I think.
11. Apply: Later in the day, ask Alan what kind of bird Ernie is. Ask him Ernie's name. (I anticipate that Alan will be intrigued with the bird and that he will want to come back over and over to watch Ernie, if only for a minute or two. Each time, I will name the type of bird and repeat Ernie's name. I think Alan will know both "parakeet" and "Ernie" before he goes home.
12. Clean-up: Not necessary. I will keep the bird cage cleaned.
13. Terminating statement: Probably not necessary. Otherwise, I'll remind Alan that Ernie is a parakeet and suggest that he might want to see a book about birds (I've brought several in) or play the lotto game.
14. Transition: See #13.
15. Evaluation: Activity, Teacher, Child: I am hoping, of course, that this will be a great success for all the children but especially for Alan. I'll write the evaluation after Ernie is brought in.

Chapter 12

THE AUDITORY LEARNER

1. His attention to visual tasks may be poor.
2. He seems bored or restless during silent filmstrips.
3. He attends more to sound than to the screen during films.
4. He may have poor handwriting.
5. His drawing or other artwork is poor.
6. Work copied from the board may often turn out badly.
7. He may have reversals or inversions in writing, or he may leave out whole words or parts of words.
8. He might prefer word games, riddles, and noisy or active toys and games to more visually oriented games, like checkers, other board games, or puzzles.
9. He may rub his eyes or show other signs of eye problems, or complain that his eyes bother him.
10. He may do poorly on written spelling, but he may be a better speller in spelling bees.
11. He may not remember much of what he has read, and he does better on material discussed in class.
12. He may read below grade level, or below the level expected for his general ability.
13. His comprehension is probably better on oral reading than on silent reading.
14. His math errors may show consistent patterns, inattention to signs, confusion of similar numerals.
15. He may do poorly on map activities.
16. He may not seem to observe things others comment on.
17. He may do poorly on sight words and flashcard drills.
18. He may be poor at visual word attack so that he confuses words which look similar.

19. He may do poorly on matching activities, but given the chance, will sort through a stack of dittoes for the clearest copy.
20. He probably dislikes ditto activities.
21. He may often skip words or even whole lines in reading and uses his finger as a pointer whenever possible.
22. He may enjoy memory work.
23. He may be a mumbler.
24. He may have trouble identifying "how many" without counting.
25. He seems brighter than his IQ test scores or achievement scores would lead you to believe.
26. His papers are probably poorly organized; often he writes the answers in the wrong blank on workbook pages, or can't find where the answers go.
27. He may seem lost on material requiring a separate answer sheet.
28. He has trouble locating words in the dictionary or index and has trouble telling time.

THE VISUAL LEARNER

1. He may seem to ignore verbal directions.
2. Questions or instructions must often be repeated, frequently in different words.
3. He may frequently have a "blank" expression on his face, or may seem to daydream during classes which are primarily verbal.
4. He may substitute gestures for words, or may seem, by his gestures, to be literally groping for a word.
5. He may have poor speech, in terms of either low vocabulary, poor flexibility of vocal patterns or articulation.
6. He may watch the teacher's lips closely, and may be distressed when he cannot see her face, such as when she is talking while writing on the blackboard or discussing a filmstrip in a darkened room.
7. He often looks to see what everyone else is doing before following instructions.
8. He may play the TV, tape or record player too loudly.
9. He may say "What?" or "Huh?" often.
10. He seems to misunderstand often.
11. He often speaks too loudly, though he may dislike speaking before the group or listening to others.
12. He prefers to "Show" aspects of "Show and Tell", and prefers filmstrips to tapes.
13. He may have trouble discriminating similar words or sounds that he hears. Bill, bell, bull, and ball may all sound the same to him, and he certainly cannot discriminate pin from pen.
14. He may do poorly in phonics-based activities.
15. He often can't remember information given verbally.
16. He may describe things in terms of visual stimuli, and omit auditory descriptive material.

17. He prefers visual games, such as board games, or active games and toys to those which involve listening or speaking.
18. His speech may be inappropriate for his age; or he may not have learned the language patterns of his home (even if the home patterns are not Standard American English).
19. He may have trouble associating sounds and objects.
20. He may substitute words similar in sound or meaning for one another.
21. He seems to know few words' synonyms commonly known by children at his age or ability level.
22. He may "get lost" in role verbalizations, even the alphabet, rote counting, or memorizing his times tables.
23. He may not enjoy music as much as he enjoys artwork.
24. He may have a speech defect; if so, it is probably an articulation problem.
25. He may respond less rapidly than his peers to unusual sounds: a faroff siren; a record player, or musical instrument in a nearby classroom.

MOTOR CONTROL

Definition: ability to control the motor or physical movement made in response to a visual, auditory, or tactile stimulus.

Fine Motor Control: the ability to coordinate fine motor muscles such as those required in eye-hand tasks, coloring, drawing, printing, writing, etc.

Gross Motor Control: the development and awareness of large muscle activity. Most common areas of development are:

1. Rolling
2. Sitting
3. Crawling
4. Walking
5. Running
6. Throwing
7. Jumping
8. Skipping
9. Dancing
10. Self-identification
11. Muscular strength

Resource for help: Remediation of Learning Disabilities by Robert E. Valett

ATTENTION

Definition: the ability to attend to or heed the situation in which one is currently involved.

Characteristics of the child with an attention disability:

1. Easily distracted by noise.
2. Hyperactive—"can't sit still."
3. Gets overly excited when there is a change in daily routine.
4. Has difficulty making transitions from one activity to another.
5. Goes from one activity to another when there is "free choice."
6. Doesn't complete work.
7. Is more upset by physiological distress than other children (hunger, physical discomfort).

DIRECTIONALITY AND SPATIAL RELATIONS

Definition: the ability to know right from left, up from down, forward from backward, and directional orientation.

Characteristics of the child with directionality and spatial relations disabilities:

1. Does not know left from right.
2. May have difficulty copying.
3. Has difficulty mastering concepts dependent upon correct sequence: reading, writing, mathematics, (place value), geography (maps), etc.
4. Lack of uniformity in writing and spacing.
5. Letters may be placed haphazardly on paper.
6. Shows reversals and incorrect sequencing of letters in reading and spelling.
7. May get lost easily; may often appear disoriented.
8. May not know location of parts of his body; may have difficulty putting on clothes or drawing figures accurately.

VERBAL EXPRESSION

Definition: the ability to understand words, to express oneself verbally, and to articulate words clearly.

Characteristics of the child with verbal expression disability:

1. Shy, seldom talks in class.
2. Tends to respond with one-word answers.
3. Cannot tell what has happened in a story he has just read.
4. When the child talks, he expresses few ideas.

CONCEPTUAL SKILLS

Definition: the ability to acquire and utilize general information from education and experience.

Characteristics of the child with conceptual skills disabilities:

1. Is unable to use concepts involving time.

2. Cannot sort pictures into categories, such as farm animals, machinery, plants, etc.
3. Cannot easily classify objects verbally (e.g., name all the animals you can).
4. Is unable to use concepts relating to feelings and emotional reactions of people.
5. Cannot easily determine similarities and differences existing between objects (e.g., How are a pig and a cow alike? How are they different?).

BEHAVIOR

Characteristics of the child with behavioral disabilities:

1. Aggressive, irritable, then remorseful.
2. Impulsive—lacks self-control, touches and handles things.
3. Withdraws—on the outskirts of activities.
4. Easily excitable, overreacts.
5. Erratic behavior. Quick changes of emotional response.
6. Hyperactive.
7. Hypoactive.
8. Short attention span compared to peers.
9. Easily distracted by noise, color, movement, activity, detail.
10. Cannot complete work independently.
11. Inappropriate or extreme laughter, tears, anger.
12. Defensiveness: denies responsibility, argumentative about obligations, rules; overreacts to demands for compliance.
13. Shows frequent frustration, irritation, reducing ability to cope with daily tasks.
14. Requires more than usual amount of individual help and attention in order to learn.
15. Attention jumps from one thought to another.
16. Repeats verbally when no longer appropriate (perseverates).

SUGGESTED READINGS

Annual editions. (1995). *Educating Exceptional Children 95/96*. Guilford, CT: The Dushkin Publishing Group.

Cook, E. R., Tessier, A., & Armbruster, B. V. (1987). *Adapting early childhood curricula for children with special needs*. Ohio: Merrill Publishing Co.

Fallon, N. H., with McGovern, J. E. (1978). *Young children with special needs*. Columbus: Charles E. Merrill Publishing Co.

Gearheart, B. R., Weishahn, M. W., & Gearheart, C. J. (1996). *The exceptional student in the regular classroom.* (6th ed.). New York: Merrill/Macmillan.

Landau, S., & McAninch, C. (May 1993). Research in review. Young children with attention deficits. *Young Children, 48*(4), pp. 49–58.

Mazzocco, M. M., & O'Conner, R. A. (November 1993). Fragile X syndrome: A guide for teachers of young children. *Young Children, 49*(1), pp. 73–77.

Raver, A. S. (1991). *Strategies for teaching at-risk and handicapped infants and toddlers*. New York: Merrill Publishing Co.

Rose, D. F., & Smith, B. J. (May 1993). Public policy report, Preschool mainstreaming: Attitude barriers and strategies for addressing them. *Young Children, 48*(4), pp. 59–66.

Watt, M. R., Roberts, J. E., & Zeisel, S. A. (November 1993). Ear infections in young children: The role of the early childhood educator. *Young Children, 49*(1), pp. 65–72.

Chapter 13

SUGGESTED READINGS

Berger, E. H. (1990). *Parents as partners in education.* (3rd ed.). Columbus, OH: Merrill/Macmillan.

Ediger, M. (1981). *Helping your child achieve in school.* ERIC Document, ED 200 314.

Gazda, G. M., et al. (1977). *Human relations development: A manual for educators.* Boston: Allyn and Bacon, Inc.

Knitzer, J., & Page, S. (May 1996). Public policy. Young children and families: The view from the states. *Young Children, 51*(4), 51–55.

National School Public Relations Association. (1973). *School volunteers: Districts recruit aides to meet rising costs, student needs.* Arlington, VA.

Chapter 14

SUGGESTED READINGS

Banks, J. A. (1979). *Teaching strategies for ethnic studies.* Boston, MA: Allyn and Bacon, Inc.

Byler, M. G. (1973). *American Indian authors for young readers.* New York: Association on American Indian Affairs.

Carkhuff, R. R., Berenson, D. H., & Pierce, R. M. (1973). *The skills of teaching: Interpersonal skills.* Amherst, MA: Human Resource Development Press.

Chesser, B., DeFrain, J., & Stinnett, N. (1979). *Building family strengths.* Lincoln, NE: University of Nebraska Press.

Fast, J. (1970). *Body language.* New York: Evans & Co.

Gazda, G. M., et al. (1977). *Human relations development: A manual for educators.* Boston: Allyn and Bacon, Inc.

Grossman, A. S. (January 1976). Children of working mothers. *Monthly Labor Review,* pp. 30–33.

Hayghe, H. (May 1976). Families and the rise of working wives—An overview. *Monthly Labor Review,* pp. 12–19.

Johnson, B. L. (April 1979). Special labor force reports summaries: Changes in marital and family characteristics of workers, 1970–1978. *Monthly Labor Review,* pp. 49–52.

Katz, W. L. (1968). *Teacher's guide to American Negro history.* New York: Quadrangle.

Kenniston, K. (1979). All our children: The American family under pressures. In *The Status of the American Family: Policies, Facts, Opinions, and Issues.* Washington, DC: National Education Association.

Kim, B. C. (1978). *The Korean American child at school and at home.* Urbana, IL: University of Illinois, School of Social Work.

Klein, T., Bittel, C., & Milnar, J. (September 1993). No place to call home: Supporting the needs of homeless children in the early childhood classroom. *Young Children, 48*(6), pp. 22–31.

Kotloff, L. J. (March 1993). Fostering cooperative group spirit and individuality: Examples from a Japanese preschool. *Young Children, 48*(3), pp. 17–23.

Linskie, R., & Rosenburg, H. (1976). *A handbook for multicultural studies in elementary schools: Chicano, Black, Asian, and Native American.* San Francisco: R & E Research Associates.

Mensher, G. B. (November 1994). A Harriet Tubman celebration: Here's how we do this annual mixed-age project. *Young Children, 50*(1), pp. 64–69.

Moore, E. K. (May 1995). Mediocre care: Double jeopardy for black children. *Young Children, 50*(4), p. 47.

No author. (March 1993). Educate yourself about diverse groups in our country by reading. *Young Children, 48*(3), pp. 13–16.

No author. (March 1993). Enriching classroom diversity with books for children, in-depth discussion of them, and story-extension activities. *Young Children, 48*(3), pp. 10–12.

The schooling of Native America. (1978). Washington, DC: American Association of Colleges for Teacher Education.

The state of Black America, 1979. (1979). New York: National Urban League.

Tachiki, A., Wong, E., Odo, F., & Wong, B. (1971). *Roots: An Asian American reader*. Los Angeles: University of California, Asian American Studies Center.

Tiedt, P. L., & Tiedt, I. M. (1979). *Multicultural teaching: A handbook of activities, information and resources*. Boston: Allyn and Bacon, Inc.

U.S. Department of the Interior (Bureau of Indian Affairs). *Indian bibliography*. Washington, DC: U.S. Government Printing Office.

Wickens, E. (March 1993). Penny's question: "I will have a child in my class with two moms—what do you know about this?" *Young Children, 48*(3), pp. 25–28.

Wigginton, E. (Ed.). The Foxfire Books. New York: Doubleday, 1972; Anchor, 1973, 1975, 1977, 1979.

Yankelovich, Skelly, & White, Inc. (1977). *Raising children in a changing society. The General Mills American family report, 1976–77*. Minneapolis: General Mills.

Yankelovich, Skelly, & White, Inc. (1979). *Family health in an era of stress. The General Mills American family report, 1978–79*. Minneapolis: General Mills.

Chapter 15

SAMPLE RATING SHEET

Student teacher's name _____   Rater's name _____

Date _____   School _____

STUDENT TEACHER EFFECTIVENESS SCALE

Excellent 1	Above Average 2	Average or Adequate 3	Needs Improvement 4	Unacceptable 5

A. Feeling Tone

Warm _____	Cool
Friendly _____	Withdrawn
Supportive _____	Authoritarian
Interacts often _____	Interacts rarely
Accepts dependency behavior _____	Does not accept dependency behavior
Physical contact often _____	Rare physical contact

B. Quality of Presentation and/or Interactions

Organized _____	Seems disorganized
Enthusiastic _____	Neutral
Flexible _____	Rigid
Clear _____	Vague
Reasonable age level _____	Unreasonable age level
Appropriate child expectations _____	Inappropriate expectations
Promotes problem solving _____	Furnishes all answers
Motivates _____	Turns off
Rewards attention to tasks _____	Ignores or negatively reinforces attending behaviors
Expands interests _____	Ignores expanding opportunities
Provides variety _____	Activities limited by lack of planning
Manages time well _____	Poor time management
Lesson planned and prepared _____	Poor or little lesson planning/preparation

Lesson smoothness _____ Poorly sequenced lesson
Lesson clean-up _____ Little or no clean-up

C. Control Techniques
Positive _____
Firm _____
Supervises all _____ Supervises only a few
Uses modeling _____
Notices accomplishment _____
Restates rules _____
Uses redirection _____
Uses many methods to change behavior _____

D. Verbal Interaction
Clear _____ Unclear
Receives children's nonverbal communication _____ Ignores
Specific directions _____ Vague directions
Questioning techniques _____
Develops concept formation _____
Volume _____
Eye contact _____

E. Housekeeping
Promotes child clean-up _____ Ignores child's ability to clean up
Replaces _____ Leaves out
Sees housekeeping tasks _____ Needs to be directed
                                                                     Seems to spend more time
Spends appropriate time _____ than necessary

F. General
Attendance _____
Well-groomed _____
Dependable _____
Total area supervision _____ Close focus
Excellent progress _____ Questionable progress
Attitude toward job _____
Performance on assignments _____
Communicative _____
Flexibility _____
Ability to take constructive suggestions _____
Could recommend as teacher aide _____
Could easily recommend as ECE teacher _____

Greatest Strengths:
Areas for Future Skills Growth:
Additional Comments:

CRITERION-REFERENCED INSTRUMENT

Field-Based Assessment Competencies

The 10 areas include:
1. Child Development Principles
2. Program Planning and Curriculum Development
3. Program Implementation and Classroom Management
4. Program Administration
5. Family and Community Relations
6. Cultural Pluralism
7. Children with Exceptional Needs
8. Assessment of Children
9. Evaluation of Program Effectiveness
10. Professional Behavior

I. *Child Development Principles*

1) Demonstrates knowledge of various theories of development and current research that are responsive to the needs of the total child.

2) Demonstrates knowledge of children from conception through age 8; with the exception that the candidate will demonstrate more in-depth knowledge about the particular age of the children in the program.

3) Demonstrates knowledge of physical development and the forces which influence it.

4) Demonstrates knowledge of social-emotional development and the forces which influence it, including the effect of family, school, society, and culture.

5) Demonstrates knowledge of personal development and the forces which influence it.

6) Demonstrates knowledge of cognitive development, including language development and creativity and the forces which influence it.

7) Demonstrates knowledge of the significance and influence of play behavior on the child's growth and development.

II. *Program Planning and Curriculum Development*

Knowledge

1) Demonstrates knowledge of child development principles in planning programs.

2) Demonstrates knowledge of factors to consider in planning an appropriate environment, indoor and outdoor, which enhances the development of children.

Application

1) Implements a curriculum based on child development principles, including the areas of: a) Large/Small Motor Activities; b) Language Arts; c) Science and Math; d) Creative Arts; e) Social Sciences; and f) Personal Development.

2) Demonstrates the ability to work as an effective member of a team in program planning.

3) Helps provide an indoor/outdoor environment which meets the needs of young children.

4) Selects and utilizes alternate teaching techniques and curriculum materials in certain situations which would stimulate and encourage active child participation.

5) Demonstrates the ability to interpret and use collected data in planning curriculum to meet the individual needs of the child.

III. *Program Implementation and Classroom Management*

Knowledge

1) Demonstrates knowledge of appropriate teaching techniques in the learning environment.

2) Demonstrates knowledge of how to facilitate effective child/adult relationships.

3) Demonstrates knowledge of play as an appropriate teaching technique.

4) Recognizes the unique contributions of staff.

Application

1) Provides children opportunities for making choices in learning, problem solving, and creative activities, whenever appropriate.

2) Utilizes play as an appropriate teaching technique.

3) Plans daily schedules which include a rhythm of physical and intellectual activities.

4) Utilizes positive suggestions in adult/child and staff relations.

5) Recognizes the importance of setting limits for children appropriate to their developmental level.

6) Models teacher behavior in accordance with expectations set for the children.

IV. *Program Administration*

Knowledge

1) Where applicable, discusses ways in which the candidate works with a governing board.

2) Can discuss philosophy of education for young children.

3) Has knowledge of licensing regulations and guidelines.

4) Has knowledge of revenue sources and conceptualization of budget priorities related to fiscal planning.

Application

1) Implements the regulations and guidelines regarding child development program operations, e.g., health, safety, and nutrition of the teacher and children; teacher/student ratios.

2) Maintains an effective record keeping system which includes information on required reports; child and family; and any other necessary information.

3) Utilizes an adequate handbook regarding personnel management.

4) Demonstrates ability to provide guidance and direction to co-worker.

5) Coordinates staff training and development programs.

6) Recommends and participates in selection and ordering of appropriate equipment and materials within the framework of the budget.

7) Develops a suggested budget for the program in one or all areas and assists the senior staff in establishing budget priorities.

V. *Family and Community Relations*

Knowledge

1) Demonstrates an understanding of the social, multicultural, and linguistically relevant patterns and parenting styles of families.

Application

1) Provides for communication with parents and community and utilizes applicable community resources.

2) Encourages parent participation and provides opportunities for parent involvement.
3) Provides for assessment of parent needs and makes arrangements for appropriate parent education and/or utilization of available resources.
4) Provides for continuity between the child's home and school experience.
5) Utilizes a wide variety of community resources which could contribute to an effective program.
6) Provides guidance to parents regarding effective ways to meet the developmental needs of children.
7) Establishes and maintains effective channels of communication with parents, including conferencing and visitation.

VI. Cultural Pluralism
Knowledge
1) Has knowledge of cultural background and needs of target populations.
2) Discusses multicultural implications for the program with staff, parents, and community members.

Application
1) Demonstrates ability to relate to parents and children from a variety of social, cultural, ethnic, and racial backgrounds.
2) Demonstrates ability to develop in the classroom an atmosphere of interest and respect for each other's culture.
3) Provides opportunities in the classroom to help children value the similarities and differences in their cultural backgrounds.
4) Demonstrates ability to design classroom activities and materials that enable children to learn about each other's cultures.
5) Makes provisions for communicating with parents and children who have limited knowledge of English.

VII. Children with Exceptional Needs
Knowledge
1) Demonstrates knowledge of the unique needs of the exceptional child.
2) Has knowledge of various forms of handicapping conditions which have an impact on child behavior.
3) Has knowledge of the sources of information regarding the legal rights of parents of exceptional children.
4) Can discuss how to implement an Individualized Educational Plan (IEP) when the need arises. (This may be demonstrated if an exceptional child is enrolled in the program.)

Application
1) Demonstrates the ability to develop a classroom atmosphere of understanding, consideration, and respect for the handicapped children integrated into the program.
2) Provides effective and appropriate methods of mainstreaming handicapped children.

3) Demonstrates teaching techniques that reflect understanding of the handicapped child.
4) Provides facilities and curriculum materials appropriate to the handicapped child.
5) Demonstrates the ability to work with the support services available for handicapped children and their families in the program.

VIII. Assessment of Children
Knowledge
1) Demonstrates knowledge of appropriate instruments and assessment techniques for infants and children and the sources from where they may be obtained.
2) Recognizes the effect of the ethnic, linguistic, and cultural backgrounds of the children on test performance and the limitations of most currently available assessment instruments.

Application
1) Utilizes long-range and short-range assessment methods.
2) Utilizes appropriate instruments and assessment techniques for infants and children.
3) Demonstrates the ability to evaluate and report a child's progress in terms of stated objectives and philosophy.
4) Demonstrates the ability to observe objectively and record information accurately.
5) Makes an effort, whenever possible, to utilize assessment instruments and techniques that are not culturally biased.

IX. Evaluation of Program Effectiveness
Knowledge
1) Demonstrates knowledge of the purposes, principles, and practices of program evaluation with emphasis upon the importance of evaluating programs for young children.
2) Demonstrates knowledge of the significant areas to be considered in program evaluation, e.g., curriculum, child motivation, peer relationships, teacher/child relationships, etc.

Application
1) Demonstrates the ability to analyze and evaluate all program elements and the effectiveness in meeting the children's developmental needs.
2) Demonstrates the ability to evaluate the effectiveness of the program with parents.
3) Utilizes effective program evaluation techniques for both long-range and short-range evaluation.
4) Utilizes evaluation results to continually improve the program if needed and to adapt to changing needs.

X. Professional Behavior
Knowledge
1) Has knowledge of the professional standards and behavior of an early childhood teacher.
2) Understands the significance and role of professional

ethics in student/teacher interactions; teacher/teacher interactions; and parent/teacher/community interactions.

3) Maintains knowledge of current information in the field of early childhood/child development education relevant to one's own professional needs.

Application

1) Continues to grow and develop professionally through coursework and continued experience.

2) Understands and performs the teaching role with professional standards and demeanor.

3) Maintains professional ethics, including but not limited to keeping the confidentiality of the child and family.

4) Demonstrates ability to work as a member of a team.

5) Demonstrates personal qualities resulting in effective functioning as a teacher of young children.

6) Uses self-evaluation on a regular basis.

Chapter 16

ADDITIONAL EXERCISE FOR CHAPTER 16
SUGGESTED ACTIVITY C.

1. Which shared activities would you have enjoyed most as a child? Why?

2. Did any shared activity seem to be planned for a structured, adult-controlled, passive-child-listening teaching style?

3. Which of shared activities do you feel would have the most children remembering and stating their address? Why?

4. Where would you place your planned activity on the following continuum?

Child choice apparent. Adequate supplies. Teacher attention and support.	Neutral teacher comments. Unclear directions. Little teacher aid.	One right way. Follow the directions. Model to copy. Child encouraged to quietly work.
Child problem solving. Shared child discussion. Shared materials.	Children copy others. Some sharing of tools.	Praise when correct. Teacher will do if child gets stuck.

SUGGESTED READINGS

Bennett, N., with Jordan, J., Long, G., & Wade, B. (1976). *Teaching styles and pupil progress.* Cambridge, MA: Harvard University Press.

Humanistic vs. traditional teaching styles and student satisfaction. (Winter 1980). *Journal of Humanistic Psychology, 20*, 1, pp. 87–90, EJ 219–357.

Instructional design and cognitive styles of teachers in elementary schools. *Perceptual and Motor Skills, 52*, 1, pp. 335–338, EJ 243–395.

Shumsky, A. (1968). *In search of teaching style.* New York: Appleton-Century-Crofts.

Silvernail, D. L. (1979). *Teaching styles as related to student achievement.* Washington, DC: NEA

Yamamoto, K. (1969). *Teaching: Essays and readings.* Boston: Houghton Mifflin Co.

Chapter 17

STUDENT TEACHER CHECKLIST

To help you evaluate your progress in achieving the developmental tasks of a student teacher (Rate yourself on each item)

F   D   C   B   A

1. Gaining firsthand knowledge of child development and behavior. Observing children's needs.
   I know each child's first and last names.
   I have observed the children in informal play situations.
   I have conferred with the teacher about personal needs of children.
2. Acquiring an understanding of the relation of the school curriculum to children's needs and the values of a democratic society.
   I have considered the appropriateness of the areas of study for the children of this age level.
   I have discussed with the teacher and college supervisor the ways in which the curriculum meets the needs of the pupils in this room.
3. Developing a professional conscience which impels him to organize the best possible learning experiences for his pupils, and to implement his own basic knowledges as necessary.
   I have demonstrated some initiative in my teaching.
   I am punctual and dependable.
   I take pride in careful workmanship—the materials I prepare for children are accurate and pleasing to the eye.
   I analyze my teaching activities each day to note strengths and needs.
   I am continually setting higher achievement goals for my teaching.
   I am really putting forth my utmost effort to do a good job.
   I allow adequate time to plan lessons and to prepare teaching materials.
   When my content background is thin, I master sufficient information to enrich the children's learning.
   My lessons are "ongoing." Each day's work grows out of needs demonstrated on the previous day.
4. Applying psychological principles of motivation and learning in teaching techniques; adapting experiences to individual differences.
   I am able to motivate all of the children most of the time or most of the children all of the time. My skill in motivation is increasing every day.
   I display sincere enthusiasm in the classroom.
   I am able to identify the needs of individual children.
   I am sympathetic and patient toward "slow growers."
   I plan ways to challenge fast-thinking children.
5. Learning to react objectively and with controlled emotions.
   In my evaluative conferences with teacher or college supervisor I am able to accept suggestions objectively.
   When a child fails to obey a school or class standard, I do not become emotionally aroused.
6. Developing an understanding of group structure: the kinds of interaction and the effect of the group upon individual children; factors which make for assimilation in or rejection by the group; the democratic control of groups of children.
   I really like these children.
   I have identified the children who have won the most acceptance by the group.
   I know why these children are most acceptable.
   I have studied the isolates in the class and can see some reasons why they are not accepted.
   I can see some progress in their acceptance because of steps I have taken.
   I believe that these children are developing a better awareness of the tenets of democratic behavior.
7. Acquiring familiarity with the best available learning aids.
   I utilize my own skills and personal resources in enriching the school experience for the pupils.

F   D   C   B   A

I take responsibility for providing effective learning materials and do not depend upon the teacher to find all of them.

I am selective in using the materials which are available and try to use those which will meet the learning goal.

8. Knowing the immediate community and utilizing its learning resources.

I have explored the community or at least the neighborhood sufficiently to become acquainted with its learning possibilities.

I have used community facilities or people to vitalize my teaching.

9. Developing skill in classroom management; in routinizing appropriate activities; and controlling physical aspects of the environment.

I get adequate rest so that I am at my best each day.

I adjust the pitch and volume of my voice in the classroom.

I begin my lessons promptly.

I watch the timing of each lesson and endeavor to stay within the schedule.

I pace the lessons so that interest is at a high pitch.

My materials are prepared and in place before I begin.

I take responsibility for the ventilation and adjustment of the physical environment without reminders from the teacher.

10. Securing pupil growth in purposing, planning, discussion, committee work, and evaluation.

I am successful in helping children to set appropriate goals.

I help children to plan activities which will permit attainment of their goals.

I encourage children to evaluate their activities in terms of their goals.

My ability to conduct discussions is improving constantly.

The supervising teacher says that I am showing real progress in formulating stimulating and effective questions.

I feel that I am increasingly alert to children's ideas and suggestions.

I help children to express themselves effectively.

11. Utilizing effective evaluation procedures in assessing his own needs and in gauging children's growth.

The supervising teacher feels that the children are making satisfactory progress under my direction.

I observe pupil reactions and development as a measure of my success.

I recognize the importance of constant evaluation for my professional growth.

I realize that I have a responsibility to make the evaluative conferences worthwhile.

I invite appraisal and suggestions.

I accept suggestions without alibiing.

I make a sincere effort to try out the suggestions I receive.

12. Meeting parents and planning with them for the guidance of their children.

I have assisted the supervising teacher in planning for a parent conference or meeting.

If permitted I have participated in a conference.

13. Getting acquainted with school services.

I am aware of all the special services which my teacher uses.

14. Learning to work cooperatively and ethically as a member of the teaching profession.

I try to be courteous in all my relationships.

I cooperate graciously with co-workers.

I do not discuss classroom happenings with anyone except the supervising teacher and the college supervisor.

Were most of your ratings in the A or B columns? Note especially the items which you rated as C or below. Try in the remaining weeks of teaching to improve in these areas.

(Reprinted by permission of the publisher, from *Success in Student Teaching* by L. Byers and E. Irish [Lexington, MA: D.C. Heath and Company, 1961].)

Chapter 18

ACCREDITATION CRITERIA (HIGH QUALITY PROGRAMS)

A. Interactions among Staff and Children

GOAL: Interactions between children and staff provide opportunities for children to develop an understanding of self and others and are characterized by warmth, personal respect, individuality, positive support, and responsiveness. Staff facilitate interactions among children to provide opportunities for development of self-esteem, social competence, and intellectual growth.

A-1. Staff interact frequently with children. Staff express respect for and affection toward children by smiling, touching, holding, and speaking to children at their eye level throughout the day, particularly at arrival and departure, and when diapering or feeding very young children. Staff actively seek meaningful conversations with children.

A-2. Staff are available and responsive to children; encourage them to share experiences, ideas, and feelings; and listen to them with attention and respect. Staff are aware of the activities of the entire group even when dealing with a smaller group; staff position themselves strategically and look up often from involvement.

A-3. Staff speak with children in a friendly, positive, courteous manner. Staff converse frequently with children, asking open-ended questions and speaking individually to children (as opposed to the whole group) most of the time. Staff include child in conversations; describe actions, experiences, and events; listen and respond to children's comments and suggestions.

A-4. Staff treat children of all races, religions, family backgrounds, and cultures with equal respect and consideration. Staff provide children of both sexes with equal opportunities to take part in all activities. Staff provide books, dolls, toys, wall decorations (photos and pictures), and recordings that reflect diverse images children may not likely see elsewhere. Staff make it a firm rule that a person's identity (age, race, ethnicity, or disability) is never an acceptable reason for teasing or rejecting. Staff initiate activities and discussions to build positive self-identity and teach the value of differences. Staff talk positively about each child's physical characteristics and cultural heritage.

A-5. Staff encourage developmentally appropriate independence in children. Staff foster independence in routine activities such as picking up toys, wiping spills, personal grooming (toileting, handwashing), obtaining and caring for materials, and other self-help skills.

A-6. Staff use positive techniques of guidance, including logical or natural consequences applied in problem situations, redirection, anticipation of and elimination of potential problems, and encouragement of appropriate behavior rather than competition, comparison, or criticism. Consistent, clear rules are developed in conjunction with children and are discussed with them to make sure they understand. Staff describe the situation to encourage children's evaluation of the problem rather than impose the solution. Staff do not force children to apologize or explain their behavior but help children recognize another child's feelings. Staff abstain from corporal punishment or humiliating or frightening discipline techniques. Food or beverage is never withheld as a discipline device.

A-7. The sound of the environment is primarily marked by pleasant conversation, spontaneous laughter, and exclamations of excitement rather than harsh, stressful noise or enforced quiet.

A-8. Staff assist children to be comfortable, relaxed, happy, and involved in play and other activities. Staff help children deal with anger, sadness, and frustration by comforting, identifying, and reflecting feelings, and helping children use words to solve their problems.

A-9. Staff recognize and encourage prosocial behaviors among children, such as cooperation, helping, taking turns, and talking to solve problems.

A-10. Staff expectations of children's social behavior are developmentally appropriate.

A-11. Children are encouraged to verbalize feelings and ideas. Adults intervene quickly when children's responses to each other become physical and discuss the inappropriateness of such responses.

SUGGESTED READING

Accreditation criteria & procedures of the National Academy of Early Childhood Programs. (1991). Washington, DC: National Association for the Education of Young Children.

Bredekamp, S. (Ed.). (1987). *Developmentally appropriate practice in early childhood education programs serving young children birth through age 8.* Washington, DC: National Association for the Education of Young Children.

Bredekamp, S., & Glowacki, S. (March 1996). The first decade of National Association for the Education of Young Children accreditation: Growth and impact on the field. *Young Children, 51*(3), 38–44.

Cost, Quality, and Outcomes Study Team. (May 1995). Cost, quality, and child outcomes in child care centers: Key findings and recommendations. *Young Children, 50*(4), 40–44.

Galinsky, E. (1990). The costs of not providing quality early childhood programs. In B. Willer (Ed.). *Reaching the full cost of quality.* Washington, DC: National Association for the Education of Young Children.

Montessori, M. (1964). *The Montessori method.* New York: Schocken Books.

National Association for the Education of Young Children. (March 1994). Public Policy Report. Creating a 21st century Head Start: Executive summary of the final report of the advisory committee on Head Start quality and expansion. *Young Children, 49*(3), 65–67.

Phillips, D. (Ed.). (1987). *Quality in child care: What does research tell us?* Washington, DC: National Association for the Education of Young Children.

Reinsberg, J. (September 1995). Reflections on quality infant care. *Young Children, 50*(6), 23–25.

Chapter 19

WORTHY WAGE ISSUES PLATFORM

The following Worth Wage Issues Platform (1994) identifies key issues of the Worthy Wage Campaign:

1. **Health Care.** Assure that there is universal and comprehensive health care coverage for *all.* The emerging national health care plan must address the unique needs of the early childhood work force and must not reduce current wage rates or place undue financial burden on early childhood programs or the work force itself.

2. **Quality improvement funds.** Insist that all new and existing federal and state funding for early care and education—including the Child Care and Development Block Grant—mandate funds specifically for quality improvements and that a portion of these funds be designated for improving compensation of the early childhood work force.

3. **Reimbursement rates.** Remove all restrictions on reimbursement rates for services that institu-

tionalize the poverty-level wages of the early childhood work force. Reimbursement rates should be equal to the cost of providing the services. This cost must include appropriate levels of compensation for the work force.

4. **Affordability to parents.** Restructure governmental assistance to parents in order for early care and education services to be more equitable. The level of support for all families must be the difference between the amount parents can afford (based on income, family size, and ability to pay) and the true cost of the service. We must eliminate the assumption that fees for services can be calculated solely on parents' ability to pay. All families and children deserve access to high-quality care, which includes justly compensated teachers and providers.

5. **Education opportunities.** Promote the necessary skills for child care employment by increasing access to higher education opportunities by the diverse population composing the early childhood work force, and ensure compensation commensurate with education. Increasing access to higher education implies that there will not be economic barriers for the trainee and that multilingual opportunities and materials will be available. Expand loan forgiveness, grants, and other programs to those currently employed in the early childhood field as well as those considering such as a career.

From *Worthy Wage News*, Vol. 2, No. 1, NCECW, Spring 1995.

Chapter 21

SUGGESTED READING

Gonzales-Mena, J. (January 1992). Taking a culturally sensitive approach in infant-toddler programs. *Young Child, 47*, 2. Washington, DC: National Association for the Education of Young Children.

GLOSSARY

ABC analysis — An observational technique in which the observer records observations in three columns, identifying *a*ntecedent, *b*ehavior, and *c*onsequence.

Absorbent mind — Maria Montessori's term to describe the capacity of young children to learn a great deal during the early years.

Abstract thinking — According to Jean Piaget, the ability to solve a variety of problems abstractly, without a need to manipulate concrete objects.

Accommodation — According to Jean Piaget, one form of adaptation, which takes place when an existing concept is modified or a new concept is formed to incorporate new information or a new experience.

Active listening — Thomas Gordon's term for the technique of reflecting back to children what they have said as a way to help them find their own solutions to problems.

Activity time — Largest block(s) of time in the early childhood program day during which children can self-select from a variety of activities.

Adaptation — Jean Piaget's term for the process that occurs any time new information or a new experience occurs.

Adventure playground — A European innovation, a type of outdoor play area in which children use a wide range of available "junk" materials to create their own environment.

Aesthetics — Enjoyment and appreciation of beauty, particularly related to all forms of art.

Aggregates — Rhoda Kellogg's term for the step in the development of art in which children combine three or more simple diagrams.

Aggression — Behavior deliberately intended to hurt others.

Allergies — Physiological reactions to environmental or food substances that can affect or alter behavior.

Anecdotal record — A method of observation involving a written "word picture" of an event or behavior.

Anxiety — A general sense of uneasiness that cannot be traced to a specific cause.

Assimilation — According to Jean Piaget, one form of adaptation, which takes place when the person tries to make new information or a new experience fit into an existing concept.

Assistant teacher — Also called aide, helper, auxiliary teacher, associate teacher, or small group leader; works under the guidance of the head teacher in providing a high quality program for the children and families in the class.

Association for Childhood Education International (ACEI) — Professional organization that focuses on issues of children from infancy to early adolescence, including those involving international and intercultural concerns.

At-risk children — Because of adverse environmental factors, for instance, poverty or low birth weight, children considered at risk for developmental delay and/or for doing poorly in school.

Attention deficit hyperactivity disorder (ADHD) — Manifested by short attention span, restlessness, poor impulse control, distractibility, and inability to concentrate.

Attachment — The child's bond with the mother, established during the first year of life.

Audience awareness — Children's growing awareness that their stories are a form of communication that should make sense to others.

Autonomy vs. Shame and Doubt — The second stage of development described by Erik Erikson, occurring during the second year of life, in which toddlers assert their growing motor, language, and cognitive abilities by trying to become more independent.

Authority stage — Stage of parenting defined by Ellen Galinsky typifying parents of young preschoolers who are defining rules as well as their own parenting role.

Autism — A socioemotional disorder of unknown origin in which the child's social, language, and other behaviors are inappropriate, often bizarre.

Babbling — The language of babies in the second half of the first year, consisting of strings of vowels and consonants that are often repeated over and over.

Basic scribbles — According to Rhoda Kellogg, the 20 fundamental markings found in all art.

Behavior management — Behavioral approach to guidance holding that the child's behavior is under the control of the environment, which includes space, objects, and people.

Behavior modification — The systematic application of principles of reinforcement to modify behavior.

Behavior setting — According to Kounin and Sherman, different environments elicit behaviors that are fitted to the setting; thus children act "schoolish" at school.

Behavioral objective — Aim or goal, usually set for an individual child, that describes in very specific and observable terms what the child is expected to master.

Behaviorism — the theoretical viewpoint, espoused by theorists such as B. F. Skinner, that behavior is shaped by environmental forces, specifically in response to reward and punishment.

Bereavement — The grief over a loss, such as after the death of a loved one.

Bibliotherapy — The use of books that deal with emotionally sensitive topics in a developmentally appropriate way to help children gain accurate information and learn coping strategies.

Bilingualism — Ability to use two languages.

Bimanual control — Ability to use both hands in tasks for which each hand assumes a different function.

Black English — Term identifying the dialect spoken by some black children, which has a complex grammatical system of its own.

Board of directors — Policy-making or governing board that holds ultimate responsibility, particularly for a not-for-profit program.

Brigance Diagnostic Inventory of Early Development-Revised — A developmental assessment tool for children from birth to age seven.

Burn-out syndrome — Condition experienced by professionals as a result of undue job stress, characterized by loss of energy, irritability, and a feeling of being exploited.

Caregiver or child care worker — Term traditionally used to describe a person who works in a child care setting.

Career lattice — Recognizes that the early childhood profession is made up of individuals with varied backgrounds; a lattice allows for both horizontal and vertical movement among positions, with accompanying levels of education, experience, responsibility, and pay.

Central processor — That aspect of the information processing model that governs and coordinates other functions such as sensory input and memory

Checklist — A method of evaluating children that consists of a list of behaviors, skills, concepts, or attributes that the observer checks off as a child is observed to have mastered the item.

Child abuse and neglect — Any action or inaction that harms a child or puts that child at risk.

Child-adult ratio — The number of children for whom an adult is responsible, calculated by dividing the total number of adults into the total number of children.

Child Advocacy — Political and legislative activism by professionals to urge consideration of social issues affecting children.

Child Development Associate (CDA) — An early childhood teacher who has been assessed and successfully proven competent through the national CDA credentialling program.

Child study movement — Occurred earlier in the 20th century in the United States when many university preschools were established to develop scientific methods for studying children.

Code of ethics — Agreed-upon professional standards that guide behavior and facilitate decision making in working situations.

Code switching — Ability to switch appropriately from one language system to another.

Cognition — The process of mental development, concerned more with how children learn than with the content of what they know.

Cognitive developmental theory — The theory formulated by Jean Piaget that focuses on how children's intelligence and thinking abilities emerge through distinct stages.

Cognitive interactionist view of language development — The view that children's language is rooted in cognitive development, requiring, for instance, ability to represent objects mentally.

Combines — According to Rhoda Kellogg, a step in the development of art in which children combine two simple diagrams.

Computer literacy — Familiarity with and knowledge about computers.

Conceptual — Montessori classroom area that focuses on academic materials related to math, reading, and writing.

Concrete Operations Period — Piaget's period covering the elementary school years.

Confidentiality — Requirement that results of evaluations and assessments be shared with only the parents and appropriate school personnel.

Conservation — Ability to recognize that objects remain the same in amount despite perceptual changes, usually acquired during the period of concrete operations.

Constructivist theory — A theory, such as that of Jean Piaget, based on the belief that children construct knowledge for themselves rather than having it conveyed to them by some external source.

Content objective — Purpose or rationale for an activity that specifies that the activity is intended to promote specific subject matter.

Conventional level of moral development — According to Lawrence Kohlberg, the stage concerned with pleasing others and respect for authority.

Conventional moral rules — Standards, which are generally culture-specific, arrived at by general consensus.

Convergent thinking — The act of narrowing many ideas into a single, focused point.

Cooing — The language of babies in the first half of the first year, consisting primarily of strings of throaty vowel sounds.

Coping strategies — Mental or physical reactions, which can be effective or ineffective, to help deal with stress.

Creative playgrounds — Outdoor play areas that use innovative materials such as tires, telephone poles, nets, and cable spools.

Criterion-referenced — A characteristic of tests in which children are measured against a predetermined level of mastery rather than against an average score of children of the same age.

Cross-modal intersensory activity — Use and integration of more than one sensory modality, for instance, matching an object that is seen visually to an identical object selected through touch only.

Cuing — A technique used to help children remember what is expected by giving them a specific signal.

Curriculum — Overall masterplan of the early childhood program reflecting its philosophy, into which specific activities are fit.

Daily living — Montessori classroom area that focuses on practical tasks involved in self- and environment-care.

Deep structure — According to Naom Chomsky, inborn understanding or underlying rules of grammar and meaning that are universal across all languages.

Deficit or impairment — A problem in development, usually organic, resulting in below-normal performance.

Denver II — A quick test for possible developmental delays in children from infancy to age six.

Developmental delay — A child's development in one or more areas occurring at an age significantly later than that of peers.

Developmental Indicators for the Assessment of Learning-Revised (DIAL-R) — A developmental screening test for children ages two to six, assessing motor, concept, and language development.

Developmental interactionist model — Foundation of the Bank Street approach, concerned with the interaction among various aspects of each child's development as well as between child and environment.

Developmental objective — Purpose or rationale for an activity that specifies that the activity is intended to promote an aspect of physical, social, emotional, or cognitive development.

Developmental test — Measures the child's functioning in most or all areas of development, although some such tests are specific to one or two areas.

Diagnostic testing — Another term for screening, which might indicate that more thorough testing should be carried out.

Diagrams — According to Rhoda Kellogg, the stage in children's art when they begin to use the six recognizable shapes, the rectangle, oval, triangle, X, cross, and the deliberate odd shape.

Dialect — A regional variation of a language that differs in some features of vocabulary, grammar, and pronunciation.

Didactic — often applied to teaching materials, indicating a built-in intent to provide specific instruction.

Direct instruction (also called programmed instruction) — A method of teaching in which the teacher determines exactly what the children should learn, devises a sequence of learning activities to teach specific information and teaches it directly by controlling the information according to children's responses.

Discipline — Generally considered a response to children's misbehavior.

Disequilibrium — According to Jean Piaget, the lack of balance experienced when existing mental structures and new experience do not fit exactly.

Divergent thinking — The act of expanding or elaborating on an idea, such as brainstorming.

Early childhood education models — Approaches to early childhood education, based on specific theoretical foundations, for instance, the behavioral, Piagetian, or Montessori view.

Early childhood teacher or educator — A specifically trained professional who works with children from infancy to age eight.

Eclectic — Describing an approach in which various desirable features from different theories or methods are selected: drawing elements from different sources.

Ecological model — A framework for viewing development that takes into account the various interconnected contexts within which individuals exist, for instance, the family, neighborhood, or community.

Educable mentally retarded — A child who has noticeable delays in most areas of development, including cognitive, but can function quite well in a regular early childhood program.

Effective praise — A form of encouragement that focuses on children's activities rather than on teacher evaluation of their work: praise that is meaningful to children rather than general or gratuitous.

Ego strength — Ability to deal effectively with the environment.

Emergent literacy — The ongoing, dynamic process of learning to read and write, which starts in the early years.

Empowerment — Helping parents and children gain a sense of control over events in their lives.

Equilibrium — According to Jean Piaget, the state of balance each person seeks between existing mental structures and new experiences.

Equipment — Large items such as furniture that represent a more expensive, long-term investment in an early childhood facility.

Event sampling — A method of observation in which the observer records a specific behavior only when it occurs.

Exosystem — According to family systems theory, that part of the environment that includes the broader components of the community that affect the functioning of the family, such as governmental agencies or mass media.

Extended family — Family members beyond the immediate nuclear family, for instance, aunts and uncles, grandparents, or cousins.

Extinction — In behavioral theory, a method of eliminating a previously reinforced behavior by taking away all reinforcement, for instance, by totally ignoring the behavior.

Eye-hand coordination — Integrative ability to use the hands as guided by information from the eyes.

Family child care homes — Child care for young children located in a private, licensed home.

Family involvement — Programs that urge parents to assist in their child's classroom, both in direct and indirect ways.

Family systems theory — A view of the family as an ever developing and changing social unit in which members constantly accommodate and adapt to each other's demands as well as to outside demands.

Fine motor development — Development of skills involving the small muscles of the fingers and hands necessary for such tasks as writing, drawing, or buttoning.

Flexibility — A measure of creativity involving the capability to adapt readily to change in a positive, productive manner.

Fluency — A measure of creativity involving the ability to generate many relevant ideas on a given topic in a limited time.

Formal Operations Period — Piaget's period covering adolescence.

Formative evaluation — Ongoing assessment to ensure that planned activities and methods accomplish what the teacher intended.

Fundamental movement phase — According to David Gallahue, the third stage of gross motor development, from ages 2 to 7, when children refine rudimentary skills so they acquire mature characteristics.

Gender identity — Identification with the same sex.

Gender stability — The recognition by children by age five to seven but absent in younger children, that sex is constant and cannot be changed.

Generativity — According to Erik Erikson, the stage of human development in which the mature adult focuses on the care and nurture of the young.

Genres — Categories or types of music, such as classical, jazz, or country.

Gifted children — Children who perform significantly above average in intellectual and creative areas.

Goal — An overall, general overview of what children are expected to gain from the program.

Gross motor development — Development of skills involving the large muscles of the legs, arms, back, and shoulders, necessary for such tasks as running, jumping, and climbing.

Guidance — Ongoing process of directing children's behavior based on the types of adults children are expected to become.

Head teacher — The person in charge of a class who is ultimately responsible for all aspects of class functioning.

High/Scope Child Observational Record (COR) — An alternative method of gathering reliable information about young children; COR utilizes teachers' notes of observations by classifying them into specific categories.

Holding grip — Placement of the hands in using a tool for drawing or writing.

Home visit — A one-on-one interaction between the teacher and the parent(s) of the child that takes place in the child's home.

Hothousing — Term taken from horticulture in which plant growth is speeded up by forced fertilization, heat, and light, refers to accelerated learning programs for young children.

Human development theory — a way to describe what happens as individuals move from infancy through adulthood, identifying significant events that are commonly experienced by all people, and explaining why changes occur as they do.

I-message — Thomas Gordon's term for a response to a child's behavior that focuses on how the adult feels rather than on the child's character.

Imagery — A relaxation technique in which a mental image such as "float like a feather" or "melt like ice" is invoked.

Ignoring — A principle of behavior management that involves removing all reinforcement for a given behavior to eliminate that behavior.

Immersion programs — An approach to teaching a second language to children by surrounding or immersing them in that language.

Individualized Family Service plan (IFSP) — Required by the 1986 Education of the Handicapped Act Amendments for handicapped children under the age of three and their families; the IFSP, often developed by a transdisciplinary team that includes the parents, determines goals and objectives that build on the strengths of the child and family.

Inductive reasoning — A guidance approach in which the adult helps the child see the consequences of a behavior on other people through logic and reasoning.

Industry vs. Inferiority — The fourth stage of development described by Erik Erikson, starting at the end of the preschool years and lasting until puberty, in which the child focuses on development of competence.

Information processing — a model of cognitive development, somewhat analogous to how a computer functions, concerned primarily with how human beings take in and store information.

Innatist view of language development — The view that inborn factors are the most important component of language development.

Interactionist view of language development — The view that language develops through a combination of inborn factors and environmental influences.

Integrated curriculum — A program that focuses on all aspects of children's development, not just cognitive development.

Interpersonal moral rules — Considered as universal, including prohibitions against harm to others, murder, incest, and theft.

Interpretive stage — Stage of parenting defined by Ellen Galinsky typifying the parent of an older preschooler or school-aged child who faces the task of explaining and clarifying the world to the child.

Initiative vs. Guilt — The third stage of development described by Erik Erikson, occurring during the preschool years, in which the child's curiosity and enthusiasm lead to a need to explore and learn about the world, and in which rules and expectations begin to be established.

Invented spelling — Used by young children in their early attempts to write by using the speech sound that most clearly fits the letters of what they want to convey.

Key experiences — In the cognitively oriented curriculum, the eight cognitive concepts on which activities are built.

Kindergarten — German word, literally meaning "garden for children," coined by Friedrich Froebel for his program for young children.

Kinesthetic sense — Information from the body's system that provides knowledge about the body, its parts, and its movement; involves the "feel" of movement without reference to visual or verbal cues.

Large group time (also called circle, story, or group time) — Time block(s) during the day when all of the children and teachers join together in a common activity.

Latch-key or Self-care children — School-aged children who, after school, return to an empty home because their parents are at work.

Lateralization — The division of the human brain, marked by a specialization in analytical and logical tasks in the left half and intuitive and creative functions in the right half.

Learning centers — (also called activity or interest areas) Where materials and equipment are combined around common activities, for instance, art, science, or language arts.

Least restrictive environment — A provision of Public Law 94-142 that handicapped children be placed in a program as close as possible to a setting designed for nonhandicapped children, while being able to meet each child's special needs.

Lesson plans — The working documents from which the daily program is run, specifying directions for activities.

Logical consequences — Rudolf Dreikurs' technique of specific outcomes that follow certain behaviors and are mutually agreed upon by teacher and children/students.

Logical thinking — According to Jean Piaget, the ability that begins to emerge around age seven in which children use mental processes to solve problems rather than relying solely on perceived information.

Long-term (or permanent) memory — In information processing theory, the vast store of information and knowledge that is held for a long time.

Macrosystem — According to family systems theory, the broadest part of the environment, which includes the cultural, political, and economic forces that affect families.

Manipulatives — Toys and materials that require the use of the fingers and hands, for instance, puzzles, beads, and pegboards.

Mapping — A map-making activity involving spatial relations in which space is represented creatively through such media as marking pens or blocks.

Materials — The smaller, often expendable items used in early childhood programs that are replaced and replenished requently.

Maturational theory — Explanation of human development dependent on information about when children achieve specific skills.

McCarthy Scales of Children's Abilities — An intelligence test, particularly used with children who are mildly retarded or who have learning disabilities.

Memory strategies — Various approaches used especially by older children and adults to help them remember information.

Mesosystem — According to family systems theory, the linkages between the family and the immediate neighborhood and community.

Metamemory — The ability to think about one's own memory.

Metropolitan Readiness Test — A test to determine whether a child is prepared to enter a program such as kindergarten.

Microsystem — According to family systems theory, that part of the environment that most immediately affects a person, such as the family, school, or workplace.

Mixed-age grouping — Programs in which children of different ages, for instance, three- to six-year-olds, are together in one class.

Mock writing — Young children's imitation of writing through wavy, circular, or vertical lines, which can be seen as distinct from drawing or scribbling.

Model — In social learning theory, those whom children imitate, particularly because of some desirable feature or attribute.

Modeling — In social learning theory, the process of imitating a model.

Montessori equipment — Early childhood learning materials derived from and part of the Montessori approach.

Moral development — The long-term process of learning and internalizing the rules and standards of right and wrong.

Multimodality — Referring to information that depends on input from several of the senses.

National Association for the Education of Young Children (NAEYC) — Largest American early childhood professional organization, which deals with issues of children from birth to age eight and those who work with young children.

Nonimmersion programs — Approach to teaching a new language that involves using both the primary and second languages, with a gradual shift from emphasis on the first to the second.

Norm-referenced — A test in which scores are determined by using a large group of same-age children as the basis for comparison, rather than using a predetermined criterion or standard of performance.

Nuclear family — The smallest family unit made up of a couple or one or two parents with child(ren).

Number concepts — One of the cognitive concepts young children begin to acquire, involving an understanding of quantity.

Nurturing stage — Stage of parenting defined by Ellen Galinsky into which the parents of an infant fit, as they form an attachment with and integrate the new baby into the family.

Object permanence — Part of Jean Piaget's theory, the recognition that objects exist, even when they are out of view; a concept that children begin to develop toward the end of their first year of life.

Objective — An aim; a specific interpretation of general goals, providing a practical and directive tool for day-to-day program planning.

Observable behavior — Actions that can be seen rather than those that are inferred.

Observational learning — In social learning theory, the process of learning that comes from watching, noting the behavior of, and imitating models.

One-to-one correspondence — A way in which young preschoolers begin to acquire an understanding of number concepts by matching items to each other, for instance, one napkin beside each plate.

Open education — A program that operates on the assumption that children, provided a well-conceived environment, are capable of selecting and learning from appropriate activities.

Open-ended materials — Early childhood materials that are flexible rather than structured and can be used in a variety of ways rather than in only a single manner.

Operant conditioning — The principle of behavioral theory whereby a person deliberately attempts to increase or decrease behavior by controlling consequences.

Organization — According to Jean Piaget, the mental process by which a person organizes experiences and information in relation to each other.

Overextension — Application of a word to a variety of related objects, especially used by toddlers.

Palmar grasp — A way of holding tools in which the pencil or crayon lies across the palm of the hand with the fingers curled around it, and the arm rather than the wrist moves the tool.

Parent-cooperative — A program staffed by one professional teacher and a rotating staff of parents

Parent education — Programs aimed at enhancing parent-child relations and improving parenting competence.

Parent-teacher conference — a one-on-one interaction between the teacher and the child's parent(s).

Parquetry blocks — Variously shaped flat blocks, including diamonds and parallelograms, that can be assembled into different patterns on a form board.

Perceived competence — Children's belief in their ability to succeed in a given task.

Personal control — The feeling that a person has the power to make things happen.

Phobia — An intense, irrational fear.

Pictorialism — According to Rhoda Kellogg, the stage in the development of art in which children draw recognizable objects.

Pincer grasp — The use of thumb and forefinger to pick up small objects; this skill develops around nine months of age.

Place identity — Considered part of self-identity because it relates to the environmental context within which a child's needs are met, competence is developed, and control over the physical world is gained.

Placement patterns — According to Rhoda Kellogg, a way of analyzing children's art by examining the 17 ways in which the total picture or design is framed or placed on the paper.

Plan-do-review cycle — The heart of the cognitively oriented curriculum through which children are encouraged to make deliberate, systematic choices with the help of teachers by planning ahead of time, carrying out, then recalling each day's activities.

Planning time — In the cognitively oriented curriculum, the time set aside during which children decide what activities they would like to participate in during the ensuing work time.

Playscapes — Contemporary, often innovative playground structures that combine a variety of materials.

Positive discipline — Synonymous with guidance, an approach that allows the child to develop self-discipline gradually.

Positive reinforcement — Application of a behavioral principle, which includes any immediate feedback (either through tangible or nontangible means) to children that their behavior is valued.

Postconventional level of moral development — According to Lawrence Kohlberg, the stage in which moral decisions are made according to universal considerations of what is right.

Pragmatics — Rules that govern language use in social contexts.

Prepared environment — Maria Montessori's term to describe the careful match between appropriate materials and what the child is most ready to learn at any given time.

Preassessment — A form of evaluation given before teaching a specific concept or topic to assess how much children know about it and to compare later how much they have learned.

Preconventional level of moral development — According to Lawrence Kohlberg, the stage during which moral decisions are made based on personal preference or avoidance of punishment.

Preoperational Period — Piaget's period covering the preschool years.

Preschematic stage — The stage in the development of art in which children have a subject in mind when they begin a picture, but in which the actual product will be an inaccurate, crude representation of the real thing.

Programmed instruction — (also called direct instruction) A method of teaching in which the teacher determines exactly what the children should learn, devises a sequence of learning activities to teach specific information, and teaches it directly by controlling the information according to children's responses.

Progressive relaxation — A technique in which various specified muscle groups are tensed then relaxed systematically.

Prosocial behaviors — Positive, commonly valued social behaviors such as sharing, empathy, or understanding.

Psychosocial theory — The branch of psychology founded by Erik Erikson, in which development is described in terms of eight stages that span childhood and adulthood, each offering opportunities for personality growth and development.

Punishment — An aversive consequence that follows a behavior for the purpose of decreasing or eliminating the behavior; not recommended as an effective means of changing behavior.

Rating scale — An assessment of specific skills or concepts that are rated on some qualitative dimension of excellence or accomplishment.

Rational counting — Distinguished from rote counting, in which the child accurately attaches a numeral name to a series of objects being counted.

Recall time — In the cognitively oriented curriculum, the time when children review their work-time activities.

Reflective abstraction — According to Jean Piaget, part of a child's self-directed activity that allows the child to think about and reflect on what he or she is doing, leading to the development of new mental abilities.

Reflexive movement phase — According to David Gallahue, the earliest stage of gross motor development during the first year; at first greatly controlled by reflexes, then gradually coming under greater voluntary control.

Reinforcement — In behavioral theory, any response that follows a behavior that encourages repetition of that behavior.

Reliability — A measure of a test indicating that the test is stable and consistent, to ensure that changes in score are due to the child, not the test.

Representation — According to Jean Piaget, the ability to depict an object, person, action, or experience mentally, even if it is not present in the immediate environment.

Resilient children — Children, who despite extremely stressful lives, appear to be stable, outgoing, and optimistic.

Rote counting — Reciting numbers from memory without attaching meaning to them in the context of objects in a series.

Rudimentary movement phase — According to David Gallahue, the second stage of gross motor development during the second year when body control is gradually developing.

Running record — A type of observation that provides an account of all of the child's behavior over a period of time.

Schemata (schema is the singular form) — According to Jean Piaget, cognitive structures into which cognitive concepts or mental representations are organized.

Schematic stage — Older children's drawings, which are more realistic and accurate than younger children's in what they depict.

Screening test — A quick method of identifying children who might exhibit developmental delay; only an indicator that must be followed up by more thorough and comprehensive testing.

Scribbling stage — The stage in the development of art in which children experiment with marks on a page.

Self-concept — Perceptions and feelings children may have about themselves, gathered largely from how the important people in their world respond to them.

Self-correcting — Learning materials such as puzzles that give the child immediate feedback on success when the task is completed.

Self-esteem — Children's evaluation of their worth in positive or negative terms.

Self-help skills — Tasks involving caring for oneself, such as dressing, feeding, toileting, and grooming.

Self-selected time-out — A technique in which children are given the responsibility for removing themselves from the classroom if they feel they are about to lose control.

Sensitive periods — Maria Montessori's term describing the times when children are most receptive to absorbing specific learning.

Sensitivity — Related to creativity, it refers to a receptivity to external and internal stimuli.

Sensorial — Montessori classroom area in which materials help children develop, organize, broaden, and refine sensory perceptions of sight, sound, touch, smell, and taste.

Sensorimotor Period — Piaget's period covering infancy.

Sensory deficit — A problem, particularly of sight or hearing.

Sensory discrimination — Involved in an activity in which one of the senses is used to distinguish a specific feature or dimension of similar materials; it might include matching or sorting by size, color, shape, sound, smell, or taste.

Sensory integration — The ability to translate sensory information into intelligent behavior.

Sensory-perceptual development — Giving meaning to information that comes through the senses.

Sensory register — In information processing theory, that part of the model describing how information initially comes to our awareness when perceived by the senses.

Seriation — A relationship among objects in which they are placed in a logical order, such as from longest to shortest.

Semantics — Related to understanding and study of word meaning.

Semantic network — The interrelationship among words, particularly related to word meaning.

Separation anxiety — Emotional difficulty experienced by some young children when leaving their mothers.

Sex cleavage — Distinct separation based on gender, evident in children at a very young age.

Shaping — In behavioral theory, a method used to teach a child a new behavior by breaking it down into small steps and reinforcing the attainment of each step systematically.

Short-term (or working) memory — In information processing theory, limited capacity for temporarily remembering information such as a telephone number.

Show-and-tell — A common group activity in which children can share something special and personal with their classmates.

Simultaneous language acquisition — A child learning two languages at the same time or before the age of three.

Slow learner — A child with mild cognitive delay and general immaturity.

Social cognition — Organization of knowledge and information about people and relationships.

Social interactionist view of language development — Theoretical view that considers language closely tied to and dependent on social processes.

Social learning theory — Theoretical view derived from but going beyond behaviorism, which considers that children learn not just from reinforcement but from observing and imitating others.

Social reinforcer — In behavioral theory, a reward that conveys approval through such responses as a smile, hug, or attention.

Socialization — The process through which children become a functioning part of society and learn society's rules and values.

Sociodramatic play — Children's dramatic or symbolic play that involves more than one child in social interaction.

Sociohistoric theory — originated by Lev Vygotsky, this theory gives prominence to the social, cultural, and historic context of child development.

Software — The "instructions" that direct a computer to perform an activity, usually stored on a disk or directly in the computer; many such programs are available for young children.

Spatial concepts — A cognitive ability involving an understanding of how objects and people occupy, move in, and use space.

Spatial relationship — The relative positions to each other of objects and people in space.

Special Time — A method for spending a few minutes a day with just one child as a way of providing unconditional attention.

Specialized movement phase — According to David Gallahue, the fourth and final stage of gross motor development, appearing around age 7 and up, when motor skills are applied to special uses, such as specific sports.

Split brain — The term that describes the brain as having two distinct sides or hemispheres, each with different functions.

Stage theorist — Any theory that delineates specific stages in which development is marked by qualitatively different characteristics and accomplishments and where each stage builds on the previous ones.

Stanford-Binet Intelligence Scale — A widely used test that yields an intelligence quotient (IQ).

Stranger anxiety — The display of fear and withdrawal by many infants beginning around six months of age, when babies are well able to distinguish their mother's face from the face of other people.

Stress — Internal or external demand on a person's ability to adapt.

Successive approximations — Breaking a complex behavior into smaller steps and reinforcing the child for each step as she comes closer to attaining the final behavior.

Successive language acquisition — Learning a second language after the age of three.

Summative evaluation — An assessment that follows a specific lesson or unit to evaluate whether the children have met the objectives.

Surface structure — According to Naom Chomsky, specific aspects of language that vary from one language to another.

Symbolic representation — The ability acquired by young children to use mental images to stand for something else.

Syntax — Involves the grammatical rules that govern the structure of sentences.

Team teaching — An approach that involves coteaching in which status and responsibility are equal rather than having a pyramid structure of authority, with one person in charge and others subordinate.

Temperament — Children's inborn characteristics such as regularity, adaptability, and other dispositions that affect behavior.

Temporal concepts —Cognitive ability concerned with the child's gradual awareness of time as a continuum.

Temporal sequencing — The ability to place a series of events in the order of their occurrence.

Time-out — Techniques in which the child is removed from the reinforcement and stimulation of the classroom.

Time-sampling — A quantitative measure or count of how often a specific behavior occurs within a given amount of time.

Total communication approach — Used with hearing impaired children, utilizing a combination of methods such as sign language, speech reading, and hearing aids.

Tripod grasp — A way of holding tools in which the pencil or crayon is held by the fingers, and the wrist rather than the whole arm moves the tool.

Trust vs. Mistrust — The first stage of development described by Erik Erikson, occurring during infancy, in which the child's needs should be met consistently and predictably.

Unconditional attention — A way of conveying acceptance to children by letting them know they are valued and liked; attention that is not given in response to a specific behavior.

Unit blocks — Most common type of blocks, precision made of hard wood in standardized sizes and shapes.

Validity — A characteristic of a test that indicates that the test actually measures what it purports to measure.

Whole language approach — Strategy for promoting literacy by surrounding children with high-quality oral and print language.

Work sampling system — Samuel Meisel's alternative method of gathering reliable information about young children, using a combination of observations, checklists, portfolios, and summary reports.

Work time — In the cognitively oriented curriculum, the large block of time during which children engage in self-selected activities.

You-message — Thomas Gordon's term for a response to a child's behavior that focuses on the child's character (usually in negative terms) rather than on how the adult feels.

Zone of Proximal Development (ZPD) — In Vygotsky's theory, this zone represents tasks a child cannot yet do by herself but which she can accomplish with the support of an older child or adult.

INDEX

Note: Page numbers followed by an *f* indicate figures.